GREAT LIVES FROM HISTORY

AMERICAN HEROES

Great Lives from History

American Heroes

Second Edition

Volume 2

Native American Leaders
Literature
Politics/Law
Medicine
Military

Editor
D. Alan Dean

SALEM PRESS
A Division of EBSCO Information Services, Inc.
Ipswich, Massachusetts

GREY HOUSE PUBLISHING

Cover photo: Chris Hurtt via iStock

Copyright © 2019 by EBSCO Information Services, Inc., and Grey House Publishing, Inc.

Great Lives from History: American Heroes, published by Grey House Publishing, Inc., Amenia, NY, under exclusive license from EBSCO Information Services, Inc.

All rights reserved. No part of this work may be used or reproduced in any manner whatsoever or transmitted in any form or by any means, electronic or mechanical, including photocopy, recording, or any information storage and retrieval system, without written permission from the copyright owner. For information, contact Grey House Publishing/Salem Press, 4919 Route 22, PO Box 56, Amenia, NY 12501.

∞ The paper used in these volumes conforms to the American National Standard for Permanence of Paper for Printed Library Materials, Z39.48 1992 (R2009).

**Publisher's Cataloging-In-Publication Data
(Prepared by The Donohue Group, Inc.)**

Names: Dean, Dewayne A., editor.
Title: American heroes / [editor, Dewayne A. Dean].
Other Titles: Great lives from history.
Description: [Second edition]. | Ipswich, Massachusetts : Salem Press, a division of EBSCO Information Services, Inc. ; Amenia, NY : Grey House Publishing, [2019] | Includes bibliographical references and index.
Identifiers: ISBN 9781642650587 (set) | ISBN 9781642653595 (v. 1) | ISBN 9781642653601 (v. 2) | ISBN 9781642653618 (v. 3)
Subjects: LCSH: Celebrities--United States--Biography. | Heroes--United States--Biography. | United States--Biography. | LCGFT: Biographies.
Classification: LCC CT214 .A47 2019 | DDC 920.073B--dc23

FIRST PRINTING
PRINTED IN THE UNITED STATES OF AMERICA

Contents

Complete List of Contents vii

Literature
Mercedes de Acosta 331
Maya Angelou 333
James Baldwin 336
Pura Belpré 339
Judy Blume 342
Giannina Braschi 344
Sandra Cisneros 347
Ta-Nehisi Coates 349
Martha P. Cotera 351
Emily Dickinson 353
Henry Louis Gates, Jr. 358
bell hooks 361
Zora Neale Hurston 363
Jhumpa Lahiri 365
Toni Morrison 368
Lola Rodríguez de Tió 370
Susan Sontag 372
Harriet Beecher Stowe 374
Walt Whitman 377
August Wilson 381

Medicine
Clara Barton 387
Martha Bernal 390
Elizabeth Blackwell 392
Deepak Chopra 396
Margaret Chung 398
Jane L. Delgado 399
Gertrude Belle Elion 402
Sanjay Gupta 405
David Ho 408
Joseph LeDoux 410
Antonia Novello 415
Susan La Flesche Picotte 417
Jonas Salk 420
Margaret Sanger 423
Nora D. Volkow 427

Military
Omar Nelson Bradley 435
Stephen Decatur 438
Mary A. Hallaren 442

Oveta Culp Hobby 444
Stonewall Jackson 447
Robert E. Lee 451
Chester W. Nimitz 455
John J. Pershing 458
Loreta Janeta Velázquez 462
Cathay Williams 464

Native American Leaders
Crazy Horse 469
Geronimo 474
Chief Joseph 477
Kamehameha I 480
Lili'uokalani 484
Wilma Mankiller 487
Nanyehi 490
Red Cloud 493
John Ross 496
Sacagawea 499
Sitting Bull 503
Sarah Winnemucca 506

Politics/Law
Madeleine Albright 511
Louis D. Brandeis 515
William J. Brennan 518
Ralph Bunche 521
Norma V. Cantú 524
Elaine L. Chao 525
Shirley Chisholm 527
Judy M. Chu 529
Clarence Darrow 531
Helen Gahagan Douglas 534
William O. Douglas 538
Tammy Duckworth 540
Geraldine Ferraro 542
Heather Fong 547
Benjamin Franklin 549
Ruth Bader Ginsburg 553
Al Gore 555
Nikki Haley 558
Alexander Hamilton 559
Learned Hand 564
Patrick Henry 567
Mazie Hirono 570

v

Charles Evans Hughes	572
Daniel Ken Inouye	577
Marí-Luci Jaramillo	580
Barbara Jordan	582
Robert F. Kennedy	586
Robert M. La Follette	590
Belva A. Lockwood	594
Huey Long	597
John Marshall	601
Thurgood Marshall	605
Vilma Socorro Martínez	608
Harvey Milk	610
Patsy Mink	613
Ralph Nader	615
Sandra Day O'Connor	617
Thomas Paine	622
Rachel Paulose	625
Colin Powell	626
Jeannette Rankin	630
Condoleezza Rice	633
Felisa Rincón de Gautier	636
Margaret Chase Smith	638
Sonia Sotomayor	642
Adlai E. Stevenson II	645
Norman Thomas	649
Earl Warren	654

Complete List of Contents

Volume 1

Publisher's Note vii
Introduction ix
Complete List of Contents xiii

Aeronautics and Spaceflight
Neil Armstrong 3
Bessie Coleman 8
Jimmy Doolittle 10
Amelia Earhart 13
John Glenn 16
Hazel Ying Lee 20
Shannon W. Lucid 22
Christa McAuliffe 25
Ellen Ochoa 27
Sally Ride 30
Alan Shepard 33
Sunita Williams 37
Orville and Wilbur Wright 39
Chuck Yeager 43

Art
Ruth Asawa 49
Judith F. Baca 51
Jean-Michel Basquiat 53
Barbara Carrasco 55
Keith Haring 56
Edmonia Lewis 58
Maya Ying Lin 60
Georgia O'Keeffe 63
Maria Tallchief 67
Martin Wong 70

Athletics
Muhammad Ali 75
Jack Dempsey 78
Lou Gehrig 82
Althea Gibson 85
Michael Jordan 88
Michelle Kwan 91
Martina Navratilova 94
Jack Nicklaus 97
Jesse Owens 100
Jackie Robinson 103
Bill Russell 106
Babe Ruth 108
Serena Williams 112
Babe Didrikson Zaharias 115

Business
Andrew Carnegie 121
Bill Gates 125
Andrea Jung 128
Indra Nooyi 130
John D. Rockefeller 132
Sheryl Sandberg 136
George Soros 138
Dave Thomas 140
Madam C. J. Walker 142

Education
Elizabeth Cabot Agassiz 149
Mary McLeod Bethune 151
Fabiola Cabeza
    de Baca Gilbert 155
Huping Ling 157
Juliette Gordon Low 159
Anne Sullivan 162
Booker T. Washington 165

Entertainment
Joan Baez 171
Lynda Carter 174
Ellen DeGeneres 176
Duke Ellington 177
Aretha Franklin 180
Katharine Hepburn 184
Billie Holiday 187
Nancy Kwan 190
Bruce Lee 192
Stan Lee 195
Dolly Parton 198
Prince 202
Fred Rogers 205
Selena 208
Nina Simone 209
James Stewart 211
Oprah Winfrey 215
Anna May Wong 218

Environment
Rachel Carson 223
Van Jones 226
Winona LaDuke 232
John Muir 234
Margaret Murie 237
Henry David Thoreau 239

Exploration
Robert D. Ballard 245
Daniel Boone 248
Richard Byrd 252
Meriwether Lewis and William
    Clark 255

Invention
Patricia Bath 263
Alexander Graham Bell 265
George Washington Carver 268
Lee De Forest 271
John Deere 276
Charles Richard Drew 279
George Eastman 282
Thomas Alva Edison 286
Thomas L. Jennings 290
Hedy Lamarr 293
Garrett Augustus Morgan 296

Journalism
Walter Cronkite 303
Ann Curry 306
Margaret Fuller 308
William Lloyd Garrison 311
Katharine Graham 316
Maria Hinojosa 319
Edward R. Murrow 321
Ida Tarbell 325

Volume 2
Complete List of Contents vii

Literature
Mercedes de Acosta 331
Maya Angelou 333
James Baldwin 336

Pura Belpré..................339
Judy Blume 342
Giannina Braschi................344
Sandra Cisneros 347
Ta-Nehisi Coates................349
Martha P. Cotera................351
Emily Dickinson 353
Henry Louis Gates, Jr................358
bell hooks 361
Zora Neale Hurston..................363
Jhumpa Lahiri 365
Toni Morrison 368
Lola Rodríguez de Tió 370
Susan Sontag..................372
Harriet Beecher Stowe 374
Walt Whitman 377
August Wilson..................381

Medicine
Clara Barton 387
Martha Bernal 390
Elizabeth Blackwell 392
Deepak Chopra..................396
Margaret Chung 398
Jane L. Delgado 399
Gertrude Belle Elion 402
Sanjay Gupta...................405
David Ho......................408
Joseph LeDoux..................410
Antonia Novello.................415
Susan La Flesche Picotte 417
Jonas Salk.....................420
Margaret Sanger................423
Nora D. Volkov 427

Military
Omar Nelson Bradley 435
Stephen Decatur................438
Mary A. Hallaren 442
Oveta Culp Hobby 444
Stonewall Jackson...............447
Robert E. Lee..................451
Chester W. Nimitz...............455
John J. Pershing 458
Loreta Janeta Velázquez..........462
Cathay Williams................464

Native American Leaders
Crazy Horse 469
Geronimo.....................474
Chief Joseph...................477
Kamehameha I 480
Lili'uokalani....................484
Wilma Mankiller 487
Nanyehi......................490
Red Cloud 493
John Ross.....................496
Sacagawea....................499
Sitting Bull....................503
Sarah Winnemucca...............506

Politics/Law
Madeleine Albright 511
Louis D. Brandeis 515
William J. Brennan 518
Ralph Bunche..................521
Norma V. Cantú................524
Elaine L. Chao 525
Shirley Chisholm 527
Judy M. Chu...................529
Clarence Darrow 531
Helen Gahagan Douglas 534
William O. Douglas 538
Tammy Duckworth 540
Geraldine Ferraro 542
Heather Fong..................547
Benjamin Franklin 549
Ruth Bader Ginsburg 553
Al Gore.......................555
Nikki Haley 558
Alexander Hamilton..............559
Learned Hand..................564
Patrick Henry 567
Mazie Hirono 570
Charles Evans Hughes 572
Daniel Ken Inouye 577
Marí-Luci Jaramillo 580
Barbara Jordan 582
Robert F. Kennedy 586
Robert M. La Follette............590
Belva A. Lockwood 594
Huey Long 597
John Marshall..................601
Thurgood Marshall 605

Vilma Socorro Martínez..........608
Harvey Milk 610
Patsy Mink 613
Ralph Nader 615
Sandra Day O'Connor.............617
Thomas Paine..................622
Rachel Paulose 625
Colin Powell...................626
Jeannette Rankin 630
Condoleezza Rice................633
Felisa Rincón de Gautier..........636
Margaret Chase Smith............638
Sonia Sotomayor................642
Adlai E. Stevenson II 645
Norman Thomas................649
Earl Warren 654

Volume 3
Complete List of Contents vii

Presidents and First Ladies
Abigail Adams 661
John Adams...................664
Dwight D. Eisenhower.............668
Betty Ford 672
Andrew Jackson 675
Thomas Jefferson 678
John F. Kennedy................682
Abraham Lincoln 686
Dolley Madison.................689
James Madison.................692
Barack Obama..................695
Eleanor Roosevelt 699
Franklin D. Roosevelt 702
Theodore Roosevelt 707
George Washington..............710

Religion
Sister Thea Bowman 717
Mary Baker Eddy 718
Barbara Harris 724
M. Hasna Maznavi...............726
Thomas Merton.................728
John R. Mott...................731
Sally J. Priesand 735
Zaid Shakir 737
Avi Weiss 738

Social Reform

Ralph David Abernathy 743
Jane Addams 746
Susan B. Anthony 750
Gloria Anzaldúa 753
Ella Baker 756
John Brown 758
Olympia Brown 762
Luisa Capetillo 765
Mary Ann Shadd Cary 767
Lourdes Casal 769
César Chávez 771
Helen Fabela Chávez 774
Kimberlé Williams Crenshaw .. 775
Dorothy Day 777
Eugene V. Debs 780
Dorothea Dix 784
Frederick Douglass 787
W. E. B. Du Bois 790
Marian Wright Edelman 793
Sue Kunitomi Embrey 797
Betty Friedan 799
Marcus Garvey 803
Emma Goldman 806
Emma González 809
Fannie Lou Hamer 811
Harry Hay 814
Aileen Clarke Hernandez 817
Samuel Gridley Howe 820
Dolores Huerta 824
Larry Itliong 829
Jesse Jackson 831
Marsha P. Johnson 834
Mother Jones 837
Frank Kameny 840
Helen Keller 843
Martin Luther King, Jr. 847
John L. Lewis 850
Malcolm X 854
Cherríe Moraga 857
Bree Newsome 859
Queen Noor 861
Rosa Parks 863
Alice Paul 866
Elizabeth Peratrovich 869
Ai-jen Poo 871
A. Philip Randolph 873
Sylvia Rivera 877
Bayard Rustin 879
Edward Snowden 881
Elizabeth Cady Stanton 883
Mary Tape 888
Reies López Tijerina 890
Sojourner Truth 892
Harriet Tubman 895
Nat Turner 898
Ida B. Wells-Barnett 899
Elie Wiesel 901

STEM

Benjamin Banneker 907
Steven Chu 909
Albert Einstein 911
Grace Murray Hopper 914
Edwin Powell Hubble 918
Mae C. Jemison 921
Katherine G. Johnson 923
Mary Golda Ross 925
Steve Wozniak 926
Chien-Shiung Wu 929

Appendixes

Chronological List of Entries ... 935
Alphabetical List of Entries 941
Subject Index 947

Literature

In the opening pages of a classic work called *On Literature*, American scholar J. Hillis Miller argued that the point of literature is simply to create imaginary worlds—and that this *matters*. The book is a passionate, articulate defense of that simple idea. Miller writes that literature changes our lives because, by immersing us in imaginary worlds, it affects the way that we see and respond. This changes our "equipment" for seeing and responding to what is in *this* world. To anyone who identifies as a reader, writers are heroes because they create these imaginary worlds for us.

American writers are uniquely situated with regards to literature understood in this way. "The United States themselves are essentially the greatest poem," as Walt Whitman wrote in his preface to *Leaves of Grass* in 1855. America was as poem because it was something still being created, a poem writing itself into existence. For Whitman, the democratic project, the essential thing about America, meant experiencing a deeper fellowship among humans than had ever existed before. In his view, America was not only a political experiment or progression, it was spiritual experiment and progression as well.

Whitman's ideas may seem naive today or even unpolitical, if we conceive of politics as essentially the business of contention rather than connection, or see progress as something primarily gained through the fight for rights. But his unique crystallization of a poetic *and* political vision was only the earliest and most explicit formulation of a synergy between ideas that has persisted and that animated a great deal of twentieth-century—and twenty-first-century—American literature as well. When James Baldwin, the great writer of African American experience, and of marginalization in general, spoke of the power of literature to create empathy, he was speaking about something profoundly political and something that touched the core of America's self-identity in the era of the civil rights movement. Also, for Baldwin, a crisis of personal self-identity and a national identity crisis could be overlapping experiences:

> It is perfectly possible — indeed, it is far from uncommon — to go to bed one night, or wake up one morning, or simply walk through a door one has known all one's life, and discover, between inhaling and exhaling, that the self one has sewn together with such effort is all dirty rags, is unusable, is gone: and out of what raw material will one build a self again? The lives of men — and, therefore, of nations — to an extent literally unimaginable, depend on how vividly this question lives in the mind.

Literature gives us opportunities to create worlds. It gives us opportunities to experience connection and empathy with people who are unlike us. And it allows us to discover, lose, or re-discover ourselves in the mirror of others or in the labyrinth of the text. These are all profound and profoundly human experiences, and we admire writers because they make these experiences and possibilities available to us. To the extent that these processes—of renewal and creation, of widening empathetic bonds, and of identity formation—overlap with the American political project, then perhaps writers can be uniquely American heroes for us.

Library stacks. (Wikimedia Commons)

MERCEDES DE ACOSTA

Writer

Born: March 1, 1893; New York City, New York
Died: May 9, 1968; New York City, New York
Area of Achievement: Literature, poetry, drama

Although Acosta's fame predominantly rests on her intimate relationships with some of the most celebrated women in art, film, and theater, she had literary success in her own right by publishing her controversial autobiography, Here Lies the Heart (1960).

EARLY LIFE

Mercedes de Acosta (mur-SAY-deez dee ah-COS-tah) was the youngest of eight children born to a Cuban father and a Spanish mother. Acosta was proud of her heritage and emphasizes in her memoir that both sides of her family had Castilian lineage. Acosta's father, Ricardo, was born in Cuba after his parents migrated from Spain to establish a coffee plantation in La Jagua. According to Acosta's dramatic account, her father led an uprising against Spanish forces in Cuba, escaped a firing squad, and ended up in the United States, where he met and married Micaela Hernandez de Alba y de Alba, who had inherited a significant family fortune. This fortune allowed the Acostas to reside in New York City's fashionable Park Avenue district.

Acosta's sister, Rita Lydig, was a prominent socialite noted for her stunning beauty and innovative fashion sense. She had her portrait painted by several famous artists of the time, including John Singer Sargeant. It was Rita who introduced Acosta to the Modernist art circles in Paris that included Igor Stravinsky, Pablo Picasso, and Sarah Bernhardt.

During World War I, Acosta was active in the Censorship Bureau and the Red Cross. She was a committed suffragette and fought for women's right to vote. She admired Isadora Duncan's attempt to liberate women from restricting corsets and other constricting styles of clothing. Until the age of seven, Acosta thought she was a boy and referred to herself as "Raphael." This sexual ambiguity would be a source of continued reflection and expression throughout her life. Acosta married Army captain and artist Abram Poole in 1920 but insisted on keeping her maiden name to retain her independence. While married, Acosta had passionate affairs with women, which she chronicled in her autobiography. She and Poole divorced

Mercedes de Acosta (Wikimedia Commons)

in 1935. Although Acosta was raised in a strict Spanish-Catholic tradition, she developed an interest in Eastern spirituality that lasted the rest of her life. Her exploration included adopting vegetarianism and traveling to India to meet Ramana Maharshi, a revered Hindu sage to whom her autobiography is dedicated.

> "*To the outward form of sex which the body has assumed, I have remained indifferent. I do not understand the difference between a man and a woman, and believing only in the eternal value of love, I cannot understand these so-called 'normal' people who believe that a man should love only a woman, and a woman love only a man. If this were so, then it disregards completely the spirit, the personality, and the mind, and stresses all the importance of love to the physical body.*"

LIFE'S WORK

Early in her career, Acosta fell in love with the theater and tried her hand as a playwright. She wrote and produced two plays as vehicles for her then-lover, Eva Le Gallienne. *Sandro Bottocelli* (1923) premiered in New York and *Jehanne d'Arc* (1925) premiered in Paris, because Acosta wanted the play to open in her heroine's own country. *Jacob Slovak*, a play about anti-Semitism, opened in 1927 to generally favorable reviews. Acosta also published three collections of poetry—*Moods: Prose Poems* (1920), *Archways of Life* (1921), and *Streets and Shadows* (1922)—and two novels, *Wind Chaff* (1920) and *Until the Day Break* (1928). However, she was unable to achieve a successful career as a poet and novelist. Critical reception to these works was generally disappointing.

Acosta had a short-lived career in Hollywood in the early 1930's under the legendary producer Irving Thalberg. An idea for her lover Greta Garbo to appear in a film wearing boy's clothes was quickly nixed (although Garbo's androgyny would be featured prominently in the 1933 film *Queen Christina*). While writing the screenplay for a film on the life of Rasputin, Acosta was asked by Thalberg to include a scene that had no basis in historical fact. She refused and was fired. None of the screenplays Acosta wrote during her time in Hollywood were produced.

After publishing her memoirs in 1960, Acosta sold her letters, photographs, and other ephemera to the Rosenbach Library and Museum in Philadelphia. Her letters from Garbo came with the stipulation that they not be made public until ten years after the death of the last surviving correspondent. The letters were released to the public in April, 2000, ten years after Garbo's death, and disappointed observers who had hoped to find among them an explicit love letter from Garbo to Acosta. Because Acosta moved in the various artistic circles of Modernist thought in the United States and Europe, her correspondents made up a veritable who's who of art, dance, film, literary, and theater worlds.

Nearly destitute at the end of her life, Acosta lived in a small two-room apartment in New York City and suffered from a variety of ailments. She felt snubbed by former lovers and friends who never forgave her for "outing" them in her autobiography. Acosta died in 1968 and is buried in Trinity Cemetery with her mother and sister.

Significance

Critics agree that Acosta never fulfilled her early promise as a writer. Her greatest literary success came with the publication of her memoir, *Here Lies the Heart* (1960), which received enthusiastic reviews although it cost her dearly in terms of her relationships. Acosta's reputation today primarily rests on the sensationalism of the celebrity women she bedded, rather than her broader role in advancing the cause of women's rights. Her forthrightness about her lifestyle during a time when the stigma of lesbianism was so pervasive is truly remarkable.

Her striking fashion sense (she favored capes, tricorn hats, and silver-buckled shoes) earned her the nickname "Black & White." Acosta continues to inspire generations of artists and writers interested in lesbian history. In a fitting tribute to Acosta's aspirations as a playwright and her cultural heritage, Odalys NanÃn, founder of Mujeres Advancing Culture History and Art (MACHA), wrote and starred in *Garbo's Cuban Lover* (2001), a play chronicling Acosta's tempestuous relationship with the elusive Hollywood star. *The Advocate* magazine listed it among the ten best plays of 2001.

Robin Imhof

The Controversy Surrounding *Here Lies the Heart*

In 1960, at the age of sixty-seven, Mercedes de Acosta published her autobiography, *Here Lies the Heart*. While the book makes no explicit reference to lesbianism, many of those who were intimate with Acosta (Greta Garbo included) never spoke to her again after its appearance. Eva Le Gallienne, who was never comfortable with her own sexual orientation, supposedly referred to the book as "Here the Heart Lies" as a way to distance herself from Acosta. In spite of those who protested that Acosta had exaggerated the nature of their relationships, much of the information Acosta revealed has been substantiated through personal correspondence and testimony from various insiders. While she often has been depicted as a predatory lesbian, there is ample evidence that Acosta also was pursued as an object of desire. Despite some inaccuracies that Robert A. Schanke noted in his biography of Acosta, *Here Lies the Heart* remains an important chronicle of same-sex female relationships during the era before Stonewall. It was reprinted in the mid-1970's and enjoyed great success, giving Acosta a renewed popularity, albeit more for her love affairs than for any of her literary accomplishments.

Further Reading

Acosta, Mercedes de. *Here Lies the Heart*. New York: William Morrow, 1960. Acosta's famous and controversial memoir.

Cohen, Lisa. "Fame Fatale." *Out* 8, no. 4 (October, 1999): 76. Lively account of Acosta's life and loves from a homosexual perspective.

Schanke, Robert A. *"That Furious Lesbian": The Story of Mercedes de Acosta*. Carbondale: Southern Illinois University Press, 2003. Schanke's scholarship calls into question some of the claims made by Acosta in her autobiography but nevertheless provides ample evidence that Acosta was much more than a mere seducer of famous women.

_____, ed. *Women in Turmoil: Six Plays by Mercedes de Acosta*. Carbondale: Southern Illinois University, 2003. Published as a companion work to the biography, Schanke, a professor of theater, rescued these plays from oblivion (only two were produced). A strong autobiographical thread runs through this collection as the female characters grapple with unfulfilling marriages and thwarted desires.

Vickers, Hugo. *Loving Garbo: The Story of Greta Garbo, Cecil Beaton, and Mercedes de Acosta*. New York: Random House, 1994. Vickers, as Cecil Beaton's official biographer and literary executor, relies on extant letters to situate this unlikely triumvirate of complicated and frustrating relationships.

Maya Angelou

Writer and entertainer

Born: April 4, 1928; St. Louis, Missouri
Died: May 28, 2014; Winston-Salem, North Carolina
Area of Achievement: Literature, poetry, film, activism

A dancer, actor, speaker, teacher, and prolific writer of poetry, books, essays, and plays, Angelou has illuminated human struggles, particularly those involving racism and civil rights. Through her stirring words, she challenges the spirit to rise above obstacles.

Early Life

Maya Angelou (MI-ah AN-jeh-lew), the second child of Bailey and Vivian (Baxter) Johnson, was born April 4, 1928, in St. Louis, Missouri. She was nicknamed Maya by her brother, Bailey, Jr., whom she adored.

When Angelou was three years old, her parents divorced, and she and her brother were sent on a train alone to Stamps, Arkansas. They were raised for the next four years by their paternal grandmother, Annie Henderson, who ran a general store. Angelou settled into a routine of chores, play, church, and school. She was an avid reader and participated in public recitations, singing, and the culture of a segregated society.

When Angelou was seven, she and her brother moved to St. Louis to live with their mother. There, Angelou experienced a fast-paced, urban culture surrounded by her prosperous maternal kin.

Shortly after settling in St. Louis, Angelou was raped. She testified against her attacker, and he was convicted and later released. When the man was beaten to death, Angelou thought her words had caused his demise. The traumatized child did not speak for approximately six years. When Angelou was eight, she and her brother were returned to their grandmother in Arkansas. Reading became Angelou's refuge. Writers such as W. E. B. Du Bois, Paul Laurence Dunbar, William Shakespeare, Edgar Allan Poe, and Charles Dickens inspired her. Eventually,

Maya Angelou (Wikimedia Commons)

she began to speak again when a favorite teacher encouraged her to read aloud the words of her beloved authors.

After Angelou completed the eighth grade, she and her brother moved to California to live with their mother. She attended the California Labor School on a dance and theater scholarship. Although she left school for a semester to work as the first African American trolley-car conductor in San Francisco, Angelou graduated from high school and a few weeks later gave birth to a son.

As an unwed teenaged mother, Angelou worked an assortment of menial jobs. After her marriage to Tosh Angelos in 1951, she formed the dance act "Al and Rita" with Alvin Ailey and won a scholarship to study African dance with Pearl Primus in New York. When the marriage ended, Angelou supported herself and her son by dancing at a strip club in San Francisco.

LIFE'S WORK

In 1954, Angelou developed a calypso act and adopted the stage name Maya Angelou. With doors opened by influential supporters, Angelou launched her singing and dancing career at St. Louis's Purple Onion Cabaret. She toured Europe with the musical *Porgy and Bess* in 1955, experiencing racism-free cultures for the first time.

In 1957, Angelou debuted in the film *Calypso Heat Wave* and recorded the album *Miss Calypso*. While she performed to support herself, Angelou's real passion was writing. She was composing song lyrics, poetry, and short stories when she met the writer John O. Killens. On his advice, Angelou moved to New York in 1959 to join the Harlem Writers Guild.

> "Without courage we cannot practice any other virtue with consistency. We can't be kind, true, merciful, generous, or honest."

Exhilarated by the flourishing black social movements, Angelou immersed herself in transformative experiences. In 1960, she cowrote and coproduced Cabaret for Freedom with Godfrey Cambridge to raise money for the Southern Christian Leadership Conference. In 1961, the organization hired her as its northern coordinator. Encouraged by her fiancé, Vus Make, Angelou performed as the White Queen in the award-winning Off-Broadway play *The Blacks*. Later in 1961, Angelou and Make moved to Cairo, where Angelou worked as associate editor with *The Arab Observer*.

Angelou's Autobiographies

Maya Angelou's autobiographies chronicle pivotal episodes of her life. While Angelou writes of deeply personal issues, such as her childhood rape in *I Know Why the Caged Bird Sings* (1970), her vividly expressed struggles with racism, sexuality, sexism, identity, and family speak to the rapidly changing culture of twentieth century America. Writing from decades-later vantage points and with novelesque plotting and dialogue, Angelou weaves in the life lessons she learned from these experiences. *Gather Together in My Name* (1974) chronicles her struggles as a single mother. *Singin' and Swingin' and Gettin' Merry Like Christmas* (1976) recounts her singing and dancing forays, particularly in Europe and Africa. *The Heart of A Woman* (1981) chronicles her early writing work with the Harlem Writers Guild and her civil rights work. *All God's Children Need Traveling Shoes* (1986) recalls her years in West Africa. *A Song Flung Up to Heaven* (2002) describes how the deaths of Malcolm X and Martin Luther King Jr., affected her. Reading like sequels to the slave narratives from the nineteenth century, Angelou's autobiographies capture both her remarkable life and the larger African American experience in twentieth and twenty-first century America.

In 1962, with her relationship ending, Angelou left Cairo to write for *The Ghanaian Times* and work at the University of Ghana. She was part of the delegation that welcomed Malcolm X to Ghana, and the two began corresponding.

In 1964, Angelou rejoined the company of *The Blacks* in Berlin. She returned to America in 1965 to work for Malcolm X, but he was killed before she began work. Heartbroken, Angelou sought solace in Hawaii near her brother and worked as a nightclub singer before moving to Los Angeles to concentrate on a writing career. To support herself, she worked in Watts until rioting devastated the city, then won a role as the nurse in *Medea* at the Theater of Being.

In 1966, Angelou returned to New York, rejoined the Harlem Writers Guild, and focused on her writing. By 1968, she had written two plays, a drama, a two-act musical, and several poems when Martin Luther King, Jr.,

Angelou receiving the Presidential Medal of Freddom from Barack Obama. (Wikimedia Commons)

asked her to join his Poor People's March. King was killed on Angelou's birthday, a few days before she was scheduled to join the march. A Writers Guild friend, James Baldwin, encouraged her to assuage her grief through writing, and Angelou began her autobiography. Later that year, she wrote and narrated the documentary series Blacks, Blues, Black! for National Education Television (now PBS) in San Francisco.

As the 1960's came to an end, Angelou continued work on her autobiography, hoping it would be a transcendent work that celebrated the human spirit while illuminating the African American experience. *I Know Why the Caged Bird Sings*, published in 1970, was a best seller. It was nominated for a National Book Award and catapulted Angelou to the forefront of a national renaissance of black achievement.

Throughout the 1970's and 1980's, Angelou experienced tremendous success, garnering awards and honorary degrees. Her poem "Just Give Me a Cool Drink of Water 'Fore I Diiie," was nominated for a Pulitzer Prize in 1972. She wrote, lectured in the United States and Great Britain, acted, and directed. She married Paul Du Feu in 1973, enrolled at the American Film Institute to study directing, and was nominated for a Tony Award for her Broadway portrayal of Mary Todd Lincoln's dressmaker. In 1974, Angelou published her second autobiography.

Ladies Home Journal named her woman of the year in 1975, and Angelou published her third autobiography in 1976. She appeared in the television miniseries adaptation of Alex Haley's *Roots* in 1977, receiving an Emmy nomination. In 1978, her documentary series Afro-Americans in the Arts won PBS's Golden Eagle Award.

Angelou's fourth autobiography was published in 1981, the year she accepted a lifetime position as Reynolds Professor of American Studies at Wake Forest University. The professorship required her to teach for one semester each year, leaving time available for writing, traveling, speaking, and participating in other projects. During the 1980's, Angelou produced books of poetry, a children's book, and her fifth autobiography. She adapted, scripted, and directed the London stage production of Moon on a Rainbow Shawl and introduced her writings to broader audiences with appearances on *The Oprah Winfrey Show*.

Throughout the 1990's, Angelou continued to work prolifically in many genres. She wrote children's books, essays, and poems and acted in television and films. She read her poem "On the Pulse of Morning" at the 1993 inauguration of President Bill Clinton. The recording of the poem won a Grammy Award. In 1995, Angelou composed and read "A Brave and Startling Truth" at the United Nations' fiftieth anniversary and "From a Black Woman to a Black Man" at the Million Man March in Washington, D.C. She appeared on television in *Touched by an Angel* and on film in *How to Make an American Quilt*. In 1996, she won a second Grammy for *Phenomenal Woman*; she appeared in the British documentary *Angelou on Burns*; and she spoke on the album *Been Found*. Angelou realized a long-held dream when she directed the major film *Down in the Delta*, released in 1998.

In 2000, Angelou received the Presidential Medal of Arts. The sixth book in Angelou's autobiography series was published in 2002, telling the story of her life in the mid to late 1960s. In 2004, Angelou published in three categories: children's books, autobiography, and essays, including *Hallelujah! The Welcome Table: A Lifetime of Memories with Recipes*. She composed and read "Amazing Peace" for the 2005 lighting of the national Christmas tree at the White House. In 2006, she acted in the film *Madea's Family Reunion* and published two books of poetry and an essay. She completed the volume *Poetry for Young People* in 2007. Angelou published *Letter to My Daughter* and received the Lincoln Medal in

2008. In 2009, she composed "We Had Him" as a tribute to Michael Jackson and was named one of *Glamour* magazine's women of the year. Maya Angelou published a new autobiography in 2013, *Mom & Me & Mom*, exploring her relationship with her mother

Significance

Angelou's deeply personal writings give voice to the twentieth century African American experience, illuminating struggles with economic inequality, civil rights, and individualism. Her eloquent descriptions and poignant human stories transcend her personal experiences to illustrate the power of the human spirit. Angelou's work addresses many themes, including abandonment, survival, identity, family, motherhood, discrimination, exploitation, and love. For these far-reaching contributions to American society and culture, President Barack Obama awarded Angelou the Presidential Medal of Freedom in 2011. Angelou died in May of 2014 at her home in North Carolina. Former President Bill Clinton and first lady Michelle Obama were among the celebrities that spoke about Angelou's career and impact at a televised memorial held in June.

Taylor Shaw, updated by Micah L. Issitt

Further Reading

Agins, Donna Brown. *Maya Angelou: Diversity Makes for a Rich Tapestry*. Berkeley Heights, N.J.: Enslow, 2006. Highly regarded biography detailing the struggles Angelou faced and overcame as a black woman growing up in a segregated society.

Angelou, Maya. *http://www.mayaanelou.com*. Angelou's official Web site offers a biography, list of her books and films, and photo and video galleries.

Courtney-Clarke, Margaret. *Maya Angelou: The Poetry of Living*. New York: Clarkson Potter, 2000. A compilation of photographs with tributes from friends of Angelou, including Coretta Scott King and Oprah Winfrey.

Gillespie, Marcia Ann, Rosa Johnson Butler, and Richard A. Long. *Maya Angelou: A Glorious Celebration*. New York: Doubleday 2008. A biography including family photographs, compiled in honor of Angelou's eightieth birthday by her friends and Rosa Johnson Butler, Angelou's niece and archivist.

Harper, Judith E. *Maya Angelou*. Mankato, Minn.: Child's World, 2010. Examines the life and accomplishments of the writer, performer, and teacher, as well as her impact on literature and black culture.

James Baldwin

Writer

Born: August 2, 1924; Harlem, New York
Died: December 1, 1987; St. Paul de Vence, France
Also known as: James Arthur Baldwin
Areas of achievement: Gay and lesbian issues; Literature; Poetry; Social issues

Baldwin came of age as a writer during the American Civil Rights movement. In his fiction, essays, and plays, he dealt forcefully with the racial issues of his time. In the process, Baldwin became a civil rights activist and spokesman who witnessed and chronicled many of the key events of the Civil Rights movement.

Early Life

James Baldwin was born in Harlem Hospital in 1924. His unmarried mother never told him the name of his biological father. Three years after Baldwin's birth, his mother, Emma Berdis Jones, married David Baldwin, a factory worker and a part-time preacher, and Emma and James took the name Baldwin. During the next fifteen years, David and Emma Baldwin had eight children and raised their family under difficult conditions during the Great Depression.

As a youth, Baldwin attended New York City public schools and tried to steer clear of the many hazards of Harlem life—drugs and alcohol, violence, and crime. His father, a strict disciplinarian, constantly warned his children of Satan's presence on the Harlem streets. Indeed, Baldwin, as he passed through adolescence, saw many of his friends succumb to drugs and crime. To shield himself from the temptations of the streets, Baldwin found two sanctuaries: the Harlem library and the church. He read voraciously and attended the Abyssinian Baptist Church in Harlem, which was led by a dynamic female preacher called Mother Horn.

At the age of fourteen, during a church service, Baldwin experienced a dramatic religious conversion that persuaded him that God had saved his soul and destined him to lead others toward salvation. He became a junior minister, offering stirring sermons in the Harlem churches. Baldwin's parents were certain that their teenage son was destined to become a great preacher, but Baldwin's religious fervor was short-lived. In the fall of 1938, Baldwin began attending DeWitt Clinton High School in the Bronx. There he met and befriended students of all faiths

James Baldwin (Wikimedia Commons)

and no faith. His high school reading material also challenged his religious beliefs, as the novels of Charles Dickens and Fyodor Dostoevski replaced his Bible. By age sixteen, Baldwin had decided that the ministry was not in his future.

Baldwin graduated from high school in 1942 and left home for the first time for a job laying railroad track in New Jersey. Away from Harlem, Baldwin experienced racial prejudice for the first time. He was denied service in restaurants and barred from the local bowling alley. After almost a year in New Jersey, Baldwin lost his job and returned to Harlem. A short time later, his stepfather died, and Baldwin felt compelled to remain in Harlem to help support his mother and younger siblings. He took odd jobs to bring money into the household, but he held fast to an ambition that had obsessed him from his student days: to become a writer.

In 1944, Baldwin sought career advice from the best known African American writer of the time, Richard Wright, author of the best-selling novel *Native Son* (1940), who was living in Brooklyn. Baldwin found Wright's address in the telephone book and made an unannounced visit. Wright, whom Baldwin greatly admired, received young Baldwin warmly and offered to read a section of a novel that Baldwin was composing based on his experiences in the Harlem churches. With Wright's assistance, Baldwin secured a grant for young writers from the Eugene F. Saxton Trust to complete the novel.

> "You think your pain and your heartbreak are unprecedented in the history of the world, but then you read. It was Dostoevsky and Dickens who taught me that the things that tormented me most were the very things that connected me with all the people who were alive, or who ever had been alive."

LIFE'S WORK

Encouraged by Wright's support and the Saxton grant, Baldwin continued to write. Early in 1947, he met Randall Jarrell, an accomplished poet and an editor with *The Nation* magazine. Jarrell assigned Baldwin some book reviews, which became Baldwin's first publications. Later that year, an editor at the journal *Commentary* invited Baldwin to write an essay on the relationship between African Americans and Jews in New York. The result, "The Harlem Ghetto," published in February, 1948, established Baldwin as a shrewd analyst of the racial landscape.

By this time, Baldwin, at the age of twenty-four, was growing restless. He felt compelled to escape from Harlem, where he was becoming claustrophobic. In 1947, Wright had left the United States to live and write in Paris. Late in 1948, Baldwin followed his role model to France, where he continued writing essays and working on that first novel. In 1949, he composed an essay titled "Everybody's Protest Novel" for a new literary journal, *Zero*. In that essay, Baldwin sharply criticized both Harriet Beecher Stowe's *Uncle Tom's Cabin* (1852), a favorite novel of his youth, and Wright's *Native Son*. The friendship between Baldwin and Wright ended shortly thereafter, but Baldwin felt that the falling out with Wright was necessary to establish his own literary voice.

Baldwin's first novel, *Go Tell It on the Mountain*, was published in 1953. The work was autobiographical, telling the story of a boy named John Grimes who grows up with a stern father in Harlem. Like Baldwin, John becomes involved with the church and undergoes a religious conversion experience that saves him from the dangers of

Baldwin lecturing in Amsterdam. (Wikimedia Commons)

the Harlem streets. The novel received excellent reviews and even earned praise from Wright.

Baldwin's years in Paris after the publication of *Go Tell It on the Mountain* were productive. He published several short stories. He completed a play, *The Amen Corner*, which premiered at Howard University in 1955. That same year, he assembled several previously published essays in a collection titled *Notes of a Native Son*. The collection marked Baldwin's growth as an essayist of the highest order. In 1956, Baldwin's second novel, *Giovanni's Room*, was published. The groundbreaking book told the tragic story of a homosexual Paris bartender. Baldwin, a nonpublic homosexual, was advised by his editor to burn the manuscript of *Giovanni's Room* rather than publish it. The novel's reception was mixed, some reviews condemning the book's subject matter and others praising Baldwin's sensitive treatment of a difficult topic.

While Baldwin was writing in Paris, great changes were taking place in the United States. In 1954, in the case of *Brown v. Board of Education*, the U.S. Supreme Court outlawed racial segregation in public schools. The following year, Rosa Parks refused to surrender her seat to a white passenger on a bus in Montgomery, Alabama, triggering a bus boycott that drew the nation's attention and propelled Martin Luther King, Jr., into a leadership position in the fledgling American Civil Rights movement. Soon afterward, a court ruling and presidential action forced the integration of Central High School in Little Rock, Arkansas. Baldwin observed these events from the safe distance of another continent.

In the fall of 1956, while school desegregation was still in the news, Baldwin picked up an American newspaper in Paris and saw a photograph of Dorothy Counts, a fifteen year- old African American student, proudly walking into a previously all-white high school in Charlotte, North Carolina. White students lined the walkway leading to the school, jeering Counts and spitting at her. Baldwin was appalled by the image. He suddenly felt guilty about living in Paris; he believed that he should have been in Charlotte or Little Rock encouraging the courageous students who were breaking down the walls of racial segregation in his homeland. He also missed his mother and siblings in Harlem.

In 1957, Baldwin returned to the United States. After a brief stop in Harlem to visit his family, Baldwin headed to the South, where he had never before traveled. He wanted to witness and chronicle the changes that were very gradually taking place in the racially segregated South. He ventured to North Carolina, Georgia, Alabama, Mississippi, and Arkansas. In Mississippi, he heard the tale of Emmett Till, an African American boy who had been brutally murdered in 1955. The Till tragedy inspired Baldwin to write a play, *Blues for Mr. Charlie*, which premiered on Broadway in 1964.

Baldwin returned to Paris to write in 1959, and for the next several years he lived there but frequently traveled to the United States to participate in important civil rights events. He embarked on a speaking tour of the South on behalf of the Congress of Racial Equality in 1963 and attended the March on Washington for Jobs and Freedom that August. In March 1965, he marched with King and others from Selma to Montgomery, Alabama, to protest that state's discriminatory voting practices.

The early 1960's were also productive writing years for Baldwin. In 1961, he published another collection of essays, *Nobody Knows My Name*. The following year, his third novel, *Another Country*, appeared in print. In 1963, Baldwin combined two previously published essays in book form under the title *The Fire Next Time*— now considered among his best nonfiction works. In 1965, he published his only collection of short stories, *Going to Meet the Man*.

After King's assassination in 1968, Baldwin became cynical about the possibility of racial reconciliation in the United States. He continued to write, publishing three more novels and several nonfiction works during the last twenty years of his life. Critics have generally found these later works less compelling than the first literary efforts

> **The Fire Next Time**
>
> First published in book form in 1963, *The Fire Next Time* comprises two essays that had previously appeared in *The New Yorker* and *The Progressive* under the titles "Letter from a Region of My Mind" and "My Dungeon Shook." The short book details James Baldwin's early life in Harlem, focusing on his religious experiences and his eventual disillusionment and departure from the Christian church, and his tentative search for a spiritual force to replace the lost religion of his youth. That exploration led him to Elijah Muhammad, leader of the Nation of Islam, which was advocating black nationalism and separatism. Muhammad saw the meeting as an opportunity to court Baldwin, already an established writer and spokesman on racial issues in the United States. Baldwin, however, after hearing Muhammad speak, rejected the Black Muslim message, asserting that the glorification of any race and the concurrent debasement of other races were a recipe for murder. *The Fire Next Time*, written in the tone of a sermon, concludes with the hope that the races will come together in America and help the nation achieve its ambitious destiny. Baldwin's final words, taken from a Negro spiritual, prophesy the punishment that God will inflict upon the nation if Americans do not end racism and inequality: "God gave Noah the rainbow sign,/ No more water, the fire next time!"

that established Baldwin's reputation. Between 1978 and 1986, Baldwin spent several years teaching as a visiting professor at Bowling Green University and at the Five Colleges in Amherst, Massachusetts. He died of cancer in France on December 1, 1987, and is buried in Hartsdale, New York.

Significance

Baldwin played a significant role in the American Civil Rights movement of the 1950's and 1960's. His best literary efforts present a sharp critique of the American racial landscape but offer the hope of racial healing. He wrote forcefully in four literary genres—novels, short stories, drama, and nonfiction—but he was at his best in personal essays that also addressed broader racial issues.

He ranks among the best American essayists of the twentieth century.

James Tackach

Further Reading

Baldwin, James. *Collected Essays*. New York: Library of America, 1998. A collection of Baldwin's major nonfiction works, including *The Fire Next Time*, *Notes of a Native Son*, and *Nobody Knows My Name*.

---. *Early Novels and Stories*. New York: Library of America, 1998. Contains Baldwin's first four novels and short fiction.

Bloom, Harold, ed. *James Baldwin*. New York: Chelsea House, 2007. A collection of critical essays on Baldwin's works.

Field, Douglas, ed. *A Historical Guide to James Baldwin*. New York: Oxford University Press, 2009. A collection of essays on Baldwin's life and works.

Leeming, David. *James Baldwin: A Biography*. New York: Knopf, 1994. A detailed biography by one of Baldwin's closest friends.

Standley, Fred L., and Louis H. Pratt, eds. *Conversations with James Baldwin*. Jackson: University Press of Mississippi, 1989. Contains more than two dozen interviews with Baldwin on his life, work, and times.

Pura Belpré

Librarian, storyteller, and writer

Born: February 2, 1903; Cidra, Puerto Rico
Died: July 1, 1982; New York City, New York
Area of Achievement: Literature, education, activism

The first Puerto Rican librarian in the New York Public Library system and an ardent advocate for social justice for Spanish-speaking communities, Belpré enjoyed a successful career as a librarian, storyteller, and children's writer, publishing the first Puerto Rican folktale for children in the United States.

Early Life

Pura Teresa Belpré Nogueras, better known as Pura Belpré (POOR-ah BEHL-pray), was born in Cidra, Puerto Rico, to Felipe Belpré Bernabe and Carlota Nogueras. She and her five siblings were surrounded by a family of storytellers who instilled a love for the rich stories and folktales handed down from generation to generation.

Pura Belpré (Wikipedia)

Belpré's family was quite nomadic, as her father was a contractor whose work took him to various parts of the island. Belpré attended primary and secondary schools in Cayey, Arroyo, Guayama, and Santurce. Often, she would spend hours exploring the natural world around her, amassing a vast storehouse of images and feelings that would later play an important role in her folktales for children.

In 1919, Belpré enrolled in the University of Puerto Rico at Rio Piedras with the intent to follow her sister's footsteps and become a teacher. However, her plans were cut short when she immigrated to New York City in August, 1920, amid the flood of Puerto Ricans entering the continental United States. She planned to attend her older sister's wedding and return to Rio Piedras. Not long after her arrival, Belpré met the African American librarian Catherine Allen Latimer at the Countée Cullen Library, a branch of the New York Public Library. Belpré was fascinated by Latimer's demeanor and skill as she interacted with numerous teenagers, and Belpré would later recall this encounter as the pivotal moment when she began considering librarianship as a career path.

LIFE'S WORK

In May, 1921, Belpré was asked by librarian Ernestine Rose to become the Spanish-speaking assistant at the 135th Street branch of the New York Public Library. She eagerly accepted the position, establishing herself as the first Puerto Rican librarian in the system. Immediately, she began training and eventually enrolled in the library school of the New York Public Library around 1925. Years later, Belpré would cite Rose and Latimer, along with librarians Ann Carroll Moore and Maria Cimino, as major influences in her professional life.

> "*Through the power of a story and the beauty of its language the child escapes to a world of his own.*"

As a librarian, she began to notice that Puerto Rican literature, particularly folktales, were absent from the library shelves. While taking a storytelling class under librarian Mary Gould Davis, Belpré was encouraged to write her first folktale—a love story from her native Puerto Rico about Pérez the mouse and Martina the cockroach. This particular story was one that she performed with handmade puppets for children during her story programs. A few years later, she was persuaded by a classmate to submit this folktale to a publisher for review. In 1932, *Pérez and Martina: A Portorican Folk Tale* was published by Frederick Warne, becoming the first Puerto Rican folktale to be published in the United States.

Throughout the late 1920's and 1930's, Belpré transferred to various branches of the New York Public Library, conducting Spanish and bilingual storytelling programs, planning community outreach efforts to Puerto Ricans, and welcoming Jewish, black, Latino, and various immigrant populations into the library. At the 115th Street branch, she hosted the first El día de reyes (epiphany) program, firmly establishing the library within the heart of the Puerto Rican and Latino community.

In 1942, Belpré traveled to Cincinnati, Ohio, to present a paper at an American Library Association conference. While there she met the famous African American composer, concert violinist, and Harlem musician Clarence Cameron White. They were married in 1943, and two years later Belpré resigned from the library to travel around the country with her husband.

Belpré's initial experiences in the library working with Spanish-speaking and Puerto Rican children and their families strongly influenced her writing and her career.

> **The Pura Belpré Awards: A Literary Celebracíon of Latino Cultures in Children's Literature**
>
> Established through the grassroots efforts of Mexican American librarians Oralia Garza de Cortés and Sandra Rios Balderrama, the Pura Belpré Awards are presented to a Latino author and a Latino illustrator who create an outstanding work of children's literature that positively represents the experiences of Latinos in the United States. From 1996 to 2008, the awards were presented biennially by their cosponsors, the American Library Association's Association for Library Service to Children and REFORMA (The National Association to Promote Library and Information Services to Latinos and the Spanish Speaking). Beginning in 2009, the award was presented annually to honor the best Latino children's books published during the previous year by a Latino author and Latino illustrator. Additional awards can be presented each year to honor other titles that are deemed worthy of recognition.
>
> The intent of the awards is to encourage Latino artists to record their cultural experiences for children and to persuade publishers to make these works available to families across the United States. The goal of honoring positive representations of Latinos furthers Belpré's mission of preserving the cultural heritage of Latino children and providing a window into Latino culture for non-Latino children. Incidentally, one of the 2009 Pura Belpré honor books, *The Storyteller's Candle = La velita de los cuentos*, by Lucia González and Lulu Delecre, is the first picture book to highlight the outreach work of Belpré. Additional information about the awards can be found in The Pura Belpré Awards: Celebrating Latino Authors and Illustrators (2006), edited by Rose Zertuche Treviño.

faced by Spanish-speaking children struggling to succeed in an English-dominant society. Belpré also understood the disappointment of not finding familiar cultural stories at the library.

From 1945 to 1960, Belpré wrote and told stories, presented lectures, and traveled with her husband. She penned many of the folktales told during her programs at the various branches of the New York Public Library. In 1946, Belpré published some of these stories as *The Tiger and the Rabbit, and Other Tales*, the first collection of Puerto Rican folktales in English published in the United States.

In June, 1960, Belpré's husband died from cancer, and shortly thereafter she returned to the New York Public Library to work as the Spanish children's specialist. For the next seven years, she traveled around New York City, assisting in the development of library programs for Puerto Rican children, conducting bilingual storytelling programs for both Puerto Rican and non-Puerto Rican populations, selecting Spanish-language children's books for library collections, and advocating for equal library services for impoverished communities.

In 1962, she began a translating career with the publication of her Spanish version of Munro Leaf's *The Story of Ferdinand*. That same year she published the picture book *Juan Bobo and the Queen's Necklace: A Puerto Rican Folk Tale*. She continued to publish original stories and translate Spanish versions of children's classics throughout the 1960's and 1970's.

In March, 1968, Belpré was forced to retire from the library because of age restrictions, but she was contracted later that year by Augusta Baker to work on a per diem basis on the South Bronx Library Project, an outreach-based program dedicated to establishing library services and collections for low-income, Spanish-speaking neighborhoods in New York City. While working on the project, Belpré traveled to branch libraries, day care centers, school libraries, and youth centers conducting puppet shows and sharing bilingual stories with children from various cultural backgrounds. In 1971, she and Mary Conwell published the professional resource *Libros en Español: An Annotated List of Children's Books in Spanish*.

Throughout her life, Belpré received notable and lifetime achievement awards for her work as a librarian, storyteller, puppeteer, advocate, and author. In May, 1982, she received the New York City Mayor's Award of Honor for Arts and Culture, and on June 30, 1982, Belpré was honored by the coordinator's council of the New York Public Library. The following day, she died in her sleep.

She had the opportunity to work one-on-one with newly arrived immigrants and poverty-stricken Americans who were trying to find their piece of the proverbial American pie. She had firsthand experience of the daily problems

In 1996, as a way to honor the librarian and her work in children's literature, the Pura Belpré Awards were established by the American Library Association and REFORMA (The National Association to Promote Library and Information Services to Latinos and the Spanish Speaking).

Significance

A quiet but passionate advocate for library services and programs for immigrant, low-income, and Spanish-speaking families, Belpré left a lasting legacy as the first Latino librarian in the New York Public Library System, the first Puerto Rican librarian in the United States, and the author of the first English editions of Puerto Rican folktales for children. Her grassroots efforts in New York City have become a shining example to future generations of librarians serving Spanish-speaking, Latino, and culturally diverse populations. At a time when race relations were tense, Belpré showcased the importance of intercultural understanding and social justice not only in her career as a librarian but also in her children's books that immortalize her passion to preserve her cultural heritage.

Jamie Campbell Naidoo

Further Reading

Centro de Estudios Puertorriqueños. *Puerto Rican Writers and Migration: Folklore, Autobiography, and History.* http://www.centropr.org/prwriters/belpre.html. This Web page, created by the Hunter College-based Centro de Estudios Puertorriqueños, provides a biographical essay about Belpré and links to numerous primary documents about her, including photographs, papers, speeches, and letters.

Hernández-Delgado, Julio. "Pura Teresa Belpré, Storyteller and Pioneer Puerto Rican Librarian." *Library Quarterly* 62, no. 4 (October, 1992): 425-440. Covers Belpré's life in Puerto Rico, her career as a librarian and storyteller, and her persistent drive to connect children from all cultures to Puerto Rican literature.

Núñez, Victoria. "Remembering Pura Belpré's Early Career at the 135th Street New York Public Library: Interracial Cooperation and Puerto Rican Settlement During the Harlem Renaissance." *Centro Journal* 21, no. 1 (Spring 2009): 53-77. Thoughtful examination of Belpré's early library work with black, Puerto Rican, and immigrant populations during the Harlem Renaissance. Highlights various archival pieces from Belpré's papers.

Sánchez González, Lisa. "Pura Belpré: The Children's Ambassador." In *Latina Legacies: Identity, Biography, and Community*, edited by Vicki Ruiz and Virginia Sánchez Korrol. New York: Oxford University Press, 2005. Overview of Belpre's work as a children's author, librarian, and storyteller, with particular emphasis on her books for children.

Judy Blume

Writer and social reformer

Born: February 12, 1938; Elizabeth, New Jersey
Area of Achievement: Literature

Blume has published books for all ages: children, young people, and adults. Her works treat in a humorous yet compassionate way such controversial subjects as religion, divorce, social exclusion, relocation, and sex. An activist for freedom to read, Blume is an opponent of censorship and book banning.

Early Life

Judy Sussman Blume (blewm), the daughter of dentist Rudolph and Esther Sussman, grew up in a Jewish family that emphasized books and reading. When Blume was in the third grade, her family moved to Florida for two years in the hope that the climate would help her older brother's health problems.

Blume took dance classes and excelled academically. At the all-girls Battin High School in Elizabeth, New Jersey, she sang in the chorus and was a features editor for the newspaper. After high school graduation, she enrolled in Boston University. When she contracted mononucleosis, however, she withdrew; she then enrolled in New York University (NYU) with a major in early childhood education.

During her junior year at NYU, she married attorney John M. Blume; they had their first child, Randy Lee (a daughter), shortly after Blume's 1961 graduation. Their son, Lawrence Andrew, was born two years later.

While she cared for the house and children, Blume began to create, write, and illustrate stories for children. Publishers, however, issued her only rejection slips. Blume enrolled at NYU in a class on writing for children and young people. As assignments in this course, Judy developed the children's book *The One in the Middle Is the Green Kangaroo* (1969) and her first draft of *Iggie's*

Judy Blume (Wikimedia Commons)

House (1970), a young adult book about a nonwhite family that moved into an all-white neighborhood. These two assignments became her first and second published books. More than twenty other books for children and young people would follow.

> "*Let children read whatever they want and then talk about it with them. If parents and kids can talk together, we won't have as much censorship because we won't have as much fear.*"

Life's Work

Although she and her husband divorced in 1975, Blume continued to write as Judy Blume. Even after her 1976-1979 marriage to physicist Thomas A. Kitchens and her third marriage on June 6, 1987, to law professor and writer George Cooper, she retained the Blume name.

Her works were a refreshing departure from the predictable, simplistic literature of the time. Many of her books—like life itself—do not have a tidy ending. Blume's writings remain popular. In addition to her work for adolescents and children, she has written three adult novels and three memoirs. Many of her volumes appear in translations; some are available in more than thirty languages. Her novels for adults include *Wifey* (1978), *Smart Women* (1984), and *Summer Sisters* (1998).

Religion—with particular emphasis on the Jewish faith—figures in many of her books, especially *Are You There God? It's Me, Margaret* (1970) and *Starring Sally J. Freedman as Herself* (1977). The last received critical reviews because of the ten-year-old girl's obsession with and mourning of the Nazi cruelties toward the Jews during the Holocaust.

Blume's writings treated frankly such sensitive topics as religion and sex. Her *Are You There God? It's Me, Margaret* appeared on the Top One Hundred List of Banned Books from the Online Computer Library Center (OCLC); several of her other books made OCLC's Top One Thousand List. To protest censorship, Blume joined the National Coalition Against Censorship (NCAC). In support, she produces posters, writes articles, speaks to groups, and encourages writers, teachers, and librarians facing criticism. All profits from her *Places I Never Meant to Be: Original Stories by Censored Writers* (2008) go to the NCAC.

Blume's books have appeared in a variety of formats: paperback, hardcover, large print, video, filmstrip, plays, animated films, film adaptations, teacher guides, television productions, and audio—some read by Blume herself. Her Fudge books were adapted for a Saturday-morning television series. Walt Disney Pictures and Blume have contracted to produce films based on some of her books, including *Deenie* (1973) and *Are You There God? It's Me, Margaret*.

Blume's honors include receiving the Young Readers Choice Award from the American Library Association (1996); earning the Distinguished Alumna Award from New York University (1996); and accepting the Eleanor Roosevelt Humanitarian Award. *Are You There God? It's Me, Margaret* became one of the all-time best sellers in paperback; by the mid-1990's it had sold some six million copies. Her *Tales of a Fourth Grade Nothing* (1972), dealing with sibling rivalry, became the third best-selling children's book of all time; more than six million paperbacks were sold by the mid-1990's. *Superfudge* (1980) was her best-selling hardcover. Blume's 1981 novel *Tiger Eyes* was made into a film in 2012, directed by Blume's son Lawrence. In 2015, Judy Blume published her fourth adult book, In the *Unlikely Event*, which was well received by critics and won a Goodreads Award.

Significance

With her books having sold eighty million copies, translated into thirty-one languages, and available in many

> **Are You There God? It's Me, Margaret**
>
> Judy Blume's third novel, *Are You There God? It's Me, Margaret*, is about a teenager trying to choose a religion. The main character, Margaret, is being pulled in several directions on this issue, by her family members and by her friends and by her curiosity. This book is characteristic of Blume's style, in which she effectively captures in print the thoughts, concerns, emotions, and speech of young characters; chooses topics vital to them; avoids a moralizing approach; uses first-person narration; and utilizes informal writing. Although Blume is a Jew, she does not push the character in this story toward the Jewish religion and does not insist that a single choice is the right one. Because of her frank handling of subjects that were usually taboo in children's and young adult literature, such as that proposed in *Are You There God? It's Me, Margaret*, Blume and her books have been subject to censorship and banning. For this reason, the writer has become a bold proponent of free speech, freedom of religion, and the freedom to read and write. Despite the controversy stirred by her works, Blume increased reading among her target audience: children and young adults. Blume's books have sold more than eighty million copies; translations appear in more than thirty languages.

formats, Blume has remained a foremost writer for children and young people since 1969. Many of her more than twenty books for them treat such sensitive topics as sex and religion—especially her Jewish faith. While some groups have tried to ban or censor her works and those of other writers, Blume openly discourages censorship, remains an activist for the freedom to read, and encourages better communication among adults, children, and young people. Her more than ninety prestigious honors and awards attest to the enduring significance of Blume's works.

Anita Price Davis, updated by Micah L. Issitt

FURTHER READING

Blume, Judy. *Letters to Judy: What Your Kids Wish They Could Tell You, a Kids Fund Project.* New York: Putnam, 1986. This collection of letters that Blume received from her readers contains some of her own comments. In this work for adults and people, Blume urges communication between adults and young people. This book helps young adults to realize they are not alone in their feelings and experiences.

Jones, Jen. *Judy Blume: Fearless Storyteller for Teens.* Berkeley Heights, N.J.: Enslow, 2009. Jones's biography of writer and social activist Blume treats the life and works of the author in 112 pages.

Nault, Jennifer. *Judy Blume.* Mankato, Minn.: Weigl, 2003. This biography of Blume, aimed at high school students, provides a life history of the writer and a review of some of the things she advocates, including the freedom to read and to write.

O'Connell, Jennifer, Meg Cabot, Beth Kendrick, and Julie Kenner. *Everything I Needed to Know About Being a Girl I Learned from Judy Blume.* New York: Pocket Books, 2009. Each essay in this collection by twenty-four women writers notes the impact Blume and her works had on the essayist's life.

Telford, Cee. *Judy Blume.* New York: Rosen Central, 2004. Telford discusses the life, the writing process and methods, the inspirations, and the work of this popular author. The book includes a biographical timeline of Blume's life, a review of some of the awards Blume has earned, a discussion and critique of some of her books, and an overview of some of Blume's beliefs.

GIANNINA BRASCHI

Puerto Rican-born poet, novelist, and essayist

Born: February 5, 1953; San Juan, Puerto Rico
Areas of achievement: Poetry; literature; sports

Known for her literary works, which examine Hispanic experiences in the United States, Braschi is especially renowned for her novel Yo-Yo Boing! The publication of this celebrated half-English, half-Spanish book generated a new genre of novels called "Spanglish."

Early Life

Giannina Braschi (jee-ah-NEEN-ah BRAHS-chee) was born in San Juan, Puerto Rico, the daughter of Euripides "Pilo" and Edmee Firpi Braschi. The Braschis were a well-to-do family. Euripides was a champion tennis player, and his wife Edmee worked as a realtor. Giannina's grandparents were also accomplished and affluent. Her maternal grandfather, Miguel Firpi, imported many of the first automobiles onto the island, while her maternal grandmother, Juanita Firpi Miranda, taught English at the University of Puerto Rico.

Following in her father's footsteps, Braschi became a champion tennis player while still an adolescent. In 1966, at the age of thirteen, she became the youngest female tennis player to win in the women's division of the U.S. Tennis Association's national tournament. After her athletic accomplishments, Braschi focused on her collegiate education and pursued opportunities abroad. Moving between Rome, Madrid, London, and Paris throughout the early 1970's, Braschi studied comparative literature at universities throughout Europe.

Enrolling in the State University of New York at Stony Brook's graduate literature program in 1974, Braschi specialized in the Golden Age of Spanish literature. This era, known as El Siglo de Oro in Spanish, refers to a literary and artistic movement within and outside of Spain, which began with Christopher Columbus's arrival in the Americas and coincided with the political ascent and subsequent fall of the Spanish Habsburg dynasty. (Though the era has no official end date, many scholars believe that Pedro Calderón de la Barca, who died in 1681, is the last writer associated with the Golden Age.) Braschi, focusing on several of the notable authors and artists of this period, completed her doctoral degree in literature in 1980.

> "Poetry must find ways of breaking distance.... all languages are dialects that are made to break new grounds."

Life's Work

Braschi's early written works were scholastic essays and books in which she discussed Spanish Golden Age writers, such as Miguel de Cervantes and Garcilaso de la Vega. Indeed, her first book examined the life and work of the Romantic poet Gustavo Adolfo Bécquer. In addition to her writing, Braschi has taught at several universities throughout the northeastern United States, including Rutgers University, the City University of New York, and Colgate University. At Colgate, she was appointed the distinguished chair of creative writing in 1997.

Braschi began writing fiction and poetry in the early 1980's, and her works were heavily influenced by the Nuyorican culture. "Nuyorican" is a combination of the words "New York" and "Puerto Rican" and refers to the Puerto Rican diaspora in, and around, New York City, which has the world's second-largest Puerto Rican population, outside of the island. The literary movement inspired by the diaspora experience examines issues of imperialism, immigration, and intergenerational conflicts within families.

Braschi published her first collection of poetry, *Asalto al tiempo*, in 1980. As much performance art as poetry, Braschi wrote, recited, and published her work entirely in Spanish, which limited her audience to Nuyoricans and literary bilingualists. A second collection of poetry, *La comedia profana*, appeared in 1985, while *El imperio de los sueños* was published in 1988. These works were noted for their use of rhythm and humor and an anti-imperialist ethos.

In 1994, Braschi's collected works were translated and published by Yale University Press in *Empire of Dreams*. Translated into English by Tess O'Dwyer, *Empire of Dreams* served as the inaugural volume for the Yale Library of Literature in Translation, an endeavor by the university to enhance access to literature written in languages other than English. This translated volume of poetry introduced Braschi to a wider audience and sparked further interest in her work.

Braschi won a National Endowment for the arts fellowship in 1997. This award undoubtedly supported her while she worked on what would become her most prominent and well-known novel, *Yo-Yo Boing!* When this novel was published in 1998, Braschi described it as a literary experiement. *Yo-Yo Boing!* is a nonlinear narrative that discards traditional concepts of literary chronology. The novel is written half in Spanish and half in English in order to capture the authenticity and emotional intensity of contemporary Nuyorican speakers. With diverse characters from different backgrounds, each speaker conveys his or her feelings and thoughts about experiences and events specific to the cultural clash between Anglo-American colonial culture and the many Latin American cultures.

Yo-Yo Boing! won critical acclaim and ushered in a new genre: the Spanglish novel. Noted primarily for a combination of English and Spanish language called "code-switching," the Spanglish novel often examines

> ## The Spanglish Novel
>
> Giannina Braschi's novel *Yo-Yo Boing!* won critical acclaim upon publication in 1998 and ushered in a new genre: the Spanglish novel. "Spanglish" is an informal term that refers to a lingual phenomenon where a speaker combines two languages in a technique called "code-switching." It is important to note that there is no one form of Spanglish. Indeed, different Latin American cultures speak different Spanglish dialects. While Puerto Rican Americans in New York speak Nuyorican Spanglish, Cuban Americans speak Cubonics, or Cuban-influenced Spanglish. In another example, Junot DÃaz's acclaimed novel *The Brief and Wondrous Life of Oscar Wao* (2007) makes use of Dominican Spanglish. The following statement is one example of Nuyorican Spanglish, taken from *Yo-Yo Boing!*: The lingual differences of the Spanglish novel are immediately apparent. However, the thematic content and the socioethnic identities of the fictional narrators can vary greatly. Often the Spanglish novel examines the cultural legacies of Hispanic cultures in contrast to, and in relationship with, Anglo-American colonial imperialism. Whatever the literary content, the Spanglish novel provides a public venue in which to examine the experiences of historically underrepresented and marginalized populations in the United States.

the cultural legacies of Hispanic cultures in contrast to, and in relationship with, Anglo-American colonial imperialism. In 1999, Braschi won the PEN American Center's Open Book Award for *Yo-Yo Boing!*, and in 2000, she received the New York Foundation for the Arts Fellowship in Fiction. After a stint as writer-in-residence at the Baltic Center for Writers and Translators, Braschi was selected as a judge of Latin American literature for the PEN American Center, the U.S. branch of a worldwide literary and human rights organization.

In 2011, Giannina Braschi debuted *United States of Banana*, her first work written entirely in English; it is a postmodern dramatic novel about the powers of the world shifting after September 11. The work is a poetic critique of 21st-century capitalism and corporate censorship. In 2012, *The Economist* cited *United States of Banana* among the best sources for bold statements on the economy: "Banks are the temples of America. This is a holy war. Our economy is our religion". *United States of Banana* takes as a springboard the collapse of the World Trade Center, the event which displaced her from the Battery Park neighborhood that became known as the Ground Zero vicinity. Braschi writes about the death of the businessman, the end of democracy, and the delusion that all men are created equal.

SIGNIFICANCE

Giannina Braschi's poetry and novels have shed light on the narratives within Nuyorican culture, and her other literary works have examined Hispanic experiences in the United States, particularly in New York City. Braschi is especially renowned for her novel *Yo-Yo Boing!*, which created the Spanglish literary genre. Her work is well-recognized, and she has received numerous honors, including the Danforth scholarship and fellowships from the Ford Foundation and the New York Foundation for the Arts; she was also named one of *El Diario La Prensa*'s Outstanding Women of 1998.

Rebecca M. Marrall

FURTHER READING

Barnstone, Willis. *Literatures of Latin America: From Antiquity to the Present*. Upper Saddle River, N.J.: Prentice Hall, 2003. Provides an overview of Latin American literature and the significance of individual writers.

Carrion, Maria M. "Geographies, Mother Tongues, and the Role of Translation in Giannina Braschi's *El imperio de los sueÃ±os*." *Studies in Twentieth Century literature* 20, no. 1 (1996): 167-191. Examines Braschi's use of language and geography in her third collection of poetry.

Fuentes, Yvonne, and Margaret Parker. *Leading Ladies: Mujeres en la Literatura Hispana y en las Artes*. Baton Rouge: Louisiana State University Press, 2006. Explores female-centric contributions to Hispanic literature and their sociocultural impact.

Goldstein, David S., and Audrey B. Thacker. *Complicating Constructions: Race, Ethnicity, and Hybridity in American Texts*. Seattle: University of Washington Press, 2007. Collection of essays examining the construction of ethnic identity and associated experiences within literature about the United States.

Sandra Cisneros

Writer and activist

Born: December 20, 1954; Chicago, Illinois
Area of Achievement: Literature, poetry, social issues

Through her poetry and her novels, Cisneros has helped to bring the Mexican American experience to the attention of mainstream American readers. She also serves as a voice for women reared in the patriarchal traditions of her culture, encouraging them to become more independent and to work for change.

Early Life

Sandra Cisneros (sihs-NEHR-ohs) was born in Chicago, Illinois, on December 20, 1954. Her father, Alfredo Cisneros del Moral, had left his home in Mexico after dropping out of college. In the United States, he gained legal status and U.S. citizenship by serving in the armed forces during World War II. After the war, he found himself in Chicago, where he met and married Elvira Cordero Anguiano, a Mexican American. They settled on Chicago's North Side, where Alfredo began working as an upholsterer. The death of a baby sister left Cisneros the only girl in the family. Since her six brothers preferred each other's company, she usually was alone; however, with her mother's encouragement, she became a voracious reader and began writing poems and stories.

Cisneros was educated at two Catholic parochial schools, St. Callistus and St. Aloysius. Her father took his family to Mexico for several months each year, so she learned a great deal about traditional life there. She also grew up completely bilingual.

Elvira played a major role in the later success of all her children, as she enrolled them in the public library and took them to museums and free concerts. A turning point for Cisneros came when she was twelve years old and her family finally moved into a house, giving her an assurance of permanence, a collection of interesting friends and neighbors, and, most important, a room of her own where she could think, read, and try her hand at writing.

In 1968, Cisneros entered Josephinum High School, a Catholic school in Chicago, where a teacher's praise impelled her to publish some of her poems and to work on the school literary magazine, eventually becoming its editor. After graduating in 1972, she used a scholarship she had won to enroll in Chicago's Loyola University, majoring in English. In her junior year Cisneros took a writing workshop, where she received valuable training in the techniques of her profession.

At the suggestion of several professors, she applied for the prestigious master of fine arts program in creative writing at the University of Iowa. She was accepted, and upon her graduation from Loyola in 1976, she made her way to the Iowa Writers' Workshop. It was at a seminar there that she had an epiphany: although her definitions of a home and a neighborhood were very different from those of her classmates, she was convinced that her people, too, deserved a place on the printed page. Cisneros had found her subject.

> "*I try to be as honest about what I see and to speak rather than be silent, especially if it means I can save lives, or serve humanity.*"

Life's Work

In 1978, with her master's degree in hand, Cisneros was ready to become a professional writer; however, it would be almost two decades before she could support herself by writing. She began working with inner-city youths at the Latino Youth Alternative High School in Chicago. During that time, she became acquainted with Chicano

Sandra Cisneros (Wikimedia Commons)

> **Esperanza and *The House on Mango Street***
>
> Sandra Cisneros's best-known work, *The House on Mango Street* (1984), is a collection of vignettes that vary from simple, colloquial narratives to poetic prose, interspersed with poetic meditations. Although it is difficult to categorize, critics agree that the book is unified by the use of a first-person narrator, Esperanza Cordera, a Mexican American girl who observes the action around her, reacts to it, and reflects upon it. Esperanza is both a character participating in the action and an outside observer, drawing conclusions about the flaws in her society, especially in its treatment of women. However, while the book ends with Mango Street essentially unchanged, Esperanza herself has come of age. She has moved from a naïve fascination with boys and sexuality to the realization that marriage and motherhood do not free women but instead condemn them to lifelong imprisonment. By choosing wise women as her advisers, Esperanza enters adulthood committed to her writing, which she sees as her route to freedom.

poet Gary Soto, who helped her publish *Bad Boys* (1980), a chapbook containing seven poems. Cisneros then became a recruiter for Loyola University. Meanwhile, she continued to work on her poetry and on the sketches that eventually would become *The House on Mango Street* (1984).

In 1982, Cisneros received a grant from the National Endowment for the Arts that enabled her to spend a year in Europe. By November, she had a manuscript ready to submit to Nicolás Kanellos of Arte Público Press, who had suggested that she compile and publish her stories. After extensive revision, in 1984, *The House on Mango Street* appeared. In 1985, it won the American Book Award of the Before Columbus Foundation, and by 2011 it had sold more than two million copies.

Over the next ten years, Cisneros worked for various institutions. She spent a year as literature director of the Guadalupe Cultural Art Center in San Antonio, Texas, then held teaching positions at California State University at Chico, the University of California at Berkeley, the University of California at Irvine, the University of Michigan at Ann Arbor, and the University of New Mexico at Albuquerque. In 1986, she won a Dobie Paisano Writing Fellowship, which enabled her to complete her first major poetry collection, *My Wicked, Wicked Ways* (1987). The next year, she won another fellowship from the National Endowment for the Arts.

In 1991, Cisneros published *Woman Hollering Creek, and Other Stories*, a collection of stories set in and around San Antonio, Texas. In addition to examining women trapped in a patriarchal culture, Cisneros touches on such issues as poverty, crime, racism, and religious faith. Woman Hollering Creek was a best seller and won the PEN Center West Award for Best Fiction of 1991, the Anisfield-Wolf Book Award, and the Lannan Foundation Literary Award.

Two books by Cisneros appeared in 1994: *Hairs* (*Pelitos*), a bilingual picture book for children, and *Loose Woman*, a collection of experimental poems. The following year, she won a MacArthur Foundation fellowship, which at last made her financially secure. Cisneros bought a house in a historic section of San Antonio, infuriated many of her neighbors by painting it bright purple, and began writing a novel, *Caramelo: Or, Puro Cuento* (2002), her most ambitious work to date. *Caramelo* is the story of Celaya Reyes, who like Cisneros herself spends her childhood in Mexico and Chicago. Celaya's attempts to disentangle truth from fiction in the extended family histories narrated by her older relatives result in some of the most humorous scenes in what critics agree is an exceptionally vivid, lively novel. *Caramelo* received the 2005 Premio Napoli Award and was nominated for England's Orange Prize.

Cisneros was awarded the Texas Medal of the Arts in 2003. In 2009, she became writer-in-residence at Our Lady of the Lake University in San Antonio. Cisneros published a new book, *Bravo Bruno* in 2011, followed the next year by *Have you Seen Marie?* In 2015 she published *A House of My Own*, which is a series of stories from Cisneros' life. In 2018 she released *Puro Amor*, a short story, through Sarabande Books. Cisneros has also contributed to a number of collected volumes, including *Things We Do Not Talk About: Exploring Latino/a Literature Through Essays and Interviews*. Her works have been translated into more than one dozen languages. She received a National Medal of Arts in 2016.

Significance

The adoption of *The House on Mango Street* as a text in schools and universities resulted in greater understanding of the problems faced by Chicanos, and when a major publishing house released *Woman Hollering Creek*, fiction by Mexican American women gained a new popularity. Through her works and through personal contacts, as well as through her foundations, Cisneros continues to work actively in support of the rights of immigrants and women.

*Rosemary M. Canfield Reisman,
updated by Micah L. Issitt*

FURTHER READING

Calderón, Héctor. "Como México no hay dos": Sandra Cisneros's Feminist Border Stories." In *Narratives of Greater Mexico: Essays on Chicano Literary History, Genre, and Borders*. Austin: University of Texas Press, 2004. Scholarly essay on themes such as gender, culture, and identity in Cisneros's writing. Map, bibliography, and index.

Cisneros, Sandra. "Muy Payasa: Conversation with Sandra Cisneros." *Interview by Nancy Sullivan.* In *Conversations with Mexican American Writers: Languages and Literatures in the Borderlands*, by Elisabeth Mermann-Jozwiak and Nancy Sullivan. Jackson: University Press of Mississippi, 2009. Cisneros discusses the autobiographical elements in her fiction, the construction of Chicano identity, and other subjects in this interview. Bibliographical references and index.

Eysturoy, Annie O. "*The House on Mango Street*: A Space of Her Own." In *Daughters of Self-Creation: The Contemporary Chicana Novel*. Albuquerque: University of New Mexico Press, 1996. Examines the Chicana's quest for the self in Cisneros's *The House on Mango Street*. Bibliographical references and index.

Kevane, Bridget. "The Fiction of Sandra Cisneros: *The House on Mango Street* (1984) and *Woman Hollering Creek* (1991)." In *Latino Literature in America*. Westport, Conn.: Greenwood Press, 2003. Offers detailed analyses of both *The House on Mango Street* and *Woman Hollering Creek*. Bibliography and index.

Rivera, Carmen Haydée. *Border Crossings and Beyond: The Life and Works of Sandra Cisneros*. Santa Barbara, Calif.: Praeger, 2009. A thorough study of the author and her works. Extensive notes, bibliography, and index.

TA-NEHISI COATES

Writer

Born: September 30, 1975; Baltimore, Maryland
Area of Achievement: Journalism; activism; social issues; civil rights

Ta-Nehisi Coates emerged as an important public intellectual with the publication of Between the World and Me *(2015) while also planting a foot firmly in the pop culture world with his work on the comic book series* Black Panther.

EARLY LIFE

Ta-Nehisi Coates—whose first name is derived from the ancient Egyptian word for Nubia—was born to William Paul Coates and Cheryl Waters on September 30, 1975. He was raised in a poor section of West Baltimore, Maryland. The crime-ridden area was the setting for the television drama *The Wire, and* much of the show's fourth season was filmed at the middle school that Coates attended.

Coates's family life was not entirely conventional. Coates has said, however, that it wasn't unusual in his neighborhood. His father had children to more than one woman, and everyone remained close, one family. Coates lived with his father, mother, and brother, while the other children lived for most of the year with their respective mothers, although they visited each other on the weekends, and when any of the boys struggled in school or posed a disciplinary problem, he was sent to live in Coates's household for a time, so that his father, could "get the kid back on track."

> "*It meant something to see people who looked like me in comic books. It was this beautiful place that I felt pop culture should look like."*

Coates' mother supported her sons by working as a schoolteacher. (When Coates misbehaved, she punished him by making him write lengthy essays, even when he was as young as six or seven.) Paul Coates, a Vietnam War veteran, was a member of the Black Panthers, and from the basement of the row house where he lived with

Ta-Nehisis Coates (Wikimedia Commons)

Waters and their two boys, he operated a small publishing company specializing in black nationalist literature and other Afrocentric volumes. Seeking to make sense of the poverty and violence he saw every day—so different from the white, suburban life he saw depicted on television—Coates avidly read those books, and it was not until he entered Howard University, a historically black university, that he began questioning some of the more fringe beliefs they inculcated in him.

Before entering Howard, Coates had struggled from time to time in school, and he started his senior year with a dismal 1.8 grade point average. The father wanted his sons to be bright and well read, and he also encouraged them to interact with other boys in the community—despite the violence and criminal activity they encountered in the process. His comfort with a wide variety of people served him well at Howard, which drew students from around the world and from every socioeconomic level and religion. Coates did not, however, graduate from Howard. He failed his British and US literature courses and, after six years of on-and-off study, he left the university in 2000 to pursue a career in journalism.

LIFE'S WORK
Coates subsequently found work at the *Washington City Paper*, then edited by the late David Carr, who went on to become a beloved figure at the *New York Times*. When not writing, Coates took a job with a food delivery service to make ends meet. After leaving the *Washington City Paper*, he bounced from job to job, working for short periods of time at *Philadelphia Weekly*, the *Village Voice*, and *Time* magazine.

As in Washington, Coates took food-delivery jobs to earn extra money. Concurrently, he wrote his memoir, which received admiring reviews when it was published in 2008. That year, he also sold a piece to the *Atlantic*. Rejected by several other periodicals, "This Is How We Lost to the White Man," which examined comedian Bill Cosby's controversial criticism of black men, impressed *Atlantic* editor James Bennet, who then hired Coates as a regular commentator. (Carr, a fan despite his criticism, had introduced the two, and Coates has noted the irony of his benefiting from the networking of two white men.)

Coates was assigned to write short blog posts for the *Atlantic*'s website on hip-hop (which he had grown to love while at Howard), politics, race, and other topics. He started an online book club focused on volumes about the Civil War and instituted a daily "open thread," on which his followers could discuss anything they liked. He quickly earned a reputation as a skilled moderator, introducing participants to new ways of thinking and firmly banning anyone he felt was uncivil.

The *Atlantic* also publishes Coates's longer essays, which have become among the most popular and thought-provoking in the magazine. "The Case for Reparations," Coates's lengthy May 2014 cover story, broke the single-day traffic record on the *Atlantic*'s website and inspired a multitude of pieces in response. Media insiders predict that he will remain on the staff of the *Atlantic* for the foreseeable future, pointing out that

Coates published his second book, *Between the World and Me*, on July 14, 2015. Written in the form of a letter to his teenaged son, the book explores America's history of racial violence and the challenges Coates faced growing up. The release had been scheduled for the fall but was moved up in response to several racially charged incidents that occurred in early 2015, including the shooting of nine African American parishioners at a church in Charleston, South Carolina, by a white supremacist. According to Benjamin Wallace-Wells, writing for *New York* magazine, novelist Toni Morrison praised Coates's work, writing, "I've been wondering who might fill the intellectual void that plagued me after James Baldwin died. Clearly, it is Ta-Nehisi Coates."

Coates has been a visiting professor at the Massachusetts Institute of Technology—a rarity for someone without an advanced degree—and in 2014 he accepted a post as a journalist-in-residence at the City University of New York. Among his laurels are a 2013 National Magazine Award for essays and criticism, a 2014 George Polk Award, and a 2015 Harriet Beecher Stowe Center Prize for Writing for Social Justice.

In 2016, Coates started work on a new run of the *Black Panther* comic book series published by Marvel. Issue #1 went on sale April 6, 2016, and sold an estimated 253,259 physical copies, the best-selling comic for the month of April 2016. The corresponding blockbuster film *Black Panther*, released in 2018 and directed by Ryan Coogler, was heavily inspired by Coates' version of the hero, especially his use of poetic dialogue.

Significance

Coates has quickly been recognized as one of the most important public intellectuals of the times, an era whose conscience is defined in large part by heightened attention to racial discrimination in U.S. society. When the *New York Times* offered Coates a job as a full-time op-ed columnist—one of the most coveted jobs in journalism—he turned down the offer. This shows, perhaps, an insight into Coates' values, his reluctance to become just another establishment voice, even as he is clearly driven by an ambition to write and to be recognized.

Of his purpose in tackling difficult and often contentious topics, he told television reporter Budd Mishkin for NY1 (15 June 2015), "You have to decide how to live morally. People ask me at the end, 'How do you feel? What do you expect to happen [after writing a piece]?' I don't expect anything to happen. I just want to be judged on the side of people who said something. When it is counted up, I don't want to be one of those people who closed my ears."

Mari Rich

Further Reading

Coates, Ta-Nehisi. *The Beautiful Struggle: A Father, Two Sons, and an Unlikely Road to Manhood.* New York: Spiegel, 2008. Print.

---. "A Last Tango with Paris." *Atlantic*. Atlantic Monthly Group, 20 June 2014. Web. 14 Sept. 2015.

---. "Ta-Nehisi Coates' 'Unlikely Road to Manhood.'" Interview by Terry Gross. *Fresh Air*. NPR, 18 Feb. 2009. Web. 14 Sept. 2015.

"Fear of a Black Pundit: Ta-Nehisi Coates Raises His Voice in American Media." *Observer*. Observer Media, 5 Mar. 2013. Web. 14 Sept. 2015.

Ip, Chris. "Ta-Nehisi Coates Defines a New Race Beat." *Columbia Journalism Review*. Columbia Journalism Rev., Nov./Dec. 2014. Web. 14 Sept. 2015.

Mishkin, Budd. "One on 1 Profile: Writer Ta-Nehisi Coates Takes the Next Big Step in His Career." *NY1*. Time Warner Cable Enterprises, 15 June 2015. Web. 14 Sept. 2015.

Roig-Franzia, Manuel. "With *Atlantic* Article on Reparations, Ta-Nehisi Coates Sees Payoff for Years of Struggle." *Washington Post*. Washington Post, 18 June 2014. Web. 14 Sept. 2015. Post, 18 June 2014. Web. 14 Sept. 2015.

Martha P. Cotera

Mexican-born activist, educator, and historian

Born: January 17, 1938; Chihuahua, Mexico
Area of Achievement: Activism, education, scholarship, women's rights

Cotera is an academic who authored groundbreaking studies that defined the pivotal role of women in Chicano political and cultural history in both Mexico and America, She also distinguished herself within Texas's Latino community by her passionate defense of civil rights and her advocacy of expanded educational opportunities for women and minorities.

Early Life

Martha Piña Cotera (MAHR-thah PEE-nah koh-TEHrah) was born Martha Piña in 1938 in Chihuahua, a Mexican state that borders Texas. One of four children, Cotera learned from her grandparents to take pride in her Mexican heritage, especially its politics. Her mother, a strong woman who raised the family, encouraged Cotera in school, where the girl excelled. Indeed, when her family immigrated to El Paso in 1946, Cotera was initially placed in the first grade but quickly tested up to the third grade. Cotera respected the opportunity to obtain an education, and in 1962 she received a B.A. in English, with a minor in history, from Texas Western College (now the University of Texas at El Paso). A year later, she married Juan Estanislao Cotera, who would become an architect, and in 1964 she accepted a position at the Texas State Library in

Martha P. Cotera (Wikimedia Commons)

Austin as both librarian and director of its archive of documents central to Texas history.

From the earliest days of her career, Cotera was committed to bettering educational opportunities for young Hispanics. To this end, in 1964 she helped form a collective of Hispanic teachers and school administrators known as Texans for the Educational Advancement of Mexican Americans. Four years later, she was instrumental in tutoring more than two hundred Hispanic students who boycotted classes in Crystal City, Texas, over discriminatory practices. In 1971, she and her husband moved to Mercedes, Texas, where she helped establish Jacinto Trevino College (later Juarez-Lincoln University), a pilot campus designed solely to prepare Hispanic students as teachers in bilingual curricula. Cotera herself completed her master's degree in education there.

Life's Work

Cotera and her husband became increasingly involved in Chicano activism, joining La Raza Unida, a political party founded in 1970 that aimed to offer Texas's large Hispanic population a viable third-party option. It was during this time that Cotera, while serving as director of the Crystal City Memorial Library, noticed what she would later term the entrenched misogyny of the Chicano Civil Rights movement, and she was moved to organize Muejeres de La Raza Unida (Women of the United Race). Through her activism, Cotera began to investigate the historic role of women in Chicano history.

After moving to Austin in 1974, Cotera worked to establish the first-ever resource bank geared to providing minority women with information about funding for community projects. The next year she accepted a post as a special collections coordinator for the Nettie Lee Benson Latin American Collection at the University of Texas at Austin, one of the nation's largest archives dedicated to a single ethnic group. Her position at the archives allowed her the opportunity to research the role of women in Hispanic culture in both Mexico and the United States. Cotera published dozens of groundbreaking articles and two landmark works: a historic survey of nearly three centuries, *Diosa y Hembra: The History and Heritage of Chicanas in the United States* (1976), and a sampling of her speeches and essays, *The Chicana Feminist* (1977). Her work, grounded in meticulous research into records sometimes centuries old, encouraged a generation of cultural studies programs which reassessed the position of women in a Chicano culture that had long been regarded as patriarchal.

> "*Racism, classism, and sexism will disappear when we accept differences and if we continue to resist loudly and clearly all racist, classist and sexist efforts on the part of other persons to enslave us.*"

In addition to her scholarly work and political activism, Cotera during two decades spearheaded pioneering causes within the Austin Latino community, organizing funding for arts programs, starting committees aimed at encouraging minority professional women, launching citywide education projects, helping fund programs for battered women and rape victims, and, most notably, establishing a first-of-its-kind database company, Information Systems Development, that focused on providing critical business information for entrepreneurs.

In addition, she became a much-sought after speaker at state and national conferences promoting women's rights and minority opportunities. Although she declined to pursue political office herself, her public advocacy of fair housing, improved public transportation, and a wider embrace of cultural diversity in public education curricula, as well as her tireless efforts on behalf of candidates sympathetic to minority rights, made her a fixture in Austin city politics.

In 1997, her twenty-five-year-old son was brutally murdered after a carjacking; he and another man were locked in the trunk of a car by two armed teenagers and subsequently drowned when the teens rolled the car into Town Lake, a reservoir in downtown Austin. Both Cotera and her husband, however, publicly advocated imprisonment rather than capital punishment for the convicted teens.

After leaving her position as archivist and bibliographer for the Benson Collection in 2009, Cotera continued to work for women and minority representation in Austin city politics. In the wake of growing concerns over long-term environmental damage to Texas and its resource-based economy, Cotera, while in her sixties, worked to help minority students who were interested in environmental studies pursue green-based career opportunities. In 2010, she was recognized with a lifetime achievement award by the Veteran Feminists of America. Through the efforts of the Latino/a Studies Program and the Fronteras Norteñas organization, "El Museo del Norte" museum project was able to receive funds from the University of Michigan Arts and Citizenship Program. Cotera, and other spear headers for the museum, are currently set on developing a "museum without walls," that can be made available to all community members in hopes to demonstrate the folk art that shows the Latino presence that has always been in the state.

Cotera's daughter, Maria Cotera, worked with her mother on the creation of a new online resource for Chicana feminism and literature, *Chicana por mi Raza*, through the University of Michigan. Martha Cotera, as a pioneer in Chicana activism, was the first person interviewed for the project.

Significance

Although her scholarly work in Chicana studies was trailblazing, Martha P. Cotera, in a long and distinguished career of activism and public advocacy of social justice issues, embodied the spirit of politics made local. Within the Austin community, she used her position in numerous advocacy groups and social agencies to encourage cultural development in order to better represent the Chicano arts, increase educational opportunities for minority children (particularly at-risk adolescents), and, perhaps most important, expand business opportunities for women and minority entrepreneurs.

Joseph Dewey, updated by Micah L. Issitt

Further Reading

Garcia, Alma M. *Chicana Feminist Thought: The Basic Historic Writings*. New York: Routledge, 1997. Brings together the key writings of feminists critical to the Chicano rights movement in the 1960's and 1970's, including Cotera.

Garcia, Juan, ed. *Mexican American Women, Changing Image*. Vol. 5 in Perspectives in Mexican American Studies. Tucson: University of Arizona Press, 1996. Wide-ranging collection of scholarly essays that address the role of women in Mexican American culture. Includes an essay by Cotera.

Torres, Eden A. *Chicana Without Apology: The New Chicana Cultural Studies*. New York: Routledge, 2003. A sweeping vision of the role of women in Chicano culture, representing the generation grounded in Cotera's scholarly work.

Emily Dickinson

Poet

Born: December 10, 1830; Amherst, Massachusetts
Died: May 15, 1886; Amherst, Massachusetts
Area of achievement: Literature

The greatest American woman poet of the nineteenth century, Dickinson lived an unusually reclusive life but led an inner life of intense, imaginative creativity that made her one of the greatest American poets.

Early Life

The sparse facts of Emily Elizabeth Dickinson's external life after her birth can be summarized in a few sentences: She spent her entire life in her family home, and died in it at the age of fifty-five. She was graduated from Amherst Academy in 1847, then attended nearby Mount Holyoke Female Seminary for one year. She traveled occasionally to Springfield and twice to Boston. In 1854, she and her family visited Washington and Philadelphia. She never married and had no romantic relationships. However, her interior life was so intense that a distinguished twentieth century poet and critic, Allen Tate, could write, "All pity for Miss Dickinson's 'starved life' is misdirected. Her life was one of the richest and deepest ever lived on this continent." It is a life that has proved a perplexing puzzle to many critics and biographers.

What led to Dickinson's monastic seclusion from society? Was it forced on her by a possessive, despotic father? Was it self-willed by her timid temperament, by rejected love, or by her neurotic need for utmost privacy while she pursued the muse of poetry? Speculation abounds, certainty eludes; nothing is simple and direct about her behavior. Perhaps the opening lines of her poem number 1129 are self-revealing:

> Tell all the Truth but tell it slant—
> Success in Circuit lies
> Too bright for our infirm Delight
> The Truth's superb surprise

At the time when Dickinson was born, Amherst was a farming village of four to five hundred families, with a cultural tradition of Puritanism and a devotion to education as well as devoutness. The Dickinsons were prominent in public and collegiate activities. Samuel Fowler Dickinson, Emily's grandfather, founded Amherst College in 1821 to train preachers, teachers, and missionaries. Edward Dickinson (1813-1874), Emily's father, was the eldest of nine children. He became a successful attorney and, at the age of thirty-two, was named treasurer of Amherst College, a position he kept for thirty-eight years. He served three terms in the Massachusetts legislature and one term as a member of Congress. Even political opponents respected him as forthright, courageous, diligent, solemn, intelligent, and reliable; he was the incarnation of responsibility and rectitude. In a letter to her brother, Dickinson mocked him (and her mother): "Father and Mother sit in state in the sitting room perusing such papers, only, as they are well assured, have nothing carnal in them."

> "*If I can stop one heart from breaking, I shall not live in vain.*"

Emily's mother, Emily Norcross (1804-1882), was born in Monson, Massachusetts, twenty miles south of Amherst. Her father was a well-to-do farmer who sent his daughter to a reputable boarding school, where she behaved conventionally, preparing herself for the respectable, rational marriage that ensued after Edward Dickinson had courted her politely and passionlessly. The

Emily Dickinson (Wikimedia Commons)

mother has received adverse treatment from most of Dickinson's biographers because of several statements the daughter wrote to her confidant, Colonel Thomas Wentworth Higginson (1823-1911):

> My Mother does not care for thought.
> I never had a mother. I suppose a mother is one to whom you hurry when you are troubled.
> I always ran Home to Awe when a child, if anything befell me. He was an awful Mother, but I liked him better than none.

Richard Sewall indicates in his magisterial two volume *The Life of Emily Dickinson* (1974) that Emily's acerbic remarks should not be taken at their surface meaning in the light of the poet's continued preference for remaining in the familial home. To be sure, Dickinson's mother read meagerly and had a mediocre mind, but she was a tenderhearted, loving person who committed herself wholly to her family and to the household's management. While she never understood her daughter's complex nature, she also never intruded on Dickinson's inner life.

Dickinson's brother Austin (1829-1895) was closest to her in disposition. Personable, sensitive, empathic, and

> ### Dickinson's "Letter to the World"
>
> This is my letter to the world,
> That never wrote to me, —
> The simple news that Nature told,
> With tender majesty.
> Her message is committed
> To hands I cannot see;
> For love of her, sweet countrymen,
> Judge tenderly of me!
>
> Source: Emily Dickinson, *Poems*, edited by Mabel Loomis Todd and T. W. Higginson (Boston, 1890).

sociable, he became an attorney, joined his father's practice, and succeeded him as Amherst's treasurer in 1873. He shared his sister's wit, taste in books, and love of nature; his vitality was a tonic for her. He married one of her schoolmates, Susan Gilbert, vivacious, worldly, and articulate.

Dickinson and her sister-in-law, living next door to each other, were in each other's homes frequently during the first years of this marriage. Dickinson had a near-obsessive concern for her immediate family and greatly desired to make of her sister-in-law a true sister in spirit. She sent Sue nearly three hundred of her poems over the years—more than to anyone else. However, a satisfyingly soulful friendship never quite materialized. To be sure, Sue's parties did keep Dickinson in at least limited circulation in her early twenties. The two women exchanged books and letters, with Dickinson occasionally seeking Sue's criticism of her poems. Dickinson, always fond of children, was particularly delighted with her nephew Gilbert; tragically, he died of typhoid fever at the age of eight; Dickinson's letter of condolence called him "Dawn and Meridian in one."

The two women's paths ineluctably diverged. Sue had a husband and, eventually, three children and was an extroverted social climber. For unknown reasons, Dickinson and Sue quarreled in 1854, and Dickinson wrote her the only dismissive letter in her correspondence: "You can go or stay." They resumed their friendship, but it proved turbulent, as did Sue's and Austin's marriage. In 1866, Sue betrayed Emily's confidence by sending her poem "A Narrow Fellow in the Grass" to the Springfield Republican, which mutilated it by changing its punctuation. "It was robbed of me," Dickinson bitterly complained.

With her natural sister Lavinia (1833-1899), Dickinson bonded intimately all her life. Like her older sister, Lavinia remained a spinster, remained at home, and outlived her family. Dickinson and Lavinia were devotedly protective of each other. The younger sister was relatively uncomplicated, steady in temperament, pretty, and outgoing. Their only quasi-serious difference centered on Vinnie's love of cats, contrasted to Dickinson's care for birds. It was Lavinia who organized the first large-scale publication of Dickinson's poems after her death.

Outside her family circle, Dickinson had only a few friends, but they mattered greatly to her—she called them her "estate" and cultivated them intensely. While still in her teens, she established a pattern that was to recur throughout her life: She sought to attach herself to an older man who would be her confidant and mentor or, to use her terms, "preceptor" or "master." These pilots would, she hoped, teach her something of the qualities that she knew she lacked: knowledge of the outer world, firm opinions and principles, sociability, and intellectual stability.

Dickinson's first candidate was Benjamin Newton (1821-1853), only nine years her senior, who was a law student in her father's office from 1847 to 1849. He served her in the roles of intellectual companion, guide in aesthetic and spiritual spheres, and older brother. He introduced her to Ralph Waldo Emerson's poetry, encouraged her to write her own, but died of consumption in his thirty-third year, before she became a serious poet. Her letters to him are not extant, but in a letter she wrote Higginson in 1862, she probably refers to Newton when she mentions a "friend who taught me Immortality—but venturing too near, himself—he never returned—."

Dickinson's first mature friendship was with Samuel Bowles (1834-1878), who inherited his father's Springfield Republican and made it one of the most admired newspapers in the United States. Bowles had a penetrating mind, warmth, wit, dynamic energy, strongly liberal convictions, and an engaging, vibrant personality. Extensively seasoned by travel, he knew virtually every important public leader and was a marvelous guest and companion. He, and sometimes his wife with him, became regular visitors in both Edward and Austin Dickinson's homes from 1858 onward.

Thirty-five of Dickinson's letters to Bowles survive, and they show her deep attachment to—perhaps even love for—him, even though she knew that he was out of her reach in every way—just as her poetry was out of his, because his taste in literature was wholly conventional. In April, 1862, Bowles left for a long European stay. Shortly thereafter, Emily wrote him, "I have the errand from my heart—I might forget to tell it. Would you please come

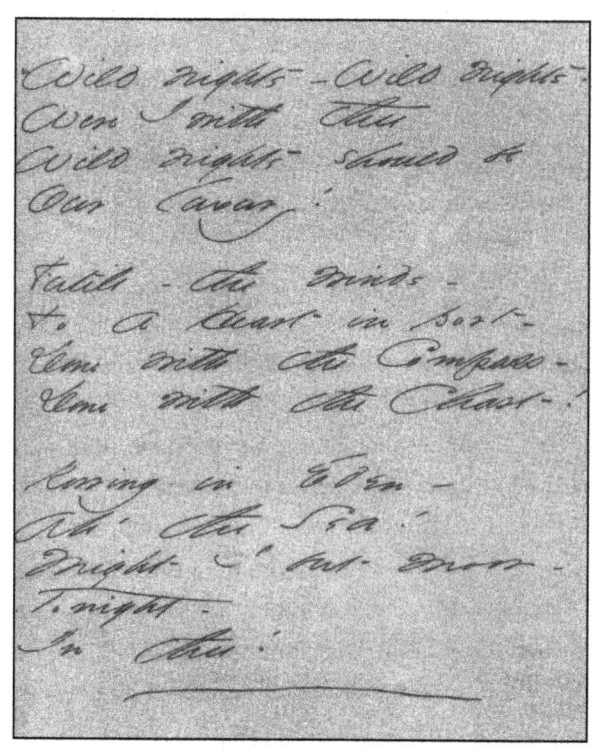

Handwritten manuscript for "Wild Nights," showing Dickinson's distinct style. (Wikimedia Commons)

home?" Then, in a second letter, "[I] t is a suffering to have a sea. . . between your soul and you." That November, the returned Bowles called at Amherst. Dickinson chose to remain in her room, sending him a note instead of encountering him.

LIFE'S WORK

The turning point in Dickinson's career as a poet, and hence in her life, came in her late twenties. Before 1858, her writing consisted of letters and desultory, sentimental verses; thereafter, particularly from 1858 to 1863, poetry became her primary activity. As far as scholars can ascertain, she wrote one hundred in 1859, sixty-five in 1860, at least eighty in 1861, and in 1862—her annus mirabilis—perhaps as many as 366, of a prosodic skill far superior to her previous achievement. What caused such a flood of creativity? Most—but not all—biographers attribute it to her unfulfilled love for the Reverend Mr. Charles Wadsworth (1814-1882).

Dickinson and Lavinia visited their father in Washington, D.C., during April, 1854, when he was serving his congressional term. On their return trip, they stopped over in Philadelphia as guests of a friend from school days and heard Wadsworth preach in the Arch Street Presbyterian Church, whose pastor he was from 1850 to April, 1862. Married and middle-aged, of rocklike rectitude, shy and reserved, Wadsworth nevertheless made an indelible impression as a "Man of sorrow" on Dickinson. He was generally regarded as second only to Henry Ward Beecher among the pulpit orators of his time. A contemporary newspaper profile described him in these terms: His person is slender, and his dark eyes, hair and complexion have decidedly a Jewish cast. The elements of his popularity are somewhat like those of the gifted Summerfield—a sweet touching voice, warmth of manner, and lively imagination. But Wadsworth's style, it is said, is vastly bolder, his fancy more vivid, and his action more violent.

It is presumed that Dickinson must have talked with Wadsworth during her Philadelphia visit. Few other facts are known: He called on her in Amherst in the spring of 1860, and again in the summer of 1880. She requested his and his children's pictures from his closest friend. In April, 1862, Wadsworth moved to San Francisco, becoming minister to the Calvary Presbyterian Society. Dickinson found this departure traumatic: She used "Calvary" ten times in poems of 1862 and 1863; she spoke of herself as "Empress of Calvary," and began one 1863 poem with the words, "Where Thou art—that is Home/ Cashmere or Calvary—the Same. . . / So I may come." With probable reference to her inner "Calvary" drama of loss and renunciation, she began at this time to dress entirely in white. By 1870, and until his death, Wadsworth was back in Philadelphia in another pastorate, but the anguished crisis he had caused her had ended by then.

After Dickinson's death, three long love letters were found in draft form among her papers, in her handwriting of the late 1850's and early 1860's. They address a "Master," and have therefore come to be called the "Master Letters." Their tone is urgent, their style, nervous and staccato. In the second of them, "Daisy" tells her "Master": "I want to see you more—Sir—than all I wish for in this world—and the wish—altered a little—will be my only one—for the skies." She invites him to come to Amherst and pledges not to disappoint him. However, the final letter shows the agony of a rejected lover, amounting to an almost incoherent cry of despair. For whom were these letters intended? Thomas Johnson and most other biographers designate Wadsworth. Richard Sewall, however, argues for Bowles, on the internal evidence that some of the images in the unsent letters parallel images in poems that Dickinson did send Bowles.

In 1861, Dickinson composed the most openly erotic of her poems, number 249, with the sea the element in which the speaker moors herself:

> Wild Nights—Wild Nights!
> Were I with thee
> Wild Nights should be
> Our luxury!
> Futile—the Winds—
> To a Heart in port—
> Done with the Compass—
> Done with the Chart!
> Rowing in Eden—
> Ah, the Sea!
> Might I but moor—Tonight
> —In Thee!

Is this poem derived from autobiographical experience— or, at least, intense longing for such experience— or is the first-person perspective no more than that of the poem's persona or speaker? Again, Dickinsonians divide on this question.

On April 15, 1862, having liked an article by Thomas Wentworth Higginson, Dickinson sent him four of her poems and a diffident note, asking him if he thought her verses were "alive" and "breathed." Trained as a minister, Higginson had held a Unitarian pulpit in Newburyport, Massachusetts, then resigned it to devote himself to social reforms, chief of which was abolitionism. He had made a reputation as a representative, influential mid-century literary critic, with particular interest in the work of female writers. The four poems Dickinson mailed him were among her best to date; in his evaluative replies, however, he showed an obtuse misunderstanding of them, as well as of her subsequent submissions, which were to total one hundred.

Dickinson undoubtedly felt a strong need for another "preceptor"—Wadsworth had just departed for San Francisco—and especially for a literary rather than romantic confidant. Higginson was to prove her "safest friend" for the remainder of her life. A warm, courteous, sympathetic man, he regarded her with mystified admiration. After their correspondence had been under way for several months, he asked her to send him a photograph. Her response was, "I had no portrait, now, but am small, like the Wren, and my Hair is bold, like the Chestnut Bur, and my eyes, like the Sherry in the Glass, that the Guest leaves." After Higginson had met her eight years later, he confirmed this self-portrait and added to it that Dickinson was a "plain, shy little person, the face without a single good feature."

Dickinson's poetry, unfortunately for both of them, was simply beyond Higginson's grasp. He immediately and consistently advised her not to seek its publication because it was "not strong enough." His critical judgments were invariably fatuous, showing deaf ears and blind eyes to her original language, syntax, meter, and rhyme. She resigned herself to his recommendation against publication but gently yet firmly ignored his strictures concerning her poems' construction. Thomas Johnson summarizes the relationship as "one of the most eventful, and at the same time elusive and insubstantial friendships in the annals of American literature."

During the late 1870's, nearing her fiftieth year, Dickinson fell in love with Otis Phillips Lord (1812-1884). He was a distinguished lawyer who, from 1875 to 1882, served as an associate justice of the Massachusetts Supreme Court. He answered Dickinson's constant need for a settled, senior friend-tutor, intellectually gifted and personally impressive; he became her last "preceptor." She had first known Judge Lord when he had called on Edward Dickinson; like her father, he was vigorous, conscientious, commanding, and highly disciplined. Their affection developed after December, 1877, when Lord's wife died. Fifteen of her letters to him survive and indicate that, over the objection of his nieces, Lord apparently offered to marry her. With her father and Bowles now dead and her mother an invalid requiring many hours of her time each week, Dickinson found considerable solace in their correspondence. However, she also knew that her reclusive life was too rigidly established for her to adapt to the major changes that marriage would require of her.

On April 1, 1882, Wadsworth, the man she had called "my closest earthly friend," died. On May 1 of that year, Lord suffered a stroke; on May 14, Dickinson wrote him a fervent letter of joy at his (temporary) recovery, assuring him of her "rapture" at his reprieve from impending death; on October 5 came news of her beloved nephew Gilbert's death; on November 14, her mother finally died, after years of serious illness. It is not surprising that Dickinson then underwent a "nervous prostration" that impaired her faculties for many weeks.

After an 1864 visit to Boston for eye treatment, Dickinson did not leave Amherst for the remainder of her life. Her withdrawal from society became gradually more marked. By 1870, she did not venture beyond her house and garden, preferring to socialize by sending brief letters, some of them accompanied by poems, flowers, or fruit. She retreated upstairs when most visitors came to call, sometimes lurking on an upper landing or around corners. While strangers regarded her eccentricities as unnatural, her friends and family accepted them as the price of her retreat into the intensity of her poetry. Perhaps her most self-revealing poem is number 303, whose first stanza declares

> The Soul selects her own Society—
> Then—shuts the Door—
> To her divine Majority—
> Present no more—

Emily Dickinson died of nephritis on May 15, 1886.

Significance

Emily Dickinson's nearly eighteen hundred poems, only seven of which saw print during her lifetime, constitute her "Letter to the World" (number 441), her real life. They establish her, along with Walt Whitman, as one of this nation's two most seminal poets. Her sharp intellectual wit, her playfulness, and her love of ambiguity, paradox, and irony liken her poetry to the seventeenth century metaphysical achievements of England's John Donne and George Herbert and New England's Edward Taylor. However, her language and rhythm are often uniquely individual, with a tumultuous rhetoric that sharply probes homely details for universal essence. She is a writer who defies boundaries and labels, standing alone as a contemporary not only of Herman Melville and Nathaniel Hawthorne but also, in the poetic sense, of T. S. Eliot, W. H. Auden, Robert Frost, Robert Lowell, and Sylvia Plath. Her work ranks with the most original in poetic history.

Gerhard Brand

Further Reading

Dickinson, Emily. *The Complete Poems of Emily Dickinson*. Edited by Thomas H. Johnson. Boston: Little, Brown, 1960. The text of the three-volume edition with the variant readings omitted.

---. *The Letters of Emily Dickinson*. Edited by Thomas H. Johnson and Theodora Ward. 3 vols. Cambridge, Mass.: Harvard University Press, 1958. The definitive editions of Dickinson's poetry and letters. They have been arranged in the most accurate chronological order possible and numbered.

---. *The Poems of Emily Dickinson*. Edited by Thomas H. Johnson. 3 vols. Cambridge, Mass.: Harvard University Press, 1955. "Including variant readings critically compared with all known manuscripts."

Habegger, Alfred. *My Wars Are Laid Away in Books: The Life of Emily Dickinson*. New York: Random House, 2001. Acclaimed literary biography. Habegger agrees with feminist critics who rejected the traditional portrayal of Dickinson as a quaint homebody; he depicts the poet as a powerful personality who transcended the strictures of her father and Victorian society. Includes analyses of Dickinson's poetry.

Kirk, Connie Ann. *Emily Dickinson: A Biography*. Westport, Conn.: Greenwood Press, 2004. Using her own primary research, Kirk paints a picture of Dickinson as a complex and busy woman who influenced American life and culture. Includes a bibliography and chronology.

Sewall, Richard B. *The Life of Emily Dickinson*. 2 vols. New York: Farrar, Straus and Giroux, 1974. By far the most comprehensive Dickinson interpretive biography. Sewall devotes his first volume to Dickinson's family, his second to her friends, and intertwines her life with both circles with great tact, sympathetic understanding, and impressive learning. The prose is clear and often eloquent. One of the most admirable modern literary biographies.

_____, ed. *Emily Dickinson: A Collection of Critical Essays*. Englewood Cliffs, N.J.: Prentice-Hall, 1963. A rich and diverse collection of critical essays, displaying an almost bewildering range of interpretive views. Such important critics and scholars as Charles Anderson, R. P. Blackmur, John Crowe Ransom, Allen Tate, and George Whicher are represented.

Henry Louis Gates, Jr.

American literary critic and scholar

Born: September 16, 1950; Keyser, West Virginia
Area of Achievement: Literature; civil rights; social issues; film and television

Gates is an influential African American literary critic, teacher, historian, filmmaker and public intellectual who is also widely known for his appearances on PBS.

Early Life

Henry Louis Gates, Jr., was born in a small West Virginia town to Henry Louis and Pauline Augusta Gates. As a child, Gates read voraciously, carefully recording his ideas in a commonplace book. When he was fifteen years

Henry Louis Gates, Jr. (Wikimedia Commons)

old, an Episcopalian priest gave him a copy of James Baldwin's *Notes of a Native Son* (1955), which catalyzed his interest in African American literature. Gates has recalled that reading this book "fueled a love of literature like nothing [he] had ever experienced before," and that he began concentrating on works by black authors.

Gates was admitted to Yale University, where in 1973 he earned his B.A. degree with high honors. Charles Davis, Gates's mentor at Yale, encouraged his study of African American literature. Gates paid tribute to his mentor with the 1982 publication of *Black Is the Color of the Cosmos*, a collection of essays by Davis and by others commemorating Davis's work. During his time at Yale, Gates received fellowship funds that enabled him to travel extensively in Africa.

Gates was awarded grants for graduate study from the Ford and Mellon foundations and entered Clare College of Cambridge University, the first black graduate student to study English there. The Nigerian poet and playwright Wole Soyinka, then a visiting professor at Cambridge, became Gates's tutor. This association was critical to the direction of Gates's thought, for Soyinka introduced him to the culture of the West African ethnic group the Yoruba, whose mythology and language patterns Gates later used in the development of his critical approach. Gates earned his M.A. from Cambridge in 1974 and his Ph.D. in 1979. He was thereupon appointed director for the African American Studies Program at Yale and assistant professor of English.

Life's Work

In his introduction to the 1983 edition of Harriet E. Wilson's *Our Nig: Or, Sketches from the Life of a Free Black*, Gates established himself as an authority on early texts by African Americans. Also in 1983, Gates published his theories on the connections between the mythology and language of the Yoruba and African and African American writings in the essay "On 'The Blackness of Blackness': A Critique of the Sign and the Signifying Monkey." This seminal essay was later expanded and published in *The Signifying Monkey: A Theory of Afro-American Literary Criticism*.

At the time Gates began his work, scholars of African American literature were focusing almost exclusively on content and on individual works as a reflection of "the black experience." Gates argued that the literature should also be examined textually for its use of language. He identified language patterns common in the works of black writers, but uncommon in works of other writers.

Central in Gates's theory is the concept of signification, which he identified as a master trope (a language pattern involving word play and an unexpected turn in the idea) in African and African American writing. Heavily influenced by deconstruction, Gates's signification includes patterns from both classical rhetoric and black vernacular, and it uses metaphor, irony, understatement, and exaggeration as well as loud-talking, specifying, testifying, and rapping. Signification presents infinite options in variations of words, phrasing, and meaning. It can tease, refuse to come to the point, use innuendo, or lie to create interest or stir up trouble.

The signifying monkey, which personifies signification in Gates's theory, is closely related to versions of Esu, the trickster god in Yoruba mythology. He is the god of interpretation and the center of circles of all possible meanings incorporated in a word or phrase. Gates has emphasized that *signifying* covers "a range of meanings and events which are not covered in . . . standard English usage."

With his insistence that works by black authors should be examined linguistically as well as for their content, Henry Louis Gates, Jr., opened a new range of perspectives on the literature. In addition to his books on critical

Asako Gladsjo, Jahmilla Wignot, Phil Bertelsen, Sabin Streeter, and Gates Jr. accept the Peabody Award for: "The African Americans: Many Rivers to Cross". (Wikimedia Commons)

theory and his editions of works of African and African American writers, Gates has contributed numerous articles to many scholarly journals.

> "*Patriotism is best exemplified through auto-critique. When you're willing to stand up within the group and say, 'It is wrong for Black people to be anti-Semitic,' or 'It is wrong for America to discriminate against persons of African descent and made them slaves and based its wealth upon free labor,' it's crucial to say that."*

On July 16, 2009, Gates returned home from a trip to China to find the door to his house jammed. His driver attempted to help him gain entrance. A passerby called police reporting a possible break-in after reporting to 911 "an individual" forcing the front door open. A Cambridge police officer was dispatched. The confrontation resulted in Gates being arrested and charged with disorderly conduct. Prosecutors later dropped the charges. The incident spurred a politically charged exchange of views about race relations and law enforcement throughout the United States. The arrest attracted national attention after U.S. President Barack Obama declared that the Cambridge police "acted stupidly" in arresting the 59-year-old Gates. Obama eventually extended an invitation to both Gates and the officer involved to share a beer with him at the White House. On March 9, 2010, Gates claimed on The Oprah Winfrey Show that he, Sgt. James Crowley, the arresting officer in the Cambridge incident, and Jonathan Johnson (Deputy Comptroller) all share a common ancestor - an ancient Irish king, Niall of the Nine Hostages.

In the twenty-first century, Gates has had a notable television career on PBS. He was the host and coproducer of *African American Lives* (2006) and *African American Lives 2* (2008). In these programs, the genealogy of prominent African Americans was explored, and the episodes featured Gates discussing the findings with his guests. Gates also hosted *Faces of America* in 2010, which extended the concept to all sorts of Americans. Beginning in 2012 Gates has hosted the PBS series *Finding Your Roots – with Henry Louis Gates, Jr.* In 2013, Gates wrote and hosted the six-part PBS series, *The African Americans: Many Rivers to Cross*, which won the 2013 Peabody Award and NAACP Image Award.

Significance

Henry Louis Gates, Jr. is a literary critic and scholar known for his important and pioneering theories about both African and African American literature. Gates's exposition of African American signification or "signifyin'" was a timely and much-praised idea in literary studies. His work for PBS in the twenty-first century has been extensive, high quality, and very popular with audiences.

Anne B. Mangum

Further Reading

Adell, Sandra. "A Function at the Junction." *Diacritics: A Review of Contemporary Criticism* 20 (Winter, 1990). Compares Gates's approach to African American literature with that of Houston Baker.

Branam, Harold. "Henry Louis Gates, Jr." In *Encyclopedia of Literary Critics and Criticism*, edited by Chris Murray. Chicago: Fitzroy Dearborn, 1999. A helpful entry on Gates that analyzes his life and career.

Bucknell, Brad. "Henry Louis Gates, Jr., and the Theory of 'Signifyin(g).'" *Ariel: A Review of International*

English Literature 21 (January, 1990). Presents a thorough analysis and discussion of Gates's ideas. Also discusses Gates's critical position in relation to the positions of other scholars who disagree with his theories.

Gates, Henry Louis, Jr. "An Interview with Henry Louis Gates, Jr." Interview by Charles H. Rowell. *Callaloo: A Journal of African American and African Arts and Letters* 14, no. 2 (Spring, 1991). Presents interesting and enlightening reflections by Gates on his ideas and his experiences.

---. "Interview with Henry Louis Gates, Jr." Interview by Jerry W. Ward, Jr. *New Literary History: A Journal of Theory and Interpretation* 22 (Autumn, 1991). Presents interesting and enlightening reflections by Gates on his ideas and his experiences.

Olney, James. "Henry Louis Gates, Jr." In *Modern American Critics Since 1955*, edited by Gregory S. Jay. Vol. 67 in *Dictionary of Literary Biography*. Detroit: Gale Group, 1988. An examination of his life and work.

bell hooks

Writer, educator, and activist

Born: September 25, 1952
Also known as: Gloria Jean Watkins; Hopkinsville, Kentucky
Area of Achievement: Education, literature, women's rights

A popular lecturer and prolific writer, hooks brought women of color into the feminist movement. Despite her academic pedigree, she writes books aimed at general audiences in hopes of effecting change in the real world.

EARLY LIFE

bell hooks was born Gloria Jean Watkins in Hopkinsville, Kentucky, to Veodis and Rosa Bell Watkins. Her father worked for the U.S. Post Office and her mother was a domestic worker. hooks grew up with five sisters and one brother. An avid reader, she was very fond of poetry and sought to become a writer. hooks received her early education in segregated schools. With the aid of scholarships, she attended Stanford University, where she studied with the feminist Tillie Olsen. At Stanford, she noticed the lack of attention to race in the feminist movement. She graduated in 1973.

In 1976, hooks earned a master's degree from the University of Wisconsin. Her first published book was a small collection of poems, *And There We Wept* (1978). She published it under the pseudonym bell hooks, the name of her maternal great grandmother, a woman known for her defiance. hooks admired this trait and adopted the name as a tribute to her ancestor. In 1981, hooks published *Ain't I a Woman: Black Women and Feminism,* a book of theory begun while she was still an undergraduate. The title is taken from a classic speech by the abolitionist Sojourner Truth. In 1983, hooks earned a doctorate from the University of California at Santa Cruz, with a dissertation on Toni Morrison.

LIFE'S WORK

Shortly after earning her doctorate, hooks published a second work of theory, *Feminist Theory: From Margin to Center* (1984). She began her first full-time teaching position, as assistant professor of Afro-American studies and English at Yale University, in 1985. In 1988, she moved to Oberlin College in Ohio, serving as associate professor of women's studies and American literature. Her third book of theory, *Talking Back: Thinking Feminist, Thinking Black,* appeared in 1989. In 1994, she was named a

bell hooks (Wikimedia Commons)

distinguished professor of English at City College of the City University of New York, where she enjoyed working with diverse students. She returned to Kentucky in 2004, accepting a position as distinguished professor in residence of Appalachian studies at Berea College. Influenced by the work of Brazilian educator Paulo Freire, hooks published her first work on education, *Teaching to Transgress: Education as the Practice of Freedom*, in 1994. This work was followed by two companion books: *Teaching Community: A Pedagogy of Hope* (2003) and *Teaching Critical Thinking: Practical Wisdom* (2009).

> "*Open, honest, truth-telling individuals value privacy. We all need spaces where we can be alone with thoughts and feelings - where we can experience healthy psychological autonomy and can choose to share when we want to.*"

A practicing Buddhist, hooks turned to spiritual concerns and the concept of love in *All About Love: New Visions* (2000), *Salvation: Black People and Love*, and *Communion: The Female Search for Love*. hooks also has published a number of children's books: *Happy to Be Nappy* (1999), *Homemade Love* (2001), *Be Boy Buzz* (2002), *Skin Again* (2004), and *Grump Groan Growl* (2008). Although most of hooks's works contain autobiographical elements, she also has published full autobiographical works: *Bone Black: Memories of Girlhood* (1997), *Wounds of Passion: A Writing Life* (1997), and *Remembered Rapture: The Writer at Work* (1999). In 2012, hooks published *Appalachian Elegy: Poetry and Place*, a series of poems about life in the wilderness. Her latest book, *Writing Beyond Race: Living Theory and Practice*, hooks discusses a path for America's evolution towards bridging racial and cultural gaps.

In addition to writing and teaching, hooks is a popular speaker who prefers question-and-answer sessions in which she can interact with her audience. Although rooted in academia, her books are written for a broad audience and are distinguished by a lack of footnotes, frequent autobiographical references, and a personable, intimate voice. In 2014, hooks founded the bell hooks Institute, in Berea, Kentucky, an unusual gallery space and learning center where hooks displays artifacts and images used in her work, displays artworks from her personal collection, and hosts intellectual discussions with academics and members of the local community.

Hooks's influence has been recognized by several publications. Utne Reader included her in its list of "One Hundred Visionaries Who Could Change Your Life." *The Atlantic Monthly* named her one of our nation's leading public intellectuals. *Publishers Weekly* called *Ain't I a Woman: Black Women and Feminism* "one of the twenty most influential women's books in the last twenty years."

SIGNIFICANCE

With *Ain't I a Woman: Black Women and Feminism*, hooks filled a gap that she identified while an undergraduate at Stanford: the exclusion of black women from the feminist movement. Much of her work also focuses on the significance of literacy, especially for women of color. As an activist interested in effecting change, hooks mainly writes for a general audience rather than for fellow academics. Although much of her early work dealt with matters of race and gender, she went on to explore liberation from all forms of domination, especially in the classroom.

Nettie Farris, updated by Micah L. Issitt

FURTHER READING

Bauer, Michelle. "Implementing a Liberatory Feminist Pedagogy: bell hooks's Strategies for Transforming the Classroom." *Melus* 25, nos. 3/4 (Fall/Winter, 2000): 265-274. Highly readable overview of hooks's teaching philosophy and how she was influenced by Paulo Freire.

Davidson, Maria del Guadalupe, and George Yancy, eds. *Critical Perspectives on bell hooks.* New York: Routledge, 2009. Collection of critical essays on the work of hooks. Includes an introduction by the editors.

hooks, bell. *Remembered Rapture: The Writer at Work.* New York: Henry Holt, 1999. Eclectic collection of autobiographical essays on writing, written over a period of twenty years.

Olson, Gary A., and Elizabeth Hirsh, eds. "Feminist Praxis and the Politics of Literacy: A Conversation with bell hooks." In *Women Writing Culture.* Albany: State University of New York Press, 1995. Lengthy interview with hooks on the significance of literacy in the feminist movement.

ZORA NEALE HURSTON

Writer and anthropologist

Hurston was the most prolific black woman writer of her time and an important figure of the Harlem Renaissance. Both as a novelist and as an anthropologist, Hurston broke new ground with her descriptions of the richly complex black cultural heritage of the United States and Caribbean basin.

Born: January 7, 1891; Nostaluga, Alabama
Died: January 28, 1960; Fort Pierce, Florida
Area of Achievement: Literature, social sciences

EARLY LIFE

Zora Neale Hurston was born in Notasulga, Alabama to Lucy Ann Potts, a former schoolteacher, and John Hurston, a carpenter and Baptist preacher. Hurston spent her early years in Eatonville, Florida. This small town was the first all-black community to be incorporated in the United States. Her father, the son of former slaves, served several terms as the town's mayor. Hurston grew up in an environment free from the racial tensions that dominated life in the South, which gave her a great deal of self-confidence. The richness of the southern black culture that surrounded her inspired much of her later work.

Hurston was an imaginative and curious child. The fifth of eight children and her mother's favorite, she was deeply affected by the death of her mother in 1904. Her relationship with her father, who attempted to curb her lively spirit, deteriorated after he remarried as she clashed violently with her stepmother. Hurston left Eatonville at the age of fourteen and began to work as a maid, but as she refused to humble herself, she did not remain long in any position. She traveled around the South as a wardrobe girl with a Gilbert and Sullivan repertory company. After leaving the company, she continued her education and completed high school at Morgan Academy in Baltimore while supporting herself as a live-in maid.

After graduating in 1918, Hurston moved to Washington, D.C., where she enrolled part-time at Howard University. She was encouraged in her writing by her teachers, who included the poet Georgia Douglas Johnson and the philosopher Alain Locke. One of her stories was printed in the magazine of the literary club at the university. In January, 1925, with the encouragement of sociologist Charles S. Johnson, who published her stories in *Opportunity: Journal of Negro Life*, Hurston moved to New York City. It was an exciting time because black writers and artists were flocking to the city to be part of the Harlem Renaissance, the black literary and cultural movement of the time. Hurston's intelligence, charm, and wit ensured her popularity. Her early stories, which prefigured her later work, featured the rural African American dialect of central Florida and its rich folklore. For Locke, Hurston's southern background provided the connection to the black folk heritage that he considered essential for the literature of the movement. Locke published one of her stories in *The New Negro* (1925) and Hurston also won second prize in a literary contest sponsored by *Opportunity: Journal of Negro Life*.

Zora Neale Hurston (Library of Congress)

> "*It would be against all nature for all the Negroes to be either at the bottom, top, or in between. We will go where the internal drive carries us like everybody else. It is up to the individual.*"

In September, 1925, Hurston began studying at Barnard College on a scholarship. She earned a bachelor's degree in 1928. While at the university, she came to the attention of the noted anthropologist Franz Boas and conducted fieldwork for him in Harlem. In 1927, Hurston married Herbert Sheen, a medical student with whom she had begun a relationship during her time at Howard. They parted company after four months, as he was not supportive of her work, and divorced in 1931.

Life's Work

Encouraged by Boas to record African American folktales and customs, Hurston traveled around Alabama and Florida gathering material. She sought sponsorship from a white patron, the wealthy socialite Charlotte Osgood Mason, who supported other Harlem Renaissance figures, including the writer Langston Hughes. In exchange for financial support, Hurston was obligated to sign a contract acknowledging her patron's ownership of her research and editorial control over its publication. The songs, customs, and folktales that she collected would later be published in *Mules and Men* (1935).

By 1932, Hurston was working with the Creative Literature Department of Rollins College in Winter Park, Florida. Some of the material she gathered in her fieldwork was featured in musical revues staged between 1931 and 1935. Plagued by financial and health problems, Hurston returned to New York but was advised by Locke, on behalf of Mason, to return to the South. Back in Eatonville, she felt restored and wrote a play, *Mule Bone*, with Hughes, but only its third act was published as they quarreled over authorship.

In 1934, her first novel, *Jonah's Gourd Vine*, was published. Written in only seven weeks, the semi-autobiographical work is set in Florida. The central character, John Buddy "Jonah" Pearson, was modeled on Hurston's father. In the same year, Hurston received a fellowship to study for a doctorate in anthropology at Columbia University. She found the terms of the fellowship restrictive and never completed the graduate degree, but she was later awarded two Guggenheim field research fellowships to study folk culture in Haiti and Jamaica.

Hurston's most acclaimed novel, *Their Eyes Were Watching God* (1937), also was written in a matter of weeks. In 1938, she released her second major anthropological work, *Tell My Horse*, was a groundbreaking study of Haitian vodoun (better known as voodoo) that, by treating it as a serious religion, sought to dispel some of the negative views surrounding it.

In 1939, a third novel was published: *Moses, Man of the Mountain*, which places the Old Testament character in the American South. In the same year, Hurston married Albert Price III. This marriage was also short-lived because of his alcoholism and abuse, and the couple divorced in 1943.

Hurston wrote an autobiography, *Dust Tracks on a Road*, that was published in 1942. The most commercially successful of her books, it was less an accurate reflection of her life than the public image she wished to present. The book won an award and Hurston was deluged with requests for magazine articles. When these began to appear in *The Saturday Evening Post*, *The Negro Digest*, and *Reader's Digest*, her often controversial views antagonized sections of the black community.

Despite the promise of her career and her recognition as a scholar and as a writer, Hurston received little financial reward from her work. She moved around the country, taking a variety of jobs to support herself. In 1948, her life took a further downward turn when Hurston, then back in New York, was arrested on suspicion of molesting a ten-year-old boy, the son of a woman from whom she had rented a room. Hurston was able to prove that she had been out of the country at the time of the alleged crime and the charges were dropped. However, the story was leaked to the press and the negative publicity had a devastating effect on her career. Seeking to escape the aftermath of the arrest, Hurston went to British Honduras, where she conducted anthropological research. A new novel, *Seraph on the Suwanee*, was published in the same year. Her only novel to feature white characters, it sold well.

After her return to the United States, Hurston worked in a series of menial jobs and was plagued by health and money problems. The advent of the Civil Rights movement in the 1950's meant her celebration of African American folk culture and her refusal to condemn the racism that nurtured it placed her out of step with the prevailing mood. A letter published in *The Orlando Sentinel* in 1955 expressing her outrage at the 1954 *Brown v. Board of Education* Supreme Court decision on desegregation of schools did not improve her image. Hurston maintained that the ruling undervalued black teachers and institutions where black children could study apart from white children.

In early 1959, Hurston suffered a stroke. Too proud to ask her relatives for help, she entered the county welfare home at Fort Pierce, Florida. She died there of hypertensive heart disease in 1960 at age sixty-nine and was buried in an unmarked grave in a segregated cemetery. Her works had gone out of print long before her death, but in the 1970's, Hurston was rediscovered by a new generation of African Americans. In 1973, the writer Alice Walker placed a granite tombstone in the cemetery in the vicinity of Hurston's unmarked grave.

SIGNIFICANCE

A strong, controversial and fiercely independent woman, in many respects Hurston was ahead of her time. She stands out from other writers of the Harlem Renaissance for her affirmation of positive aspects of the lives of ordinary black people who had little interaction with whites and therefore no sense of oppression. Hurston rose from obscurity to become the first African American to graduate from Barnard College. A notable scholar, she published two important anthropological studies of African American and Caribbean folklore and became a member of the American Folklore Society, the American Anthropological Society, the American Ethnological Society, the New York Academy of Sciences, and the American Association for the Advancement of Science.

Christine Ayorinde

FURTHER READING

Boyd, Valerie. Wrapped in Rainbows: The Life of Zora Neale Hurston. New York: Scribner, 2003. A well-researched and readable account of Hurston's life and work.

Hemenway, Robert E. Zora Neale Hurston: A Literary Biography. Introduction by Alice Walker. Urbana: University of Illinois Press, 1977. This well-researched study includes unpublished letters, manuscripts, and interviews with people who knew Hurston.

Hurston, Lucy Anne. Speak, So You Can Speak Again: The Life of Zora Neale Hurston. New York: Doubleday, 2004. A facsimile collection of memorabilia and reminiscences by Hurston's niece. Includes a recording of Hurston speaking and singing.

Hurston, Zora Neale. Dust Tracks on a Road: An Autobiography. 1942. Reprint. New York: HarperCollins, 1991. Hurston's autobiography is presented here with a new foreword by Maya Angelou.

Kaplan, Carla, ed. Zora Neale Hurston: A Life in Letters. New York: Doubleday, 2002. A collection of Hurston's letters from the 1920's to the 1950's.

JHUMPA LAHIRI

British-born Indian novelist and writer

Born: July 18, 1967; London, England
Birth name: Nilanjana Sudeshna Lahiri
Area of Achievement: Literature

Writer Jhumpa Lahiri is best known for winning the 2000 Pulitzer Prize for fiction for her first book of short stories, Interpreter of Maladies, *about the immigrant experiences of second-generation Indian Americans. Her second book, a novel called* The Namesake *(2003), also garnered critical acclaim and was made into a movie in 2006 Since 2015, Lahiri has taught creative writing at Princeton University.*

EARLY LIFE

Jhumpa Lahiri (JOOM-puh lah-HEER-ee) was born Nilanjana Sudeshna Lahiri in London, England, on July 18, 1967, to Bengali immigrants Amar and Tapati Lahiri. A librarian at the London School of Economics, Amar Lahiri had become discouraged with his job by the time his daughter was two years old. The Lahiri family

Jhumpa Lahiri (Wikimedia Commons)

immigrated to the United States, where he accepted a library position at the Massachusetts Institute of Technology (MIT).

In 1970, the Lahiri family settled in South Kingstown, Rhode Island, where Lahiri's father took employment at the University of Rhode Island as a professor librarian. Lahiri's mother took a job as a teacher of the Bengali language. Nicknamed Jhumpa in kindergarten, Lahiri assumed the pet name for life and, from an early age, was confronted with a divided ethnic identity.

The Lahiri family never fully integrated into the culture of the United States. Lahiri's parents held close connections to their traditional Indian roots, speaking Bengali in the home, cooking traditional dishes, and observing Indian customs. However, during their frequent trips to India, Lahiri was considered the American, despite being born in the United Kingdom. From an early age, Lahiri was aware that she straddled two worlds and was perceived as different by each community. Whether in the United States or in Kolkata, Lahiri felt herself an outsider, a feeling that would carry into her work as a writer.

Lahiri's early memories of hearing her maternal grandfather tell stories aloud resonated in her love for reading and writing. As early as seven years old, Lahiri started putting pen to paper. A shy child, Lahiri found comfort in reading and writing stories. She wrote ten-page "novels" at playtime with her like-minded friends. Her experiences in India coupled with her life in Rhode Island only increased her curiosity and fueled her imagination.

After graduating from South Kingstown High School at the age of eighteen, Lahiri applied for and gained US citizenship. In 1989, Lahiri earned a BA in English literature at Barnard College in New York City. Only after Lahiri graduated from college and took on odd jobs in a bookstore and as a research assistant did she regain her interest in writing. In 1992, she began to write stories again.

Lahiri continued her education, earning multiple advanced degrees at Boston University, including an MFA in creative writing, an MA in English literature, an MA in comparative studies in literature and the arts, and, in 1997, a PhD in Renaissance studies. Lahiri accepted a fellowship at the Fine Arts Work Center in Provincetown, Massachusetts, in 1997, and taught creative writing at both Boston University and the Rhode Island School of Design. Lahiri eventually settled in Brooklyn, New York, with her husband, journalist Alberto Vourvoulias-Bush, and their two children, Octavio and Noor.

Jhumpa Lahiri's *Interpreter of Maladies*

A collection of nine short stories, *Interpreter of Maladies* won Jhumpa Lahiri the 2000 Pulitzer Prize for Fiction, and she became not only the youngest but the first South Asian winner of this most sought after award. The stories describe the experiences of Indians, Indian immigrants transplanted to the United States, and Indian Americans born and raised in the United States, like Lahiri herself. Recurring themes include cultural and personal isolation, loneliness, conflict in relationships, reconciliation of dual identity, second-generational rebellion, gender roles, and miscommunication between couples. Set in India, the title story Interpreter of Maladies describes the sexual tension between Indian tour guide Mr. Kapasi and Indian American Mrs. Das, whose interest is piqued when she learns her guide works as a translator between doctors and Gujarati patients—an "interpreter of maladies." Mrs. Das spurns Mr. Kapasi when he perceptively interprets the maladies of Mrs. Das's family.

LIFE'S WORK

Jhumpa Lahiri started her fiction-writing career as early as seven years old. Her story *The Adventures of a Weighing Scale* won a small prize in elementary school. However, it was not until graduate school that she made serious contributions to the world of short-story fiction. She made regular contributions to *The New Yorker*, and her fictional works appeared in journals and magazines including the *Agni Review, Salamander, Harvard Review, Epoch, Louisville Review*, and *Story Quarterly*.

Previously a little-known writer, Lahiri emerged on the writing scene in 1999, when she published her first book of short stories titled *Interpreter of Maladies*. At the age of thirty-two, she surprised the literary world when she won the 2000 Pulitzer Prize for fiction for the short-story collection, gaining the distinction of being the youngest author ever to receive the prestigious literary award and for being the first South Asian writer to be awarded this coveted American prize. Subsequently, Lahiri was named by *The New Yorker* as one of the twenty best writers under the age of forty.

In 2003, Lahiri published her first novel, *The Namesake*, a thirty-year drama of a Bengali couple who journey from Kolkata, India, to Boston, Massachusetts, to raise the next generation of Indian Americans. The characters in the book struggle with identity in a new country, much as Lahiri's own family did. Originally published as a novella, *The Namesake* was named among *The New York Times*'s notable books of 2003 and one of the best books of the year by *USA Today* and *Entertainment Weekly*. In 2007, *The Namesake* was adapted to screen by Indian film director Mira Nair.

> "You can't have a hit every time. The main thing is to keep on working and not be afraid to take risks. It's better to do something that's not perfect and successful every time. It's important to be fearless and move forward, to learn from what went wrong."

Lahiri's *Unaccustomed Earth*, a second collection of short stories on the theme of the Bengali American immigrant experience, debuted in 2008 with equal success, rising to number one on *The New York Times* 'bestseller list.

Lahiri's writing garnered numerous awards. In 1993, she was awarded the TransAtlantic Award from the Henfield Foundation. She was given both the O.Henry Award and the PEN/Hemingway Award for the short story *Interpreter of Maladies* in 1999. In 2000, she received the Addison M. Metcalf Award from the American Academy of Arts and Letters and *The New Yorker* Debut of the Year for *Interpreter of Maladies*. In 2002, she was awarded a Guggenheim Fellowship. Her third book, *Unaccustomed Earth*, won the Frank O'Connor International Short Story Award in 2008 and the Asian American Literary Award in 2009.

In 2010, Lahiri was asked to sit on the Committee on the Arts and Sciences, a presidential advisory committee that provides the White House with guidance on arts and sciences developments. Lahiri's next novel, *The Lowland*, published in 2013, was nominated for both the Man Booker Prize in fiction and the National Book Award for Fiction. The novel won the DSC Prizefor South Asian Literature.

Generally speaking, Lahiri's writing has been favorably reviewed for its well-crafted language, powerful prose, well-developed characters, and themes of South Asian immigrant displacement and identity. Lahiri's work has been viewed as a refreshing addition to classic American literature.

Significance

An Indian American writer of Bengali origin, Jhumpa Lahiri was hailed as one of the twenty best writers in the early twenty-first century. A second-generation South Asian American writer, Lahiri won the 2000 Pulitzer Prize for fiction for her first book of short stories, *Interpreter of Maladies*, an award previously given to the likes of novelists Ernest Hemingway, William Faulkner, and John Steinbeck. Praised for writing with careful precision and explosive detail and in a direct, understated style, Lahiri narrates her stories about Indian American immigrants living in the United States and their second-generation children who struggle with double ethnic consciousness.

Lahiri's works have been read by millions worldwide and have been translated into various languages, including Bengali, Spanish, Japanese, Persian, and Swedish. In 2014, Lahiri won the National Humanities Medal in recognition of her accomplishments in literature.

Tamara M. Valentine, updated by Micah L. Issitt

Further Reading

Bala, Suman, ed. *Jhumpa Lahiri, the Master Storyteller: A Critical Response to "Interpreter of Maladies."* New Delhi: Khosla, 2002. Print. An anthology of thirty critical responses to and scholarly reviews of Lahiri's stories.

Brians, Paul. "Jhumpa Lahiri: Interpreter of Maladies (2000)." *Modern South Asian Literature in English.* Westport: Greenwood, 2003. 195-204. Print. Literature as Windows to World Cultures. A chapter introducing Lahiri as one of fifteen postcolonial South Asian English-language authors and offeringa critical review of Interpreter of Maladies.

Huang, Shuchen Susan. "Jhumpa Lahiri (1967-)." *Asian American Short Story Writers: An A-to-Z Guide.* Ed. Guiyou Huang. Westport: Greenwood, 2003.125-33. Print. Places Lahiri within the context of forty-nine contemporary Asian American short story writers. Contains a biography, major works and themes, critical reception, and a bibliography.

Lahiri, Jhumpa. "Trading Stories: Notes from an Apprenticeship." *New Yorker.* Condé Nast, 13 June 2011. Web. 15 Feb. 2012. An autobiographical essay that explores Lahiri's search for identity in the author's own words.

Rajan, Gita. "Ethical Responsibility in the Inter subjective Spaces: Reading Jhumpa Lahiri's Interpreter of Maladies and A Temporary Matter." *Transnational Asian American Literature: Sites and Transits.* Ed. Shirley Geok-lin Lim, et al. Philadelphia: Temple UP, 2006. 122-41. Print. An analysis of the characters' resolutions of ethical issues as they construct a transnational social identity.

TONI MORRISON

Writer

Born: February 18, 1931; Lorain, Ohio
Area of Achievement: Literature; Social issues

Morrison has been lauded as one of the most complex and mature authors of her time. Her ability to bring complicated historical issues to life has earned her numerous awards, including a Pulitzer Prize for Beloved *and a Nobel Prize in Literature.*

Toni Morrison (Wikimedia Commons)

EARLY LIFE

Toni Morrison was born Chloe Anthony Wofford to George and Ramah Willis Wofford on February 18, 1931. Morrison's parents had moved to Ohio from the South seeking better social and economic prospects for their family. Her father, who had been mistreated in childhood by whites, taught Morrison to distrust them. Morrison's parents and maternal grandmother also taught her the value of stories, often spinning tales for her and her siblings.

Morrison's high school years were spent studying literature and Latin. She graduated from Howard University, where she shortened her name to Toni, in 1953 with a bachelor's degree in English, then from Cornell University in 1955 with a master's in English. During the next few years, she taught at Texas Southern University and Howard. While teaching at Howard in 1957, she met Harold Morrison, a fellow faculty member. They were married the next year and divorced in 1965 after having two sons. Shortly after the birth of her second son, Morrison took a job as an editor.

LIFE'S WORK

Morrison wrote her first novel, *The Bluest Eye* (1970), while working as an editor. She felt unfulfilled in her career, so she began to write a tragic story about a little girl who longs to have blue eyes. The novel was lauded as sophisticated and complex. By the time Morrison's second novel, *Sula,* was published in 1973, she was considered a writer worth watching. *Sula* was nominated for the National Book Award in 1974. By 1977, Morrison had won the National Book Critics Circle's Fiction Award and the American Academy and Institute of Arts and Letters Award, and published *Song of Solomon* (1977).

The 1980's were an important decade for Morrison. *Tar Baby* was published in 1981. She left her editing job and took another teaching position, this time at State University of New York, Albany. In 1986, her first play, *Dreaming Emmett,* debuted. One year later, *Beloved* was published. The novel won the Pulitzer Prize for fiction in 1988. Morrison was inducted into the American Academy of Arts and Letters the same year.

Morrison held the Robert F. Goheen Chair in the Humanities at Princeton University from 1989 until her retirement in 2006. After the late 1990s, Morrison stopped regularly offering writing workshops and instead conceived and developed the prestigious Princeton Atelier, a program that brings together talented students with critically acclaimed, world-famous writers and performing artists. The students work together with the artists to produce works of art that are presented to the public after one semester of collaboration. In November 2017, Princeton re-dedicated the West College building as Morrison Hall in her honor.

During the 1990's, Morrison took her writing in new directions. Although she continued writing fiction, she branched into criticism and lyrics as well. One of her best known collections of critical essays, *Playing in the Dark: Whiteness and the Literary Imagination*, was published in 1992. Her novel *Jazz* was published the same year. For this novel especially, and her body of work generally, Morrison was awarded the Nobel Prize in Literature in 1993. As the decade progressed, she returned to editing with *Race-ing Justice, En-Gendering Power: Essays on Anita Hill, Clarence Thomas, and the Construction of Social Reality* (1992) and co-edited *Birth of a Nation'hood: Gaze, Script, and Spectacle in the O. J. Simpson Case* (1997). Four sets of lyrics were also published in this decade: *Honey and Rue* (1993), *Four Songs* (1994), *Sweet Talk* (1997), and *Spirits in the Well* (1998). *Paradise*, another novel, was published in 1998, and *The Big Box*, a children's book Morrison co-wrote with her younger son, Slade, was published in 1999.

President Barack Obama talks with Presidential Medal of Freedom recipient Morrison in the Blue Room of the White House, May 29, 2012. (Wikimedia Commons)

> "*Passion is never enough; neither is skill. But try. For our sake and yours forget your name in the street; tell us what the world has been to you in the dark places and in the light. Don't tell us what to believe, what to fear. Show us belief's wide skirt and the stitch that unravels fear's caul.*"

In the 2000's, Morrison continued to write novels, music lyrics, children's books, and nonfiction. She wrote the libretto for *Margaret Garner* (2005), an opera based on *Beloved*, and released the novel *A Mercy* in 2008.

In 2010, as she was working on her novel Home, Morrison's son Slade dies of pancreatic cancer. This put a stop to her work for many months. Home was eventually published in 2012 and was dedicated to her son. Morrison's eleventh novel, God Help the Child, was published in 2015.

Significance

Morrison's ability to create complex characters, confront deep social issues, address history and community, and convey the lyricism of the oral tradition makes her writing an important part of the African American literary canon. Critics have explored themes such as abuse, incest, passion, and history in her work, as well as technical aspects such as narrative technique and imagery. Morrison's writing also is important because it crosses traditional boundaries, ranging from realism to naturalism and lyrical modernism. Influenced by predecessors such as James Baldwin and William Faulkner, Morrison also can be seen as a descendant of authors such as Richard Wright and Zora Neale Hurston. As a result, her own writing has played an influential role in American literature.

In 2012, Oberlin College in Ohio became the base of the Toni Morrison Society, an international literary society dedicated to scholarly research of Morrison's work. In 2016, the college received a grant to complete a documentary film about Morrison's intellectual and artistic vision, titled The Foreigner's Home. The film incorporated footage shot by Morrison's oldest son Harold, who also consulted on the film.

Along with her Pulitzer Prize and Nobel Prize in Literature, Morrison has been awarded the National

Humanities Medal in 2000, the Norman Mailler Prize in 2009, the Library of Congress Creative Achievement Award for Fiction in 2011, the Presidential Medal of Freedom in 2012, and the PEN/Saul Bellow Award for Achievement in American Fiction in 2016.

Theresa L. Stowell

Further Reading

Beaulieu, Elizabeth Ann. *The Toni Morrison Encyclopedia*. Westport, Conn.: Greenwood Press, 2003. Contains detailed coverage of Morrison's works, including information on characters, themes, topics, and settings. Entries range from one sentence to several pages depending on topic. Easy-to-read format makes this a valuable resource.

Conner, Marc C., ed. *The Aesthetics of Toni Morrison: Speaking the Unspeakable*. Jackson: University Press of Mississippi, 2000. Collection of eight essays dealing with issues such as aesthetics, language, the grotesque, and loss in Morrison's novels.

Gates, Henry Louis, Jr., and K. A. Appiah, eds. *Toni Morrison: Critical Perspectives Past and Present*. New York: Amistad, 1993. Comprehensive collection of critical analysis of Morrison's works. Includes reviews of her first six novels, sixteen critical essays, and four interviews.

Tally, Justine, ed. *The Cambridge Companion to Toni Morrison*. New York: Cambridge University Press, 2007. Thirteen critical essays on topics such as language, characters, memory, the black community, and narrative technique in Morrison's works. Includes a helpful further reading section and index.

Lola Rodríguez de Tió

Puerto Rican-born poet and activist

Born: September 14, 1843; San German, Puerto Rico
Died: November 10, 1924; Havana, Cuba
Area of Achievement: Poetry, activism, women's rights

Rodríguez de Tió, a revered figure in Cuban and Puerto Rican history, was a nineteenth-century lyric poet who fought for the independence of both countries. As a member of the ruling elite, her work on behalf of opportunities for women made her one of Latin America's most influential early feminists.

Early Life

Lola Rodríguez de Tió (TEE-oh) was born Dolores Rodríguez de Astudillo y Ponce de León in San Germán, into a family belonging to Puerto Rico's ruling class. Her father was Don Sebastian Rodríguez de Astudillo, one of the founders of the Puerto Rican Bar Association and holder of a magisterial deanship; her mother was Doña Carmen Ponce de León, a descendant of Ponce de León, the famous explorer and first colonial governor. Rodríguez de Tió attended religious schools and studied with private tutors in her home, often present for the nearby gatherings of the assorted intellectuals and politicians meeting with her father. Her well-educated mother managed the child's education, and though it was rare at the time for a woman to be an intellectual, Rodríguez de Tió, as a comfortable member of Puerto Rico's ruling elite, also found support and encouragement in her literary endeavors from the poet Ursula Cardona de Quinones.

Bonacio Tío Segarra, a journalist and poet, married Rodríguez de Tió when she was twenty. Sources suggest that the two had a modern relationship as partners in life and politics, and politically the couple worked against the corruption and brutality in Puerto Rico under Spain's colonial government. Tío Segarra recognized and supported Rodríguez de Tió's gift for lyricism and wrote the preface

Lola Rodríguez de Tió (Wikimedia Commons)

to her first published poetry collection. As advocates of radical nationalist beliefs, the two together experienced harassment and tribulation once the Spanish authorities became aware of their work.

Life's Work

Rodríguez de Tió published her first book of poetry, *Mis cantares*, in 1876. The book sold 2,500 copies. Prior to that, the fiery lyric piece "La Borinquena," composed for a traditional melody, established Rodríguez de Tió's reputation and caused her to be deported after she read it out loud at a literary gathering in her own home. The song's development as the national anthem happened gradually from its original form as a song of romantic love, into the resulting chant to liberty and a symbol of patriotism.

Because of their rebellious stance against tyranny, Rodríguez de Tió and her husband were forced to live in exile at various times over the years, first in Venezuela, then Cuba, then New York City. Wherever they went, they worked for Puerto Rican and also Cuban independence and formed alliances with the artistic and intellectual communities in each city. In Venezuela, for example, they met Eugenio María de Hostos, a brilliant patriot who became an important influence on Rodríguez de Tió. While in New York City, Rodríguez de Tió began intense political contact with José Martí and other Cuban political exiles, creating the Cuban Revolutionary Party in 1895. Rodríguez de Tió served in the leadership of the clubs Rius Rivera in 1896 and Caridad in 1897. When she returned to Cuba in 1899, she spent the rest of her life working for social justice and the improvement of the situation of Cuban women.

> "*The woman who studies and reads arrives at such a state of consciousness that she finds in herself the feeling of confidence that takes her with a firm and certain step towards independence and supreme happiness.*"

Rodríguez de Tió published three books: *Mis cantares* (*My Songs*) in 1876, *Claros y nieblas* (*Bright Intervals and Mist*) in 1885, and *Mi libro de Cuba* (*My Book on Cuba*) in 1893. Some sources have recounted that Fidel Castro quoted from one of her well-known poems, "Cuba and Puerto Rico," in a 1966 speech, but that he attributed the poem to Martí. Still, Rodríguez de Tió's poetry expresses her affection for both Puerto Rico and her adopted homeland. She died on November 10, 1924, in Havana, Cuba, at the age of eighty-one.

Significance

Considered a leading literary figure and a national hero, Rodríguez de Tió was named to the Cuban Academy of Arts and Letters in 1910 and Patron of the Galician Beneficent Society in 1911. She has been called Puerto Rico's most distinguished nineteenth-century lyric poet, and as the most prominent female Puerto Rican Romantic poet she certainly stands tall. However, Rodríguez de Tió's activism and political engagement truly set her apart from other patriots of her generation. With her stalwart dedication to Romanticism in tandem with her fierce militancy, Rodríguez de Tió embodied the tension between the legacy of Spain's Golden Age and Spanish authoritarian colonialism.

Jan Voogd

Further Reading

Babin, Maria Teresa, and Stan Steiner, eds. *Borinquen: An Anthology of Puerto Rican Literature*. New York: Knopf, 1974. Discusses the process and impact of Rodríguez de Tió's "Song of Borinquen" and its relationship to the national anthem of Puerto Rico.

Rodríguez de Tió, Lola. *Mis cantares*. Reprint. Alexandria, Va.: Alexander Street Press, 2005. An example of poetry originally published in the 1880's but recently more available as new editions of her work have been produced in electronic format and printon- demand.

---. *Obras completas*. 4 vols. San Juan: Instituto de Cultura Puertorriquena, 1968-1971. Difficult to find but forms the cornerstone of understanding Rodríguez de Tió's artistry.

---. *Poesías patrióticas, poesías religiosa; Cantares, nieblas y congojas; and Mi libro de Cuba*. Barcelona: Ediciones Rumbos, 1967, 1968. Originally published in the 1800's, these are examples of work republished in Spain during the 1960s.

Ruiz, Vicki, and Virginia Sanchez Korrol. *Latina Legacies: Identity, Biography, and Community*. New York: Oxford University Press, 2005. Includes an entire chapter on Rodríguez de Tió and the struggle for freedom in Puerto Rico.

Susan Sontag

Writer

Born: January 16, 1933; New York City, New York
Died: December 28, 2004; New York City, New York
Area of Achievement: Literature

Sontag, a novelist, short-story writer, filmmaker, and human rights activist, is noted for her provocative essays. She was among the first American intellectuals to make legitimate the study of popular culture and cinema.

Early Life

Susan Sontag (SAHN-tag) was the first daughter of Mildred and Jack Rosenblatt, both of whose parents were assimilated, nonobservant European Jews who had immigrated to the lower East Side of Manhattan. While Sontag's parents operated a fur export business in China, she and her younger sister remained in New York with their grandparents. After Sontag's father died in 1938, her mother relocated to Tucson, Arizona, and in 1945 married Army Air Corps captain Nathan Sontag, whose last name Susan took as her own.

The family moved to Los Angeles, where Sontag attended high school, graduating early at the age of fifteen. Receiving little attention from her mother, Sontag spent much time living within herself and her thoughts; gifted with a great love of learning and a powerful mind, her voluminous reading led her to imagine a large and liberal life as a writer and thinker in a great urban center. More specifically, she hoped for an ideal life in New York City, writing essays for *The Partisan Review*, a liberal political and literary magazine founded in the 1930s by Jewish intellectuals.

Sontag attended the University of California, Berkeley, for a semester, and then in 1950 she moved on to the University of Chicago, where, at age seventeen, she met and married twenty-eight-year-old sociologist Philip Rieff after a whirlwind courtship of just ten days. In 1952, Sontag gave birth to their son, David. After receiving a B.A. from the University of Chicago, Sontag did graduate work at Harvard and Oxford Universities and at the Sorbonne in Paris, where she developed a lifelong love of European culture. Divorcing Rieff upon her return from Paris in 1958, Sontag moved with her son to New York City, where she taught at various universities, worked as an editor at *Commentary* magazine, and fulfilled her ambition to write for the venerable *Partisan Review*. Her bold and stylish essays for that increasingly traditional journal, however, expressed the audacious spirit of a new era and marked her as a voice that belonged to an emerging generation of American intellectuals.

"Compassion is an unstable emotion. It needs to be translated into action, or it withers."

Life's Work

Rather than seeking a conventional academic career, Sontag lived and worked within New York City literary and intellectual circles. She introduced new energies into this intelligentsia through essays that reflected the irreverent and radical energies of the 1960s, and in many ways she remained identified with that era. Of particular note is her 1966 book of essays *Against Interpretation*, which questioned conventional critical judgments, advocating a more transgressive countercultural sensibility. She advised a greater concern with surreal and sensual experience than with ordinary analysis, and she shocked her fellow intellectuals by taking pop culture and film seriously. In the most important essay in this collection, "Notes on Camp," she suggested that the modern temper

> ## Innovative Essays
>
> Susan Sontag came to prominence in the 1960s and 1970s through her adventurous essays, which dared to give careful consideration not only to thinkers and writers associated with high culture but also to film, popular art, pornography, and the homosexual counterculture. These essays took a canonical place among a new wave of free-spirited experiments in music, art, film, and literature in American society. Spanning five decades, her essays not only addressed important literary subjects but also championed the avant-garde, furthered the cause of human rights, and examined such topics as photography and the psychology of illness.
>
> Sontag is known for her essay titled "Notes on Camp," in which she characterized the modern temper as a fruitful dialectic between an aesthetic, sensual, and free-spirited counterculture and the conscientious and morally exacting sobriety she associated with her own Jewish tradition. Although a scholar who began her career in the academic world, Sontag achieved renown for her undaunted and independent intellect that ranged restlessly beyond the borders of established conventions. She significantly enriched the American cultural landscape through her pioneering cultural criticism and her analysis and advocacy of such major twentieth-century European thinkers as Georg Lukacs, Simone Weil, Roland Barthes, Elias Canetti, Walter Benjamin, Antonin Artaud, E. M. Cioran, and W. G. Sebald.

was the product of an exquisite interaction between a spontaneous gay subculture and traditional Jewish moral seriousness.

These and subsequent essays established Sontag's identity as an adventurous polymath, mixing topics such as drugs, pornography, and science fiction with astute considerations of major European writers such as Georg Lukacs, Simone Weil, Roland Barthes, Elias Canetti, Walter Benjamin, Antonin Artaud, E. M. Cioran, and W. G. Sebald—none of whom had previously enjoyed recognition in the United States. During these early years, Sontag also made four films and published novels and short fiction. Statuesque and photogenic, with intense dark eyes and long dark hair, Sontag's beauty, intellect, sophistication, and avant-garde credentials made her one of her era's major celebrities. She particularly consolidated her credentials as a cultural radical and public intellectual when she traveled to Hanoi, the capital of North Vietnam, afterward publishing a controversial book critical of American society.

Continuing her fascination with the camera, in 1977 Sontag published *On Photography,* which considered the impact of the photograph and which won that year's National Book Critics Circle Award. At this time Sontag also underwent arduous treatments for advanced breast cancer, which led to another major book, 1978's *Illness as Metaphor,* an examination of the cultural and psychological aspects of cancer and tuberculosis.

Although earlier Sontag had supported the Communist regimes of North Vietnam and Cuba, a political reconsideration led to her speaking in support of the Polish Solidarity movement in 1982 and to her denunciation of Soviet Communism. When she served as president of the PEN American Center from 1987 to 1989, her work as a political activist continued through her support of author Salman Rushdie when he was targeted for assassination by a conservative Muslim cleric; she also campaigned on behalf of other mistreated or jailed writers around the world. Arguably her most engaged political action consisted of her stay in the city of Sarajevo from 1993 to 1996, where, in the thick of the war and on behalf of the Bosnian people, she directed a theatrical production of Samuel Beckett's masterpiece, *En attendant Godot* (1952; Waiting for Godot, 1954).

Despite the extraordinary success of her essays, Sontag considered herself at heart a writer of fiction. Her two historical novels were particularly successful; her final novel, *In America,* won the National Book Award in 2000. While Sontag avoided any form of identity politics, whether it be based on gender, religion, or sexuality, in the 1990s she formed a romantic partnership with the photographer Annie Leibovitz. During this decade, Sontag was treated again for cancer; in 2004 she died of leukemia. She is buried in Montparnasse Cemetery in Paris.

SIGNIFICANCE

Sontag was among the most famous and highly regarded American intellectuals of the twentieth century. Her inspired cultural criticism addressed the artistic, social, and spiritual changes in her society after World War II, and she epitomized a new sensibility associated with a greater sense of personal, political, and philosophical freedom. She was among the first intellectuals to make legitimate the study of popular culture and cinema, and she enriched and shaped America's cultural climate through her authoritative analyses of important European writers and thinkers. The controversies engendered by Sontag's work are a measure of its power and also speak to her reputation as a daring, passionate, and engaged thinker. Decades of sustained and serious creativity produced novels, short stories, films, plays, and, especially, influential essays on the important topics of her time, including communism, fascism, the Vietnam War, human rights, the AIDS crisis, film, photography, postmodern literature, philosophy, and art.

Margaret Boe Birns

FURTHER READING

Ching, Barbara, and Jennifer A. Wagner-Lawlor, eds. *The Scandal of Susan Sontag.* New York: Columbia University Press, 2009. Essays examine Sontag as a pop icon, filmmaker, playwright, director, novelist, essayist, and traveler. Photographs and illustrations.

Lopate, Phillip. *Notes on Sontag.* Princeton, N.J.: Princeton University Press, 2009. Discussion of Sontag and her work by a writer who knew her; places special emphasis on her status as a cultural mover and shaker and as a brilliant essayist.

Poague, Leland. *Conversations with Susan Sontag.* Oxford: University Press of Mississippi, 1995. More than twenty interviews with Sontag, spanning 1967 to 1993, tracking the development of her thinking and her career as a writer, filmmaker, and novelist.

Rollyson, Carl. *Reading Susan Sontag: A Critical Introduction to Her Work.* Chicago: Ivan R. Dee, 2001. An analysis of Sontag's novels, essays, and her work in film and theater by her first biographer. Chronology and glossary of terms used in her essays.

_____, and Lisa Paddock. *Susan Sontag: The Making of an Icon.* New York: W. W. Norton, 2000. The first full-length biography and critical study of Sontag and her work. Discussion of Sontag's personal and family life, sexuality, illnesses, and status as a famous intellectual.

HARRIET BEECHER STOWE

Novelist

Born: June 14, 1811; Litchfield, Connecticut
Died: July 1, 1896; Hartford, Connecticut
Area of Achievement: Literature, social reform, women's rights

Stowe was the author of Uncle Tom's Cabin, *which almost certainly had the greatest social and political impact on the United States of any book ever published. In attacking slavery as a threat to the Christian family, her novel helped to abolish that institution, and many people credit it with helping to bring on the Civil War.*

EARLY LIFE

Harriet Beecher Stowe was the daughter of Lyman Beecher, a stern New England Calvinist preacher whose image of a God who predestined humans to heaven or hell left a mark on his children, and one of her brothers was Henry Ward Beecher, the famous Brooklyn preacher. The fact that Harriet's mother died when she was four made her father's influence even more important. By the age of six and a half, the young "Hattie," as she was known to her family, had memorized more than two dozen hymns

Harriet Beecher Stowe (National Archives and Records Administration)

and several long chapters in the Bible. As an adult, however, she would substitute for her father's dogmas a religion of hope that stressed the love and compassion of Christ rather than the divine judgment that her father preached. Some people hold that she "feminized" her father's religion. Throughout her life, she retained a strong sense of religious mission and zeal for social improvement.

At the age of twelve, Harriet moved to Hartford to live with her older sister Catharine, a purposeful woman who had started the Hartford Female Seminary. Harriet attended Catharine's school and stayed on as a teacher and guardian of young children. In 1832, she moved with her family to Cincinnati, Ohio, where her father had been offered the post as president of the new Lane Theological Seminary. Three years after arriving in Cincinnati (in January, 1836), Harriet Beecher married Calvin Stowe, a Lane professor.

These years in the West prepared Stowe for her later career. She had eight children between 1836 and 1850, and if she and Calvin had not alternated taking "rest cures" in Vermont over the years, she might have had more. In 1834, Harriet won a fifty-dollar prize for "A New England Sketch," which was published in the *Western Monthly Magazine*. From that point on, the members of her family saw her as a person of literary promise, even though she claimed that this activity was only a way of supplementing the always meager family income. In 1842, Calvin wrote to his wife, "[My] dear, you must be a literary woman. It is written in the book of fate."

While in Cincinnati, Harriet also experienced the intense emotions aroused by the slavery issue during these years. On one visit to a Kentucky plantation, she saw slaves whom she later used as models for some of the characters in *Uncle Tom's Cabin*. In 1836, a local mob attacked the print shop of an abolitionist in the city, and the struggle between the abolitionists and the moderates at Lane eventually drove her father to retire and her husband to take a job at Bowdoin College in Maine in 1850.

LIFE'S WORK

When President Abraham Lincoln met Harriet Beecher Stowe in the fall of 1862, he greeted her as "the little lady

An illustration of Eva and Topsy from Uncle Tom's Cabin. (Library of Congress)

who made this big war." He was not alone in believing that the publication of Stowe's *Uncle Tom's Cabin* (1852) had been a crucial event in arousing the antislavery sentiments that led to the outbreak of the American Civil War in 1861. Although *Uncle Tom's Cabin* was not the best novel of the nineteenth century, it certainly had the greatest impact. *Uncle Tom's Cabin* sold 300,000 copies the year it was published, and Stowe's great work helped to end slavery by personalizing that "peculiar institution." Slavery was wrong, the novel argued, because it was unChristian. More specifically, slavery tore children from their mothers and thus threatened the existence of the Christian family. It has been said that *Uncle Tom's Cabin* was "a great revival sermon," more effective than those of her father. Harriet herself later wrote that the book was written by "the Lord Himself.... I was but an instrument in his hands."

Each of the main characters in this melodramatic novel displayed virtues and vices that were important to Stowe. The main character, Tom, was sold by a kind master, Mr. Shelby, to a second one, Augustine St. Clare, who had ambiguous feelings about slavery and planned to free Tom. Before he could do so, St. Clare was killed and Tom was sold to a singularly evil man, Simon Legree, who finally beat Tom to death when the slave refused to tell him the hiding place of two slaves who were planning to escape.

Aside from Tom, the strongest characters in the novel were female. The slave Eliza, also sold by Mr. Shelby, escaped with her son (who would have been taken from her) by jumping across ice floes on the Ohio River. She and her husband George were finally reunited in Canada. Little Eva, the saintly and sickly child of Augustine St. Clare, was a Christlike figure who persuaded her father to free Tom before she herself died. Mary Bird, the wife of an Ohio senator, shamed her husband into helping Eliza when she sought comfort at their home. Senator Bird violated the Fugitive Slave Law of 1850— which he had helped to pass and which required northerners to return escaped slaves— by helping Eliza. Ophelia, a cousin of Augustine St. Clare who came from Vermont to help him care for his invalid wife and child, was the model of a wellorganized homemaker who was especially proud of her neat kitchen. Another courageous female was the slave Cassy, who quietly poisoned her newborn with opium after she had had two other children sold away from her.

> "When you get into a tight place, and everything goes against you till it seems as if you couldn't hold on a minute longer, never give up then, for that 's just the place and time that the tide'll turn."

It was no accident that so many of the heroes in *Uncle Tom's Cabin* were women motivated by a Christian love of neighbor or that the most dramatic events in the novel focused on the way slavery destroyed families. *Uncle Tom's Cabin* was particularly effective in arousing antislavery sentiment and particularly infuriating to southern defenders of slavery, precisely because it dramatically attacked one of the strongest arguments of slaveholders, the religious one that saw slavery as an essential part of the patriarchal system of authority established by God and sanctioned by Scripture. For Stowe, Christianity began at home with a strong family. Any institution that undermined the family was necessarily unchristian.

In many ways, Harriet Beecher Stowe was a lay preacher whose writings were sermons. Like some other nineteenth-century advocates of women's rights, Stowe believed that women were morally superior to men. She did not believe that women should govern the country or replace men in the world of business, but rather that they should set a moral example for society through their control of the "domestic sphere," where they could influence society by shaping the lives of their children. Stowe advocated greater equality between the men's sphere and the women's sphere. Women deserved greater respect because most of them—slave or free—were mothers, and therefore they had a greater understanding of both love and the "sacredness of the family" than men did.

In some of her later novels, especially *Pink and White Tyranny: A Society Novel*, *My Wife and I* (both 1871), and *We and Our Neighbors* (1875), Stowe continued to argue that women could improve the world by being guardians of morals in the home. She was not a "radical" advocate of full social equality for women, and she was critical of reformers such as Elizabeth Cady Stanton and Susan B. Anthony. Despite her active professional career as a writer, which made her the principal wage earner in the family after 1853, Stowe continued to maintain that she wrote only to supplement the family income. She also continued to write novels in which strong women—for example, Mary Scudder in *The Minister's Wooing* (1859) and Mara in *The Pearl of Orr's Island* (1862)—acted as female ministers who taught their families the path to salvation from the well ordered kitchen that was, in effect, a domestic pulpit. This complex woman continued to publish until she was nearly seventy. Although Uncle Tom's Cabin had a greater impact on American history than any other single novel, Harriet Beecher Stowe's literary reputation rests on those novels that portrayed life in the New England villages of her youth: *The Pearl of Orr's Island*, *Oldtown Folks* (1869), and *Poganuc People: Their Loves and Lives* (1878). Although peopled by stern Calvinist ministers and wise, compassionate women, these works were not consciously written to correct a social injustice, as was *Uncle Tom's Cabin*. In 1873, Stowe used some of her income to buy a large home in Hartford, Connecticut, where she and Calvin spent their last years. Calvin died in 1886, ten years before his sometimes controversial wife.

SIGNIFICANCE

Harriet Beecher Stowe will always be remembered primarily as the author of *Uncle Tom's Cabin*, which helped to end slavery in the United States and to spark the bloodiest war in American history. During the 1850s and 1860s, she remained one of the most popular American writers. Many of her works were first serialized in the *Atlantic Monthly* and then published as books, which earned her a steady and comfortable income.

Historians now recognize that Harriet Beecher Stowe's contribution to American history goes beyond these accomplishments. Although one cannot view this traditionally religious woman as a modern feminist, she did play an important role in women's history. Writing was one of the few "respectable" careers open to women in nineteenth-century America, because women could write at home and legitimately argue that their work was necessary to supplement family income. It is somewhat ironic that Stowe's fiction, which powerfully affected the course of events outside the "domestic sphere," was written to earn greater respect for women as leaders of the home and family. It is also interesting that a century after Stowe's reputation was at its peak, Betty Friedan's pathbreaking book *The Feminine Mystique* (1963) would attack the central idea of Harriet Beecher Stowe: that women's primary role should be to lead and shape the home and family.

It is a tribute to Harriet Beecher Stowe that Friedan's work was necessary. Stowe softened the harsh Calvinism of her father by emphasizing a religion of love more congenial to women; she also defended a separate "sphere" for female activity in American life. It can be argued that both of these things were necessary to raise the status of women in America. That, in turn, made it easier for other women to demand later the greater freedom that women enjoy in the United States a century after Stowe's death.

Ken Wolf

Further Reading

Adams, John R. *Harriet Beecher Stowe*. New York: Twayne, 1963.

Ammons, Elizabeth, ed. *Critical Essays on Harriet Beecher Stowe*. Boston: G. K. Hall, 1980.

Crozier, Alice. *The Novels of Harriet Beecher Stowe*. New York: Oxford University Press, 1969.

Degler, Carl N. At Odds: *Women and the Family in America from the Revolution to the Present*. New York: Oxford University Press, 1980.

Douglas, Ann. *The Feminization of American Culture*. New York: Doubleday, 1988.

Hedrick, Joan D. *Harriet Beecher Stowe: A Life*. New York: Oxford University Press, 1994.

Stowe, Harriet Beecher. *Uncle Tom's Cabin*. New York: Bantam Books, 1981.

White, Barbara A. *The Beecher Sisters*. New Haven, Conn.: Yale University Press, 2003.

Wilson, Robert Forrest. *Crusader in Crinoline: The Life of Harriet Beecher Stowe*. Reprint. Westport, Conn.: Greenwood Press, 1972.

Walt Whitman

Poet

Born: May 31, 1819; West Hills, New York
Died: March 26, 1892; Camden, New Jersey
Area of Achievement: Literature: poetry

The first true poet of American English, Whitman created a language to express the spirit of American democracy and used that language to shape a vision of a new continent that still fires the American imagination.

Early Life

Walt Whitman was born in a two-story, cedar-shingled house that his father had built about thirty miles east of New York City on Long Island. He was born in the same year as his fellow writers Herman Melville and James Russell Lowell. His father's family, as he recalled them, "appear to have been always of democratic and heretical tendencies." Walter Whitman, Sr., had been born on the day of the storming of the Bastille in France in 1789 and trained his sons as radical democrats, identifying with independent farmers and laborers and regarding financiers and power brokers as "the enemy." His mother's family were of Dutch ancestry, inclined to the freethinking tradition of the Quakers, and Whitman ascribed his creative impulses to her non-bookish sense of practical learning. He felt that her combination of the "practical and the materialistic" with the "transcendental and cloudy" might be the source of his own contradictory instincts.

The family moved from the rural regions of Long Island to Brooklyn in 1823. Already a bustling market town, Brooklyn was the third largest city in the United States by 1855 with a population of 200,000. The elder Whitman hoped to make a fortune in real estate, but he lacked the shrewdness to prosper in a speculative arena, and the Whitman family moved about once every year for the next decade.

A mediocre student but an avid reader, young Walt went to work for the *Long Island Patriot*, a local newspaper, at the age of twelve in 1831. He became a journeyman printer, but a fire in the printing district forced him out of work, and a quarrel with his father ended the possibility of any work on the family farm. He took a series of jobs as a country schoolteacher between 1836 and 1841, but only a few of his quarter-year appointments were renewed. He established a warm relationship with many of his students, but his explosive temper and

Walt Whitman (Library of Congress)

stubborn insistence on the validity of his ideas led to frequent clashes with the school authorities. Whitman moved back to New York City in 1841, but continued arguments with his father impelled him to take lodgings in a boardinghouse in lower Manhattan.

Between school assignments, Whitman had published his earliest known writing, an item entitled "Effects of Lightning," in the August 8, 1838, issue of the *Long Island Democrat*. The rather rough and motley group of people he met in the boardinghouse district became the models for some of the characters in his first novel, *Franklin Evans* (1842), the story of a farmer's apprentice from Long Island who comes to New York. Whitman also published about a dozen short stories—mostly in the manner of Edgar Allan Poe or Nathaniel Hawthorne—between 1841 and 1845, and while the stories are derivative and sentimental, his work during this time convinced him that he could be a writer.

Although Whitman continued to maintain close contact with his family, often acting as a third "parent" with his younger siblings, he was now an independent young man making his way in the world. He stood nearly six feet tall, weighed about 180 pounds, had large hands and feet, a broad nose, full lips, and in later life, a bristling beard. He walked with a confident stride, could leap easily aboard a moving Broadway stage, and appeared at ease with the rugged, masculine presence he projected. As his close friend John Burroughs observed, however, there was also "a curious feminine undertone in him which revealed itself in the quality of his voice, the delicate texture of his skin, the gentleness of his touch and ways."

By 1848, Whitman had worked for ten different newspapers, most prominently as the editor of the Brooklyn *Daily Eagle*, and was an active citizen in Brooklyn political affairs, even writing lumbering patriotic verse when the occasion required it. His involvement with the Democratic Party in Brooklyn drew him into the rapidly developing debate over slavery during the 1840's, and his stand on the explosive issue of free soil led to his firing in 1848 from the *Daily Eagle*. Through his contacts in the field of journalism, he was able to work briefly as an editor of the New Orleans *Crescent* while that paper was reorganized during the early part of 1848, his first trip to the South. Upon his return to New York, he rented a storefront in lower Manhattan with the plan of setting himself up as a kind of lecturer and "universal authority," a "Professor of Things in General" like the hero of Thomas Carlyle's *Sartor Resartus* (1833–1834), a book he found fascinating. Apparently, there was no public demand for his wisdom.

During the late 1840's and the early 1850's, Whitman continued with real estate work, renovating buildings with his family, including considerable carpentry work. He enjoyed the swirl of intellectual life in New York, counting young painters, actors, and writers among his friends. He attended numerous lectures (including Ralph Waldo Emerson's famous address "The Poet"), kept up with original theories in the sciences (phrenology, hydrology), studied archaeology as an interested layman and would-be Egyptologist, debated new philosophical constructs (Fourierism), and listened enthusiastically to music of all sorts, from American folk music to the celebrated "Swedish Nightingale" Jenny Lind. He recalled these times as "days of preparation; the gathering of the forces"; the preparation he referred to was for the creation and publication of his masterpiece, *Leaves of Grass* (1855–1892).

Life's Work

Whitman claimed that he had begun "elaborating the plan of my poems... experimenting much, writing and abandoning much" in 1847, but his assertion that he began "definitely" writing the poems down in 1854 seems closest to the actual facts. The first "notes" that Whitman made for the poems usually consisted of flashes of illumination, revelations of the self and its relationship to the world. He had no guide for the form of these poems, regarding most of the prominent poets of his day as negative examples. Henry Wadsworth Longfellow's enormously popular *The Song of Hiawatha* (1855) he thought had, at best, a "pleasing ripply" effect. Whitman invented a style that was appropriate for his subject, demonstrating that form is an extension of content or an expression of content, and proving the wisdom of Henry David Thoreau's contention that American poetry is nothing but "healthy speech."

> "*This is what you shall do: Love the earth and sun and the animals, despise riches, give alms to everyone that asks, stand up for the stupid and crazy, devote your income and labor to others, hate tyrants, argue not concerning God, have patience and indulgence toward the people, take off your hat to nothing known or unknown, or to any man or number of men...*"

On May 15, 1855, just before his thirty-sixth birthday, Whitman registered the title *Leaves of Grass* and brought the copyright notice to the printing office of Thomas and Joseph Rome. He had been working steadily there throughout that spring, continuing to write and revise while he helped to set type and read the proofs. He not only wrote but also designed, produced, published, and eventually promoted the book that, as Justin Kaplan says, "for nearly forty years [he] made the center of his life, the instrument of health and survival itself." There were 795 copies of the first edition, and two hundred were bound in cloth at a unit cost to Whitman of thirty-two cents, while the remaining copies were given a cheaper binding. The manuscript remained in the Rome brothers' print shop until it was burned accidentally in 1858 "to kindle the fire" as Whitman remarked laconically. On the frontispiece, there was a portrait, uncaptioned, of a bearded man, hand on his hip, hat rakishly askew. Ten pages of prose were followed by eighty-three of poetry, and on page 29, the anonymous author revealed himself:

> Walt Whitman, an American, one of the roughs,
> a kosmos
> Disorderly, fleshy and sensual... eating and drinking
> and breeding
> No sentimentalist... no stander above men and women or
> apart from them... no more modest than immodest.

Whitman was a tireless champion of his own work, but of all of his acts of self-promotion, his most successful and in some senses his most audacious was his gift of *Leaves of Grass* to Ralph Waldo Emerson, the philosopher-poet king of American letters. Emerson replied from Concord, Massachusetts, on July 21, 1855, in a five-page tribute, in which he expressed his enthusiasm for the poetry and saluted the poet "at the beginning of a great career." Many other reviews were less generous, some extremely negative ("a mass of stupid filth"), but praise from people such as Henry David Thoreau, Charles Eliot Norton, and others was sufficient encouragement for the poet.

Whitman was already preparing the second edition of *Leaves of Grass* in 1855 and 1856, composing the first draft of his great poem "Crossing Brooklyn Ferry" (then known as "Sundown Poem") during this time. He continued to supply friendly journals with information about and anonymous reviews of his work, and supplemented his income by writing and selling articles to various newspapers. At Christmas, 1859, he published "Out of the Cradle Endlessly Rocking," then titled "A Child's Reminiscence," which was one of the new poems included in the 1860 edition.

Perhaps because of Emerson's compliments, a Boston publisher, Thayer and Eldridge, offered to produce the second edition of *Leaves of Grass*, and although Emerson cautioned Whitman about some of the sexually suggestive poetry (arguing that unimpeded sales of the book depended on public acceptance), Whitman felt that the book would have to stand as it was. "I have not lived to regret my Emerson no," he stated. He did discard the prose preface, retitled some of the poems, revised several and added 124 new ones, producing a thick volume of 456 pages, bound in orange cloth and stamped with symbolic devices. Now, he thought that *Leaves of Grass* was being "really published" for the first time. This time, the frontispiece was a portrait by a friend that presented Whitman wearing a coat, wide collar, expansive tie, and a grave, intent expression. The book's reception was important to Whitman, but events of a larger magnitude captured his attention.

In February, 1861, Whitman saw Abraham Lincoln, already a proto-heroic image for him of the New Man of the West, when the president traveled up Broadway to stay at the Astor. In April of that year, 250,000 people filled the streets to welcome Major Robert Anderson, a soldier at Fort Sumter. The nation was moving toward civil war, and Whitman's admiration for Lincoln and his cause, plus his brother George's rather impetuous enlistment, tempted the poet himself momentarily to consider military service.

At the age of forty-two, Whitman recognized that he had neither the qualifications nor the disposition to be a soldier. Instead, his instinct for involvement in the great anguish of the Union, and his instinct to offer comfort to young men suffering, led him to New York hospitals, where he worked as a nurse (80 percent of the nurses were male). When his brother was wounded, he traveled to Virginia and shared mess and tent with George for a week. He was trying to earn a living by publishing occasional articles at this time, but when he returned to Washington, he wrote to Emerson that he had ended his "New York stagnation," and he began to try to find a government job. He spent the war years tending the wounded and casually seeking a political appointment, and in 1864, after a lifetime of exceptional health, he suffered a collapse as a result of stress, hypertension, and depression. He was never quite as vigorous again. He succeeded in obtaining a job as a government clerk in 1865, but after Lincoln's death, the new administration swept his friends out and he lost his job.

In October, 1865, Whitman published *Drum Taps*, including the poem "O Captain! My Captain!" his most successful poem during his lifetime, and the superb "When Lilacs Last in the Dooryard Bloom'd," the one poem not included in an anthology celebrating Lincoln a few years later. He was rehired by the government to work in the attorney general's office in 1866 and saw his good friend William O'Connor offer strong support for his work in a sixty-page pamphlet, *The Good Gray Poet* (1866), and in a positive review in the *New York Times*. His work was beginning to develop a favorable reputation in Europe that surpassed the public estimate of his accomplishments in the United States. As a kind of rejoinder to his old intellectual antagonist Carlyle, he published *Democratic Vistas* in 1871, agreeing with Carlyle's pessimistic view of the "present" but envisioning a positive future for his country. As a kind of poetic counterpart to *Democratic Vistas*, he also completed *Passage to India* (1871), in which he described materialistic concerns giving way to spiritual enlightenment.

Whitman suffered a stroke in January, 1873. His mother died in May of that year, a severe blow, and he was discharged from his government job in July. Another stroke occurred in February, 1875, but it did not keep Whitman from his enthusiastic plans for a centennial edition of *Leaves of Grass*, as well as readings and essays commemorating the event. His recollections of his wartime experiences were published in *Specimen Days and Collect* in 1882 and 1883, which also contained his thoughts on the natural world. In 1884, Whitman bought a house on Mickle Street in Camden, New Jersey, and slept under his own roof for the first time in his life. He lived there for eight years, remaining true to the emblem on his writing table, "Make the Works," through that time. In January, 1892, only two months before his death, he had prepared an announcement for what has become known as the "Death-Bed" edition of *Leaves of Grass*, and in his last years, he became, in the words of Allen Ginsberg, "lonely old courage teacher" to his friends and admirers.

SIGNIFICANCE

According to Justin Kaplan, *Leaves of Grass* contained "the most brilliant and original poetry yet written in the New World, at once the fulfillment of American literary romanticism and the beginnings of American literary modernism." As much as he contributed to American literature, however, Whitman's contributions to American cultural life were equally great. At a time when the arts in the United States were still held in a kind of patronizing thrall by European antecedents, Whitman claimed equality for American experience and demonstrated the dominion of singularly American creation. He liberated poetry from its narrow British inclination toward narrative and ode and closed the gap between poetry and its audience.

Similarly, Whitman resisted the tyranny of fashion by his insistence on the beauty of ordinary citizens of the republic and gave Americans a sense of the finest aspects of their own character through his definitive admiration for the open, easy, accepting nature of American life and social commerce. He celebrated the individual, saw the strength of the singular amid the surging crowds of American cities, and at the same time, caught the spirit of American pride in its growing industrial and technological might.

Whitman was reared a quasi-Quaker and followed no standard doctrine or specified religion, but his poetry is based on the best precepts of Christianity—a sympathy whose scope is universal and inclusive, stemming from a predisposition to love and understand. Nevertheless, he was also a kind of pagan, a lover of many gods, ecumenical and free of prejudice and bigotry in his writings, a feature all the more impressive for his personal struggle to overcome some of the more ingrained cultural assumptions of his day.

When the bridge near Camden was named for Whitman, objections from self-designated "Christians" and "Patriots" that Whitman's books were not properly moral echoed the criticism of his own time. Whitman's unabashed expressions of erotic ardor, especially the images of love emphasizing handsome young men, confounded the noxious Puritan strain still virulent in American life, but his sense of love, like his sense of religion, was not limited by any sectarian preference. Rather, his emphasis on social liberty, individual freedom, and artistic integrity, culminating in his archetypal image of the American nation always on the entrance of an open road, stands as a reminder of American strength as a country. As Guy Davenport says, Whitman has been woven into Americans' myth of themselves as their "greatest invention in literature" and as their "lyric voice." As his life and time fade into the glories of a heroic past, his poetry remains as an emblem of his country's beautiful innocence at the dawn of its creation.

Leon Lewis

Further Reading

Allen, Gay Wilson. *The Solitary Singer: A Critical Biography of Walt Whitman*. New York: New York UP, 1967. Print.

Bloom, Harold, ed. *Walt Whitman*. Philadelphia: Chelsea, 2003. Print.

Brasher, Thomas L. *Whitman as Editor of the Brooklyn "Daily Eagle."* Detroit: Wayne State UP, 1970. Print.

Dandeles, Gregory M. "The Laurel Tree Cudgel: War and Walt Whitman in Allen Ginsberg's 'America.'" *Journal of American Culture* 36.3 (2013): 221–29. Print.

Davenport, Guy, ed. *The Geography of the Imagination*. Berkeley: North Point, 1981. Print.

Hummer, T. R. "The Intimacy of Walt Whitman's 'America.'" *Slate*. Slate, 19 Mar. 2013. Web. 4 Nov. 2014.

Kaplan, Justin. *Walt Whitman: A Life*. New York: Simon, 1980. Print.

Martin, Justin. *Rebel Souls: Walt Whitman and America's First Bohemians*. Boston: Da Capo, 2014. Print.

Miller, James E., Jr., ed. *Walt Whitman's "Song of Myself": Origin, Growth, Meaning*. New York: Dodd, 1964. Print.

Reynolds, David S. *Walt Whitman*. New York: Oxford UP, 2005. Print.

Traubel, Horace. *With Walt Whitman in Camden*. Vol. 1. Boston: Small, 1906. Print.

---. *With Walt Whitman in Camden*. Vol. 2. New York: Appleton, 1908. Print.

---. *With Walt Whitman in Camden*. Vol. 3. New York: Kennerly, 1914. Print.

---. *With Walt Whitman in Camden*. Vol. 4. Philadelphia: U of Pennsylvania P, 1953. Print.

---. *With Walt Whitman in Camden*. Vol. 5. Carbondale: Southern Illinois UP, 1964. Print.

Whitman, Walt. *The Correspondence*. Ed. Edwin Haviland Miller. 6 vols. New York: New York UP, 1961–1977. Print.

Zweig, Paul. *Walt Whitman: The Making of the Poet*. New York: Basic, 1984. Print.

August Wilson

Playwright

Born: April 27, 1945; Pittsburgh, Pennsylvania
Died: October 2, 2005; Seattle, Washington
Area of Achievement: Literature; theater

Wilson's award-winning plays earned him acclaim as one of America's leading playwrights. His most extraordinary theatrical achievement is the completion of the Pittsburgh Cycle *in 2005. This is an epic 10-play cycle chronicling African American experience in each decade of the 20th century, chiefly as lived by his fictional families in Pittsburgh's Hill district, where he himself came of age.*

Early Life

August Wilson was born in Pittsburgh, Pennsylvania, in 1945. The son of a white father who was rarely around his family and a black mother who struggled to raise her six children on welfare and her meager income from janitorial jobs, Wilson learned at first hand about the hardships and prejudice facing black people in American society.

When the family moved to a predominantly white neighborhood, bricks were thrown through their windows, and Wilson's schools days at Central Catholic High School were clouded by the racial epithets he often found scrawled on his desk. Wilson's mother, a proud, determined woman who insisted that her children spend time each day reading, imbued young August with a sense of pride and self-esteem.

August Wilson (Getty Images)

Wilson's formal schooling ended in the ninth grade. Refusing to believe that a well-researched and footnoted paper that Wilson submitted could be his own work, his teacher gave him a failing grade. Wilson tore up the paper and never returned to school, choosing instead to educate himself at the local public library, where he read extensively on a wide range of subjects. There, he discovered for the first time the works of black authors such as Langston Hughes, Ralph Ellison, and Richard Wright.

Wilson's teens were for him a time of great anger and frustration, which found occasional release in outbursts of rage as he and his friends smashed the black lawn jockeys that they found in front of white homes. During the 1960's, Wilson joined several Black Power organizations, and for many years he adopted a militant stance toward society's racial injustices.

> *"I write the black experience in America, and contained within that experience, because it is a human experience, are all the universalities."*

He supported himself during this period with a brief stint in the Army and by working as a short-order cook and a stock clerk. A keen observer of the world around him, he also began storing up the details of life in the black community that would later inform his plays, lending to them the authenticity that has made them successful.

LIFE'S WORK

Wilson's career as a writer began almost by chance when he was twenty. His older sister paid him twenty dollars to write a college term paper for her, and he used the money to buy himself a used typewriter. Still supporting himself with odd jobs, Wilson began writing poetry and became associated with the Black Arts movement in Pittsburgh. In 1968, he and playwright Rob Penny founded the Black Horizon Theater, where he worked as a producer and director.

Wilson began writing one-act plays in the early 1970's, but it was not until 1978 when he moved to St. Paul, Minnesota, that he began writing his first full-length play, *Jitney* (1979), the first entry in his ten-play dramatic cycle about African American life in the twentieth century United States. It was also during this period that Wilson met and married his second wife, Judy Oliver. From his earlier marriage he had a daughter, Sakina.

In 1979, Wilson began submitting plays to the O'Neill National Playwrights Conference. When his first four submissions were rejected — the conference rejected *Jitney* twice — Wilson found himself reassessing his previous efforts and embarking on a new project that would test the true depth of his writing talents. The result, *Ma Rainey's Black Bottom*, was accepted by the O'Neill Conference and given a staged reading in 1982.

It was there that Wilson met the conference's artistic director, Lloyd Richards. A powerful force within the American theater community, Richards was for many years the dean of the Yale University School of Drama and the director of the school's acclaimed repertory theater, as well as the first African American ever to direct a play on Broadway. Their meeting led to an ongoing collaboration between writer and director that would contribute greatly to Wilson's subsequent work.

At Richards's urging, Wilson applied for and received numerous grants and fellowships that allowed him to concentrate his efforts solely on his writing. Wilson's plays had their original stagings under Richards's direction at the Yale Repertory Theater before moving on to other regional theaters and to Broadway.

Ma Rainey's Black Bottom opened on Broadway in 1984 and received the New York Drama Critics Circle Award, and Wilson followed it in 1987 with *Fences*, which received four Tony Awards, the Drama Critics Circle Award, the first American Theater Critics Association New Play Award, and the Pulitzer Prize in drama.

Fences was followed by *Joe Turner's Come and Gone* in 1988 and *The Piano Lesson* in 1990, both of which received the Critics Circle Award. *The Piano Lesson* also brought Wilson his second Pulitzer Prize. In 1992, *Two Trains Running*, which received the Critics Circle Award and the American Theater Critics Association New Play Award, opened on Broadway.

In 1997, his early play *Jitney* was revived at the Crossroads Theatre in New Brunswick, New Jersey, and received enthusiastic reviews. The following year, Wilson received the Edward Albee Last Frontier Playwright Award. He collaborated with Victor Walker and others to form the African Grove Institute at Dartmouth College, where he also taught during the 1998 academic year. In 1999, Wilson completed *King Hedley II*, which had its premiere at the Pittsburgh Public Theatre. The play went on to Broadway, where it was about to be closed after twenty-four preview performances and seventy-two regular performances. When it was nominated for a Tony as best play of 2001, however, its run was extended for another ten weeks.

Wilson completed the last play of his decade-by-decade assessment of African American life in the United States, *Radio Golf*, within months of his death in 2005. It was presented at the Mark Taper Forum in Los Angeles in September, 2005. Wilson succumbed to liver cancer on October 2, 2005.

Summary

Wilson's groundbreaking plays chronicling the black experience in the twentieth century, above all in the *Pittsburgh Cycle* or the *Century Cycle*, brought a vital new voice to the American theater. The stories that he told and the complex characters that he created offered powerful dramatic portraits of lives that have often been marginalized or forgotten altogether. Believing that only by embracing their history can African Americans find a true sense of their heritage, Wilson drew on important periods in black history as background material for his plays.

In 2016, Denzel Washington directed the film adaptation of *Fences*, released on Christmas Day. The film was universally lauded, chosen as one of the top 10 films of the year by the American Film Institute, and nominated for four Academy Awards, including Best Picture, Best Actor, Best Supporting Actress, and Best Adapted Screenplay. Viola Davis ended up winning Best Supporting Actress for her portrayal of Rose Lee Maxson.

Further Reading

Bloom, Harold. *August Wilson* (Bloom's Modern Critical Views). Chelsea House, New York: 2009.

Bogumil, Mary L. *Understanding August Wilson*. Columbia: University of South Carolina Press, 1999.

Bryer, Jackson & Hartig, Mary. *Conversations with August Wilson* (Literary Conversations). Jackson, UP of Mississippi, 2006.

Elkins, Marilyn, ed. *August Wilson: A Casebook*. New York: Garland, 1994..

Pereira, Kim. *August Wilson and the African-American Odyssey*. Champaign: University of Illinois Press, 1995.

Snodgrass, Mary Ellen. *August Wilson: A Literary Companion* (Mcfarland Literary Companions). McFarland, 2004. Print.

Medicine

Medicine as we recognize it day depends on insights that were gained mostly in the nineteenth century. The first vaccine was created just before the arrival of that century, in 1796, when Edward Jenner developed a method for administering a vaccine for smallpox. Other vaccines were invented in the late nineteenth century; vaccines for cholera, rabies, anthrax, tetanus, dyphtheria, whooping cough, and tuberculosis were all available before the century was out. The syringe was invented in 1853. The stethoscope was invented in 1816, and the familiar uniform of scrubs and face masks came into existence thanks to the discovery by Louis Pasteur in 1857 that germs cause disease. Ether was first used as a general anesthetic in 1842. Modern drug development began in earnest in the nineteenth century, and the most famous of them all—Aspirin—was developed just before the close of that century in 1899.

As medicine increased dramatically in scientific rigor and complexity, medical education underwent similar changes. The first medical school in the United States opened in 1765 at the College of Philadelphia. Harvard Medical School opened in 1782. In the early days, the educational component was meant to supplement the traditional apprenticeship model for obtaining medical training. This continued for many years. It wasn't until the Johns Hopkins Medical School was established in 1898 that medical education became thoroughly rigorous and based on the model of a university education.

Nursing was established as a profession in the nineteenth century, too. Its origins are generally traced to the pioneering humane, professional, and scientific reforms of Florence Nightingale. Nursing was one of the few professions available to women in the era. One especially ambitious and humanitarian American nurse, Clara Barton, went on to establish the American Red Cross in 1877.

Most of the figures in this section either performed research that led to important medical breakthroughs or they were—or are—involved in some way in public health or advocacy. A few exceptions to this pattern are historic "firsts." Thus, Elizabeth Blackwell is noted as the first woman to have received a medical degree in the United States, and Susan La Flesche Piccotte, an Omaha Native American doctor and reformer, is recognized as the first Native American to have earned a medical degree, etc.

Dr. George Stiles (right), medical researcher at George Washington University, in laboratory with two assistants, 1912. (Library of Congress)

Clara Barton

Nursing pioneer

Born: December 25, 1821; North Oxford, Massachusetts
Died: April 12, 1912; Glen Echo, Maryland
Area of Achievement: Medicine, social reform

After devoting half of her life to humanitarian pursuits, Barton became the key figure in establishing the American Red Cross.

Early Life

Clarissa Harlowe Barton (known as Clara) was influenced by her parents' liberal political attitudes. The youngest child, Clara had identity problems that worsened when she showed interests in academic and other pursuits considered masculine. Farm work and nursing relatives who were ill, however, led her increasingly to connect approval and praise to helping others.

In 1836, Barton began teaching school. She was a gifted teacher who chose to enforce discipline through kindness and persuasion at a time when physical force was the standard. During the next decade, Barton developed quite a reputation as she moved from town to town, taming obstreperous students and leaving for another challenge. As she gained self-confidence, she began to have an active social life, though she never married. Tired of teaching and concerned that her own education was inadequate, she enrolled at the Clinton Liberal Institute in Clinton, New York, at the end of 1850. She studied for a year, but as an older student, she felt out of place and made few friends.

Unable to afford more school and unwilling to be dependent on her family, Barton went to live with friends in New Jersey. In 1852, she persuaded authorities to offer free public education by allowing her to open a free school. Although she was initially unpaid, Barton eventually made the school such a success that she was offered a salary and the opportunity to expand her program. As the school grew, however, the school board decided that a man should be placed in charge and paid more than any women involved. Frustrated and angry, Barton moved to Washington, D.C., in search of new opportunities in 1854.

Barton found work as a clerk in the Patent Office, where the commissioner was willing to give women positions. For several years Barton made good money and earned respect for her efficiency despite the resentment of her male colleagues. Shifting political fortunes forced

Clara Barton (Library of Congress)

Barton to leave her post in 1857. For three years, she lived at home in Massachusetts before returning to the Patent Office in 1860.

> "*I may be compelled to face danger, but never fear it, and while our soldiers can stand and fight, I can stand and feed and nurse them.*"

Life's Work

With the outbreak of the Civil War in 1861, Clara Barton began the humanitarian work that would occupy the rest of her life. Federal troops were arriving in Washington without baggage or food. She began to gather and distribute supplies to ease their distress. Her efforts quickly grew to include battlefield assistance in helping the wounded at the beginning of the war. Because the military had badly underestimated medical needs, Barton's individual effort gathering supplies and caring for the wounded at battles such as Fredericksburg proved immensely valuable. By the end of 1862, however, the Army was becoming better organized and the work of amateurs was no longer significant. Barton also had problems getting official support and recognition because, unlike Barton, most volunteers were more harm than help. The Army could not accept one volunteer while denying others. Barton, as she often did, became defensive, taking every rebuke, regardless of the source, personally.

After the war, Barton undertook a project to identify missing soldiers and inform their families of their fates. Her efforts included a trip to Andersonville prison where, with the help of a former inmate who had kept the death roll, Barton supervised the identification and marking of some 13,000 graves. Despite some success, Barton's work in tracing missing soldiers resulted in identification of less than 10 percent of the missing.

During her pursuit of these activities, Barton confronted two difficulties of a sort typical of her career. One problem arose because the Army was also attempting to find missing soldiers. Barton sought sole control of the whole effort, but this control was not granted and she feuded with the officer in charge. Barton possessed a zeal for efficiency that made her reluctant to share responsibility or credit. This attitude prevented her from delegating authority and provoked hostility among many people who actually wanted to help her. The second problem was a result of poor accounting. She could not provide details of expenses, leaving herself open to charges of malfeasance.

Memorial to Barton at the Antietam National Battlefield site. (Wikimedia Commons)

Although she was always more interested in field work than administration, Barton was unwilling to share power with someone who would handle paperwork. She paid little attention to tracking the disbursement of donated funds and poured her own limited resources into her projects even though she could produce no receipts. There is no evidence that she sought personal gain. Nevertheless, her poor accounting resulted in repeated complaints that ultimately came back to haunt her during her work with the Red Cross.

Barton's involvement with the Red Cross began in Europe, where she met some of the organization's leaders and learned that the United States had not ratified the Treaty of Geneva (1864) that had created the organization. Barton was invited to assist in the work of the International Red Cross during the Franco-Prussian War of 1870-1871. Her experiences gave her a new perspective on the suffering of civilians during war—she had worked almost entirely on behalf of soldiers in the Civil War. Friendship with Grand Duchess Louise of Baden, a Red Cross leader, resulted in Barton working six months in Strasbourg. She was convinced of the value of the Red Cross and determined that supporting self-help was better than handouts. She held these convictions the rest of her life.

In 1872, Barton returned to the United States, after suffering a nervous breakdown that some regarded as partially psychosomatic. Retiring from public life to stay in a sanatorium eventually improved her health. In 1877, she decided to form an American Red Cross society to gather funds to help victims of the Russo-Turkish War. She received permission from the International Red Cross, and began a campaign to secure American ratification of the Treaty of Geneva. U.S. government officials, however, insisted that because the country observed the tenets of the treaty, there was no reason for a formal alliance.

Barton lobbied diligently for ratification. She sought help from friends in Washington, D.C., cultivated the press, and relied upon her friendship with members of the Grand Army of the Republic, a Civil War veterans group that had honored her. To increase awareness of the work of the Red Cross, Barton made peacetime disaster relief a priority. Progress was slow, but the treaty was ratified in 1882. Her group was officially recognized by the government, paving the way for it to be associated with the International Red Cross. This recognition helped Barton launch her next campaign: to make the American Association of the Red Cross the central relief agency in the United States.

The 1880's and 1890's were times of heroic effort for Barton. Her labor was certainly greatly increased by her refusal to yield any share of control, and, during the decades of her presidency, she and the Red Cross were essentially synonymous. She wanted the national agency to be the center of a network of state groups, but she was frequently drawn away from organizing to oversee field work and was hampered by continual shortages of funds. She also spent much of 1883 running a women's prison at the request of Benjamin Butler,Butler, Benjamin the former Union general who had become governor of Massachusetts. Assisting Butler with his political problems concerning the funding of the progressive prison, Barton established that the costs were mostly appropriate, despite sloppy administrative work. Unfortunately, her efforts on Butler's behalf diverted Barton's attention from the urgent demands of Red Cross work.

For the rest of her life, however, Barton devoted herself almost exclusively to Red Cross work. She traveled, seeking funds and public support—sometimes for herself as well as her cause—and attended annual meetings of the International Red Cross, where she was accepted as a delegate when no other woman was even allowed on the convention floor. She was a hero to feminists, whose cause she supported, although never so vigorously as to cause hostility toward the Red Cross. Field work continued to beckon, including relief efforts in the wake of floods in the Ohio and Mississippi River valleys in 1884 and an earthquake in Charleston, South Carolina, in 1886. She allowed the head of the New Orleans chapter to lead an effort in a yellow fever epidemic around Jacksonville, Florida, only to find that the nurses he took resembled camp followers more than caregivers. This incident confirmed her determination to do everything herself.

Barton received praise from the press for relief efforts in the wake of the 1889 Johnstown flood, but she was later greatly criticized for not keeping track of expenditures. Some of the expenses appear to have been inappropriate, though not fraudulent, but her lack of receipts made defense against such criticism almost impossible. Barton hoped to parlay the Johnstown success into government funding for the Red Cross as the official agency for coordinating wartime relief. This effort stalled, however, and she turned her attention to efforts to alleviate a Russian famine.

By the mid-1890's, relief funds were at a low ebb and criticism of her poor accounting hampered the activities of both the American and international organizations. Although Barton was in her seventies and her energy was beginning to decline, she repudiated every criticism, attacked critics, and continued. In 1896, she went to Turkey to aid Armenians suffering from Turkish atrocities. She secured permission from the Turkish sultan to send Dr. Julian Hubbell, one of her most loyal collaborators, into Armenia, where he had significant success.

Back in the United States, she found appeals from Cuban civilians suffering in the struggle against Spain. Because the U.S. government wanted to keep out of the situation, little was being done to provide relief. Eventually, Barton went to survey the situation with a committee of relief agencies. When the head of another agency criticized her work and tried to supplant her, Barton returned to the United States and got her rival discredited. By the time she returned to Cuba, however, the Spanish-American War (1898) had begun. The New York Red Cross chapter, which, along with several others, had been acting almost autonomously, provided necessary assistance to stateside military hospitals, and the California chapter sent aid to the Pacific front in the Philippines. Barton headed for Cuba, eventually leaving without official sanction. Although intending to help civilians, her team stumbled into a battle fought by the Rough Riders. To her delight, Barton found herself nursing soldiers again. Important work with civilians followed, and the Red Cross proved its value.

The organization's efforts during the Spanish-American War and its aftermath did lead to legislation granting a federal charter to the American Red Cross in 1900. In the end, however, this success was also Barton's downfall. Concerned that donations were in decline, some members of the Red Cross organized independent efforts during Barton's absence and were reluctant to relinquish control to her. The crisis came after a hurricane in Galveston, Texas, in September of 1900.

Barton launched relief efforts without consulting the organization's new board of directors, and her bookkeeping was so lackadaisical that the national treasurer resigned rather than defend her expenditures. The struggle went on for several years, becoming more acrimonious because Barton came to regard her critics as personal foes. Finally, Barton was forced to resign all ties to the Red Cross in 1904. She did retain quarters at a house in Maryland that had been built largely with her own money and had served as Red Cross headquarters during the final years of her presidency. Continuing to support public health efforts and the woman's rights movement, Barton alternated living in Maryland and in North Oxford, Massachusetts, until her death in April, 1912.

Significance

Clara Barton established the American Red Cross almost singlehandedly. Earlier efforts to do so had failed, and the nation lacked a major disaster relief agency. Rival organizations did arise, but most were launched later in imitation of Barton's efforts. Barton's prodigious labor and self-sacrifice on behalf of establishing the American Red Cross ultimately earned for her the recognition she desired, yet she never allowed her ego to prevent her from giving unstintingly of her work and wealth to those who needed help.

That ego did, however, cause problems. The combination of childhood insecurity and individual success in the Civil War rendered Barton incapable of working equally with others. She preferred to work with trusted aides who deferred to her authority, and she seemed to interpret any initiative outside her control as a personal affront. This caused Barton much disquiet and slowed the growth of the Red Cross. Although most if not all the charges made against her personally were without merit, it cannot be denied that had she shared leadership with someone who was willing to do the vital paperwork much more progress could have been made. Furthermore, Barton's reputation would not have been sullied. Nevertheless, her crusading spirit on behalf of nursing reform created for Barton an impressive legacy.

Fred R. van Hartesveldt

Further Reading

Barton, Clara. *The Story of My Childhood.* Reprint. New York: Arno Press, 1980. Although it was intended to be the first chapter of an autobiography and hence covers only Barton's first years, this work is a valuable source given the influence of her childhood on her character.

Barton, William E. *The Life of Clara Barton.* 2 vols. Boston: Houghton Mifflin, 1922. An old-fashioned and uncritical biography, but filled with details and information often missing in modern studies.

Burton, David H. *Clara Barton: In the Service of Humanity.* Westport, Conn.: Greenwood Press, 1995. Sympathetic yet critical biography, which suggests that Barton's dedication to helping people in need was not entirely selfless. While he recounts the many examples of Barton's heroism and generosity, the author also portrays his subject as a self-centered and thin-skinned personality.

Dulles, Foster Rhea. *The American Red Cross.* New York: Harper & Brothers, 1950. Written by an excellent historian, this valuable work provides background on Barton and her work with the Red Cross.

Oates, Stephen B. *A Woman of Valor: Clara Barton and the Civil War.* New York: Free Press, 1994. Best known for his biographies of Abraham Lincoln, Oates provides a vivid account of Clara Barton's early career during the Civil War years. While revealing Barton's drive to succeed and her skill in generating public support for her relief efforts, Oates's detailed narrative also illuminates her difficult personality and strained emotional life, thus providing a welcome corrective to older, less critical accounts.

Pryor, Elizabeth B. *Clara Barton: Professional Angel.* Philadelphia: University of Pennsylvania Press, 1987. Although informed by the author's research into numerous primary sources, this biography suffers somewhat from a lack of critical distance in its approach, as suggested by its subtitle.

Ross, Ishbel. *Angel of the Battlefield: The Life of Clara Barton.* New York: Harper & Brothers, 1956. A reasonable biography, though somewhat dated. Like most of the work on Barton, this volume is adulatory in its approach.

Martha Bernal

Psychologist and educator

Born: April 13, 1931; San Antonio, Texas
Died: September 28, 2001; Black Canyon City, Arizona
Area of Achievement: Child psychology

Bernal was the first woman of Mexican heritage to receive a doctorate in clinical psychology from an American university. She became a leading researcher on methods of correcting behavioral problems in children and an expert in the training of psychologists on minority and multicultural issues.

Early Life

Martha Bernal (behr-NAHL) was born in San Antonio, Texas, and raised in El Paso by her parents, Alicia and Enrique de Bernal, who emigrated from Mexico during the Mexican Revolution. Her parents instilled in her traditional Mexican values, including an emphasis on the importance of family. The family spoke Spanish at home. When Bernal enrolled in elementary school unable to speak English, she began learning about discrimination toward Mexican culture. She experienced difficulties growing up in a bicultural community from this young age because interaction among children of different races was discouraged.

Bernal graduated from El Paso High School and desired more formal education, a choice that was not typical for Mexican women, who generally were encouraged to then marry and raise families. Although resistant, her parents eventually agreed to Bernal's wishes and financially supported her while she attended Texas Western College, now known as the University of Texas at El Paso.

After graduating from college with a bachelor's degree in psychology, Bernal continued her education by earning a master of arts degree from Syracuse University in New York (1955). She subsequently obtained a doctoral degree in clinical psychology from Indiana University in 1962. As a woman, Bernal was not allowed to participate in research projects with her psychology professors and often considered dropping out because of this gender discrimination. By persevering, Bernal became the first Mexican American woman to earn a doctorate in clinical psychology.

> "After 1979, I wanted to conduct research that had bearing on central issues affecting ethnic minorities. For this reason, my previous research seemed dissatisfying. It became necessary to change research fields, and I struggled for several years to carve out a new minority mental health research area for myself."

LIFE'S WORK

Bernal had great difficulty obtaining her first academic job because institutions only wanted to hire male psychologists. Instead, she completed a two-year postdoctoral fellowship in human psychophysiology through the U.S. Public Health Service at the University of California at Los Angeles (UCLA). With this added experience, Bernal eventually obtained her first academic position in 1969 as assistant professor at the University of Arizona at Tucson.

Bernal returned to UCLA's Neuropsychiatric Institute to begin her scientific research. She was awarded a grant by the National Institute of Mental Health (NIMH) to study learning theory and classical conditioning in children with behavior problems, most notably autism. Her research concentrated on altering the parents' behavior by teaching them skills and lessons to help change their children's behavior. Bernal believed that children with autism did not have an innate cause for their disorder but rather had learned their behaviors. For this work, Bernal was bestowed several National Research Service Awards from the NIMH and is cited as one of the first psychologists to study this subject in an empirical manner.

After several years at UCLA, Bernal relocated to the University of Denver to continue her work. There she evaluated the efficacy and validity of her previous studies. In addition to her professional research, Bernal became more involved in minority issues regarding race and gender discrimination after attending the influential Conference on Chicano Psychology (1973). Bernal refocused her scientific research in order to make it more applicable to minority issues. She also acted as an advocate for minorities and professionally sought the help of the American Psychological Association to bring attention to minority issues in the profession. In 1979, the NIMH gave Bernal another National Research Science Award to educate psychologists about multicultural issues.

Bernal's initial findings regarding diversity in the psychology field were not encouraging: training programs lacked appropriately sensitive multicultural lectures and curricula, had little to no minority students enrolled, and did not employ minority professors. She completed a second postdoctoral fellowship through the Ford Foundation in which she studied ways to eliminate these disparities. In 1986, Bernal moved to Arizona State University, where she focused on marriage counseling of minority couples when mental illness was diagnosed in the wife. Additionally, it was at Arizona State University that she performed much of her groundbreaking work on how identities are established in Mexican American children and families. The research has been hailed as pioneering because of the creative and new interview approaches used in an attempt to understand how ethnicity is created and transmitted from influences such as parents, families, other adults, and peers.

Bernal raised awareness of multicultural issues by speaking at many professional conferences. She spoke at the 1972 Vail Conference on Training in Psychology and the Lake Arrowhead National Conference of Hispanic Psychologists (1979). She was influential with drafting the bylaws of the Board of Ethnic Minority Affairs (1979) and helped establish the National Hispanic Psychological Association (1979), now known as the National Latino/a Psychological Association, of which she eventually became president. Bernal was appointed to the Commission on Ethnic Minority Recruitment, Retention and Training (1994) and served on the board for the Advancement of Psychology in the Public Interest (1996-1998).

Bernal's Work on Negative Stereotypes of Mexican Americans

Martha Bernal focused much effort on cultural education to overcome stereotypes that persons of Mexican heritage are criminals, violent, and drug users. Her research attempted to provide a greater understanding and respect of the Mexican culture and to discourage the exploitation of its people. While at Arizona State University, Bernal created a method of measuring ethnic identity called the Ethnic Identity Questionnaire. Bernal used this tool to interview Mexican and Mexican American children and families. The research brought to light common feelings and thoughts, including how Mexican identity is influenced and formed and how American society can better appreciate Mexican culture. She published the findings of these studies in a book titled *Ethnic Identity: Formation and Transmission Among Hispanics and Other Minorities* (1993), as well as in several peer-reviewed scientific journals. Bernal frequently lectured about her research findings in order to raise multicultural awareness. For three years, she also coordinated an annual Ethnic Identity Symposium to address these issues.

Among the noteworthy awards that Bernal received are the Distinguished Life Achievement Award from Division 45 of the Society for the Psychological Study of Ethnic Minority Issues (1979), the Hispanic Research Center Lifetime Award (1979), the Pioneer Senior Women of Color Honor (1999), the Carolyn Attneave Diversity Award for lifelong contributions to ethnic minorities psychology (1999), and the Award for Distinguished Contributions to the Public Interest from the American Psychological Association (2001).

After three separate occurrences of cancer over two decades, Bernal died of lung cancer at seventy years of age. The Martha E. Bernal Memorial Award at Arizona State University was established in her honor.

Significance

Bernal overcame cultural and gender discrimination in her youth and throughout her career. She convinced not only her family but also her colleagues that Mexican women could become productive and successful in the professional and academic worlds. Although Bernal's early career path was not focused on ethnicity or minority issues, she realized the importance of these issues and fought for more than twenty years in order to incorporate them into the field of psychology. Bernal's groundbreaking research on minority populations serves as a basis for the now-common multicultural studies classes in undergraduate and graduate psychology and counseling programs.

Janet Ober Berman

Further Reading

Bernal, Martha E. "Behavioral Feedback in the Modification of Brat Behaviors." *The Journal of Nervous and Mental Disease* 148, no. 4. (April, 1969): 375-385. Bernal's initial clinical research findings on how to modify children's behavior problems using classical conditioning.

Bernal, Martha E., and George P. Knight. *Ethnic Identity: Formation and Transmission Among Hispanics and Other Minorities.* Albany: State University of New York Press, 1993. Details Bernal's research findings on multicultural awareness and the development of ethnic identification.

Bernal Martha E., et al, eds. "Mexican American Identity." Mountain View, Calif.: Floricanto Press, 2005. Edited by Bernal and colleagues, this book focuses on how society, politics, and public policy influence views of Mexican Americans and how Mexican identity is established.

Vasquez, Melba J. T. "The Life and Death of a Multicultural Feminist Pioneer: Martha Bernal (1931-2001)." *The Feminist Psychologist Newsletter* 30, no. 1 (Winter, 2003). A tribute to Bernal's life and work, chronicling the struggles Bernal faced both professionally and personally as a Mexican American woman in the field of clinical psychology.

Elizabeth Blackwell

Physician

Born: February 3, 1821; Bristol, England
Died: May 31, 1910; Hastings, England
Area of Achievement: Medicine, women's rights

As the first woman to receive a degree from an American medical school, Elizabeth Blackwell became a leading figure in the drive to open the field of medicine to women.

Elizabeth Blackwell (Wikimedia Commons)

EARLY LIFE

Elizabeth Blackwell was born on February 3, 1821, in a small town near Bristol, England. The third of nine surviving children of Samuel and Hannah Blackwell, Elizabeth joined a family heavily influenced by the progressive and reformist values held by her father. In addition to being a successful sugar refiner, Samuel Blackwell was an outspoken member of his community, having wedded the practice of his Puritan faith with the support of various liberal causes, such as women's rights, temperance, and the abolition of slavery.

> *"If society will not admit of woman's free development, then society must be remodeled."*

The destruction of his refinery by fire in 1832 led Samuel Blackwell to move his family to America. After a few years spent in New York and New Jersey, the Blackwells came to settle in Cincinnati, Ohio, in May, 1838. Pursued to the end by his monetary troubles, Samuel Blackwell died in August of that year, leaving Hannah, her two eldest daughters, and Elizabeth responsible for providing for the family. They were able to do so by opening what would become a successful boarding school, where Elizabeth spent the first four of her seven years as a teacher.

It was during these seven years, which also included one year in Kentucky and two more in North and South Carolina, that Elizabeth Blackwell began to grow frustrated at the limits of the teaching profession, both in its poor remuneration and its low social status. She also became aware of her growing aversion to the idea of marriage, an institution which, at the time, imposed even greater restrictions than did teaching on the women who entered into it. These realizations became important factors in Blackwell's decision to pursue a career in the highly respected field of medicine, a field so utterly dominated by men that no woman had ever before received a diploma from an American medical school.

LIFE'S WORK

It was during her final two years teaching in the Carolinas that Elizabeth Blackwell, within the personal libraries of the distinguished physicians John and Samuel Dickson, began her study of medicine. These years of self-education served to prepare Blackwell for her move, in May of 1847, to Philadelphia, the home of several well-respected medical schools to which she would subsequently apply. This application process forced Blackwell to confront the institutional prejudices of the day. Although they were often supported by sympathetic faculty members, her applications were rejected by every medical school in Philadelphia and New York as well as by several rural colleges of much less stellar reputations. It was only when the administration of Geneva Medical College in upstate New York put her application up for review by the all-male student body that Blackwell's determination won her a chance for a legitimate education. Presented with a woman's name, the students had thought the submission was a joke and passed it unanimously.

Immediately upon beginning her studies, Blackwell experienced the scorn of both townspeople and fellow students alike. Even the women within the community were taken aback by what they perceived as brash and unfeminine behavior by Blackwell in her pursuit of medical training, and she was often made aware that the idea of a woman physician upset many of those who would one day benefit from the course of action she was endeavoring to take. Gradually, however, Blackwell's intelligence and doggedness won her great measures of respect from important faculty members and the other students with whom she worked.

After completing an internship in 1848 at the Philadelphia Hospital and writing a thesis based on her

Historical street marker in Syracuse, New York honoring Blackwell at the site of Geneva college, no SUNY Upstate Medical School. (Wikimedia Commons)

experiences there, Blackwell emerged from her course work with a focus that would last throughout her professional career: the importance of preventative care in the form of improved personal hygiene. With this focus established and her studies complete, Blackwell received her medical degree from Geneva Medical College on January 23, 1849. She became the first woman in the United States to ever earn such an honor and was ranked first in her graduating class.

Before she was to begin her career in earnest in New York in August of 1851, Blackwell spent a year and a half abroad, in both England and France, with the intention of enhancing her education. Though received graciously by the medical community in England and invited by prominent staff members of several hospitals to tour their grounds, Blackwell found that in France the only kind of advanced training available to her was as a midwife.

This period in Blackwell's life is most notable for the eye disease she contracted from a patient during her midwives' course at La Maternité in Paris, the resulting loss of sight in one eye dashed her hopes of ever becoming a surgeon. Through these trials, Blackwell's strength of character enabled her to overcome adversity. Toward the end of her stay in Europe, she returned to England and gained valuable clinical experience under the supervision of Dr. James Paget at St. Bartholomew's Hospital. In retrospect, the setbacks she experienced in this interlude abroad helped steel Blackwell for the resistance she encountered in her attempts to establish herself as a practicing physician in New York.

For a woman doctor during the 1850's, merely finding a place in which to practice proved a near impossibility. Blackwell's applications to city dispensaries for positions in the pediatric wards were flatly rejected, as were her requests to visit the female wards of a city hospital. These rejections were handed down despite her rather impressive array of degrees and recommendations. Even more indicative of this era's prejudice was Blackwell's inability even to rent a space of her own for private practice. No landlord would lease a space for such a disreputable practice, knowing that every other tenant who might be sharing a building with a "female physician" (the contemporary euphemism for "abortionist") would be forced to move or be shamed.

While overcoming these obstacles and patiently awaiting the growth of her practice, Blackwell succeeded in publishing a series of lectures on hygiene in 1852. Later, in 1853, Blackwell opened a dispensary for the poor, supported by funds she raised herself. Four years later, her dispensary became the New York Infirmary for Women and Children, the first hospital completely organized and operated by women. Outside her professional life, Blackwell in 1853 took on the responsibility of adopting a seven-year-old orphan named Katherine Barry who would remain her closest relation for the rest of her days.

In her battle to open the infirmary in 1857, Elizabeth Blackwell was joined by two other women doctors: her younger sister, Emily, who had followed Elizabeth into the profession, and Marie Zakrzewska, a Polish émigré who had been educated at Western Reserve College (later Case Western Reserve University) and who would become the resident physician at the infirmary until 1859. Once this hospital was established, Blackwell's next major goal was to create a medical college for women with a commitment to rigorous preparation and to the cause of good hygiene. Before this goal was to materialize, however, Blackwell departed in August of 1858 for a one-year stay in Great Britain, where she both practiced medicine and lectured, and also made the acquaintance of such admirers as Dr. Elizabeth Garrett and Florence Nightingale.

Upon Blackwell's return to the United States, her plans were interrupted by the outbreak of the Civil War, during which she became involved in a committee concerned with the status of care for soldiers and also helped to select and train nurses going out into the field. Finally, in 1868, Blackwell brought her quest to fruition as she founded the Woman's Medical College of the New York Infirmary and served as the first chair of hygiene at the college. (The college eventually became part of Cornell's medical school in 1899, after the university decided to grant admission to women.)

In 1869, Elizabeth Blackwell left the United States to live and work in Great Britain. At first, she took up residence in London, where she practiced privately until she accepted a position at the New Hospital and London School of Medicine for Women in 1875. As a result of her ill health, Blackwell was forced to retire after just one year. Leaving London, she moved with Katherine Barry to Hastings, where Blackwell spent most of her last thirty years. Never one to remain idle for long, Blackwell spent these days writing books, essays, and articles addressing a wide variety of topics, but especially focusing on the issues of medicine and morality. She also visited the continent and traveled to the United States in 1906. In 1907, she suffered injuries as a result of falling down some stairs at her summer house in the Scottish highlands. Blackwell died at her seaside home in Hastings in 1910 and was buried in Scotland.

Significance

It would not be difficult to present Elizabeth Blackwell's achievements as a list of breakthroughs in the process of opening the field of medicine to women. As the first woman to ever receive a degree from an American medical school, the founder of the first hospital run solely by women, and the founder of one of the earliest medical colleges for women, Blackwell stands as a distinguished pioneer in the fight for a woman's right to become a practicing physician.

To focus on her breakthroughs alone, however, would unfairly limit the scope of Blackwell's contribution. From the moment she decided to pursue her degree, Blackwell committed herself to more than mere medicine. Desiring a greater status than was afforded by traditional feminine pursuits and seeking a level of freedom that she could find nowhere else, Blackwell chose to challenge the various obstacles that hindered women from pursuing professional careers. Medicine was the avenue she selected in order to accomplish her ultimate goal of advancing the opportunities available to women. Immersed in her era's atmosphere of social activism, Blackwell dedicated her work and her writings to causes of morality and equality. The breadth of Elizabeth Blackwell's influence is amply illustrated by the names of those individuals—people as various as Herbert Spencer and Florence Nightingale, as Dante Gabriel Rossetti and George Eliot—who came to admire and respect Blackwell's ideas and accomplishments.

Bonnie L. Ford

Further Reading

Abram, Ruth J., ed."Send Us a Lady Physician": *Women Doctors in America, 1835-1920.* New York: W. W. Norton, 1986. Compiled to accompany a museum exhibit, this collection of essays celebrates the pioneering spirit of early women physicians and describes the experience of women in the health professions during the nineteenth and early twentieth centuries.

Blackwell, Elizabeth. *Pioneer Work in Opening the Medical Profession to Women.* Reprint. Amherst, N.Y.: Humanity Books, 2004. Originally published in 1895, this work consists of autobiographical sketches that delineate the enormous struggle Blackwell had to endure in order to enter and graduate from medical school. It is clear that she was fully conscious of her historical role.

Brown, Jordan. *Elizabeth Blackwell.* New York: Chelsea House, 1989. This biography is part of the publisher's American Women of Achievement series. Although primarily intended for young adult readers, the book provides an excellent introduction to Blackwell's life and examines the various issues that confronted her in her quest to provide opportunities for women in the medical profession.

Hume, Ruth Fox. *Great Women of Medicine.* New York: Random House, 1964. Hume devotes her first chapter to Blackwell and offers the reader a compact biography that emphasizes Blackwell's early life and career in the United States until her retirement in England.

Morantz-Sanchez, Regina. "Feminist Theory and Historical Practice: Rereading Elizabeth Blackwell." *History and Theory* 31 (December, 1992): 51-69. A scholar analyzes Blackwell's writings to demonstrate how the discussion of scientific topics in these works reflected Blackwell's feminist concerns.

Ross, Ishbel. *Child of Destiny: The Life Story of the First Woman Doctor.* New York: Harper & Row, 1949. Ross wrote a full-length biography of Blackwell with the aid of interviews with family members. Full of fascinating detail, the book chronicles Blackwell's work as well as her personal life and her many associations with major figures of the nineteenth century. It places her within the reform movement of the era.

Wilson, Dorothy Clarke. *Lone Woman: The Story of Elizabeth Blackwell, the First Woman Doctor.* Boston: Little, Brown, 1970. Novelist, dramatist, and biographer, Dorothy Clarke Wilson brings her dramatic skills to enliven this solid biography that is based on family reminiscences and papers as well as extensive research in primary sources.

DEEPAK CHOPRA

Indian-born American physician

Born: October 22, 1946; New Delhi, India
Area of Achievement: Health and medicine; television and radio

Deepak Chopra, an American physician born in India, is a best-selling writer and popular public speaker whose work centers on mind/body medicine and health, spirituality, quantum mechanics, and Ayurveda, a traditional medicine system native to India. Ayurveda in the West is largely classified as alternative medicine.

Deepak Chopra (Wikimedia Commons)

EARLY LIFE

As a youth, Chopra yearned to become a journalist or actor, but he was later inspired to become a physician by a character in the Sinclair Lewis novel *Arrowsmith*. Chopra completed his medical education at the All India Institute of Medical Sciences in New Delhi. He began his medical career as an endocrinologist, obtaining certification in internal medicine with a specialty in endocrinology. However, Chopra later shifted to a career focused in alternative medicine. Before embarking on his own productive medical career, Chopra studied, for several years, with Maharishi Mahesh Yogi, who developed Transcendental Meditation and is regarded as the guru of the movement associated with the technique.

Chopra moved to the United States in 1968 and completed his medical internship and residency in New Jersey, Massachusetts, and Virginia. He obtained his medical license in Massachusetts in 1973 and another in California in 2004. During his early career, Chopra also served as a professor, both at Tufts University and at Boston University. In addition, he was chief of staff at Boston Regional Medical Center. He later went on to establish a private practice. He has been a longtime member of many respected societies, including the American College of Physicians, the American Medical Association (AMA), and the American Association of Clinical Endocrinologists.

LIFE'S WORK

In 1985, Chopra met Maharishi Mahesh Yogi. The well-known alternative practitioner offered to mentor Chopra in the study of Ayurveda. Soon after studying with the Maharishi, Chopra was appointed founding president of the American Association of Ayurvedic Medicine. He later was named the medical director of the Maharishi Ayurveda Health Center for Stress Management and Behavioral Medicine.

Chopra was later appointed executive director of the Sharp Institute for Human Potential and Mind-Body Medicine. Around 1993, he moved with his family to Southern California. The following year, Chopra formally left the Transcendental Meditation movement, reportedly making this decision after his former mentor accused him of trying to compete with his position and to obtain the qualification of "guru."

Chopra resigned from the Sharp Institute in 1996. With David Simon, a medical doctor and an authority in mind/body medicine, he founded the Chopra Center for

Well Being in La Jolla, California. The center offers courses in Ayurveda and other alternative medicine techniques. In recent years, some notable institutions (such as the AMA and the University of California) have granted education credits for physicians studying at the center.

Chopra had written more than eighty books that have been translated into dozens of languages. These books are concerned with New Age spirituality, alternative medicine, and peace, among other topics. More than twenty have been New York Times best sellers. He has sold more than twenty million copies worldwide. Chopra also has hosted a weekly radio show, in which he interviewed scientists and others working in alternative medicine. He has been vocal about his opposition to the over-prescribing of drugs and to drug dependency, especially after the death of his friend, singer-songwriter Michael Jackson.

> "There are no extra pieces in the universe. Everyone is here because he or she has a place to fill, and every piece must fit itself into the big jigsaw puzzle."

Chopra has received various awards for his work in alternative medicine. Esquire magazine named him one of the "top ten motivational speakers" in the United States. He has served as an adviser to the National Ayurveda Medical Association since 2002, and in 2005 he was also appointed senior scientist at the Gallup Organization. In addition, he has served as an adjunct professor at the Kellogg School of Management at Northwestern University. Chopra also contributes significantly to various media, acting as a columnist for the *San Francisco Chronicle* and *The Washington Post*, and he regularly contributes to Intent.com and the HuffingtonPost.com.

Significance

Like other alternative and complementary medicine practitioners, Chopra has many critics. Some opponents of his work argue that he misleads and exploits the ill. In particular, critics claim that he creates false hope in the weak, deterring them from seeking traditional, possibly more effective, medical care. Furthermore, some of his critics argue that much of Chopra's popularity comes from his public speaking abilities, not from his teachings. Chopra has said that "perfect health is a matter of choice." *Business Week* indicated that one of Chopra's main teachings is that health can be improved by ridding oneself of negative emotions and by developing intuitive communication with one's own body.

As of 2015, Chopra has written 80 books, 21 of them *New York Times* bestsellers, which have been translated into 43 languages. His book *The Seven Spiritual Laws of Success* was on the *New York Times* Best Seller list for 72 weeks.

Brandy Weidow, M.S.

The Maharishi and Transcendental Meditation

Deepak Chopra first met the Maharishi Mahesh Yogi in 1985. The Maharishi had for three decades been the exponent of Transcendental Meditation (TM). He introduced his technique in 1955, touring worldwide to present it. The Maharishi attracted widespread influence in the West, not least because The Beatles and other celebrities took an interest in him. Chopra quickly absorbed TM teaching and became interested in the Maharishi's promotion of Ayurvedic medicine. The term *ayurveda* means "longevity" in Sanskrit. Ayurveda, also called Vedic philosophy, stresses balance, exercise, meditation, and massage, as well as the healing properties of things found in nature. Chopra has acknowledged that the Maharishi inspired him to see how the use of meditation can help slow the aging process. However, by 1994, Chopra had severed his connections with the official TM movement, as he saw it a hindrance to developing his own brand of Vedic philosophy.

Further Reading

Chopra, Deepak. "Medicine's Great Divide: The View from the Alternative Side." *American Medical Association Journal of Ethics* 13.6 (2011): 394–98. Print.

---. *Perfect Health: The Complete Mind/Body Guide*. Rev. ed. New York: Harmony, 2001. Print.

---. *Reinventing the Body, Resurrecting the Soul: How to Create a New You*. New York: Three Rivers, 2010. Print.

Ninivaggi, Frank John. *Ayurveda: A Comprehensive Guide to Traditional Indian Medicine for the West*. Westport: Praeger, 2008. Print.

Margaret Chung

Physician

Born: October 2, 1889; Santa Barbara, California
Died: January 5, 1959; San Francisco, California
Areas of achievement: Medicine, government and politics

Margaret Chung was the first American-born Chinese woman physician in the United States. She was also responsible for organizing and inspiring members of the armed forces in the fight against the occupying Japanese forces in China during World War II.

Early Life

Margaret Chung was born on October 2, 1889, in Santa Barbara, California. Her mother, Ah Yane, had emigrated from China in 1874 at a young age. At age eleven, Ah Yane was arrested in a San Francisco brothel, removed from her guardians' care, and transferred to the Chinese Presbyterian Mission Home. Margaret's father, Chung Wong, arrived in California in 1875 as a teenager, eventually establishing himself as a merchant of imported Chinese goods. Ah Yane and Chung Wong likely met through their work with Presbyterian missionaries and, in November of 1888, the couple married and relocated to Santa Barbara. Less than a year later, their first child, Margaret, was born.

Racial discrimination made life difficult for the Chung family, and Chung Wong's retail business eventually failed, forcing him to file for bankruptcy and to take on manual jobs as a fruit vendor, ranch foreman, and truck driver. When Margaret was about ten years old, her father became bedridden by rheumatism and her mother became increasingly weakened from tuberculosis.

As the oldest of eleven children, Margaret assumed most of the responsibility for caring for her parents and siblings and took a job at a restaurant to supplement her father's income. Through her determination and hard work, she earned enough money from scholarships and odd jobs to put herself through college and medical school.

Life's Work

In 1916, Margaret Chung graduated from the University of Southern California's College of Physicians and Surgeons. She completed her residency at Kankakee State Hospital in Illinois, specializing in surgery, psychiatry, and criminology. Following her father's death in 1917, Chung returned to Southern California and began work as a staff surgeon at the Santa Fe Railroad Hospital, eventually establishing a small practice in Los Angeles.

In 1922, Chung moved to San Francisco and established a private practice there, slowing expanding it as she gained the respect of the local community. Despite the move, she nevertheless maintained her practice in Los Angeles, making frequent trips by plane between the two cities and eventually attracting a large clientele of Hollywood celebrities. In 1925, Chung became one of the founding physicians of Chinese Hospital in San Francisco's Chinatown, which was one of the first modern medical clinics in the neighborhood. Through her practice, Chung established many important connections and loyal friendships and was known to host dinners for her clients at her home.

In 1931, Chung was responsible for conducting the medical examinations of seven young aviators in the navy reserve. She quickly took the men under her wing and began hosting them and their friends at her home. As more such servicemen established ties with Chung, they began calling her Mom Chung. Because Chung was unmarried, the group began referring to themselves as her "fair-haired bastards." By 1941, Mom Chung had

Margaret Chung (Wikimedia Commons)

"adopted" more than one thousand "sons" in the army and navy. Through her many connections, Chung recruited the first two hundred American aviators of the Flying Tigers, the volunteer group of American aviators who flew combat missions for China against the Japanese.

> "Women of every nation, every country, should learn medicine, so that they can teach the women of their countries and their races how to care for themselves and their children—how to improve the coming generation."

After the Japanese attack on Pearl Harbor, Hawaii, in December 1941, Chung helped to organize and ship emergency supplies to the naval base and received recognition from President Harry S. Truman for her efforts. Throughout World War II, Chung provided encouragement and support to her "sons" stationed overseas through personalized letters and gifts. She also made a number of radio broadcasts and speeches promoting the war effort. Chung was also instrumental in lobbying for the creation of the Naval Women's Reserve (known at the time as WAVES) in 1942. In 1945, Chung was presented the People's Medal by the Chinese government for her tireless efforts to support China throughout the war. Chung died on January 5, 1959, after battling a long illness.

Significance

Though Margaret Chung is best remembered for her efforts to support the Allied forces during World War II, she pioneered across both racial and gender lines and challenged widespread prejudicial attitudes regarding the abilities of women and Asian Americans. Through her personal, professional, and political efforts, Chung not only bridged the gap between disparate communities, but also worked tirelessly for the greater good. She is remembered for her patriotism and for her tireless efforts to support her community and her country.

Mary Woodbury

Further Reading

Miller, Johnny. "Margaret Chung, a One-Woman USO in WWII." *SFGate*. Hearst Communications, 4 Jan. 2009. Web. 12 Jan. 2012. A compilation of news clips from the past one hundred years, including a segment about Chung's involvement in the war effort during World War II.

Wu, Judy Tzu-Chun. *Doctor Mom Chung of the Fair-Haired Bastards: The Life of a Wartime Celebrity*. Berkeley: U of California P, 2005. Print. A thorough biography of Chung's life and career, supplemented by sociological analysis of the status of Chinese American women in the United States during Chung's lifetime.

---. "'The Ministering Angel of Chinatown': Missionary Uplift, Modern Medicine, and Asian American Women's Strategies of Liminality." *Asian/Pacific Islander American Women: A Historical Anthology*. Ed. Shirley Hune and Gail M. Nomura. New York: New York UP, 2003. 155–71. Print. A chapter providing historical context for and details of Chung's professional achievements.

---. "Was Mom Chung a 'Sister Lesbian'?" *Journal of Women's History* 13.1 (Spring 2001): 58–82. Print. Examines the sociological and historical impact of Chung's racial, gender, and sexual identities.

Jane L. Delgado

Cuban-born activist, psychologist, and entrepreneur

Born: June 17, 1953; Havana, Cuba
Area of Achievement: Activism; psychology; business

As the first female president and chief executive officer of the National Alliance for Hispanic Health, Delgado is an outspoken advocate in the Hispanic community on healthcare issues. She was instrumental in leading the first research efforts to study how Hispanic individuals differ in their healthcare needs from people of other ethnic backgrounds.

Early Life

Jane L. Delgado (dehl-GAH-doh) was born to Lucila Aurora Navarro Delgado, a factory worker, on June 17, 1953. Her mother emigrated with Delgado and her sister from Cuba to Brooklyn, New York, in 1955. Delgado credits her mother as a role model who instilled important educational and life lessons. Because she spoke only a little English, Delgado initially struggled in school but was able to learn quickly. She graduated high school two years early and at the age of sixteen enrolled at the State

University of New York at New Paltz. Delgado graduated with a bachelor of science degree in 1973.

While still enrolled in school, Delgado began working for the Children's Television Workshop, first as the assistant to the auditor and then as children's talent coordinator on *Sesame Street* (1973-1975). In 1975, Delgado earned master of arts degrees in personality psychology and social psychology from New York University. She then attended the State University of New York at Stony Brook for a doctorate in clinical psychology, which she earned in 1981. She concurrently earned a master of science degree in urban policy sciences from Stony Brook's W. Averell Harriman School for Management and Policy.

Life's Work

During her doctoral work, Delgado joined the U.S. Department of Health and Human Services in 1979. She served as a senior policy analyst and dealt with national health issues. She cowrote a report on minority health in 1985, demonstrating a lack of health data—such as on life expectancy, adult-onset chronic diseases, and birth defects—in the Hispanic population compared with other ethnic groups.

In 1985, Delgado became the first Latina to serve as president and chief executive officer of the National Alliance for Hispanic Health (NAHH), formerly known as the Coalition of Spanish-Speaking Mental Health Organizations. The NAHH is the nation's oldest and largest Hispanic nonprofit organization serving the community's health needs. Delgado oversees the organization's national staff and operations. In 1987, she and the NAHH used the aforementioned report on health data disparities to convince the National Center for Health Statistics to collect health care information on the Hispanic population, specifically Mexican Americans, Puerto Ricans, and Cuban Americans. The Hispanic Health and Nutrition Examination Survey (HHANES) findings were the first published series of scientific journal articles related to Hispanic health, socioeconomic, and demographic data. These articles were of paramount importance in allowing national and community policy and program changes to target Hispanic individuals.

Delgado is passionate about improving environmental health. Under the NAHH, Delgado has sponsored programs such as the Health and Environment Action Network, which aims to clean up the nation's dirtiest cities by providing children with environmental monitors that electronically track pollutant data. In 2009, Delgado became the first Latina appointed to the board of directors of the Mickey Leland National Urban Air Toxics Research Center (NUATRC), a research facility focused on air quality. She serves on the Environmental Protection Agency's Clean Air Act advisory council and is a founding board member of the Ocean Awareness Project, which provides community education regarding the ocean and environmental factors affecting it.

In addition to environmental health, Delgado and the NAHH have focused their efforts on health insurance for the uninsured, publicly backing President Barack

---

National Coalition of Hispanic Health and Human Services Organization

The mission of the National Alliance for Hispanic Health (NAHH), also known as the National Coalition of Hispanic Health and Human Services Organization, is to improve the health and well-being of the Hispanic community. The NAHH, led by Jane L. Delgado since 1985, provides services to more than 15 million individuals annually. The organization advocates for comprehensive health care, promotes cultural education, and increases public knowledge and awareness of Hispanic health issues. The NAHH conducts research and provides information to individuals through community groups, universities, foundations, and government agencies. Some NAHH programs include Su Familia Helpline, a national bilingual family health information service; Cuidando con Cariño, a phone line to provide information on end-of-life care issues; a Medicare Part D hotline for insurance questions; and ¡Vive to Vida!, an exercise program.

In 2000, Delgado made philanthropy a focus for the NAHH. The organization also emphasizes education in the Hispanic community. In 2008, it announced the NAHH/Merck Ciencia Hispanic Scholars Program, which awards annual scholarships to Hispanic students pursuing science, technology, engineering, or math. The NAHH was named one of the best nonprofit organizations for which to work by *The NonProfit Times* in 2010. Truly committed to health, the NAHH does not accept funding from alcohol or tobacco companies.

Obama's health-care reform package. Delgado is a member of the Advisory Panel on Medicare Education and the national advisory council for Rosalynn Carter's Task Force on Mental Health. She is an adviser to the March of Dimes and the American Academy of Family Physicians. She serves on the boards of the Kresge Foundation, Patient Safety Institute, Lovelace Respiratory Research Institute, and the Alaska Native Heritage Center in Anchorage. Delgado also advocates for the use of computers and technology in health care.

> *"I believe that the most important thing in life is not about any one individual but about the greater good. Sometimes it is essential to create some discomfort to remind people of that. Concepts such as 'winning' or 'rugged individualism' can promote a selfish or self-interested culture."*

Delgado has written several books on Hispanic health. *¡Salud! A Latina's Guide to Total Health* (1997) is the first health book written by and for the Hispanic female population. She also published *The Latina Guide to Health: Consejos and Caring Answers* (2009). Delgado attempts to present medical information in an upbeat and understandable manner when describing conditions that are of particular concern to Hispanic populations.

The numerous awards bestowed to Delgado include the Food and Drug Administration Commissioner's Special Citation (1995), Community Leadership Award from the Puerto Rican Family Institute (1996), and the 2004 National Hispanic Woman of the Year Award. She has twice been named by *Hispanic Business* to its list of One Hundred Most Influential Hispanics in the United States (1998 and 2002). Delgado resides in Washington, D.C., with her husband, Mark A. Steo, and daughter, Elizabeth Ann Steo.

In 2000, *Ladies Home Journal* named Delgado one of seven "Women to Watch," among other "unsung heroines who are forging ahead to improve our health. Delgado was honored in 2005 by the Hispanic Heritage Foundation with their Award for Education, recognizing her contributions to innovation in the use of technology in health care. In 2008 Delgado was honored as one of the Health Heroes for 2008 by *WebMD Magazine* and in 2007 was listed among the 100 most influential Hispanics by *People En Español*. In 2015 she received the FDA Commissioner's Special Citation the Dr. Harvey Wiley Award (highest award to a civilian)[11] In 2010, Ladies Home Journal named Delgado one of its "Ladies We Love." In 2016 Latino Leaders named her to the 101 Most Influential Latinos in the U.S.

SIGNIFICANCE

Delgado has done groundbreaking work, from her early push to colect health statistics on the Hispanic population to her books that translate this research into advice for the common reader. She works tirelessly on issues for which she has a passion and has dedicated many years to the NAHH. Delgado aims to make inclusiveness a norm by mentoring young individuals of all backgrounds at the organization. She also has reached out to a younger generation by blogging her thoughts and comments on important topics on the NAHH Web site.

Janet Ober Berman

FURTHER READING

Delgado, Jane L. *The Latina Guide to Health: Consejos and Caring Answers*. New York: Newmarket Press, 2009. Focusing on pertinent medical findings in the Hispanic population, such as incidences of mental health disorders and other chronic diseases.

---. *¡Salud! A Latina's Guide to Total Health*. Rev. ed. New York: HarperCollins, 2002. This new edition of Delgado's first book details the significant health challenges facing Hispanic women, including topics such as pregnancy, menopause, cancer, diabetes, and exercise.

_____, et al. "Hispanic Health and Nutrition Examination Survey: Methodological Considerations." *American Journal of Public Health* 80 Supplement. (December, 1990): 6-10. The first publication of the HHANES findings with the original data regarding health issues specifically related to the Hispanic population.

Metger, Raphael, et al. "Environmental Health and Hispanic Children." *Environmental Health Perspectives* 103, Supplement 6. (1995): 25-32. An NAHH research article on the importance of studying environmental health hazards in the Hispanic population.

Gertrude Belle Elion

Biochemist and pharmacologist

Born: January 23, 1918; New York City, New York
Died: February 21, 1999; Chapel Hill, North Carolina
Area of Achievement: Medicine, science and technology

Elion invented a revolutionary drug research methodology that focused on how normal and abnormal cells reproduce. This enabled her to develop target-specific drugs that killed or suppressed abnormal cells or pathogens without damaging normal cells.

Early Life

Gertrude Belle Elion (EHL-ee-on) was born into a religious and scholarly family in New York City in 1918. Her father, Robert Elion, had emigrated from Lithuania when he was twelve. Descended from a long line of rabbis, he became a dentist. Elion's mother, Bertha Cohen, was fourteen when she emigrated from Russia, and her family included biblical scholars. Elion and her younger brother Herbert had a happy childhood and received a sound education in the public schools. An outstanding student who had an insatiable desire for knowledge in all subjects, Elion especially enjoyed science books. She admired inventors, such as Louis Pasteur and Marie Curie.

A turning point in Elion's life occurred when she was fifteen years old and her beloved grandfather died a slow, agonizing death from cancer. Elion vowed to find a cure for the disease. In 1933, she became a chemistry major at Hunter College, the women's branch of the City College of New York. Fortunately, Hunter College was free and Elion had high grades. Otherwise, she would not have been able to attend college, since her family had become bankrupt during the stock market crash of 1929.

In 1937, Elion graduated with highest honors. A doctorate was required to become a chemical researcher, so Elion applied for scholarships or assistantships to graduate schools. Her applications were rejected, and jobs in research labs were scarce. She applied for a laboratory position for which she was qualified, but the interviewer thought a woman would be too distracting. At this point, Elion finally realized that there was gender discrimination in the sciences.

Eventually, she found work as a lab assistant, without pay at first. By 1939, she had some savings and was able to start graduate school at New York University, where she was the only female in the chemistry class. She earned a master of science degree in chemistry in 1941.

Gertrude Belle Elion (Wikimedia Commons)

Life's Work

Meanwhile, another tragedy occurred. In 1941, her fiancé, Leonard Canter, died of acute bacterial endocarditis, an infection of the inner lining of the heart. Penicillin, which would have saved his life, was not used as a drug until years later. She never married, and this personal loss further intensified her lifelong desire to cure diseases.

After World War II began, men were called to support the war effort, and more jobs became available to women. There was a shortage of industrial chemists, so Elion was able to find work as a quality-control chemist for the Quaker Maid Company in 1942. She learned about instrumentation, but the work was repetitive: She checked the acidity of pickles, the color of mayonnaise, and the mold levels of fruit. After a year and a half, she found a research job synthesizing sulfonamides at Johnson and Johnson, but the laboratory closed after six months.

In 1944, Dr. George Hitchings hired Elion to be his research assistant at Burroughs Wellcome (now GlaxoSmithKline), a pharmaceutical company in Tuckahoe, New York. From the beginning, Hitchings was impressed with Elion, and she was fascinated by his research in nucleic acid biochemistry. Thus began one of the most productive and famous collaborations in history. Hitchings encouraged her to follow her instincts, work independently, and publish papers. Although he guided Elion and reviewed her papers, he listed her name first on papers she wrote. She would continue that tradition with her own assistants in the future. Over the course of her career, she published more than 225 papers. Hitchings and Elion worked together for more than four decades and revolutionized medicine and pharmacology. Their research involved immunology, microbiology, and virology, as well as organic chemistry.

The traditional method for developing new drugs was a trial-and-error process in which new compounds were tried out on a target, usually a mouse. Hitchings and Elion used a new rational scientific approach requiring less time and speculation. They focused on how cells reproduce at various stages and studied the differences between the biochemistry of normal human cells and those of bacteria, tumors, and other pathogens (diseasecausing agents).

> *"People ask me often (was) the Nobel Prize the thing you were aiming for all your life? And I say that would be crazy. Nobody would aim for a Nobel Prize because, if you didn't get it, your whole life would be wasted. What we were aiming at was getting people well, and the satisfaction of that is much greater than any prize you can get."*

In 1944, biochemist Oswald Avery discovered that deooxyribonucleic acid (DNA) was the carrier of genetic information (genes and chromosomes). However, it was not until 1953 that James Watson and Francis Crick discovered the double helix structure of DNA. Thus, not

---

Purinethol

Gertrude Belle Elion changed the way drugs are discovered with the new methodology that she and Hitchings created. They compared normal and abnormal cell metabolism and reproduction and then created antimetabolites to interfere with the life cycle of abnormal cells without harming normal cells. Elion focused on the purine bases (adenine and guanine), which are two of the four bases that are part of the larger nucleic acid (DNA) molecule, which carries genetic information.

Using this methodology in 1950, Elion synthesized a cancer drug, diaminopurine, which interfered with the metabolism of leukemia cells (abnormal white blood cells). It produced a complete remission in an acutely ill leukemia patient who had a relapse after two years and died. Saddened, Elion then made and tested over one hundred compounds. Finally, she substituted a sulfur atom for the oxygen atom on a purine molecule and made 6-mercaptopurine (6-MP), the first effective leukemia drug.

Elion's 6-MP (marketed as Purinethol in the United States) was the first childhood leukemia drug capable of causing a complete, though temporary, remission. Before the development of this drug, 50 percent of all children with acute leukemia died within three to four months. Eventually, a combination of 6-MP with other drugs could effectively cure childhood leukemia. By the early 1990's, the 6-MP therapy could cure 80 percent of patients with acute lymphoblastic leukemia. 6-MP also suppressed the immune system, which had implications for organ transplant surgery. In 1959, Robert Schwartz tested 6-MP on rabbits injected with a foreign compound, and the drug prevented their immune systems from producing antibodies. Then, the British surgeon Roy Calne used 6-MP on dogs receiving kidney transplants; the dogs given the drug outlived the dogs who did not receive 6-MP.

Elion remembered that she had synthesized azathioprine (Imuran), a complex version of 6-MP, and that this related compound did not affect cancer cells but was a better immunosuppressant than 6-MP. Calne then used Imuran for a successful organ transplant on a collie named Lollipop. Using the same drug, Dr. Joseph Murray performed the first successful kidney transplant between unrelated people in 1962. In the 1960's, Elion also developed allopurinol (Zyloprim), another compound related to 6-MP. This drug was effective for treating gout and many diseases occurring in South America.

much was known about nucleic acids at that time, but Hitchings and Elion understood that DNA was the essence of life and that all cells required nucleic acids to reproduce. Nucleic acids carry the information each living thing inherits from its parents. That information tells the cell how to carry out its activities and is coded in small molecules called bases.

Elion and Hitchings realized that if they slightly changed the natural bases, or DNA building blocks, in a cell so that the altered bases could not be used to make new nucleic acids, then these new bases would act as antimetabolites, chemicals that prevent cell metabolism. Mistaking these antimetabolites for natural bases and incorporating them, viruses, cancer cells, and pathogens would be poisoned and unable to reproduce or carry out their own chemical activities, thus stopping the spread of disease without harming normal cells. Elion and Hitchings called these false bases "rubber donuts" because they looked real but did not work.

In 1950, at the age of thirty-two, Elion synthesized two cancer drugs, diaminopurine and thioguanine, by using these methods. She also developed 6-mercaptopurine (Purinethol), the first effective treatment for childhood leukemia. Through the years, she invented many other life-saving drugs: azathioprine (Imuran), the first immunosuppressive agent used for organ transplants; allopurinol (Zyloprim) for gout; pyrimethamine (Daraprim) for malaria; trimethoprim (Septra) for meningitis, septicemia, and bacterial infections of the urinary and respiratory tracts; and acyclovir (Zovirax) for viral herpes.

Elion retired in 1983 but remained active in education and scientific organizations. Along with Hitchings and Sir James Black, she received the 1988 Nobel Prize in Physiology or Medicine. In 1991, she received the National Medal of Science and also became the first woman to be included in the National Inventors Hall of Fame. Although she never had time to finish her doctorate, George Washington University, Brown University, the University of Michigan, and other schools awarded her honorary doctorates. Elion died at the age of eighty-one on February 21, 1999.

Significance

The new drug-making methodology developed by Elion and Hitchings led to new drugs no one had ever thought possible. The holder of forty-five patents, Elion invented or helped develop the first effective drugs for an extraordinary range of diseases. When she discovered a compound, she explored all its implications and used it to find more information and to discover compounds against other diseases. Her innovative approach profoundly affected the whole field of drug development and became the standard in pharmaceutical research.

Elion's immunosuppressive drug, Azathioprineazathioprine, which could be used to prevent a patient's immune system from rejecting a transplanted organ as a foreign invader, made organ transplant surgery possible. Transplant operations have since become routine. By 1990, over 200,000 kidney transplants had been performed worldwide. In 2006, there were over 17,000 kidney transplants in the United States and an overall total of over 28,000 transplants, including pancreas, liver, intestine, kidney-pancreas, heart, heart-lung, and lung. By May, 2008, there were 99,258 people on the waiting list for an organ.

Elion's antiretroviral drug led to her research laboratory's development of azidothymidine (AZT), the first

Elion and Dr. George Hitchings worked steadily from the 1940s through to the 1980s and shared a Nobel Prize for their rational drug design work at the Burroughs Wellcome Research Laboratories in the USA. (Wellcome Images)

drug treatment for acquired immunodeficiency syndrome (AIDS), in 1984. Until 1991, AZT was the only drug approved for the treatment of AIDS. Her developments in cancer drugs have had a lasting impact on cancer research. She laid the foundation for the discovery of future cancer treatments, such as nelarabine (Arranon), a cancer drug licensed in the United States in 2005 to treat certain rare forms of leukemia and lymphoma when patients have exhausted standard options. The multitude of drugs invented by Elion continue to save countless lives every day throughout the world, and her humanistic spirit inspired future generations of scientists.

Alice Myers

FURTHER READING

Ambrose, Susan A., et al. *Journeys of Women in Science and Engineering: No Universal Constants.* Philadelphia: Temple University Press, 1997. Based on interviews and written in the first person, this extensive collection of stories tells how eighty-eight women found their life's work and the challenges they faced. Includes a case study of Elion. Illustrated, with bibliography and index.

Brokaw, Tom. *The Greatest Generation.* New York: Random House, 1998. Celebrated broadcast journalist Tom Brokaw explores the concept of "hero" in biographies of both ordinary and famous Americans of the Great Depression and the World War II eras. Illustrated. Index.

Hutchison, Kay Bailey. *Leading Ladies: American Trailblazers.* New York: Harper, 2007. Celebrates the accomplishments and struggles of American women in traditionally male-dominated fields. A chapter on winners of the Nobel Prize in science includes a biographical portrait of Elion. Illustrated, with bibliography and index.

McGrayne, Sharon Bertsch. *Nobel Prize Women in Science: Their Lives, Struggles, and Momentous Discoveries.* Secaucus, N.J.: Carol, 1993. Very readable and well-researched biographies of fourteen female scientists who overcame gender discrimination as both students and researchers to accomplish groundbreaking scientific work. Illustrated. Notes and index.

Sherman, Irwin. *Twelve Diseases That Changed Our World.* Washington, D.C.: ASM Press, 2007. This historical examination of twelve diseases includes a chapter on AIDS that discusses Elion's antiviral work. Bibliography and index.

Yount, Lisa. *Contemporary Women Scientists. New York: Facts On File, 1994.* Elion is one of ten women profiled in this sensitive study of the obstacles facing female scientists. Illustrated, with bibliography and index.

SANJAY GUPTA

Physician, journalist

Born: October 23, 1969; Novi, Michigan
Areas of achievement: Journalism, medicine

Neurosurgeon Sanjay Gupta is the Emmy Award–winning chief medical correspondent for the Cable News Network (CNN). In addition to saving lives on the operating table, his medical reporting educates American audiences about advances in medical technology and the medical challenges that people face during catastrophes.

EARLY LIFE

Sanjay Gupta was born in Novi, Michigan, a suburb of Detroit, to Subhash and Damyanti Gupta. His parents and his older brother, Yogesh, immigrated from India to Michigan in the 1960s to work as engineers for the Ford Motor Company. His mother was one of the first female engineers to work for Ford.

Gupta graduated from Novi High School and, at the age of seventeen, enrolled in the accelerated Interflex medical program at the University of Michigan in Ann Arbor. Interflex combined premedical studies and medical school into a six-year program. Gupta attended medical school at the University of Michigan and received his MD in 1993. He selected neurological surgery as his specialty and completed his neurosurgery residency at the University of Michigan Medical Center. Following his residency, Gupta received a fellowship in neurosurgery at the University of Tennessee's Semmes-Murphey clinic.

From 1997 to 1998, Gupta served as a White House Fellow and worked as a special adviser to First Lady Hillary Rodham Clinton. He wrote speeches on health care and helped Clinton research medical policy. He was offered the chance to work for CNN in 1998, but Gupta decided to return to Michigan instead.

LIFE'S WORK

In 2000, Gupta became a partner at the Great Lakes Brain and Spine Institute in Jackson, Michigan. In 2001, he

Sanjay Gupta (Wikimedia Commons)

moved to Atlanta, Georgia, to work at Grady Memorial Hospital. He eventually became associate chief of the neurosurgery service, as well as an assistant professor of neurosurgery at Emory University School of Medicine in Atlanta.

In the summer of 2001, Gupta joined CNN as a medical journalist. He led CNN's reporting on the anthrax scares following the terrorist attacks of September 11, 2001. Even though Gupta thought he would primarily work as an off-the-air consultant, his natural smile and easygoing manner quickly made him one of CNN's most popular reporters.

At the start of the Iraq War in 2003, Gupta traveled to Kuwait and then to Baghdad, Iraq, as an embedded journalist with the Navy's Devil Docs medical unit. He provided live coverage of the desert operating rooms during the American-led invasion of Iraq. Since the Devil Docs did not have a neurosurgeon, they asked Gupta to perform operations on Iraqis and American soldiers who had suffered head traumas. Gupta participated in five life-saving surgeries while embedded in Iraq. Fellow journalists criticized Gupta for practicing medicine while reporting on it. He had, according to his critics, violated a tenet of journalistic ethics by crossing the line between reporting the story and being the story. That year, Gupta won the Humanitarian Award from the National Press Photographers Association.

In 2004, the Atlanta Press Club named Gupta the Journalist of the Year. On May 15 of the same year, Gupta married Rebecca Olson, a family-law attorney. As of 2011, Gupta and his wife have three daughters, Sage Ayla, Sky Anjali, and Soleil Asha.

In 2006, the president of the CBS, Sean McManus, came to a formal agreement with CNN that allowed Gupta to file up to ten reports a year for the television-news programs *Evening News with Katie Couric* and *60 Minutes*. This agreement allowed Gupta to remain at CNN as the network's chief medical correspondent and keep his post as associate chief of neurosurgery at Grady Memorial Hospital, while also occasionally reporting for CBS.

On the July 9, 2007, episode of CNN's *Situation Room*, Gupta aired a fact-check segment of Michael Moore's controversial 2007 documentary *Sicko*. Moore's film heavily criticized the American health-care system, unfavorably comparing it to the socialized health-care systems of Canada, England, France, and Cuba. In his segment, Gupta stated that Moore, an advocate of socialized medicine, had "fudged facts." Moore was interviewed live on CNN immediately following Gupta's segment, and he accused Gupta of bias in favor of pharmaceutical companies. The next day, Gupta debated Moore on the program *Larry King Live*.

CNN announced on January 9, 2009, that Gupta had been offered the position of surgeon general by President Barack Obama. Some health-care professionals and journalists reacted favorably to this news, since Gupta's exemplary communication skills and previous experience with government would make him a natural candidate for this post. Others felt that Gupta had often displayed poor medical judgment and was too closely connected to drug companies to be an objective surgeon general. Michigan congressman John Conyers Jr., a friend of Michael Moore, wrote a letter opposing Gupta's nomination. In March of that same year, Gupta withdrew his name from consideration, citing the strain the job would have on his family.

In 2009, the American Medical Association's Medical Communications Conference awarded Gupta the Health Communications Achievement Award. That same year, the National Association for Multi-Ethnicity in Communications presented Gupta with its Mickey Leland Humanitarian Award.

During his reporting in Haiti following the January 2010 earthquake, Gupta received a call from the aircraft carrier USS *Carl Vinson* that an earthquake victim, a 12-year-old girl, was aboard and needed a neurosurgeon. Gupta, a pediatric surgeon, Henri Ford, and two U.S. Navy doctors removed a piece of concrete from the girl's skull in an operation performed aboard the *Vinson*.

In addition to his regular work on television-news programs, Gupta has also appeared as a guest on programs such as *The Daily Show with Jon Stewart*, *Real Time with Bill Maher*, and *The Oprah Winfrey Show*. He has also published a regular column in *Time* magazine. On April 28, 2012, Gupta was awarded an honorary Doctor of Humane Letters degree for his accomplishments in the medical field. He also gave the commencement address at the spring commencement ceremony held in the University of Michigan Stadium. On June 12, 2016, Gupta addressed the Oregon Health & Science University graduating class of 2016.

> "The worst crime of all would be that a mistake happens and no one talks about it or learns from it. So, as unsettling as it is to think about, these mistakes, complications and unexpected outcomes get discussed openly, and everyone hopefully gains something from it."

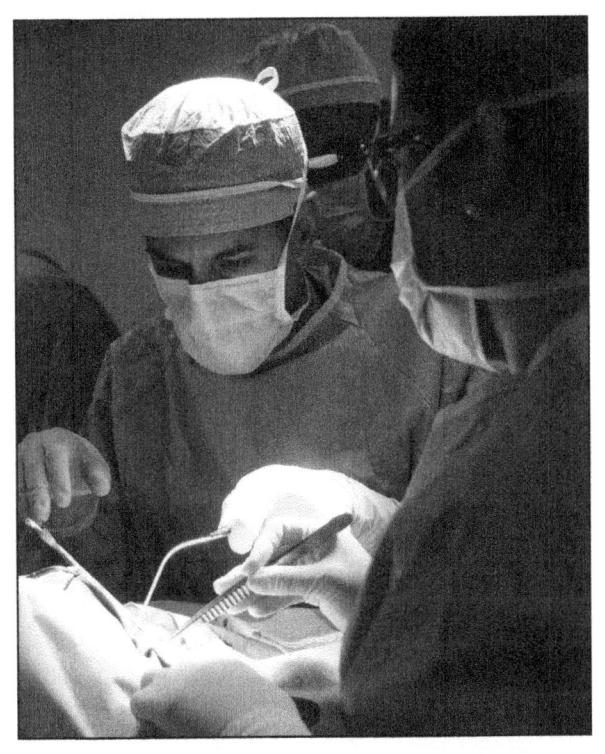

Gupta, left, and Lt. Cmdr. Kathryn Berndt, a Navy surgeon, perform surgery on a 12-year-old Haitian girl with a severe head injury aboard the Nimitz-class aircraft carrier USS Carl Vinson (CVN 70). Sugeons removed a piece of concrete from the child's brain caused by the earthquake in Haiti. (Wikimedia Commons)

Significance

Gupta is an accomplished neurosurgeon known for taking the complexities of his field and presenting them in an easily understandable form to a mass audience. He has done for medicine what astrophysicist Neil deGrasse Tyson has done for astronomy and cosmology, which is to communicate a highly technical field of science to the educated public in an enthusiastic and comprehensible manner.

Nevertheless, Gupta has also received criticism for his medical reporting. Several critics have alleged that Gupta shows a "pro-screening bias" and has a tendency to champion medical tests before satisfactory evidence has accumulated to warrant their routine use. Others have questioned the adequacy of Gupta's medical judgments, as well as the degree of entanglement between his reporting and the drug companies that sponsor his news programs. One of the greatest criticisms of Gupta is his tendency to practice medicine while reporting on-site. He did this in Iraq and Haiti, and journalists have said that he needs either to be an on-site physician or an on-site reporting journalist, not both.

Despite these criticisms, Gupta's mastery of medical journalism was on display in 2011 when Arizona congresswoman Gabrielle Giffords survived after being shot in the head in Tucson, Arizona. People were flummoxed by how someone could have survived such an injury. By using models of the human brain and skull on television, Gupta explained the complicated injury in the clear and tactful manner for which he was known. His strong communication skills and upbeat personality have made him a trusted source for medical information and a favorite reporter for many American television news-watchers.

Michael A. Buratovich

Further Reading

Cruz, Gilbert. "Surgeon General: Sanjay Gupta." *Time*. Time, Inc., 8 Jan. 2009. Web. 20 Feb. 2012. A brief article outlining Gupta's background and professional accomplishments. Also contains several quotes from and by Gupta.

Gupta, Sanjay. *Chasing Life: New Discoveries in the Search for Immortality to Help You Age Less Today.* New York: Wellness Central, 2008. Print. A mixed discussion of potential future cures and health advice to stay healthy and live longer.

---. *Cheating Death: The Doctors and Medical Miracles That Are Saving Lives Against All Odds.* New York: Wellness Central, 2010. Print. Relates several harrowing stories of physicians whose fast thinking saved the lives of patients who, under normal circumstances, would have died.

DAVID HO

Taiwanese American medical researcher

Born: November 3, 1952; Taichung, Taiwan
Also known as: Ho Da-i
Area of Achievement: Medicine; STEM

Scientist David Ho made significant contributions to our understanding of HIV/AIDS and the mechanisms by which it reproduces in the human body. His work led to the development of the anti-retroviral therapy that is currently used to treat the disease, and he has been at the forefront of the search for a vaccine.

EARLY LIFE

David Ho was born Ho Da-i in Taichung, Taiwan, on November 3, 1952. His father, Paul Ho, was born in Jungshi province, located north of Canton, in China. Paul Ho moved to Taiwan to become a teacher, and there he met David's mother, Sonia Ho. In 1957, Paul Ho immigrated to the United States to pursue an advanced degree in engineering. His wife and two sons, David and Phillip, joined him in 1965, the year that U.S. immigration laws were reformed under President Johnson to remove quotas for non-European immigrants. The three arrived with six suitcases between them and no other belongings.

When David Ho arrived in the United States, he was twelve years old and spoke no English. He went through a difficult period of adjustment and later spoke of the "culture shock" he experienced coming from Taiwan to the United States. The two countries are culturally different, but Ho also noted that the United States was far more economically developed. For example, Taiwan's busy streets were full of bicycles, while in the United States they were full of automobiles. Ho had been an excellent student in Taiwan. But in the United States, because he didn't speak English, some of his teachers and some of the other students thought that he was unintelligent. Thanks in part to his youth, Ho became fluent in English in about a year's time. Later in life, Ho attributed his tendency towards introversion to this isolating experience when he was young. Ho also focused his energies on mathematics and science and excelled in those areas because they are less culturally specific than other school subjects like English or social studies.

In 1970, Ho became a United States citizen. After high school, Ho attended the California Institute of Technology where he received a bachelor of science degree in physics in 1974. After college, Ho moved to Boston to attend medical school at the Harvard-MIT Division of Health Sciences and Technology.

LIFE'S WORK

David Ho is best known for his significant contributions, over many years, to HIV/AIDS research. He is one of the most important scientists working in that field. Ho first encountered HIV/AIDS when he was a resident at Cedars-Sinai Medical Center in Los Angeles in 1981. There

David Ho (Wikimedia Commons)

he personally saw three of the first five patients to die from what was later identified as AIDS. Before dying, the patients—all of them young men—very quickly lost weight, developed pneumonia, experienced seizures and dementia, and developed cancers. The course of their illness was measured in only weeks and months. And within the next year, Ho saw about fifty more cases. Nobody knew at that time about the virus that causes AIDS; nobody knew what was killing these men. Theories ranged from a rare cancer to allergies to drug abuse to sexually transmitted disease. Not yet thirty years old and at the start of his career, Ho decided to devote himself to researching the disease and looking for a cure.

Ho became a Harvard University research fellow in 1982. In 1986, he returned to Los Angeles to be an assistant professor at UCLA Medical School. Then, in 1990, he moved to New York City to become the chief executive officer and the scientific director of the Aaron Diamond AIDS Research Center (ADARC), which was founded by wealthy philanthropist Irene Diamond. ADARC is the largest privately-funded research center devoted to HIV/AIDS research in the world.

In the 1980s, Ho was among the first scientists to identify what came to be called the human immuno-deficiency virus, or HIV. (The virus was first identified by Luc Montagnier in France and Robert Gallo in the United States, and the two shared a Nobel Prize for their work.) Ho's most significant achievement was to show how HIV replicates in the body. Ho was the first scientist to show that HIV grows and replicates in certain immune cells called macrophages. He also showed that the virus replicates very, very quickly, overwhelming the immune systems of its victims. This disproved the theory that the virus lived for many years in infected patients and only slowly replicated and caused disease. Ho showed, too, that the virus produces many genetic mutations when it replicates. This aspect of the virus made the task of developing effective drug treatments a particular challenge.

Ho's research paved the way for the drug cocktails that over time have become the mainstay for keeping people with HIV healthy. Ho has received numerous honors and awards; in 1996, he was named *Time* magazine's "Man of the Year." He received the Presidential Citizen's Medal by President Bill Clinton in 2001 and was inducted into the California Hall of Fame in 2006.

> "*There is no question that good treatment is not only right medically and ethically, but also smart financially.*"

Significance

Ho's accomplishments in the HIV/AIDS research field have been of the highest importance; in addition to being one the first to identify the virus, Ho discovered exactly how the virus replicates in the body. Ho has been the director of the Aaron Diamond AIDS Research Center (ADARC) since 1990 and a professor at Rockefeller University in Manhattan since 1996.

Ho has spoken often of his experiences as a Chinese-American immigrant. In 2003, he was the subject of a Bill Moyers special program on PBS called *Becoming American: The Chinese Experience*. In addition to his work with numerous institutions in the United States, Ho is also an honorary professor at Peking Union Medical College, the Chinese Academy of Medical Sciences, the Chinese Academy of Sciences, the University of Hong Kong, Wuhan University, and Fudan University.

D. Alan Dean

Further Reading

Wilkinson, Alec. "Please Leave David Ho Alone." *Esquire*. March 1, 1999. https://classic.esquire.com/article/1999/3/1/please-leave-david-ho-alone. Accessed Dec. 15, 2018.

"Becoming American: The Chinese Experience." Bill Moyers Interview with David Ho. https://www.pbs.org/becomingamerican/ap_pjourneys_transcript3.html. Accessed Dec. 15, 2018.

Holt, Nathalia. *Cured: The People Who Defeated HIV*. New York: Penguin, 2014.

Wainberg, Mark. "Understanding HIV Pathogenesis Through Virus and Lymphocyte Dynamics: An Expert Interview With Dr. David Ho." *Medscape HIV/AIDS*. 2006;12(1). https://www.medscape.org/viewarticle/532151. Accessed Dec. 28, 2018.

Xiaojian Zhao, Edward J.W. Park Ph.D. "David Ho." *Asian Americans: An Encyclopedia of Social, Cultural, Economic, and Political History: Vol. 1*. ABC-Clio: Santa Barbara, 2013.

JOSEPH LEDOUX

Neuroscientist, educator and writer

Born: December 7, 1949; Eunice, Louisiana
Area of achievement: Neuroscience

Joseph LeDoux's revolutionary work on fear and the thousands of studies it has inspired have shed light on the neurological bases of fear-related disorders in humans, including phobias and post-traumatic stress disorder (PTSD), and have pointed to potential treatments as well.

EARLY LIFE

Joseph Edward LeDoux Jr. was born on December 7, 1949 in Eunice, a town in Louisiana's Cajun country. He has a younger sister, Bonnie. His father, J. E. "Boo" LeDoux, and mother, the former Elizabeth Priscilla Buller, owned a butcher shop; his mother kept the accounts and wrapped the meat that his father cut. Until LeDoux was about 12, the family lived above the shop. As a child LeDoux would ride his bike through the neighborhood, selling pigs' feet for a nickel. In the shop he prepared cow brains for sale, each time peeling away the outer membranes and then, with his fingers, removing the bullet, deep within, that had killed the cow. LeDoux thought about what the animals felt during their last moments. "I had a sense of soul or spirit and wondered about the cow—even though religion taught that animals don't have souls, it still kind of perplexed me," he recalled to *Current Biography*. "Did they feel anything? Did they think anything?" Young LeDoux greatly feared the venomous water moccasins ubiquitous in the bayous. Another of his fears, David Dobbs wrote for *Scientific American Mind*, was that he might get "stuck" in "sleepy" Eunice forever.

LeDoux, whose parents were strict Roman Catholics, attended Catholic schools, served as an altar boy in his church, and until age 13 planned to enter the priesthood. "In eighth grade," he told *Current Biography*, "I guess the hormones kicked in and I got interested in girls. And the priest thing was out the window." Next he aimed at a career as a folk musician and then, after hearing the Beatles and other pioneering rockers, as a rock musician. Soon he was playing electric guitar for his high-school rock-and-roll band, the Countdowns; he also served as a disc jockey at a local radio station. LeDoux's parents, however, who grew up poor during the Great Depression, wanted him to become a businessman and told him that they would pay for his college education only if he studied business.

LeDoux earned a B.S. degree in that field at Louisiana State University (LSU) in Baton Rouge in 1971 and remained at LSU to pursue a master's degree in marketing, which he considered to be the least boring aspect of business. He became interested in human psychology—for example, "why people bought stuff they didn't really need," he told Dobbs. While enrolled in a class taught by Robert Thompson, he grew fascinated by the psychology of learning, memory, and motivation. Before long LeDoux began helping with research on rats in Thompson's lab, and his name appeared as a co-author on four of Thompson's published papers. LeDoux earned an M.S. degree from LSU in 1974.

Determined to pursue a doctorate in neuroscience, LeDoux read widely in psychology. In part because he had almost no training in biology, he was rejected by all but one of the dozen graduate schools to which he applied. The acceptance came from the State University of New York (SUNY) at Stony Brook, after Thompson recommended LeDoux to an acquaintance of his—Michael S. Gazzaniga, who taught at SUNY-Stony Brook from 1973 to 1978. Gazzaniga told Dobbs that LeDoux had "a long-hair ponytail, and maybe some wouldn't have thought him impressive. But there are people who walk in and you see right away they have it. Joe was one." Gazzaniga became LeDoux's adviser.

A few years earlier Gazzaniga had made a revolutionary discovery through his research on split-brain patients—people who had undergone a surgical procedure in which the corpus callosum, the largest bundle of nerves that connects the two hemispheres, was completely severed, to reduce the symptoms of severe epilepsy; thus, the higher-level portions of the two hemispheres could no longer communicate. As with all people, external signals sent from the left eyes of those with split brains go to the brain's right hemisphere, and signals from the right eye go to the brain's left hemisphere, the latter of which contains the brain's language center (the part responsible for reading, writing, and speech). Both hemispheres of split-brain patients are aware of what is being seen, but the patients can talk only about objects that the right eye has observed. When Gazzaniga covered the right eyes of split-brain patients, they were not able to express verbally what they were looking at. But, he discovered, they *could* respond *nonverbally*. For example, if the patients were looking at a picture of an apple only through their left eyes—which transmit the visual signal to their right hemispheres—they are not able to say, "That is an apple." But if given a bag containing various objects, they were able to select the object (the apple) that matched the picture if they used their left hands, which received a signal from their right hemispheres.

One day, LeDoux recalled to Carlin Flora for the *NYU Alumni Magazine* (Spring 2008, on-line), Gazzaniga remarked to him, "Gee, there's not much research on emotion out there." Keeping in mind the results of the split-brain experiment, LeDoux and Gazzaniga designed a similar experiment that focused on emotions. Their split-brain patient was unusual in that although he could speak only "through his left hemisphere," he could read with both. When the patient's right eye (and left hemisphere) were shown words, he could say the word aloud and convey its emotional significance—that is, how he felt about it ("good" or "bad"). Predictably, when the patient's right eye was covered and only his brain's right hemisphere received visual signals, he could not say the word. Nevertheless, he could convey how the word made him feel. For example, he said "good" when he saw "mother" and "bad" when he saw "devil," even though he could not say "mother" or "devil" aloud to identify those words. The emotional information (the way the stimuli made him feel) traveled from one hemisphere to the other hemisphere because the anterior commissure—which connects the left and right amygdalae, which are crucial for emotional processing—was still intact. The emotional processing occurred without the patient's being consciously aware of what the stimulus (the printed word, in that case) was. In other words, the processing occurred unconsciously. Those findings are described in LeDoux's Ph.D. dissertation, "The Split Brain and the Integrated Mind," as well as in the book *The Integrated Mind* (1978), which he co-wrote with Gazzaniga, and in *The Emotional Brain* (1996).

> "*Unfortunately, one of the most significant things ever said about emotion may be that everyone knows what it is until they are asked to define it.*"

LIFE'S WORK

After he received his Ph.D. degree in psychology from SUNY-Stony Brook, in 1977, LeDoux joined Cornell University Medical College, in New York City, as a National Institutes of Health (NIH) postdoctoral fellow in the Department of Neurology. He became an instructor at the college in 1979 and was promoted to assistant and then associate professor in 1980 and 1986, respectively. Earlier, in 1978, he had started working in the laboratory of the world-renowned neurobiologist Donald J. Reis, who told him, he recalled to John Brockman, that he "could do whatever I wanted as long as I recorded blood pressure" on his study animals—rats—as a contribution to Reis's investigations of the brain's influence on the autonomic nervous system.

LeDoux chose rats as subjects in his study of the neurological basis of emotion, because for both ethical and practical reasons, he could not use humans in studies in which parts of brains were deliberately rendered nonfunctional. More recently LeDoux has also made use of functional imaging of brains—scans that record brain activity over specified periods of time—which can supplement but not replace work with nonhumans. "The animal work...gives the framework for interpreting the snapshots we get from human imaging studies," LeDoux told Brockman.

With his physiological studies of rats, LeDoux "launched into a new field alone," Gazzaniga told Carlin Flora. "His training with me was in testing patients, so he had to go back and learn basic neuroscience, learn how to make lesions in the brain. It was like getting another Ph.D." LeDoux's first application for a grant, in the mid-1980s, which offered as the title of his research project "The Neural Basis of Emotion," was rejected on the grounds that emotion cannot be studied physiologically. In 1985, after LeDoux changed the title to "The Neural Pathways Underlying Emotional Conditioning"—indicating the behavioral component of his project—and made a few other small changes, the National Institute of Mental Health (NIMH), a division of the NIH, awarded him the grant. (The NIMH has renewed that grant ever since. LeDoux's work has also been supported by other NIMH grants, along with funding from sources including the National Science Foundation and the American Heart Association.)

LeDoux chose to study fear because the outward and physiological expressions of fear in the face of sudden threats are present among most animal species. For example, the sudden appearance of a predator will cause a prey animal to become motionless (freeze in place) for a fraction of a second and then flee, with an accelerated heartbeat and the release of stress hormones into the bloodstream. "All animals have to be able to detect and respond to danger, regardless of the kind of cognitive architecture they have," LeDoux told John Brockman. "This is as true of bees and worms and snails, as it is of fish, frogs, birds, rats, and people." Physiological manifestations of such emotions as love or hope, by contrast, are as yet difficult or impossible to pin down.

In his experiments on rats, LeDoux used conditioned learning, a technique introduced by the Russian physiologist Ivan Pavlov in the 19th century. Pavlov would repeatedly give dogs meat right after ringing a bell, and within a short time the dogs would start salivating immediately upon hearing the bell, before or without smelling the meat. The odor of meat elicits salivation automatically; salivation in response to a ringing bell is called a conditioned response. In LeDoux's experiments with conditioned learning, the rats would soon ignore a repeated, nonthreatening tone; they would freeze and arch their backs and their hearts would beat faster when their feet were subjected to mild electric shocks accompanied by the sound; after a sufficient number of repetitions of sound and shock, they would freeze, and their heartbeats accelerate, upon hearing the sound alone, without the shock.

LeDoux set out to determine which parts of the brain's auditory system are involved in that sort of conditioning. "It's a matter of connecting the dots in the brain," he said to *Current Biography*. In rats, humans, and other vertebrate species, sound waves move through the ear and are converted to electrochemical signals that travel to three parts of the brain in succession: the auditory midbrain, the auditory thalamus, and the auditory cortex (that is, the parts of the midbrain, thalamus, and cortex connected with hearing). When LeDoux disrupted the functioning of the last part of the auditory pathway, the auditory cortex, in his rats' brains (by means of induced lesions), fear conditioning proceeded exactly as it had before. That result showed that, contrary to what scientists had universally believed, the auditory cortex—which is necessary for *consciousness* of an external auditory stimulus—is not necessary for producing an emotional response to a sound. That discovery was LeDoux's first major contribution to neuroscience. Like the study he conducted on split-brain patients, his series of experiments with rats showed that emotions (as revealed physiologically) can operate outside the realm of consciousness and without the involvement of higher brain centers, which are involved in thinking and reasoning.

As spelled out in a series of papers in the mid-1980s co-authored by Reis and others, LeDoux discovered that destruction of the auditory thalamus and of the auditory midbrain *did* prevent learned conditioning in rats. Next, by means of a tracer chemical injected into each rat's thalamus, he determined that an auditory signal is carried to several subcortical regions. By cutting off the connections between the thalamus and each of those regions, LeDoux found that only one of them was necessary for fear conditioning in rats. That single exception was the amygdala—in particular, the part known as the lateral amygdala—in either of the hemispheres. (Subsequent studies, some of which used brain-scan technology, have linked the amygdalae to additional emotions, including anger, sadness, and disgust, and LeDoux and others have detected subtle differences in the functions of the left and right amygdalae.)

In subsequent studies of conditioned learning, LeDoux and his colleagues focused on a portion of the cortex called the prefrontal cortex, which in humans is associated with complex cognitive functions. Normally, after a rat develops an association between, say, the sound of a bell and an electric shock, the association can be unlearned (that is, forgotten) if the rat repeatedly hears the bell without being shocked. In that circumstance, in scientific jargon, "extinction" of the learned response has occurred. LeDoux discovered that cutting the connections between the prefrontal cortex and the systems that bring auditory signals to the brain did not interfere with fear conditioning, but that without those connections, the stimulus never lost its power—extinction became impossible. In the latter case, LeDoux and others later found, every time the rats were subjected to the stimulus (the sound of the bell), thus triggering the retrieval of their "fear" memory, particular neurons in the amygdala underwent molecular changes, including the synthesis of new proteins—changes that could be detected after the memory went back into storage. Thus, during the recall process a memory is affected by the person's mood as well as cognitive and emotional information (conscious and unconscious) acquired since the event that is being remembered. The new proteins, in effect, "update" the memory when it is stored again.

Those findings have had major implications for the treatment of an array of anxiety disorders in humans. Scientists in other labs have used LeDoux's discoveries of "evolving" memories to help war veterans or victims of violent assaults who suffer from PTSD. The scientists instructed their patients to write about their traumatic experiences in detail and then read silently what they had written. Immediately afterward, the patients were given a drug that interfered with protein synthesis involving the memory they had actively recalled. The next time the patients read their accounts of their traumas, their memories were less intense, indicating that the memories had reentered storage in a weakened state. Theoretically, given sufficiently potent drugs and enough time, their painful memories can be erased altogether.

After leaving Cornell, in 1989, LeDoux joined New York University, where he taught courses in neuroscience and psychology and continued his research. He was promoted to professor in 1991 and was named the Henry and Lucy Moses Professor of Science in 1996; since 2005 he has also held the title University Professor. In addition, since 2007 he has directed the Emotional Brain Institute, in Orangeburg, New York, whose work is supported by both NYU and the Nathan Kline Institute for Psychiatric Research. His investigations have greatly expanded knowledge about the amygdala: its structure and functions at the macroscopic level (parts observable with the naked eye); its structure and functions at the microscopic level, including its various populations of neurons, how they are organized, and how they function; projections that connect the amygdala to other parts of the brain; changes that take place in it during conditioned learning, including protein synthesis during retrieval and storage of memories; its modes of chemical and electrical signaling at synapses; its receptors for glucocorticoids and other hormones; and patterns of gene expression within it. In the past two decades, LeDoux has published upwards of 120 peer-reviewed professional papers with dozens of colleagues, among them Claudia R. Farb, Lizabeth M. Romanski, Glenn E. Schafe, and Karim Nader. The papers have appeared in an array of publications whose names indicate the breadth of LeDoux's work—*Brain Research*; *Journal of Neuroscience*; *Journal of Comparative Neurology*; *Genes, Brain and Behavior*; *Learning and Memory*; *Journal of Traumatic Stress*; *Neuropharmacology*; *Current Molecular Pharmacology*; *Synapse*; *Frontiers in Neural Circuits*; and *Psychoneuroendocrinology*, to name a few.

LeDoux has written two books for informed lay readers and specialists alike: *The Emotional Brain: The Mysterious Underpinnings of Emotional Life* (1996) and *Synaptic Self: How Our Brains Become Who We Are* (2002). *The Emotional Brain* offers a history of the scientific study of emotion and a detailed survey of LeDoux's work, insights, and hypotheses up to that point. According to Keith Oatley, the book is "in tune with what psychologists know about emotions and learning,...and...directly applicable to understanding anxiety, the most common ingredient of emotional disorders. It's a terrifically good book." Years later a writer for the *Economist* noted that *The Emotional Brain* had "helped to inspire what is today one of the liveliest and most controversial areas of economic research: neuroeconomics," which combines psychology, economics, and neuroscience to determine how people make financial decisions. In *Synaptic Self* LeDoux described in detail the functioning of the brain at the cellular level—in particular, the thousands of tiny gaps, called synapses, between one neuron and its neighbors, where signals are transmitted from one to another, and he discussed how the connections among brain cells contribute to conscious and unconscious aspects of our personalities. In a blurb for its book jacket, Daniel Goleman, the author of *Emotional Intelligence*, described *Synaptic Self* as "a brilliant manifesto at the cutting edge of psychology's evolution into a brain science...[from] one of the field's preeminent, most important thinkers." "Covering an avalanche of neuroscientific research," Gilbert Taylor wrote for *Booklist*, as quoted on Amazon.com, *Synaptic Self* "is surely the most accessible contemporary work for those interested in the brain's effect on personality."

The Emotional Brain earned glowing reviews. Paul Gross described it for the *Wilson Quarterly* as "an outstanding specimen of the accessible science book" and concluded, "I have not seen a more readable and compelling account of ongoing brain science and its implications for what it means to be human." In an assessment for the *American Journal of Psychiatry*, Sergio Paradiso wrote that although *The Emotional Brain* is about "hard science," it "reads like a novel with a plot as thrilling as those of Agatha Christie." Using as examples experiences familiar to nonexperts, such as fears associated with car accidents, LeDoux explained that connections from the amygdala to the cognitive systems of the brain are stronger than connections from the cognitive systems to the amygdala. That is why, while conscious control of emotion and feeling is weak, emotion and feeling can easily overwhelm consciousness; in other words, it is much easier for feelings to overwhelm our thoughts than for our thoughts to push away unwanted feelings.

There is "an imperfect set of connections between cognitive and emotional systems in the current stage of evolution of the human brain," LeDoux wrote in *Synaptic Self*. "This state of affairs is part of the price we pay for having newly evolved cognitive capacities that are not yet fully integrated into our brains." "Our brain has not evolved to the point where the new systems that make complex thinking possible can easily control the old systems that give rise to our basic needs and motives, and emotional reactions...," he further explained. "Doing the right thing doesn't always flow naturally from knowing what the right thing to do is."

The theme of *Synaptic Self*, in LeDoux's words, is "You are your synapses. They are who you are," or, as William Calvin put it in an admiring review for *Nature*, "The synapses are the seat of self." In another enthusiastic assessment, Richard J. Davidson wrote for *Science*, "The book's central message is that the self is the product of patterns of interconnectivity among neurons in the brain. Who we are is in large part learned through experience and much of this information is stored implicitly, in ways that affect our behavior but are not fully accessible consciously." LeDoux told *Current Biography* that one major point in *Synaptic Self* is that "nature and nurture are not different but two ways of doing the same thing, which is wiring synapses. The synapse is both the way through which nature operates on personality and through which experience operates on personality... The brain is adaptive and malleable. To say that personality is a function of the brain does not mean that it's a hardwired function. Learning is an important part of brain wiring, as is genetics."

In 2015 LeDoux emphasised the notion of survival functions mediated by survival circuits, the purpose of which is to keep organisms alive (rather than to make emotions). For example, defensive survival circuits exist to detect and respond to threats, and can be present in all organisms. However only organisms that can be conscious of their own brain's activities can feel fear. Fear is a conscious experience and occurs the same way as any other kind of conscious experience: via cortical circuits that allow attention to certain forms of brain activity. He argues the only differences between an emotional and non-emotion state of consciousness are the underlying neural ingredients that contribute to the state. These ideas and their implications for understanding the neural foundations of pathological fear and anxiety are explained in his 2015 book, *Anxious: Using the Brain to Understand and Treat Fear and Anxiety*. In this he says "Fear and anxiety are not biologically wired... They are the consequence of the cognitive processing of nonemotional ingredients."

In 2018 LeDoux further said that the amygdala may release hormones due to a trigger (such as an innate reaction to seeing a snake), but "then we elaborate it through cognitive and conscious processes." He differentiated between the defense system, which has evolved over time, and emotions such as fear and anxiety. He points out that even simple organisms such as bacteria move in response to threats; "It's in the brain to allow an organism, whether it be a bacterium or a human, to detect and respond to danger. It's not in the brain to create feelings like fear and anxiety."

SIGNIFICANCE

As recently as a few decades ago, nearly all psychologists, psychiatrists, and neuroscientists thought that emotions could not be studied as biological, chemical, physical, or physiological phenomena. Insights regarding emotions, they believed, could be gained only through analyses of people's descriptions of their thoughts and dreams (the kind of work conducted by such pioneering psychiatrists as Sigmund Freud, Carl Jung, and Karen Horney) or analyses of observed behavior among non-human animals (research associated with the naturalist Charles Darwin and such animal psychologists as Konrad Lorenz and Harry F. Harlow). LeDoux—along with a few others—has overturned those beliefs. "His investigations of the links between the brain's structure and emotions have helped to give this field scientific respectability," the University of Toronto psychologist Keith Oatley wrote for *New Scientist*.

LeDoux's work with rats has led him to conclude that attempts to locate in the brain a single, "all-purpose" emotional system (long known as the limbic system) have failed because most likely a single system does not exist. "I've come to think that emotions are products of different systems, each of which evolved to take care of problems of survival, like defending against danger, finding mates and food, and so forth," LeDoux explained to John Brockman for the *Edge*. "These systems solve behavioral problems of survival. Detecting and responding to danger requires different kinds of sensory and cognitive processes, and different kinds of motor outputs, different kinds of feedback networks, and so on, than finding a mate or finding food. Because of these unique requirements, I think different systems of the brain are going to be involved in the different kinds of emotions."

LeDoux also emphasizes that so-called emotional memories, which are unconscious, are distinct from memories of emotions and feelings, which are conscious. He told Brockman, "I think it's safe to say fear behavior preceded fear feelings in evolution... In this sense, animals were unconscious, unfeeling, and non-linguistic before they were conscious, feeling, and linguistic... I'm trying to understand the things about emotions that are similar in humans and other animals so that I can work on emotions through the brain."

LeDoux is also the guitarist, lead singer, and songwriter of the rock band the Amygdaloids, a quartet of neuroscientists. The band's latest album, *Theory of My Mind* (2010), features guest musicians including the singer/songwriter Roseanne Cash. The lyrics in the Amygdaloids songs focus on such brain-related topics as memory, emotion, and free will.

At present, LeDoux is seeking to find out more about what happens to memories in the brain after they are retrieved, how the brain goes from unconscious reaction to conscious action, and components of individual differences in fear reactions. He is working on a textbook titled "An Introduction to Brain, Mind and Behavior."

LeDoux is a fellow of the New York Academy of Sciences and the American Academy of Arts and Sciences. His other honors include awards from the NIMH, the American Psychological Association, and the Fyssen Foundation. He lives in New York City with his wife, Nancy Princenthal, an art critic and contributing editor at the magazine *Art in America*. Their son Milo is a student at Merton College, Oxford University, in England. Their first son, Jacob, is deceased.

FURTHER READING

Dreifus, Claudia. "A CONVERSATION WITH/Joseph LeDoux; Taking a Clinical Look at Human Emotions." *The New York Times*, The New York Times, 8 Oct. 2002, www.nytimes.com/2002/10/08/health/a-conversation-with-joseph-ledoux-taking-a-clinical-look-at-human-emotions.html.

Flatow, Ira, and Joseph LeDoux. "The Amygdaloids Mix Neuroscience And Rock 'N' Roll." *Talk of the Nation*, National Public Radio, 9 July 2010.

LeDoux, Joseph. "The Amygdala Is NOT the Brain's Fear Center." *Psychology Today*, Sussex Publishers, 10 Aug. 2015, www.psychologytoday.com/us/blog/i-got-mind-tell-you/201508/the-amygdala-is-not-the-brains-fear-center.

---. *Anxious: Using the Brain to Understand and Treat Fear and Anxiety*. Pemguin Books, 2016.

---. "Coming to Terms with Fear." *PNAS*, National Academy of Sciences, 25 Feb. 2014, www.pnas.org/lookup/doi/10.1073/pnas.1400335111.

---. *Synaptic Self: How Our Brains Become Who We Are*. Penguin Books, 2002.

---. *The Emotional Brain: The Mysterious Underpinnings of Emotional Life*. Simon & Schuster, 1996.

Oatley, Keith. "Review : Survival of the Cowardly." *New Scientist*, New Scientist, 4 Jan. 1997, www.newscientist.com/article/mg15320634-500-review-survival-of-the-cowardly/.

Shiromani, Peter, and Terrence Keane. *Post-Traumatic Stress Disorder Basic Science and Clinical Practice*. Edited by Joseph E. Ledoux, Humana Press, 2009.

ANTONIA NOVELLO

Physician and U.S. surgeon general (1990-1993)

Born: August 23, 1944; Fajardo, Puerto Rico
Area of Achievement: Medicine; government and politics

As a public health advocate for women, children, and minorities, Novello became the first Hispanic and first woman to serve as United States surgeon general. Her policies aimed to decrease the incidence of pediatric acquired immunodeficiency syndrome (AIDS) and eliminate health-care disparities, particularly in the Latino community.

EARLY LIFE

Antonia Coello Novello (noh-VEH-loh) was born on August 23, 1944, in Fajardo, Puerto Rico. She was the oldest of three children born to Ana Delia Flores Coello, a schoolteacher, and Antonio Coello. Her parents later divorced, and her mother remarried. Her father died when Novello was eight years old.

Novello was born with megacolon, a birth defect affecting the large intestine. She was not able to receive surgical treatment until she was eighteen years old because her family could not afford transportation to the surgical hospital. Medical treatments at her local hospital instilled in Novello an empathy for patients and inspired her medical career. Novello credits her mother with modeling strong educational values by teaching her math and science and encouraging her to overcome obstacles such as her illness.

Antonia Novello (Wikimedia Commons)

Heeding her mother's advice, Novello graduated from high school when she was only fifteen years old. She attended the University of Puerto Rico at Río Piedras on a scholarship and earned a bachelor of science degree (1965). Novello pursued a medical education at the University of Puerto Rico School of Medicine at San Juan, from which she graduated in 1970. During medical school, Novello's favorite aunt died of renal failure, thus stimulating Novello to study renal diseases. She moved to the University of Michigan Medical Center in Ann Arbor for her internship, residency, and a fellowship in nephrology in the Department of Internal Medicine (1970-1973). She was the first woman at the medical center to be named intern of the year. Novello relocated to Georgetown University School of Medicine to complete another fellowship in the Department of Pediatrics from 1973 to 1976.

Life's Work

After the fellowship, Novello entered pediatric private practice in Springfield, Virginia, and became a staff physician at Georgetown University Hospital. In 1978, she joined the Public Health Service Commission Corps (PSCHH) and became project officer at the National Institute of Arthritis, Metabolism, and Digestive Diseases. Novello completed a master's degree in public health at Johns Hopkins University's School of Hygiene and Public Health (later renamed the Bloomberg School of Public Health) in 1982. She was promoted to assistant surgeon general of PSCHH in 1986 and also served as the deputy director and coordinator for AIDS research at the National Institute of Child Health and Human Development, where she published research on pediatric AIDS.

Novello was appointed fourteenth surgeon general of the United States by President George H. W. Bush in 1990. She was both the first Hispanic person and first woman to hold this position. As surgeon general, Novello focused on health care for women, children, and minorities. She raised awareness regarding the maternal transmission of AIDS to newborns, created a workshop that led to the formation of the National Hispanic/Latino Health Initiative, spearheaded the removal of cartoon images from cigarette advertisements, mandated identification checks for the purchase of tobacco products, and discouraged alcohol distribution to minors. She resigned from the position in 1993.

In 1993, Novello was named the PSCHH's special representative for health and nutrition to the United Nations Children's Fund (UNICEF), a position she held until 1996. She subsequently accepted a position as visiting professor of health policy and management at the Johns Hopkins University School of Hygiene and Public Health. New York governor George Pataki then appointed Novello state commissioner of health in 1999. She served for seven years, but was later charged with governmental fraud and theft for using state funds for personal errands. She pleaded guilty to one lesser charge and paid a restitution fee and a fine and completed community service with low-income patients at a New York health clinic.

> "*I believe that fortitude is key. More than anything, be consistent. Go at it. Go at it. Go at it. When you succeed, don't forget the responsibility of making somebody else succeed with you.*"

Novello has received the Public Health Service Commendation Medal, Public Health Service Outstanding Service Medal, Hispanic Heritage Award for Leadership, James Smithson Bicentennial Medal, and Legion of Merit

Medal. In 2006, she was a finalist for *Hispanic Business* magazine's woman of the year award (2006).

In 2008, Novello was named vice president of women and children health and policy affairs at Disney Children's Hospital at Florida Hospital in Orlando, where she concentrates on family health and preventing illness. She married Joseph R. Novello, a former U.S. Navy flight surgeon and psychiatrist, in 1970, but the couple eventually divorced.

Significance

Novello overcame childhood illness and poverty to become one of the country's most successful public health leaders. She turned what could have been a discouraging medical diagnosis into motivation to help others gain equal access to health care. Novello is one of the most influential Latino role models in health care and continues to work to improve care for minorities.

Janet Ober Berman

Further Reading

Novello, Antonia C. "Cancer, Minorities, and the Medically Underserved: A Call to Action." *Journal of Cancer Education* 21, no. 1 Supplement (Spring, 2006): S5-S8. Transcript of a lecture detailing Novello's approach to eliminating health disparities in minorities.

Novello, Antonia C., et al. "Final Report of the United States Department of Health and Human Services Secretary's Work Group on Pediatric Human Immunodeficiency Virus Infection and Disease: Content and Implications." *Pediatrics* 84, no. 3 (September, 1989): 547-555. Influential paper on pediatric AIDS that brought attention to Novello's work and led to her appointment as surgeon general.

Olmstead, Mary. *Antonia Novello*. Chicago: Raintree, 2004. Basic biography for younger readers, focusing on Novello's tenure as surgeon general.

Wade, N. A., et al. "Decline in Perinatal HIV Transmission in New York State (1997-2000)." *Journal of Acquired Immune Deficiency Syndromes* 36, no. 5 (August, 2004): 1075-1082. Article detailing the success of public health policies in declining rates of newborns with human immunodeficiency virus (HIV).

Susan La Flesche Picotte

Native physician

Born: June 17, 1865; Omaha Reservation, Nebraska
Died: September 18, 1915; Walthill, Nebraska
Area of achievement: Medicine

As the first female Native American physician, Picotte served her tribe as medical missionary and community leader for twenty-five years.

Early Life

Susan La Flesche Picotte (lah-flehsh pee-koh) was born to chief Joseph La Flesche (also known as Iron Eye), the son of a French fur trader, and Mary Gale La Flesche (also known as One Woman), the daughter of a white army surgeon and his Omaha wife. Adopted by Omaha chief Big Elk, Iron Eye succeeded him as one of the two principal chiefs of the tribe in 1853. The La Flesches believed that some accommodation to the ever-advancing white world was essential if their tribe were to survive. Susan, the youngest of Iron Eye's four remarkable daughters, grew up in a family much influenced by assimilation-oriented

Susan La Flesche Picotte (Wikimedia Commons)

missionaries. Her parents converted to Christianity, adopted the white man's lifestyle, and encouraged their children to seek formal education. Picotte's oldest sister, Susette (Bright Eyes), ultimately gained fame as a speaker, journalist, and Indian rights advocate; Rosalie enjoyed a successful business career in the livestock industry; and Marguerite became a teacher among the Omahas.

Reared on the reservation, Picotte attended agency day schools run by Quaker and Presbyterian missionaries. At the age of fourteen, she and seventeen-year-old Marguerite traveled to New Jersey to attend boarding school at the Elizabeth Institute for Young Ladies, returning home to Nebraska two and a half years later. From 1882 to 1884, Picotte taught at the mission school before continuing her education at the Hampton Normal and Agricultural Institute in Virginia. Established in 1868 to educate freed slaves (and later, Indians as well), Hampton emphasized vocational training; however, the sisters could read and write English fluently and were encouraged to pursue an academic program. Picotte was graduated second in her class in 1886. Urged to study medicine by the school physician, Dr. Martha Waldron, she eagerly accepted a scholarship to Woman's Medical College of Pennsylvania. On March 14, 1889, Picotte was graduated at the head of her class of thirty-six women, becoming the first female Native American to acquire a medical degree.

LIFE'S WORK

Following a four-month internship at Women's Hospital in Philadelphia, Picotte accepted the position of government physician to the Omaha agency school. Of all the Nebraska tribes, the Omahas were considered the most successful in trying to accommodate to white ideas of "progress." The Omaha Allotment Act of 1882 had divided much of the reservation into individual farms, and more and more Indian families were sending their children to the agency school. Despite this seeming progress, drought, grasshoppers, unscrupulous white neighbors, and inept government agents all combined to create desperate poverty among the Omahas. With this social upheaval and deprivation came malnutrition and disease. Influenza, dysentery, and tuberculosis were endemic on the reservation, as were periodic outbreaks of cholera, smallpox, diphtheria, and typhoid fever. Within weeks of her arrival, the twenty-four-year-old Picotte also took on the arduous task of treating the entire adult population, giving her a patient load of more than twelve hundred.

The size of the reservation thirty by forty-five miles and the absence of paved roads forced Picotte to travel huge distances by horse and buggy or on horseback, often in severe weather. In 1891, the Women's National Indian Association, which had financed her medical training, asked her to take on additional duties as their medical missionary to the tribe. That same year, she gained membership in the Nebraska State Medical Society. Soon she experienced the first of several bouts with osteomyelitis, a painful infection of her facial bones that later caused deafness and eventually led to her premature death. Exhausted and temporarily bedridden by the disease, she resigned as agency doctor in October of 1893.

Despite her frail health and enormous professional responsibilities, Picotte became increasingly involved in tribal and family affairs during the 1890's. Ever the missionary, she taught Sunday school at the Presbyterian church, acted as interpreter for non-English-speaking Omahas, and worked closely with Marguerite to upgrade sanitary conditions on the reservation. To everyone's surprise, on June 30, 1894, she married Henry Picotte, an uneducated French-Sioux from the Yankton Agency and a brother of Marguerite's late husband, Charles. The Picottes settled for a time in Bancroft, on the southern edge of the reservation, where Henry farmed the La Flesche allotment and Picotte had two sons: Caryl, born in 1895, and Pierre, born in 1898. While rearing her children and caring for her ailing mother, she continued to practice medicine, treating both Indian and non-Indian patients. Before long she was also nursing Henry, whose excessive drinking undermined his health and ultimately caused his death in 1905.

> *"It is vital that every child in Nebraska, whether native, white, immigrant or offspring of former slave, be afforded an opportunity to learn."*

For Picotte, the scourge of alcoholism went beyond the boundaries of a personal family tragedy. Her father had waged a successful campaign against whiskey peddlers and liquor consumption on the Omaha reservation. After Iron Eye's death in 1888, however, the situation deteriorated. Picotte eventually came to regard "demon rum" as the principal health hazard threatening her people. In temperance lectures, newspaper articles, and letters to government officials, she argued that alcohol abuse not only increased violence and crime but also made her tribespeople easy prey for all sorts of deadly diseases, especially tuberculosis and pneumonia.

Moreover, she charged, local politicians and bootleggers routinely used whiskey to cheat tribal members out of their allotments. She lobbied the Bureau of Indian Affairs (BIA) for stricter enforcement of the 1897 congressional ban on selling liquor to Indians. By 1906, she had convinced the secretary of the interior to ban all liquor sales in any new town carved out of the Omaha reservation.

Picotte and her sister Marguerite (who had remarried) bought property in the new town of Walthill, where, in 1906, they each built modern homes. Over the next nine years, Picotte actively participated in the civic and professional life of the community, despite her own failing health. The Presbyterian Board of Home Missions hired her as their missionary to the Omahas, the first nonwhite to hold such a post. She served several terms on the Walthill Board of Health, during which time she led campaigns to eradicate the communal drinking cup and the household fly as agents of disease. She organized the Thurston County Medical Association, served a three-year term as state chair of the Nebraska Federation of Women's Clubs' public health committee, and began an intensive study of tuberculosis.

In 1909, the Omaha tribe sought Picotte's help in solving serious problems arising out of the allotment system. By law, individual allotments were to be held in trust by the government for twenty-five years, until Native American owners were deemed sufficiently "assimilated" to handle their own financial affairs. Meanwhile, government red tape and dictatorial agency control deprived tribal members of desperately needed trust funds. Making matters worse, the BIA instituted new restrictions in 1909; consolidated the Omaha and Winnebago agencies; and announced plans to extend the trust period an additional ten years, despite the Omahas' high literacy rate and well-educated leadership. Picotte wrote a series of blistering newspaper articles protesting the BIA's conduct. In February of 1910, barely recovered from a near-fatal attack of neurasthenia, she headed up a tribal delegation sent to Washington, D.C., to fight the new policies. Unsuccessful in getting the old agency restored, Picotte did persuade the secretary of the interior to cancel the ten-year trust extension, thus granting most Omahas control over their own property.

Picotte's main dream was to erect a centrally located hospital where she could provide better medical care for her Indian patients. Through her efforts, the Presbyterian Church provided $8,000, and Quakers gave an additional $500. Marguerite and her husband donated the land, and various other friends agreed to purchase the equipment. After Walthill Hospital opened in January of 1913, Picotte was able to practice there for only two years. The bone disease in her face and neck spread, taking her life on September 18, 1915. Her funeral was conducted jointly by Presbyterian clergy and a tribal elder; the medical facility she built was renamed the Dr. Susan Picotte Memorial Hospital.

SIGNIFICANCE

As practicing physician, missionary, social reformer, and political leader, Susan La Flesche Picotte had a profound effect on the lives of her people. By 1915, there was scarcely an Omaha alive who had not been treated by her; even those who did not embrace all of her reformist ideals trusted her. As the Omahas' unofficial but clearly recognized spokesperson, Picotte defended their interests in the white world, even as she devoted her energies to their physical well-being at home. Beyond modern medical care, public health improvements, and vigorous leadership, she provided her tribe and the larger world with a vibrant example of what late nineteenth century reformers hoped to accomplish with their assimilationist policies. Like her father, Picotte believed that education, Christian principles, and legal rights were the key to her tribe's advancement. That she and her non-Indian mentors underestimated the difficulties facing American Indians and overestimated the virtues of forced acculturation does not detract from her achievement. Susan Picotte walked with grace in two worlds; assimilated into middle-class mainstream American culture, she never abandoned her tribal roots or her overriding concern for her people. Few women, Indian or white, have left such an indelible mark on their communities.

Constance B. Rynder

FURTHER READING

Clark, Jerry E., and Martha Ellen Webb. "Susette and Susan La Flesche: Reformer and Missionary." In *Being and Becoming Indian: Biographical Studies of North American Frontiers*, edited by James A. Clifton. Chicago: Dorsey Press, 1989. Contrasting the lives of the two best-known La Flesche sisters, the authors conclude that both women were thoroughly assimilated into white culture; Susan, however, participated more directly in tribal life and harbored less bitterness toward non-Indians.

Green, Norma Kidd. *Iron Eye's Family: The Children of Joseph La Flesche*. Lincoln, Neb.: Johnsen, 1969. The pioneering work on the La Flesche family, and still the best source of detailed information on Picotte's life. Green explores the achievements of three generations of this large and fascinating clan. Included are the children of Iron Eye's secondary wife, Ta-in-ne, as well as a glimpse of the adult lives led by Picotte's two sons, Caryl and Pierre.

Hauptman, Laurence M. "Medicine Woman: Susan La Flesche, 1865-1915." *New York State Medical Journal* 78 (September, 1978): 1783-1788. Focuses on Picotte's experiences in medical school, emphasizing her enthusiasm and scientific curiosity. Hauptman makes good use of her correspondence to convey the image of a supremely self-confident young woman who also possessed a wry sense of humor.

Mathes, Valerie Sherer. "Dr. Susan La Flesche Picotte: The Reformed and the Reformer." In *Indian Lives: Essays on Nineteenth- and Twentieth-Century Native American Leaders,* edited by L. G. Moses and Raymond Wilson. Albuquerque: University of New Mexico Press, 1985. Mathes portrays Picotte's life and work as a manifestation of the late nineteenth century female reform tradition. This article also gives the most up-to-date diagnosis of the physician's own perplexing health problems.

Milner, Clyde A. *With Good Intentions: Quaker Work Among the Pawnees, Otos, and Omahas in the 1870's.* Lincoln: University of Nebraska Press, 1982. Places the La Flesche family's advocacy of accommodation in the larger context of the Quaker- inspired "Peace Policy" adopted by the government in 1869. For the Omahas' role within this framework, Milner relies heavily on a landmark study of the tribe published in 1911 by Picotte's half brother, ethnologist Francis La Flesche.

Tong, Benson. *Susan La Flesche Picotte, M.D.*: Omaha Indian Leader and Reformer. Norman: University of Oklahoma Press, 1999. Interpretive biography focusing on Picotte's ability to move between two disparate cultures her Omaha Indian life in the West and the world of college, medical school, and politics in the East.

Wilson, Dorothy Clarke. *Bright Eyes: The Story of Susette La Flesche, an Omaha Indian.* New York: McGraw-Hill, 1974. Romanticized biography of Picotte's older, more famous sister. There is little material here on Susan herself, but more on her mother, Mary Gale, than is available elsewhere.

JONAS SALK

Physician and scientist

Born: October 28, 1914; New York City, New York
Died: June 23, 1995; La Jolla, California
Area of Achievement: Medicine

Salk's development of the first effective vaccine against polio led to the control of a disease that annually killed or paralyzed thousands of children.

EARLY LIFE

Jonas Salk (sawlk) was born in New York City in 1914, the first of three sons of Jewish Russian immigrants Daniel and Dora Press Salk. While Jonas Salk's mother envisioned a rabbinical career for her son, his interests as a youth were in the political arena: He wanted to attend law school with the goal of running for Congress. An exceptional student, Salk applied to and was accepted into Townsend Harris High School, which offered an accelerated academic program. Salk graduated at the age of fifteen and enrolled at the City College of New York (CCNY).

CCNY was noted for its rigorous programs and

Jonas Salk (Wikimedia Commons)

outstanding academic atmosphere. Equally significant for immigrant families, the school charged no tuition. While a freshman, Salk decided a career in law was not for him, and he embarked on a career in medicine. His particular interest was in medical research rather than developing a standard medical practice.

Salk's early years in New York overlapped with the increasingly serious development of poliovirus epidemics. Poliomyelitis was an ancient disease, but the etiological agent had only been isolated by Karl Landsteiner in Vienna several years earlier. The first major epidemic in the United States occurred in 1916. More than nine thousand children were affected in New York City, with more than two thousand deaths. There is no evidence the outbreak directly affected the Salk family, but certainly the prevalence of the devastating disease would have had some influence on Salk's interest in medical research.

Salk enrolled in New York University Medical School in the fall of 1934. He quickly became interested in the field of chemistry, and his meticulous work in the laboratory came to the attention of his professor, Robert Keith Cannan. Cannan routinely offered research positions to his outstanding students, and when an offer was made to Salk it was quickly accepted, even though it would delay his graduation. While Salk's initial work addressed methods of purifying bacteria, he also began preliminary work on the inactivation of viruses with formaldehyde.

LIFE'S WORK

Salk received his medical degree in 1939. In June of that year, Salk married Donna Lindsay, a young woman studying social work at Smith College whom he met while she was vacationing in Woods Hole, Massachusetts. Lindsay's father, the head of a relatively wealthy family, agreed to the marriage on two conditions: first, that Salk would get his medical degree, and, second, that Salk would take a middle name. Lindsay's father chose for him the initial "E," and Salk decided his name would become Jonas Edward Salk.

Salk entered his medical internship in March, 1940, at Mount Sinai Hospital in Manhattan, only blocks from where he was born. Despite the completion of his work in 1942, Salk found his opportunities were limited; university or medical school positions for Jews were subject to unwritten quotas. Furthermore the United States was at war, and physicians were needed in the armed services. However, while in medical school, Salk had become acquainted with the chairman of the microbiology department, virologist Thomas Francis, who had subsequently joined the University of Michigan as chairman of the Department of Epidemiology. Francis was working on an influenza vaccine and offered a position in the department to Salk. Salk accepted and began research in developing his first successful viral vaccine—against influenza.

In the fall of 1947, Salk was offered a permanent position at the University of Pittsburgh, replacing Dr. Walter Schlesinger as the head of what was loosely termed a virology laboratory at Municipal Hospital, in a room situated next to the morgue. However, the university was willing to carry out extensive renovations, including an increase in laboratory space, and Salk accepted the offer.

By the late 1940's polio epidemics had become an annual summer ritual, and the incidence of the disease continued to rise. Salk began to focus on polio as his area for research, and with grants provided by the Mellon Foundation, and increasingly from the National Foundation for Infantile Paralysis, he brought together a research team and purchased the necessary laboratory materials. His first major success was the determination that poliovirus

The first polio vaccine arrives in Holland. (Wikimedia Commons)

strains consisted of only three major types rather than the hundred or more that had been suspected. Often overlooked, this discovery meant a vaccine could be directed against a manageable number of viral variants.

> *"I look upon ourselves as partners in all of this, and that each of us contributes and does what he can do best. And so I see not a top rung and a bottom rung — I see all this horizontally — and I see this as part of a matrix. And I see every human being as having a purpose, a destiny, if you like. And what my hope is that we can find some way to fulfill the biological potential, if you like — the destiny that exists in each of us — and find ways and means to provide such opportunities for everyone. Now at the moment the world is suffering from large numbers of people who have no purpose in life — for whom there is no opportunity — and that's sad."*

Two approaches to develop the vaccine represented the primary sources of contention between competing laboratories. Dr. Albert Sabin, for many years one of the leading researchers in virology and working at Children's Hospital in Cincinnati, argued that a killed virus vaccine, Salk's approach, was not only less effective than a live attenuated vaccine but also potentially dangerous. Salk argued that a vaccine composed of formalin-killed virus, when prepared properly, not only was safe but also was effective in immunizing recipients. Preliminary vaccine trials, initially by Salk on himself and his family, followed by larger trials with children, supported this viewpoint. In what was considered the largest public health trial in history, nearly two million children participated during the spring of 1954 in a program under the auspices of Francis and the University of Michigan to test the efficacy of Salk's vaccine.

On April 12, 1955, in the Rackham Building on the University of Michigan campus, Francis and Salk released the results of the trial. The vaccine was shown to be between 80 and 90 percent effective in protecting children against polio.

Salk moved to La Jolla, California, in 1962. He spent his last years in research at the Salk Institute for Biological Studies, carrying out research to fight cancer and AIDS. In 1995, Salk died of heart failure.

Conquering Polio

During the early 1950's, the major polio epidemics in the United States resulted in nearly sixty thousand cases each year. More than three thousand died and nearly twenty-two thousand developed mild to severe paralysis during the course of each outbreak, with cases overwhelmingly among children. The numbers never represented the fear within the population that grew during "polio season" in the summer months. The Salk polio vaccine was not a cure for the disease; nor did it prove to be 100 percent effective. However, it did prove to be remarkably safe when proper procedures were followed. By 1957 an estimated 100 million doses of the vaccine were distributed throughout the United States, and within three years after the Salk vaccine was licensed, the annual incidence of polio in the United States was reduced by nearly 90 percent.

The oral polio vaccine created by Albert Sabin was licensed in 1961, and the combination of the Salk and Sabin vaccines resulted in the elimination of polio in the United States by 1979, and soon the disease was eradicated throughout much of the world. The Salk vaccine played a major role in this accomplishment, with an estimated 500,000 annually being spared the consequences of the disease.

SIGNIFICANCE

The development of Salk's inactivated viral vaccine disproved the notion, prevalent among virologists of the time, that vaccines prepared from killed viruses could not provide adequate protection against the agent. Certainly this fear had precedents: During the 1930's, several versions of killed polio vaccines actually resulted in development of the disease in some children. However, despite an accident by one laboratory that prepared the vaccine improperly, Salk's vaccine was shown to be both safe and effective.

Salk's vaccine was eventually superseded by the attenuated viral vaccines developed by Salk's rival, Albert Sabin, and most current viral vaccines are prepared either by attenuation or through recombination techniques creating protein conjugates. However, the techniques utilized by Salk have been applied in development of several forms of killed vaccines directed against certain types of hepatitis and viral encephalitis.

Richard Adler

FURTHER READING

Allen, Arthur. *Vaccine: The Controversial Story of Medicine's Greatest Lifesaver*. New York: W. W. Norton, 2008. The history of vaccine discovery and development. The author moves from the stories behind eradication or control of diseases to the controversies associated with vaccination itself.

Kluger, Jeffrey. *Splendid Solution: Jonas Salk and the Conquest of Polio*. New York: G. P. Putnam's Sons, 2004. Both a detailed biography of Salk and the scientific story behind development of the poliovirus vaccine. An excellent source for those interested in the in-fighting between Salk and Sabin.

Offit, Paul A. *The Cutter Incident: How America's First Polio Vaccine Led to the Growing Vaccine Crisis*. New Haven, Conn.: Yale University Press, 2007. Cutter Laboratories in Berkeley, California, was one of six pharmaceutical companies licensed to make the Salk vaccine. Mistakes in quality control resulted in contaminated batches of vaccine, and nearly two hundred people contracted the disease; of these, eleven died.

Oshinsky, David. *Polio: An American Story*. New York: Oxford University Press, 2005. While emphasis in the book is placed on the respective roles of Salk and Sabin, the author also brings to light lesser known individuals in the story of polio.

MARGARET SANGER

Health educator

Born: September 14, 1879; Corning, New York
Died: September 6, 1966; Tuscon, Arizona
Area of Achievement: Public health, women's rights, social reform, education

Through the establishment of low-cost birth control clinics, including the first such clinic in the United States, Sanger made birth control information and contraceptive devices available to American women of all social classes.

EARLY LIFE

Margaret Sanger (SAN-gur) was the sixth of eleven children born to poor Irish parents. Her mother died at the age of forty, and Sanger always believed that her mother's premature death was a consequence of excessive childbearing. During her mother's illness, Sanger acted as a nurse and also helped care for her younger siblings. Sanger enjoyed a close relationship with her father, who worked as a headstone carver. Higgins advised his resourceful children to use their minds to make a contribution to the world and to try to leave it better than they found it.

As a young girl, Sanger formed the conclusion that poverty, illness, and strife were the fate of large families, whereas small families enjoyed wealth, leisure, and positive parental relationships. Being from a large family, Sanger always felt inferior, and she longed to be rich and comfortable.

After the death of her mother, Sanger decided to become a nurse. During her final training at a Manhattan hospital, she met an architect named William Sanger, who fell in love with her at first sight. Sanger married Bill Sanger in 1902 after a six-month courtship. Over the next few years, Bill continued his work as an architect and Margaret stayed home with their three children. Sanger's restlessness and boredom in her role as a housewife led to her return to obstetrical nursing in 1912. She felt a need to regain her personal independence, and her mother-inlaw agreed to move in and take care of the children. At the same time, Sanger began attending socialist meetings in Greenwich Village. She observed forceful speakers, such as Emma Goldman, who were rethinking the position of women and the future of worldwide political and economic systems. Sanger was considered a shy, delicate woman who rarely voiced her opinion at meetings.

Sanger's speaking debut was as a substitute before a group of working women. Her topic was family health. The working women liked Sanger's demeanor and believed what she said. Throughout her life, much of Sanger's impact was attributable to her personal appearance: She was petite, feminine, and demure. Sanger invariably gained support after the publication of her picture in the newspaper. Although her appearance was described as Madonna-like, Sanger was single-minded, stubborn, and intolerant; she was also charming, personable, and energetic. Sanger's personality was such that people either worshiped her or despised her.

Margaret Sanger (Library of Congress)

Life's Work

During her years as an obstetrical nurse, Sanger frequently made house calls to the Lower East Side of New York City to attend poor women who were giving birth or experiencing complications from self-induced abortions. These women were worried about the health and survival of the children they already had and were desperate to find a way to stop having more children. They would beg Sanger to tell them "the secret" of the rich women and would promise that they would not tell anyone else. Sanger would suggest coitus interruptus or the use of condoms, but she quickly realized that the women rejected initiating these methods, placing contraceptive responsibility on men. Sanger herself never believed in male-oriented contraceptives because she saw men as opponents, rather than partners, in the struggle for conception control.

A turning point in Sanger's life occurred when she met a young mother of three named Sadie Sachs. Sanger was called to nurse Sachs during the sweltering summer of 1912. Sachs had attempted an abortion and was near death when Sanger was called to the apartment. Two weeks later, Sachs was finally out of danger. She believed that another pregnancy would kill her and she pleaded with the attending physician to help prevent another pregnancy. The doctor callously told Sachs that she could not expect to have her cake and eat it too. His only suggestion, jokingly added, was that she have her husband, Jake, sleep on the roof. After the doctor left, She turned to Sanger, who was more sympathetic than the doctor but who had no better suggestion for contraception. Sanger promised the anguished woman that she would return at a later date and try to provide helpful information. Sanger did not return, and three months later she was again summoned to the Sachs apartment. Sachs was in critical condition from another abortion attempt, and this time she died minutes after Sanger arrived. Sanger was burdened with guilt over her death and resolved that she would find out how to prevent conception so that other women would be spared the pain, suffering, and heartache of unwanted pregnancies.

> "The basic freedom of the world is woman's freedom. A free race cannot be born of slave mothers. A woman enchained cannot choose but give a measure of that bondage to her sons and daughters. No woman can call herself free who does not own and control her body. No woman can call herself free until she can choose consciously whether she will or will not be a mother."

After two years of research, including a trip to France, Sanger decided to publish a journal aimed at working women that would encourage them to rebel and to insist on reproductive freedom. It was at this time that Sanger coined the term "birth control." In 1914, the first issue of *The Woman Rebel* was published. Birth control Although Sanger advocated that women limit births, she was prohibited by Anthony Comstock from explaining to women the precise methodologies for limiting births. Comstock was the head of the New York Society for the Suppression of Vice, and Sanger had experienced problems with him several years earlier when she wrote articles for *The Call*, a labor publication. Sanger's health-oriented column on venereal disease was aimed at adolescent girls, but Comstock refused to allow the column to be published. He had been instrumental in seeing that no obscene materials were distributed through the United States mail, and Comstock made it clear to publishers of *The Call* that he considered Sanger's article obscene and that its publication would result in immediate revocation of their mailing permit. Both Sanger and Comstock wanted to protect

America's young people. Comstock sought to protect the young by distancing them from information on venereal disease, while Sanger thought that the protection of the young could best be achieved by exposing them to and educating them about the realities, dangers, and treatment of venereal disease.

Thousands of women responded to Sanger's articles in *The Woman Rebel*, once again pleading for information about the prevention of pregnancy. Sanger wrote a pamphlet called "Family Limitation" that provided practical, straightforward information in language that women of all social classes could understand. Sanger included descriptions and drawings of suppositories, douches, sponges, and the cervical pessary. Sanger also advocated sexual fulfillment for women, which was a radical idea in the early 1900s. After twenty refusals, Sanger found a printer for "Family Limitation".

With the help of friends, Sanger began distributing the pamphlet and was arrested immediately. The possibility of prison was overwhelming to Sanger at this time, so she sailed for Europe before she came to trial, leaving her husband and children behind. She settled in London and was accepted into the intellectual circle of people on the vanguard of sexual and contraceptive thought. Sanger discovered that the Netherlands, because of an emphasis on child spacing, had the lowest maternal death rate and infant mortality rate in the world. In addition, contraceptive clinics had been in operation for thirty years. When Sanger visited the Netherlands, she received trained instruction on the fitting and insertion of the diaphragm, which came in fourteen sizes. Sanger became convinced that she not only would have to overcome the restraint on free speech in the United States but also would have to provide women with access to trained people, preferably physicians, who could fit them with contraceptives.

Sanger returned to the United States to stand trial, but the charges against her were dismissed. Anthony Comstock had died while she was away, and the mood of the people was now supportive of Sanger.

In October of 1916, Sanger opened the nation's first birth control clinic. The clinic provided birth control and venereal disease information and birth control instruction. Most important, the clinic kept detailed medical records and case histories of patients. Although Sanger and her sister Ethel Byrne were imprisoned for their role in the new birth control clinic, public sentiment was in their

---

Sanger's Defiance

In a 1916 pamphlet, *The Fight for Birth Control*, Margaret Sanger explained why she became involved in the effort to educate American women about contraception and told of the battles she faced in publishing *The Woman Rebel* in 1914.

"During fourteen years experience as a trained nurse, I found that a great percentage of women's diseases were due to ignorance of the means to prevent conception. I found that quackery was thriving on this ignorance, and that thousands of abortions were being performed each year—principally upon the women of the working class. Since the laws deter reliable and expert surgeons from performing abortions, working women have always been thrown into the hands of the incompetent, with fatal results. The deaths from abortions mount very high.

"I found that physicians and nurses were dealing with these symptoms rather than their causes, and I decided to help remove the chief cause by imparting knowledge to prevent conception, in defiance of existing laws and their extreme penalty. I sent out a call to the proletarian women of America to assist me in this work, and their answers came by the thousands. I started The Woman Rebel early in 1914. The first issue of the magazine was suppressed. Seven issues out of nine were suppressed, and although sent out as first-class mail, the editions were confiscated. The newspapers—even the most radical— declined to give this official tyranny any publicity.

"In August, 1914, a Federal Grand Jury returned three indictments against me, based on articles in the March, May and July issues of *The Woman Rebel*. The articles branded as "obscene" merely discussed the question and contained no information how to prevent conception. But the authorities were anxious to forestall the distribution of this knowledge and knew that this could only be done by imprisoning me. I decided to avoid the imprisonment, at least until I had given out the information. One hundred thousand copies of a pamphlet, "Family Limitation," were prepared and distributed, and I sailed for England."

Sanger and her sister Ethyl Byrne on the steps of a courthouse in Brooklyn, New York, on January 8, 1917. This photo was taken during a trial accusing Sanger and others for opening a birth control clinic in New York. Both were found guilty. (Wikimedia Commons)

favor. In the next few years, Sanger began publishing the *Birth Control Review*, a scientific, authoritative journal intended for health care professionals. In 1921, Sanger organized the first national birth control conference, which attracted physicians from all over the country.

Margaret and Bill Sanger were divorced in 1920, and in 1922 Margaret married a wealthy businessman named Noah Slee. Slee contributed many thousands of dollars to his wife's cause but always stayed in the background of her life. Sanger was a national figure by this time and a frequent speaker who enthralled her audience. She traveled internationally and made a great impact on the birth control movements in both Japan and India. In her efforts to establish international unity, Sanger established a World Population Conference, and years later, in 1952, the International Planned Parenthood Federation.

Throughout her career, Sanger lamented the absence of a safe, easy, effective contraceptive. She believed that some sort of contraceptive pill would best meet the needs of women, and she called such a pill her "holy grail." When she discovered that scientists John Rock and Gregory Pincus were experimenting with hormonal methods of contraception, Sanger convinced Mrs. Stanley McCormick, a wealthy widow, to provide funding for Rock and Pincus to continue their research for a contraceptive pill.

Sanger continued to be an active force in the birth control movement until very late in her life. As a nursing home patient in Tucson, Arizona, she was irascible and stubborn and insisted that since she was rich and smart she would do exactly as she pleased. She did just that until she died in 1966 of arteriosclerosis, one week before her eighty-seventh birthday.

Significance

In her lifetime, Sanger was jailed eight times, yet she never relented in her efforts to promote, and democratize access to, birth control. The medical records of patients visiting Sanger's birth control clinic provided the basis for the initial studies on the effects of child spacing on maternal health and marital satisfaction. These records also yielded information on the efficacy of various birth control methods for different groups of women.

Sanger's early efforts to distribute contraceptive information were condemned by the church, the press, and the medical profession. Her belief that sex is a normal part of human life that requires a rational response led her to search for easy and safe contraceptives that would allow women to choose maternity while attaining freedom through control of their bodies. Sanger believed that in some way every unwanted child would be a social liability, and that a society should try to maximize its social assets by having children that are wanted by their parents. Sanger insisted that the best measure of the success of her work was in the reduction of human suffering.

Availability of contraceptive information and birth control devices has had widespread implications for Americans, both individually and collectively. Maternal death rates and infant mortality rates have declined, child spacing spans have increased, and total family size has decreased. Control of conception is a subject taught in classes throughout the country, and American women and men take for granted the fact that contraceptives are sold in drugstores and are easily obtained from physicians. As a result of the achievements of Sanger, control of conception has become a reality for many women throughout the world.

Lesley Hoyt Croft

Further Reading

Chandrasekhar, Sripati. *"A Dirty Filthy Book": The Writings of Charles Knowlton and Annie Besant on Birth Control and Reproductive Physiology*. Berkeley: University of California Press, 1981. Includes essays by Sanger's American and British predecessors who laid the foundation for her work. Provides an account of the Bradlaugh-Besant trial in 1877 and its impact on the British birth rate.

Davis, Tom. *Sacred Work: Planned Parenthood and Its Clergy Alliances*. New Brunswick, N.J.: Rutgers University Press, 2005. Recounts how Planned Parenthood allied with members of the clergy, beginning with Sanger's efforts to include clergymen in the organization's efforts to dispense public information about contraceptives.

Douglas, Emily Taft. *Pioneer of the Future*. New York: Holt, Rinehart and Winston, 1970. A thorough work documenting the milestones of Sanger's life. Good in-depth account of research, events, and individuals who gave Sanger the basic knowledge, ideas, and encouragement from which to proceed.

Franks, Angela. *Margaret Sanger's Eugenic Legacy: The Control of Female Fertility*. Jefferson, N.C.: McFarland, 2005. Describes Sanger's ideas many of which are still debated about birth control, eugenics, sterilization, and population control.

Gray, Madeline. *Margaret Sanger: A Biography of the Champion of Birth Control*. New York: Richard Marek, 1979. Excellent, well-researched biography with one of the few in-depth examinations of Sanger's later years, including her addiction to Demerol.

Kennedy, David M. *Birth Control in America: The Career of Margaret Sanger*. New Haven, Conn.: Yale University Press, 1970. Focuses on Sanger's public career in the United States and illuminates American society in the years prior to 1945. Describes the social context in which Sanger worked and the attitudinal, behavioral, and institutional responses she evoked.

Sanger, Margaret. *Margaret Sanger: An Autobiography*. New York: Dover, 1971. A factual description of the life of the author without much insight and introspection. Describes people who influenced Sanger, including the C. V. Drysdales and Havelock Ellis in England, and Aletta Jacobs, birth control pioneer in the Netherlands.

---. *Motherhood in Bondage*. New York: Brentano's, 1928. Reprint. New York: Pergamon Press, 1956. Composed of letters written to Sanger by women desperate to discover a method of preventing conception. Tragic, heart-wrenching accounts.

---. *Woman and the New Race*. New York: Brentano's, 1920. Attempts to convince working-class women that control of reproduction is the key to a healthier, more satisfying life and a better world. Advocates rebellion to gain access to contraceptive information.

Nora D. Volkow

Neuroscientist; federal-agency administrator; educator

Born: March 27, 1956; Mexico City, Mexico
Area of Achievement: Neuroscience

Nora Volkow has been recognized by the medical and research communities for her significant contributions to our understanding of addiction.

Early Life

Nora Dolores Volkow was born on March 27, 1956 in Mexico City, Mexico. Her father, Esteban Volkov, was a Russian-born chemist who worked in the pharmaceutical industry. Her mother, Palmira Fernandez, was a fashion designer; a native of Spain, she fled to Mexico in the 1930s, during the Spanish Civil War. Volkow has an older sister, Veronica, a translator, poet, and essayist, and younger twin sisters: Patricia, a physician and AIDS specialist, and Natalia, an administrator at Mexico's National Institute of Statistics. (All the siblings changed the last letter of their surname from "v" to "w.")

Volkow and her sisters were raised in the very house where one of their great-grandfathers, the Russian revolutionary Leon Trotsky (1879-1940), was assassinated. Trotsky (born Lev Bronstein) settled in Mexico City in 1937, after the Soviet dictator Joseph Stalin sent him into exile. After he came to Mexico, Trotsky and Natalya, his second wife, shared a house with another couple—the artists Diego Rivera and Frida Kahlo. Conflict spurred by the suspicion that Trotsky was having an affair with Kahlo

Nora D. Volkow (Wikimedia Commons)

led the Trotskys to move to a house nearby, on Calle Viena.

Soon afterward, in 1939, Nora Volkow's father, then named Vsevolod Platonovich Volkov, the son of one of Trotsky's two daughters from his first marriage, came to Mexico City to live with his grandfather. Then about 13 years of age, he had no other living relative except a half-sister whom he did not meet until decades later; his mother had committed suicide, and every other member of his family had died in Stalin's purges or prison camps or under unexplained, suspicious circumstances. One day in August 1940, Volkov came home to learn that Trotsky had been severely wounded in his study by a Soviet agent wielding an ice axe; his grandfather died the next day. Volkov continued to live in the house on Calle Viena; years later, after changing his given name to Esteban, he brought his wife to live there. (According to some sources, he has also used the name Esteban Volkov Bronstein.)

As youngsters growing up in the house on Calle Viena (the building is now part of the Trotsky Museum), Volkow and her sisters would play with Trotsky's clothes and look through his books and papers. "My father didn't know about that," Volkow said. "He would have been very upset. But children are children." From a very early age, Volkow knew about her great-grandfather's assassination, largely through information imparted by people (most of them strangers to the Volkovs) who had been drawn to visit the house by their interest in Trotsky. "As little girls, whenever somebody rang the bell and asked us to guide them through the house, we did so, and that was a privilege," Natalia Volkow told Bill Snyder for the Vanderbilt University Medical Center magazine *Lens* (February 2006, on-line). "We usually took a long time talking to them—listening to them." But Volkow and her sisters did not discuss Trotsky with their father; his memories made talking about his grandfather too painful for him.

Volkow was a curious, perceptive child and an avid reader. She spent hours watching people interact on the streets of Mexico City. She was fascinated, she recalled, by the "diversity of behavioral responses in both animals and humans" and by how "the brain can generate fear, pain, love, language." What most interested her was how people relate to one another, everyone from a mother and her child or two strangers passing each other on the street. She also spent a lot of time observing the behavior of stray dogs and people's interactions with them and the ways in which members of ant colonies work together.

Volkow completed her secondary-school education at the private, English-language Modern American School in Mexico City. When she graduated, in 1974, she was fluent in French and German as well as Spanish and English. She then took undergraduate courses as well as medical instruction at the Universidad Nacional Autonoma de Mexico (National Antonomous University of Mexico), in Mexico City. Volkow was particularly interested in cardiology and biochemistry—especially the latter's application to cancer research—but her fascination with human behavior remained: she knew that she would ultimately pursue psychology and neuroscience. "Clearly," she said, "when I went to medical school, I went with the brain in mind."

LIFE'S WORK

Volkow earned an M.D. degree in January 1981; she ranked first in her class of 2,000 at her graduation and won the the Premio Robins Award for best medical student of her generation. About a month later Volkow read an article in *Scientific American* (October 1980) about the three-dimensional brain-imaging technique known as positron emission tomography (PET), in which scientists used scanners to track radioactive chemicals, called tracers, injected into patients suffering from Alzheimer's disease, epilepsy, the effects of strokes, and drug addiction. Different tracers were used to illuminate the parts of the brain involved in different activities. The technique was significant because scientists could learn noninvasively (that is, without surgery) about the functioning of the brains of people and animals. Reading the article marked a turning point in Volkow's life: she felt so excited about the prospect of using the technology that she abandoned her plans to pursue a postgraduate degree at the Massachusetts Institute of Technology and resolved to gain acceptance to the residency program in psychiatry at New York University (NYU). As partners in a collaborative program with Brookhaven National Laboratory, NYU Psychiatry Department researchers had access to the laboratory's PET scanners. With that goal she traveled to New York and secured an interview with the Psychiatry Department's chairman, Robert Cancro. In a conversation with Guy Gugliotta, Cancro recalled meeting Volkow: "It was clear she was bright, anxious, enthusiastic and you could see the drive." While at NYU Volkow earned the Laughlin Fellowship Award as one of the 10 outstanding psychiatric residents in the U.S.

> "*Whether coming from the perspective of neuroscience or meditation, our aim is to understand how we can encourage self-control, manage our emotions, and offer children a purposeful life that will prevent substance abuse.*"

Volkow's first professional paper, about the use of brain-imaging equipment for detecting cancerous brain tumors, reflected her medical training in Mexico. She soon turned her interest to schizophrenia, a psychiatric disorder that fascinated her: "It intrigued me because [the disorder] produces disruptions across a wide variety of processes," among them perception and reasoning; many schizophrenics suffer from hallucinations and delusions over which they have no control.

Chance led Volkow to turn from studying schizophrenia to researching drug addiction. In 1984 she left New York to take the post of assistant professor at the University of Texas Health Science Center at Houston; she also served as an attending physician at the university-affiliated Memorial Hermann Hospital. Although the hospital had imaging equipment, the patient population did not include schizophrenics. But there were many cocaine addicts. Abuse of certain drugs, such as alcohol, cocaine, and methamphetamine, produces psychosis in some people; symptoms of psychosis, as in schizophrenia, often include audio or visual hallucinations and/or delusional thinking. For that reason drug abusers would be suitable subjects for research for Volkow, who wanted to "get inside the process of psychosis."

Volkow was one of the first people—possibly the first—to use PET scans to examine the brains of drug addicts. She was surprised by what she found: as indicated by impaired blood flow, there was clear damage in their brains, similar to the destruction caused by small strokes. That was an "eye opener," Volkow said; the prevailing belief was that cocaine was a relatively safe drug, but the brain-imaging data she had collected showed that it was not. Volkow had also used general neuropsychological tests to evaluate her subjects. The addicts had performed relatively well on those tests, which measured such cognitive functions as memory and reaction time. Volkow concluded that the tests were not capable of detecting the brain damage that the PET scans revealed; moreover, such tests overlooked such phenomena as social intelligence, emotional intelligence, and multitasking abilities. Volkow's evidence notwithstanding, the medical community initially rejected her findings, because neuropsychological testing was well-established, whereas PET was a new technology. "In the beginning, I had a lot of trouble getting that data published," Volkow recalled. She commented to Bill Snyder, "When you go against the current it takes time to change its course." Three years passed before an article describing her research was published; entitled "Cerebral Blood Flow in Chronic Cocaine Users: A Study with Positron Emission Tomography," it appeared in the *British Journal of Psychiatry* in May 1988. Its three co-authors included the physicist Stephen Adler, whom Volkow married during her time in Texas.

Earlier, in 1987, Volkow had joined the Brookhaven National Laboratory, in Upton, New York, as an associate scientist with the Department of Medicine. She remained at the laboratory for 16 years, conducting research as director of the nuclear-medicine division (1994-2003), director of the NIDA/DOE Imaging Center (1997-2003), and associate director of life sciences (1999-2003). In addition to cocaine, Volkow investigated addictions to alcohol, nicotine, heroin, and methamphetamine. All those addictions involve dopamine, a neurotransmitter in the brain that plays a crucial role in desire, decision making, and motivation. The two most significant factors with regard to one's susceptibility to addiction are genes and environment: those with naturally high levels of dopamine receptors are much less likely than others to exhibit compulsive behavior when exposed to potentially rewarding stimuli—that is, they are much less likely to become addicts. Environmental factors, such as the availability of drugs and approval of their use among members of a person's family and social circle, also play important roles. For those reasons some but not all people who use drugs become addicted.

Dopamine transmits information to brain cells via the synapses, which exist at either end of each cell; the cells absorb the new information by means of receptors. Volkow and her colleagues found that there are "common changes in the brains of people regardless of the drug that they take... And we showed that [for people addicted to drugs cited above] there was a decrease in the levels of dopamine receptors in their brains." Furthermore, Volkow and her colleagues discovered that the abuse of such drugs leads to abnormalities in the orbitofrontal cortex—a region in the brain's frontal lobes that allows us to attribute values to actions, people, and things. Such abnormalities can lead to potentially devastating effects, such as the destructive decision to continue or even intensify drug abuse. Ordinarily, if a person is hungry, the orbitofrontal cortex of the brain will give food a higher "value"—make it a higher priority—than at other times; once the person is no longer hungry, the "value" that person attributes to the food becomes negligible or nil. Among drug abusers, Volkow's studies have shown, the orbitofrontal cortex is in effect hijacked, which leads the addicts to place an extraordinarily high value on consuming the desired drug. Moreover, damage to that brain region disrupts those people's ability to behave appropriately in social situations, which may lead to social isolation, continued drug abuse, and criminal activity.

Although the drugs mentioned above have many effects in common, they also have different effects, because the molecular composition of each is different from that of the others. Cocaine is especially harmful in that it kills brain cells, by interfering with blood circulation in the brain; the drug known as ecstasy (also called E) interferes with the workings of the neurotransmitter serotonin, which is very important in mood regulation; and methamphetamine has an especially devastating effect on processes involving dopamine.

In a study of effects on the brain of methamphetamine use that Volkow conducted with Joanna Fowler and nine others, their subjects consisted of two groups: one contained 15 methamphetamine addicts who had been using the drug for at least two years and who had stopped using it for at least two weeks prior to the experiment, and the other comprised 21 people who had never used the drug.

When, using PET scans, Volkow and her colleagues compared levels of dopamine in the addicts and the nonaddicts, they found that the former subjects' dopamine levels were more than 20 percent lower than those in the other group in areas of the brain crucial for movement, concentration, and motivation. Volkow and her colleagues published those findings in the March 2001 issue of the *American Journal of Psychiatry*.

In the mid-1990s Volkow and her colleagues started using MRI in addition to PET scans in their research. PET scans and MRI complement each other: PET scans reveal molecular functions and activity and changes in function and activity at the cellular level; MRI shows the structure of parts of the body—their size and shape—but does not provide information about function. Volkow has used both techniques in another area of research: her investigations of the heavy use or abuse of prescription drugs, including medications, such as Ritalin, extensively used to treat attention deficit and hyperactivity disorder (ADHD). In one study Volkow compared the brains of subjects injected with Ritalin (whose chemical structure is similar to that of amphetamine) with those of subjects injected with cocaine. The results, as Volkow wrote in a paper published in the *Archives of General Psychiatry* (Volume 52, Number 6, 1995), showed that the distribution of Ritalin in the brain was almost "identical to that of cocaine." In addition, both Ritalin and cocaine peaked a few minutes after injection: that is, the effects of both reached their maximums after a few minutes (between four and 10 minutes with Ritalin, between two and eight minutes with cocaine). The only significant difference between the two drugs revealed in that particular study, Volkow wrote, was that Ritalin took more than four times as long—90 minutes—as cocaine to leave the body. Ritalin is commonly prescribed to children who have been diagnosed with ADHD. However, Volkow pointed out, children (and adults) take the drug orally in pill form, not by means of injections or by snorting it, and the chemicals in pills metabolize differently from those that are injected or snorted; therefore, similarities between Ritalin and cocaine should not necessarily be used to condemn Ritalin as unsuitable as a treatment for ADHD.

In 2003 Elias Zerhouni, the director of the National Institutes of Health (NIH), appointed Volkow to the post of director of the National Institute on Drug Abuse (NIDA). Volkow was initially apprehensive, concerned that her new post would leave her little time for research, but she decided that she could not pass up an opportunity to make an impact on policy as well as science. (She still conducts

Dr. Antonello Bonci, National Institute on Drug Abuse, Intramural Scientific Director briefs (left to right), Dr. Thomas Ross, Dr. Volkow and Maryland Congressman John Sarbanes August 25, 2015, at the Bayview Campus in Baltimore, Maryland. (Wikimedia Commons)

research at Brookhaven as an NIH intramural scientist, usually for several days each month.) Principal activities at NIDA, whose budget in 2011 was $1.09 billion, include using state-of-the-art technologies to further understanding of the anatomy and physiology of the brain, behavioral development, and addiction and its consequences; uncovering genetic and environmental factors that predict vulnerability to addiction and effectiveness of treatments; addressing health disparities and vulnerabilities among different populations (such as adolescents, members of minorities, and people in prison); applying knowledge gained from basic and cognitive neuroscience to develop improved prevention and treatment strategies; developing and testing new medications and behavioral therapies to treat addiction; and studying the links between addiction and other diseases, especially HIV/AIDS.

Volkow believes that although addiction is a brain disease, its presence does not absolve addicts from all responsibility for their behavior. She also emphasizes, however, that we need a subtle and serious reevaluation of long-held and widely accepted concepts of addiction. "A sick person is still responsible to seek treatment and sustain it for as long as needed, just as a patient with AIDS has to take responsibility for seeking and staying in treatment," Volkow wrote in an e-mail message to Current Biography. (That message and a Current Biography phone interview with Volkow are the sources of all quotes in this article unless otherwise indicated.) "There is an important nuance in the case of addiction, though, in which, like for some other psychiatric conditions, the very foundations of free will and sound decision making might be severely impaired, dramatically lowering the ability of these patients to recognize their condition and lay out a rational plan to deal with it—at least to begin with. This is why it is so important for society to walk away from the stigma, recognize addiction for what it is and devise and deploy rational and humane ways of dealing with this devastating disease."

Significance

Since the 1990s, and now as director of NIDA, Volkow has warned that many children are misdiagnosed as having ADHD (and consequently receive drugs that they do not need), while other children who have ADHD, particularly in minority communities, are not diagnosed properly or at all, and as a result become more likely to abuse drugs. The solution, Volkow has said, is to improve diagnosis and treatment. Volkow has studied neurological phenomena associated not only with drugs but with obesity. Her research has produced evidence that compulsive eaters have low levels of dopamine receptors in their brains and that their orbital frontal cortexes show signs of damage. However, it is important to note, Volkow said, that what motivates the drive to eat is more complex than what motivates the drive to take drugs. We eat not only for pleasure but also for calories and nutrition; furthermore, she added, "food addiction" is not an officially recognized disorder, while compulsive eating is; the latter can lead to obesity and various health problems.

Society often looks down on and misunderstands people suffering from psychiatric disorders, such as schizophrenia and bipolar disorder. That is true to an even greater extent regarding drug addicts, who suffer from what Volkow calls "a disease of the brain that produces a loss of your ability to exert control." "By far, the biggest obstacle that I [have] had to contend with in my career in general and as the NIDA director in particular," Volkow wrote, "is the stigma that society attaches to drug abuse and addiction. This stigma permeates every social domain and has many negative effects, which include the suboptimal involvement of the healthcare system in the management of substance use disorders and the continuous reluctance on the part of the pharmaceutical industry to invest [in] the research necessary for the development of effective addiction medications. On a different level, we are challenged by the fragmentation of the substance abuse field, which has pitted those who favor biological approaches for the treatment of substance use disorders (SUDs) against those who oppose them; those who support legalization of drugs to help combat crime vs. those who are against such efforts for fear of increasing the magnitude of the drug problem, and those who support the notion of addiction as a brain disease against those who believe that addiction is squarely a moral failure of an individual. These obstacles have impeded the dialog around substance abuse and addiction and prevented effective treatments from reaching those who need them."

Volkow served as associate professor in the Department of Psychiatry at the State University of New York (SUNY) at Stony Brook from 1991 to 2003 and as associate dean at the School of Medicine at SUNY-Stony Brook from 1997 to 2003. Volkow is the first person from the NIH to visit the Dalai Lama at his residence in Dharamshala, Himachal Pradesh, India. During this 2013 visit, Volkow took part in a dialogue with the Dalai Lama about addiction science, as part of a five-day conference sponsored by the Mind and Life Institute. In 2014, Volkow was a featured speaker at TEDMED, the annual multidisciplinary gathering where leaders from all sectors of society come together to explore the promise of technology and potential of human achievement in health and medicine. Volkow's talk focused on the parallels between compulsive overeating and drug addiction.

Fowler told Bill Snyder that "people just glom onto [Volkow]. She's like pouring out ideas all day... She can take a problem and very easily see through it; see relationships, simplify things." Volkow maintains a residence in Chevy Chase, Maryland. A former competitive swimmer, she runs several miles daily. She also paints, "to break my patterns of thinking," she told Guy Gugliotta.

FURTHER READING

"Dr. Nora D. Volkow Named New Director of NIDA." *NIDA Archives*, National Institute on Drug Abuse, 23 Jan. 2003, archives.drugabuse.gov/news-events/news-releases/2003/01/dr-nora-d-volkow-named-new-director-nida.

Duenwald, Mary, and Nora D. Volkow. "A CONVERSATION WITH: NORA VOLKOW; A Scientist's Lifetime of Study Into the Mysteries of Addiction." *New York Times*, New York Times, 13 Aug. 2003, www.nytimes.com/2003/08/19/health/conversation-with-nora-volkow-scientist-s-lifetime-study-into-mysteries.html.

Flatow, Ira, and Nora D. Volkow. "Science and the Origins of Addiction." *Talk of the Nation*, National Public Radio, 16 June 2006.

Gugliotta, Guy. "Revolutionary Thinker." *The Washington Post*, WP Company, 21 Aug. 2003, www.washingtonpost.com/archive/lifestyle/2003/08/21/revolutionary-thinker/107f99c4-56fd-4d7f-8df8-184ae8bd15e2/?utm_term=.e0dc3026135a.

Snyder, Bill. "Nora Volkow: Two Paths to the Future." *Lens*, Vanderbilt University Medical Center, Feb. 2006, www.mc.vanderbilt.edu/lens/article/?id=129.

"Why Do Our Brains Get Addicted?" Performance by Nora Volkow, *TEDMED*, TED, 2014, www.tedmed.com/talks/show?id=309096.

Wingert, Pat. "Nora Volkow." *Newsweek*, 13 Mar. 2010, www.newsweek.com/nora-volkow-105459.

Zuger, Abigail. "A General in the Drug War." *The New York Times*, The New York Times, 13 June 2011, www.nytimes.com/2011/06/14/science/14volkow.html.

Military

Heroic qualities are traditionally linked to the martial virtues. The word "hero," from the Greek ἥρως (hérōs), originally referred to figures from ancient mythology who were warriors and fighters. Achilles, an archetypal *Greek hero, was the* most formidable fighter in the Trojan War and the central character in Homer's *Iliad*. Herakles (in Roman Latin, Hercules) was a mythological hero famous for accomplishing the Twelve Labors of Hercules and for conducting several war-like campaigns. In all cases, physical strength, courage, valor in battle, and the vanquishing of enemies were the qualities considered heroic.

Unlike ancient Greek heroism, American military heroism goes hand and hand with the value of patriotism. America's military heroes exhibit the traditional martial qualities of heroes in the service of the nation, and thus the history of American military heroism is closely linked to the history of the nation and its wars. The Continental Army was approved on June 14, 1775, and, under the leadership of George Washington, it lasted until the end of the Revolutionary War. The United States military was established in an act passed by the United States Congress on September 29, 1789, the last day of its first session, although the dates often given for the founding of the United States Army, the Marine Corps and the United States Navy are the dates of their establishment under the revolutionary regime—that is, 1775. The Air Force was established in 1947.

This section highlights a number of figures, often lesser-known, of interest to readers of history. It also seeks to be inclusive and representative of the important role that women and minorities have played in the United States military.

U.S. Air Force Airmen from the 720th Special Tactics Group jump out of a C-130J Hercules aircraft during water rescue training. (Julianne Showalter, U.S. Air Force)

Omar Nelson Bradley

Military leader

Born: February 12, 1893; Clark, Missouri
Died: April 8, 1981; New York city, New York
Primary conflict: World War II (1939-1945)

Bradley provided stability and continuity within the U.S. military establishment during the critical period following the end of World War II and the onset of the Cold War.

Early Life

Omar Nelson Bradley was born to John Smith Bradley, a schoolteacher, and Sarah Elizabeth Hubbard Bradley, a homemaker. Though "desperately poor," to use Bradley's words, his family took in the two daughters of his mother's sister when the latter died, and they became his "sisters." A second son was born to the Bradleys but died of scarlet fever before his second birthday.

Bradley's father, who supplemented the modest income he received from his teaching with what odd jobs he could find, contracted pneumonia and died in January, 1908. The family moved to Moberly, where Bradley attended high school and became interested in Mary Quayle, the daughter of his Sunday school teacher and his future wife. Having been graduated in 1910 with good grades, "but not the highest," Bradley planned to become a lawyer, though he was uncertain as to how he would fund his education. His Sunday school superintendent suggested that he consider the U.S. Military Academy at West Point in New York.

Bradley took the advice, competed for and won an appointment to West Point, and entered the academy in 1911. In later life, he would remark that the four years spent at West Point were "among the most rewarding of my life." Considering the subsequent career that sprang from those four years, one might say that the country as a whole was handsomely rewarded as a result of Bradley's decision.

When he was graduated from West Point in 1915, Bradley stood 44th in a class of 164. He later confessed that his affinity for sports Bradley played on the varsity football and baseball teams might have detracted from his academic performance. Bradley's class would gain fame as the one that "the stars fell on." Bradley, who would ultimately wear five of those stars, was always proud of a

Omar Nelson Bradley (Wikimedia Commons)

complimentary entry in his senior yearbook, which described "his most promising characteristic" as "getting there. . . . " The words of praise came from fellow classmate Dwight D. Eisenhower, who was himself destined to wear five stars and be twice elected president of the United States.

Life's Work

Following graduation, Bradley was assigned to duty with the Fourteenth Infantry Regiment at Fort Laughton near Seattle, Washington. He was later transferred to Douglas, Arizona, but did not join the Pershing expedition into Mexico. On December 28, 1916, Bradley, by then a first lieutenant, married his high school sweetheart, Mary Quayle. Four months later, the United States entered World War I. Convinced that his career would suffer irreparable harm if he did not see duty in France, Bradley desperately tried to secure assignment to a combat unit. He never succeeded; instead he spent the war guarding copper mines in Montana. When he was finally ordered to report for overseas duty, his destination was not France

Meeting of the Supreme Command, Allied Expeditionary Force, London, 1 February 1944. Left to right: Lieutenant General Omar Bradley, Commander in Chief 1st US Army, Admiral Sir Bertram H Ramsay, Allied Naval Commander in Chief, Expeditionary Force, Air Chief Marshal Sir Arthur W Tedder, Deputy Supreme Commander, Expeditionary Force, General Dwight D. Eisenhower, Supreme Commander, Expeditionary Force, General Sir Bernard Montgomery, Commander in Chief, 21st Army Group, Air Chief Marshal Sir Trafford Leigh-Mallory, Allied Air Commander in Chief, Expeditionary Force, Lieutenant General Walter Bedell Smith, Chief of Staff to Eisenhower. (Wikimedia Commons)

but Siberia. Fortunately, those orders were canceled, and Montana suddenly looked much better than it had before.

Like most career officers, Bradley found duty in the peacetime army to be rather routine and advancement quite slow. He spent five years teaching in one capacity or another, one year as an instructor in the ROTC program at South Dakota State University and four years in the math department at West Point. He became a father during his tour at West Point, when Mary gave birth to a daughter, Elizabeth. An earlier stillborn birth and complications arising during the second pregnancy convinced the Bradleys that they should have no more children.

After completing his tour at West Point in 1923, Bradley attended infantry school at Fort Benning, Georgia, for one year and was then assigned to duty in Hawaii for three years. While there he met George S. Patton, then serving as chief intelligence officer of the Hawaiian Division and described by Bradley as "one of the most extraordinary men military or civilian I ever met."

Returning to the United States in 1928, Bradley attended the Command and General Staff School at Fort Leavenworth, Kansas, after which he had a choice of assignments between Fort Benning and West Point. He chose the former, later recalling that it was "the most important decision of my life." While at Benning he attracted the attention of George C. Marshall, who would later, as chief of staff of the Army, prove to be instrumental in Bradley's rapid rise to high command during World War II. In fact, after attending the Army War College and serving another four years at West Point, Bradley served under Marshall following Marshall's appointment as chief of staff in April, 1939. When, in late 1940, Marshall offered Bradley command of the Eighty-second Division, he became the second in his class to get two stars and the first to command a division.

Like so many of his colleagues, Bradley first attracted widespread public attention during World War II. Though he never reached the pinnacle of command achieved by Eisenhower or assumed the almost legendary proportions of the flamboyant Patton, he carved his own special place in United States military history as the "G.I. General." Newsman Ernie Pyle, whose cartoons and reports made household names of many wartime personalities, confessed that it was a challenge to write about Bradley because he was so "damn normal." Rather tall and solidly built, Bradley was never described as handsome. In his late forties when the United States entered the war, he was balding and bespectacled, conveying a congeniality not usually associated with a combat general.

Bradley was not assigned to overseas duty until February, 1943, when he joined Eisenhower in North Africa. For a brief time he served as deputy commander of the United States II Corps under George S. Patton and later assumed command of that unit when Patton was called to head Seventh Army operations in the Sicilian campaign. Bradley again served under Patton in Sicily, where he became disillusioned with his superior's methods both on and off the battlefield. Patton's involvement in the infamous slapping incidents in Sicily, in which he struck two enlisted men who were suffering from battle fatigue, cost him any chance he might have had for immediate advancement. Consequently, when Sicily was safely in Allied hands, it was Bradley who was chosen to command

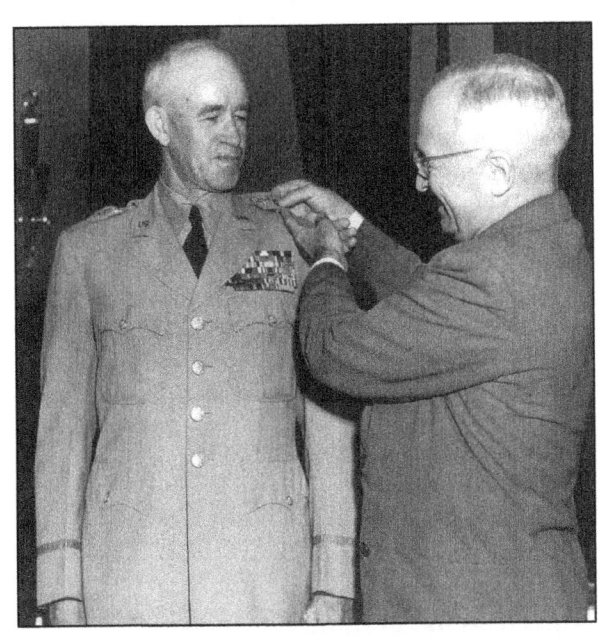

President Harry S. Truman promotes General Bradley to five-star rank, 22 September 1950. (Wikimedia Commons)

American forces in the next major operation of the war Normandy while Patton remained behind.

Bradley played a key role in Operation Overlord, first as commander of the American First Army and later as head of the Twelfth Army Group, on an equal footing with Britain's field marshal Bernard Law Montgomery. In an ironic twist, Patton, who assumed command of the newly activated Third Army on August 1, 1944, was now subordinate to Bradley. This proved to be a workable combination when Bradley the strategist and Patton the tactician combined to parlay Operation Cobra into a theater-wide breakout, leading to the eventual liberation of most of northern France. Bradley proved to be an asset to Eisenhower in more ways than one. He not only demonstrated great competence as a strategist and battlefield manager but also held a tight rein on Patton and frequently served as a buffer between him and the equally irascible Montgomery.

As the war in Europe drew to a close, Bradley did not have to worry about a new assignment. Marshall, Eisenhower, and President Harry S. Truman were unanimous in the opinion that he should be made head of the Veterans Administration. In August, 1945, Bradley assumed the new duties of his office and all the headaches that went with it chief among them being administration of the G.I. Bill and upgrading the quality of medical care for veterans. He found his job to be challenging and rewarding, deriving the greatest satisfaction from the improvements made in the quality of medical care that veterans received.

In February, 1948, Bradley left the Veterans Administration to become chief of staff of the Army, a post he held for about eighteen months before becoming chairman of the Joint Chiefs of Staff in August, 1949. This was the position he held when the so-called Cold War turned hot in Korea in June, 1950. Bradley's view that the United States was right to intervene in Korea while not seeking to expand the war in Asia represented a consensus within the military; his often quoted statement that a wider war in Asia would be "the wrong war, at the wrong place, at the wrong time, and with the wrong enemy" succinctly summarized the military's position. This conviction put him at odds with General Douglas MacArthur, then commander of United Nations forces in Korea, but ultimately it was Bradley's viewpoint that prevailed.

> "Wars can be prevented just as surely as they can be provoked, and we who fail to prevent them must share the guilt for the dead."

The Korean War ended in 1953 during Bradley's tour as chairman of the Joint Chiefs of Staff, and shortly thereafter he resigned from full-time active service. Ceremonial duties as one of the nation's senior military statesmen took some of his time, but most of it was devoted to his business interests. He served for a while as chair of the board of the Bulova Watch Company and was a director on several other corporate boards. In 1965, Bradley's wife died, and for several months he suffered from severe depression. In September, 1966, he married Kitty Buhler, a gregarious Hollywood screenwriter, who, despite being thirty years his junior, remained devoted to him until his death in April, 1981.

Significance

Bradley was the product of rural, mid-western America the values of which were always reflected in his career. Cognizant of his own modest beginnings, he identified and sympathized with the plight of the common soldier. He successfully made the transition from combat general to administrator and from total war, as required by World War II, to the concept of limited war, as imposed by the constraints of the Cold War. His career spanned two world wars and the Korean conflict. During World War II, his professional military talents had carried him to the position of Army Group command. He ultimately wore five stars as general of the Army and served as head of the Veterans Administration, chief of staff of the Army, and chairman of the Joint Chiefs of Staff. Who could doubt, to paraphrase Eisenhower, that the farm boy from Missouri had truly "gotten there"?

Kirk For Jr.

Further Reading

Blumenson, Martin. *Patton: The Man Behind the Legend, 1885-1945.* New York: William Morrow, 1985. This book offers insights into Patton's candid assessment of Bradley, first as a subordinate and later as a superior. Patton displays great respect for Bradley while objecting strenuously to some of his military decisions.

Bradley, Omar N. *A Soldier's Story.* New York: Henry Holt, 1951. Published during Bradley's tenure as chairman of the Joint Chiefs of Staff, these wartime memoirs, though informative, reflect the restrictions imposed on Bradley by his official position and government classification of many World War II documents.

Bradley, Omar N., and Clay Blair. *A General's Life.* New York: Simon & Schuster, 1983. Begun as an autobiography and subsequently completed by Blair after the general's death, this is the only work that entirely covers Bradley's life and career.

Chandler, Alfred D., Jr., and Louis Galambos, eds. *The Papers of Dwight David Eisenhower.* 11 vols. Baltimore: Johns Hopkins University Press, 1970-1979. Bradley and Eisenhower confronted many common problems from different perspectives both during and after World War II. These volumes are useful and illuminating for both periods.

Eisenhower, Dwight D. *Crusade in Europe.* Garden City, N.Y.: Doubleday, 1948. Eisenhower's wartime memoirs contain much information on Bradley and the major campaigns in which he participated. Eisenhower's appreciation of Bradley's talents is apparent.

Jordan, Thomas M. "Battle Command: Bradley and Ridgway in the Battle of the Bulge." *Military Review* 90, no. 2 (March/April, 2000): 95. Describes the role of Bradley and Lt. General Matthew Ridgway in the Battle of the Bulge in Germany in 1944.

Muench, James F. *Five Stars: Missouri's Most Famous Generals.* Columbia: University of Missouri Press, 2006. Profiles five American generals from Missouri, including Bradley.

Pogue, Forrest C. *Ordeal and Hope, 1939-1943* and *Organizer of Victory, 1943-1945.* Vols. 2-3 of *George C. Marshall*, 3 vols. New York: Viking Press, 1963-1966. Perhaps more than any other, Marshall was instrumental in Bradley's rapid climb to Army Group command in 1944. The works cited here cover only the war years.

Weigley, Russell F. *Eisenhower's Lieutenants: The Campaigns of France and Germany, 1944-1945.* Bloomington: Indiana University Press, 1981. A brilliant work describing the last major military campaigns of the European war. This book evaluates Bradley's skills as a strategist while inviting comparisons with his colleagues, British and American.

Stephen Decatur

American naval commander

Born: January 5, 1779; Sinepuxent, Maryland
Died: March 22, 1820; Washington, D.C.
Primary conflict: War of 1812 (1812-1815)

The most colorful and successful open-sea naval commander of his time, Decatur was a national hero of the Barbary Wars and the War of 1812. However, despite his military accomplishments, his career had made little impact on naval policy and strategy.

Early Life

Stephen Decatur's father, Stephen, was a seafaring man who earned his living as a merchant ship captain and, during the American Revolution, as a privateer. Decatur was a sickly child during his early years. At the age of eight, suffering from a prolonged and severe cough, he accompanied his father on a voyage to the French port of Bordeaux. His malady, probably whooping cough, disappeared.

Because his father was at sea much of the time, Decatur was raised in Philadelphia, Pennsylvania, by his mother, Ann, who sent him to the Episcopal Academy and later to the University of Pennsylvania in the hope that he would become either a clergyman or a scholar. However, despite his health problems and his mother's wishes, Decatur craved the active over the contemplative life. As a young man, he was 5 feet 10 inches in height, possessed a muscular build, and had a handsome countenance with an aquiline nose.

Stephen Decatur (Wikimedia Commons)

Decatur first worked as a clerk in 1796 for Gurney and Smith, a Philadelphia shipping company, but after the United States Navy was established on April 30, 1798, and a naval war had commenced with France, Decatur, through his father's influence, secured a midshipman place on the newly constructed ship, the *United States*. Built in Philadelphia, this forty-four gun frigate was familiar to Decatur. Its captain, John Barry, was both a friend and professional colleague of Decatur's father.

The reasons for Decatur's determination to join the Navy are unclear. Perhaps it was the lure of adventure presented by the new United States Navy and the war with France, or perhaps he wanted to follow his father's nautical footsteps. A more murky reason was the apparent result of Decatur's attack upon a prostitute who had solicited him. He struck her with a blow that was powerful enough to kill her. To avoid a prison sentence for their client, Decatur's lawyers assured the court that Decatur would join the Navy.

Life's Work

Decatur's first real taste of glory occurred in 1804 during the Barbary Wars, when, as captain of the schooner *Enterprise* in Commodore Edward Preble's Mediterranean squadron, he captured a Barbary slave ship, the *Mastico*. Renamed the *Intrepid*, it was 60 feet in length with a 12-foot beam. A scheme was devised to burn the former U.S. frigate *Philadelphia*, which had run aground and been captured by the Tripolitans. Decatur chose a crew of seventy-four volunteers who would sail the *Intrepid* into Tripoli Harbor under the guise of a Barbary ship seeking repairs from a recent storm. The Americans were to board, burn, and escape, leaving the *Philadelphia* in ashes. It was a daring plan well suited to Decatur's adventuresome temperament.

Although delayed for one week because of severe weather, the attack, when executed at dusk on February 16, 1804, was a huge success. Decatur's crew sailed within a few yards of the *Philadelphia* before they were found out. They quickly overcame the defenders, many of whom feared for their lives and jumped overboard. During the next thirty minutes, twenty Tripolitans were killed, combustibles were laid and ignited, the attackers returned to the *Intrepid*, and the *Philadelphia* was engulfed in flames. During all of this, only one of Decatur's sailors was wounded. Burning the *Philadelphia* assured Decatur's role as a hero. He was promoted to captain at the age of twenty-five, the youngest American naval officer to attain that rank. Lord Horatio Nelson called the attack "the most bold and daring act of the age." President Thomas Jefferson presented Decatur with a sword and words of praise.

Later that same year, Decatur's brother, James, was killed by the commander of a Tripolitan gunboat, who shot James when he was boarding the already surrendered vessel. Along with ten others, Decatur tracked down the commander and killed him after some brutal hand-to-hand fighting. During the melee, Decatur's life was saved by a sailor who intentionally absorbed a blow that would have killed Decatur.

At the conclusion of the Tripolitan phase of the Barbary Wars, Decatur returned home, where he broke with his former fiancé and met and married Susan Wheeler, the daughter of the mayor of Norfolk, Virginia. She was a popular and beautiful young woman who had already rejected advances made by Vice President Aaron Burr and Jerome Bonaparte.

Decatur served in various naval positions during the six years from 1806 to 1812. In 1807 he served on the court martial panel that suspended Captain James Barron, Decatur's erstwhile friend and former tutor, from the Navy for five years because of his behavior as captain of the *Chesapeake*. Barron was found guilty for failing to adequately prepare his ship for action against the British ship the *Leopard* and thereby humiliating the United States Navy by demonstrating its inability to prevent the seizure of four British Royal Navy deserters, three of whom were Americans impressed earlier by the British. Another more personal reason for the deterioration and ultimately fatal culmination of Decatur's and Barron's relationship was the latter's implied criticism of Decatur's attraction to Susan Wheeler when Decatur already had a fiancé in Philadelphia. Decatur thought that it was none of Barron's concern.

> *"Fortunately for our country, every man stands upon his own merit."*

When Great Britain and the United States went to war in 1812, the still young United States Navy consisted of just sixteen warships. Decatur was captain of one of them, the familiar *United States*. Sailing alone between the Azores and Madeira, he sighted the *Macedonian*, a British frigate. The U.S. ship was larger and now carried fifty-four 24-pound guns, compared to the *Macedonian*'s forty-nine 18 pounders. Ironically, this very encounter had been discussed prior to the war by Decatur and Captain John Carden, commander of the *Macedonian*. Despite the heavier gun advantage of the *United States*, Carden had argued that his ship would prevail because its crew was more experienced and because the *Macedonian* was a more maneuverable vessel.

As it turned out, even though Carden had the wind advantage, he failed to recognize the *United States* and instead assumed it was a smaller frigate with guns of lesser range and shot than his own. Carden's tactics played into Decatur's hands by allowing Decatur to press his advantage of more guns and greater destructive shot. Carden surrendered the *Macedonian* after losing one-third of his three-hundred-man crew in a two-hour fight, while seven were killed and five wounded aboard the *United States*. Decatur's reputation as a hero reached its summit. The government also awarded him thirty thousand dollars in prize money. Decatur's achievements during the remainder of the war were a good deal less dramatic, although his status as a genuine American hero remained high.

By tightening their blockade along the Atlantic coast, the British were able to prevent most ships from entering and sailing from U.S. ports. On January 14-15, 1815, unaware that the war had ended three weeks earlier, Decatur

Decatur's conflict with the Algerine at Tripoli. (Wikimedia Commons)

attempted to liberate his ship, the *President*, by escaping from New York Harbor. Heavy winds caused the ship to run aground for two hours and compelled Decatur to make a fifty-mile run along the Long Island coast. Four British warships chased him, and, although the frigate *Endymion* had to retire because of battle damage, the remaining British ships forced his surrender. British losses were less than half of the twenty-four Americans killed and the fifty-five who were wounded. Despite the defeat, Decatur maintained his status as a hero. A naval court of inquiry not only exonerated him but also determined that the surrender of the *President* was an American victory.

Two months after the Treaty of Ghent, which ended the War of 1812, the United States was at war again, this time with Algiers. Decatur, now a commodore (at that time the highest rank in the United States Navy), assembled a squadron of ten ships, including three frigates, one of which was the *Macedonian*. After capturing the Algerine flagship and killing the grand admiral of the Algerine fleet, Decatur's entire squadron sailed into Algiers Harbor. A treaty favorable to the United States was the result. Additional concessions were later made by Tunis as well. Decatur was the principal negotiator in both cases.

After returning home, Decatur was appointed to the three-member Board of Naval Commissioners. The Decaturs (they had no children) moved to Washington, D.C., where Decatur continued to contribute to naval affairs.

Decatur died as he had lived: defending his honor. The cashiered Barron returned to the United States from Denmark in 1818 and unsuccessfully applied for reinstatement in the U.S. Navy. Barron blamed the Board of Naval Commissioners and Decatur in particular. He initiated a correspondence with Decatur that ended when Barron challenged Decatur to a duel. They met at Bladensburg, Maryland, on March 22, 1820. Although Decatur, an excellent pistol marksman, aimed to wound his opponent, Barron aimed to kill—and succeeded. Shot in the groin, Decatur died twelve hours later. Congress adjourned to attend Decatur's funeral, naval officers wore crepe for thirty days, guns on ships at Washington and Norfolk fired at thirty-minute intervals, and numerous eulogies were presented by people of all ranks and classes. President James Monroe and his cabinet marched in the funeral procession.

Barron was finally reinstated in 1824. He was given command of the Philadelphia Navy Yard and later the Norfolk Navy Yard. He died in 1851 at the age of eighty-three.

Significance

Decatur's contributions to the United States were revered a great deal more during his lifetime than by subsequent generations of Americans. Although no naval history of the post-Revolutionary War period would be complete without devoting considerable attention to Decatur, his heroic accomplishments, impressive as they were, made a limited impact on naval policy and strategy. Early nineteenth century Americans needed a hero to help represent and justify their nation's brief history and its full membership among contemporary nations. Decatur was the right person at the right place at the right time. Perhaps his dedication to his country was best expressed by a toast he made at a dinner held in his honor in 1816: "Our Country! In her intercourse with foreign nations, may she always be in the right, but our country right or wrong."

John Quinn Imholte

Further Reading

Anthony, Irvin. *Decatur*. New York: Charles Scribner's Sons, 1931. Anthony's book is subjective but remains one of the few book-length biographies of Decatur. Includes much personal detail.

Blassingame, Wyatt. *Stephen Decatur: Fighting Sailor*. Champaign, Ill.: Garrard, 1964. This volume is suitable for early elementary students.

De Kay, James Tertius. *A Rage for Glory: The Life of Commodore Stephen Decatur, U.S.N*. New York: Free Press, 2004. A comprehensive, popular biography. De Kay, a naval historian, recounts the origins of Decatur's fierce patriotism and provides new details about his death.

Guttridge, Leonard F., and Jay D. Smith. *The Commodores*. New York: Harper & Row, 1969. This volume includes pithy accounts of Decatur and Barron, along with other high-ranking naval officers. Especially valuable for the Bladensburg duel.

Lewis, Charles Lee. *The Romantic Decatur*. Philadelphia: University of Pennsylvania Press, 1937. This is the standard book-length biography of Decatur. For the most part, Lewis remains objective throughout the book.

Schroeder, John H. "Stephen Decatur: Heroic Ideal of the Young Navy." In *Command Under Sail: Makers of the American Naval Tradition*, edited by James C. Bradford. Annapolis, Md.: Naval Institute Press, 1985. Most of this overview of Decatur's naval career is supported by primary sources.

Tucher, Glenn. *Dawn Like Thunder: The Barbary Wars and the Birth of the U.S. Navy*. Indianapolis: Bobbs-Merrill, 1963. Tucher details Decatur's participation in the Barbary Wars.

Tucker, Spencer. *Stephen Decatur: A Life Most Bold and Daring*. Annapolis, Md.: Naval Institute Press, 2005. A biography, in which Tucker relates Decatur's military achievements to the rise of the United States Navy in the nineteenth century. In his description of Decatur's raid at Tripoli Harbor, Tucker explains how Decatur's heroism set a new standard of courage for future naval officers.

Mary A. Hallaren

Military leader

Born: May 4, 1907; Lowell, Massachusetts
Died: February 13, 2005; McLean, Virginia
Primary conflict: World War II (1939-1945)

The third director of the Women's Army Corps, Hallaren expanded opportunities for women in the U.S. armed forces during and after World War II. Through her efforts, women moved from auxiliary status to permanent status as regular service members. Furthermore, she was the first woman commissioned an officer in the regular Army.

Early Life

Mary A. Hallaren (HAHL-ehr-ehn), director of the Women's Army Corps from 1947 until 1953, was born in Lowell, Massachusetts, to John J. Hallaren and Mary A. (Kenney) Hallaren. Her parents were Irish immigrants who lived in the Pawtucketville section of Lowell. She attended public schools in Lowell, graduating from Lowell High School. She received a teaching degree from Lowell Teachers College in 1927 and taught middle school in Lexington for fifteen years before she entered the military.

Teaching meant that Hallaren had summers free for travel. She hitchhiked and backpacked through the United States and the rest of the world. She started by traveling to national parks in the United States. After seeing most of the country, she toured Canada and Mexico, then traveled through Europe and South America. Hallaren was in Munich, Germany, one summer when she crossed paths with Adolf Hitler. The Nazi leader was virtually unknown in the United States, but already was a sensation in Germany. Hallaren remembered that Hitler received a thunderous reception in the Munich town square, but he did not make a strong impression on her. On a hike through Rome, she drew a crowd by wearing pants. (Italians had not seen many women wearing pants.) She was known by her students and her fellow teachers as the Hitchhiking Teacher.

Life's Work

Hallaren's adult life can be divided into her military career and her post-retirement service work. Shortly after the United States entered World War II, the U.S. Army created the Women's Army Auxiliary Corps (WAAC).

Mary A. Hallaren (Wikimedia Commons)

U.S. Representative Edith Nourse Rogers had introduced a bill in Congress that led to the WAAC's establishment. Oveta Culp Hobby was its first director.

Hallaren followed her brothers into the Army and enlisted in 1942. She had been asked by an Army recruiter about her height. (Hallaren claimed to be five feet tall, but she was likely a few inches shorter.) The recruiter wondered what such a short person could do in the Army, and Hallaren replied, "You don't have to be six feet tall to have a brain that works."

In August, 1942, she was selected to be in the first class of the WAAC Officer Candidate School at Fort Des Moines, Iowa. Hallaren's first job was assistant WAAC commandant at the Second WAAC Training Center in Daytona Beach, Florida, and she trained the First WAAC Separate Battalion. Hallaren's battalion was sent to Europe in July, 1943, the first women's battalion to receive orders to serve overseas in the European theater of World War II. Hallaren began service in Europe as the WAAC staff director attached to the U.S. Eighth and Ninth Air Forces. Upon arrival in England, her unit was divided into companies for service with several Army Air Corps units. The women initially were assigned to jobs as clerks, telephone operators, cooks, and drivers. By the end of the first year, however, they were filling two hundred different jobs, including cryptographer.

Ironically, Hallaren's passion for hiking played a small part in the history of her battalion. At one time during the battalion's tour of duty, the troop ship carrying the WAAC personnel between European ports had been forced to remain docked while Army intelligence officers investigated an alleged tie between one of the WAAC soldiers and the Hitler Youth. Years later, Hallaren learned that she was the one facing investigation. She was under suspicion because the German hiking club she had joined earlier eventually folded into the Hitler Youth.

> "*To me there was no question that women should serve.*"

From June, 1945, to June, 1946, Hallaren served as the WAAC staff director for the European Theater of Operations. Her work and leadership abilities attracted the attention of the Allied supreme commander, Dwight D. Eisenhower. When the fighting ended in Europe, General Eisenhower asked Hallaren to oversee the transition of the Women's Army Auxiliary Corps to the Women's Army Corps (WAC), which was to become a permanent part of the military establishment. Hallaren was promoted to colonel in May, 1947, the first woman commissioned in the regular Army. It also was the highest rank that could be held by a woman at the time. Many under Hallaren's command referred to her as the Little Colonel.

Recalled to Washington, Hallaren worked to encourage Congress to upgrade the official status of women in the military and make them a permanent part of the armed services. Her proposal, which became the Women's Armed Services Integration Act of 1948, first met with strong resistance, especially among members of the House Armed Services Committee. The committee tried to rework the legislation so that it would limit women's status in the service and permit service only in time of national crises (that is, as temporary staff only). Working with former service members, Hallaren indirectly led a lobbying campaign that flooded the offices of members of the Armed Services Committee. The committee eventually agreed that women should become a permanent part of the military, thus forming the Army WACs and the Navy WAVES (Women Accepted for Volunteer Emergency Service). Colonel Hallaren, the first woman commissioned an officer in the regular Army, served as WAC director from December, 1948, through May, 1953.

Hallaren retired from the Army in 1960. During her years of service, she received numerous citations including the Bronze Star, the Army Commendation Medal, the Legion of Merit, the Croix de Guerre, and the Legion of Honor. Five years after retiring from active military service, Hallaren started a third career. A friend had told her about Women in Community Service (WICS), a national nonprofit organization created by a coalition of five women's groups: American GI Forum Women, Church Women United, National Council of Catholic Women, National Council of Jewish Women, and National Council of Negro Women. WICS had been seeking an executive director, and Hallaren took the job. She led the organization for fourteen years. She also was instrumental in the creation of the Women in Military Service for America Memorial at Arlington National Cemetery in Virginia. Hallaren died on February 13, 2005, of complications from a stroke.

SIGNIFICANCE

Hallaren was a pioneer in expanding the role of women in American society. She engaged apparent obstacles with courage, good humor, and a strong sense of curiosity. U.S. representative Barbara A. Mikulski, a Democrat from Maryland, introduced a bill in 1978 to promote Hallaren to brigadier general on the retired list. In her floor statement, Mikulski summed up Hallaren's career, indicating that her military career would not have been limited had Hallaren been a man.

In spite of her many successes, Hallaren maintained a sense of humility. On October 5, 1996, she was inducted into the American Women's Hall of Fame. She accepted the honor with pride and humility, saying that she was a good citizen who had only done a good job in the Women's Army Corps and with WICS.

John David Rausch

FURTHER READING

Brokaw, Tom. *The Greatest Generation*. New York: Random House, 1998. A brief profile of Colonel Hallaren, as one of the many Americans who served in the military during World War II. Illustrated.

Dean, Mensah. "Activist's Army of Victories for Women." *Washington Times*, October 10, 1996, p. 8. This profile was written when Hallaren was inducted into the National Women's Hall of Fame. It is an excellent, concise summary of her careers as a schoolteacher, military officer, and social activist.

Morden, Bettie J. The Women's Army Corps, 1945-1978. Washington, D.C.: Center of Military History, United States Army, 1990. A detailed examination of the development of the Women's Army Corps from the end of World War II through the end of WAC's existence. Hallaren reviewed the manuscript of the book and her role as a WAC leader is discussed throughout.

Nathan, Amy. Count on Us: American Women in the Military. Washington, D.C.: National Geographic Society, 2004. This book, written for elementary and middle school audiences, examines the role of women in the American military from the Revolutionary War through the 2003 invasion of Iraq. Colonel Hallaren's career is discussed briefly.

Weiner, Josephine. The Story of WICS. Washington, D.C.: Women in Community Service, 1979. A detailed examination of the development of WICS as a nongovernmental organization implementing social policy across the United States.

Witt, Linda."A Defense Weapon Known to Be a Value": Servicewomen of the Korean War Era. Hanover, N.H.: University Press of New England, 2005. This book reviews the role of women in the military during the period immediately before the Korean conflict and during that conflict. A brief sketch of Colonel Hallaren's career appears in the book.

OVETA CULP HOBBY

Politician and businesswoman

Born: January 19, 1905; Killeen, Texas
Died: August 16, 1995; Houston, Texas
Area of Achievement: Government and politics, women's rights, military affairs, business and industry
Primary conflict: World War II (1939-1945)

As a U.S. Army officer, cabinet member, and business leader, Hobby was a pioneer for American women in many areas of public life. In her job as the first secretary of Health, Education, and Welfare she helped to institutionalize the department so that it became an important and necessary Washington fixture. She also helped develop the Women's Army Auxiliary Corps during World War II and was its first head.

EARLY LIFE

Oveta Culp Hobby (oh-VEH-tah kulp HOH-bee) was born to Isaac William Culp and Emma Hoover Culp. Her father was an attorney who was first elected to the Texas state legislature in 1919; her mother was a homemaker who was active in the woman suffrage movement. From her earliest childhood, Hobby's father took a personal interest in her training and schooling. Isaac Culp instilled an interest in public life in Hobby and convinced her that her gender did not constitute a barrier to any ambition she might have had. It was still somewhat unusual for a woman of her day, even one of the educated classes, to attend college. Not only did Hobby complete her undergraduate work at Mary Hardin-Baylor College, but she also studied law at the main campus of the University of Texas.

At a very young age and only partly through the influence of her father, Hobby began securing positions in the law, business, and government matrix of Texas. At the age of twenty, she was working as assistant city attorney in Houston. For several years, she served as parliamentarian, or chief clerk, for the lower house of the Texas state legislature, a position that enabled her to make extensive contacts in Texas politics. She made some use of these

Oveta Culp Hobby (Library of Congress)

contacts when she decided to run for the legislature as a Democrat in 1929. Despite her efforts, she was not elected; women in electoral politics were to be more truly a phenomenon of her children's generation. On February 23, 1931, Hobby took a more conventional step when she married William P. Hobby, about thirty years her senior, publisher of the *Houston Post*, and a former governor of Texas.

Life's Work

Marriage, however, did not mean retirement to domesticity and obscurity for Hobby, as it did for many women of the period. Hobby immediately threw herself into both the business and editorial aspects of her husband's newspaper business. Starting out as a research editor, she moved steadily up the hierarchy of the newspaper until 1938, when she was named executive vice president. These were not ceremonial positions; Hobby's husband, busy managing other sectors of his extensive business interests, delegated much of his responsibility for the *Post* to his wife.

Houston during the 1930's was a much smaller city than it became later in the century, and the Post was in many ways a small, regional newspaper. Hobby made efforts to modernize the newspaper and bring it to the level of sophistication achieved by dailies on the East Coast. She placed a premium on intelligent coverage of women's issues, adding a woman editor to the staff to cover the activities and interests of women. Aside from her newspaper work and her devotion to her children, Hobby was particularly active within the Texas chapter of the League of Women Voters.

Hobby first attained national prominence with the beginning of American involvement in World War II. The United States government realized immediately after the onset of the war that this conflict would be more "total" than previous ones. It would affect not only soldiers fighting the war but also civilians living and working on the home front. Realizing that women would be more actively involved in the war effort than before, the government sought the assistance of recognized women leaders to help coordinate this involvement. Hobby was recruited to be the head of the women's division of the War Department's Bureau of Public Relations. This mainly involved liaison work between the army and female family members of servicemen, and therefore fell short of giving women full equality in the war effort. The War Department soon realized the inadequacy of this situation, and, in the spring of 1942, the Women's Army Auxiliary Corps (WAAC) was established to mobilize the talents and energy of women. Because of her work with Army Chief of Staff George C. Marshall to plan the WAAC, Hobby was the natural choice to head this corps and, as such, was given military rank, first as a major, and then, more appropriately considering the status of her role, as a colonel.

World War II was one of the great watersheds in the democratization of American society. Most, if not all, of this democratization was unintentional. The government did not set out to use the war to enfranchise women and African Americans, yet staffing needs compelled the government to make use of their talents to serve the war efforts. Hobby's tenure at the WAAC saw the most thorough emergence of American women into the public sphere in history. Once it was realized that the contribution of women was indispensable to the war effort, their social marginalization was far less viable. The increasing significance of women was recognized when the "auxiliary" was dropped from the name of the corps in the middle of the war. By 1945, Hobby's efforts with the WAC had become nationally known, and, next to Eleanor Roosevelt, Hobby became the second most important woman in the American war effort.

After the war, Hobby returned to her duties at the *Houston Post*, but her interest in Washington affairs continued. In 1948, she advised the commission headed by former President Herbert Hoover on reducing waste in government bureaucracy. Surprisingly, her continuing interest in politics was no longer centered on the Democratic Party. In the Texas of Hobby's girlhood, it had been culturally mandatory for a Texan to be a Democrat, since Texas, like many southern states, was dominated by a virtual one-party system. During her years in Washington, D.C., however, Hobby was increasingly drawn to the Republican Party, especially after its transformation under the leadership of Thomas E. Dewey. Under Dewey, the Republicans accepted most of Franklin D. Roosevelt's New Deal social policies, while being more friendly to the free market and to capitalist initiative than were the Democrats. Hobby, a businesswoman as well as a liberal, was particularly sympathetic to this point of view. In addition, since they did not depend as heavily on the political influence of southern conservatives and urban party bosses as did the Democrats, the Republicans could theoretically be more responsive in alleviating the oppression of African Americans. As a result, although she continued to support local Democratic candidates, Hobby actively campaigned on behalf of Republican presidential candidates in 1948 and again in 1952.

Hobby (right) talks with Auxiliary Margaret Peterson and Capt. Elizabeth Gilbert at Mitchel Field in New York. (Library of Congress)

Although Dewey suffered an upset loss in his 1948 presidential race against incumbent Harry Truman, the Republicans won in 1952 with the election of former general Dwight D. Eisenhower. By this time, Hobby was solidly in the Republican camp. When it came time for the new president to make his appointments, Eisenhower remembered Hobby's wartime service and asked her to be the director of the Federal Security Agency. This agency coordinated the various government efforts directed at securing the health and comfort of American citizens. Socially concerned Democrats had long wanted to give this agency cabinet-level status, but it was the Eisenhower administration, often attacked for its conservatism, that presided over the agency's elevation as the Department of Health, Education, and Welfare (HEW). After her appointment as secretary of this department was approved in 1953, Hobby became the second woman to serve in the cabinet. (Frances Perkins, secretary of labor in the Roosevelt administration, was the first.)

Hobby had enormous ambitions for the department, not all of which were realized during her tenure. She considered plans for overhauling the nation's medical insurance system, proposing legislation that would have established a federal corporation to provide financial backing for private low-cost medical plans. Although her proposals were defeated as a result of staunch opposition by the American Medical Association and fiscal conservatives in Congress, many elements of her plan received renewed attention during the 1990's under President Bill Clinton. Hobby also wished to focus more attention on the plight of the disadvantaged and economically subordinated, a highly unpopular cause during the prosperous 1950's. So much of the budget was being spent on Cold War defense projects that funding for the projects Hobby wished to undertake was simply not available.

Despite these difficult challenges, Hobby performed her job with dynamism and diligence. She was particularly instrumental in the widespread distribution of Jonas Salk's polio vaccine. As one of the few highly visible women in public life in the 1950's, she made a decided impression on young women growing up at the time. She seemed responsible, capable, optimistic, someone equipped for the challenges of the political world. Although she had only been in office for two years when she resigned to take care of her ailing husband on July 13, 1955, Hobby had made important contributions during her tenure at HEW.

Hobby did not rest on her laurels after her retirement from government. Taking over the executive reins at the *Houston Post*, she presided over its development into a large metropolitan daily, acquiring the latest in technological equipment to help the paper keep pace with the exponential growth of Houston itself. She also oversaw the expansion of the Post media empire into the new realms of radio and, especially, television. She served as cofounder of the Bank of Texas and was invited to serve on the boards of several corporations, including the Corporation for Public Broadcasting. Hobby also developed more interests in the cultural sphere, accumulating an impressive collection of modern art, including paintings by Pablo Picasso and Amedeo Modigliani. Although Hobby did not pursue public office herself, she did have the satisfaction of seeing her son, William, Jr., elected as lieutenant governor of Texas in 1972 and serve twelve years in that position. In 1978, she became the first woman to receive the George Catlett Marshall Medal for Public Service from the Association of the United States Army in recognition of her contributions during World War II.

Hobby continued to be a prominent and muchbeloved figure on the local Houston scene. In the later years of her life, her business success and family fortune made her one of the richest women in the United States. She could look back on a remarkable and unmistakably American life.

SIGNIFICANCE

It is difficult to isolate one specific mark Hobby made on American history, if only because her long life saw her excel in so many pursuits. Her wartime service helped pave the way for the promotion of women to a position of full equality in the military as well as in civilian society. Her business success proved that women not only could direct a large corporate concern but also could transform and expand that concern at an age when many business executives typically settled into retirement.

> "*Regard each man, each woman, as an individual, not as a Catholic, a Protestant, or a Jew; not as an Indian, American, or European. Like or dislike a person for his own intrinsic qualities—not because he belongs to a different race or subscribes to a different religion. Dignify man with individuality.*"

Nevertheless, it was arguably in her cabinet role as the first secretary of Health, Education, and Welfare that Hobby made her most enduring contribution. Hobby started her cabinet position off on a good footing, helping institutionalize it so that it (and, more important, the concerns it represented) became a Washington fixture. The Eisenhower cabinet of which Hobby was a member was derided at the time as consisting of "eight millionaires and a plumber," but it was in fact composed of many remarkable personalities, four of whom survived well into the 1990's: Attorney General Herbert Brownell, Secretary of Agriculture Ezra Taft Benson, Attorney General William Rogers, and Hobby herself. Perhaps slighted by the Democratic bias of many historians, the Eisenhower cabinet was, especially in terms of domestic policy, a progressive force. Hobby's presence was crucial in shaping this tendency. Hobby's cabinet service also firmly established the tradition of women being present in the cabinet. Under Roosevelt, the Democratic Party had been most associated with the equality of women. Hobby's presence in a Republican cabinet meant that drawing on the abilities of Americans of either gender became a bipartisan concern. Every future woman cabinet member owed her position, in a way, to Hobby's achievements.

Margaret Boe Birns

FURTHER READING

Beasley, Maurine H., and Sheila J. Gibbons. *Taking Their Place: A Documentary History of Women and Journalism.* Washington, D.C.: American University Press, 1993. This book provides an impression of the history of women in journalism before, during, and after Hobby's newspaper years.

Clark, James Anthony. *The Tactful Texan: A Biography of Governor Will Hobby.* New York: Random House, 1958. This biography of Hobby's husband provides information on Hobby's early career.

Eisenhower, Dwight D. *The White House Years: Mandate for Change, 1953-1956.* Garden City, N.Y.: Doubleday, 1963. The first volume of Eisenhower's presidential memoirs makes frequent mention of Hobby in her role as head of the Department of Health, Education, and Welfare.

Howes, Ruth, and Michael Stevenson, eds. *Women and the Use of Military Force.* Boulder, Colo.: Lynne Rienner, 1993. This book considers the theoretical issues accompanying women's service in the military.

Hutchison, Kay Bailey. *American Heroines: The Spirited Women Who Shaped Our Country.* New York: William Morrow, 2004. U.S. senator Hutchison provides profiles of women who made history. Includes a profile of Hobby.

Lyon, Peter. *Eisenhower: Portrait of the Hero.* Boston: Little, Brown, 1974. Emphasizes Hobby's role as the nation's top health care official.

Whisenhunt, Donald W., ed. *The Human Tradition in America Between the Wars, 1920-1945.* Wilmington, Del.: SR Books, 2002. A collection of biographical essays describing how a wide range of Americans coped with the significant changes in American society that occurred from 1920 through 1945. Includes an essay on Hobby.

STONEWALL JACKSON

Military leader

Born: January 21, 1824; Clarksburg, Virginia
Died: May 10, 1863; Guinea Station, Virginia
Primary conflict: Civil War (1861-1865)

The ablest and most renowned of Robert E. Lee's lieutenants, Jackson led daring marches and employed do-or-die battle tactics that resulted in key victories that helped to sustain the Confederacy through the first two years of the Civil War.

Early Life

Thomas Jonathan Jackson was born in a hilly, heavily forested region of what later became West Virginia that was sparsely populated by the Scotch-Irish settlers who were his forebears. Self-reliance was thrust upon the boy at an early age; the third of four children, he was orphaned by the age of seven. Taken in by an uncle, Cummins Jackson, he grew up in a farm environment in which he acquired numerous practical skills but little schooling. Even as a teenager, however, Jackson clearly demonstrated the traits of physical courage, uncompromising moral integrity, and high ambition serviced by an iron will. Resolved to improve his lot by education, Jackson obtained an appointment to the United States Military Academy at West Point. The shambling young man from the hills cut a poor figure among the generally more sophisticated and better educated cadets. Yet, impervious to taunts, he earned the respect of his classmates by perseverance and phenomenal concentration, finishing seventeenth in a class of fifty-nine.

Shortly after he was graduated in 1846, Jackson was ordered to Mexico as a second lieutenant of artillery. He took part in the siege of Veracruz and distinguished himself in several battles during the advance on Mexico City in the summer of 1847. Jackson's courage and effectiveness brought admiration from his superiors and a rapid succession of promotions; by the end of the war, at the age of twenty-two, he had attained the rank of brevet major. A photograph taken of him at that time shows a man with a trim figure (Jackson stood about five feet, ten inches, and weighed about 150 pounds) and a pleasant, earnest face characterized chiefly by the firm set of the mouth and clear, deep-set eyes that gaze out solemnly beneath a prominent brow. (The flowing beard that would give Jackson the appearance of an Old Testament prophet was to come later.)

Assigned to Fort Hamilton, New York, in 1848, Jackson entered the routine existence of a peacetime army garrison for the next two years. During this time, however, he became more and more deeply involved in religious pursuits. Jackson came to think of his rather frail health, with its persistent digestive disorders, as a visitation of Providence to lead him into more righteous ways. He was baptized, unsure whether he had been as a child, and from that time on, the course of his life was

Stonewall Jackson (Library of Congress)

inseparable from his sense of consecration to the will of the Almighty.

Life's Work

In the spring of 1851, an instructor's position at the Virginia Military Institute, founded twelve years earlier on the model of West Point, became available. Jackson was nominated for it, and, bored with his work as a peacetime army officer, he resigned his commission and reported to Lexington in July, 1851, to take up the duties of a professor of natural philosophy (or, in modern terminology, general science) and artillery tactics for the next nine years.

Not by any account an inspiring teacher, Jackson nevertheless mastered topics in which he had no formal credentials, thereby earning at least the grudging respect of his students. Jackson also came to be regarded as something of an eccentric for his rigid ways and odd personal mannerisms—for example, his habit of frequently raising his left arm, ostensibly to improve circulation, and his silent grimace serving in place of a laugh—which would be remarked on by his troops during the Civil War and give color and distinction to the legend of "Old Jack."

Settled in his new life, Jackson turned his thoughts to marriage. Seeking a wife from the religious community of Lexington, in 1853 he married Eleanor Junkin, the daughter of the Reverend Dr. George Junkin. The union was tragically brief; Eleanor died the next year in childbirth. Two years later and after a summer tour of Europe that restored him from the lethargy of mourning, Jackson courted and married Mary Anna Morrison, the daughter of another clergyman, who would remain his devoted wife until his death and would eventually bear him a daughter.

> "Captain, my religious belief teaches me to feel as safe in battle as in bed. God has fixed the time for my death. I do not concern myself about that, but to be always ready, no matter when it may overtake me. Captain, that is the way all men should live, and then all would be equally brave."

Life for the Jacksons during the next three years was characterized by affection, tranquillity, and a mutual sense of religious purpose (Jackson was by now a deacon of the Presbyterian Church and maintained a Sunday school for black slaves). The impending events of the Civil War were to bring all that to an end. Although not a champion of either slavery or secession, Jackson felt loyalty deeply rooted to his native soil, and when Virginia seceded from the Union, his course was clear.

In April, 1861, Jackson was commissioned a colonel in the newly formed Confederate army and took command at Harpers Ferry. Within three weeks, he distinguished himself by establishing strict military order for the rather undisciplined garrison of raw, untrained soldiers and by capturing a large number of Northern locomotives and freight cars for use by the Confederate army.

Some three months later, Jackson earned the sobriquet of "Stonewall" at the Battle of First Manassas (or Bull Run). In this opening major conflict of the war, an army of some thirty-five thousand Federal troops under General Irvin McDowell marched south from Washington to crush the rebellion. On July 21, after some preliminary fighting, McDowell made his main attack near Manassas Junction. As the defending Confederates fell back toward Jackson's brigade, which was holding the ridge above Bull Run, General Barnard E. Bee rallied his troops with the cry "Look yonder! There is Jackson and his brigade standing like a stone wall!" Later in the day, it was Jackson's brigade that broke the Union line with a furious bayonet charge, thus halting General McDowell's offensive and forcing a rethinking of strategy in Washington.

Jackson at Bull Run. (Library of Congress)

With a huge increase in the Union army, the new strategy called for a seaborne assault upon Richmond via the Jamestown Peninsula, led by George McClellan (a classmate of Jackson at West Point) and supported by a secondary force coming down the Shenandoah Valley under the command of Nathaniel Prentiss Banks. Jackson, now a major general, correctly surmised that a diversion up the Shenandoah Valley would not only neutralize Banks but also threaten Washington and thus divert troops from McClellan's peninsular offensive. Beginning in March, 1862, Jackson led his troops in a succession of battles renowned in military history as the Valley Campaign. Utilizing the tactics of deception, rapid forced marches, and hit-and-run assaults and retreats, Jackson blunted the Federal advance down the Shenandoah Valley, alarmed Washington, and consequently stalled McClellan's attack upon Richmond.

Jackson's victories continued to inspire the South and dismay the North during the year 1862. In August, Jackson played the pivotal role in defeating the new Union offensive led by General John Pope at the Second

Battle of Manassas. In December, at the Battle of Fredericksburg, he and James Longstreet shared the responsibility for the Confederate victory over the forces of General Ambrose Burnside.

In the spring of 1863, the Union forces, under yet another commander, Joseph "Fighting Joe" Hooker, gathered for a massive offensive upon Richmond. Robert E. Lee, outnumbered two to one, decided to risk his defense on a hazardous division of his forces, with a corps led by Jackson, now a lieutenant general, tasked with flanking Hooker's army. On the evening of May 2, 1863, the unsuspecting Union Eleventh Corps was routed by Jackson's attack some four miles west of Chancellorsville. Darkness brought a lull to the fighting, during which Jackson and a small staff reconnoitered the battlefield to determine a route for a further Confederate advance. Returning to its own lines, however, Jackson's scouting party, in one of the great ironic moments of history, was mistaken for a Union cavalry patrol and fired upon. Hit by several musket balls, Jackson fell, his left arm shattered. Amputation failed to save his life, and on May 10, 1863, he succumbed to pneumonia. His last words uttered in a final, sublime moment of lucidity were, "Let us cross over the river and rest under the shade of the trees."

SIGNIFICANCE

Jackson's death was a mortal blow to the Confederacy. In subsequent battles in the eastern theater, the absence of his leadership was sorely missed; Lee was to remark later that if he had had Jackson at Gettysburg, he would have won that crucial battle. Beyond such speculation, however, there is no doubt that the loss of such an inspiring leader—by far the most popular commander on either side—seriously undermined Confederate morale.

Jackson's charismatic popularity was the product of both his brilliant generalship and his singular force of character. Merciless in driving his own troops and ruthless in pursuit of his enemy, he nevertheless was admired by both for his legendary courage, integrity, and lack of egoistical motive. Lee venerated his memory, referring to him as "the great and good Jackson."

Jackson's battles (in particular, the Valley Campaign) have been studied as models by successive generations of military students in the United States and Europe. Jackson understood and applied the principles of mass and maneuver as well as any commander in history, concentrating his forces at decisive points against numerically superior but more dispersed opponents. Beyond his significance as a tactical genius, however, "Stonewall" passed early into the realm of national epic, defining an ideal of valor for generations of American youths.

Charles Duncan

FURTHER READING

Chambers, Lenoir. *Stonewall Jackson*. 2 vols. New York: William Morrow, 1959. Comprehensive, detailed biography. A lucid, graceful writer, Chambers brings admirable clarity and insight to his subject.

Churchill, Winston L. S. *The American Civil War*. New York: Fairfax Press, 1985. A reprint of the chapters on the American Civil War in Churchill's four-volume *A History of the English Speaking Peoples* (1956-1958). In any edition, Churchill's brief history of the Civil War is a masterpiece and focuses especially well on the significance of Jackson's role.

Clark, Champ. *Decoying the Yanks: Jackson's Valley Campaign*. Alexandria, Va.: Time-Life Books, 1984. As the title suggests, primarily a history of Jackson's Shenandoah Valley Campaign in the spring of 1862. Contains, however, a good short biography of Jackson in his early years as well. Lavishly illustrated with contemporary photographs, paintings, and drawings, the book gives a vivid account of the most spectacular achievement of Jackson's generalship.

Farwell, Byron. *Stonewall: A Biography of General Thomas J. Jackson*. New York: W. W. Norton, 1992. Thorough, balanced, and well-written account of Jackson's life.

Henderson, G. F. R. *Stonewall Jackson and the American Civil War*. 2 vols. New York: Longmans, Green, 1898. A classic biography of Jackson. Henderson's thoughtful, elegant study has gone through numerous editions and is still, after more than three-quarters of a century, a valuable resource cited in virtually every work on Jackson that has appeared since its publication.

Robertson, James I., Jr. *Stonewall Jackson: The Man, the Soldier, the Legend*. New York: Macmillan, 1997. Robertson, a Civil War historian, recounts the details of Jackson's life and military career, depicting his subject as a great military strategist and a man of strong religious faith.

Tate, Allen. *Stonewall Jackson, the Good Soldier*. New York: Minton, Balch, 1928. Reprint. Ann Arbor: University of Michigan Press, 1957. Short biography for the general reader by a leading southern man of letters. Tate's Confederate sympathies date the book but also provide an interesting partisan slant; he excoriates Jefferson Davis for not unleashing Jackson at decisive points that might have turned the tide for the Confederacy.

Vandiver, Frank. *Mighty Stonewall*. New York: McGraw-Hill, 1957. Comprehensive, well-balanced one-volume biography of Jackson by a respected Civil War historian. Vandiver's research is thorough, while his lively, anecdotal presentation brings to life the historical events for the reader.

Wheeler, Richard. *We Knew Stonewall Jackson*. New York: Thomas Y. Crowell, 1977. Extremely useful, well-conceived book of excerpts from contemporary accounts of Jackson linked by the author's commentary. In effect, an economical, accurate, short biography in which the author's sources speak for themselves.

ROBERT E. LEE

Military leader

Born: January 19, 1807; Stratford Hall, Virginia
Died: October 12, 1870; Lexington, Virginia
Also known as: Bobby Lee, Uncle Robert, Marse Robert, Granny Lee, King of Spades, Old Man, Marble Man
Primary conflict: Civil War (1861-1865)

Perhaps the finest military tactician of his generation, Lee commanded the Army of Northern Virginia so brilliantly during the American Civil War that he helped to prolong the life of the Confederacy.

EARLY LIFE

One of the famous Lees of Virginia and fifth of seven children, Robert Edward Lee was born at the family estate of Stratford. His father, Colonel Henry "Light Horse" Harry Lee, had served with distinction as a cavalryman in the Revolutionary War and later as governor of Virginia, although he was financially insecure. His mother, Anne Hill Carter Lee, belonged to another aristocratic Virginia family. The family moved to Alexandria in Robert's fourth year, and he attended the local schools there. Because of the long absences and then the death of his father, Robert gradually took over the major care of his invalid mother. This intimate relationship shaped young Lee's character as one of quiet dignity, high moral integrity, and personal strength.

Desiring to emulate his father and to obtain a free education, Lee attended the United States Military Academy at West Point, where he performed as an outstanding cadet and was graduated second in a class of forty-six in 1829. Entering the engineer corps, he built and maintained coastal fortifications and river works. In June, 1831, he married his childhood friend Mary Anne Randolph Custis, the great-granddaughter of the wife of George Washington, at the opulent Custis estate at Arlington. Their marriage strengthened Lee's deep roots in his native state, though his devotion to his country enabled him to resist the temptation to settle down to the life of a country squire at Arlington, which he managed even while posted elsewhere, and where his seven children were reared. He ably performed the mundane tasks of a peacetime army engineer and held the rank of captain at the outbreak of the Mexican War in 1846.

LIFE'S WORK

Lee's genius as a field officer emerged during the Mexican War and placed him in the public eye. He received the brevet rank of major for his performance as a staff officer in the early campaigns, after which he transferred to

Robert E. Lee (National Archives and Records Administration)

the staff of General Winfield Scott for the major invasion of central Mexico. Lee contributed materially to the capture of Veracruz in April, 1847; through his ability and bravery in placing artillery and reconnoitering in several battles, he was promoted to brevet lieutenant colonel. After the attack on Chapultepec, in which he was wounded, he became brevet colonel. Soon, however, Lee returned to routine duties, constructing fortifications near Baltimore and then, during 1852-1855, improving the course of study at West Point as superintendent. His reward was a transfer out of engineering to the Second Cavalry Regiment, with the rank of lieutenant colonel, policing the Indians in west Texas. In July, 1857, he assumed the colonelcy of the regiment. Home on leave during the fall of 1859, Lee was ordered to subdue John Brown's force, which had occupied the armory at Harpers Ferry (then part of Virginia) in Brown's stillborn attempt to incite a slave uprising in the South. After accomplishing the task, Lee returned to his regiment and, in 1860, assumed command of the Department of Texas.

Lee and his Confederate officers in their first meeting since Appomattox, taken at White Sulphur Springs, West Virginia, in August 1869, where they met to discuss "the orphaned children of the Lost Cause". This is the only from life photograph of Lee with his Generals in existence, during the war or after. (Wikimedia Commons)

A mild-mannered, even gentle officer with an excellent physique and devoted to the army and the flag, Lee dutifully obeyed his orders to return to Washington upon the secession of Texas from the Union in February, 1861. The next month, he was made colonel of the First Cavalry. By any measure the most able officer in the army, he was the logical choice to command the forces necessary to subdue the southern rebellion, a command offered him by the Lincoln administration upon the outbreak of the Civil War in mid-April, 1861. Following the secession of Virginia and considerable soul searching, however, Lee decided that his loyalty rested with his home state, whereupon he resigned his commission on April 23. He was given command of the Virginia militia and was soon appointed brigadier general in the new Confederate Army. Within months, his normal dark hair and mustache would be replaced by a full beard and hair completely grayed, the result no doubt of his awesome responsibilities.

Promoted to the full rank of general during the summer, one of five initially appointed, Lee first advised President Jefferson Davis in organizing the Confederate Army. He took command of the forces attempting to hold West Virginia in the Confederacy in August but was soundly defeated the next month at Cheat Mountain. Early in November, he assumed command of the coastal defenses of South Carolina, Georgia, and eastern Florida. Shortages of troops there led him to establish a strong defense against potential Union naval and amphibious penetrations. His strategy was faulty, however, because the Union had no intention of invading the interior in that quarter and instead attacked and successfully occupied key coastal positions merely for use as blockading stations for the navy.

Lee was recalled early in March, 1862, to help Davis organize the defenses of Richmond against the advance of General George B. McClellan's army in the Peninsular Campaign. When the commander of the defending army, General Joseph E. Johnston, was wounded at Fair Oaks, Lee was given command on June 1, and he quickly reorganized his forces into the Army of Northern Virginia, a name he created. He masterfully countered McClellan's forces in the Seven Days' Battles, concluded on July 1, then swung north to defeat the army of General John Pope at the Second Battle of Bull Run in late August. Crossing the Potomac, Lee attempted to gain the support of Marylanders but was stopped by McClellan in the Antietam campaign in September. He concluded the year by repulsing the bloody Union assaults on his well-placed army at Fredericksburg in December.

Lee's true genius in tactics lay in erecting field fortifications and in his remarkable ability to operate from the interior position—that is, to shift his forces between different points in his lines that were threatened by the larger numbers of the opposing Union armies. This tactic was best demonstrated in his stunning victory at Chancellorsville in May, 1863, when his army was half the size of that of the enemy. His greatest gamble occurred when he invaded Pennsylvania a month later. Frustrated from trying to turn the Union flanks at Gettysburg in July, he tried a frontal assault—"Pickett's charge"—that was virtually annihilated by the Army of the Potomac under General George G. Meade. As a result of this defeat, Lee was thereafter confined to the strategic defensive.

> "*Madam, don't bring up your sons to detest the United States government. Recollect that we form one country now. Abandon all these local animosities, and make your sons Americans.*"

Lee fought a steadily losing battle against the vastly greater numbers and better-equipped troops of General Ulysses S. Grant's armies in the Wilderness Campaign during the spring of 1864. Lee's men, inspired largely by his towering leadership, stopped every bloody assault, but Lee was obliged to retreat each time, lest the larger Union forces turn his flank and cut him off from Richmond. As a result, Lee withdrew into the defenses of that city and adjacent Petersburg, to withstand what turned out to be a nine-month-long siege. Near its end, in February, 1865, he was finally made general in chief of all Confederate armies. It was, by this time, too late. He placed Johnston in command of the only other remaining major army, in the Carolinas; then, in April, he attempted to escape a fresh Union offensive at Petersburg to link up with Johnston. Grant cut him off at Appomattox Courthouse in Virginia, where Lee surrendered on April 9, effectively ending the Civil War. His three sons were with him, two of them major generals, one a captain.

Having lost his home at Arlington, which became the national cemetery, Lee assumed the presidency of Washington College at Lexington, Virginia, in October, 1865. For the next five years, in weakened health, he served effectively not only as a college administrator but also as a quiet symbol of reunion and restoration, burying the passions of the wartime bitterness and thereby setting an example for the defeated South. Following his death, the college was renamed Washington and Lee in his honor.

SIGNIFICANCE

Robert E. Lee became a legend in his own time, first to the embattled peoples of the South and, eventually, to the nation at large. He symbolized the plain fact that, rather than treason, the cause of the Confederacy had represented the playing out of the final contradiction of the American nation. North and South, geographically, economically, and socially distinct, could no longer coexist within the fabric of the Constitution. The southern plantation aristocracy, agrarian and founded upon slavery, had become an anachronism in the modern, industrialized Western world. Its ultimate survival could be obtained only by arms, in which contest Lee had been the supreme champion. His stately character, bearing, and professionalism represented the ideal of southern society. Though he had opposed slavery, secession, and even war as a final political solution, like so many of his generation, he had had to make the tragic, fateful decision to stand by his neighbors in defense of the only way of life they knew. In defeat, he accepted the course of history without rancor.

The contrast between Lee's conduct and that of his Union counterparts reflected the great shift in social values marked by the Civil War. He ordered his troops to abstain from plundering civilian property, failing to understand—unlike Grant, William T. Sherman, and Philip H. Sheridan—that the modern war that they were all waging was a harbinger of a new age of mass conflict,

Lee mounted on Traveller, his famous "war horse." (Wikimedia Commons)

aimed at breaking civilian resistance with the use of modern industrialized machine weapons, thus destroying the socioeconomic institutions of an enemy. No better example of the adage that the Civil War was the last great war between gentlemen could be found than in the person of Robert E. Lee himself, the perfect gentleman of the long-past Age of Reason that had spawned his noble family.

Lee's achievements on the field of battle, however, established him as one of the greatest army commanders in history. Not merely an inspiring leader, he made correct, informed judgments about his enemy, then struck decisively. As a theater strategist defending his beloved Virginia, he became a master of the mobile feint, thanks largely to several able lieutenants. Stonewall Jackson's fast-moving so-called foot cavalry thrust into the Shenandoah Valley to draw away troops from McClellan during the Peninsular Campaign. J. E. B. Stuart's cavalry rode circles around the Union armies in every campaign. However, both these commanders were killed, in 1863 and 1864, respectively. Jubal A. Early's drive up the valley the latter year might have succeeded but for the determined riposte of Grant and Sheridan. In grand strategy, however, Lee was not adept, having misjudged Union intentions along the south Atlantic coast early in the war and never having the authority to mastermind Confederate fortunes until near the end of the struggle. He did not attempt to influence Davis beyond the Virginia theater.

Had Lee not been outnumbered most of the time, one can only conjecture what might have been the outcome of the war: As a tactician, he had no match in the Union army. The fatal flaw lay in the nature of the Confederacy itself, a politically loose grouping of rebelling states, devoid of effective central leadership. After Gettysburg, observed one of Lee's generals on the eve of Appomattox, the men had been fighting simply for him.

Clark G. Reynolds

FURTHER READING

Blount, Roy, Jr. *Robert E. Lee: A Penguin Life*. New York: Lipper/Viking, 2003. Concise biography, written from the perspective of a southerner. Particularly strong in detailing Lee's life after the Civil War.

Connelly, Thomas L. *The Marble Man: Robert E. Lee and His Image in American Society*. New York: Alfred A. Knopf, 1977. An excellent interpretative analysis of Lee's reputation as a southern and national hero during and since the Civil War.

Dowdey, Clifford. *Lee*. Boston: Little, Brown, 1965. An excellent one-volume treatment of Lee's career, adding new materials and interpretations of Lee's performance at Gettysburg.

Fellman, Michael. *The Making of Robert E. Lee*. New York: Random House, 2000. Intellectual biography, focusing on Lee's psychology and ideas on race, slavery, and other issues. Describes how Lee struggled to reconcile his Christian virtue, humility, and sense of duty with his desire for success and fame.

Flood, Charles Bracelen. *Lee: The Last Years*. Boston: Houghton Mifflin, 1981. The best analysis of Lee's actions and achievements during the last five years of his life, including his reactions to the late war.

Freeman, Douglas Southall. *R. E. Lee*. 4 vols. New York: Charles Scribner's Sons, 1934-1935. The definitive biography, which dissects Lee's career with such detail and careful interpretation as to become the standard work for all students of Lee.

Johnson, Robert Underwood, and Clarence Clough Buel, eds. *Battles and Leaders of the Civil War*. 4 vols. New York: Century, 1887. The most comprehensive and reliable source of reminiscences of key Civil War leaders, including many of Lee's subordinates and opponents, with complete lists of the opposing armies and navies, down to the regimental and ship level. Excellent maps and illustrations.

Lee, Robert E. *Recollections and Letters of General Robert E. Lee by His Son Capt. Robert E. Lee*. 2d ed. Garden City, N.Y.: Doubleday, Page, 1924. An invaluable memoir, especially useful for insights into Lee's family relationships.

---. *The Wartime Papers of R. E. Lee*. Edited by Clifford Dowdey and Louis Manarin. Boston: Little, Brown, 1961. Primary source material drawn from official records and private sources that offer insights into Lee's character and abilities as a commander.

Sanborn, Margaret. *Robert E. Lee*. 2 vols. Philadelphia: J. B. Lippincott, 1966-1967. A sound popular history based on the usual abundant primary and secondary sources.

Thomas, Emory M. *Robert E. Lee: A Biography*. New York: W. W. Norton, 1995. Comprehensive, analytical biography by a prominent Civil War historian. Thomas focuses on Lee as a person, portraying him as a man of many paradoxes.

Chester W. Nimitz

Military leader

Born: February 24, 1885; Fredericksburg, Texas
Died: February 20, 1966; Yerba Buena Island, California
Area of Achievement: Military (Navy)
Primary conflict: World War II (1939-1945)

Nimitz commanded American forces in the Pacific during World War II and played a crucial role in winning the important and difficult Battle of Midway. After the war, he became chief of Naval Operations.

Early Life

Chester William Nimitz (NIH-mihtz) was the son of Chester B. Nimitz and Anna Henke Nimitz. Although his father had died before he was born and the family was never well-off financially, he enjoyed a happy childhood with his cherished and hardworking mother and his not-so-hardworking but happy-go-lucky stepfather (who was also his uncle), William Nimitz. Perhaps the most important male influence on the boy, however, was that of his grandfather, Charles Henry Nimitz, who filled his mind with tales of nautical adventure. Despite such talk of the sea, Nimitz's ambition as a teenager was to become a soldier, so impressed was he by officers from the Army post at Fort Sam Houston. There were no vacancies at West Point, however, so he attended the United States Naval Academy instead, and was graduated on January 30, 1905, seventh in a class of 114.

Blond and handsome, kindly and humorous, above all capable of laughing at himself when the need arose, young Nimitz was prime material for a happy marriage; yet nuptials did not occur until April 9, 1913, when he wed Catherine B. Freeman of Wollaston, Massachusetts. They had four children: Catherine, Chester, Anna, and Mary.

Life's Work

Nimitz's early interests were in engineering and submarines. During World War I, he served on an oiler and also with the submarines, ending the war as a lieutenant commander. In the postwar period, he had the usual kinds of assignments that rising officers enjoyed: attendance at the Naval War College, teaching in ROTC, service with battleships, and command of a cruiser. He never became an aviator, a fact that might have caused problems for a lesser man during World War II, when he was called on to command an aircraft carrier-oriented fleet. Nimitz became an admiral in 1938 and in 1939 took charge of the Bureau of Navigation, the office that controlled personnel assignments.

This latter post gave him access to President Franklin D. Roosevelt, who, along with almost everyone else, took a liking to the new admiral. In early 1941, Roosevelt offered Nimitz command of the Pacific Fleet, but he declined because of lack of seniority a lucky move: Had he accepted the offer, he, instead of Admiral Husband E. Kimmel, might have had to take the blame for the disaster at Pearl Harbor later that same year.

After the invasion at Pearl Harbor, Kimmel was dismissed and Nimitz was named to replace him as Commander in Chief Pacific (CINCPAC), as of December 31, 1941. From his desk in Pearl Harbor, Nimitz would lead all the American forces, Army as well as Navy and Marines, in the North, Central, and South Pacific areas; he also was in direct command of all naval units in those areas by virtue of wearing a different hat. Thus, in a sense, he was his own boss, being both theater commander and theater naval chieftain. This arrangement worked well, but did not eliminate all command problems in the war against Japan.

Chester W. Nimitz (Wikimedia Commons)

Nimitz signs as Supreme Allied Commander during the formal surrender ceremonies on the USS Missouri in Tokyo Bay on September 2, 1945. Directly behind him are (left-to-right): General Douglas MacArthur; Admiral William Halsey, USN, and Rear Admiral Forrest Sherman, USN. (Wikimedia Commons)

One of Nimitz's difficulties was with General Douglas MacArthur, commander of the Southwest Pacific Area (SWPA). MacArthur wanted his theater to be the scene of the principal thrust against Japan, even if that meant reducing Nimitz's activity to nothing. Probably MacArthur would have been happiest if Nimitz and his theater had been put under SWPA command. The Navy Department would never have allowed either the lesser or the greater of MacArthur's ambitions to come true, but Nimitz had to operate throughout the war with the knowledge that the Army in general, and MacArthur in particular, wanted a greater share of material and command.

Nimitz also had to contend with his own boss, Admiral Ernest J. King, chief of Naval Operations and commander in chief of all American warships around the world. King was a ferocious man, just as harsh as Nimitz was kindly, and he worried about CINCPAC's aggressiveness. King thought that Nimitz might not be willing to dismiss those who fell short of perfection; he also wondered at first about Nimitz's willingness to take enormous risks in fighting the Japanese. Perhaps the real problem was that King could not resist the temptation to become personally involved in running the Pacific war. Another thing that bothered King about Nimitz was the latter's reluctance to do battle against MacArthur. King was responsible for upholding the Navy's prerogatives in the face of demands from his equals in the highest councils of war the British, the Army, and the Army Air Forces; therefore, he could not afford to be affable, or so he seems to have reckoned. Nimitz, on the other hand, outranked all the generals and admirals in his own theater and was not in a position to thwart MacArthur's plans directly; he, therefore, could approach the war in a more genial frame of mind. For all that, King and Nimitz made a good team, each compensating for the other's rare moments of bad judgment.

Since Nimitz was tied for the most part to his desk, the battles in his theater were conducted either by commanders at sea or on the invaded islands: Admirals Frank Jack Fletcher, William F. Halsey, and Raymond A. Spruance, and Marine generals A. Archer Vandegrift and Holland M. Smith, among others. Nevertheless, as commander in chief, Nimitz bore the ultimate responsibility for their campaigns, except insofar as King himself sometimes determined the overall strategy and except for the times when Halsey's services were lent to MacArthur.

"*God grant me the courage not to give up what I think is right even though I think it is hopeless.*"

Undoubtedly, the most important battle in which Nimitz's role was most personal and crucial was that fought near the island of Midway in 1942. The Pacific Fleet was much inferior to that of Japan, and so it was vital for the Americans, if they were to hold Midway, to know what the Japanese intended to do. Fortunately, Nimitz could tap the resources of a brilliant cryptologist, Lieutenant Commander Joseph J. Rochefort, Jr., who had recently broken the Japanese naval code and thereby was able to predict the enemy's plan. It was Nimitz himself, however, who had to decide whether to believe Rochefort's evidence, and it was also Nimitz who next had to convince a headstrong King that Rochefort was right. Even after that, there were plans to be made and risks to be taken. It was Nimitz who decided not to use the United States' elderly battleships in the coming fight because they would only get in the way; a non-aviator, he nevertheless put his faith in his aircraft carriers. It was Nimitz who decided on the deployment of those carriers, although Fletcher and Spruance were in command afloat. The result of all these plans and decisions, along with the skill and luck of those on the scene, was an overwhelming American victory, one of the great turning points of the war.

Nimitz was farther removed from the controls during the battles on and around Guadalcanal in August and November, 1942. These were King's pet projects, and conducted on the scene by the South Pacific commanders, who reported to Nimitz. Though close victories, they served to confirm the verdict of Midway: From then on, it was not a question of whether the United States would win the war against Japan but of how soon and at what cost. If Nimitz took too long or spent too much American blood, the public might demand that MacArthur be given the lion's share of men, material, and tasks. Nimitz was responsible more than any other person for his forces moving ahead rapidly and, for the most part, with no more bloodshed than necessary. His campaigns in the Gilberts, the Marshalls, the Marianas, Iwo Jima (Iwo To), and Okinawa were all successful. During the reconquest of the Philippines, however, Nimitz was in general an onlooker: Halsey still reported to him but was operating according to MacArthur's plan. Thus, there was no unity of command during the Battle of Leyte Gulf (October 23-26, 1944); the only common commander of all American forces at Leyte was President Roosevelt himself. Nimitz did intervene once to correct an unfortunate move by Halsey.

World War II ended with Nimitz and MacArthur accepting Japan's surrender, both of them now wearing the five stars of the new American ranks, respectively fleet admiral and general of the Army; this was an honor shared by only five other officers as of V-J Day.

On December 15, 1945, Nimitz succeeded King as chief of Naval Operations. It was a time of demobilization, but the biggest issue facing the new chief was that of unification of the services. Although CINCPAC's joint command had worked well, and although command disunity had bedeviled the Leyte Gulf campaign, Nimitz nevertheless agreed with most Navy men in objecting to unification on the national level. Sailors feared that the new Air Force might try to take over the Navy's aerial component, while the Army, having lost its airplanes, might attempt to seize control of the Marine Corps as compensation. However, when Congress "unified" the services in 1947, the Navy Department retained its airplanes and the Marines. Nimitz deserves some of the credit for his department's victory: He had made himself welcome at the White House of President Harry S. Truman, a man who, unlike Roosevelt, had originally favored the Army.

Although five-star officers do not retire in the usual sense, Nimitz nevertheless went off active duty in December, 1947. In 1949, however, Truman offered to reappoint him as chief of Naval Operations in the wake of the so-called Admirals' Revolt against the Defense Department, an incident touched off by Navy-Air Force rivalry. What Truman wanted was a conciliator, but Nimitz declined the offer. Instead, he spent his retirement as regent of the University of California, as United Nations plebiscite administrator for Kashmir (1949-1950), and as roving ambassador for the United Nations (1950-1952). In the late 1950's, he helped E. B. Potter edit an important textbook of naval history, *Sea Power: A Naval History* (1960).

By 1965, Nimitz was suffering from osteoarthritis and pneumonia; the latter had bothered him off and on for many years despite his generally robust condition. Strokes and heart failure followed, and he died in San Francisco on February 20, 1966.

President Roosevelt in conference with General MacArthur, Admiral Nimitz (standing), and Admiral Leahy, while on tour in Hawaiian Islands. (Wikimedia Commons)

Significance

Despite King's occasional misgivings, Nimitz's career proves that nice guys do not necessarily finish last. He fully deserved his elevation to five-star rank for his all-important role in the Battle of Midway and his more distant but still vital part in subsequent American Pacific victories. His postwar services also justified the honor. Although he disliked controversy, and therefore did not subsequently write his memoirs or even allow a biography in his lifetime, he nevertheless was able to carry out the duties of a great commander without inordinate displays of ego or temper. Whether such a pleasant man could have held off the War Department and the British in Washington during World War II is another question, but perhaps the American Joint Chiefs of Staff and the Anglo-American Combined Chiefs of Staff would have benefited from his reasonable and amiable presence. He was too quiet a man to make good "copy" for the press, as was the case with some other famous World War II commanders, but he achieved as much greatness or more.

Karl G. Larew

Further Reading

Buell, Thomas B. *Master of Sea Power: A Biography of Fleet Admiral Ernest J. King*. Boston: Little, Brown, 1980. This book does not rank with E. B. Potter's biography of Nimitz, but it is quite worthwhile and helps the reader to see Nimitz from the point of view of Washington and London.

Dull, Paul S. *The Imperial Japanese Navy, 1941-1945*. Annapolis, Md.: Naval Institute Press, 1978. This is a highly successful attempt to see the war in the Pacific from the Japanese navy's viewpoint.

Hoyt, Edwin P. *How They Won the War in the Pacific: Nimitz and His Admirals*. New York: Lyons Press, 2000. Examines how the top admirals worked together during World War II, concentrating on Nimitz. Describes Nimitz's strategy for winning the war in the Pacific and how his wisdom, strength, and ability to remain calm during times of great stress made him a great admiral.

James, Dorris Clayton. *The Years of MacArthur: Volume II, 1941-1945*. Boston: Houghton Mifflin, 1975. A gigantic, brilliant biography. James accomplishes the nearly impossible: He provides a balanced, fair treatment of one of America's most controversial leaders.

Morison, Samuel E. *The Two-Ocean War: A Short History of the United States Navy in the Second World War*. Boston: Little, Brown, 1963. Admiral Morison, himself a professional historian, oversaw the production of the Navy's multivolume official history of World War II; this is a one-volume distillation of that effort.

Potter, E. B. *Nimitz*. Annapolis, Md.: Naval Institute Press, 1976. This is a long but well-written, authoritative, and masterful biography by an eminent naval historian. It is by far the most important source for any sketch of Nimitz's life.

Potter, E. B., and Chester W. Nimitz, eds. *Sea Power: A Naval History*. Englewood Cliffs, N.J.: Prentice-Hall, 1960. A useful textbook covering all the history of naval warfare.

Prange, Gordon W., Donald M. Goldstein, and Katherine V. Dillon. *Miracle at Midway*. New York: McGraw-Hill, 1982. One of Prange's posthumous books, perhaps a bit flawed because it was put together after his death; nevertheless, it provides interesting and dramatically told insights concerning Nimitz's most famous battle.

Spector, Ronald H. *Eagle Against the Sun*. New York: Free Press, 1985. A well-balanced, well-written, and up-to-date account of the Pacific war by a highly respected, rising young historian.

John J. Pershing

Military leader

Born: January 13, 1860; Laclede, Missouri
Died: July 15, 1948; Washington, D.C.
Primary conflict: World War I (1914-1918)

A career soldier, Pershing was ready when called on to lead the American Expeditionary Force to Europe in World War I, helping preserve democracy in the first global conflict.

Early Life

The eldest of John Pershing and Elizabeth Pershing's nine children, John Joseph Pershing was born in the year preceding the outbreak of the Civil War. Tensions ran high in this midwestern state, and Pershing's father suffered for his staunch support of the Union, which he served as a sutler. Pershing early aspired to a career in law, and initially his goal appeared attainable. A brief period of

John J. Pershing (Wikimedia Commons)

postwar prosperity, however, soon gave way to virtual bankruptcy for the family, and when Pershing's father gave up storekeeping to work as a traveling salesperson, John took to farming and odd jobs. One of them, as janitor for the nearby black school in Prairie Mound, led to a permanent position as a teacher there. In 1882, he attended the Normal School in Kirksville, obtaining a bachelor's degree in elementary didactics. That same year, he took the test for appointment to the United States Military Academy and received a nomination. To meet the age limitation for entrants, he changed his birth month from January to September.

After a month in a Highland Falls, New York, preparatory school, Pershing enrolled with 129 other young men at West Point. Somewhat older than his classmates, he commanded their respect, holding his five-foot ten-inch frame ramrod-straight and casting a stern glance at the world from steel-gray eyes; the mustache and silvered hair would come later. Pershing proved an adequate student and a first-rate leader, whom schoolmates elected class president each year. In each of his four years, he held the top position for cadets, culminating in his selection as first captain of the Corps of Cadets in his final year. In 1886, he was graduated and commissioned a second lieutenant of cavalry.

> "*A competent leader can get efficient service from poor troops, while on the contrary an incapable leader can demoralize the best of troops.*"

LIFE'S WORK

A career as a soldier did not hold great promise in the late nineteenth century. Pershing spent his first years with the Sixth Cavalry, fighting in the last of the Indian Wars. Later, he commanded a troop in the Tenth Cavalry, an all-black unit with whom Pershing gained unusually good rapport. His service on the frontier was broken by a tour at the University of Nebraska, where he transformed a slovenly cadet corps into one of the country's finest detachments of college trainees. During his off-duty time, he earned a law degree and gave serious thought to resigning.

In 1898, he returned to his alma mater as a tactical officer, instructing West Point cadets in the fundamentals of soldiering. In that year, troubles with Spain over Cuba erupted into a war, and Pershing sought duty with the force being organized to invade the Caribbean island. Unable to go to Cuba as a cavalryman, Pershing obtained a temporary assignment as a quartermaster. In that position, he gained important insight into the follies of the army's system for providing supplies to its line units. That lesson was stored away for future use in Europe during the first global conflict of the twentieth century.

Pershing was promoted to captain in 1901, fifteen years after he was commissioned. Because promotions were based on seniority, he expected little further advancement. The early years of the new century saw him in the Philippines, leading American soldiers in a pacification effort against nationals who resisted the United States government's efforts to bring Western-style democracy to the islands. Pershing earned a reputation as a successful negotiator with Philippine leaders, and his remarkable march around Lake Lanao was noted not only in the Philippines but also in Washington, D.C. A tour on the newly formed general staff gave Pershing the opportunity to meet the woman he would eventually wed: Frances

Warren, daughter of Wyoming senator Francis E. Warren, a Republican and member of the Senate's military committee. Pershing and Frances were married in January, 1905, and left almost immediately for Japan, where Pershing was to serve as a military observer during the Russo-Japanese War.

In 1906, Pershing's efforts on behalf of his country were generously rewarded. In an unusual move, President Theodore Roosevelt nominated the captain for promotion to brigadier general, allowing him to jump over almost a thousand officers senior to him and bypass the field grade ranks (major, lieutenant colonel, and colonel). The new general spent much of the next decade in the Philippines, returning to the United States for assignment at the Presidio, San Francisco, in 1914. Almost immediately, Pershing left for El Paso, Texas, to organize a force that would invade Mexico to capture the bandit Pancho Villa.

Pershing and Secretary of State for War and Secretary of State for Air Winston Churchill in conversation in London on the day of the Victory Parade on 19 July 1919. (Wikimedia Commons)

While Pershing was in Texas, his family, which now included three daughters and a son, remained in California. On August 26, 1915, tragedy struck the Pershings. Coals ignited wax on the ground floor of their wood-frame quarters, and Frances and the three girls perished in the ensuing fire; only Pershing's son, Warren, was saved. With stoic courage, Pershing made his way to California, accompanied the bodies to Wyoming for burial, then returned to his troops on the Mexican border.

The Punitive Expedition that Pershing commanded from 1915 to 1917 was ostensibly organized in retaliation for raids conducted by Villa within the United States city of Columbus, New Mexico. Pershing's force of twenty thousand men traversed the Mexican desert for months, while political negotiations continued between President Woodrow Wilson and the various factions trying to seize permanent control of the government in Mexico. The force withdrew in 1917, when the war in Europe forced Wilson to shift his attention to that region of the world.

In May, 1917, Pershing was notified that he had been selected to organize an American force for duty with the Allied forces in Europe. Hastily assembling a small staff, he traveled to England and then to France, where he spent a year shaping a force that would ultimately consist of more than one million Americans. Handpicked subordinates wrestled with problems of obtaining supplies, coordinating troop movements, quartering the divisions and separate units, feeding and clothing the newly arrived recruits, and training men to survive as individuals and fight as units. Pershing's time was occupied in constant inspections and in wrangling with Allied commanders, especially marshals Philippe Pétain of France and Douglas Haig of England, both of whom wanted to detail small American units for duty with French and British units already employed on line against the Germans. Convinced that Americans should fight in American units, commanded by American officers, Pershing held out against their constant requests. Only reluctantly did he finally commit some battalions of the First Infantry Division for duty with the French. His strategy paid off in the late summer of 1918, when the American First Army achieved smashing victories against the Germans along the Saint-Mihiel salient and then in the Meuse-Argonne area of France.

The entrance of American forces into the war helped deal the final death blow to Germany's hopes for conquest. In November, 1918, the Germans agreed to the terms of surrender, and Pershing was faced with the problems of dismantling the huge military machine he had worked so hard to assemble. For the better part of the next two years, he was engaged in returning troops to America and drafting detailed reports of the actions of his army during the war.

In 1920, Congress passed a law designating Pershing general of the armies, allowing him to keep the four-star rank that had been bestowed on him temporarily while he was in command of the American Expeditionary Force

(AEF). There was some talk of Pershing running for president, and he allowed his name to appear on the ballot in the Nebraska primary as a favorite-son candidate; a poor showing convinced him, however, to abandon that campaign. In July, 1921, President Warren G. Harding and Secretary of War John Weeks named Pershing chief of staff of the army. In that position, the hero of World War I fought a three-year battle against the Congress and a large contingent of American people who wanted to return the American military to its prewar position: small and poorly funded. Pershing argued (in vain) for larger permanent forces and an active program to train men for future service through the National Guard and Army Reserve. Despite his pleas, the size of the army shrunk, its budget dwindled, and its capability to mobilize evaporated.

In September, 1924, Pershing retired. The following years were far from quiet ones, though, since duty with various government commissions kept the general busy. In 1924, he served with the delegation trying to resolve the Tacna-Arica boundary dispute between Peru and Chile. He later served with the American Battle Monuments commission and continued to provide sage advice to his successors in the office of the chief of staff. In 1936, Pershing became seriously ill, but he recovered and once again offered his services to the country when America became embroiled in World War II. President Franklin D. Roosevelt sought his advice, and in fact Pershing helped convince the president to keep General George C. Marshall in Washington, D.C., rather than let him assume field command in Europe. Marshall, a protégé of Pershing who had been a key staff officer in the AEF, often consulted his mentor during World War II.

Pershing received special honors when the Congress ordered a medal struck in his honor in 1946. He died on July 15, 1948. In accordance with his wishes, he was buried at Arlington National Cemetery, under a simple headstone, among the soldiers whom he had led in "the Great War."

SIGNIFICANCE

Pershing's lifelong career of service to his country has secured for him a place among American military heroes. The epitome of the American soldier-leader, he was purposely self-effacing when placed in political circles, remaining true to the principle of military subordination to civilian control with great conviction. His efforts as a stern disciplinarian, a brilliant organizer of large forces, and a staunch believer in the capabilities of the American soldier were a vital element in the Allied success in World War I. In addition, his consistent support for the citizen-soldier helped set the model for future generations of planners and shaped the future of American military organization for the remainder of the century. Finally, his sagacious tutelage of subordinates such as George C. Marshall and George S. Patton provided America the military leadership it needed to rise to the challenge posed by Adolf Hitler and his confederates in World War II.

Laurence W. Mazzeno

FURTHER READING

American Military History. Washington, D.C.: Office of the Chief of Military History, 1969. Official history of American military involvement at home and abroad; includes accounts of the Indian Wars, the Punitive Expedition in Mexico, and World War I, providing excellent background and highlighting Pershing's contributions when in command.

Goldhurst, Richard. *Pipe, Clay and Drill: John J. Pershing: The Classic American Soldier*. New York: Reader's Digest Press, 1977. A solid biography that places Pershing's actions within the larger context of American political enterprises. Detailed chapters on the Punitive Expedition.

Grotelueschen, Mark Ethan. *The AEF Way of War: The American Army and Combat in World War I*. New York: Cambridge University Press, 2007. Examines the American Expeditionary Force's doctrine and methods of fighting, including Pershing's command of the force.

Liddell-Hart, Basil Henry. *Reputations Ten Years After*. Boston: Little, Brown, 1930. Liddell-Hart's chapter on Pershing provides an antidote to hagiographic portraits that were popular immediately after the war and points out Pershing's difficulties in dealing with high-ranking officials of Allied forces.

O'Connor, Richard. *Black Jack Pershing*. Garden City, N.Y.: Doubleday, 1961. An objective biography, highly readable and informative, of modest length.

Smythe, Donald. *Guerrilla Warrior: The Early Life of John J. Pershing*. New York: Charles Scribner's Sons, 1973. A detailed, scholarly account of the early years of Pershing's life through his participation in the Punitive Expedition.

---. *Pershing: General of the Armies*. Bloomington: Indiana University Press, 1986. Smythe's definitive biography of Pershing focuses on Pershing's role as commander in chief of the American Expeditionary

Force in World War I and his tenure as chief of staff of the army.

Vandiver, Frank. *Black Jack: The Life and Times of John J. Pershing.* 2 vols. College Station: Texas A & M University Press, 1977. A comprehensive biography, based largely on records in the Library of Congress, National Archives, and other collections. Places Pershing's actions in the context of America's coming of age as a world power.

Weigley, Russell A. *A History of the United States Army.* New York: Macmillan, 1967. A scholarly yet highly readable account of the growth of the American military establishment; chapter on World War I provides excellent summary of Pershing's actions and an assessment of his accomplishments as commander of the American Expeditionary Force.

Welsome, Eileen. *The General and the Jaguar: Pershing's Hunt for Pancho Villa, a True Story of Revolution and Revenge.* New York: Little, Brown, 2006. Recounts Pancho Villa's attack on Columbus, New Mexico, in 1916, and General Pershing's subsequent search for Villa.

Loreta Janeta Velázquez

Cuban-born soldier

Born: June 26, 1842; Havana, Cuba
Died: 1923
Primary conflict: Civil War (1861-1865)

After the outbreak of the American Civil War, Velázquez disguised herself as a man and joined the Confederate army. She fought in several battles, only being discovered as a woman after she was injured. She also worked as a spy for the Confederacy, infiltrating the U.S. Secret Service.

Early Life

The majority of information known about Loreta Janeta Velázquez (loh-REH-tah jah-NEH-tah veh-LAHS-kehz) comes from her autobiography, *The Woman in Battle,* published in 1876. She was born in Havana, Cuba, on June 26, 1842. Her father was a Spanish government official and her mother was French American. Velázquez had three older brothers and two older sisters. In 1844, the family moved from Cuba to Mexico (to an area that is now part of Texas), where her father owned plantations. Her father fought for Mexico in the Mexican-American War and became very bitter toward Americans.

After the war, the family moved back to Cuba. In her memoirs, Velázquez recalls that she always wanted to be a man when she was a child; she idolized Joan of Arc. Velázquez was educated by an English governess until 1849, when she was sent to Catholic school in New Orleans. While there, she lived with an aunt, who spent two years teaching her to read, write, and speak English. Velázquez had an arranged engagement to a Spanish man named Raphael. However, she felt trapped and did not love him. Instead, she fell in love with William, the boyfriend of her schoolmate, and eloped with him. They were married April 5, 1856, when Velázquez was just fourteen years old. She returned to her aunt's home and kept the marriage a secret until the following October. She had her first child in 1857 before following her husband westward. By 1860, they had three children and were living in St. Louis. The third baby died shortly after birth; the two older children died later that year of fever.

Life's Work

Political, economic, and social tensions within the United States had been rapidly growing in the years before the 1860 election. The election of Abraham Lincoln as president led to the secession of a number of Southern states, which formed the Confederate States of America. Velázquez's husband, William, was from Texas, so he resigned from the U.S. Army after Texas's secession on February 1, 1861, to join the Confederate army. William

Loreta Janeta Velázquez (Wikimedia Commons)

was sent to Richmond shortly after the couple's fifth wedding anniversary.

Velázquez had a Memphis tailor make her two Confederate uniforms, adding extra padding inside the coat to conceal her shape. Upon reaching New Orleans, Velázquez needed a disguise that was more comfortable. She got a French tailor to make six wire-net shields to disguise her body. She also used a false mustache and beard to disguise herself as Lieutenant Harry Buford. Velázquez then traveled to Arkansas and recruited 236 men for a regiment. She claims to have delivered the regiment to her husband in Florida for him to command. William was killed a few days later in a training accident.

Failing to purchase a commission into the army, Velázquez fought as an independent officer, which she felt gave her more freedom. She was wounded during the First Battle of Bull Run (Manassas, Virginia) on July 21, 1861, the first major battle of the war. Her injuries were not severe, and she refused medical attention out of fear of being discovered. After the battle, Velázquez went to Washington, D.C., dressed as a woman, to become a spy. She even claimed to have met Lincoln. Velázquez returned to the army as Lieutenant Buford whenever she grew tired of dressing as a woman. In her memoirs, she brags about the attention she received from other women while disguised as Buford. During the Battle of Shiloh, Velázquez claims to have fought valiantly as Buford and spied as a woman at night. She claims to have gotten close enough to Ulysses Grant that she could have killed him but felt it would have been murder. While helping bury the dead, she was wounded by a shell and discovered to be a woman by the army doctor.

Giving up on her army career, Velázquez obtained a British passport and allegedly became a drug smuggler and blockade runner. She then says that the Confederate government hired her to infiltrate the Union's Secret Service as a double agent. According to Velázquez, she was hired by the Secret Service and assigned to discover a Confederate spy—herself. This position allowed her to travel freely throughout the Union. While doing so, Velázquez attempted to organize a rebellion among Confederate prisoners of war. In the last months of the war, she traveled to Ohio, Canada, London, and Paris, arriving in New York City the day after General Robert E. Lee's surrender in April 1865.

After the war, Velázquez traveled through Europe and the former Confederacy. She married her third husband and moved to Venezuela but returned shortly after his death. It was in Texas that she wrote and published her memoirs in 1876. Velázquez wrote the book in order to earn enough money to support herself and her son. The book drew heavy criticism and skepticism; among the most vehement of its critics was Confederate General Jubal Early. Despite having lost her notes, Velázquez's tome is more than six hundred pages long and includes details about the weather and specific conversations. There also is no record of a Harry Buford serving in the Confederate army. Some historians believe that she used the alias Alice Williams, who was reported to have fought as Lieutenant Henry Beford or Bensford. Others claim

---

Women Who Fought as Men in the U.S. Civil War

During a time before equal rights for the sexes, military jobs were restricted to men. Women who wanted to aid the war effort joined Sanitary Commissions, aid groups, or became nurses. However, for some women, being confined to a hospital was not enough. These women, like Loreta Janeta Velázquez, became spies or disguised themselves as men in order to enlist in the armed forces. It is unclear from the war records how many women fought in the war; estimates range from hundreds to thousands. Most of them were from the poorer classes, in their late teens or early twenties, and first-generation Americans or immigrants themselves. Sarah Rosetta Wakeman and Jennie Hodgers enlisted for the money, in order to feed their families. Many others, like Malinda Blalock and Frances Clayton, followed their husbands and boyfriends to war. The death of husbands and loved ones also led some women, such as Charlotte Hope, to enlist, hoping to avenge the deaths. Some of the women, like their male counterparts, joined for the sole purpose of adventure. Ones like Velázquez enlisted because of a strong sense of patriotic duty, which sometimes included the belief of being the second Joan of Arc. A number of women were discovered while trying to enlist, others when they were wounded or became ill, and some not until their death. After being detected, the women were arrested, sent home, or forced to work as nurses. If discovered after being captured, they often were the first prisoners exchanged or sent back across the lines wearing dresses.

that Velázquez heard the stories of Williams and passed them off as her own. The book cannot be proven or disproven but appears to be at least a highly fictionalized version of the truth. Velázquez is believed to have died in 1897, but little is known about her outside of her memoirs.

SIGNIFICANCE

Velázquez saw the American Civil War as her chance to live out her dream of being a man and fighting for a cause like her hero, Joan of Arc. Her defiance of the gender norms of her era allowed her to experience a very different life, one filled with excitement and adventure. Her memoirs have made her one of the most well-known women who fought and spied for the Confederacy and one of the most famous Cuban Americans to do so as well.

Jennifer L. Campbell

FURTHER READING

Hall, Richard. *Women on the Civil War Battlefront.* Lawrence: University Press of Kansas, 2006. A well-researched work written by a pioneer in the field that discusses the various roles women played during the Civil War: as soldiers, spies, nurses, scouts, and smugglers.

Velázquez, Loreta Janeta. *The Woman in Battle.* Richmond, Va.: Dustin, Gilman and Company, 1876. Reprint. Charleston, S.C.: Nabu Press, 2010. Velázquez recounts her adventures during the Civil War as Harry Buford, a spy, double agent, and blockade runner. She also includes her family history and life before and after the war. Much of her book is considered factually suspect.

Winkler, H. Donald. *Stealing Secrets.* Naperville, Ill.: Cumberland House, 2010. A work focusing on female spies during the Civil War, including Velázquez. The author discusses how these woman helped change the course of the war. Based on newspapers, journals, diaries, letters, and memoirs from the war.

CATHAY WILLIAMS

Soldier

Born: September 1844; Independence, Missouri
Died: 1893; Trinidad, Colorado
Also known as: William Cathay
Primary conflict: Civil War (1861-1865)

An African-American woman and a former slave, Cathay Williams enlisted in the United States Army posing as a man in 1866. She served for two years before she was discovered and discharged.

EARLY LIFE

Not much is known of Cathay Williams's life. She was born into slavery, the child of an enslaved woman and a free man, in Independence, Missouri, in 1844. As a young woman, she was a house slave on a plantation near Missouri's capital, Jefferson City. At the outset of the Civil War, Missouri was in a unique position; a slave-owning state since its founding in 1821, it was initially populated by Southerners who had traveled up the Mississippi River. The Missouri Compromise of 1820 allowed Missouri to be the sole exception to the rule that Louisiana Purchase territory north of 36°30' latitude was to remain free of slavery. The demographics in Missouri changed somewhat in the decades following its founding as more and more non-slave-owning Germans and other immigrants moved into the state. However, by the census of 1860, there were still over 115,000 slaves counted—almost ten percent of the population—and the majority of whites in Missouri still identified with the Southern states.

In the summer of 1861, Union troops entered Missouri, occupying Jefferson City. The passage of the Confiscation Act of 1861 meant that any property or material that was being used to support the Confederacy could be seized by Union forces. The Act was unclear about the status of slaves who were taken in this manner, and many of them were impressed into service for the Union troops. (Remember that the Emancipation Proclamation wasn't signed until nearly eighteen months later, in January 1863.) Cathay Williams was among the slaves who were seized as contraband and impressed into service. She was seventeen years old.

Life's Work

Williams spent the next few years traveling with the 8th Indiana Volunteer Infantry Regiment, under the command of Colonel William Plummer Benton. Working as a laundress and a cook, she accompanied the troops on long marches through Arkansas, Louisiana, and Georgia. In Arkansas, she was present at the Battle of Pea Ridge in March 1862. She was also present for parts of the Red River Campaign, sometimes called the Red River Expedition, a series of battles fought along the *Red River* in Louisiana that took place between March and May in 1864. She also marched with the troops under General Phillip Sheridan heading north into Virginia's Shenandoah Valley later that same year.

When the war was over, Williams had no home to return to. We can only speculate about why she returned to the Army, this time as a soldier. Working for and living with the soldiers during the war may not have been an easy life, but it was familiar to her. Further, she knew that soldiers received salaries and had a degree of respect in society that a freed female slave could probably never achieve. During her time working as a servant for the Union soldiers, she would have encountered African-Americans who were soldiers. By the time the war ended in 1865, nearly 180,000 black men had served as soldiers in the Union Army—about ten percent of the total fighting force. Half of them were former slaves (or "contraband," just like Williams).

We know that Williams enlisted at St. Louis on November 15, 1866, using the name "William Cathay." There were no extensive physical examinations for recruits in that period. Her enlistment papers state that William Cathay was twenty-two years old with "black eyes, black hair, black complexion," and that "he" was 5 feet 9 inches tall. She joined on the same day as a friend and a cousin, both young men, who were aware of her ruse and evidently went along. She served with them in the same regiment, the 38th United States Infantry Regiment, one of six African-American regiments that were authorized in 1866 for the defense of the frontier during the Indian Wars. The black soldiers of this era came to be known as "Buffalo soldiers," a nickname probably originally given to them by Native Americans. From Kansas, the troops of the 38th Infantry Regiment marched over 500 miles to New Mexico, where they served protecting white settlers from Native American raids.

Not long after enlisting, Williams acquired smallpox. She was hospitalized for a time before catching up to her fellow soldier in either Kansas or New Mexico. She learned to shoot a gun, to clean it, to perform garrison and guard duty, and other tasks that would have been required of soldiers, and there is no evidence to suggest that she was unable to perform her duties. On the other hand, we know that she was ill frequently, and she was hospitalized four times for various ailments during her time as a soldier.

In October 1868, Williams was sick once again, and she growing tired of playing a soldier. The details are not clear, but either the physician discovered that she was a woman or she told the physician that she was. Williams was discharged on October 14, 1868, with a certificate of disability; she was not discharged dishonorably. She stayed in Fort Union and resumed working as a cook and a laundress. Later, she moved to Pueblo, Colorado, and then Trinidad, Colorado, where she worked as a dress maker. She passed away in Trinidad in 1893.

> "*They were partly the cause of my joining the army. Another reason was I wanted to make my own living and not be dependent on relations or friends.*"

Significance

In 1876, the story of Williams's life became known when the *Daily Times* of St. Louis published a piece by an enterprising reporter called "She Fought Nobly: The Story of a Colored Woman Who Served as an Enlisted Soldier during the Late War." The story made her a local celebrity for a time in her town in Colorado, but otherwise she was largely forgotten to history. Even the date of her death was not recorded and remains unknown. The motivation for Williams's decision to become a soldier also remains obscure, but it was surely undertaken for personal reasons not public ones. Williams is interesting to us today more than she was to readers in the nineteenth century. We cannot help but see her as a pioneer in ongoing struggles—the women's movement, the civil rights movement—whereas in the nineteenth century, her story was just a curiosity. Almost everything that we know about Williams derives from that one tantalizing newspaper article that was largely forgotten after its publication in 1876. Whatever else Cathay Williams's story signifies, it should remind us of the extent to which history is written on the basis of changing winds of interest and meaning.

D. Alan Dean

Further Reading

Glasrud, Bruce A. and Michael N. Searles (eds). *Buffalo Soldiers in the West: A Black Soldiers Anthology*. Corpus Christi, TX: Texas A&M University Press, 2007.

Pennington, Reina. *Amazons to Fighter Pilots - A Biographical Dictionary of Military Women*. Westport, Connecticut: Greenwood Press, 2003.

Tucker, Phillip Thomas. *Cathy Williams: From Slave to Female Buffalo Soldier*. Mechanicsburg, PA: Stackpole Books, 2002.

Native American Leaders

Native Americans are the indigenous peoples who lived in North America when Europeans arrived. Large numbers of indigenous peoples died following the arrival of European settlers, sometimes from diseases, many others through wars or forced migrations. Native American history in the modern period is largely a tale of suffering and upheaval. Cultural loss, separation from ancestral homelands, the trauma of children being taken away and sent to boarding schools and other negative experiences have all left profound marks on Native American memory.

Today there are more than five hundred distinct Indian nations recognized by the United States government. Some of these are designated by the familiar term "tribe," while others are called nations, bands, pueblos, or native villages. A surprising number—over two hundred—are located in Alaska. The rest are located in thirty-five different states. Each is ethnically, culturally, and linguistically unique, although many are closely related. The largest tribes today—in descending order of size—are the Cherokee, the Navajo, the Choctaw, the Sioux, the Chippewa, the Apache, the Blackfoot, the Iroquois, the Pueblo, and the Creek.

In recent times, Native Americans worked hard to recover and preserve cultural traditions that give their communities a sense of identity and purpose. Native American leaders from the past are sometimes figures admired for the courage with which they resisted colonization and for the savvy with which they negotiated English culture while upholding their own. Some significant modern Native American leaders, such as Winona LaDuke, have been passionate about a vision for economics for their community that is rooted in the Native American worldview and in traditional values like respect for the earth. Many would agree that the challenge facing Native American communities today is how to develop tools and concepts that will allow them to address social and economic challenges while remaining within the tribal system and following traditional Native values.

A banner at Oceti Sakowin camp at Standing Rock during the Dacota Access Pipeline protests. Mni Wiconi means Water is Life. (Wikimedia Commons)

Crazy Horse

Lakota leader

Born: 1842?
Died: September 5, 1877; Fort Robinson, Nebraska
Area of achievement: Warfare and conquest

The greatest of the Lakota (Sioux) war chiefs, Crazy Horse led his people in a valiant but futile struggle against domination by the white Americans and white culture. He fought to the last to hold his native land for the Indian people.

Early Life

Crazy Horse's Lakota(Sioux) name was Tashunca-uitko. Little is known of his early life; even the date of his birth and the identity of his mother are uncertain. He was probably born in a Lakota camp along Rapid Creek in the Black Hills during the winter of 1841-1842. Most scholars believe that his mother was a Brule Lakota, the sister of Spotted Tail, a famous Brule chief. His father, also called Crazy Horse, was a highly respected Oglala Lakota holy man. Tashunca-uitko was apparently a curious and solitary child. His hair and his complexion were so fair that he was often mistaken for a captive white child by soldiers and settlers. He was first known as "Light-Haired Boy" and also as "Curly." At the age of ten, he became the protégé of Hump, a young Minneconjou Lakota warrior.

> "*Treat the earth well: it was not given to you by your parents, it was loaned to you by your children. We do not inherit the Earth from our Ancestors, we borrow it from our Children.*"

When he was about twelve years old, Curly killed his first buffalo and rode a newly captured wild horse; to honor his exploits, his people renamed him "His Horse Looking." One event in Crazy Horse's youth seems to have had a particularly powerful impact on the course of his life. When he was about fourteen, His Horse Looking witnessed the senseless murder of Chief Conquering Bear by the troops of Second Lieutenant J. L. Gratton and the subsequent slaughter of Gratton's command by the Lakota. Troubled by what he had seen, His Horse Looking

Crazy Horse (Wikimedia Commons)

went out alone, hobbled his horse, and lay down on a high hill to await a vision. On the third day, weakened by hunger, thirst, and exposure, the boy had a powerful mystical experience that revealed to him that the world in which men lived was only a shadow of the real world.

To enter the real world, one had to dream. When Curly was in that world, everything seemed to dance or float—his horse danced as if it were wild or crazy. In this first crucial vision, His Horse Looking had seen a warrior mounted on his (His Horse Looking's) horse; the warrior had no scalps, wore no paint, was naked except for a breech cloth; he had a small, smooth stone behind one ear. Bullets and arrows could not touch him; the rider's own people crowded around him, trying to stop his dancing horse, but he rode on. The people were lost in a storm; the rider became a part of the storm with a lightning bolt on his cheek and hail spots on his body. The storm faded, and a small red-tailed hawk flew close over the rider; again the people tried to hold the rider back, but still he rode on.

By the time he revealed this vision a few years later, His Horse Looking had already gained a reputation for great bravery and daring. His father and Chips, another holy man, made him a medicine bundle and gave him a red-tailed hawk feather and a smooth stone to wear.

When Curly went into battle thereafter, he wore a small lightning streak on his cheek, hail spots on his body, a breech cloth, a small stone, and a single feather; he did not take scalps. He was never seriously wounded in battle. His Horse Looking's father, in order to honor his son's achievements, bestowed his own name, Crazy Horse, upon the young man (he then took the name Worm) and asserted to his people that the Lakota had a new Crazy Horse, a great warrior with powerful medicine.

The Gratton debacle had one immediate effect other than the vision: It resulted in brutal reprisals by the Bluecoats. On September 3, 1855, shortly after Crazy Horse had experienced the vision, General W. S. Harney attacked the Brule camp in which Crazy Horse was living with Spotted Tail's people. The soldiers killed more than one hundred Indians (most of them women and children), took many prisoners, and captured most of the Lakota horses. Crazy Horse escaped injury and capture but was left with an abiding hatred of the whites. Because the major white invasion of the West did not begin until after the Civil War, Crazy Horse spent his youth living in the traditional ways: moving with the seasons, hunting, and warring with the other plains Indians.

LIFE'S WORK

The solitary boy grew into a strange man who, according to Black Elk,

> would go about the village without noticing people or saying anything.... All the Lakotas (Sioux) liked to dance and sing; but he never joined a dance, and they say nobody heard him sing.... He was a small man among the Lakotas and he was slender and had a thin face and his eyes looked through things and he always seemed to be thinking hard about something. He never wanted many things for himself, and did not have many ponies like a chief. They say that when game was scarce and the people were hungry, he would not eat at all. He was a queer man. Maybe he was always part way into that world of his vision.

Crazy Horse and the Oglala north of the Platte River lived in relative freedom from the white man's interference until 1864. From the early 1860's, however, there was ever-increasing pressure from white settlers and traders on the U.S. government to guarantee the safety of people moving along the Oregon Trail and Santa Fe trail and to open the Bozeman Road that ran through the Lakota country.

The military began preparations early in 1865 to invade the Powder River Indian country; General Patrick E. Connor announced that the Indians north of the Platte "must be hunted like wolves." Thus began what came to be known as Red Cloud's War, named for the Lakota chief who led the Lakota and Cheyenne warriors. General Connor's punitive expedition in 1865 was a failure, as were subsequent efforts to force the free Indians to sign a treaty. In 1866, General Henry B. Carrington fortified and opened the Bozeman Road through Lakota territory. By 1868, having been outsmarted, frustrated, and beaten again and again by Red Cloud's warriors, the United States forces conceded defeat, abandoned the forts, closed the Bozeman Road, and granted the Black Hills and the Powder River country to the Indians forever.

Crazy Horse rose to prominence as a daring and astute leader during the years of Red Cloud's War. He was chosen by the Oglala chiefs to be a "shirt-wearer" or protector of the people. All the other young men chosen were the sons of chiefs; he alone was selected solely on the basis of his accomplishments. Crazy Horse played a central role in the most famous encounter of this war. On December 21, 1866, exposing himself repeatedly to great danger, he decoyed a troop of eighty-one of Colonel Carrington's men, commanded by Captain William J. Fetterman, into a trap outside Fort Phil Kearny. All the soldiers were killed.

Red Cloud's War ended in November, 1868, when the chief signed a treaty that acknowledged that the Powder River and Big Horn country were Indian land into which the white man could not come without permission. The treaty also indicated that the Indians were to live on a reservation on the west side of the Missouri River. Red Cloud and his followers moved onto a reservation, but Crazy Horse and many others refused to sign or to leave their lands for a reservation; Crazy Horse never signed a treaty.

As early as 1870, many whites who were driven by reports of gold in the Black Hills began to venture illegally into Indian territory. Surveyors for the Northern Pacific Railroad protected by United States troops also invaded the Black Hills in order to chart the course of their railway through Indian land. Crazy Horse, who became

Representation of a fight scene with Crazy Horse in the Battle of Little Bighorn, drawn by the Oglala-Lakota-Sioux Amos Bad Heart Bull (Tatanka Chante Shicha) after 1890. (Wikimedia Commons)

the war chief of the Oglala after Red Cloud moved onto the reservation, led numerous successful raids against the survey parties and finally drove them from his lands. The surveyors returned in 1873; this time they were protected by a formidable body of troops commanded by Lieutenant Colonel George A. Custer.

In spite of a series of sharp attacks, Crazy Horse was unable to defeat Custer, and the surveyors finished their task. In 1874, Custer was back in Indian territory; he led an expedition of twelve hundred men purportedly to gather military and scientific information. He reported that the hills were filled with gold "from the roots on down"; the fate of the Indians and their sacred hills was sealed. Not even the military genius of their war chief, their skill and bravery, and their clear title to the land could save them from the greed and power of the white men.

During the years between the signing of the 1868 treaty and the full-scale invasion of Indian lands in 1876, Crazy Horse apparently fell in love with a Lakota woman named Black Buffalo Woman, but she was taken from him through deceit and married another man, No Water. Crazy Horse and Black Buffalo Woman maintained their attachment to each other over a period of years, causing some divisiveness among the Lakota and resulting in the near-fatal shooting of Crazy Horse by No Water. Crazy Horse eventually married an Oglala named Tasina Sapewin (Black Shawl) who bore him a daughter. He named the child They Are Afraid of Her, and when she died a few years later, he was stricken with grief.

Because of the reports concerning the great mineral wealth of the Black Hills, the U.S. government began to try to force all the Indians to move onto reservations. On February 7, 1876, the War Department ordered General Philip Sheridan to commence operations against the Lakota living off of reservations. The first conflict in this deadly campaign occurred March 17, when General George Crook's advance column under Colonel Joseph J. Reynolds attacked a peaceful camp of Northern Cheyennes and Oglala Lakota who were on their way from the Red Cloud Agency to their hunting grounds. The survivors fled to Crazy Horse's camp.

Crazy Horse took them in, gave them food and shelter, and promised them that "we are going to fight the white man again." Crazy Horse's chance came in June, when a Cheyenne hunting party sighted a column of Bluecoats camped in the valley of the Rosebud River. Crazy Horse had studied the soldiers' ways of fighting for years, and he was prepared for this battle. General Crook and his pony soldiers were no match for the Lakota and Cheyenne guided by Crazy Horse. Crook retreated under cover of darkness to his base camp on Goose Creek.

After the Battle of Rosebud (June 17), the Indians moved west to the valley of the Greasy Grass (Little Bighorn) River. Blackfoot, Hunkpapa, Sans Arc, Minneconjous, Brule, and Oglala Lakota were there, as well as the Cheyenne—perhaps as many as fifteen thousand Indians, including five thousand warriors. The soldiers had originally planned a three-pronged campaign to ensnare and destroy the Indians. Crook's withdrawal, however, forced General Alfred Terry to revise the plan. On June 22, he ordered Colonel John Gibbon to go back to the Bighorn River and to march south along it to the Little Bighorn River. Custer and the Seventh Cavalry were to go along the Rosebud parallel to Gibbon and catch the Indians in between. General Terry, with the remaining forces, would trail them and provide whatever support was necessary. General Terry expected that Gibbon and Custer would converge and engage the enemy on June 26.

General Custer and his troops arrived on June 25, and Custer elected to attack the Indian encampment without waiting for Gibbon's column. His rash decision was fatal to him and to the Seventh Cavalry. The Lakota and

Cheyenne, led by Crazy Horse and Gall, Sitting Bull's lieutenant, crushed Custer; more than 250 soldiers died. Perhaps Crazy Horse and Gall could have defeated the troops of Gibbon and Terry as well, but they were not committed to an all-out war, as were the whites, and they had had enough killing, so they moved on, leaving the soldiers to bury their dead.

The Battle of the Little Bighorn is recognized as a great moment in the history of the Lakota nation, but it also proved to be a sad one, for it confirmed the U.S. government's conviction that in spite of the Treaty of 1868, the free Indians must be either confined to a reservation or annihilated. In the brutal days that were to follow, Crazy Horse clearly emerged as the single most important spiritual and military leader of the Lakota.

The federal government's response was swift: On August 15, Congress enacted a new law that required the Indians to give up all rights to the Powder River country and the Black Hills. Red Cloud and Spotted Tail succumbed to what they took to be inevitable and signed documents acknowledging that they accepted the new law. Sitting Bull and Gall fought against the forces of General Crook and Colonel Nelson Miles during the remainder of 1876 but decided to take their people to Canada in the spring of 1877. Crazy Horse alone resolved to stay on his own lands in the sacred Black Hills.

General Crook led an enormous army of infantry, cavalry, and artillery from the south through the Powder River country in pursuit of Crazy Horse, and Colonel Miles led his army from the north, looking for the Oglala war chief. Crazy Horse was forced to move his village from one place to another in order to avoid the Bluecoats. He had little ammunition or food, the winter was bitterly cold, and his people were weary. In December, he approached Colonel Miles's outpost and sent a small party of chiefs and warriors with a flag of truce to find out what the colonel's intentions were. The party was attacked as it approached the outpost; only three Lakota survived. Miles's brutal intentions were made quite clear, and Crazy Horse was forced to flee again.

Colonel Miles caught up with the Lakota on January 8, 1877, at Battle Butte; in spite of his lack of ammunition and the weakened condition of his warriors, Crazy Horse was able, through bravery and superior tactics, to defeat Miles. Crazy Horse and his band escaped through the Wolf Mountains to the familiar country of the Little Powder River. The soldiers decided to cease their military operations until spring, but they redoubled their efforts to persuade the Indians to surrender. Numerous emissaries were sent throughout the northern lands with pack trains of food and gifts to tempt the suffering Lakota and Cheyenne into coming in to the security of the agencies.

Many small bands yielded to these entreaties, but Crazy Horse only listened politely and sent the messengers home. His fame and his symbolic value to the Indians grew daily; the longer he resisted, the more important he became to the thousands of Indians now confined to reservations. When Spotted Tail himself came to entice them to give up, Crazy Horse went off alone into the deep snows of the mountains in order to give his people the freedom to decide their own fate. Most chose to stay with their leader, but Spotted Tail did persuade Big Foot to bring his Minneconjous in when spring came.

In April, General Crook sent Red Cloud to plead with Crazy Horse and to promise him that if he surrendered, the Lakota would be given a reservation in the Powder River country, where they could live and hunt in peace. At last, Crazy Horse gave in; the suffering of his people was so great, the prospects of renewed conflict with Crook and Miles so grim, and the promise of a Powder River reservation so tempting that he led his band to the Red Cloud Agency, arriving in an almost triumphal procession witnessed by thousands on May 5, 1877.

Predictably, Crazy Horse did not like living at the agency, and General Crook did not make good on his promise of a Powder River reservation. Black Shawl died, and Crazy Horse married Nellie Larrabee, the daughter of a trader. The more restive Crazy Horse became, the more concerned the government became, and the more vulnerable the chief was to the plots of his enemies. Wild rumors that Crazy Horse planned to escape or to murder General Crook circulated.

The government officials decided that it would be best to arrest and confine the war chief. On September 4, 1877, eight companies of cavalry and four hundred Indians, led by Red Cloud, left Fort Robinson to arrest Crazy Horse and deliver him to the fort. Crazy Horse attempted to flee but was overtaken and agreed to go and talk with Crook. When it became clear to him that he was not being taken to a conference but to prison, Crazy Horse drew his knife and tried to escape. He was restrained by Little Big Man and other followers of Red Cloud, and Private William Gentles bayoneted him. He died during the early hours of September 5; his father, Worm, was at his side. Crazy Horse's parents were allowed to take the body; they rode into the hills and buried their son in a place known only to them.

Later that fall, the Lakota were forced to begin a journey eastward to the Missouri River and a new reservation/prison. Among the thousands of Indians were

Crazy Horse's Oglala. After approximately seventy-five miles of travel, the Oglala, two thousand strong, broke from the line and raced for Canada and freedom. The small cavalry contingent could only watch as these Lakota fled to join Sitting Bull—manifesting, in their refusal to submit to the white man, the spirit of Crazy Horse.

Significance

Crazy Horse, like numerous other Indian patriots, was a martyr to the westward expansion of the United States, to the unity and technological superiority of the white culture, to its assumed racial and cultural superiority, and to the greed of white Americans. He also seems to have been a truly exceptional and admirable man; he was the greatest warrior and general of a people to whom war was a way of life. He provided a powerful example of integrity and independence for the Indians during a very difficult period of their history; he never attended a peace council with the whites, never signed a treaty, never even considered giving up his lands: "One does not sell the earth upon which the people walk." Furthermore, he seems to have been a basically selfless man who was genuinely devoted to the greater good of his people, to protecting his native land and his traditional way of life. To quote Black Elk:

> He was brave and good and wise. He never wanted anything but to save his people, and he fought the Wasichus (the whites) only when they came to kill us in our own country.... They could not kill him in battle. They had to lie to him and kill him that way.

When Crazy Horse was born, the Lakota were a strong, proud, and free people; they were skilled horsemen and masters of war and hunting. The rhythms of their lives were the rhythms of the seasons and of the game they hunted. They venerated nature and cherished individual freedom and achievement. When Crazy Horse died, the Lakota were still proud, but they were no longer truly strong or free. Freedom, independence, and cultural integrity were realities for Crazy Horse in his youth, but particularly after the tragic battle at Wounded Knee in December, 1890, freedom and independence and integrity as a people have only been dreams for the Lakota—dreams in which the legend and spirit of Crazy Horse, fierce, intelligent, indomitable, continue to play a vital part, as is evidenced by Peter Matthiessen's choice of a title for his angry and eloquent 1983 study of the contemporary struggles of the Lakota: *In the Spirit of Crazy Horse*.

Hal Holladay

Further Reading

Ambrose, Stephen E. *Crazy Horse and Custer: The Parallel Lives of Two American Warriors*. New York: Anchor Books, 1996. Ambrose, a historian who has written several popular biographies and military histories, examines the similarities between Crazy Horse and Custer.

Andrist, Ralph K. *The Long Death: The Last Days of the Plains Indians*. New York: Macmillan, 1964. The story of the military conquest of the plains Indians, the Lakota as well as others. A vivid, meticulous, and well-written survey. Excellent maps.

Brown, Dee. *Bury My Heart at Wounded Knee: An Indian History of the American West*. New York: Holt, Rinehart and Winston, 1971. A revisionist history of the West from 1860 to 1890 told from an Indian point of view. Crucial to a full understanding of American history and the destruction of the culture and civilization of the American Indian. Crazy Horse's story is one of many.

Connell, Evan S. *Son of the Morning Star: Custer and the Little Bighorn*. San Francisco: North Point Press, 1984. An intelligent and thorough reconstruction of what might have happened and why at the Little Bighorn on June 25, 1876. A fascinating study of the major participants in that historic battle, focusing on Custer.

Hinman, Eleanor. "Oglala Sources on the Life of Crazy Horse." *Nebraska History* 57, no. 1 (1976). Interviews with Oglala Indians who witnessed various events in the life of Crazy Horse. Provides particularly interesting insights into his conduct in battle, his feud with No Water, and his death.

Josephy, Alvin M., Jr. *The Patriot Chiefs: A Chronicle of American Indian Resistance*. New York: Viking Press, 1958. The life stories of outstanding Indian leaders, including Crazy Horse, Tecumseh, and Chief Joseph. A good brief biography. Places Crazy Horse's struggle in the context of the heroic and tragic resistance of Indians to the white man throughout North America.

Marshall, Joseph, III. *The Journey of Crazy Horse: A Lakota History*. New York: Viking Press, 2004. Marshall, a Lakota who was raised on the Rosebud Sioux Reservation, drew on the recollections of his grandfather and other oral histories to produce this biography.

Neihardt, John G. *Black Elk Speaks*. Lincoln: University of Nebraska Press, 1961. A fascinating document that contains the life story of an Oglala holy man as told by himself. Black Elk was a member of Crazy Horse's tribe and was present at the Little Bighorn, as well as at

Fort Robinson when Crazy Horse was killed. Invaluable insights into the Lakota culture and way of life.

Olson, James C. *Red Cloud and the Sioux Problem*. Lincoln: University of Nebraska Press, 1965. Well-documented appraisal of Indian affairs in the Western plains during the 1860's and the 1870's. Thorough account of relations between the Lakota and the federal government. Judicious treatment of contending leaders.

Sajna, Mike. *Crazy Horse: The Life Behind the Legend*. New York: John Wiley & Sons 2000. Detailed biography, offering new perspectives on Crazy Horse's role in the battle at the Little Bighorn and his eventual surrender and murder.

Sandoz, Mari. *Crazy Horse: The Strange Man of the Oglalas*. New York: Alfred A. Knopf, 1941. A comprehensive and authoritative biography in which the author attempts to tell not only the chief's story but also that of his people and culture. Told from Crazy Horse's point of view.

Vaughn, Jesse W. *Indian Fights: New Facts on Seven Encounters*. Norman: University of Oklahoma Press, 1966. A flawed study of seven significant battles that occurred between 1864 and 1877 in Wyoming and Montana. Vaughn's accounts of the Fetterman Massacre and Major Reno's part in the Battle of the Little Bighorn are quite useful.

GERONIMO

Apache leader

Born: June 1, 1829
Died: February 17, 1909; Fort Sill, Oklahoma
Area of Achievement: Warfare

Through two decades, Geronimo was the most feared and vilified person in the Southwest, but in his old age, he became a freak attraction at fairs and expositions. His maligned and misunderstood career epitomized the troubles of a withering Apache culture struggling to survive in a hostile modern world.

EARLY LIFE

Although the precise date and location of Geronimo's (jeh-RAHN-ih-moh) birth are not known, he was most likely born around June, 1829, near the head of the Gila River in a part of the Southwest then controlled by Mexico. Named Goyathlay (One Who Yawns) by his Behonkohe parents, the legendary Apache warrior later came to be called Geronimo—a name taken from the sound that terrified Mexican soldiers allegedly cried when calling on Saint Jerome to protect them from his relentless charge.

Geronimo's early life, like that of other Apache youth, was filled with complex religious ritual and ceremony. From the placing of amulets on his cradle to guard him against early death to the ceremonial putting on of the first moccasins, Geronimo's relatives prepared their infant for Apache life, teaching him the origin myths of his people and the legends of supernatural beings and benevolent mountain spirits that hid in the caverns of their homeland.

Through ritual observances and instruction, Geronimo learned about Usen, a remote and nebulous god who, though unconcerned with petty quarrels among men, was the Life Giver and provider for his people. "When Usen created the Apaches," Geronimo later asserted, "he also created their homes in the West. He gave to them such

Geronimo (Library of Congress)

grain, fruits, and game as they needed to eat.... He gave to them a climate and all they needed for clothing and shelter was at hand." Geronimo's religious heritage taught him to be self-sufficient, to love and revere his mountain homeland, and never to betray a promise made with oath and ceremony.

Geronimo grew into adulthood during a brief period of peace, a rare interlude that interrupted the chronic wars between the Apache and Mexican peoples. Even in times of peace, however, Apache culture placed a priority on the skills of warfare. Through parental instruction and childhood games, Geronimo learned how to hunt, hide, track, and shoot—necessary survival skills in an economy based upon game, wild fruits, and booty taken from neighboring peoples.

Geronimo also heard the often repeated stories of conquests of his heroic grandfather Mahko, an Apache chief renowned for his great size, strength, and valor in battle. Like his grandfather, Geronimo had unusual physical prowess and courage. Tall and slender, strong and quick, Geronimo proved at an early age to be a good provider for his mother, whom he supported following his father's premature death, and later for his bride, Alope, whom he acquired from her father for "a herd of ponies" stolen most likely from unsuspecting Mexican victims. By his early twenties, Geronimo (still called Goyathlay) was a member of the council of warriors, a proven booty taker, a husband, and a father of three.

Life's Work

In 1850, a band of Mexican scalp hunters raided an Apache camp while the warriors were away. During the ensuing massacre, Geronimo's mother, wife, and three children were slain. Shortly after this tragedy, Geronimo had a religious experience that figured prominently in his subsequent life. As he later reported the incident, while in a trancelike state, a voice called his name four times (the magic number among the Apache) and then informed him, "No gun can ever kill you. I will take the bullets from the guns of the Mexicans, so they will have nothing but powder. And I will guide your arrows." After receiving this gift of power, Geronimo's vengeance against Mexicans was equaled by his confidence that harm would not come his way.

While still unknown to most Americans, during the 1850's, Geronimo rose among the ranks of the Apache warriors. A participant in numerous raids into Mexico, Geronimo fought bravely under the Apache chief Cochise. Although wounded on several occasions, Geronimo remained convinced that no bullet could kill him. It was during this period that he changed his name from Goyathlay to Geronimo.

> "I cannot think we are useless or Usen would not have created us. He created all tribes of men and certainly had a righteous purpose in creating each."

War between the U.S. government and the Apache first erupted in 1861 following a kidnapping-charge incident involving Cochise. The war lingered for nearly a dozen years until Cochise and General Oliver Otis Howard signed a truce. According to the terms of the agreement, the mountain homeland of the Chiricahua (one of the tribes that made up the Apache and Geronimo's tribe) was set aside as a reservation, on which the Chiricahua promised to remain.

Following Cochise's death in 1874, the United States attempted to relocate the Chiricahua to the San Carlos Agency in the parched bottomlands of the Gila River. Although some Apache accepted relocation, Geronimo led a small band off the reservation into the Sierra Madre range in Mexico. From this base, Geronimo's warriors conducted raids into the United States, hitting wagon trains and ranches for the supplies needed for survival.

In 1877, for the first and only time in his life, Geronimo was captured by John Clum of the United States Army. After spending some time in a guardhouse in San Carlos, Geronimo was released, being told not to leave the reservation. Within a year, however, he was again in Mexico. Although a fugitive, he was blamed in the American press for virtually all crimes committed by Apache "renegades" of the reservation.

Upon the promise of protection, Geronimo voluntarily returned to the San Carlos Agency in 1879. This time, he remained two years until an unfortunate incident involving the death of Noch-ay-del-klinne, a popular Apache religious prophet, triggered another escape into the Sierra Madre. In 1882, Geronimo daringly attempted a raid into Arizona to rescue the remainder of his people on the reservation and to secure for himself reinforcements for his forces hiding in Mexico. This campaign, which resulted in the forced abduction of many unwilling Apache women and children, brought heavy losses to his band and nearly cost Geronimo his life. The newspaper

Geronimo (right) and his warriors from left to right: Yanozha (Geronimos's brother-in-law), Chappo (Geronimo's son of 2nd wife) and Fun (Yanozha's half brother) in 1886 (Wikimedia Commons)

coverage of the campaign also made Geronimo the most despised and feared villain in the United States.

In May, 1883, General George Crook of the United States Army crossed into Mexico in search of Geronimo. Not wanting war, Geronimo sent word to Crook of his willingness to return to the reservation if his people were guaranteed just treatment. Crook consented, and Geronimo persuaded his band to retire to San Carlos.

Geronimo, however, never adjusted to life on the reservation. Troubled by newspaper headlines demanding his execution and resentful of reservation rules (in particular, the prohibition against alcoholic drink), Geronimo in the spring of 1885 planned a final breakaway from the San Carlos Agency. With his typical ingenuity, Geronimo led his 144 followers off the reservation. Cutting telegraph lines behind him, he eluded the cavalry and crossed into Mexico, finding sanctuary in his old Sierra Madre refuge. Although pursued by an army of five thousand regulars and five hundred Apache scouts, Geronimo avoided capture until September, 1886, when he voluntarily surrendered to General Nelson Miles. (He had agreed to a surrender to General George Crook in March but had escaped his troops.)

Rejoicing that the Apache wars were over, the army loaded Geronimo and his tribesmen on railroad cars and shipped them first to Fort Pickens in Florida and then to the Mount Vernon Barracks in Alabama. Unaccustomed to the warm, humid climate, so unlike the high, dry country of their birth, thousands of the Apache captives died of tuberculosis and other diseases. In 1894, after the government rejected another appeal to allow their return to Arizona, the Kiowa and Comanche offered their former Apache foes a part of their reservation near Fort Sill, Oklahoma.

Geronimo spent the remainder of his life on the Oklahoma reservation. Adapting quickly to the white man's economic system, the aged Apache warrior survived by growing watermelons and selling his now infamous signature to curious autograph seekers. Although the government technically still viewed him as a prisoner of war, the army permitted Geronimo to attend, under guard, the international fairs and expositions at Buffalo, Omaha, and St. Louis. In 1905, Theodore Roosevelt even invited him to Washington, D.C., to attend the inaugural presidential parade. Wherever Geronimo went, he attracted great crowds and made handsome profits by selling autographs, buttons, hats, and photographs of himself.

In February, 1909, while returning home from selling bows and arrows in nearby Lawton, Oklahoma, an inebriated Geronimo fell from his horse into a creek bed. For several hours, Geronimo's body lay exposed. Three days later, the Apache octogenarian died of pneumonia. As promised, no bullet ever killed him.

Significance

The Industrial Age of the late nineteenth century altered the life patterns of American farmers and entrepreneurs, women and laborers. No groups, however, were more affected by the forces of modernization than were the Native American Indians. Geronimo's tragic career as warrior and prisoner epitomized the inevitable demise of an ancient Apache culture trapped in a web of white man's history.

Although a stubbornly independent and uncompromising warrior, Geronimo symbolized to countless Americans the treacherous savagery of a vicious race that could not be trusted. Highly conscious of his wrath and unrelenting hatred, the American public never knew the deeply religious family man who yearned to abide in his mountain homeland.

During his last twenty-three years of captivity, the legend of Geronimo grew, even as the public's hatred of the once-powerful Apache mellowed into admiration. Always a good provider, Geronimo established for himself a profitable business by peddling souvenirs and performing stunts at Wild West shows. A living artifact of a world that no longer existed, Geronimo became the comic image of the tamed American Indian finally brought into white man's civilization.

Terry D. Bilhartz

FURTHER READING

Adams, Alexander B. *Geronimo: A Biography.* New York: G. P. Putnam's Sons, 1971. A well-researched history of the Apache wars that contains much material on Mangas Coloradas, Cochise, and other warriors as well as Geronimo. Replete with documentation of the connivance, blunders, and savagery that characterized the removal of the Apache from their homelands, this biography exposes the limitations of General Nelson Miles and the inexperience of the white leadership in Indian affairs.

Betzinez, Jason, with Wilbur Sturtevant Nye. *I Fought with Geronimo.* Harrisburg, Pa.: Stackpole Books, 1960. Another first-hand narrative account of the Apache wars written by the son of Geronimo's first cousin. Includes stories told more than half a century after the event. An entertaining primary source, but it must be used with caution.

Brown, Dee. "Geronimo." *American History Illustrated* 15 (May, 1980): 12-21; 15 (July, 1980): 31-45. The best article-length introduction to the life of Geronimo. A lively and sympathetic overview of the career of this clever Apache warrior.

Clum, Woodworth. *Apache Agent: The Story of John P. Clum.* Boston: Houghton Mifflin, 1936. Reprint. Lincoln: University of Nebraska Press, 1978. A story of the only man who ever captured Geronimo. Written from the notes of John Clum, a man who hated Geronimo with a passion. Biased yet entertaining account.

Cozzens, Peter, ed. *Eyewitnesses to the Indian Wars, 1865-1890: The Struggle for Apacheria.* Harrisburg, Pa.: Stackpole Books, 2001-Â Â Â Â . This book is the first in a five-volume series containing army reports, diaries, news articles, and other contemporaneous accounts of Indian wars. This volume focuses on military campaigns against the Apaches, with part five, "Chasing Geronimo, 1885-1886," containing accounts of Geronimo's escape and eventual surrender.

Davis, Britton. *The Truth About Geronimo.* New Haven, Conn.: Yale University Press, 1929, 1963. An entertaining narrative filled with humorous and thrilling incidents written by an author who spent three years in the United States Army attempting to locate and capture this Apache warrior.

Debo, Angie. *Geronimo: The Man, His Time, His Place.* Norman: University of Oklahoma Press, 1976. The best of the many Geronimo biographies. Carefully researched and documented, this balanced account portrays Geronimo neither as villain nor as hero, but as a maligned and misunderstood individual trapped in an increasingly hostile environment. Highly recommended.

Faulk, Odie B. *The Geronimo Campaign.* New York: Oxford University Press, 1969. A reassessment of the military campaign that ended with the surrender of Geronimo in 1886. Includes much information collected by the son of Lieutenant Charles B. Gatewood, who arranged the surrender and was one of the few white men Geronimo trusted.

Geronimo. *Geronimo: His Own Story.* Edited by S. M. Barrett and Frederick Turner. New York: Duffield, 1906. The personal autobiography dictated by Geronimo to Barrett in 1905. A chronicle of Geronimo's grievances, in particular against the Mexican nationals. Includes informative sections on Apache religion, methods in dealing with crimes, ceremonies, festivals, and appreciation of nature.

Kraft, Louis. *Gatewood and Geronimo.* Albuquerque: University of New Mexico Press, 2000. A biography of Geronimo and Lieutenant Charles B. Gatewood, a cavalryman posted in Arizona who was criticized by the military and civilians for his equitable treatment of Apaches.

CHIEF JOSEPH

Nez Perce leader

Born: March 3, 1840; Walloaw Valley, Oregon
Died: September 21, 1904; Colville Indian Reservation, Washington
Area of Achievement: Warfare

The leader of his people in the Nez Perce War of 1877, Chief Joseph attempted to retain for his people the freedoms enjoyed prior to white American interest in their lands. Although he ultimately failed to preserve his people's independence, he became an enduring symbol of the fortitude and resilience of Native Americans.

Chief Joseph (National Archives and Records Administration)

EARLY LIFE

Chief Joseph (Heinmot Tooyalakekt in his native tongue, which translates as Thunder-Rolling-in-the-Mountains) was born to Old Joseph (Tuekakas) and Asenoth. His exact birthdate is unknown, but he was baptized Ephraim on April 12, 1840, by the Reverend Mr. Henry H. Spalding, who maintained a Presbyterian mission at Lapwai in the heart of Nez Perce country. This area, which comprises parts of Idaho, Oregon, and Washington, contains some of the most desirable land in the United States. As such, white Americans desired the land upon which the Nez Perce and other bands of Indians lived.

In 1855, the U.S. government greatly reduced the holdings of all tribes and bands in the northwestern United States in a series of treaties at the Council of Walla Walla, called by the governor of the Washington Territory, Isaac Stevens. In those treaties, the Neemeepoo (meaning the people) or Nez Perce (pronounced nez purse) agreed to what amounted to a 50 percent reduction of their territory. The Nez Perce were able to keep this much of their land because the whites were not yet interested in the wild and remote country of west-central Idaho and northwestern Oregon. The Nez Perce had been exposed to Christianity as early as 1820. The existence of Christian names indicates that many practiced that religion. Chief Joseph was, or was generally believed to have been, baptized and named Ephraim. It would fall to him, a kind and gentle man, to deal with the problems—initially encroachment and then expropriation—which threatened the lands of his fathers.

The troubles of the Nez Perce began in 1861, when gold in quantity was discovered along the Orofino Creek, a tributary of the Clearwater. Old Joseph attempted to keep the prospectors from the land but finally accepted the inevitable and sought to supervise rather than prohibit the activity. This plan failed. Once the area had been opened, many whites entered. In violation of the agreements, and of the treaties of 1855, which prohibited such white encroachments, some whites turned to farming.

The results were surprising. The government, rather than forcing the whites to leave, proposed an additional reduction of the Nez Perce lands. The federal government indicated that as much as 75 percent of the holdings should be made available for white settlement. Old Joseph refused; his refusal apparently split the Nez Perce peoples. Some of them agreed to the reduction. Aleiya, called Lawyer by the whites, signed the agreement that the Joseph faction of the Nez Perce would refer to as the thief treaty. Hereafter, the Nez Perce were divided into the treaty and nontreaty bands. Old Joseph refused to leave the Wallowa Valley, where his nontreaty Nez Perce bred and raised the Appaloosa horse.

Old Joseph died in 1871, and, at his parting, he reminded his eldest son, Heinmot Tooyalakekt, or Young Joseph, Chief Joseph was as adamant in his refusal to sell or part with the land as had been his father, but he realized the power and inconstancy of the U.S. government. In 1873, President Ulysses S. Grant issued an executive order dividing the area that the whites were settling between the whites and the Nez Perce. In 1875, however, Grant opened the entire region to white settlement. In 1876, he sent a commission to see Chief Joseph. The decision had been made to offer Joseph's band of non-treaty Nez Perce land in the Oklahoma Indian Territory for all of their Idaho holdings.

What transpired as a result of this decision has been termed by Jacob P. Dunn, Jr., in *Massacres in the Mountains* (1886), "the meanest, most contemptible, least justifiable thing that the United States was ever guilty of...." Chief Joseph refused the offer to move to Oklahoma. General Oliver Otis Howard arrived with orders to enforce the presidential decision. General Howard proposed a swift compliance with those orders. Joseph realized that his Nez Perce could not long stand against a government and an army determined to take their land and move them. Accordingly, a council of chiefs, including Joseph's younger brother Ollokot (a fine warrior), White Bird, Looking Glass, and the Wallowa prophet, Toohoolhoolzote, reached the decision to go to Canada rather than to Oklahoma. General Howard, however, declared that "the soldiers will be there to drive you onto the reservation...."

LIFE'S WORK

The Nez Perce War of 1877 is misnamed. It would be more appropriate to label it a chase. It is the story of Chief Joseph's attempt to lead his people to the safety of Canada, where the geography and the climate were more similar to the traditional lands than were those of Oklahoma. The United States Army, under orders to deliver the Nez Perce to the Indian Territory, would pursue Chief Joseph's band during the 111-day war/chase that eventually found Joseph winding over fourteen hundred miles through the mountains. His attempt to elude the military would fail because of nineteenth century technology rather than his lack of ability.

> "If the white man wants to live in peace with the Indian he can live in peace. There need be no trouble. Treat all men alike. Give them the same laws. Give them all an even chance to live and grow. All men were made by the same Great Spirit Chief. They are all brothers. The earth is the mother of all people, and all people should have equal rights upon it."

Hostilities began when a member of White Bird's band of Nez Perce, Wahlitits, wanting to avenge the death of his father at the hands of white men, and two other youths, killed four white men. Apparently, some whites were of the opinion that only a war would guarantee the removal of the Nez Perce from the land, and some of them had been trying for some time to provoke that war. The men killed by Wahlitits had been the first white men killed by Nez Perce in a generation.

Joseph's reaction to the killings was one of regret and the realization that only flight would preserve his people. General Howard's reaction was to move immediately not only against White Bird's people but also against all the non-treaty Nez Perce. The initial engagement on June 17, 1877, was between two troops of the First Cavalry (about ninety men) under Captains David Perry and Joel Trimble. The cavalry was accompanied by eleven civilian volunteers. One of those civilian volunteers fired at the Nez Perce truce team. This action led to a short, unplanned, disorganized fight during which the Nez Perce, under Ollokot, killed thirty-four cavalry. (Important also was the capture of sixty-three rifles and many pistols.)

This initial defeat led Howard, fearing a general uprising of all Nez Perce—treaty and non-treaty alike—to call for reinforcements. Troops from all over the United States were quickly dispatched, including an infantry unit from Atlanta, Georgia, to the Washington Territory. Joseph's strategy was to seek protection from the Bitterroot Mountain range, where traditional cavalry tactics would be neutralized. Leading his approximately five hundred women and children and 250 warriors, he moved over the Lolo Trail, crossed the Bitterroots, and then, hoping to avoid detection, moved southward to the vicinity of the Yellowstone National Park, which he crossed in August, 1877. Joseph then swung northward into present-day Montana, hoping to reach Canada undetected. Seeking the security of the Bearpaw Mountains, Joseph moved his people as quickly as the women and young could travel. They were not quick enough: The Bearpaws would be the location of the final encounter with the military.

Joseph was not a military strategist; Ollokot was. Joseph urged that they try to reach Canada. Ollokot, Toohoolhoolzote, Looking Glass, and other chiefs preferred to fight. Battles had been joined several times along the route. At the Clearwater (July 11), at Big Hole (August 9-10), at Camas Meadows (August 16), at Canyon Creek (September 13), and at Cows Creek (September 23), sharp engagements were fought. Each resulted in Joseph's band eluding capture but with irreplaceable losses. The military, meanwhile, was receiving reinforcements in large numbers. Especially important was the arrival of Colonel Nelson Miles with nearly six hundred men, including elements of the Second and Seventh cavalries.

About thirty miles from the Canadian border, the Nez Perce halted, believing that they had succeeded in eluding the army and had the time to rest. Joseph was wrong: The telegraph and the railroad had outflanked him. Colonel Miles caught the Nez Perce unprepared on September 30, on the rolling plains of the Bearpaw Mountains. Joseph's band, hopelessly outnumbered, held out until October 4. After a hastily convened, makeshift council, Joseph decided to surrender. On October 5, he rode to the headquarters of Miles and General Howard, who had arrived in force the day before, and handed his rifle to Howard, who, in turn, passed it to Colonel Miles—still in command of the operation.

Joseph's surrender was apparently based upon an assumption that his people could return to the Lapwai. This was not to be. The Nez Perce were loaded onto boxcars and transported to the Oklahoma Indian Territory. In this new climate and country, many of the remaining Nez Perce died. Joseph repeatedly begged for permission to return to the northwestern hunting grounds. Partial success came in 1885, when Joseph was allowed to return with his people to the Colville Reservation in Washington. Thereafter, every attempt on Joseph's part to effect a return to the Lapwai was unsuccessful. Joseph died on September 21, 1904, on the Colville Indian Reservation.

Significance

Chief Joseph of the Nez Perce was a dignified leader of his people. A man who loved the land of his ancestors, he attempted to retain it. His defiance of the U.S. government was a gallant, almost successful, effort. His failure marked the end of the wars of the Northwest and was the last important Indian resistance except for the Battle at Wounded Knee Creek. The removal of the Nez Perce to reservations marked the end of freedom as the American Indians had known it. As Joseph said, "you might as well expect the rivers to run backward as that any man who was born free should be content when penned up and denied liberty."

Richard J. Amundson

Further Reading

Allard, William Albert. "Chief Joseph." *National Geographic* 151 (March, 1977): 408-434. A well-illustrated, concise, balanced, readily available source.

Andrist, Ralph K. *The Long Death: The Last Days of the Plains Indians*. New York: Macmillan, 1964. Includes a well-written, sympathetic chapter on the Nez Perce. Especially valuable for detailing the reasons for the decision to go to Canada.

Beal, Merrill D. *"I Will Fight No More Forever": Chief Joseph and the Nez Perce War*. Seattle: University of Washington Press, 1963. A carefully written, well-illustrated account that gives special attention to the hostilities.

Brown, Dee. *Bury My Heart at Wounded Knee: An Indian History of the American West*. New York: Holt, Rinehart and Winston, 1970. A classic study of white-Indian relationships that must be read by the serious student. It contains an excellent account of Chief Joseph and his attempted flight to Canada. White motivation in the contest is perhaps overstated.

Chalmers, Harvey, II. *The Last Stand of the Nez Perce: Destruction of a People*. New York: Twayne, 1962. Contains a valuable glossary of characters and a balanced account of the hostilities.

Dunn, Jacob P., Jr. *Massacres of the Mountains: A History of the Indian Wars of the Far West*. New York: Harper & Brothers, 1886. A chapter devoted to what Dunn argues was an injustice committed by the U.S. government. Many later sources rely upon his analysis.

Josephy, Alvin M., Jr. *The Patriot Chiefs: A Chronicle of American Indian Leadership*. Harmondsworth, England: Penguin Books, 1958. One of the few sources that deals with Chief Joseph as an individual. The account of the war is excellent.

Miles, Nelson A. *Personal Recollections and Observances*. Chicago: Werner, 1896. The final days of the Nez Perce recounted by the officer in the field commanding the United States military. Unsympathetic toward Joseph's motivation.

Moeller, Bill, and Jan Moeller. *Chief Joseph and the Nez Perces: A Photographic History*. Missoula, Mont.: Mountain Press, 1995. Color photos and text depict the places in Idaho and Montana where the Nez Perce Indians camped, followed trials, and sought refuge from government troops between June and October, 1877.

Moulton, Candy. *American Heroes: Chief Joseph, Guardian of the People*. New York: Forge Books, 2005. Well-documented biography, recounting Chief Joseph's attempt to lead his people to safety in Canada and his subsequent diplomatic initiatives to regain his people's homeland.

Park, Edwards. "Big Hole: Still a Gaping Wound to the Nez Perce." *Smithsonian* 9 (May, 1978): 92-99. Deals with a serious setback during the great chase of 1877.

Kamehameha I

King of the Hawaiian Islands (r. 1804-1819)

Born: c. 1736; Kohala, Hawaii
Died: May 8 or 14, 1819; Kona, Hawaii
Areas of Achievement: Government and politics, military

Through his prowess, astute leadership in battle, and adroit use of European advisers, ships, and weapons, Kamehameha overcame his rival and united the Hawaiian Islands for the first time in their history. In the process, he

Kamehameha I (Wikimedia Commons)

made himself their king and founded a dynasty that helped the islands preserve their independence from European and American rule through most of the nineteenth century.

Early Life

Because Kamehameha (kah-may-HAH-may-HAH)—whose Hawaiian name means the "lonely one" or the "silent one"—was born before the European arrival in the Hawaiian Islands, and therefore before there were any written records, scholars must rely on native tradition for information about his birth. Estimates of his birth year vary from 1736 to 1758, but the modern consensus favors 1758. Kamehameha's mother was Kekuiapoiwa, and his father was Keoua, although there is a story that his real father was Kahekili, king of Maui.

Kamehameha was described by European contemporaries as being well over six feet tall, athletically built, and savage in appearance. He was a member of the chiefly caste, the *alii*, who ruled despotically over the common people. The *alii* were considered to have descended directly from the gods and possessed varying degrees of divinity. The highest *alii* were those who were born to a high-ranking chief and his sister—a system reminiscent of ancient Egypt. Hawaiians worshiped a number of gods, including Kane, the god of creation; Ku, the war god; and Lono, the fertility god. Life was governed by many prohibitions and strict rules for behavior known as the *kapu* (taboo). A priestly caste had charge of worship in the *heiau*, or open stone temples.

Kamehameha's father, Keoua, died young, and from then on Kamehameha was reared at the court of his uncle, Kalaniopuu, the king of Hawaii. It was during this period that Captain James Cook happened upon the Hawaiian Islands, which he called the Sandwich Islands in honor of John Montagu, fourth earl of Sandwich. Cook came first to Kauai and Niihau in 1778, and in 1779 entered Kealakekua Bay near Kailua on the lee side of Hawaii. The Hawaiians at first considered Cook to be the god Lono, but an unfortunate series of events disillusioned them, and he was killed in a skirmish on the shore of Kealakekua Bay. Kamehameha accompanied Kalaniopuu during a visit to one of Cook's ships and even spent the night there, but he seems not to have been present when Cook died.

> "*E na'i wale nō 'oukou, i ku'u pono 'a'ole pau.*" ("Prevail/continue my pono (righteous) deeds, they are not yet finished.")

Life's Work

When Kalaniopuu died, he left the kingship to his son Kiwalao, who undertook a system of land distribution unfavorable to Kamehameha and the other chiefs of Kona. After a bloody battle at Mokuohai in 1782 in which Kiwalao was killed, and with the assistance of an eruption of the volcano Kilauea that wreaked havoc with other opposing forces and showed them that Pele (the goddess of volcanoes) was against them, Kamehameha gained control over all of Hawaii.

When King Kahekili died in 1794, he controlled all the islands of the Hawaiian chain except Hawaii, Kauai, and Niihau. With the assistance of foreign ships and weapons, Kamehameha soon conquered Maui, Molokai, Lanai, and Kahoolawe. In 1795 he proceeded to Oahu—which now had Kalanikupule, Kahekili's brother, as its king—and landed his forces at Waikiki and Waialae. They drove Kalanikupule's forces up the Nuuanu Valley and forced the bulk of them to fall to their deaths from cliffs.

Kalanikupule escaped but was later captured and sacrificed to the war god Kukailimoku.

Kamehameha now ruled all the Hawaiian Islands except for Kauai. He soon started preparations for an invasion of Kauai, and in the spring of 1796, he headed toward the island with a large flotilla of canoes. However, rough seas forced him to turn back and postpone his invasion. Hearing that a rebellion was taking place in Hawaii, he returned there to squelch it. He spent the next six years in Hawaii, during which time he assembled a formidable fleet of double canoes and a number of small schooners constructed by European carpenters. With these ships and a large supply of European weapons, he sailed to Oahu in 1804. However, his invasion plans were frustrated again, this time by a terrible plague (probably cholera) that was brought by foreign ships. The population of Oahu was devastated, and large numbers of Kamehameha's army also succumbed. Kamehameha himself was stricken but managed to survive.

Kamehameha I at Spear Practice (Wikimedia Commons)

Kamehameha continued to plan his invasion of Kauai and even acquired a large ship, the *Lelia Byrd*, to lead the assault. He also entered into negotiations with the island's king, Kaumualii, to solve the problem without battle. An American captain, Nathan Winship, persuaded the two kings to meet on board his ship, the *O'Cain*, and Kaumualii submitted to Kamehameha's sovereignty on the condition that he could retain his position until death.

Now Kamehameha reigned over all the islands, apparently the first to do so. He was an absolute dictator but used his power wisely. He divided up the lands in such a way that no chief had enough power to be tempted to rebel and appointed governors to administer each island. He issued decrees that made life safer and often worked at menial tasks to set an example for his people to follow. He appointed a Hawaiian named Kalanimoku (known as Billy Pitt after the British prime minister William Pitt) as chief executive officer.

During Kamehameha's lifetime, foreign visitors to the Hawaiian Islands became increasingly numerous. The first ships to appear after Cook's unfortunate visit were those captained by George Vancouver, who had been a member of Cook's crew. Vancouver visited the islands in 1792, 1793, and 1794. He brought cattle and goats and other commodities to the islands but refused to provide any arms. He persuaded Kamehameha to cede the Hawaiian Islands to Britain, although Kamehameha apparently believed that he was entering into a defensive alliance in the hope that he would get help against his enemies. In any event, Britain made no effort to follow through, but a close connection between Britain and the "Sandwich Islands" continued. This is symbolized by the Hawaiian flag, which bears the Union Jack in the upper left corner.

Although most of the ships that visited Hawaii during this period were traders searching to replenish their ships, there were occasional visits of a different stripe. Anton Schäffer, a German surgeon in the employ of the Russian-American Company, was sent to Hawaii to recover or receive compensation for a Russian cargo lost from a ship wrecked off Kauai. Schäffer got grandiose ideas and attempted, with the help of Kaumualii, to establish Russian outposts in Kauai and Oahu. He was repulsed by the Hawaiians with the assistance of the Americans in Honolulu and was forced to make his escape by hiding on a ship to Canton.

When the Europeans first visited the Hawaiian Islands, they were able to obtain valuable goods from the native Hawaiians for baubles or for small pieces of iron, which were especially prized because they could be made into fishhooks or daggers. Fresh water, hogs, and other food items were needed. As time went by, the Hawaiians became aware of the value of their commodities, and prices went up accordingly. Kamehameha himself secured great amounts of goods in barter and even large amounts of hard money, which he retained in storehouses in Kailua, Lahaina, and Honolulu.

Kamehameha had a total of twenty-one wives, but his favorite was Kaahumanu, by whom he had no children. Kamehameha married Keopuolani for dynastic purposes when she was about thirteen years old. Keopuolani and Kamehameha had three children who survived, one of whom, Liholiho, was designated as the heir to the kingdom. Kamehameha spent most of his last years in Kailua, although he occasionally traveled to the other parts of his realm. In 1819, he contracted a malady that no one could cure, and on May 19, he died. His body was treated in the usual way for *alii:* His bones were stripped of their flesh and hidden somewhere in a cave by one of his faithful retainers.

Significance

Only a few monarchs in world history have received the appellation "great." Kamehameha, by uniting all of the Hawaiian Islands under his sway and keeping his land independent of foreign dominance, probably deserves such a title. He was flexible enough to adapt to the changing times but still retained his way of life under the taboo system. If he was sometimes harsh and cruel by contemporary standards, he was also kind and generous. During his brief reign as Kamehameha II, his son Liholiho, upon the urging of Kaahumana (a *kuhina nui*, or prime minister), put a dramatic end to the taboo system by publicly eating with the women, which had been strictly forbidden. After Liholiho's death (by measles during a trip to England), Kaahumanu remained as regent until Liholiho's brother came of age, and she saw to it that the remnants of the taboo system were destroyed. In 1819, the same year that Kamehameha died, the missionaries came to Hawaii and transformed Hawaiian life forever.

Henry Kratz

Further Reading

Daws, Gavan. *Shoal of Time: A History of the Hawaiian Islands*. New York: Macmillan, 1968. Reprint. Honolulu: University of Hawai'i Press, 1974. Daws's book, the best one-volume history of Hawaii, contains an excellent section on Kamehameha and his times, starting with Cook's discovery of the islands. It is very readable, with copious endnotes and an excellent bibliography.

Desha, Stephen. *Kamehameha and His Warrior Kekuhaupi'o*. Translated by Frances N. Frazier. Honolulu: Kamehameha Schools Press, 2000. Orginially published as a magazine serial in the Hawaiian language during the early 1920's, this book recounts the epic tale of King Kamehameha and a warrior named Kekuhaupi'o. An engaging saga for younger readers that includes a great deal of information about Hawaiian history and culture. Glossary and detailed index.

Kuykendall, Ralph S. *The Hawaiian Kingdom 1778-1854: Foundation and Transformation*. Honolulu: University of Hawai'i Press, 1938. This first volume of Kuykendall's monumental history of Hawaii contains an extensive account of Kamehameha's life and the history of Hawaii since Cook's appearance there. The book also includes an appendix discussing Kamehameha's controversial birth year.

Malo, David. *Hawaiian Antiquities*. Translated by Nathaniel B. Emerson. 2d ed. Honolulu: Bishop Museum Press, 1951. This volume, written by a native Hawaiian in the Hawaiian language, was translated in 1898 by one of the great experts on Hawaiian culture. It contains a wealth of information about virtually every aspect of Hawaiian life before the European discovery, including old Hawaiian folktales and chants.

Mellen, Kathleen Dickenson. *The Lonely Warrior: The Life and Times of Kamehameha the Great of Hawaii*. New York: Hastings House, 1949. This is a well-researched and readable biography. Mellen used oral sources of Hawaiian traditions along with written sources and was aided in her work by Kawena Pukui, a distinguished scholar of Hawaiian culture and language employed by the Bishop Museum. The book contains several useful maps, including one denoting the battle on Oahu that ended at Nuuanu Pali.

Morrison, Susan. *Kamehameha: The Warrior King of Hawai'i*. Honolulu: University of Hawai'i Press, 2003. Brief biography written for younger readers.

Mrantz, Maxine. *Hawaiian Monarchy: The Romantic Years*. Honolulu: Aloha Graphics, 1973. This forty-seven-page booklet gives a quick summary of the monarchy by providing short biographies of all of the monarchs from Kamehameha I to Lili'uokalani. It also contains portraits of all the monarchs, as well as other interesting photographs.

Tregaskis, Richard. *The Warrior King: Hawaii's Kamehameha the Great*. New York: Macmillan, 1973. Tregaskis relies heavily on unauthenticated sources and his own imagination to write what amounts to a fictionalized biography. Nevertheless, the main facts are there, and the book contains genealogical tables, a map of the Hawaiian Islands, sixteen pages of reproductions of contemporary paintings, and a useful bibliography.

Lili'uokalani

Queen of Hawaii (r. 1891-1892)

Born: September 2, 1838; Honolulu, Hawaii
Died: November 11, 1917; Honolulu, Hawaii
Area of Achievement: Politics, music

The last monarch of the Hawaiian kingdom, Lili'uokalani struggled futilely to preserve her people's independence against the pressures of American annexation.

Lili'uokalani (Wikimedia Commons)

Early Life

Born into Hawaii's royal family, Lili'uokalani (leh-LEE-ew-o-kah-LAH-nee) was the daughter of a chief named Kapaakea and his wife, Keohokalole. Kapaakea was one of the fifteen counselors of the king, Kamehameha III. Immediately after her birth, she was adopted into another family. A woman named Konia was her foster mother, and her foster father was a chief named Paki. This practice of adoption was the custom among the leading families of Hawaii; it was a way to cement alliances among the chiefs, who were the nobility of Hawaii. All of Lili'uokalani's ten brothers and sisters were also adopted into and reared by other families. When Lili'uokalani was four years old, she was enrolled in the Royal School, a boarding school run by American missionaries. The students of this school were all members of the royal extended family, which was made up of the families of the king and chiefs. In this school, Lili'uokalani learned English and was taken to church every Sunday, but she said that she never got enough to eat. The school closed in 1848, when Lili'uokalani was ten years old, and after that she attended a day school also run by American missionaries. Learning was important to Lili'uokalani throughout her life.

After Paki's death in 1855, Lili'uokalani continued to live in his home, along with her sister Bernice and Bernice's husband, Charles R. Bishop. The Bishops were to be a major influence on Lili'uokalani's life.

Although at one time she was engaged to be married to Lunalilo (also known as Prince William), who would become king in 1873, she ultimately was married to the son of an Italian-born sea captain and a New England woman. The man was named John O. Dominis, and the marriage took place on September 16, 1862. The couple began their married life at Washington Place, the estate built by the groom's father for his family. This was to remain Lili'uokalani's private residence throughout her life.

Much of Lili'uokalani's adulthood before her accession as queen was spent on benevolent work for native Hawaiians. She was also a composer of music, and she wrote more than one hundred songs, including several Christian hymns, but is best known for the famous Hawaiian song "Aloha 'Oe." In 1887, she attended Queen Victoria of England's Jubilee celebration as an honored guest. She never had any children.

Life's Work

A year after Lili'uokalani's marriage, King Kamehameha IV died, on November 30, 1863. Because the young king had recently lost his only son to illness, there was no direct heir to the throne. According to the Hawaiian Constitution of 1852, the king's brother was elected as the new monarch by the cabinet, the privy council, and the *kuhina nui* (the queen, who served as coruler with the Hawaiian king). He became known as Kamehameha V. By the time he died in 1872, a new constitution had been passed (in 1864) that gave the king the right to choose his own successor. The successor he had named, however, his sister Princess Victoria, had died in 1866, and he had named no one else.

Now it was up to the Hawaiian legislature to elect a new king from among the nobility. This was when Lili'uokalani's former fiancé, Lunalilo, ascended the throne. He lived only a year longer, however, and also died without naming an heir. This time, Lili'uokalani's brother Kalakaua was elected, and in 1877 she was chosen as heir to the throne. She served as regent from January to October of 1881 while the king was making a trip around the world, which gave her a taste of what it would later be like to be queen. She took this role again in 1890 and 1891 while the king was in California on a trip meant to restore his failing health. He died in January of 1891, however, leaving his sister Lili'uokalani as queen.

Lili'uokalani was proclaimed queen on January 29, 1891, at the age of fifty-two. She inherited a government that had been, throughout the nineteenth century, a mixture of Hawaiian tradition, British constitutional ideals, Victorian influence, and American interference brought by missionaries, adventurers, and politicians. Symbolic of this mixture were the combinations of names held by the Hawaiian nobility. (Lili'uokalani was also known as Lydia Kamakaeha Paki and Mrs. John O. Dominis.) This mixture was strengthened by the frequency of intermarriage between Hawaiians and people of European American extraction, of which Lili'uokalani's own marriage was an example.

Lili'uokalani's brother, influenced by American businesspeople, had led Hawaii on a course toward ruin by trying to return to a more despotic form of government. This led to revolution in 1887 and to increased American influence, because in the new constitution of that year members of the nobility were to be elected by voters of large income and property, which in practice meant large numbers of Americans and others of foreign birth or ancestry. Hawaii was also under the grip of an economic depression as a result of the McKinley Tariff Act, which removed tariffs on other importers of sugar to the United States. Because sugar had become the center of Hawaii's economy, this act devastated the island nation.

This was the situation the new queen faced: political turmoil and economic difficulty. Her solution was to strengthen the monarchy. Lili'uokalani was firmly opposed to the Constitution of 1887, which was far more democratic than previous constitutions had been. At the same time, the political strife and economic difficulties in the islands made the idea of annexation by the United States look rather appealing to some Hawaiians, and by 1892 there were secret organizations working toward that end.

After an attempt by the queen to promulgate a new constitution giving the monarchy more power, in January, 1892, a revolutionary committee took over the government and ended the monarchy, setting up a provisional government until a union with the United States could be worked out. The queen assented against her will, in order to avoid bloodshed, and retired to Washington Place. A treaty of annexation by the United States was drawn up and signed by the provisional government on February 14, 1893. It had not been acted upon, however, by the Senate of the United States by the time Grover Cleveland became president a few days later. A friend of Lili'uokalani, Cleveland had received a letter from her about the coup d'état. After his inauguration, he withdrew the treaty from the Senate's consideration and launched a lengthy investigation into the matter. Meanwhile, the provisional government remained in power.

> "*I could not turn back the time for political change, but there is still time to save our heritage. You must remember never to cease to act because you fear you may fail.*"

When it became clear that annexation was not imminent, a constitutional convention in 1894 set up what was to be the Republic of Hawaii. Lili'uokalani protested to both the United States and Great Britain, but to no avail. An attempt to restore the monarchy was quickly squelched, leading to Lili'uokalani's arrest and conviction on charges of treason. She was imprisoned in the Iolani Palace and forced to sign abdication papers. Hawaii was officially annexed to the United States on August 12, 1898, but the republic continued to govern the islands under the authority of the president of the United States.

Lili'uokalani was pardoned in 1896, and in that year she traveled to the United States to visit her late husband's relatives, trying to forget her sorrows over recent events. She returned in August of 1898, her enthusiastic welcome home showing how much support she still retained among both native-born and foreign-born Hawaiians.

While in the United States, she wrote her autobiography, *Hawaii's Story by Hawaii's Queen* (1898), as well

Lili'uokalani on a country visit with a hale pili in the background. (Wikimedia Commons)

as translating an ancient Hawaiian poem. Lili'uokalani died on November 11, 1917, in Honolulu, Hawaii.

Significance

Although her reign was Hawaii's last as an independent nation, Lili'uokalani's impact on Hawaii's history cannot be denied. Because she was part of a tradition in which women played important roles, she never questioned her right to rule. Although she believed in a strong monarchy, Lili'uokalani organized institutions for the improvement of the health, welfare, and education of her native Hawaiian compatriots. She was an educated woman who valued learning, and she was both an author and a composer. A native Hawaiian, she was also an enthusiastic participant in the Victorian-inspired society of her times. Her downfall was her accession to the throne at a time when her tiny kingdom, influenced as it was by both European and American values and politics, could no longer remain independent. Although she resigned herself to Hawaii's annexation to the United States, she never agreed with the idea, always remaining convinced of the value of national autonomy for her islands.

Lili'uokalani is something of a tragic figure. Trained and educated as a potential ruler, passionate about her country and her people, a woman of cosmopolitan learning and taste, she nevertheless came to power at a time when her method of rule came into conflict with the movement of history.

Eleanor B. Amico

Further Reading

Kuykendall, Ralph S., and A. Grove Day. *Hawaii: A History, from Polynesian Kingdom to American State*. Englewood Cliffs, N.J.: Prentice-Hall, 1948. The parts of this book labeled books 3 and 4 (chapters 11 through 12) give a helpful chronicle of the events of the latter years of the Hawaiian kingdom. They help the reader understand the background to the situation that Lili'uokalani inherited, as well as the outcome of her own reign.

Lili'uokalani. *Hawaii's Story by Hawaii's Queen*. Rutland, Vt.: Tuttle, 1964. The queen's autobiography is the best source for learning about her early life. Although it is somewhat rambling, it is invaluable because it gives Lili'uokalani's perspective on events in her own words. It ends with her return from the United States in 1898.

Loomis, Albertine. *For Whom Are the Stars?* Honolulu: University of Hawai'i Press, 1976. A highly readable and sympathetic account of the end of the Hawaiian monarchy, discussing the revolution and events leading up to it, the first failure to annex Hawaii to the United States, the founding of the republic, the rebellion of 1895, and the queen's arrest and trial.

"Native Hawaiians Seek Redress for U.S. Role in Ousting Queen." *The New York Times*, December 11, 1999, p. A20. A report about a group of Hawaiians seeking redress for the U.S. involvement in Lili'uokalani's overthrow. Discusses then-president Bill Clinton's apology for the incident.

Russ, William Adam, Jr. *The Hawaiian Republic, 1894-98, and Its Struggle to Win Annexation*. Selinsgrove, Pa.: Susquehanna University Press, 1961. This book follows up on Russ's earlier book (below). This volume analyzes the years of the Hawaiian Republic, between the time of Lili'uokalani's abdication and Hawaii's annexation by the United States.

---. *The Hawaiian Revolution, 1893-94*. Selinsgrove, Pa.: Susquehanna University Press, 1959. Analyzes in readable detail the events of the revolution that deposed Queen Lili'uokalani. It also examines the involvement of the United States and American interests in the overthrow of Hawaiian autonomy.

Tate, Merze. *The United States and the Hawaiian Kingdom: A Political History*. New Haven, Conn.: Yale University Press, 1965. This book focuses on the period of Hawaiian history that included Lili'uokalani's life and work: 1864 to 1898. Chapters 4 through 7 deal specifically with various events of her reign: her attempt to change the constitution, the revolution of 1893, and annexation by the United States.

Young, Lucien. *The Real Hawaii: Its History and Present Condition*. New York: Doubleday & McClure, 1899. An eyewitness account of the revolution of 1893 and the events that followed. The author was on a ship stationed at Honolulu at the time. Written to discount the reports of James H. Blount, the envoy of Lili'uokalani to President Cleveland, the book gives an account of Hawaiian culture, history, and economy as well as of the revolution and its aftermath.

WILMA MANKILLER

Principal chief of the Cherokee Nation

Born: November 18, 1945; Tahlequah, Oklahoma
Died: April 6, 2010; Tahlequah, Oklahoma
Area of Achievement: Native American affairs, government and politics, women's rights, social reform

As the first woman principal chief of the Cherokee Nation of Oklahoma, or of any major American Indian tribe, Mankiller renewed a long tradition of female leadership in Cherokee affairs. She coupled feminist ideas with Cherokee tradition to form a strong tribe with a renewed spirit of independence.

EARLY LIFE

Wilma Mankiller was born in the W. W. Hastings Indian Hospital in Tahlequah, Oklahoma. Her mother was Clara Irene Sitton, who was of Dutch-Irish descent, and her father was Charley Mankiller, a full Cherokee; they had married in 1937. Mankiller was the sixth of eleven children. The family lived on Mankiller Flats in Adair County, northeastern Oklahoma. Mankiller Flats was an allotment of 160 acres that had been given to John Mankiller, Charley's father, in 1907, when Oklahoma became a state.

The name "Mankiller" was a Cherokee military title that had to be earned, like that of the armed forces ranks of major or captain. Mankiller's great-great-great-grandfather, Mankiller of Tellico, earned the title in the eighteenth century and then established it as a family surname. (During her days as chief, Mankiller often told white males that she had earned the name herself.) Tellico is in eastern Tennessee and was part of the original Cherokee Nation. The Mankillers and most other Cherokee were forcibly moved to the Indian Territory, later the State of Oklahoma, along the infamous Trail of Tears in 1838-1839.

The first eleven years of Wilma's life were spent on Mankiller Flats and within traditional Cherokee culture. In 1956, however, the Mankiller family moved to San Francisco, California, as part of a government relocation plan to move American Indians to large cities and into mainstream American life. Life in San Francisco was shocking to the family, especially for the Mankiller children, but they soon adjusted.

On November 13, 1963, Mankiller married Hugo Olaya, a member of a wealthy Ecuadoran family, who was then a student in San Francisco. Two daughters, Felicia and Gina, were born to the couple before differences in lifestyles led to a divorce in 1974. During these years,

Wilma Mankiller. (Wikimedia Commons)

Wilma had earned a degree from San Francisco State College (now university).

Mankiller was poignantly reminded of her Cherokee background again when, in 1969, a group of American Indians occupied Alcatraz Island in San Francisco Bay to gain support for American Indian rights. Alcatraz was considered indigenous territory, and Mankiller and many others in her family participated in that occupation, in which Mankiller's life of political activism began.

Mankiller's father, who had become a longshoreman and a union organizer in California, died in 1971. Charley always had encouraged his children, especially Wilma, to read books, which were always in abundance in their home. His body was returned to his native Adair County for burial. Wilma heard older Cherokee men say that her father had "come back" home. The emotions of the day of her father's burial seemed to be a signal for family members to return, one by one, to Oklahoma. Mankiller returned in 1975, a year after her divorce. Only two older brothers remained in California.

Living in two worlds, Mankiller's life mirrored that of Nancy Ward, an eighteenth century Cherokee who had earned the title Beloved Woman and who also had lived in the white world as well as the Cherokee. Like Ward, Wilma was able to combine the best of Cherokee tradition with the best of European-American civilization. Mankiller's balanced philosophy led her to contribute greatly to the welfare of the Cherokee Nation.

LIFE'S WORK

Mankiller began her work to improve American Indian life before she left California. In 1974, with Bill Wahpapah, she cofounded the American Indian Community School in Oakland. However, her return to Oklahoma marked the beginning of her full-time service to her people.

The Cherokee Nation of Oklahoma, with 55,000 acres of northeastern Oklahoma and a federally recognized "enrollment," or population, of about 250,000 people, was ranked second only to the Navajo in size among American Indian tribes in the United States. When Oklahoma became a state in 1907, the traditional tribal government of the Cherokee was dissolved. This created a unique political organization, neither a reservation nor an autonomous government, with unique political and social problems and concerns. Mankiller now began directing her energy toward solving those problems

Mankiller's first regular job with the Cherokee Nation began in 1977 as an economic-stimulus coordinator. Her job was to guide as many people as possible toward university training in such fields as environmental science and health and then to integrate them back into their communities. She soon became frustrated with the slow-moving male-dominated bureaucracy of the Cherokee Nation, a bureaucracy she believed had been imposed on them by whites and which was supported by the insecurity of Cherokee men forced to live in a white-dominated society.

Before Europeans came to North America, Cherokee women such as Ward occupied leadership roles in tribal affairs. The original Cherokee Nation was matrilineal, and the name Beloved Woman was given to those who performed extraordinary service. Women had a major voice in choosing chiefs and in other tribal affairs. The first Europeans to contact the Cherokee accused them of having a "petticoat government." After this contact, the influence of Cherokee women began to decrease. In her autobiography *Mankiller: A Chief and Her People* (1993), Mankiller declared her belief that the Trail of Tears, combined with the tremendous strain of relocation in the West, was the final step in the forced development of a more subservient position for women.

A significant development in 1971 helped to open the way for a return to more female participation in Cherokee affairs. A revision of the tribal constitution provided that, for the first time since Oklahoma statehood in 1907, the principal chief would be elected by the people of the tribe rather than being appointed by the president of the United States. An entirely new constitution in 1976 solidified that change and provided for the election of a new fifteen-member tribal council.

In 1979, after working for two years as an economic stimulus coordinator, Mankiller was made a program development specialist and grant writer. Her immediate success in this position, especially in writing grant proposals, brought her to the attention of the tribal council and Principal Chief Ross Swimmer. This phase of her work was soon interrupted by tragedy. On November 9 she was seriously injured in a head-on collision on a country road. The driver of the other car was Sherry Morris, a white woman who was a very close friend of Mankiller. Morris was killed. Within a year of the accident, Mankiller developed a rare form of muscular dystrophy.

These back-to-back experiences caused Mankiller to reach more deeply into her Cherokee background and led to a change in her philosophy of life. In 1981, although still undergoing physical therapy, she was able to return to her work with the Cherokee Nation, and she did so with her old energy. In that year she helped establish the

Cherokee Nation Community Development Department and became its first director.

> *"In Iroquois society, leaders are encouraged to remember seven generations in the past and consider seven generations in the future when making decisions that affect the people."*

The next step in Mankiller's career came in 1983, when Chief Swimmer asked her to join his reelection ticket as his deputy chief. This request was unusual for two reasons: Mankiller was a woman, and she was a liberal Democrat; Swimmer was a conservative Republican. After first declining, Mankiller accepted the offer as a way to help her people.

One of Mankiller's opponents for deputy chief was Agnes Cowan, the first woman to serve on the tribal council. Mankiller was surprised when gender became an immediate issue in the campaign. The hostility she faced included the slashing of her car tires and death threats. She fought the negative campaigning by conducting a positive and cheerful campaign based primarily on her past service to the Cherokee people. The victory for the Swimmer-Mankiller ticket meant that, on August 14, 1983, Mankiller became the first female deputy chief in Cherokee history.

In 1984, Deputy Chief Mankiller participated in a significant meeting a reunion between the Cherokee Nation of Oklahoma and the Eastern Band of the Cherokee from North Carolina. The Eastern Band had descended from those who escaped the Trail of Tears by hiding in the mountains. This meeting, the first full tribal council since 1838, was held at Red Clay in Tennessee, on the Georgia state line. Red Clay was the last capital of the original Cherokee Nation. At that reunion, an eternal flame was lit and still burns at Red Clay. In her autobiography, Mankiller emphasized the tremendous historical and emotional impact that this event had on the Cherokee people.

A major career surprise for Mankiller came in 1985, when U.S. president Ronald Reagan nominated Chief Swimmer as assistant secretary for the Interior Department's Bureau of Indian Affairs. As a result, on December 14, Mankiller became the first woman principal chief of the Cherokee Nation. Without hesitation she declared that economic growth would be the primary goal of her administration. She described her guiding theory as bubble-up economics, in which the people themselves would plan and implement projects that would benefit the tribe in future years. In a famous quotation, she reminded her people that, in traditional Iroquois society, from which the Cherokee descended, leaders considered seven generations past and seven generations future when making major decisions.

Until the next scheduled election in 1987, Chief Mankiller, governing without a mandate from the people, faced strong opposition that limited her real power. In October of 1986, while considering whether to run for a full term, Mankiller had married Charlie Soap, a full Cherokee who she had met in 1977. She described her new husband as the most well-adjusted male she had ever known. It was Soap who persuaded her to run in the 1987 election, which she won in a runoff. Because the Cherokee Nation had now returned to the strong female leadership of its past, Chief Mankiller described her election as a step forward and a step backward at the same time.

Although Mankiller's first full term was successful in terms of economic progress, her level of personal involvement was curtailed by a resurgence of kidney disease from which she had suffered for many years. This led to a kidney transplant in June, 1990. The donor was Mankiller's older brother, Don. By 1991, only a year after her transplant, Chief Mankiller had sufficiently recovered to run for a second full term. She won that election by an overwhelming 82 percent of the vote. The same election put six women on the fifteen-member tribal council. With a resounding voice, the Cherokee had returned to their ancient tradition of shared gender leadership. Mankiller's work of improving the everyday lives of her people continued during her second term of office. During her ten years as chief, the population of the Cherokee Nation of Oklahoma increased from 55,000 to 156,000 people.

Mankiller's impact reached far beyond the borders of the Cherokee Nation. In 1988, she was named Alumnus of the Year by San Francisco State University. This was followed, in 1990, by an honorary doctorate from Yale University. In 1993, Mankiller gave a well-known speech at Sweetbriar College, "Rebuilding the Cherokee Nation," in which she reviewed the progress made by the tribe and expressed her hopes for its future. Poor health forced Mankiller to retire from her position in 1995. A fitting tribute to her wide-ranging influence was the election of Joyce Dugan as the first female chief of the Eastern Band of the Cherokee in North Carolina.

In her years after retirement, Mankiller continued her work, including much literary output, as a political, cultural, and social leader of the Cherokee and as a spokesperson for the rights of all women. Mankiller contributed to the 2004 book *Every Day Is a Good Day*, a collection of essays on the lives of indigenous women, and the 2008 book *Reflections on American Indian History*. Mankiller was diagnosed with pancreatic cancer in 2010, and died in April of that year. In 2013, the film *The Cherokee Word for Water*, told the story of Mankiller's political career.

The honors bestowed upon her, in addition to her 1993 induction into the National Women's Hall of Fame, are proof of her lasting influence. Other honors include Woman of the Year from *Ms.* magazine (1987); the John W. Gardner Leadership Award, Independent Sector (1988); the Indian Health Service Award, U.S. Public Health Service (1989); and the Oklahoma State University Henry G. Bennett Distinguished Service Award (1990). The Presidential Medal of Freedom, the nation's highest civilian honor, was bestowed on her by President Bill Clinton in 1998.

Significance

Mankiller's leadership led to both tangible and intangible changes for the Cherokee Nation. The most significant tangible changes were the benefits for the Cherokee that came from the development of the U.S. Department of Commerce, which was created soon after Mankiller's 1987 victory. The Commerce Department helps to coordinate the business enterprises of the Cherokee tribe and is mandated to balance tribal income with the needs of tribal members; this, in turn, creates jobs and profits. The intangible results include a renewed spirit of independence for all Cherokee and a renewed confidence that Cherokee women once again could influence the destiny of the tribe. In 1990, Mankiller signed a historic self-governance agreement that authorized the Cherokee Nation to administer federal funds that previously had been administered by the Bureau of Indian Affairs in Washington, D.C. The same year saw a revitalizing of tribal courts and tribal police as well as the establishment of a Cherokee Nation tax commission.

Glenn L. Swygart, updated by Micah L. Issitt

Further Reading

Edmunds, R. David., ed. *The New Warriors: Native American Leaders Since* 1900. Lincoln: University of Nebraska Press, 2001. Features a variety of American Indian leaders, including Mankiller, as part of a generation who rose to the challenges of the twentieth century.

Janda, Sarah Eppler. *Beloved Women: The Political Lives of Ladonna Harris and Wilma Mankiller*. De Kalb: Northern Illinois University Press, 2007. A fascinating look at the two American Indian activists Mankiller and Harris who were at the forefront of American Indian relations with the U.S. government and in tribal development. Focuses on how feminism coupled with a sense of "Indianness" shaped the political lives of the two leaders.

Mankiller, Wilma. *Every Day Is a Good Day: Reflections by Contemporary Indigenous Women*. New York: Fulcrum, 2004. Mankiller and eighteen other indigenous women of the Americas discuss their lives and those of their people, living in a Eurocentric world.

---. *Mankiller: A Chief and Her People*. New York: St. Martin's Press, 1993. This autobiography is by far the best source for Mankiller's life, career, and philosophy. Includes many excellent photographs of the Mankiller family, other key individuals, and major events in Mankiller's life.

_____, et al., eds. *The Readers' Companion to U.S. Women's History*. New York: Houghton Mifflin, 1998. Among the five editors of this volume, Mankiller is listed first. In addition to several references to her in other essays, she contributed two essays: on the Iroquois Confederacy and on feminism.

Van Viema, David. "Activist Wilma Mankiller Is Set to Become the First Female Chief of the Cherokee Nation." *People Weekly*, December 2, 1985. Based on an interview with Mankiller by Michael Wallis, this article conveys the initial impression she had of her new job as chief. Reveals Mankiller's identification with her Cherokee roots.

Wallace, Michele. "Wilma Mankiller." *Ms.*, January, 1988. Wallace emphasizes the role of women in Cherokee history. Also covered is Mankiller's philosophy of leadership and her influence on women's rights in general. Includes her plans for Cherokee progress.

Nanyehi

"Beloved woman" of the Cherokee

Born: c. 1738; Monroe County, Tennessee
Died: c. 1822; Benton, Tennessee
Also known as: Nancy Ward
Area of achievement: Native American leader

Nanyehi (Wikimedia Commons)

A prominent Native American woman of the eighteenth century, Nanyehi (also called Nancy Ward) was a Cherokee leader who worked on behalf of her people during a period of intense white colonization.

Early Life

Little is known about the childhood of Nanyehi. She was born at Chota, a Cherokee site near the Little Tennessee River, in approximately 1738. The Cherokee were among the "five civilized tribes" (so-called from the point of view of eighteenth- and nineteenth-century Europeans). They were one of a group of Native Americans descended from the Mississippian culture, a civilization that flourished from about 800 to 1600. The Mississippian culture extended from eastern New York and western Pennsylvania down into the southeastern United States and past the Mississippi River into eastern portions of the Midwest. They lived in organized towns, constructed vast earthworks and streets, lived in buildings, grew crops, including maize and beans, and were typically matrilineal societies—meaning that family affiliation was counted through the mother's line, not the father's. The Mississippian people suffered a decline that began before contact with white colonizers. It is believed that a series of droughts, along with increasingly violent warfare between various Mississippian groups, resulted in a significant loss in population.

Chota was an important town recognized as the capital city of the Cherokee. It was also an important trading town, and English traders resided there throughout the mid-eighteenth century. Nanyehi was born into an important Cherokee family, known as the Wolf clan, and her mother, Tame Deer, was the sister of Chief Attakullakulla. Because of the near-constant warfare with other tribes, the French and Indian War (1753–1763) then being waged in the region, and the occasional skirmishes with white colonizers, Nanyehi grew up acquainted with threats and violence of all kinds.

Life's Work

Nanyehi married Kingfisher of the Deer clan and they had two children, Fivekiller and Catherine. Once, during a battle against the Creek Indians in 1755, Nanyehi hid behind a log near her husband and aided him in battle. It is said that she took his bullets (in that era likely balls of lead) and chewed on them to give them jagged edges so that they would theoretically inflict more damage. When her husband was shot and killed, Nanyehi took his gun, and, shouting a Cherokee war-cry, she charge the Creek forces. Her valor helped lead the Cherokee to a victory, and she was later given the title Ghigau or "beloved woman" by the tribe. As a Ghigau, Nanyehi was a member of the Cherokee's General Council—the only woman in that role—and she wielded great power.

> "You know that women are always looked upon as nothing; but we are your mothers; you are our sons. Our cry is all for peace; let it continue. This peace must last forever. Let your women's sons be ours; let our sons be yours. Let your women hear our words."

In the 1750s, Nanyehi married an English trader named Bryant Ward who was residing among the Cherokee. They lived together in Chota and had a daughter together, Elizabeth. Marriage as understood in modern, developed societies is not a universal institution; its definition changes with history and across cultures. For the Cherokee, for example, marriage was not a lifelong arrangement. Thus, the fact that Ward had been married previously to an English woman—who was still alive in South Carolina— was not an issue for the Cherokee.

The tomb of Nanyehi, known by her English name Nancy Ward, and her brother and son. (Wikimedia Commons)

When Ward decided to go back to South Carolina, he remained close to Nanyehi and their daughter Elizabeth, and the two women would occasionally travel to South Carolina to visit Ward and his family there. As a result of her relationship with Ward, Nanyehi developed an interest in, and an appreciation for, the culture of the white settlers.

In the 1760s, the Cherokees allied with the British colonists against the French. The colonists built forts in the region with the blessing of the Cherokees, and the colonists agreed to defend the Cherokee against Creeks and Choctaws. By now, frontiersmen were streaming into that part of Appalachia from the east, usually by traveling overland from Virginia to Fort Duquesne in present-day Pittsburgh, and then boat down the Ohio River in the direction of the Mississippi. Violence between whites and Native Americans was common on the frontier, and, as a result of an incident in which several frontiersmen killed a group of Cherokees, the Cherokees turned against the colonists. It was in this period that Nanyehi met a woman named Mrs. William Bean, who had been taken captive by the Cherokee. Rather than kill her, Nanyehi nursed her back to health and brought her to live in her home. Mrs. Bean taught Nanyehi how to work a loom. Mrs. Bean was also allowed to bring two dairy cows into the Indian settlement, introducing the use of dairy and dairy farming to the Cherokees. Thanks to this experience, in later years, Nanyehi would become a successful rancher of cattle.

During the Revolutionary War, the Cherokees were divided in their sympathies. Some wanted to ally with the British so that they could fight with British help against the white settlements. Others wanted to foster conditions for peaceful coexistence with the white settlers; Nanyehi was among the latter. During the 1770s and 1780s, Nanyehi occasionally warned white settlers as well as colonial American soldiers about imminent attacks so that they could either flee or resist the Indian attack without experiencing a slaughter. She hoped that the violent cycle of retaliation could be broken.

In 1785, Nanyehi was a tribal leader representing the Cherokee at the signing of the Treaty of Hopewell. She spoke eloquently there in favor of peace and friendship, then passed the traditional peace pipe to the American delegation. The treaty established a western border for the colonists, promised the recall of existing white homesteaders from Cherokee lands, and gave the Cherokees the right to punish those who refused to leave voluntarily. However, the treaty was ignored almost from the start.

Over the following years, Cherokee land was both taken away and voluntarily sold to whites, and the Cherokee themselves underwent drastic changes in lifestyle and economics. Nanyehi, now an elderly woman, was still the respected head of the Cherokee Women's Council, and she often spoke eloquently to her people about the need to maintain control of their lands. In 1819, against Nanyehi's advice, the Cherokee sold a large portion of their land to the United States. Forced to leave Chota as a result, she settled on the Ocoee River near Benton, Tennessee, where she opened an inn. She died there in 1822.

Significance

Nanyehi, an important Cherokee figure of the eighteenth century, has long been of interest to historians of Native American culture and the American frontier. She has attracted attention from American feminists as well. Representing the remnants of a less patriarchal civilization, Nanyehi held the traditional title Ghigau or "beloved woman," and she sat the Council of Chiefs for the Cherokee. She was also the head of the Cherokee Women's

Council. Her position gave her authority over the prisoners who were captured in battles and skirmishes, something she put to good use when she spared the life Mrs. Bean and learned from her how to weave cloth and raise dairy cattle before releasing her.

Nanyehi was well-known and respected in her lifetime by the white settlers who lived in Cherokee territory. Also called by her adopted English name Nancy Ward, she promoted friendly relations between Cherokees and whites, helped negotiate the Treaty of Hopewell, and lobbied her people not to sell their lands to colonizers. Living at a time of tremendous upheaval in Cherokee civilization, she introduced dairy farming and other material and economic novelties into Cherokee life.

D. Alan Dean

FURTHER READING

Carney, Virginia Moore. *Eastern Band Cherokee Women: Cultural Persistence in Their Letters and Speeches.* Knoxville, TN: University of Tennessee Press, 2005.

Green, Rayna, *Women in American Indian Society*, Chelsea House, 1992.

McClary, Ben Harris. "The Last Beloved Woman of the Cherokees." *Tennessee Historical Society Quarterly* 21 (1962): 352–64.

Purdue, Theda. *Cherokee Women: Gender and Culture Change, 1700–1835.* Lincoln, NE: University of Nebraska Press, 1998.

RED CLOUD

Oglala Lakota leader

Born: 1822; North Platte, Nebraska
Died: December 10, 1909; Pine Ridge, South Dakota
Area of Achievement: Warefare, tribal leadership

Red Cloud led the Lakota (Sioux) Indians through a difficult period, effectively resisting the onrush of American westward advance and later helping the Lakota make the transition to reservation life under American rule.

EARLY LIFE

Red Cloud was born into the Oglala subtribe of the Teton branch of Lakota, or Dakota people (more popularly known as Sioux) on the high plains of what is now Nebraska. His father, a headman in the Brulé subtribe, was named Lone Man, and his mother was Walks-as-She-Thinks, a member of the Saone subtribe. There is disagreement over the origins of the name Red Cloud. Some sources contend that it was a family name used by his father and grandfather, while others claim that it was coined as a description of the way his scarlet-blanketed warriors covered the hills like a red cloud.

Little is known about Red Cloud's early life. His father died when he was young, and he was reared in the camp of Chief Old Smoke, a maternal uncle. He undoubtedly spent his boyhood learning skills that were important to Lakota men at the time, including hunting, riding, and shooting. Plains Culture Indians sometimes conducted raids against enemies, and Red Cloud joined his first war party and took his first scalp at the age of sixteen. Thereafter, he was always quick to participate in expeditions against Pawnee, Crows, or Ute. Other Oglala frequently retold Red Cloud's colorful exploits in battle. During a raid against the Crows, he killed the warrior guarding the ponies and then ran off with fifty horses. This was a highly respected deed among Plains Indians, whose horses were central to their way of life. On an expedition against the Pawnee, Red Cloud killed four of the enemy—an

Red Cloud (National Archives and Records Administration)

unusually high number in a type of warfare in which casualties were normally low.

During the early 1840's, most Oglala bands camped around Fort Laramie on the North Platte River, where they could obtain a variety of goods from white traders. Red Cloud was part of a band known as the Bad Faces, or Smoke People, under the leadership of his uncle, Old Smoke. Another band in the area, the Koya, was led by Bull Bear, the most dominant headman among the Oglala and commonly recognized as their chief. The two groups frequently quarreled. One day in the fall of 1841, after young men of both sides had been drinking, a member of the Bad Faces stole a Koya woman. Bull Bear led a force to the Bad Face camp and shot the father of the young man who had taken the woman. The Bad Faces retaliated, and when a shot to the leg downed Bull Bear, Red Cloud rushed in and killed him. This event led to a split among the Oglala that lasted for many years. It also elevated Red Cloud's standing among the Bad Faces, and shortly after the incident he organized and led a war party of his own against the Pawnee.

Soon after recovering from wounds suffered in that raid, Red Cloud married a young Lakota woman named Pretty Owl. Sources disagree as to whether he thereafter remained monogamous or took multiple wives, a common practice among prominent Lakota. There is no agreement on how many children he fathered, although five is the number most accepted by scholars. Over the next two decades, Red Cloud's reputation and status continued to grow. By the mid-1860's, he was a ruggedly handsome man of medium stature with penetrating eyes and a confident and commanding presence. He was also a band headman and a leading warrior with an increasing following among the Bad Faces. Lakota social and political structure was decentralized; no one person had authority over the whole group. Instead, certain leaders were recognized as chiefs on the basis of ability and achievement. An important member of his band, at this time Red Cloud was not yet a chief.

Life's Work

In the several decades before the Civil War, traders began operating in Lakota territory, followed by wagon trains, telegraph construction, and more. The Lakota welcomed most of the traders and at least tolerated most of the wagon trains, even though whites disrupted hunting by killing indiscriminately and chasing many animals away from traditional hunting grounds. By the closing years of the Civil War, American traffic across the northern plains increased even further. The discovery of gold in the mountains of Montana in late 1862 enticed more whites to cross Lakota land, leading to friction and occasional clashes. The final straw came when the government sent soldiers in to build forts and protect passage along a popular route known as the Bozeman Trail that linked Montana with the Oregon Trail.

> "*I am poor and naked, but I am the chief of the nation. We do not want riches but we do want to train our children right. Riches would do us no good. We could not take them with us to the other world. We do not want riches. We want peace and love.*"

In 1865, many Lakota, including Red Cloud, took up arms in resistance. Several Lakota leaders signed a treaty in the spring of 1866 that would open the Bozeman Trail, but Red Cloud and his many followers held out, insisting on a removal of soldiers. The government tried to ignore Red Cloud for a time, but the Lakota almost completely closed down travel and obstructed efforts to construct the forts. This was the high point in Red Cloud's career as a military strategist. He led his men to a number of victories, most notably the annihilation of Captain William J. Fetterman and eighty-two soldiers in an incident known to whites as the Fetterman Massacre and to Indians as the Battle of a Hundred Slain. In November of 1868, when, after negotiations, the army withdrew the troops and abandoned the forts, Red Cloud finally ended the war.

This victory increased Red Cloud's standing among his people, although he still was not the Lakota's exclusive leader. The U.S. government, however, assumed that he was the head chief and dealt with him as such. During the late 1860's, there was talk of creating a reservation for the Lakota, and Red Cloud surprised everyone by announcing that he would go to Washington, D.C., and talk about the idea.

Some have argued that Red Cloud was motivated by a desire to gain the status among the Lakota that he already enjoyed in the view of federal officials. On the other hand, he may have realized that since many white Westerners opposed a reservation and preferred the extermination of Indians, a reservation, combined with the withdrawal of troops from all Lakota lands, an important objective to Red Cloud, might be the best compromise he could achieve. He and twenty other Lakota leaders were escorted to the nation's capital in 1870 with great ceremony. Red Cloud did not win everything he wanted, but he

Two Oglala chiefs, American Horse (wearing western clothing and gun-in-holster) and Red Cloud (wearing headdress), shaking hands in front of teepee, probably on or near Pine Ridge Reservation. (Library of Congress)

clearly emerged as the most famous Native American of his time. He was applauded by many easterners who sympathized with Indians and saw Red Cloud as a symbol of justifiable response to white advance.

In 1871, Red Cloud settled on the newly created reservation, at the agency named after him. Then, only a few years later, gold was discovered in the Black Hills portion of the reserve, and the government pressured the Lakota to sell the area. When negotiations broke down, events quickly escalated into the Sioux War of 1876-1877. With one eye on the government, Red Cloud publicly opposed the armed action undertaken by some Lakota to stop the flood of prospectors onto their lands, but privately he seemed to sanction such moves.

Red Cloud frequently became embroiled in political battles with federal agents on the reservation. He tried to win whatever provisions and concessions he could to ease his people's suffering, and he resisted government efforts to break down traditional cultural and political life. When many Lakota became involved in the controversial Ghost Dance in 1889-1890, Red Cloud avoided early commitment to or open encouragement of participation. Many dancers, however, believed that they indeed had his support. Red Cloud's frequent compromise position and his seeming cooperation with government agents sometimes made him suspect among some of his people, and, as a consequence, his influence steadily eroded. He died on the reservation on December 10, 1909.

Significance

Red Cloud emerged as a military and political leader at a dramatic and tragic time in the history of the Lakota people. Onetime powerful nomadic buffalo hunters, they were going through far-reaching changes. American westward advance constricted their land base, destroyed the buffalo upon which their economy depended, and ultimately brought about their impoverishment. Moreover, government attempts to destroy traditional Lakota ways of life on the reservation, while never completely successful, resulted in cultural shock.

For a time, Red Cloud resisted militarily as effectively as any Native American leader ever had. Then, when American domination became clear, he attempted delicately to balance the two worlds of Indian and white, hoping to win the best results possible for his people under the circumstances. This was a difficult task, and he did not satisfy everyone. He was attacked from both sides—by whites for not doing more to encourage his followers to assimilate into the white world, and by some Lakota for being too willing to give in to government authorities.

Red Cloud stood as a symbol to many Indians (and some whites) of strong defense of homelands and culture, while to other whites he epitomized the worst in Indian treachery and savagery. For both sides, the name Red Cloud conveyed immense power and meaning. During the 1960's and 1970's, with the rise of the Red Power movement and a rejuvenation of Indian culture, he again became a symbol—this time to a generation of young Indian (and sometimes white) political activists who found inspiration in what they saw as his defiance in the face of unjust authority.

Larry W. Burt

Further Reading

Allen, Charles Wesley. *Autobiography of Red Cloud: War Leader of the Oglalas*. Edited by R. Eli Paul. Helena: Montana Historical Society Press, 1997. Red Cloud gave an oral account of his life to a historian in 1893, and Allen later prepared a manuscript with Red

Cloud's recollections. The manuscript languished in the offices of the Nebraska State Historical Society for decades until it was published by the Montana Historical Society in 1997.

Cook, James H. *Fifty Years on the Old Frontier.* New Haven, Conn.: Yale University Press, 1923. Neither scholarly nor complete in its coverage of Red Cloud, it does contain some interesting, colorful, and firsthand descriptions of the Lakota leader and some of his exploits by a prominent frontiersman and close friend.

DeMallie, Raymond J., ed. *The Sixth Grandfather: Black Elk's Teachings Given to John G. Neihardt.* Lincoln: University of Nebraska Press, 1984. Does not focus on Red Cloud's life specifically, but provides direct accounts of various events in his life, especially surrounding the 1875-1876 Black Hills controversy, as told by Black Elk and other Lakota participants to poet John Neihardt.

Goodyear, Frank H., III. *Red Cloud: Photographs of a Lakota Chief.* Lincoln: University of Nebraska Press, 2003. Red Cloud was photographed many times because he believed these photographs helped him serve as a mediator between the Oglala Lakota and the federal government. This book contains more than eighty photographs by Mathew Brady, Edward Curtis, and other photographers. It also features a biographical and historical analysis written by Goodyear.

Hyde, George E. *Red Cloud's Folk: A History of the Oglala Sioux Indians.* Norman: University of Oklahoma Press, 1937. Less complete and authoritative than the more recent book by James C. Olson, but generally well written and reliable. Focuses on the earliest period of which historians have any knowledge of Lakota history to about the end of the Sioux War of 1876-1877.

---. *A Sioux Chronicle.* Norman: University of Oklahoma Press, 1956. A continuation of *Red Cloud's Folk* that carries the story of the Oglala to the tragedy at Wounded Knee in 1890. Contains less information about Red Cloud, because his role was diminishing by the end of the nineteenth century. However, it does offer useful material on Red Cloud's part in Lakota history after the creation of the reservation during the 1870's.

Olson, James C. *Red Cloud and the Sioux Problem.* Lincoln: University of Nebraska Press, 1965. The best and most complete account of Red Cloud. Except for some background information on the Lakota and Red Cloud's early life, it begins with the period immediately after the Civil War and ends with the death of Red Cloud in 1909.

Robinson, Doane. *A History of the Dakota or Sioux Indians.* Aberdeen, S.D.: News Printing, 1904. Reprint. Minneapolis, Minn.: Ross and Haines, 1958. First printed by the South Dakota State Historical Society in 1904, this book bears the mark of scholarship in an earlier era in its attitude toward Indians. It is so factually solid and complete that it still stands as an important source for information on Red Cloud.

Utley, Robert M. *The Last Days of the Sioux Nation.* New Haven, Conn.: Yale University Press, 1963. An excellent history of the events surrounding the famous Massacre of Wounded Knee, including material about Red Cloud's participation in that event that reveals something about his role in Lakota society in 1890.

JOHN ROSS

Part-Cherokee leader

Born: October 3, 1790; Turkeytown, Alabama
Died: August 1, 1866; Washington, D.C.
Area of Achievement: Tribal leadership

As a leader of the Cherokee nation during its ordeal of forced removal and civil war, Ross is the supreme example of nineteenth century Native American statesmanship.

EARLY LIFE

Born in a Cherokee settlement in Alabama, John Ross was by blood only one-eighth Cherokee. His mother, Mollie McDonald, was the granddaughter of a Cherokee woman, but his father, the trader Daniel Ross, and all of his mother's other ancestors were Scottish. His father, while securing a tutor for his children and sending Ross to an academy near Kingston, Tennessee, did not want to stamp out his children's Cherokee identity, and his mother gave him a deep sense of loyalty to the tribe, to their ancient lands and traditions, and to the ideal of Cherokee unity. As a son of three generations of Scottish traders, Ross early showed an interest in business. In 1813, he formed a partnership with Timothy Meigs at Rossville, near modern Chattanooga, and two years later another with his brother Lewis Ross; during the Creek War of 1813-1814, when Cherokee warriors fought in Andrew Jackson's army, he did a lucrative business filling

John Ross (Wikimedia Commons)

government contracts. During the Creek War, he served as adjutant in a company of Cherokee cavalry.

By the mid-1820's, his increasing involvement in the political affairs of the Cherokee nation caused him to abandon business. In 1827, he settled at Coosa, Georgia, thirty miles from the new Cherokee capital at New Echota, and established himself as a planter, with a substantial house, orchards and herds, quarters for his twenty slaves, and a lucrative ferry.

Ross served as a member of four Cherokee delegations to Washington between 1816 and 1825 and was president of the tribe's National Committee in 1818, when it resisted the attempt of Tennessee to persuade the tribe to surrender their lands in that state. In 1822, he was a cosigner of a resolution of the National Committee that the Cherokee would not recognize any treaty that surrendered Cherokee land. In 1823, Ross earned for himself the undying loyalty of the majority of the tribe when he rejected a bribe offered by federal commissioners and publicly denounced them in a meeting of the National Committee.

Life's Work

Ross was president of the convention that in 1827 produced the Cherokee constitution. This document, in its assignment of powers to three branches of government, its bicameral legislature, and its four-year term for the principal chief, was modeled on the Constitution of the United States. In 1828, he was elected principal chief, an office that he held until his death, and in 1829 he went to Washington on the first of many embassies that he undertook in that capacity.

The Cherokee established their republic within the context of an ongoing struggle to maintain their traditional claims against state governments, particularly that of Georgia. In 1802, Georgia had ceded to the United States its western territory (what later became Alabama and Mississippi) in exchange for a promise that all Native Americans would be removed from Georgia. A substantial number of Cherokee, accepting removal, surrendered their land rights and moved west. (One of them was the great Cherokee genius Sequoya, who gave his people a syllabary for their language.)

With the inauguration of Andrew Jackson, who was determined to send the Cherokee west, and the discovery of gold on Cherokee land, it was clear that removal was almost inevitable. Ross was determined to exhaust every legal and political recourse, however, before submitting to the superior physical might of the U.S. government. Though Jackson was willing to assert the power of the federal government—even if it meant war—to put down any movement in South Carolina for "nullification" of the Constitution, he declared that in the Cherokee case he would not interfere with state sovereignty. As a result, his Indian Removal Bill of 1830 included the provision that any Native American who chose not to remove was subject to state law. Georgia therefore refused to recognize the legitimacy of the Cherokee republic and made no effort to prevent white squatters from moving into the Cherokee country. These official attitudes and the chaos caused by the gold rush produced a state of anarchy in which, on one occasion, Ross himself barely escaped assassination.

By 1833, pressure by the government of Georgia and by the Jackson administration was producing dissension among the Cherokee themselves. John Ridge, son of an influential Cherokee family, and Elias Boudinot, editor of the *Cherokee Phoenix*, were both working for acceptance of removal and were thus undermining the efforts of Ross, who wanted the tribe to resist removal, and if it were inevitable, to accept it only on the best possible terms.

In 1835, returning from a trip to Washington, Ross found his land and house occupied by a white man, who was able to present a legal title granted by Georgia. In the same year, the Ridge faction signed the Treaty of New Echota, accepting removal. In spite of the fact that it was signed by only a handful of Cherokee, in spite of opposition by the Cherokee who had already settled in the West,

Ross' home, now a historical site, in Rossville, Georgia. (Wikimedia Commons)

in spite of a protest signed by fourteen thousand Cherokee, and in spite of Henry Clay's opposition in the Senate, it was approved by the Senate in May, 1836, and signed by Jackson.

> "*In truth, our cause is your own; it is the cause of liberty and of justice; it is based upon your own principles, which we have learned from yourselves; for we have gloried to count your [George] Washington and your [Thomas] Jefferson our great teachers;*"

Under the conditions of the treaty, the Cherokee were given two years to prepare for removal, and Ross spent that time in further hopeless efforts to persuade the government to give the entire Cherokee people opportunity to accept or reject the treaty. The removal itself was flawed by looting, arson, and even grave-robbing by white squatters; disease was inevitable in the stockades that served as holding pens; of the thirteen thousand people who were removed, probably four thousand, including Ross's wife, died on the "Trail of Tears."

In his first years in Oklahoma, Ross devoted all of his energies to his efforts to unite three Cherokee factions: his own Nationalist followers, the Ridge-Boudinot faction that had accepted removal, and the Old Settlers, who had formed their own government and did not want to merge with the easterners. In July, 1839, a convention wrote a new constitution, virtually the same as that of 1827, and passed the Act of Union, which was ratified by all parties.

In spite of Ross's efforts for Cherokee unity, extremists in his own party exacted the traditional Cherokee penalty for selling tribal lands when they murdered Ridge and Boudinot. Ross was not involved in these crimes and did not condone them, but they were a source of disharmony in the tribe as long as he lived, and they were the primary reason that he had difficulty negotiating a new treaty with the government in an attempt to guarantee Cherokee claims to their Oklahoma lands. Ross had opposed removal because he knew that if the government were allowed to confiscate the Georgia lands they could confiscate lands in Oklahoma later. The government refused to agree to guarantees, however, because the followers of Ridge and Boudinot claimed that Ross was responsible for the murders; finally, in 1846, the Polk administration signed a treaty acceptable to all parties.

On September 2, 1844, Ross married Mary Bryan Stapler, daughter of a Delaware merchant, who bore him two children. The period from the 1846 treaty until the Civil War was a relatively happy time for Ross and for his people. He prospered as a merchant, raised livestock, and contributed much of his wealth to charities on behalf of poor Cherokee; under his guidance, seminaries and a Cherokee newspaper were established.

Though, by 1860, Ross owned fifty slaves, he opposed slavery on principle, and this issue during the 1850's was another source of tribal dissension, his full-blood followers opposing it and the mixed-bloods favoring it. When the war began and agents were working among the Oklahoma tribes on behalf of the Confederacy, Ross favored neutrality and adherence to the 1846 treaty. Only when the neighboring tribes accepted a Confederate alliance and the Cherokee nation was virtually surrounded was Ross willing to accept an alliance. However, in June, 1862, when Union forces finally arrived from Kansas, he welcomed them, though he and his family were forced to leave the Cherokee country as refugees when the Union forces withdrew. His four sons by his first wife served in the Union Army, and one of them died in a Confederate prison.

For the next three years, Ross was in the East working to persuade the Lincoln administration to send federal troops to the Cherokee country and to feed the six thousand pro-Union Cherokee who had taken refuge in Kansas. The last year of the war was a particularly unhappy time for him because of the illness of his wife, who died in July, 1865.

When Ross died on August 1, 1866, he was in Washington negotiating a peace treaty with the U.S. government and fighting the efforts of the Cherokee faction that had been pro-South in the war to get federal approval of a permanently divided tribe. The treaty that was proclaimed ten days after his death was his last contribution to the cause of Cherokee unity.

SIGNIFICANCE

John Ross was passionately devoted to the ancestral homeland of the Cherokee and to their cultural traditions, but when he recognized that removal might be inevitable he submitted to it in order to reestablish a unified Cherokee nation on the frontier; his people's achievement of a remarkable blend of tribal traditions and white man's political and economic methods was his greatest monument. Though he was "by blood" only one-eighth Cherokee, he grew up as a Cherokee, identified with the Cherokee people, and devoted his life to the great cause of tribal unity. The Cherokee tragedy, which remains permanently fixed as one of the most disgraceful acts of the American people, stands in contrast to the life of the man who was probably the most distinguished Native American political leader of the nineteenth century and who resembles Lincoln both in his political skills and in his vision of union as the only basis for peace and justice.

Robert L. Berner

FURTHER READING

Eaton, Rachel Caroline. *John Ross and the Cherokee Indians*. Chicago: University of Chicago Press, 1921. A doctoral dissertation that concentrates on the Cherokees' political ordeal during Ross's lifetime. Essentially accurate, though apparently written without access to all the early documents.

Jahoda, Gloria. *The Trail of Tears*. New York: Wings Books, 1995. Recounts the Cherokees' forced removal and resettlement west of the Mississippi River.

McLoughlin, William G. *After the Trail of Tears: The Cherokees' Struggle for Sovereignty, 1839-1880*. Chapel Hill: University of North Carolina Press, 1993. Examines the social, cultural, and political history of the Cherokee Nation in the forty years after the tribe was forced to resettle in Oklahoma. Describes Ross's leadership during this period.

Meserve, John Bartlett. "Chief John Ross." *Chronicles of Oklahoma* 13 (December, 1935): 421-437. A brief but balanced account of Ross's life, though flawed by several errors in detail.

Moulton, Gary. *John Ross: Cherokee Chief*. Athens: University of Georgia Press, 1978. The best and most nearly definitive account of Ross's life and political struggles. Most useful because of its copious notes, which provide all the apparatus necessary for further study.

Starkey, Marion L. *The Cherokee Nation*. New York: Alfred A. Knopf, 1946. A semipopular account of Cherokee history from the beginnings to removal, with a final chapter devoted to later events. Written from the point of view of the missionaries to the Cherokee and perhaps overly sympathetic to the Treaty Party.

Wardell, Morris L. *A Political History of the Cherokee Nation, 1838-1907*. Norman: University of Oklahoma Press, 1938. A scholarly account of the Cherokee from removal to Oklahoma statehood. Refers to Ross in passing.

Woodward, Grace Steele. *The Cherokees*. Norman: University of Oklahoma Press, 1963. The best general account of the full range of Cherokee history, from first white contact to the late twentieth century. A fuller and much more balanced history than Starkey's book.

SACAGAWEA

Lemhi Shoshone explorer

Born: May 1788; Lemhi River Valley, Idaho
Died: December 20, 1812
Area of Achievement: Exploration

Sacagawea was the only woman who accompanied the Lewis and Clark Expedition in its exploration of the territory acquired through the Louisiana Purchase, but as the expedition's primary guide and interpreter, she played a major role in its success.

Sacagawea (Wikimedia Commons)

EARLY LIFE

Sacagawea (sahk-ah-jah-WEE-ah) was born into a band of northern Shoshone Indians, whose base was the Lemhi Valley of central Idaho. Her name translates as "Bird Woman" (Hidatsa) or "Boat Pusher" (Shoshonean). The northern Shoshone, sometimes referred to as Snake Indians (a name given them by the French because of the use of painted snakes on sticks to frighten their enemies), were a wandering people, living by hunting, gathering, and fishing. As a child, Sacagawea traveled through the mountains and valleys of Idaho, northwest Wyoming, and western Montana. In 1800, at about age twelve, Sacagawea and her kin were encamped during a hunting foray at the Three Forks of the Missouri (between modern Butte and Bozeman, Montana) when they were attacked by a war party of Hidatsas (also called Minnetarees), a Siouan tribe; about ten Shoshone were killed, and Sacagawea and several other children were made captives. Sacagawea was taken to reside with the Hidatsas at the village of Metaharta near the junction of the Knife and Missouri Rivers (in modern North Dakota).

Shortly after her capture, Sacagawea was sold as a wife to fur trader Toussaint Charbonneau. A French-Canadian who had developed skills as an interpreter, Charbonneau had been living with the Hidatsas for five years. At the time that Sacagawea became his squaw, Charbonneau had one or two other Indian wives.

All that is known of Sacagawea for certain is found in the journals and letters of Meriwether Lewis, William Clark, and several other participants in the expedition of the Corps of Discovery, 1804-1806, along with meager references in other sources. The Lewis and Clark party, commissioned by President Thomas Jefferson to find a route to the Pacific and to make scientific observations along the way, traveled on the first leg of their journey up the Missouri River to the mouth of the Knife River, near which they established Fort Mandan (near modern Bismarck, North Dakota) as their winter headquarters. The site was in the vicinity of Mandan and Hidasta villages. Here the expedition's leaders made preparations for the next leg of their journey and collected information on the Indians and topography of the far West.

LIFE'S WORK

Sacagawea's association with the Lewis and Clark expedition began on November 4, 1804, when she accompanied her husband to Fort Mandan. She presented the officers with four buffalo robes. Charbonneau was willing to serve as interpreter, but only on condition that Sacagawea be permitted to go along on the journey. After agreeing to those terms, Lewis and Clark hired Charbonneau. At Fort Mandan on February 11, 1805, Sacagawea gave birth to Jean-Baptiste Charbonneau. Thus, along with the some thirty men, the "squaw woman" and baby became members of the exploring group.

The expedition set out from Fort Mandan on April 7, 1805. Charbonneau and Sacagawea at different times were referred to in the journals as "interpreter and interpretess." Sacagawea's knowledge of Hidatsa and Shoshonean proved of great aid in communicating with the two tribes with which the expedition primarily had contact. Later, when the expedition made contact with Pacific coast Indians, Sacagawea managed to assist in communicating with those peoples even though she did not speak their language. Her services as a guide were helpful only when the expedition sought out Shoshone Indians in the region of the Continental Divide in order to find direction and assistance in leaving the mountains westward. Carrying her baby on her back in cord netting, Sacagawea stayed with one or several of the main groups of explorers, never venturing out scouting on her own. Little Baptiste enlivened the camp circles, and Clark, unlike Lewis, became fond of both baby and mother.

Several times on the westward journey Sacagawea was seriously ill, and once she and Charbonneau were nearly swept away in a flash flood. In May of 1805, Sacagawea demonstrated her resourcefulness by retrieving many valuable articles that had washed out of a canoe during a rainstorm. Lewis and Clark named a stream "Sâh-câ-ger we-âh" (*Sah ca gah we a*), or "bird woman's River," which at a later time was renamed Crooked Creek. Not the least of Sacagawea's contributions was finding sustenance in the forests, identifying flora that Indians considered edible. She helped to gather berries, wild onions, beans, artichokes, and roots. She cooked and mended clothes.

On reaching the Three Forks of the Missouri, Sacagawea recognized landmarks and rightly conjectured where the Shoshone might be during the hunting season. A band of these Indians was found along the Lemhi River. Sacagawea began "to dance and show every mark of the most extravagant joy... sucking her fingers at the same time to indicate that they were of her native tribe." The tribe's leader, Cameahwait, turned out to be Sacagawea's brother (or possibly cousin). Lewis and Clark established a cordial relationship with Sacagawea's kinsmen and were able to obtain twenty-nine horses and an Indian guide through the rest of the mountains.

As it came down from the mountains, the exploring party made dugout canoes at the forks of the Clearwater River, and then followed an all-water route along that stream, the Snake River, and the Columbia River to the Pacific coast. At the mouth of the Columbia River, just below present Astoria, Oregon, the adventurers built Fort Clatsop, where they spent the winter. Sacagawea was an important asset as the expedition covered the final phase of the journey. "The wife of Shabono our interpreter," wrote William Clark on October 13, 1805, "reconsiles all the Indians, as to our friendly intentions a woman with a party of men is a token of peace."

Besides her recognition of topography that aided in finding the Shoshones, Sacagawea's other contribution as guide occurred on the return trip. During the crossing of the eastern Rockies by Clark's party (Lewis took a more northerly route), Sacagawea showed the way from Three Forks through the mountains by way of the Bozeman Pass to the Yellowstone River. Lewis and Clark reunited near the junction of the Missouri and the Yellowstone. Sacagawea, Charbonneau, and infant Baptiste accompanied the expedition down the Missouri River only as far as the Hidatsa villages at the mouth of the Knife River. On April 17, 1806, they "took leave" of the exploring group. Clark offered to take Sacagawea's baby, whom Clark called "Pomp," with him to St. Louis to be reared and educated as his adopted son. Sacagawea, who consented to the proposal, insisted that the infant, then nineteen months old, be weaned first.

With the conclusion of the Lewis and Clark expedition, details about Sacagawea's life become sketchy. In the fall of 1809, the Charbonneau family visited St. Louis. Charbonneau purchased a small farm on the Missouri River just north of St. Louis from Clark, who had been named Indian superintendent for the Louisiana Territory. In 1811, Charbonneau sold back the tract to Clark. Sacagawea yearned to return to her homeland. Charbonneau enlisted in a fur trading expedition conducted by Manuel Lisa. In April of 1811, Sacagawea and Charbonneau headed up river in one of Lisa's boats. One observer on board at the time commented that Sacagawea appeared sickly.

Sacagawea left Jean-Baptiste Charbonneau with Clark in St. Louis. On August 11, 1813, an orphan's court appointed Clark as the child's guardian. Sacagawea's son went on to have a far-ranging career. At the age of eighteen, he joined a western tour of the young Prince Paul Wilhelm of WÃ¼rttemberg, and afterward went to Europe, where he resided with the prince for six years. The two men returned to America in 1829, and again explored the western country. Jean-Baptiste thereafter was employed as a fur trapper for fifteen years by the American Fur Company. He later served as an army guide during the Mexican War. Joining the gold rush of 1849, Jean-Baptiste set up residence in Placer County, California. Traveling through Montana in May of 1866, he died of pneumonia.

There once was a lively controversy over the correct determination of the date and place of Sacagawea's death. Grace Raymond Hebard, a professor at the University of Wyoming, published the biography *Sacajawea* in 1933, in which she went to great lengths to prove that Sacagawea died on April 9, 1884. Hebard traced the alleged wanderings of the "Bird Woman" to the time that she settled down on the Wind River Reservation in Wyoming. Hebard made a substantial case, based on oral testimony of persons who had known the "Bird Woman"; the hearsay related to known details of the Lewis and Clark expedition. Hebard also relied upon ethnological authorities.

At the heart of the controversy is a journal entry of John Luttig, resident fur company clerk at Fort Manuel. On December 20, 1812, he recorded: "this Evening the Wife of Charbonneau, a Snake Squaw died of a putrid fever she was a good and the best Women in the fort, aged abt 25 years she left an infant girl." It is known that Sacagawea had given birth to a daughter, Lizette. The Luttig journal was not published until 1920. Hebard claimed that the death notice referred to Charbonneau's other

Shoshone wife, Otter Woman. The issue, however, seems put to rest by the discovery in 1955 of a document in William Clark's journal dated to the years 1825 to 1828. Clark's list of the status of members of his expedition states: "Se car ja we au Dead." Nevertheless, the notion that Sacagawea lived until the 1880's continues to have support.

Significance

Sacagawea had a fourfold impact on the Lewis and Clark expedition. Though she viewed much of the country the group traversed for the first time, her geographical knowledge was most important in locating the Shoshones in the Rocky Mountains and directing Clark's party through the Bozeman Pass. At crucial instances her services as a translator were essential, and she served as a contact agent. Perhaps, most of all, as an Indian mother with a young baby, she dispelled many of the fears of the Indians encountered on the journey, particularly the fear that the expedition might harm them.

Sacagawea may be credited as a primary factor in ensuring the success of the Lewis and Clark expedition. Sacagawea also contributed to the uplifting of morale. Throughout the venture she exhibited courage, resourcefulness, coolness, and congeniality. The presence of mother and baby encouraged a certain civilized restraint among the members of the party. Henry Brackenridge, who met Sacagawea in April of 1811, said that she was "a good creature, of a mild and gentle disposition." Clark expressed regrets at the end of the expedition that no special reward could be given to Sacagawea. In many ways she was more valuable to the expedition than her husband, who ultimately received compensation for their efforts.

Sacagawea's place in history was long neglected. Interest in her life, however, gained momentum with the centenary celebrations of the Lewis and Clark expedition during the early twentieth century and especially with the rise of the suffrage movement, which saw in Sacagawea a person of womanly virtues and independence. Eva Emery Dye's novel, *The Conquest: The True Story of Lewis and Clark* (1902), did much during the course of its ten editions to popularize an exaggerated role of Sacagawea on the famous journey of discovery.

Sacagawea attracted new attention in 2000, when the U.S. Mint began issuing a new dollar coin with her image on the front. Images of American Indians had been used on many earlier coins—such as the "Indian head" penny and the "buffalo" nickel—but new Sacagawea dollar was the first coin to feature the image of a specific Indian person.

Harry M. Ward

Further Reading

Anderson, Irving. "A Charbonneau Family Portrait." *American West* 17 (Spring, 1980): 4-13, 58-64. Written for a popular audience, this article provides a thorough and reliable account of the lives of Sacagawea, her husband Toussaint, and her son Jean-Baptiste.

Chuinard, E. G. "The Actual Role of the Bird Woman." *Montana: The Magazine of Western History* 26 (Summer, 1976): 18-29. Emphasizes the role of Sacagawea as a guide and contact agent and challenges the exaggeration of her actual accomplishments.

Clark, Ella E., and Margot Edmonds. *Sacagawea of the Lewis and Clark Expedition*. Berkeley: University of California Press, 1979. Includes discussion of Sacagawea's life and the efforts made to popularize her legend. Although they provide a relatively accurate account, the authors choose to accept the discredited theory that Sacagawea lived until 1884.

Howard, Harold P. *Sacajawea*. Norman: University of Oklahoma Press, 1971. A balanced biography aimed at a general audience, this work attempts to sort out fact from legend in the life of Sacagawea.

Hunsaker, Joyce Badgley. *Sacagawea Speaks: Beyond the Shining Mountains with Lewis and Clark*. Guilford, Conn.: Two Dot Books, 2001. Sacagawea recounts her experiences with the Corps of Discovery. Hunsaker uses oral tradition, scholarly research, anecdotes, and other materials to compile Sacagawea's first-person narrative.

Jackson, Donald, ed. *Letters of the Lewis and Clark Expedition, with Related Documents, 1783-1854*. 2d ed. 2 vols. Urbana: University of Illinois Press, 1978. Contains a variety of letters, journal entries, and other papers relevant to the activities of the expedition. Sheds some light on the contribution of the Charbonneau family.

Nelson, W. Dale. *Interpreters with Lewis and Clark: The Story of Sacagawea and Toussaint Charbonneau*. Denton: University of North Texas Press, 2003. Examines the contributions of Toussaint and Sacagawea to the Lewis and Clark expedition. Nelson seeks to rehabilitate Toussaint's character and reputation.

Perdue, Theda, ed. *Sifters: Native American Women's Lives*. New York: Oxford University Press, 2001. Chapter 4 in this collection of biographies focuses on the myth and reality of Sacagawea's life.

Ronda, James P. *Lewis and Clark Among the Indians*. Lincoln: University of Nebraska Press, 1984. This scholarly study examines the contact made between the Lewis and Clark expedition and the Indians. Provides insights into Sacagawea's contributions to the success of the expedition. Includes an appendix that evaluates various books and articles about Sacagawea.

SITTING BULL

Hunkpapa Lakota holy man

Born: March 1, 1831; Grand River, Dakota Territory
Died: December 15, 1890; Standing Rock Indian Reservation, South Dakota
Areas of achievement: Government and politics, warfare and conquest

One of the outstanding icons of nineteenth century Indian defiance of American expansion, Sitting Bull led his Lakota (Sioux) people from their zenith in the middle of the nineteenth century to the decline of their culture in the face of superior technology and numbers of the whites.

Sitting Bull (Library of Congress)

EARLY LIFE

Sitting Bull was born Tatanka Iyotanka in a village a few miles below where Bullhead, South Dakota, now stands. During his first fourteen years, his Lakota (Sioux) friends called him Slow, a name he earned because of his deliberate manner and the awkward movement of his sturdy body. The youth grew to manhood as a member of the Hunkpapa tribe, one of seven among the Teton Lakota, the westernmost division of the Sioux Confederation. His people thrived as a nomadic hunter-warrior society. As an infant strapped to a baby-board, he was carried by his mother as the tribe roamed the northern Plains hunting buffalo. At five years, he rode behind his mother on her horse and helped as best he could around the camp. By the age of ten, he rode his own pony, wrapping his legs around the curved belly of the animal (a practice that caused him to be slightly bowlegged for the remainder of his years). He learned to hunt small game with bow and arrows and to gather berries. He reveled in the games and races, swimming and wrestling with the other boys. His was an active and vigorous life, and he loved it.

The warrior dimension of Lakota male life came more into focus as the boy grew. The Tetons concentrated most of their wrath on the Crow and Assiniboin Indians at first, and the whites at a later time. The hub of Lakota society centered on gaining prestige through heroic acts in battle. Counting coups by touching an enemy with a highly decorated stick was top priority. The Lakota lad learned his lessons well, and, at the age of fourteen, he joined a mounted war party. He picked out one of the enemy, and, with a burst of enthusiasm and courage, he charged the rival warrior and struck him with his coup stick. After the battle, word of this heroic deed spread throughout the Hunkpapa village. The boy had reached a milestone in his development; for the remainder of his life, he enjoyed telling the story of his first coup. Around the campfire that night, his proud father, Jumping Bull, gave his son a new name. He called him Sitting Bull after the beast that the Lakota respected so much for its tenacity. A buffalo bull was the essence of strength, and a "sitting bull" was one that held his ground and could not be pushed aside.

In 1857, Sitting Bull became a chief of the Hunkpapa. He had ably demonstrated his abilities as a warrior, and his common sense and his leadership traits showed promise of a bright future for him. Although his physical appearance was commonplace, he was convincing in argument, stubborn, and quick to grasp a situation. These traits gained for him the respect of his people as a warrior and as a statesman.

> *"I wish it to be remembered that I was the last man of my tribe to surrender my rifle."*

LIFE'S WORK

Sitting Bull's leadership qualities were often put to the test in his dealings with the whites. During the 1860's, he skirmished with the whites along the Powder River in Wyoming. He learned of their method of fighting, and he was impressed with their weapons. In 1867, white commissioners journeyed to Lakota country to forge a peace treaty. They also hoped to gain Lakota agreement to limit their living area to present-day western South Dakota. While his Jesuit friend Father Pierre De Smet worked to gain peace, Sitting Bull refused to give up his cherished hunting lands to the west and south and declined to sign the Treaty of 1868. Other Lakota, however, made their marks on the "white man's paper," and the treaty became official.

Developments during the 1870's confirmed Sitting Bull's distrust of the white men's motives. Railroad officials surveyed the northern Plains during the early 1870's in preparation for building a transcontinental railroad that would disrupt Lakota hunting lands. In 1874, the army surveyed the Black Hills, part of the Great Sioux Reservation as set up by the treaty, and, in the next year, thousands of miners invaded this sacred part of the Sioux reserve when they learned of the discovery of gold there. The tree-covered hills and sparkling streams and lakes were the home of Lakota gods and a sacred place in their scheme of life. The whites had violated the treaty and disregarded the rights of the Lakota. Sitting Bull refused to remain on the assigned reservation any longer and led his followers west, into Montana, where there were still buffalo to hunt and the opportunity remained to live by the old traditions.

As many other Lakota became disgruntled with white treatment, they, too, looked to Sitting Bull's camp to the west as a haven from the greedy whites. In this sense, he became the symbol of Lakota freedom and resistance to the whites, and his camp grew with increasing numbers of angry Lakota.

The showdown between Lakota and whites came in 1876. The U.S. government had ordered the Lakota to return to their reservations by February of 1876, but few Indians abided by this order. The government thus turned the "Sioux problem" over to the army with instructions to force the Indians back to the agencies. In the summer of 1876, General Alfred H. Terry led a strong expedition against Sitting Bull's camp. The Indian chief had a premonition of things to come when he dreamed of blue-clad men falling into his camp. Soon, he would learn the significance of this portent. A detachment of cavalry from Terry's column under the command of Lieutenant Colonel George A. Custer attacked Sitting Bull's camp. The forty-five-year-old chief rallied his men, and they defeated Custer, killing more than three hundred soldiers, including their leader.

Although the Lakota had won the Battle of the Little Bighorn, they decided that it was time to leave the area and divide up into smaller groups in order to avoid capture. Many additional soldiers were ordered into the northern Plains, and they spent the remainder of the summer and fall chasing and harassing the fleeing Lakota. While other groups of Lakota eventually returned to their agencies, Sitting Bull led his people to Canada, where they resided until 1881. Even though the Canadian officials refused to feed the Lakota, the latter were able to subsist in their usual manner of hunting and gathering until 1881, when the buffalo were almost gone. Because of homesickness and a lack of food, Sitting Bull finally surrendered to United States officials, who kept him prisoner at Fort Randall for two years.

By 1883, Sitting Bull had returned to his people at Standing Rock Agency in Dakota Territory and soon became involved in unexpected activities. In that same year, the Northern Pacific Railroad sponsored a last great buffalo hunt for various dignitaries, and Sitting Bull participated. In the next year, he agreed to tour fifteen cities with Colonel Alvaren Allen's Western show. Sitting Bull was portrayed as the Slayer of General Custer, but the stubborn Indian chief found this label inaccurate and distasteful. In 1885, Sitting Bull signed with Buffalo Bill Cody's Wild West Show and traveled in the eastern United States and Canada during the summer. He sold autographed photographs of himself and eventually gave

Sitting Bull and Buffalo Bill, Montreal, 1885. (Wikimedia Commons)

away most of the money he made to poor white children who begged for money in order to eat. At the end of the season, the popular Buffalo Bill gave his Indian friend a gray circus horse and large white sombrero as a remembrance of their summer together.

During the latter part of the decade, Sitting Bull returned to Standing Rock, where he settled into reservation life. The Hunkpapa still cherished him as their leader, much to the dismay of agent James McLaughlin, who sought to break the old chief's hold over his people.

In 1890, Wovoka, a Paiute Indian prophet from Nevada, began to preach a message that most Indians prayed was true. He dreamed that he had died and gone to Heaven. There, he found all the deceased Indians, thousands of buffalo, and no whites. The Indian prophet taught that, in order to achieve a return to the old ways of life, the Indians had only to dance the Ghost Dance regularly until the second coming of the Messiah, who would be in the form of an Indian. The Ghost Dance spread rapidly throughout much of the West, and soon Lakota were following Wovoka's teachings. Sitting Bull had his doubts about the new religion, but he realized that it disturbed the whites and in particular agent McLaughlin, and so he encouraged his people to dance.

The events that followed brought about the death of Sitting Bull as well as the military and psychological defeat of the Lakota. Cautious Indian officials deplored the fact that the Lakota were dancing again. Sitting Bull, the symbol of the old culture, was still their leader, and they decided to arrest him. McLaughlin chose Lakota Indians who served in the Agency Police Force to apprehend Sitting Bull. They came to his hut to seize him during the night of December 15, 1890, and a scuffle broke out. The fifty-nine-year-old chief was one of the first to be killed. In the dust and confusion of the struggle, fourteen others died. Several days later, other Lakota who had left their reservation were stopped at Wounded Knee Creek, and a scuffle again broke out with the white soldiers, who were trying to disarm them and to force them back to the agency. When the fighting was over on that cold December day, 153 Lakota had died and the dream of a return to the old way of life was lost forever.

SIGNIFICANCE

Sitting Bull, the proud leader of the Hunkpapa, had died along with many of his people. He had served his people well as a feared warrior and respected chief. He had fought against Indians and whites, including sixty-three coups against unfortunate Indians. The whites had suffered their worst defeat when they attacked his village. Although the old chief was unable to fight, he proved his inspirational mettle to the people. During his last years, he continued to serve as a model for his followers, although in a losing cause.

Technology and the overwhelming white population were forces that even the stubborn Lakota leader could not subdue. Gone were the days of nomadic camp life, horseback riding, and buffalo hunting. Also gone were the memories of courtships and polygamous marriages: White Americans hoped to convert the Lakota tribesmen into Christian yeoman farmers. By 1890, the frontier phase of American history had passed, and citizens confronted the problems of immigration from southern and eastern Europe, the growing urbanization, and the massive industrialization that would make the United States a world leader. The Lakota life that was so well adapted to the Plains environment was gone forever.

John W. Bailey

Further Reading

Adams, Alexander B. *Sitting Bull: An Epic of the Plains*. New York: G. P. Putnam's Sons, 1973. A richly detailed popular account of Sitting Bull's life, with a good description of the various divisions and tribes of the Lakota.

Anderson, Gary Clayton. *Sitting Bull and the Paradox of Lakota Nationhood*. New York: Longman, Addison Wesley, 1996. Biography focusing on the challenges Sitting Bull faced in leading the Lakota people.

Bailey, John W. *Pacifying the Plains: General Alfred Terry and the Decline of the Sioux, 1866-1890*. Westport, Conn.: Greenwood Press, 1979. Follows Sitting Bull's career in the period after the Civil War, with particular emphasis on his role as the leader of the non-reservation Lakota and their conflict with the military during the 1870's.

Johnson, Dorothy M. *Warrior for a Lost Nation: A Biography of Sitting Bull*. Philadelphia: Westminster Press, 1969. A readable book based upon limited research. Includes Sitting Bull's pictographs or calendar of winter counts that recorded his feats in battle.

Utley, Robert M. *The Lance and the Shield: The Life and Times of Sitting Bull*. New York: Ballantine Books, 1994. A definitive biography that portrays Sitting Bull as a complex leader.

---. *The Last Days of the Sioux Nation*. New Haven, Conn.: Yale University Press, 1963. An excellent book that focuses on the death of Sitting Bull and the Wounded Knee battle of 1890. The author illustrates how the Lakota suffered a military and psychological conquest that saw their demise after the failure of the Ghost Dance.

Vestal, Stanley. *Sitting Bull: Champion of the Sioux, a Biography*. Boston: Houghton Mifflin, 1932. Rev. ed. Norman: University of Oklahoma Press, 1957. The most reliable biography of Sitting Bull, based upon oral and documentary research. The author was closely associated with the Plains Indians since his boyhood and proved to be a careful student of their culture.

Sarah Winnemucca

Northern Paiute writer and lecturer

Born: c. 1844; Humboldt Lake, Nevada
Died: October 16, 1891; Henry's Lake, Idaho
Also known as: Sarah Hopkins Winnemucca, Sally Winnemucca, Thocmetony ("Shell Flower")
Area of achievement: Writing, Indigenous rights

Author of Life Among the Piutes: Their Wrongs and Claims *(1883), Sarah Winnemucca was an influential advocate for Native American rights and one of the most accomplished Native American women in history.*

Early Life

Sara Winnemucca's father, known as Chief Winnemucca, was a tribal leader of the Northern Paiutes. When she was born, sometime around 1844, the Paiutes and another tribe called the Washos were the only inhabitants of what is now western Nevada. As a member of a line of tribal

Sarah Winnemucca (Wikimedia Commons)

leaders, Sarah Winnemucca enjoyed a privileged upbringing among the Paiutes. Also known as the Numa, her people were nomadic, roaming across the land of Nevada with the changing seasons. Her grandfather, Chief Truckee, was the first Paiute to work cooperatively with newly arrived whites. He fought with the Americans against the Mexicans for control of California. Winnemucca's father, however, was less comfortable with pursuing friendly relations with the white colonizers.

When she was six years old, she accompanied her grandfather on a trip to California. That was her first exposure to white people. When she was thirteen, she briefly became a servant in the household of an American military official, Major Ormsby, in Nevada. She returned to her tribe following an incident of mistreatment. When she was sixteen, she and her sister Elma traveled to California to attend a convent school in San Jose, but she remained there for only a few weeks. During these years of cultural upheaval and travels, Sarah Winnemucca learned to speak English and Spanish as well as three Indian dialects.

Life's Work

In Sara's lifetime, the land of her people was colonized with increasing intensity as white settlers arrived in droves to settle on their territory. Nevada became part of the United States with the Treaty of Guadalupe Hidalgo in 1848. At first part of the Utah Territory, it became its own territory in 1861 before being admitted as the thirty-sixth state in 1864. In these years, the Paiutes, who had in earlier times roamed freely across vast stretches of land, were confined to reservations. The disruption to their way of life was profound. First they were confined to the Pyramid Lake Reservation in Nevada, then they were moved to the Malheur Indian Reservation in Oregon. Later, they were sent to Yakima, Washington. When the tribe was moved to Pyramid Lake, they were expected to abandon their nomadic way of life and to live in a town like white people. They were forced to farm for their survival, but they were provided with little or no training. Worse, the land was arid. While at Pyramid Lake, many Paiutes died of starvation.

Sarah, building on connections established by her grandfather and taking on a leadership role in her community, spoke on their behalf with United States military leaders at Camp McDermit in Nevada. She described their desperate situation and begged the United States to help. Eventually, because of her efforts, supplies arrived at the reservation, saving hundreds of lives.

Sarah then became an interpreter in the employ of the United States military. It was a difficult position. By working with the colonizers, Winnemucca was often able to obtain decent treatment for the Paiutes, but it divided her loyalty and there were conflicts. She was eventually fired when the reservation came under the administration of a new agent, William Rinehart, with whom she could not get along. In 1878, she worked for the United States Army during the Bannock War, a small war fought against the Bannock tribe who were Paiutes but culturally similar to the Northern Shoshone. A group of Bannock Indians had captured her father, and Winnemucca traveled on horseback over 200 miles, without sleep, to reach them. Her work mediating between the Indians and the United States military was noted on the front page of the *New York Times* in an article with the headline, "A Brave Indian-Squaw, Sarah, Daughter of the Paiute Head Chief, Penetrates to the Hostiles' Camp and Rescues Her Father and Brothers."

> "When I think of my past life, and the bitter trials I have endured, I can scarcely believe I live, and yet I do; and, with the help of Him who notes the sparrow's fall, I mean to fight for my down-trodden race while life lasts."

In 1880, Sarah traveled to Washington DC with her father to meet the secretary of the interior, Charles Schurz to plead for better treatment on behalf of her people. In particular, they sought permission for them to return to the Malheur reservation. Although they were granted permission, the return never materialized. Because of incidents like this, some among the Paiutes were skeptical of Sarah's collaborationist approach, and they accused her of being interested in advancing herself personally. Three years later, she wrote *Life Among the Piutes* in English and addressed to a white audience. Nevertheless, in the book she responded to her people's accusations against her, writing, "You have a right to say I have sold you. It looks so. I have told you many things which are not my own words, but the words of the agents and the soldiers… they were the words of the white people, not mine."

Sarah became a celebrity on the East coast when she began to receive financial support from Elizabeth Palmer Peabody and Mary Peabody Mann, two prominent women from an important New England family. They funded speaking engagements in which Sarah dressed in native attire and spoke before well-to-do white audiences, describing her life and the hardships experienced by her people. Giving over 400 speeches in New England, she had occasion to meet important literary and political figures like the Supreme Court Justice Oliver Wendell Holmes and the writers Ralph Waldo Emerson and John Greenleaf Whittier. Sarah did this for only a few years, however, before growing disillusioned.

She returned to the West and opened a school where she taught Paiute children English and instructed them in trades that they could use to survive in white American culture. The school was never well-funded and it closed soon after opening. She retired to live with her sister Elma in Montana where she died a few years later in 1891. She was forty-seven years old.

Significance

Winnemucca's life was spent straddling white and native cultures and attempting to translate between them. Her liminal position in this regard is an example of what W.E.B. Du Bois, in the context of African-American experience, would later call "double consciousness": the conflicted or mixed identity in the psycho-social experience of members of subordinated groups. As a result of her efforts to navigate between two cultures, Winnemucca was sometimes held in deep suspicion by both.

Her most important legacy is her book, *Life Among the Piutes*. More than an autobiography, it is an important document describing the westward expansion of white settlements seen from the point of view of Native Americans. The book was also the first ever published by a Native American woman.

D. Alan Dean

Further Reading

Boardman, Kathleen and Gioia Woods, eds. *Western Subjects: Autobiographical Writing in the North American West*. Salt Lake City: University of Utah Press, 2004.

Garceau-Hagen, Dee, ed. *Portraits of Women in the American West*. New York: Routledge, 2005.

Hopkins, Sarah Winnemucca. *Life Among the Piutes: Their Wrongs and Claims*. Reno, NV: University of Nevada Press, 1994.

Zanjani, Sally. *Sarah Winnemucca (American Indian Lives)*. Lincoln, NE: Bison Books, 2004.

Politics/Law

It's sometimes said that political figures today can never have the heroic status that (some) politicians had in the past—men like John F. Kennedy or Franklin Delano Roosevelt. The contentious nature of recent politics, the willingness to dig for dirt or expose private lives, and an unwillingness to give the benefit of the doubt—these things have made it difficult for political figures to be idolized to the extent that they once were. This shouldn't cause us to turn away from what is admirable about men and women in American politics, however, or to dismiss politics as dirty and divisive. The United States is a political entity. As such, politics is, first of all, something that has united and unites us. And, although not all Americans hold the same views, the vast majority subscribe to American ideals like liberty, equality, democracy, individualism, unity, and diversity.

Among other things, the figures in this section chart the expansion of liberty and equality over the course of American history. It features a large number of "firsts" in the progress of women and minorities in public life. Shirley Chisholm was the first African American Congresswoman. Judy Chu was the first Chinese-American to be elected to Congress. Thurgood Marshall was the first African American on the United States Supreme Court. Antonia Novello was the first Hispanic Surgeon General. They have made differences in American politics and law in cases such as *Brown* vs. *Board of Education* and on legislation like the *Education Amendments* of 1972, whose Title IX bans sex discrimination in schools.

James Earle Fraser's statue The Contemplation of Justice, *which sits on the west side of the United States Supreme Court building, on the north side of the main entrance stairs. The sculpture was installed in 1935.* (Matt H. Wade via Wikimedia Commons)

Madeleine Albright

Secretary of State, ambassador to the U.N.

Born: May 15, 1937; Prague, Czechoslovakia
Area of Achievement: Government and politics, Diplomacy

As ambassador to the United Nations and as the first woman to hold the office of U.S. secretary of state, Albright helped shape a foreign policy emphasizing an activist but not unilateral role for the United States.

Early Life

Madeleine Albright was born Marie Jana Korbel in Prague, Czechoslovakia, shortly before Nazi Germany took control of the country. Her father, Josef Korbel, was an intellectual and a member of the Czech diplomatic corps. Her mother, Anna Speeglova Korbel, was the daughter of a prosperous family. Albright had two siblings: Katherine Korbel Silva and John Joseph Korbel. Albright's grandparents were Jewish, and three of them died in the Holocaust a fact Albright revealed only after her appointment as secretary of state. Her parents converted to Roman Catholicism, apparently to escape persecution, and Albright grew up celebrating Christian rituals such as Christmas and Easter.

Albright's earliest experiences were shaped by World War II. When German agents took power in Czechoslovakia in 1938, her father, an outspoken opponent of the Nazis, was targeted for execution. While Josef Korbel tried to get false diplomatic papers that would get his family out of the country, he and his wife walked the streets of Prague with the infant Albright, making sure they stayed in public places where the Nazis would not assault him. They were able to escape to England. Albright later recalled staying in London air-raid shelters and sleeping under a steel table during bombing raids. During her stay, she became fluent in English. After the war, the Korbel family returned briefly to Prague. Josef soon resumed his diplomatic career, which took him to Belgrade, Yugoslavia, and then to New York, where he was assigned a position at the United Nations.

While the Korbels were in New York, Czechoslovakia experienced another coup; the communists took charge and Josef Korbel was once again a wanted man. The family was granted political asylum in the United States, and in 1949 they moved to Colorado, where Josef became a professor of international relations at the University of Denver. A respected scholar and the author of many books on diplomacy, Josef Korbel was Albright's first major intellectual authority. She has attributed many of her views to her father's influence.

Madeleine Albright (Wikimedia Commons)

In Colorado, Albright attended a small private high school. She won a scholarship to Wellesley College in Massachusetts, where she majored in political science, edited the college newspaper for a year, and campaigned for Democratic presidential candidate Adlai Stevenson. In 1959, she graduated with honors.

Only three days after graduation, Albright married Joseph Medill Patterson Albright, the heir of a prominent newspaper family. They moved to Chicago, where he was employed with the *Chicago Sun-Times*. Albright, however, was told that as a journalist's spouse, she would never be hired by a newspaper. Instead, she worked briefly in public relations for the *Encyclopedia Britannica* before the family moved to New York City in 1961. During the next six years, Albright gave birth to three daughters: twins, named Alice and Anne, and Katherine. She also enrolled in the graduate program in public law and government at Columbia University.

LIFE'S WORK

Albright has credited her success to her willingness to work hard. While she pursued graduate study and raised a family, she typically awoke at 4:30 a.m. and worked late into the night. She earned a master's degree, a certificate in Russian studies, and, in 1976, a doctorate. Her dissertation concerned the role of the press in the 1968 crisis in Czechoslovakia, during which dissidents tried to end Soviet control of the country. The dissertation, like much of her later career and writing, would combine her fascinations with journalism and foreign policy. At Columbia, Albright studied with Professor Zbigniew Brzezinski, who directed the Institute on Communist Affairs. Along with her father, Brzezinski would be one of Albright's most important intellectual mentors.

> "When we're trying to solve difficult national issues it's sometimes necessary to talk to adversaries as well as friends. Historians have a word for this: diplomacy."

In 1968, Albright's husband was transferred to Washington, D.C., where he became the bureau chief of Newsday. Albright became involved with her daughters' private school, for which she organized several successful fund-raising projects. As a result, a friend recommended her as a fund-raiser for Senator Edmund Muskie's campaign for the 1972 Democratic presidential nomination. Although Muskie did not win the nomination, he hired Albright to serve as the chief legislative assistant in his Senate office. She was especially involved in assisting Muskie with his duties as a member of the Senate Foreign Relations Committee.

When Jimmy Carter was elected president in 1976, he appointed Brzezinski to be his national security adviser. Brzezinski brought Albright onto the staff of the National Security Council, where she worked as congressional liaison. When Ronald Reagan became president in 1981, Albright moved from governmental service to a position as senior fellow in Soviet and Eastern European Affairs at the Center for Strategic and International Studies. In 1982, Albright and her husband separated, and she began to devote herself wholeheartedly to her career as a foreign policy analyst and advocate. With the support of a fellowship from the Smithsonian Institution's Woodrow Wilson Center for Scholars, she published *Poland: The Role of the Press in Political Change* (1983).

In 1982 Albright joined the faculty of Georgetown University, where she remained until 1993 and where she returned after her service as secretary of state. Her experience as a faculty member was a decided success. She served as a professor of international affairs and directed the school's Women in Foreign Service program. She was named teacher of the year on four occasions. While on the Georgetown faculty, Albright began inviting a variety of guests from academia, the diplomatic service, journalism, and politics to her home for discussions of international issues. Among those who attended Albright's "salons" was the governor of Arkansas, Bill Clinton; among the topics was the shape that U.S. foreign policy might take when the Democrats regained the White House.

Albright coordinated foreign policy for Democratic presidential nominee Walter Mondale and vice presidential nominee Geraldine Ferraro during the 1984 campaign. Four years later, she was senior foreign policy adviser and a major speechwriter for Democratic candidate Michael Dukakis. During the next four years, Albright served as president of the Center for National Policy, a Democratic think tank and a resource for members of Congress, where she dealt principally with Eastern European affairs. She was also involved with the Georgetown Leadership Seminar, an annual session for government officials, bankers, journalists, and military officers. Albright was a frequent guest on the public television program Great Decisions, which provided a chance to reach a larger audience with her views on international affairs.

When Bill Clinton ran for president in 1992, Albright helped to write the foreign policy sections of the Democratic party platform as well as position papers for the nominee. She was, therefore, an obvious choice for a diplomatic post in the Clinton administration. In December, 1992, the president-elect named her U.S. Ambassador to the United Nations and made her a member of his cabinet.

Albright brought great energy to her role at the United Nations. She traveled to the capital of every member nation of the Security Council, visited Somalia when U.S. troops were stationed there, and went to 18 Bosnia, where she strongly advocated greater American involvement in the conflict with Serbia. In 1995, she attended the U.N. Conference on Women, held in China, where she spent a day escorting First Lady Hillary Clinton. She also led the First Lady on a tour of Prague in 1996.

Albright increased the visibility of the seven women ambassadors to the United Nations by organizing lunches for them. She also led the effort to oust Secretary-General

Boutros Boutros-Ghali from his leadership post. Boutros-Ghali was intensely unpopular with conservatives in the U.S. Congress, and her opposition to him later helped to win Senate approval for her appointment as secretary of state. While serving in the United Nations, Albright remained closely tied to the decision-making process in Washington, D.C., where she attended cabinet meetings and sessions of the National Security Council's principals' group.

After Clinton was reelected in 1996, it soon became apparent that Secretary of State Warren Christopher would step down from his post. The president considered several former senators and career diplomats to fill the position, but he eventually chose to nominate Albright. She was easily confirmed by the Senate, which supported her nomination by a vote of 99-0.

As secretary of state, Albright faced instability in many areas of the world, financial crises that had diplomatic repercussions, and a reconsideration of relations with some of the United States' friends and adversaries. For example, in the Middle East, hostile relations with Iraq continued as Saddam Hussein apparently persisted in threatening his neighbors and in resisting United Nations inspections of his country's weapons capabilities. The United States maintained a hard line against the Iraqi leader while trying to ease the hardships endured by the people of that country. On the other hand, a dialogue emerged between the United States and Iran, with Secretary Albright suggesting that the two former adversaries might look for common ground. She encouraged the Israelis and Palestinians to continue their peace process and negotiate the future of the disputed territories.

With respect to Europe, Albright was an enthusiastic supporter of an expansion of the North Atlantic Treaty Organization (NATO) to include Poland and the Czech Republic and of the Good Friday agreement to resolve the political and religious conflicts in Northern Ireland. She advocated a strong multilateral response to the crisis in Bosnia, including a U.S. "police" presence, economic assistance, and punishment of war criminals. Albright also encouraged economic assistance to Russia to avert a political and economic emergency there. The secretary of state visited a number of African nations, as well as important Asian countries such as Korea, Japan, and China. In addition to reaffirming support for the United States' traditional allies, she explicated President Clinton's policy that promoted expanded trade with China while keeping the issue of human rights on the diplomatic agenda. In light of the nuclear tests conducted by India and Pakistan, Albright called for both countries to sign the Comprehensive Test Ban Treaty and reaffirmed the administration's desire that the U.S. Senate ratify the treaty. She also urged Congress to provide assistance through the International Monetary Fund to Indonesia and other countries experiencing economic crises and to appropriate funds to pay the United States' obligations to the United Nations.

Unlike some of her predecessors who saw foreign policy as a very personal achievement, Albright believed in developing a highly competent team to carry out the U.S. diplomatic agenda. For example, during Albright's term in the Department of State, Richard Holbrooke, who had negotiated the Dayton Agreement to resolve the Bosnian crisis, became ambassador to the United Nations. Albright described Holbrooke's appointment as part of her program to surround herself with strong people. Albright was also involved in promoting the humanitarian element in international development efforts, focusing on the connections between economic investments and everyday family life in less-developed countries.

Albright was particularly aware of the connection between the status of women around the world and its implications for U.S. foreign policy. She pressed for Senate ratification of the Convention on the Elimination of All Forms of Discrimination Against Women (CEDAW) and emphasized the need to stabilize birth rates, educate women, and involve them in international development efforts. She used her office to promote the empowerment of women as an integral element in achieving peace and prosperity and to attempt to increase the representation of women in diplomatic service. Albright saw herself as part of a network of female foreign ministers, many of whom became acquainted through their service in the United Nations. In response to questions about how she was viewed by leaders of countries whose cultures did not recognize the equality of women, Albright stated that she was always viewed with the highest respect. She noted that having a woman represent the most powerful country in the world was a message in itself.

Albright left the State Department in 2001 when Republican president George W. Bush took office. Since leaving her cabinet post, Albright has written two books, a memoir called *Madame Secretary* (2003) and *The Mighty and the Almighty: Reflections on America, God, and World Affairs* (2006), which considers the role of religion in world affairs. She also formed a strategic consulting firm, the Albright Group, resumed her faculty position as a professor at the Georgetown School of Foreign Service, held an appointment as distinguished scholar at the University of Michigan, and served on the board of

Albright, flanked by Secretary of State John Kerry and former Secretaries of State Hillary Rodham Clinton and Colin L. Powell (not pictured), delivers remarks at a reception celebrating the completion of the U.S. Diplomacy Center at the U.S. Department of State in Washington, D.C. on January 10, 2017. (Wikimedia Commons)

directors of the New York Stock Exchange. She has traveled abroad widely with organizations promoting human rights. In the latter role, Albright led a 2006 delegation to Africa as part of the Commission on Legal Empowerment of the Poor. She also served as a foreign observer of the 2007 Nigerian elections in conjunction with her involvement with the National Endowment for Democracy.

Albright strongly criticized the conduct of the Bush administration for its arrogance and unilateralism. She has argued that the war in Iraq is the worst disaster in American foreign policy and that its unintended consequences undermine the future security of the Middle East. Albright contends that the United States, rather than operating independently, must form partnerships with other nations to address vital issues of energy, environmental conditions, and terrorism. In Albright's view, terrorism is a method used by diverse groups to achieve their political goals. Unless Americans learn what terrorism is intended to accomplish, fighting a "war" on the method will be futile. She has said that to regain the trust of other nations, the United States must display not only its military power but also its power to do good. In her view, because the biggest problem in the world is the gap between the rich and the poor, addressing that gap should be an American priority.

As a political scientist, Albright has described the world as being in the process of a systemic change, whereby the old dominance of nation-states is challenged by larger forces such as globalization and by fragmentation through ethnic separatism and the power of actors who are not nations, such as the leaders of militant religious movements. Thus the system is far more chaotic than it was during the relative stability of the Cold War. Such a time of change requires a moral and multilateral foreign policy

In 2009, NATO Secretary General Anders Fog Rasmussen asked Albright to Chair a Group of Experts focused on developing NATO's New Strategic Concept, and in 2012 she received the Presidential Medal of Freedom, the nation's highest civilian honor, from President Obama. Albright continues her work at Georgetown as the first Michael and Virginia Mortara Distinguished Professor of Diplomacy and through her involvement in various organizations, including as Chair of both the National Democratic Institute for International Affairs and the Pew Global Attitudes Project.

Significance

Prior to Albright's appointment as secretary of state, no woman had held such a high position in the U.S. diplomatic service. Only one woman, Jeane Kirkpatrick, had preceded Albright as ambassador to the United Nations. Albright assumed the secretary of state's post with a reputation for being candid, and she was also outspoken about affirming her identity as a woman. Immediately after assuming her post, she noted that the secretary of state's office had been designed with a male occupant in mind: It was equipped with conveniences such as racks for men's suits and drawers for socks. Albright noted that apparently, she did not fit the traditional image of the secretary of state.

With respect to foreign policy, Albright was an enthusiastic advocate of the assertive use of U.S. power and influence if not military engagement. She stated that her "mind-set is Munich"; in other words, her view was formed by the experience of Czechoslovakia. At Munich in 1938, diplomats from Great Britain and France effectively handed control of her native country over to Adolf Hitler in return for his promise to cease aggression. Hitler then promptly took over Czechoslovakia, continued his conquests, and provoked World War II. In Albright's view, the lesson of Munich was that nations should not compromise with aggression; however, she always held that diplomacy must precede and would often avert conflict.

As secretary of state, Albright was a severe critic of nations charged with violations of human rights, including Cuba, Iraq, and Iran. On the other hand, she had to find ways to balance disapproval of China's internal repression with efforts to promote trade with the world's most populous country. During her tenure, the Department of State faced instability in Russia, conflicts in the Middle East, and tensions caused by the expansion of NATO, but the United States was able to avoid military involvement in any major foreign conflicts. She was a severe critic of the Bush administration's unilateral approach to international affairs and especially to its conduct in the war in Iraq.

Albright had an important influence in two areas of public life: as a model of a woman who achieved success in a nontraditional role and as a major architect of American foreign policy at the end of the twentieth century.

Mary Welek Atwell

FURTHER READING

Albright, Madeleine. *Madame Secretary: A Memoir.* New York: Miramax Books, 2003. Albright relates the story of her private life and career, focusing on her time as ambassador to the United Nations and as the first female secretary of state. She integrates her theoretical approach to international affairs with anecdotes and descriptions of world figures.

---. *Memo to the President Elect: How We Can Restore America's Reputation and Leadership.* New York: HarperCollins, 2008. Drawing on her experience as adviser to two presidents and as a key figure in four presidential transitions, Albright explains how to select a first-rate foreign policy team, how to avoid the pitfalls that plagued earlier presidents, how to ensure that decisions, once carefully made, are successfully implemented, and how to employ the full range of tools available to a president to persuade other countries to support U.S. objectives, while addressing the top international conflicts of the time.

---. *The Mighty and the Almighty: Reflections on America, God, and World Affairs.* New York: HarperCollins, 2006. Albright argues that effective foreign policy requires a recognition and an understanding of the importance of religion in international politics. She asserts the importance of finding common ground among religious traditions as an important tool in building peaceful relations.

---. *Prague Winter: A Personal Story of Remembrance and War, 1937-1948.* New York: Harper-Collins, 2013. Albright recounts the story of her formative years in Czechoslovakia during the tumult of Nazi occupation, World War II, fascism, and the onset of the Cold War.

Dobbs, Michael. *Madeleine Albright: A Twentieth-Century Odyssey.* New York: Henry Holt, 1999. Written by a reporter for The Washington Post, this journalistic biography emphasizes Albright's European background and her life experiences as well as her career in public service.

Gibbs, Nancy. "The Many Lives of Madeleine."*Time*, February 17, 1997. Gibbs writes that Albright's rise to the highest governmental position of any woman in U.S. history resulted from her political strategy, determination, diplomatic prowess, and perfectionism.

Lippman, Thomas. *Madeleine Albright and the New American Diplomacy.* Boulder, Colo.: Westview Press, 2000. Lippman, a reporter for The Washington Post who traveled with Secretary of State Albright for more than two years, focuses on her role in that office. He describes Albright's campaign for the position, her frustrations with the Middle East peace process, and her efforts to ensure a democratic government in the Russian Federation.

Sciolino, Elaine. "Madeleine Albright's Audition."*The New York Times Magazine,* September 22, 1996. Sciolino evaluates Albright's career as a key member of Clinton's foreign policy team and discusses her chances of becoming secretary of state.

LOUIS D. BRANDEIS

Lawyer, U.S. Supreme Court justice (1916-1939), and Zionist leader

Born: November 13, 1856; Louisville, Kentucky
Died: October 5, 1941; Washington, D.C.
Areas of Achievement: Law; social issues

Brandeis devised the "Brandeis brief," in which social and economic facts became part of the argument to justify legal reform. As a Supreme Court justice, he was noted for his eloquent and persuasive opinions in free-speech cases.

Louis D. Brandeis (Library of Congress)

EARLY LIFE

Louis D. Brandeis (BRAN-dis) was born in Louisville, Kentucky, on November 13, 1856. His parents, Adolph and Frederika Brandeis, were middle-class Czech Jews who emigrated to the United States in 1849. Two other Czech families to whom they were related—the Dembitzes and the Wehles—came on the same ship. After a brief sojourn in Madison, Indiana, they settled in Kentucky. The families started two successful businesses. Although not wealthy, they lived in comfortable surroundings. The home was bilingual; Brandeis's parents viewed German as the language of the arts and culture. The works of Friedrich Schiller and Johann Wolfgang von Goethe were read aloud in German to the children, and Brandeis's mother frequently played the compositions of Wolfgang Amadeus Mozart on the piano. Brandeis was heavily influenced by a much-admired uncle, Lewis Dembitz, a lawyer. He later adopted "Dembitz" as his middle name to honor his uncle.

The family did not observe Jewish ritual or traditions or celebrate the Jewish holidays. Brandeis attended the German-English Academy for a solid grounding in German and then the Louisville Male High School, where his grades put him at the top of his class. Shortly after his graduation, the family took an extended trip to Europe. During this European visit, Brandeis attended three terms at the Annen-Realschule in Dresden. In the fall of 1875, after his return to the United States, he entered Harvard Law School, where he again excelled.

Brandeis found life in Cambridge and Boston to his liking Although he practiced briefly in St. Louis after his graduation from Harvard, he returned to Boston in 1879 and formed a law partnership with Samuel D. Warren, one of his close friends from Harvard Law School.

LIFE'S WORK

The firm of Warren and Brandeis was immediately successful. It practiced commercial and business law primarily. Brandeis's special strength was mastering the facts of a case in great detail. This often enabled him to suggest litigation-avoiding solutions to business disputes. Warren and Brandeis became Boston's leading law firm, and the partners became wealthy. Brandeis's increasing prominence and his growing reputation as an innovator and reformer in the law brought many cases of broader social and economic significance to the firm. The most important of these was *Muller v. Oregon* (1908). This case tested the constitutionality of an Oregon statute establishing maximum hours of labor for women. Under the Supreme Court's precedents at the time, the statute would have been unconstitutional. Brandeis marshaled medical and other socioeconomic facts to prove that the law was rationally connected to reality and to the state's interest in promoting public health. The form of the brief Brandeis devised became known as the "Brandeis brief." His victory in *Muller v. Oregon* catapulted him to the highest level of the American bar.

> *"Fear of serious injury cannot alone justify suppression of free speech and assembly. Men feared witches and burnt women. It is the function of speech to free men from the bondage of irrational fears."*

Brandeis was also interested in social and economic reform by political means. He had started out as a Republican, had supported Theodore Roosevelt in 1904, but left the Republican Party after the election of William Howard Taft in 1908. In 1912, he was deeply involved in the presidential campaign as a supporter of and adviser to Woodrow Wilson. On Wilson's election, it was widely rumored that Brandeis would receive a high administrative post in the new administration. Apparently Wilson had considered Brandeis for the post of attorney general, but at least in part because of virulent objections from the business community, some of them probably anti-Semitic in origin, the appointment was not offered. Brandeis continued as an independent adviser to the president on antitrust, banking, and other business and labor issues.

After the death of Justice Joseph Lamar in 1916, President Wilson nominated Brandeis to fill the vacancy on the Supreme Court. A bitter four-month confirmation struggle ensued. Brandeis was opposed by the business community and by anti-Semitic forces, both explicit and veiled. He was charged with being a socialist and with unethical behavior as an advocate. The charges proved to be unfounded. Although for a time it appeared that the nomination would fail, the Senate acted to confirm his appointment on June 1, 1916. Brandeis took his seat on the Supreme Court on June 5, 1916. He was to serve for twenty-three years.

Although Brandeis was a nonobservant Jew, his other main interest outside the law was Zionism. He was a leader in the Zionist Organization of America from 1910 until his death, and although for a time he was at odds with the movement's leadership, his faith in the Zionist ideal never wavered. He also attempted to do what he could—with no more success than anyone else—to devise practical means of assisting European Jews threatened by the Nazi rule in Germany. He continued his active assistance to Zionism even after this appointment to the Supreme Court, an extrajudicial activity that would be frowned upon today.

As associate justice of the Supreme Court, Brandeis made his primary mark as a dissenter. He and Oliver Wendell Holmes were widely celebrated as champions of free speech, and the eloquence and power of their opinions have never been surpassed in American constitutional history. Brandeis's long struggle—eventually successful—against the Court's practice of striking down state economic and social legislation as violations of "liberty of contract" under the due process clause of the Fourteenth Amendment is less well known, but it remains one of his main contributions to the canon of American law. He also fought against the use of antitrust statutes to prevent or to punish the organization of labor unions. This battle, too, was eventually won.

Brandeis and the First Amendment

"Brandeis and Holmes dissenting" was commonly noted in free-speech cases before the United States Supreme Court in the 1920's and 1930's. Both justices were celebrated for their opposition to restrictions on speech. The dissents written by Justice Oliver Wendell Holmes were better known to the public and widely admired for their passion in defense of free-speech values. However, it was the craftsmanlike approach of Louis Brandeis that the Supreme Court later adopted. In effect, he established the right to free speech that Americans enjoy today.

The original constitutional rule for free speech was the famous "clear and present danger test." If a speech or publication presented a clear and present danger of resulting in some evil that the government had the power to prevent, then the speaker could be punished. It was the opinions of Justice Brandeis that ultimately persuaded later courts to put real teeth into the test. In case after case, Brandeis insisted that the "danger" has to be real and substantial; it has to be danger to the safety of the state itself, not just danger of riot or property destruction. Moreover, he argued that the prosecution in a free-speech case has to show that the words used were an actual incitement to imminent lawless action. If it were otherwise, then any criticism of the government's programs could subject the critic to criminal penalties. In *Whitney v. California* (1927), Brandeis's best-known free-speech opinion, he pointed out that restrictions on speech usually spring from fear: "Men feared witches and burnt women."

In 1939, Brandeis, then eighty-three, began to feel himself failing physically and mentally. His retirement on February 13, 1939, evoked hundreds of letters to the editor and newspaper editorials praising his work and his life. Many came from people who had formerly been his political adversaries. He lived quietly in retirement with his wife until his death after a heart attack in October, 1941.

SIGNIFICANCE

Brandeis's work on the Supreme Court remains significant because issues he considered important were carried into law. For example, because of his efforts, the people in the United States have the most freedom in the world in the areas of speech and press rights. The constitutional tests the Court uses derive directly from Brandeis's free-speech opinions. In the area of economic regulation Brandeis's views have also prevailed. Brandeis believed in capitalism, but he was opposed to banks and corporations growing too big because he feared that concentrations of capital would distort democratic processes.

As an assimilated American Jew, Brandeis and his support of Zionism inspired other assimilated Jews to remember their heritage, and his prominence helped create the atmosphere of public support for the state of Israel when it was founded.

Robert Jacobs

FURTHER READING

Burt, Robert A. *Two Jewish Justices: Outcasts in the Promised Land*. Berkeley: University of California Press, 1988. Burt attempts to discern what role the Jewishness of Justices Louis Brandeis and Felix Frankfurter played in their conduct on the Court.

Gal, Allon. *Brandeis of Boston*. Cambridge, Mass.: Harvard University Press, 1980. Traces the development of Brandeis's political and Zionist thought.

Halpern, Ben. *A Clash of Heroes: Brandeis, Weizmann, and American Zionism*. New York: Oxford University Press, 1987. Extensive discussion of Brandeis's role in the Zionist movement and his conflict with Weizmann over the future direction of the Zionist movement.

Mason, Alpheus Thomas. *Brandeis: A Free Man's Life*. New York: Viking Press, 1946. This biography draws heavily on Brandeis's papers and the recollections of his immediate family.

Strum, Philippa. *Louis D. Brandeis: Justice for the People*. Cambridge, Mass.: Harvard University Press, 1984. A brief overview of Brandeis's life and work.

Urofsky, Melvin I. *Louis D. Brandeis: A Life*. New York: Random House, 2009. A thorough biography of Brandeis, integrating his family, legal, political, and Zionist activities.

WILLIAM J. BRENNAN

Associate justice of the United States (1956-1990)

Born: April 25, 1906; Newark, New Jersey
Died: July 24, 1997; Arlington, Virginia
Area of Achievement: Law

The most influential liberal voice of the U.S. Supreme Court during the second half of the twentieth century, Brennan wrote many of the Court's landmark opinions in the areas of criminal procedures, First Amendment freedoms, equal protection, gender equality, and personal autonomy.

EARLY LIFE

The second of eight children whose parents were Irish immigrants, William J. Brennan was profoundly influenced by his hardworking father, who rose from a coal shoveler in a brewery to become a city commissioner and director

William J. Brennan (Library of Congress)

of public safety. Growing up in a working-class milieu, Brennan identified with poor people and favored labor unions. Adopting his father's liberal social philosophy and work ethic, Brennan made excellent grades in school while he worked at a large number of jobs, beginning in grade school and continuing through his college years.

Brennan majored in business and finance at the University of Pennsylvania, graduating with honors in 1928. The week before graduation, he married Marjorie Leonard, who worked in order to finance his legal education at the Harvard Law School, where he graduated in 1931. Admitted to the New Jersey bar the next year, he embarked on a career as a labor lawyer at a prominent law firm, where he was named a partner in 1937. Following the outbreak of World War II, he entered the U.S. Army as a major in 1942 and left the service as a colonel in 1945.

Life's Work

Returning to civilian life, Brennan was a leading voice in the court reform movement of New Jersey. In 1949, he was appointed a trial judge, and three years later he was appointed to the Supreme Court of the state. As a judge, he was a strong supporter for the rights of criminal defendants, and he criticized McCarthy-period excesses in speeches around the state. In 1956, President Dwight D. Eisenhower nominated Brennan as associate justice for appointment on the U.S. Supreme Court. Eisenhower's advisers convinced him that the appointment of a Roman Catholic Democrat from the Northeast would help Republicans gain votes in some of the closely divided states. In the Senate, Senator Joseph McCarthy was the person to oppose the nomination. Eisenhower would later refer to his choice of Brennan as one of his two major mistakes, the other being the selection of Chief Justice Earl Warren.

Despite Brennan's junior status, he quickly emerged as one of the most brilliant and influential of the justices. Quickly joining the Court's liberal wing, he would write a large percentage of the Warren Court's landmark decisions. However, Brennan usually took a more cautious and nuanced approach than did his liberal colleagues, avoiding absolute statements in favor of a "balancing" of competing legal values. Even his critics acknowledged the care and thoughtfulness of his writings.

Many of Brennan's more important judicial opinions dealt with issues of equal protection. In *Cooper v. Aaron* (1958), he asserted federal judicial supremacy in reaction to the "massive resistance" to desegregation orders in the South. His opinion for the Court in *Baker v. Carr* (1962) provided the foundation for the "reapportionment revolution," based on the principle of "one person, one vote." In the case of *Green v. School Board* (1968), Brennan rejected a "freedom of choice" plan that preserved racially segregated schools, and he insisted that school districts had the obligation to bring about desegregated schools. Brennan's *Green* ruling provided the basis for later decisions approving court-ordered busing plans, which he would consistently endorse.

Brennan also wrote many of the landmark First Amendment opinions, particularly in the area of free expression. His opinion in *Roth v. U.S.*(1957), for example, explicitly recognized for the first time that some forms of pornography were constitutionally protected. Although the opinion recognized that states might criminalize "obscenity," he defined obscenity so narrowly that it became very difficult to prosecute. In *New York Times v. Sullivan* (1964), Brennan's opinion for the Court recognized the constitutional right to criticize public officials without the threat of libel suits, based on "the principle that debate on public issues should be uninhibited, robust, and wide open." Rejecting the idea of absolute immunity from libel, however, he allowed officials to sue for "actual malice," which he defined as reckless and deliberate disregard for the truth. His majority opinion in *Goldberg v. Kelly* (1970) recognized welfare as a form of property for constitutional purposes, which meant that it could not be terminated except through fair procedures.

Beginning in the 1970's, as the Supreme Court became more conservative, Brennan and Thurgood Marshall were the strongest proponents of judicial liberalism. In *Gregg v. Georgia* (1976), they were the only justices to dissent and argue that capital punishment was inherently unconstitutional. On most constitutional and statutory issues, the two justices disagreed with the conservative William H. Rehnquist, who was appointed chief justice in 1986. In an increasingly polarized Court, Brennan worked tirelessly to attempt to achieve a liberal majority. In *Texas v. Johnson* (1989), he spoke for a 5 to 4 majority in striking down laws that criminalized the desecration of the flag of the United States.

Brennan was the Court's most outspoken proponent of gender equality. In the landmark case of *Craig v. Boren* (1976), his opinion for the majority recognized gender-based classifications would be subject to heightened scrutiny, which meant that any discrimination against women was likely to be found unconstitutional. Brennan, nevertheless, was a consistent defender of affirmative action programs that involved preferences on the basis of gender or race in order to counteract the effects of prior discrimination. He was also a strong supporter of the controversial "right of privacy," which included a woman's right to obtain an abortion, despite his active membership in the Catholic Church, which opposes abortion.

Brennan sometimes wrote very caustic dissents, and he occasionally became involved in public controversy. In the *South Texas Law Review* (1986), he responded to Attorney General Edwin Meese and other critics who accused him of "judicial activism," or rendering judgments based on ideological preferences rather than the literal words of the U.S. Constitution or the original intent of the Framers. Referring to these criticisms as "little more than arrogance cloaked as humility," he argued the Court should uphold the fundamental purpose of the Constitution, which was to promote the "human dignity of every individual." His approach was based on the concept of a "living Constitution," which assumes that the meaning of the Constitution changes as culture evolves. His conservative colleague Antonin Scalia described his jurisprudence as "results-oriented."

> "*The genius of the Constitution rests not in any static meaning it might have had in a world that is dead and gone, but in the adaptability of its great principles to cope with current problems and current needs.*"

Significance

Brennan exercised a profound impact on the Supreme Court during the second half of the twentieth century. During his tenure of thirty-four years, he authored 1,360 opinions, second in number only to those written by Justice William O. Douglas. In addition to his contributions as a researcher and writer, he was recognized as being unusually effective in negotiating with other justices to form a majority. Chief Justice Warren described him as "a prodigious worker and a master craftsman" who served as "a unifying influence on the bench and in the conference room."

Brennan was strongly committed to an activist Court that would not hesitate to take a strong stand in favor of the principles and values of judicial liberalism. While he avoided absolutist positions, he could be counted on to vote in favor of individual liberties, equality for minorities, the rights of criminal defendants, and personal autonomy in matters such as marriage and sexuality. Few of his opinions have been overturned, and he is widely recognized as one of the most articulate and thoughtful writers in the history of the Court.

Thomas Tandy Lewis

Further Reading

Goldman, Roger, and David Gallen. *Justice William J. Brennan, Jr.: Freedom First*. New York: Carroll & Graf, 1994. A scholarly and sympathetic analysis of Brennan's life and his career in jurisprudence.

Irons, Peter. *Brennan versus Rehnquist: The Battle for the Constitution*. New York: Alfred A. Knopf, 1994. Written by a prominent liberal lawyer, this book presents an excellent comparative analysis of two strong ideological voices that dominated the Supreme Court for many years.

Marion, David. *The Jurisprudence of Justice William J. Brennan: The Law and Politics of "Libertarian Dignity."* New York: Rowman & Littlefield, 1997. A close analysis arguing that Brennan's career represented the most important judicial force of the century, promoting an expansion of individual rights and human dignity.

Michelman, Frank. *Brennan and Democracy*. Princeton, N.J.: Princeton University Press, 1999. Written by an admiring former law clerk, this rather difficult book analyzes Brennan's views on the substantive and procedural aspects of modern democratic theory.

O'Brien, David M., ed. *Judges on Judging: Views from the Bench*. 2d. ed. Washington, D.C.: CQ Press, 2004. A collection of writings on judicial processes by justices of various courts in the United States. Includes two essays by Brennan: "The Constitution of the United States: Contemporary Ratification" and "Guardians of Our Liberties State Courts No Less than Federal."

Richards, Robert D. *Uninhibited, Robust, and Wide Open: Mr. Justice Brennan's Legacy to the First Amendment*. Boone, N.C.: Parkway, 1994. A relatively short account of Brennan's opinions on the major categories relating to freedom of expression, which he considered the "cornerstone of the democracy."

Schwartz, Bernard, and E. Joshua Rosenkranz, eds. *Reason and Passion: Brennan's Enduring Influence*. New York: W. W. Norton, 1997. Collection of interesting essays on a variety of topics written by journalists, legal scholars, and six Supreme Court justices.

Urofsky, Melvin I. *The Warren Court: Justices, Rulings, and Legacy*. Santa Barbara, Calif.: ABC-CLIO, 2001. An examination of the Supreme Court with Warren as chief justice. Includes profiles of the justices, including Brennan, the Court's discussions of its decisions, and an appraisal of its influence.

Ralph Bunche

Diplomat, political scientist, and civil rights leader

Born: August 7, 1903; Detroit, Michigan
Died: December 9, 1971; New York, New York
Also known as: Ralph Johnson Bunche
Areas of Achievement: Civil rights; Diplomacy; Education; Government and politics

During his distinguished career, Bunche promoted the Civil Rights movement, helped to organize the United Nations, worked as a mediator in numerous conflicts, and was awarded the Nobel Peace Prize.

Early Life

Ralph Johnson Bunche was born into a poor family in Detroit, Michigan, in 1903. His father, Fred Bunch, a barber, was frequently unemployed, and his mother, Olive Johnson Bunch, who contracted tuberculosis around 1912, was a member of a large extended family. In 1915, the family moved to Albuquerque, New Mexico, where they lived with Bunche's light-skinned grandmother, Lucy Johnson. In 1916, Fred left his wife and two children in search of work, promising to call for them when he found work, but Bunche never saw him again. In 1917, his mother died from tuberculosis. The night she died, he later recalled, "she had asked for milk and there was none in the house because I had drunk it up." Lucy Johnson assumed responsibility for raising the two children. They moved to South Central Los Angeles at a time when the region was beginning its economic decline.

Bunche always was an excellent student. At Jefferson High School, he was on the debate team, played basketball, worked as a paperboy, and was valedictorian of the class of 1922. His graduation address was titled "Our New Responsibility." He later attributed his "spirit of competition" to his grandmother's constant insistence "to let them, especially white folks, know that you can do anything they can do." Despite the economic challenges of the family, his grandmother insisted that he attend college. He enrolled at the University of California at Los Angeles (UCLA), where he was president of the debating society, a writer for the school newspaper, and a star basketball player. In 1927, he was awarded a B.A. with a major in political science, graduating summa cum laude and as class valedictorian.

The next year, Bunche started work toward a master's degree in political science at Harvard University. He had a tuition scholarship and earned his living expenses by working at a secondhand bookstore. His determination to outperform the other students created much stress, and he became addicted to cigarettes. Although offered a scholarship to pursue a Ph.D., Bunche declined in order to teach and organize a political science department at Howard University, the nation's premier black institution of higher learning. His colleagues at Howard included philosopher Alain Locke, sociologist E. Franklin Frazier, and the first black president of the school, Mordecai Wyatt Johnson. In 1929, Bunche took a leave of absence to earn a doctorate at Harvard, and while there he married Ruth Ethel Harris, one of his Howard students. In 1934, he was awarded a Ph.D. for his dissertation on the decolonization of the French empire in Africa, which won the Toppan Prize for the year's best dissertation in the field of government. During the next two years, a scholarship

Ralph Bunche (Wikimedia Commons)

> ### Bunche's Nobel Peace Prize
>
> Ralph Bunche was awarded the Nobel Peace Prize in 1950 for his central role in mediating the truce that ended the Arab-Israeli War of 1949. His involvement in the conflict began in 1946, when the secretary-general of the United Nations, Trygve Lie, commissioned him to assist the committee that recommended Palestine be portioned between Arabs and Jews. Soon after fighting broke out in 1948, Bunche served as assistant to U.N. mediator Folke Bernadotte, and after Bernadotte's assassination, Bunche replaced him. The negotiations dragged on for eleven months, taking place mostly on the island of Rhodes. Bunche became an expert on the conflict and exercised a combination of persuasion, determination, and patience. After negotiating Israeli agreements with Egypt, Lebanon, and Jordan, he announced on June 24, 1949, that Israel and Syria had accepted his compromise proposals. Representatives signed an armistice near Mishmar Ha Yarden, Israel, on July 20. Bunche later said that his success was partially attributable to a "coolness of temper and attitude of objectivity when dealing with human sensitivities and irrationalities." When informed that he had won the Nobel Peace Prize, he at first wanted to decline the honor, saying he should not be given an award for doing a job for which he had been paid, but U.N. officials insisted that the award would help to publicize the organization's contributions to peace. Bunche devoted his Nobel address to the importance of U.N. efforts to preserve world peace. He was the first person of African ancestry to receive the prestigious award.

allowed Bunche to do postgraduate study in African anthropology at the London School of Economics and the University of Cape Town in South Africa.

LIFE'S WORK

In 1936, Bunche returned to his teaching and administrative activities at Howard University. During this period, he was committed to a quasi-Marxian ideology and was a contributing editor of *Science and Society: A Marxian Quarterly*. His first book, *World View of Race* (1936), predicted that the future would see many class-based wars between the haves and have-nots. In 1938, he began working with Swedish economist Gunnar Myrdal, who had funding from the Carnegie Corporation to study the status of African Americans. Bunche was responsible for substantial parts of the monumental work *An American Dilemma: The Negro Problem and Modern Democracy* (1944), which would later make a significant contribution toward the Civil Rights movement. In doing field research for the study, Bunche spent considerable time in the South. One of the valuable fruits of the research was his long monograph *The Political Status of the Negro in the Age of FDR*, which was published in 1973.

> "*To suggest that war can prevent war is a base play on words and a despicable form of warmongering. The objective of any who sincerely believe in peace clearly must be to exhaust every honourable recourse in the effort to save the peace. The world has had ample evidence that war begets only conditions which beget further war.*"

When the United States entered World War II in 1941, Bunche left academia to do research on African colonial affairs for the Office of Strategic Services (OSS). Among other tasks at OSS, Bunche wrote the manual used by U.S. troops for fighting in North Africa. In early 1944, he was transferred to the U.S. Department of State, and he was soon promoted to the Office of Political Affairs as head of the division concerned with trusteeships. In this capacity, he actively participated in many of the high level meetings responsible for negotiating the charter of the United Nations (U.N.), and he was the first African American to serve on the U.S. delegation to the General Assembly. By this time, his ideological commitment had changed from Marxist socialism to democratic liberalism, and he disagreed with many of his earlier writings.

In 1946, the Secretary General of the United Nations, Trygve Lie, appointed Bunche as director of the Trusteeship Division, a position Bunche held for the next nine years. His greatest achievement during this period was negotiating the 1949 truce that ended the first Arab-Israeli War, for which he was awarded the Nobel Peace Prize. Bunche was promoted to under-secretary general of the United Nations in 1955; his title was changed to under-secretary general for special political affairs in 1957.

In 1956, Bunche's mediation during the Suez Canal

Bunche greeting people at the Civil Rights March on Washington. (National Archives and Records Administration)

Crisis helped secure an agreement on the stationing of U.N. emergency forces to supervise the Egypt-Israeli border. Shortly thereafter, he was actively involved in negotiations to end the violent civil war in the former Belgian Congo (now known as the Democratic Republic of the Congo) and helped to prevent the dissolution of the fragile new country. During this complex conflict, some militant African Americans attacked him as an "Uncle Tom" because of his refusal to give unqualified support to the popular nationalist leader, Patrice Lumumba, and some people blamed him for Lumumba's tragic death. In subsequent years, Bunche was frequently the U.N.'s primary troubleshooter in attempts to mediate peace settlements in places such as Cyprus, Yemen, and Kashmir.

Throughout his busy career, Bunche was a strong supporter of the Civil Rights movement. In August, 1963, he was one of the speakers at the momentous March on Washington, although his address was overshadowed by Martin Luther King, Jr.'s "I Have a Dream" speech. In March, 1965, despite suffering from chronic phlebitis, Bunche joined King and Ralph Abernathy to lead the Alabama march between Selma and Montgomery. When the group arrived at Montgomery, Bunche gave a speech denouncing the flying of the Confederate flag over the state capitol and declared that "peace in the world can be built only upon the principle and practice of equal rights and status for all peoples, respect and dignity for all men." After this speech, he received a considerable amount of hate mail.

Bunche's schedule at the United Nations kept him away from home on many occasions, and he often expressed guilt for not spending more time with his family. On October 6, 1966, his thirty-three-year-old daughter Jane died, almost certainly by suicide, and Bunche apparently felt that he was partly to blame for the tragedy. The shock of her death probably promoted the rapid deterioration of his own health. In addition to struggling with diabetes since 1958, Bunche increasingly suffered from phlebitis, diminished eyesight, and kidney failure. When he tried to resign for health reasons in 1967, Secretary General U Thant persuaded him that his continued presence was essential. By May, 1971, Bunche's many illnesses had made it impossible for him to attend meetings, although he continued to hold his position until that summer. He died in New York Hospital on December 9 at the age of sixty-eight.

Significance

Many monuments and buildings honor Bunche's career and achievements. In 1980, the park across from the United Nations headquarters was renamed the Ralph Bunche Park, and a fifty-foot-high stainless-steel obelisk, *Peace Form One*, designed by Daniel Larue Johnson, was installed to celebrate his efforts for peace. In 1982, the U.S. Postal Service issued a postage stamp in his memory. In 1997, the library of the U.S. Department of State, the federal government's oldest library, was named the Ralph J. Bunche Library. Although Bunche's name was not well known in the early twenty-first century, he was one of the most accomplished diplomats in history. His most important achievement was helping to bring about the armistice of the Arab-Israeli War in 1949, but he also was instrumental in promoting settlements in numerous other disputes throughout the world. His part in the creation of the United Nations was substantial. By setting an example of courage, moderation, and reason, Bunche also made a positive contribution to the Civil Rights movement. Finally, his research and writings, particularly his study of African Americans during the New Deal era, remain valuable works of scholarship.

Thomas Tandy Lewis

Further Reading

Abrams, Irvin. *The Nobel Peace Prize and the Laureates: An Illustrated History, 1901-2001.* Boston: G. K. Hall, 2001. The chapter on Bunche provides a useful discussion of his role in negotiating an end to the Arab-Israeli War of 1949.

Henry, Charles P. *Ralph Bunche: Model Negro or American Other?* New York: New York University Press, 1999. A scholarly and readable work, emphasizing how Bunche's ideas about race and class changed in reaction to circumstances.

_____, ed. *Ralph J. Bunche: Selected Speeches and Writings.* Ann Arbor: University of Michigan Press, 1995. A valuable anthology with helpful historical introductions by an expert on Bunche's life and career.

Keppel, Ben. *The Work of Democracy: Ralph Bunche, Lorraine Hansberry, and Kenneth Clark.* Boston: Harvard University Press, 1995. An interesting analysis of how and why each of these three individuals became symbols of the early Civil Rights movement.

Pearson, Lester B. "Unforgettable Ralph Bunche." *Reader's Digest* 102 (March 1973): 89-93. Expression of appreciation from the Canadian Nobel laureate who worked with Bunche at the United Nations. Rivlin, Benjamin, ed. *Ralph Bunche, the Man and His Times.* New York: Holmes & Meier, 1990. Valuable collection of essays about various aspects of Bunche's diverse career.

Urquhart, Brian. *Ralph Bunche: An American Life.* New York: W. W. Norton, 1993. Definitely the most complete and interesting account of his life and career, written by a longtime friend and colleague at the United Nations—the basis for a long documentary distributed by William Greaves Productions.

Norma V. Cantú

Lawyer, educator, and activist

Born: November 2, 1954; Brownsville, Texas
Areas of achievement: Law; education; activism

As an attorney for the Mexican American Legal Defense and Educational Fund (MALDEF) and the U.S. Department of Education, Cantú worked to ensure equal educational opportunities for Latino students.

Early Life

Norma V. Cantú (kahn-TEW) was the oldest of six children raised in a bilingual Mexican American family in Brownsville, Texas. Cantú's mother was a homemaker who went back to school and became a public school teacher and then an assistant principal. Her father Federico drove a milk truck and then became a postal carrier. Cantú's grandfather, who had little formal education, instilled in her the importance of acquiring an education, and Cantú was an excellent student. In 1971, after attending high school for just three years, she graduated with honors from Brownsville High School. Cantú majored in English and education at Pan American University (now the University of Texas-Pan American), from which she received a B.A. degree, summa cum laude, in December, 1973. The following year she taught English in Brownsville. In 1977, at the age of twenty-two, Cantú became the second Hispanic woman to graduate from Harvard University when she earned her degree from the Harvard Law School. She began her legal career in the office of the Texas attorney general, where she worked on the nursing home task force from 1977 through 1978. She then taught English in San Antonio, Texas, in 1979.

Life's Work

Also in 1979, Cantú took a job as a trial and appellate lawyer for the Mexican American Legal Defense and Educational Fund (MALDEF). Four years later, she became the national director for MALDEF's Education Litigation and Advocacy Project, and she was the organization's regional counsel and education director from 1985 to 1993. At MALDEF, Cantú was the lead council for many education-centered lawsuits, including litigation supporting equal educational funding for Latino students, mandatory school busing, and equal educational opportunities for disabled students, minorities, and English-language learners. An aggressive litigator, Cantú took legal action against the state of Texas for alleged discrimination in its public school funding formula and in higher education. As an advocate for policies supporting affirmative action, Cantú was challenged by those who did not share her belief in the need for these policies.

On March 5, 1993, President Bill Clinton nominated Cantú to be the U.S. Department of Education's assistant secretary for civil rights. After being sworn in on May 24, 1993, Cantú worked to run an efficient administration. Her goals included streamlining the department, supporting bilingual education, promoting race-based scholarships, improving equal educational opportunities, and promoting greater opportunities for female athletes. She created and enforced federal policies and guidelines and advised the secretary of education on civil rights issues. She had the right to withhold funding from educational institutions that violated federal civil rights statues. She also investigated and resolved more complaints than previous administrations had handled and hired more bilingual staff.

From 1998 to 2001, Cantú was a representative of the U.S. State Department for the International Commission on the Child. After she retired from government work, she was a visiting professor of law and education at the University of Texas, where she taught graduate writing seminars in education and courses about politics and policies in education, school reform, and disability law. She was a frequent guest lecturer at other universities, a speaker at several national conferences, and a member of the editorial board of the *Texas Hispanic Journal on Law and Policy*, published by the University of Texas's law school.

As she progressed in her profession, Cantú maintained her connections with the Hispanic community, often taking a proactive stance and lecturing on social equality, particularly equal opportunity in education, health issues, and the value of affirmative action. In 2002, she co-founded the Mexican American Legislative Leadership Foundation, which provided opportunities for students to work with the Texas legislature.

Cantú is the author of "Emerging Legal Issues: A Proposed Agenda for Advocacy for Hispanics," one of the essays in *Latino Empowerment: Progress, Problems, and Prospects* (1988). Her awards include the University of Texas-Pan American Distinguished Alumnus Award (1996), the National Association of Collegiate Women Athletic Administration Honor Award (1996), and the 2004 Spirit of Excellence Award from the American Bar Association'sÂ Commission on Racial and Ethnic Diversity in the Profession.

SIGNIFICANCE

As an aggressive litigator, civil rights advocate, and educator, Cantú has demonstrated a hard drive and a keen interest in providing opportunity to the disadvantaged. The first Latina assistant secretary for the U.S. Department of Education's Office of Civil Rights did not forget her heritage. Her efforts created more student scholarships and experiential opportunities, provided better prospects for female athletes, reduced harassment of minority students, and fostered equality in education. She shared her experiences and knowledge in her publications and in her university classes.

Cynthia J. W. Svoboda

FURTHER READING

Glaze, Melissa. "Latino Focus: Norma Cantú; In Recognition of Norma Cantú." *Texas Hispanic Journal of Law and Policy* 9, no. 1 (Fall, 2003): 2-5. An overview of Cantú's background, her work with MALDEF and the Office of Civil Rights, and her teaching career.

Healy, Patrick. "A Lightning Rod on Civil Rights." *Chronicle of Higher Education* 46, no. 4 (September 17, 1999): A42-A44. Scrutinizes Cantú's strategies and the controversial issues involving her political and legal career.

Hoff, David J. "In the Line of Fire." *Education Week* 17, no. 15 (December 3, 1997): 30-36. Provides an overview of the impact of affirmative action on Cantú's education, her major career accomplishments, and her position in the Office of Civil Rights. Includes comments from her critics.

Pell, Terence J. "A More Subtle Activism at the Office of Civil Rights. *Academic Questions* 10, no. 3 (Summer1997): 82-89. Covers Cantú's appointment with the Office of Civil Rights, the office's function, and her work for the office.

ELAINE L. CHAO

Taiwanese-born businesswoman and government official

Born: March 26, 1953; Taipei, Taiwan
Full name: Elaine Lan Chao
Area of Achievement: Government and politics, business, economics

Elaine L. Chao is best known as the first Asian woman to serve as a member of a US president's cabinet. She served in the administration of US President George H. W. Bush.

EARLY LIFE

Elaine L. Chao was born Hsiao-lan Chao on March 26, 1953, in Taipei, Taiwan. She is the daughter of James S. C. and Ruth Mulan Chu Chao. In 1961, Chao immigrated to the United States with her mother and five younger siblings, joining her father who had arrived a few years earlier. The family settled in Long Island, New York, where Chao's father started a shipping business. When she came to the United States, Chao did not know English.

Elaine L. Chao (Wikimedia Commons)

However, she learned the language with the help of her father and through rigorous study.

After completing high school in 1971, Chao enrolled at Mount Holyoke College, where she studied economics. After graduating from college, Chao began working for Foremost Maritime Corporation, where she specialized in logistics and finance. She later attended the Harvard Business School, earning an MBA in 1979. In 1993, she married US senator Mitch McConnell of Kentucky.

> "We want to make sure that workers know their rights and that employers know their obligations. That is the best way to protect workers"

Life's Work

Chao was hired as a transportation finance specialist for Citibank in 1979. Four years later, Chao served for one year as a White House Fellow in the Office of Policy Development. After completing her fellowship, she served as vice president of Bank America Capital Markets Group from 1984 until 1986, when she was selected to serve as deputy maritime administrator at the United States Department of Transportation. During the 1984 presidential election, Chao served as a member of President Ronald Reagan's campaign staff. When Federal Maritime Commission Chairman Ed Hickey died in 1988, Reagan appointed Chao as Hickey's successor.

During the 1988 presidential campaign of George H. W. Bush, Chao served on the Women for Bush-Quayle and Asian Americans for Bush-Quayle organizations. After winning the election, President George H. W. Bush appointed Chao to serve as the deputy secretary of the Department of Transportation. She remained at the Department of Transportation until 1991, when she left to become director of the Peace Corps. Under Chao's leadership, the Peace Corps expanded its outreach to include countries in the former Soviet Union.

When the Clinton administration came to power in 1992, Chao left the Peace Corps to become chief executive officer (CEO) of the United Way of America, a position she held until 1996. As CEO, Chao led the United Way out of a fiscal disaster that threatened its future. When her tenure at the United Way ended, Chao became a fellow at the Heritage Institute, where she served as editor of its journal, *The Policy Review*.

After five years away from the government sector, Chao returned to political office as a member of the presidential cabinet. Appointed by President George W. Bush in 2001, she became the first Asian American to serve as US secretary of labor. As the labor secretary, Chao ushered in many reforms related to pension plans, overtime pay, and ergonomics. She remained with the Department of Labor until 2009. After leaving the Department of Labor, Chao returned to the Heritage Foundation.

Significance

Through hard work, determination, and the support of her family, Chao triumphed over social and cultural barriers to achieve a successful career in business and government. Her leadership has had a significant impact on the institutions where she has worked.

Michele T. Fenton

Further Reading

ElaineLChao.com. Elaine L. Chao, 2009. Web. 10 Jan. 2012. Official website of Elaine Chao. Includes a biography, photographs, and videos, as well as articles written and speeches given by Chao.

Roston, Eric. "Ten Questions for Elaine Chao." *Time* 14 Dec. 2005: 6. Print. An interview about Chao's work as US secretary of labor, the aftermath of Hurricane Katrina, the concerns regarding pension plans, and job creation.

United States. United States Senate Committee on Health, Education, Labor, and Pensions. *First Session on Nomination of Elaine Chao to be Secretary of Labor.* Washington: GPO, 2001. Print. A transcript of the US Senate confirmation hearing held to decide whether to accept or reject President George W. Bush's nomination of Elaine Chao as the new secretary of labor.

Shirley Chisholm

Representative from New York (1969-1983), presidential candidate, and educator

Born: November 30, 1924; New York City, New York
Died: January 1, 2005; Ormond Beach, Florida
Area of Achievement: Education, government and politics

Chisholm was the first African American woman to serve in Congress and to run for president of the United States. She was a student activist, a New York state legislator, an active member of Congress, and an outspoken presidential campaigner who said she felt more discriminated against as a woman than as an African American.

Early Life

Shirley Anita St. Hill Chisholm (CHIHZ-ohlm) was born in Brooklyn, New York, one of eight children of Guyanan immigrant Charles St. Hill and Barbados native Ruby Seale. When Chisholm was three, she and three sisters were sent to live with their grandmother in Barbados for eight years. She attributed her later success to the strict British education she received there. Back in Brooklyn, she attended Girls' High School, graduated cum laude in sociology as a scholarship student at Brooklyn College in 1946, and received a master's degree in elementary education from Columbia University in 1952. She was married to Jamaican private investigator Conrad O. Chisholm from 1949 to 1977 (they divorced) and to Buffalo businessman Arthur Hardwick from 1977 until his death in 1986.

Chisholm worked in New York City as a teacher at Mount Calvary Child Care Center, as director of the Friends Day Nursery, and at Hamilton-Madison Child Care Center. From 1959 to 1964, she served as an educational consultant in the city's Bureau of Child Welfare. She became an activist as a member of Brooklyn College's Harriet Tubman Society and went on to serve as a board member for the Brooklyn Home for Aged Colored People, a member of the Brooklyn branch of the National Association for the Advancement of Colored People (NAACP), a volunteer at the Democratic Women's Workshop, and a member of the League of Women Voters and Bedford-Stuyvesant Political League.

Although her forthright and outspoken manner made her unpopular with local Democratic Party leaders, her community work helped her win election to two terms in the New York state legislature, where she worked to pass bills providing scholarships and remedial training for poor African American students, state funding for day care centers, and unemployment insurance for domestic workers. She also supported a bill that eliminated the practice of stripping tenure from woman teachers who took maternity leave. In 1968, Chisholm won a seat in Congress by a large margin over a prominent liberal white Republican civil rights leader. Her campaign slogan,

Shirley Chisholm (Library of Congress)

"Unbought and Unbossed," became the title of her first book, published in 1970, and the basis for a later PBS documentary.

Life's Work

Chisholm started her first term in the U.S. House of Representatives with characteristic courage. Named to the Forestry Subcommittee of the Agriculture Committee, she protested on the floor of the House that there were no forests in Bedford-Stuyvesant for her to represent and that she wanted to serve on committees that dealt with racism, poverty, and urban decay. Within weeks she was named to the Veterans' Affairs Committee. In her seven terms in the House, she also was appointed to the Education and Labor Committee and ultimately became the only woman on the Rules Committee. Throughout her tenure, she opposed war and defense expenditures and worked for employment, housing, education, and anti-hunger programs for the poor. She also worked against laws and customs that limited women's careers and supported abortion rights and the Equal Rights Amendment. Her women's liberation views made her a popular speaker on college campuses. She also was an active member of its Congressional Black Caucus.

> "The Constitution they wrote was designed to protect the rights of white, male citizens. As there were no black Founding Fathers, there were no founding mothers — a great pity, on both counts. It is not too late to complete the work they left undone. Today, here, we should start to do so."

In 1972, Chisholm decided to run for president. She fought to appear on television's *Face the Nation* alongside three other Democratic hopefuls, George McGovern, Henry Jackson, and Ed Muskie. In recognition of her efforts, fellow candidate Hubert Humphrey assigned his delegates to her at the Democratic National Convention, where the party named McGovern as its candidate. Chisholm had not expected to win the nomination, but in her 1973 book *The Good Fight,* she declared that someone had to do it first, and while her attempt did not open the door to women or African Americans, it pushed it ajar. She was named woman of the year by Clairol in 1973.

Chisholm retired from Congress in 1982. From 1983 to 1987, she was Purington Professor of politics and women's studies at Mount Holyoke College in Massachusetts, taking a year off (1985) to serve as a visiting scholar at Spelman College. In 1984, she cofounded the National Political Congress of Black Women and became its first president. Chisholm was a member of the advisory council of the National Organization for Women (NOW) and an honorary committee member of the United Negro College Fund. In 1988, she worked for the presidential campaign of Jesse Jackson. She continued to support early sex education in order to combat teenage pregnancy, urged more African Americans to become college professors, and opposed the Persian Gulf War in 1991, the same year she moved to Florida. In 1993, President Bill Clinton nominated her for the position of ambassador to Jamaica, but she declined because of declining health. That year, she was inducted into the National Women's Hall of Fame.

Chisholm died January 1, 2005, in Florida after a series of strokes.

Significance

In 1968, Chisholm became the first African American woman to be elected to Congress, and in 1972, she became the first major-party black candidate for president and the first woman to run for the Democratic presidential nomination (Margaret Chase Smith previously tried for the Republican nomination). She was outspoken about racial and economic conditions in the United States and what she considered the waste of war, as well as about her role as a trailblazer for future African Americans and women. Her significance was acknowledged even before Hillary Clinton and Barack Obama battled for the Democratic presidential nomination in 2008. In 2002, scholar Molefi Kctc Asante included Chisholm on his list of One Hundred Greatest African Americans.

Chisholm is celebrated in lyrics to many hip-hop songs such as "Nobody Beats the Biz" (1988) by Biz Markie, "Maaaad Crew" (1999) by Redman and Method Man, "Spread" (2003) by Andre 3000 of Outkast, "Mama and Me" (2005) by Nellie McKay, and "George Bush Is the Prez" (2006) by L. L. Cool J.

Chisholm's book *Unbought and Unbossed* was expanded and rereleased in 2010. It describes her 1968 campaign for the hotly contested new Seventeenth District congressional seat in a largely African American and Hispanic section of New York City. Her advantage was having worked for years for its citizens as an educator and New York state assemblywoman, her ability to speak Spanish on the campaign trail, and her self-styled "Fighting Shirley Chisholm" image. In the PBS documentary based on *Unbought,* Chisholm expressed her wish to be remembered after her death as someone who dared to be a catalyst of change.

Erika E. Pilver

FURTHER READING

Brownmiller, Susan. S*hirley Chisholm: A Biography.* New York: Simon & Schuster, 1972. A personal portrait of Chisholm and the people in her life, from Barbados to Congress.

Chisholm, Shirley. *The Good Fight.* Orlando, Fla.: Houghton, 1973. Chisholm describes her 1972 campaign for the Democratic nomination for president.

---. *Unbought and Unbossed.* Boston: Houghton Mifflin, 1970. Rev. ed. Edited by Scott Simpson. Washington, D.C.: Take Root Media, 2010. Chisholm's autobiography has been expanded with analyses by Donna Brazile, Shola Lynch, and others exploring Chisholm's impact and legacy.

Duffy, Susan, ed. *Shirley Chisholm: Bibliography of Writings by and About Her.* Metuchen, N.J.: Scarecrow Press, 1988. Books, speeches, ERIC documents, newspaper articles, campaign material, and letters.

Falk, Erika. *Women for President: Media Bias in Eight Campaigns.* Urbana: University of Illinois Press, 2008. Examines and analyzes media coverage of Chisholm's campaign along with those of seven other female presidential candidates.

Gutgold, Nicola D. "Shirley Chisholm: 'Ms. Chis.'" *Paving the Way for Madam President.* Lanham, Md.: Lexington Books, 2006. Detailed biography and analysis of Chisholm's political career, especially her presidential campaign.

Hicks, Nancy. *The Honorable Shirley Chisholm: Congresswoman from Brooklyn.* New York: Lion Books, 1971. A small volume in descriptive style and featuring many quotations from Chisholm, concentrating on her early years in Congress and reflecting strongly her determined and feisty nature.

Winslow, Barbara. *Shirley Chisholm: Catalyst for Change.* New York: Routledge, 2013. Part of the Lives of American Women series, this book focuses on Chisholm's lifelong advocacy for fair treatment, access to education, and equal pay.

JUDY M. CHU

Representative from California (2009-present) and educator

Born: July 7, 1953; Los Angeles, California
Area of Achievement: Government and politics, Education

After working for twenty years in education as a college professor and three years as a school-board member, Judy Chu moved on to a political career. She served as mayor of Monterey Park and as a representative in the California State Assembly before becoming the first Chinese American woman elected to the US Congress.

EARLY LIFE

Judy May Chu was born in Los Angeles to May and Judson Chu. May had immigrated to the United States from China after the 1945 War Brides Act temporarily repealed the ban on Chinese immigration imposed earlier by the Immigration Act of 1924. She became a cannery worker, whereas Judson, a native of California, worked as an electrical technician for Pacific Bell.

Judy Chu began her studies at the University of California, Santa Barbara and then transferred to the University of California, Los Angeles (UCLA), where she obtained a BA in mathematics. She then attended the California School of Professional Psychiatry and earned a PhD in clinical psychology. As a student, Chu gravitated toward the newly emerging Asian American courses, learning about the many contributions to society and politics made by Chinese and Japanese immigrants despite their facing hardships and discrimination, something her family had experienced firsthand. She also became more aware of the possibilities for women in leadership roles.

In 1973, Chu helped develop and teach one of the first courses in Asian American women's studies at UCLA. The course was a challenge, as few curriculum materials were available at the time. After receiving her doctorate, she taught community college classes for twenty years at Los Angeles City College and East Los Angeles College, and from 1985–88, she served on the Garvey School District Board of Education in Rosemead, California.

LIFE'S WORK

During the late 1980s, an influx of Asian immigrants caused racial tensions in Monterey Park to escalate. To counteract animosity and promote diversity in their

Judy M. Chu (Wikimedia Commons)

community, Chu and her husband, attorney Mike Eng—whom she had met at UCLA and married in 1978—cofounded the Coalition for Harmony and its community-wide Harmony Month. The project was so successful that the UCLA Alumni Association awarded Chu its Public Service Award.

In 1988, feeling drawn to civic duty, Chu successfully ran for Democratic councilwoman on the Monterey Park City Council, thus beginning her career in politics. During her thirteen years on the council, Chu was elected mayor three times.

In 2001, Chu was elected to the California State Assembly to represent the Forty-Ninth District, a position she had unsuccessfully campaigned for two other times. The Forty-Ninth District includes the cities of El Monte, Monterey Park, San Marino, and nearby locations in the San Gabriel Valley. While serving on the assembly, she chaired the Appropriations Committee, the Budget Subcommittee on Health and Human Services, and the Select Committee on Hate Crimes. She also served on committees that dealt with the environment, tax amnesty, language access, and other issues. In 2006, when her term on the assembly expired, she successfully ran for a position on the California Board of Equalization, while her husband succeeded her as representative for the Forty-Ninth District.

In 2009, Chu defeated her Republican opponent, Monterey Park City Councilmember Betty Chu, in a special election held to replace Hilda Solis, the congressional representative for California's Thirty-Second District. Backed by Solis, who had been appointed US secretary of labor under President Barack Obama, Chu drew support from California's Latino population as well as the state's Asian and Caucasian voters.

While serving in Congress, Chu largely aligned herself with the Democratic platform, including its support for women's rights and gay rights, as evidenced by her vote for H.R. 2965, also known as the Don't Ask, Don't Tell Repeal Act of 2010, and her vote against the Stupak Amendment to H.R. 3962, which would prohibit health-insurance companies from paying for abortions if they received any federal subsidies. She also introduced or cosponsored many bills that deal with education, the environment, and other social-justice issues, including H.R. 2902, the Equal Access to Quality Education Act of 2011; H.R. 1310, the Clean Water Protection Act; and H.R. 676, the Expanded and Improved Medicare for All Act. She served as a member of the House Committee on the Judiciary; the House Committee on Small Business; and the Subcommittee on Crime, Terrorism, and Homeland Security, among other committees.

Significance

Chu was the first Chinese American woman elected to the US Congress and only the fifth woman of Asian American heritage to be so elected. She holds a special allegiance to Asian American causes, sponsoring bills such as H. Res. 243, Celebrating Asian/Pacific American Heritage Month, and H. Res. 282, Expressing the Regret of the House of Representatives for the Passage of Discriminatory Laws against the Chinese in the United States, including the Chinese Exclusion Act.

Sally Driscoll

Further Reading

Chu, Judy. "Asian American Women's Studies Courses: A Look Back at Our Beginnings." *Asian American Women: The Frontiers Reader*. Ed. Linda Trinh Võ, et al. Lincoln: U of Nebraska P, 2004. Print. Presents Chu's firsthand knowledge about the roots of Asian American women's studies and their influence on higher education and society in the United States.

"US Congresswoman Judy Chu: Serving California's 32nd District." *Congresswoman Judy Chu*. Judy Chu, n.d. Web. 19 Jan 2012. Offers videos, voting records, press releases, photographs, and other professional and biographic information about Chu.

Rojas, Aurelio. "Asian Americans Flex Political Muscle." *Sacramento Bee* 22 May 2001: A3. Print. Details Chu's rise in popularity with Latinos as she became known for building coalitions that spanned diversity and promoted unity.

Clarence Darrow

Lawyer

Born: April 18, 1857; Kinsman, Ohio
Died: March 13, 1938; Chicago, Illinois
Areas of Achievement: Law, literature

The most renowned defense attorney of his time, Darrow won a number of significant verdicts in difficult cases, including the Scopes trial, while espousing unpopular causes.

Early Life

The fifth of eight children (one of whom died in infancy), Clarence Darrow (DAH-roh) was born in Kinsman, a small town in northeastern Ohio. His father, Amirus Darrow, was a carpenter who increasingly supplemented his income by working as an undertaker; he was also an avid reader who scattered books on all subjects throughout the house. In addition to his own commitment to reading and self-instruction, young Darrow owed some of his later outlook to his father's unorthodoxy and skepticism toward revealed religion. His mother, Emily Eddy Darrow, bestowed much attention on him and, until her death when he was fifteen, had great hopes for his success. He was educated at a local school and spent his summers playing baseball or working on a farm. At the age of sixteen, Darrow enrolled at Allegheny College, in Meadville, Pennsylvania; he gave up his studies there after a year and for a time was employed as a schoolteacher. In 1877, he spent a year at the University of Michigan's law school. Apparently, Darrow grew weary of formal education, and he spent a further year working and studying at a law office in Youngstown, Ohio. After a brief and apparently perfunctory oral examination, Darrow was admitted to the Ohio bar, at the age of twenty-one.

With his career now fairly started, Darrow took a fancy to Jessie Ohl, the daughter of a prosperous mill keeper, and after an involved courtship, they were married in 1880; their son Paul was born three years later. Darrow opened law offices in Andover and then in Ashtabula, Ohio; although few cases came his way, in 1884 he was elected borough solicitor, or prosecutor. Darrow had already campaigned actively for the national Democratic Party. He chafed at a small-town existence and thought it likely that his legal career would advance further in a large city. Accordingly, in 1887, he moved with his family to Chicago, where social and political strife had already given the city some notoriety.

Life's Work

For a time, Darrow served on the legal staff of the city of Chicago, and he also obtained a position as corporation counsel for the Chicago and North Western Railway. Increasingly disaffected with the venality and easy ethics of

Clarence Darrow (Library of Congress)

his employer, he took another job with a law firm and began to specialize in cases with social implications. After the mayor of Chicago was shot to death, Darrow tried unsuccessfully, in an appeal, to save the assassin from the gallows. In 1894, widespread disorders accompanied a massive strike of the Pullman Company's railroads; Darrow offered his services but was unsuccessful in his efforts to defend Eugene V. Debs from charges of criminal conspiracy.

> *"To disband the armies and destroy the forts, to diffuse love and brotherhood, and peace and justice in the place of war and strife, could tend only to the building up of character, the elevation of the soul, and the strength and well-being of the state."*

Darrow also attempted a sortie into national politics but was defeated when he ran for the U.S. Congress as a Democrat in 1896. As his professional commitments mounted, Darrow became estranged from his wife, Jessie, and they were quietly divorced in 1897. His remarriage, to Ruby Hamerstrom in 1903, seemed to put his personal life on a firmer footing. For a time, Darrow considered a literary career; he produced works that dealt with crime and social ills, as well as *Farmington* (1904), a semiautobiographical novel.

In 1898, Darrow took up another criminal conspiracy case, brought against Thomas I. Kidd and other leaders of a woodworkers' union in Wisconsin; he persuaded a jury that Kidd could not be held responsible for incidental acts of union violence that the leaders had neither foreseen nor encouraged. Elected to the Illinois legislature in 1902, Darrow continued to take labor cases, and he served as counsel for the United Mine Workers of America at United States Anthracite Coal Arbitration Commission hearings in Scranton, Pennsylvania.

Social concerns continued to attract him; in 1907, he won acquittal for William D. Haywood, of the Western Federation of Miners, who had been charged with complicity in the bombing death of a former governor of Idaho. In 1911, in another case involving union violence, Darrow defended James B. and John J. McNamara, who had planted dynamite in the *Los Angeles Times* building; the resulting explosion had killed twenty-one people. Pleading his clients guilty and pointing out that they had not intended to cause any loss of life, Darrow prevailed on a jury to spare the lives of the defendants; one was sentenced to life imprisonment and the other received fifteen years in prison. After this trial, Darrow himself was charged with jury bribery, and he assisted in his own defense. During the proceedings, the testimony of detectives and police informants was discredited, and he retained his freedom.

Darrow often gave the impression of studied casualness; he was tall, large boned, with prominent cheekbones, a sharp beaklike nose, and an overhanging forehead. He had light-blue eyes that, according to his contemporaries, could be animated by kindness or contracted in anger and outrage. In his gait, he seemed to slump forward; frequently during arguments, an unruly shock of hair would fall over his eyes. His clothes, though well tailored, seemed invariably unpressed, and Darrow claimed that he usually slept in them. His voice was deep, resonant, and slightly rasping. He was a born debater, skilled at the parry and thrust of cross-examination. His summations were moving and masterfully devised treatises on morality and the law, which frequently attracted overflow audiences into the courtroom.

Darrow was a confirmed skeptic, whose views were tempered by humanity and an instinctive sympathy for the downtrodden. He inveighed against the death penalty, which he considered a barbaric relic of more intolerant ages. An openly avowed agnostic, he sometimes contended that life had no meaning. Frequently, he took controversial cases for the sake of defendants and ideas that were out of public favor. Much of his success derived neither from factual expertise nor from technical mastery of the law; rather, he was determined and generally able to sway juries and judges with deeply felt moral appeals.

As word of his prowess spread, Darrow attracted numerous clients. Many times, he took their cases simply because he did not have the heart to turn them away. About certain issues he felt deeply; in 1920, he invoked the guarantee of freedom of speech in his unsuccessful defense of twenty Chicago communists. Abhorrence of the death penalty prompted him, in 1924, to defend Nathan F. Leopold, Jr., and Richard Loeb, who had carried out the wanton and senseless murder of a fourteen-year-old boy. Darrow pleaded his clients guilty and in a lengthy, heartfelt plea, kept them from execution. To protest the rising tide of fundamentalism, in 1925 he took the case of John T. Scopes, who was charged with violation of a Tennessee statute against teaching evolution in the public schools. Although ultimately the defendant was fined, Darrow arranged a dramatic courtroom confrontation by examining counsel for the prosecution, William Jennings

Bryan; in the process, Darrow pointed up the inconsistencies that resulted when biblical literalism was applied to the problems of science.

For many years, Darrow had been outraged by racial inequality; by his own account his most satisfying case came with his defense, in 1926, of a black family in Detroit. While defending their house against an angry, rampaging mob, Dr. Ossian Sweet and his sons had fired on their assailants, killing one man and wounding another. By evoking the atmosphere of extreme prejudice against them and demonstrating the severe provocation that beset the Sweets, Darrow obtained a verdict of self-defense. In 1927, he won acquittal for two antifascist Italian émigrés who had killed two of their political opponents during a quarrel in New York.

Darrow read widely and had an abiding interest in science, literature, and social thought; he also propounded his views readily and augmented his income by taking part in platform debates. Against some of the well-known figures of his day, Darrow defended agnosticism, condemned Prohibition and capital punishment, and morbidly contended that life was not worth living. He also considered retirement from the practice of law. By this time, his son Paul had established a career in business and was in no sense inclined to emulate his famous father's professional pursuits. For nine months in 1929 and 1930, Darrow and his wife traveled extensively on a vacation in Europe.

Darrow's last major case, which he claimed he took because he wanted to visit Hawaii, was a defense of Lieutenant Thomas Massie and three others in 1932. They had killed one of the men who had allegedly raped Massie's wife. At length, verdicts of manslaughter were returned against the defendants; in an agreement with the prosecution, Darrow and his colleagues obtained executive clemency for their clients in return for dismissals of the indictments still pending in the rape cases.

In 1934, Darrow was called to Washington and made chair of the National Recovery Administration Review Board. Decidedly uncomfortable in this position, he contended that the government was acting as much to sanction as to control the growth of combinations in business. After a year, he resigned. Failing health was accompanied by increasing despondency; Darrow made few public appearances, and some of those close to him felt that his death, when it came on March 13, 1938, must also have brought relief.

Significance

During his lifetime, Darrow served as defense attorney in nearly two thousand cases; more than one hundred of them were for charges of murder. At one time, Darrow estimated that he had represented one-third of his clients without payment; many other cases were taken to protest what he regarded as cruelty and injustice. His most celebrated cases have become a permanent part of the nation's legal lore, and his summations have been taken as models of expository speaking.

In important respects, Darrow was unique, and he spoke for the unpopular and the outcast during an age before legal consensus had delineated the rights of the accused. Some of his abiding concerns, such as opposition to the death penalty, are still warmly debated. Although he did little to advance the technical growth of the law, his stance of strident advocacy is still cited in recalling some of the most memorable courtroom confrontations in American legal practice.

J. R. Broadus

Further Reading

Darrow, Clarence. *Closing Arguments: Clarence Darrow on Religion, Law, and Society*. Edited by S. T. Joshi. Athens: Ohio University Press, 2005. A collection of Darrow's writings on philosophy and religion, law and crime, and politics and society.

---. *Crime, Its Cause and Treatment*. New York: Thomas Y. Crowell, 1922. This work constitutes the most extensive single statement of Darrow's views on crime and penology. He argues that heredity and environment create most criminals; crime would be reduced by improving social conditions. Darrow maintains that, for the most part, punishment is meant not to deter criminal acts, but to satisfy society's primal longings for vengeance.

---. *The Story of My Life*. New York: Grosset and Dunlap, 1932. Brash, irreverent retelling of Darrow's life in law, which becomes markedly world-weary toward the end. Interspersed among accounts of his famous cases are excursions into science, religion, and criminology. This work is valuable not so much for its discussion of particular clients or trials some are dealt with rather sketchily as for its evocation of the issues and concerns that moved Darrow.

Leopold, Nathan F., Jr. *Life Plus Ninety-Nine Years*. Garden City, N.Y.: Doubleday, 1958. The memoirs of one of Darrow's most celebrated clients, this work deals largely with the author's trials and imprisonment. Early in the book, Leopold writes admiringly of

Darrow's work during his Chicago murder trial of 1924; he also mentions Darrow's visits and continuing concern during his incarceration.

Ravitz, Abe C. *Clarence Darrow and the American Literary Tradition*. Cleveland, Ohio: Press of Western Reserve University, 1962. Early in his career, literature was a sometime avocation for Darrow, and this study points to the relationship between his legal theories and his ventures into fiction and literary criticism. Many of his early writings dealt with crime and industrial accidents; the themes of these now nearly forgotten productions foreshadowed concerns he also voiced in the courtroom and in his later, nonfiction works.

Scopes, John T., and James Presley. *Center of the Storm*. New York: Holt, Rinehart and Winston, 1967. The defendant during the famous Tennessee trial of 1925, Scopes discusses his beliefs on evolution, science, and religion. He describes Darrow as the second most influential person in his life, after his father, and depicts at length the unusual but incisive defense his attorney offered.

Stone, Irving. *Clarence Darrow for the Defense*. 1941. New ed. New York: New American Library, 1971. A popular biography on a broad canvas, this work is dated in some ways but was also written close to the events it describes. It is sufficiently thorough and detailed still to warrant consultation. Darrow's major trials and triumphs are set forth at length, at times projecting a heroic image. Darrow's personal papers, published materials available at the time, and interviews with nearly two hundred contemporaries and associates of the great advocate were used in the preparation of this work.

Tierney, Kevin. *Darrow: A Biography*. New York: Thomas Y. Crowell, 1979. A sober and clear study that assesses Darrow's limitations as well as his strengths. Factual problems in some of Darrow's cases, and also his inconsistencies as a thinker, are presented along with his many achievements. While in no way disparaging, this closely argued and well-documented work delineates the one-sided qualities that indeed contributed so much to Darrow's greatness.

Vine, Phyllis. *One Man's Castle: Clarence Darrow in Defense of the American Dream*. New York: Amistad, 2004. Vine recounts the murder trial of Ossian Sweet, an African American physician who purchased a home in a white area of Detroit in the 1920's.

Weinberg, Arthur, and Lila Weinberg. *Clarence Darrow: A Sentimental Rebel*. New York: G. P. Putnam's Sons, 1980. A thorough and well-rounded though somewhat uncritical modern biography. Darrow's own trial for jury bribery is treated at some length. The relationship between his great cases and his manner of thinking is developed through each stage of his career; along the way tribute is paid to his espousal of unpopular causes. This work draws extensively on court records, Darrow's own writings, and unpublished papers of Darrow and several of his associates.

HELEN GAHAGAN DOUGLAS

Representative from California (1945-1951) and social reformer

Born: November 25, 1900
Died: June 28, 1980
Area of Achievement: Social reform, government and politics, civil rights, theater and entertainment

Both personally and as a U.S. representative from California, Douglas advocated for civil liberties and opportunities for oppressed minorities. She became only the third woman elected to Congress from California and the first who did not take her congressional seat from a deceased husband.

EARLY LIFE

Helen Gahagan Douglas (HEH-lehn geh-HAY-gehn DUHG-lahs) was born Helen Mary Gahagan in Boonton, New Jersey, where her parents briefly rented a home so that her father could supervise a construction project nearby. Her twin brothers had been born two years earlier, and a sister and brother would follow in 1902 and 1910. She grew up in Brooklyn, New York, in a comfortable household with strong-willed parents intent on imbuing their children with strong moral and educational ideals. Her father, Walter, was an engineer who founded his own construction company in 1899 and prospered from the outset. A graduate of the Massachusetts Institute of Technology, he read insatiably and filled the Gahagan house with shelves of books. Helen's mother, Lillian, had been reared on the Wisconsin frontier. She was a country schoolteacher before her marriage, and her beauty,

Helen Gahagan Douglas (Wikimedia Commons)

optimistic outlook, and exquisite singing voice were inherited by her elder daughter.

Douglas had the benefit of the accoutrements of affluence during her childhood. These included a summer home in Vermont, a family trip to Europe when she was twelve, accompanying her mother to the opera (which, ironically, Douglas disliked intensely), and private schools. The first of these was the Berkeley School for Girls, which was located only a block from the Gahagans' home. It was at this school that her interest in acting blossomed under the direction of her drama teacher, Elizabeth Grimball. Her grades were mediocre in subjects unrelated to performing, but she studied intensely for a college preparatory school. She matriculated at Barnard College in New York to be close to the stage and her drama instructor.

Douglas would spend only two years at Barnard College before her debut into the Broadway theatrical world. Her impressive performances in school productions and an Off-Broadway play led director William A. Brady, Jr., to cast her as the ingenue in *Dreams for Sale* by Owen Davis in 1922. Over the extremely strong protests of her father, who insisted that she complete her education, Douglas accepted.

Douglas quickly became a star. Her generally favorable reviews led to contracts with Brady and other well-known producers and assured her a niche in the roster of leading ladies of the 1920's stage. Practically every new theatrical season brought a new role, and she toured the country in roles she established in New York. She was the subject of much press coverage, not only for her acting talent but also for her great beauty.

Douglas's ambition to perform ultimately led in another direction. During the run of a New York play in 1926, she began to take vocal lessons from a Russian émigré, Madame Sophia Cehanovska. For the next several years, Douglas would devote time, money, and trips to Europe to the pursuit of performing operatic roles with leading companies, a pursuit that was never as successful as her Broadway acting career.

Douglas's performance in the 1930-1931 Broadway production of *Tonight or Never* by Lili Hatvany was important for a number of reasons. The play was her only collaboration with the legendary David Belasco (he would die during its run), her father died during the same run, and she married her costar, Melvyn Douglas. By the end of 1931, she had moved from New York to the West Coast, where Melvyn began his career in motion pictures. Except for some brief performing engagements, Helen would not live in New York again until after her immersion in and forced withdrawal from another career of a very different type.

Life's Work

The first task for Douglas and her husband, on reaching California, was to establish a new way of life in new surroundings. Melvyn had a studio contract with Metro-Goldwyn-Mayer (MGM), and Douglas was busy with singing lessons and performances on the West Coast stage in both acting and singing roles. Although Douglas would have the opportunity to read dozens of film scripts in search of suitable parts, her efforts to find strong roles or to receive reasonable financial offers were stymied. She appeared in only one picture, *She* (1935), a film later considered a "classic" for its overblown production and acting rather than for any positive contributions to the cinematic arts.

The hectic pace of life on the dramatic and sound stages for the couple soon led both to seek a respite. They accomplished this by traveling around the world in 1933. A few months after their return home, Douglas gave birth to their first child, Peter. A daughter, Mary Helen, would follow five years later. Douglas continued her theatrical performances and vocal training, and the family settled into a new home built on three acres in the hills above the Hollywood Bowl.

Two significant events contributed to Douglas's involvement in political causes. The first involved her awakening to conditions in Germany and Austria during a concert tour there in 1937. She ultimately canceled several engagements on the tour after encountering anti-Semitism directed against the pianist who was traveling with her. Although she was not Jewish, her husband Melvyn was, so she regarded these sentiments as a personal affront.

Back in California, Douglas became involved in Democratic Party campaign activities in 1938. Her husband had joined in the statewide gubernatorial and congressional campaign efforts; at first, she merely accompanied him to meetings. After becoming acquainted with social and economic conditions firsthand, however, she began to take the lead in organizing efforts to assist migrant workers. As a result of their activities on behalf of California Democrats, the Douglases were invited to visit President Franklin D. Roosevelt and First Lady Eleanor Roosevelt in the White House in 1939. Douglas was greatly impressed by Eleanor Roosevelt, who became for her something of a political mentor and role model.

Douglas's intelligence and capacity for hard work, as well as her friendship with the First Lady, led to her rapid rise within the leadership of the Democratic Party in California. In 1940, she was selected as the state's Democratic national committeewoman. In that capacity, she attended the party's national convention, where she was an enthusiastic supporter of a third term for Roosevelt. Following Roosevelt's reelection, Douglas was appointed vice chair and head of the Women's Division for the California State Democratic Party. Her efforts for Southern California Democratic candidates in 1942 contributed to party successes there in spite of Republican victories throughout the rest of the state.

Douglas's high visibility in state Democratic politics made her a natural choice for the congressional race in the Fourteenth District in 1944, when popular congressmember Thomas Ford announced his retirement. Although she did not live in the largely workingclass district in central Los Angeles, she campaigned thoroughly there and won the nomination in the May primary. Prior to the general election, Douglas delivered a principal address before the Democratic National Convention in Chicago, in which she reviewed the accomplishments of the Roosevelt administrations. In the fall campaign, she followed the lead of Democrats nationally in identifying her programs with Roosevelt and the New Deal, a strategy that produced a narrow victory. She became only the third woman elected to Congress from California and the first who did not take over her seat from a deceased husband.

In Washington, D.C., Douglas adhered to the same formula that had produced political success in California. She maintained a grueling schedule, largely eschewed social events, and applied her keen mind to the process of absorbing all available information on issues pending before Congress. Her legislative interests lay in two areas, one involving foreign affairs, the other domestic. She secured an appointment to the House Foreign Affairs Committee, which is usually an unimportant body, since only

U.S. National Bureau of Standards director Edward Uhler Condon (1902-1974); U.S. Senator Brien McMahon (1903-1952); U.S. Representative Helen Gahagan Douglas (1900-1980); Harvard College Observatory astronomer Harlow Shapley (1885-1972); and William Hammatt Davis (1879-1964), former Chairman of the War Labor Board, at an event sponsored by Science Service. In late 1945, Senator McMahon was developing the Atomic Energy Act of 1945, which established the U.S. Atomic Energy Commission. (Wikimedia Commons)

the Senate ratifies treaties. Nevertheless, with negotiations under way for the postwar international organization that became the United Nations, Douglas believed that the House as well as the Senate would play an integral role in the increased nationwide commitment to internationalism. Membership on the House Foreign Affairs Committee would provide a forum for activities designed to ensure world peace. In domestic affairs, Douglas's natural inclinations were bolstered by the makeup of her congressional district. She lent support throughout the postwar period to legislation benefiting organized labor and African Americans and other minorities.

> "Character isn't inherited. One builds it daily by the way one thinks and acts, thought by thought, action by action. If one lets fear or hate or anger take possession of the mind, they become self-forged chains."

Through her diligence, her charismatic appeal, and her high visibility in the press, Douglas became a leading figure in California politics. Following her second reelection, in 1948, her congressional seat seemed to be secure; she and her supporters now looked to a greater challenge the seat in the U.S. Senate held by the conservative Democrat Sheridan Downey. Following the incumbent's withdrawal from the 1950 primary, Douglas won the nomination in spite of vicious attacks on her internationalist position as being procommunist.

The smear tactics begun in the Democratic primary intensified in the general election, when Douglas faced Congressman Richard M. Nixon. In an election that has since become famous for the infamous dirty tricks of the Nixon campaign, Douglas was removed from public office. In her autobiography some thirty years later, she wryly remarked that "There's not much to say about the 1950 campaign except that a man ran for the Senate who wanted to get there, and didn't care how."

Douglas's life after politics was spent partly in the public eye, since she continued to speak in favor of causes such as world peace. She campaigned for Democratic presidential candidates Lyndon B. Johnson in 1964 and George McGovern in 1972. During the last three decades before her death from cancer in 1980, she was certainly not forgotten, but neither was she occupying her accustomed place in the limelight.

Significance

In a number of respects, Douglas had an enviable life and a great deal of good fortune. She became a famous actor almost overnight, not only because of her talent but also because of her great beauty. Capitalizing on her acting fame, she became a force in politics through intelligence and hard work. Although her fame boosted her political career at the outset, it eventually became a liability to Douglas as a politician seriously intent on pursuing an important agenda. She constantly downplayed her glamour in order to be taken seriously.

She was able, in the end, to use the press attention focused on her to advance an international and domestic social program that was liberal, enlightened, and forward-looking. She did not hesitate to challenge bigotry, isolationism, and red-baiting. Although her public service was cut short because of Nixon's malicious campaign against her in 1950, she stood as a symbol for other intelligent, forthright, public-spirited women and men to emulate.

Richard G. Frederick

Further Reading

Douglas, Helen Gahagan. *The Eleanor Roosevelt We Remember.* New York: Hill & Wang, 1963. In her autobiography, Douglas clearly indicated that Eleanor Roosevelt was a major influence in her decision to become a political activist. This book, a tribute to Roosevelt, contains photographs from a variety of sources and an admiring text by Douglas.

---. *A Full Life.* Garden City, N.Y.: Doubleday, 1982. An engaging autobiography in which the author thoroughly discusses her family life, stage experiences, and involvement in political affairs.

Douglas, Melvyn, and Tom Arthur. *See You at the Movies: The Autobiography of Melvyn Douglas.* Lanham, Md.: University Press of America, 1986. A posthumously published autobiography that focuses on the author's acting career and includes occasional anecdotes about his wife's careers and their marriage.

Lowry, Margaret M. S. "Pretty and Therefore 'Pink': Helen Gahagan Douglas and the Rhetorical Constraints of U.S. Political Discourse." *Rhetoric Review* 22, no. 3 (2003): 282. Lowry's feminist and rhetorical analysis examines Douglas's 1946 speech "My Democratic Credo." She concludes that Douglas adapted a "masculine" discourse to create the image of a rational, authoritative representative.

Mitchell, Greg. T*ricky Dick and the Pink Lady: Richard Nixon Versus Helen Gahagan Douglas Sexual Politics* and the Red Scare, 1950. New York: Random House, 1998. Mitchell examines the California Senate campaign of 1950.

Morris, Roger. *Richard Milhous Nixon: The Rise of an American Politician.* New York: Henry Holt, 1990. Includes the fullest description and analysis of the 1950 Senate campaign in California. Especially valuable for establishing the context of California politics. Morris covers the Douglas and Nixon primary campaigns as well as the general election.

Scobie, Ingrid Winther. *Center Stage: Helen Gahagan Douglas, a Life.* New York: Oxford University Press, 1992. A thorough biography by a professional historian who conducted research in manuscript and oral history collections around the country. Scobie also met with and interviewed the Douglases.

WILLIAM O. DOUGLAS

Associate justice of the United States (1939-1975)

Born: October 16, 1898; Maine Township, Minnesota
Died: January 19, 1980; Bethesda, Maryland
Area of Achievement: Law

As the longest-serving justice in the history of the U.S. Supreme Court, Douglas was reputed as an outspoken advocate of civil rights and liberties during his thirty-six years on the Court. In particular, he played a critical role in establishing a constitutional right to privacy and developing broad protections for freedom of speech.

EARLY LIFE

William O. Douglas, the son of a minister, was born in the small town of Maine, Minnesota. At the age of three, his family moved to California and two years later to Yakima, Washington, the town where he would grow up. Douglas, just five years old when his father died after stomach surgery, grew up in modest circumstances. His mother struggled to provide for him and his two younger siblings. From an early age, Douglas held many jobs, such as picking fruit and delivering newspapers. His outstanding performance in high school earned for him a scholarship to Whitman College in Walla Walla, Washington. After graduating from college, he taught high school for a brief time before earning his law degree from Columbia University in New York.

After serving as a law professor at Columbia and Yale, Douglas entered government service when Franklin D. Roosevelt became president of the United States in 1933. Roosevelt appointed Douglas to serve as chair of the Securities and Exchange Commission (SEC), the government agency that regulated and investigated corporations' sale of stock. Douglas chaired the agency until March, 1939, when Roosevelt selected the forty-year-old Douglas for the U.S. Supreme Court. Because the U.S. Constitution does not limit the term of service for Supreme Court justices, many justices serve for life. As the youngest appointee in the twentieth century, Douglas was on the Court for thirty-six years and helped decide several thousand cases.

LIFE'S WORK

Associate Justice Douglas helped to initiate a significant shift in the Court's focus during Roosevelt's presidency. Roosevelt's long tenure as president (1933-1945) allowed

William O. Douglas (Library of Congress)

him to appoint many replacements for justices who retired or died. At the time of Roosevelt's death in 1945, eight of the nine justices on the Court, including Douglas, were his appointees. Douglas joined the other Roosevelt appointees in shifting the Court's focus from cases analyzing the legality of social programs and economic regulation to devoting much of its attention to defining individual rights and liberties. It was during Douglas's tenure as a justice that the Court made many of its most important decisions concerning racial equality, freedom of speech, and the rights of criminal defendants.

Douglas voted consistently in interpreting the Constitution as a document protecting the rights of individuals and limiting the government's authority to control people's lives. Studies of Supreme Court decision making found that Douglas, more frequently than any other justice of the twentieth century, favored individuals in their disputes with the government over civil rights and liberties, especially those cases concerning the First Amendment rights of freedom of speech and religion.

Douglas was a prolific author of judicial opinions. He often wrote the dissenting opinion in those cases in which he disagreed with the Court's decision. He dissented in those cases in which a majority of justices supported governmental authority over claims of individuals' rights. For example, in *Miller v. California* (1973) he dissented against the Court's efforts to create definitions for permissible obscenity and pornography because he believed that the First Amendment broadly protected people's right to express themselves with words and pictures, even if those expressions were offensive to others. Similarly, he dissented during the 1950's, in cases such as *Dennis v. United States* (1951), when the majority of justices permitted the government to prosecute and imprison people for teaching and advocating a political philosophy of communism. In *Terry v. Ohio* (1968), when the Court permitted police officers to stop and frisk people on the streets after observing suspicious behavior, Douglas was the lone justice to argue that there must be concrete evidence of criminal misconduct and not mere suspicion before police can interfere with a person's liberty simply to be on a street.

Justice Douglas also wrote important majority opinions. In *Skinner v. Oklahoma* (1942), for example, Douglas wrote the decision that prohibited states from imposing forced sterilization on persons convicted of crimes. His most famous and controversial majority opinion came in *Griswold v. Connecticut* (1965), the case that announced the existence of a constitutional right to privacy. Although the word "privacy" does not appear in the Constitution, Douglas wrote that the right to privacy is older than the Constitution itself and can be recognized by reading between the lines of other provisions concerning search and seizure, freedom of association, and other rights. The reasoning in Douglas's opinion in *Griswold* was later used by the Court to establish rights concerning abortion (*Roe v. Wade*, 1973), the private sexual conduct of gay and lesbian adults (*Lawrence v. Texas*, 2003), and other controversial matters. Many critics claim that Douglas went too far in *Griswold* by inventing a right to privacy that does not exist in constitutional law.

Douglas gained a reputation as a fiercely independent justice who was not afraid to express his political views and conclusions about legal matters. In one memorable episode, lawyers approached him during the Court's summer recess to challenge the legality of President Richard M. Nixon's decision to expand U.S. military action in Cambodia during the Vietnam War. Douglas drafted a temporary order prohibiting Nixon from further bombing in Cambodia, but the other justices quickly communicated with each other and unanimously overruled Douglas, thus preventing a major confrontation between the Court and the president (*Holtzman v. Schlesinger*, 1973).

> "*The liberties of none are safe unless the liberties of all are protected.*"

The books he wrote about freedom, democracy, and American society clearly show Douglas's independence and legal philosophy. His writings were controversial because critics believed that he was encouraging antiwar protestors and civil rights activists to rebel against society during the 1960's. Indeed, his non-judicial writings were used by Congress member Gerald R. Ford in 1970 in his unsuccessful bid to persuade federal lawmakers to impeach Douglas and remove him from the Court. The impeachment effort was also fueled by the Nixon administration's desire to seek revenge against political liberals after the U.S. Senate refused to confirm two conservative southern judges whom Nixon had sought to appoint to the Court. Douglas's independence continued even after he retired from the Court in 1975 because of a debilitating stroke. He unsuccessfully sought to initiate a new policy that would permit retired justices to continue to participate in the Court's deliberations in selected cases.

Significance

Douglas contributed significantly to the expansion of constitutional rights for Americans in the middle decades of the twentieth century. As an associate justice from 1939 to 1975, he participated in many of the Court's most famous, and infamous, decisions, including the prohibition on governmental racial discrimination in *Brown v. Board of Education*; the provision of free speech protection for inflammatory, antigovernment speeches in *Brandenburg v. Ohio* (1969); and the requirement that police officers inform suspects of their rights prior to questioning (*Miranda v. Arizona*, 1966). Douglas's own opinion in *Griswold v. Connecticut* (1965) established the constitutional right to privacy and laid the foundation for subsequent Court decisions protecting individuals' personal choices against intrusion by government. Because he was both the Supreme Court's longest-serving justice and its most outspoken advocate of individual liberty and free expression, Douglas's influence reached thousands of decisions that shaped, and will shape, the evolving definition of constitutional rights.

Christopher E. Smith

Further Reading

Ball, Howard, and Phillip J. Cooper. *Of Power and Right: Hugo Black, William O. Douglas, and America's Constitutional Revolution*. New York: Oxford University Press, 1992. Analysis of Douglas's contributions to constitutional law and his legacy as a Supreme Court justice. Focuses on specific issues, including racial discrimination, freedom of speech, and freedom of religion.

Douglas, William O. *The Court Years, 1939-1975*. Vol. 2 in *The Autobiography of William O. Douglas*. New York: Random House, 1981. Focuses on Douglas's role in decision making on the Supreme Court.

---. *Go East Young Man: The Early Years The Autobiography of William O. Douglas*. New York: Random House, 1974. Contains a first-person account of Douglas's childhood, education, and early career. Later authors have challenged the honesty and accuracy of certain aspects of Douglas's retelling of the details of his early life.

Murphy, Bruce Allen. *Wild Bill: The Legend and Life of William O. Douglas*. New York: Random House, 2003. A comprehensive biography of Douglas. Presents a critical view of Douglas's unfulfilled aspirations for political office and his efforts to shape his public image.

O'Brien, David M. *Storm Center: The Supreme Court in American Politics*. 6th ed. New York: W. W. Norton, 2003. Analysis of the history and internal operations of the Supreme Court. Includes discussion of Douglas's role on the Court and his participation in the Court's decision making.

Tammy Duckworth

Representative (2013-2017) and Senator (2017-present) from Illinois

Born: March 12, 1968; Bangkok, Thailand
Area of Achievement: Government and politics, Military

Tammy Duckworth joined the United States Army Reserves while a doctoral student at Northern Illinois University. Despite losing both legs while serving in Iraq, Duckworth has served her country as an officer and civil servant. She has worked as an advocate for injured and disabled soldiers in the armed forces.

Early Life

Tammy Duckworth was born Ladda Tammy Duckworth on March 12, 1968, in Bangkok, Thailand. Her parents were Frank and Lamai Duckworth. Duckworth's father, an American, had served in the US Marines and worked for the United Nations. Her mother was a native of Thailand. Eventually, Duckworth's family moved to Honolulu, Hawaii, where she attended McKinley High School.

After completing high school, Duckworth attended the University of Hawaii, where she majored in political science. She later served as a Smithsonian Fellow and went on to earn a master's degree in international affairs from George Washington University. It was during her time at George Washington University that Duckworth took an interest in the military and joined the school's Reserve Officer Training Corps (ROTC) program. The Duckworth family has a longstanding tradition of military service; since the American Revolution, at least one member of the family has served in the Armed Forces.

In 1991, Duckworth was admitted to Northern Illinois University as a doctoral student. In 1992, Duckworth became a commissioned officer in the United States Army Reserve. A year later, she married Bryan W. Bowlsbey. In 2001, Duckworth was hired by Rotary International as

Tammy Duckworth (Wikimedia Commons)

manager of the organization's clubs in the Asia Pacific Region.

LIFE'S WORK

In 2003, Duckworth was called to active military duty for Operation Iraqi Freedom. While serving in Iraq, Duckworth flew helicopter missions for the US Army. On November 12, 2004, as she returned from an assignment, Duckworth's UH-60 Blackhawk was struck by a rocket-propelled grenade (RPG). Although she and her crew landed the helicopter safely, Duckworth was gravely injured. Her right arm was shattered, and both legs were lost. She later recovered at Walter Reed Army Medical Center. While there, Duckworth received several medals, including a Purple Heart.

In 2006, Henry Hyde, then serving as US representative for the Sixth Congressional District of Illinois, announced his retirement. While the Republican Party endorsed Peter Roskam as Hyde's replacement, the Democratic Party endorsed Tammy Duckworth. Despite a valiant effort, Duckworth lost the race to Roskam. However, another opportunity in government opened up when then-governor of Illinois Rod Blagojevich named Duckworth director of the Illinois Department of Veterans Affairs in November 2006.

During her time at the Illinois Department of Veterans Affairs, Duckworth instituted Veterans Adaptive Activities Day, the Illinois Warriors Assistance Program, and the GI Loan for Heroes mortgage program. In 2008, she was named Woman of the Year by the Asian American Bar Association of Illinois, chosen National Outstanding Disabled American Veteran of the Year by the Disabled American Veterans (DAV), and asked to be one of several speakers at the 2008 Democratic National Convention.

In 2009, President Barack Obama appointed Duckworth as the assistant secretary of Veterans Affairs for Public and Intergovernmental Affairs. During her tenure as assistant secretary, Duckworth established the Office of New Media and the Office of Tribal Government Relations, along with several outreach programs for veterans. Duckworth left the Veterans' Administration on June 13, 2011. Several weeks after her resignation, she announced her intention to run for the US House of Representatives for the newly created Eighth Congressional District of Illinois.

> "*We must be an inclusive nation that respects and supports all of its citizens: a nation that doesn't give up on anyone who hasn't given up on themselves.*"

Duckworth defeated former Deputy Treasurer of Illinois Raja Krishnamoorthi for the Democratic nomination on March 20, 2012, then faced incumbent Republican Joe Walsh in the general election. Duckworth received the endorsement of both the *Chicago Tribune* and the *Daily Herald*. On November 6, 2012, Duckworth defeated Walsh 55%–45%. She became the first disabled woman to be elected to the U.S. House of Representatives, and the first member of Congress born in Thailand. She was sworn into office on January 3, 2013. Duckworth won re-election to the House in 2014, defeating Republican candidate Larry Kaifesh with 56% of the vote.

On March 30, 2015, Duckworth announced that she would challenge incumbent U.S. Senator Mark Kirk for his seat in the 2016 Senate election in Illinois. Duckworth defeated fellow Democrats Andrea Zopp and Napoleon Harris in the primary election on March 15, 2016. During a televised debate on October 27, 2016, Duckworth talked about her ancestors' past serving in the United States military. Kirk responded, "I'd forgotten that your parents came all the way from Thailand to serve George Washington." The comment led to the Human Rights Campaign withdrawing their endorsement of Kirk and switching it to Duckworth, stating his comments were "deeply offensive and racist." On November 8, Duckworth defeated Kirk 54 percent to 40 percent to win the Senate seat.

In January 2018, following a federal government shut down after the Senate could not agree on a funding bill, Duckworth responded to President Trump's accusations that the Democrats were putting "unlawful immigrants" ahead of the military:

> I spent my entire adult life looking out for the well-being, the training, the equipping of the troops for whom I was responsible. Sadly, this is something that the current occupant of the Oval Office does not seem to care to do — and I will not be lectured about what our military needs by a five-deferment draft dodger. And I have a message for Cadet Bone Spurs: If you cared about our military, you'd stop baiting Kim Jong Un into a war that could put 85,000 American troops, and millions of innocent civilians, in danger.

Duckworth became the first U.S. Senator to give birth while in office in 2018. Shortly afterward, rules were changed so that a Senator has the right to bring a child under one year old on the Senate floor and breastfeed them during votes. The day after those rules were changed, Maile became the first baby on the Senate floor when Duckworth brought her.

SIGNIFICANCE

Despite the injuries she suffered during Operation Iraqi Freedom, Duckworth persevered and refused to let disability stop her from pursuing her dreams, serving her country, and living a full and active life.

Throughout her career, Duckworth has worked tirelessly to promote the rights of disabled veterans. She has instituted outreach and assistance programs to meet the needs of those permanently injured in the line of duty, as well as programs to reduce homelessness among veterans.

FURTHER READING

Goodin, Emily. "Politics Hotline Extra: Reporters from around the World Are Flocking to Illinois's Sixth Congressional District to Cover the Open Seat Campaign between Democrat Tammy Duckworth and Republican Peter Roskam." *National Journal* 38.42 (2006): 70. Print. Discusses the race between Duckworth and Roskam for the seat vacated by Congressman Henry Hyde.

Krigman, Eliza. "Duckworth's New Mission." *National Journal* 41.30 (2009): 61. Print. Briefly discusses what Duckworth hopes to accomplish in her role as assistant secretary of Veterans Affairs for Public and Governmental Affairs.

McKelvey, Tara, and Laurie Campbell. "Faces from the Front Lines." *Marie Claire* 13.3 (2006): 134. Print. An interview of several talking about their experiences as soldiers in the Iraq War. Duckworth describes the attack on the helicopter she was the injuries she suffered, and her plans for the future.

O'Brien, Michael, and Cameron Joseph. "Former Obama Officer to Run for House Seat: Redistricting in Illinois Could Boost Duckworth's Chances." *Hill* 18.98 (2011): 13. Print. A brief article discussing Duckworth's second bid for a seat in the US House of Representatives.

Silver, Cary. "Reaching for the Sky." *Rotarian* 184.4 (2005): 32–35, 45. Print. An article in which Duckworth talks about her life since being injured in Iraq, her road to recovery, her inspiration to others, and her plans for the future.

United States. Cong. Senate. Committee on Veterans' Affairs. *Nominations of the 111th Congress, Part I.* 111th Cong., 1st sess. S. Doc. Washington: GPO, 2009. 126–67. Print. Transcript of the US Senate confirmation hearing held on Duckworth's nomination as the assistant secretary of Veterans Affairs for Public and Intergovernmental Affairs.

GERALDINE FERRARO

Representative from New York (1979-1985), Vice presidential candidate and, Ambassador

Born: August 26, 1935; Newburgh, New York
Died: March 26, 2011; Boston, Massachusetts
Area of achievement: Government and politics

In 1984, Ferraro, a member of the U.S. House of Representatives, became the first woman to be nominated to the vice presidency by a major political party.

Geraldine Ferraro (Wikimedia Commons)

Early Life

Geraldine Ferraro (fer-RAH-roh) was born to an Italian American family in Newburgh, New York, on August 26, 1935. Her father, Dominick Ferraro, operated a nightclub in Newburgh. In 1944, he was arrested and charged with operating a numbers racket. He died of a heart attack the day he was to appear for trial.

Antonetta Corrieri Ferraro, the major influence on Geraldine's early life, was left to rear her two children alone. She and the children left Newburgh to make ends meet; they relocated in a modest home in the somewhat less desirable South Bronx. Education was traditionally a way up and out for the children and grandchildren of immigrant families, and Antonetta Ferraro worked hard as a seamstress to provide an education for her children. Geraldine Ferraro attended Marymount Manhattan College and was graduated in 1956. She worked as a schoolteacher to support herself while attending law school at night and received her law degree from Fordham University in 1960, the same year she married John Zaccaro, a real estate developer. In honor of her mother, Ferraro kept her maiden name.

In the years that followed, three children were born to Ferraro and her husband. Although she passed the New York bar examination in 1961, she chose to practice law part-time while rearing her children. It was not until 1974 that she entered public service and accepted a post as an assistant district attorney in Queens County, New York, specializing in cases involving women, children, and the elderly.

Life's Work

Running as a Democrat, Geraldine Ferraro was elected to the United States Congress in 1978, then reelected in 1980 and 1982. During those years she devoted her considerable energies to serving her working-class district in Queens, New York, by obtaining federal assistance for roads and subways, pure water and pollution control, control of illicit drugs, and other urban issues.

As one of the few women in Congress there were only eleven Democrats and six Republicans in 1979 and a total of twenty-four women in 1983 she also became an obvious symbol for the feminist movement that had begun to transform American society. Ferraro denied that she wanted to be solely a women's representative, but she did speak out on the feminization of poverty, the discrimination affecting salaries and pensions awarded to men versus women, and the problems of single-parent households headed by women.

Ferraro was not the first woman to have made her mark in Congress. In 1916, Jeannette Rankin was the first woman elected to Congress, and she voted against American involvement in both world wars. Pat Schroeder of Colorado and Barbara Milkulski of Maryland were two Democratic representatives rising to prominence at the same time as Ferraro. Outside Congress, women were also achieving positions of political power. By the 1980's, Sandra Day O'Connor sat on the United States Supreme Court, Elizabeth Dole and Margaret Heckler were in the cabinet, Dianne Feinstein was the mayor of San Francisco, and many male politicians were asking their female colleagues to speak for them in election campaigns.

The year 1984 was a presidential election year, and the conservative Republican Ronald Reagan was running for reelection. Most observers believed it would be a difficult challenge to defeat the former actor, who enjoyed notable popularity as president and was recognized for his skills of communication. After enduring a bruising series of primaries, Walter Mondale, former vice president under Jimmy Carter and onetime senator from Minnesota, emerged as the leading Democratic challenger and came to the San Francisco convention in July with the Democratic presidential nomination assured. The only remaining question was who would be his vice presidential running mate.

> "*Some leaders are born women.*"

Traditionally, vice presidential candidates have been selected to bring balance to the ticket. With Mondale's roots in the upper Midwest, it could be expected that he might well choose someone from one of the big coastal states such as New York or California. Age, experience, and ideology could also play a part. In the past, however, balancing gender had never been seriously considered, and the Democratic and Republican parties had never chosen a female candidate for either the presidency or the vice presidency. When he appeared before the National Women's Political Caucus in 1983, Mondale himself had indicated that he would consider a woman as his vice presidential candidate if he received the Democratic nomination.

In November of 1983, several influential women met with Ferraro in hopes that she would consent to accept the vice presidential nomination if it were offered. Other Democratic women had been considered, but most were rejected as unsuitable because of geography, their stand against abortion, their brief tenure in elective office, or their lack of national and foreign policy experience. Ferraro nicely complemented Mondale: an Italian American Catholic from urban New York, she had completed three terms in Congress representing a conservative ethnic and blue-collar constituency. Ferraro had struck a balance between her role as a wife and a mother of three children and her career as a politician. She had also made an impact within Democratic Party circles. In her position as secretary of the Democratic Caucus in 1982, Ferraro had served as House liaison to the National Party Conference; in 1984, she was the chair of the Platform Committee at the Democratic National Convention and oversaw the selection of presidential and vice presidential nominees.

The prospect of a woman as the Democratic vice presidential nominee was widely discussed. In June of 1984, Time magazine featured Ferraro and Feinstein on the cover as possible candidates. By the end of the month, there was considerable pressure on Mondale to choose a woman as his running mate: The National Organization for Women (NOW) was seemingly threatening a convention fight if a woman was not selected. Mondale, however, did not have to be threatened. Always supportive of women's issues, Mondale knew that as a long-shot candidate against a popular incumbent he had little to lose and possibly much to gain by choosing a woman running mate. Many, including some Republicans, believed that a woman nominee would attract significant numbers of votes to the Democratic ticket.

On July 19, 1984, Ferraro made history when she was nominated as the Democratic vice presidential candidate. She and Mondale knew that the campaign would not be easy, but they believed that Reagan was vulnerable both on his foreign policy, which they deemed too belligerent toward the Soviet Union and therefore a danger to world peace, and on the domestic issues of unfairness and lack of opportunity for the less privileged members of American society. Unfortunately for Ferraro, much of the ensuing campaign revolved not around the issues of public policy but rather around herself and her personal history.

Sadly, it might have been predicted that a woman candidate would be treated differently, and not only by representatives from the opposite political party. Ferraro had difficulties with Mondale's own campaign staff, and other problems arose which, she argued, would not have occurred if she had been a man. More troubling were claims that she had acted unethically and perhaps illegally in the financing of her first congressional campaign, with her congressional disclosure statements, and with her family's past taxes and tax returns. These negative issues quickly dominated her campaign. She questioned whether such charges would have received such credence and publicity if she were a male candidate. Her husband was initially willing to release his financial statement but not his personal tax returns, which he had been filing separately for several years. His reluctance to release this information led to charges that he had something sinister to hide. Over the next several weeks, accusations were made that Zaccaro's father had rented office space to an underworld figure and that Zaccaro himself had borrowed money from an estate in which he was the legal conservator. In late August, after the various tax and financial statements were finally made available for public scrutiny, Ferraro held an open press conference in the attempt to put the issue to rest. This tactic was only partially successful.

Ferraro was also criticized by members of the Roman Catholic hierarchy for her stand in favor of personal choice in the controversial matter of abortion. This, too, she believed reflected a double standard: Male Roman Catholic politicians had not been personally criticized for similar stands on the abortion issue, and in the past, Catholic bishops had generally abstained from political comment. Given the Mafia stereotype closely connected to the image of the Italian American community in the popular mind, Ferraro also was exposed to charges that she and her husband and their families had ties to organized crime. What was most galling for Ferraro was that other Italian American politicians did not come to her defense. The final blow to Ferraro's dignity was the report in October that her father had been arrested shortly before his death, charged with participation in a numbers racket.

Ferraro and Walter Mondale in Fort Lauderdale, FL during the 1984 campaign. (Wikimedia Commons)

Despite these personal attacks and the physical challenges of the 1984 campaign, Ferraro found her activities to be highly rewarding. In three months, Ferraro traveled more than fifty-five thousand miles and spoke in eighty-five cities. Her campaign raised $6 million for the national Democratic ticket. Crowds were invariably large and enthusiastic wherever she appeared. In November, however, the country voted overwhelmingly for Ronald Reagan and George H. W. Bush. The polls and political commentators had early predicted the outcome, and Ferraro realized that she and Mondale were going to lose even before election day. In the aftermath of the election, polls indicated that most women voters, like their male counterparts, chose the Reagan-Bush ticket over Mondale and Ferraro. In reality, most voters vote for the presidential candidate rather than the vice presidential candidate, and Mondale was not a match for the charismatic Reagan.

After the 1984 campaign, Ferraro chose to keep a low political profile and passed up the opportunity to challenge Senator Alphonse D'Amato, the incumbent Republican from New York, in 1986. The previous year she had published her autobiography, *Ferraro: My Story*. It sold moderately well. Still under public scrutiny, her husband pleaded guilty to overstating his net worth in getting a loan and was sentenced to community service. Later, Ferraro's son, John, a college student, was arrested on cocaine charges. In 1990, Ferraro chose to campaign aggressively on behalf of female Democratic candidates in New York.

Ferraro launched her own political comeback in 1992, when she entered the New York Democratic primary as a candidate for the United States Senate. Competing against three other candidates in the primary, Ferraro faced a tough battle. Typically upbeat and optimistic to the end, Ferraro finished second, less than 1 percentage point and fewer than ten thousand votes behind the winner, New York State attorney general Robert Abrams, who was ultimately defeated in the general election, but ahead of New York City comptroller and former congresswoman Elizabeth Holtzman and the Reverend Al Sharpton. She again sought the New York Democratic senatorial nomination in 1998, but she was the runner-up to Congressman Charles Schumer, who defeated the Republican incumbent, D'Amato.

President Bill Clinton chose Ferraro to represent the United States at the United Nations, a position she held with the rank of ambassador. From 1993 until 1996 she served as a member of the United Nations Commission on Human Rights. In addition to her feminist commitments, Ferraro continued her involvement in foreign policy issues, becoming a member of the Council of Foreign Relations and the National Democratic Institute of International Affairs; she also served on the board of the National Organization of Italian American Women. A witty and incisive speaker, Ferraro was a popular media figure and cohosted the Cable News Network (CNN) show *Crossfire* for several years during the mid-1990's, where she was the liberal voice to balance the conservative John Sununu, former chief of staff to President George H. W. Bush.

In 1998, Ferraro was found to be suffering from multiple myeloma, a common form of blood cancer. Initially she kept her illness from public knowledge, but believing that as a public figure she could become a spokesperson for research and fund-raising for the disease, she became active in the Multiple Myeloma Research Foundation and testified before the Senate. Ferraro was also active in several management and consulting businesses. Of the three Zaccaro children, John and Laura Anne Lee became a lawyer and a pediatrician, respectively, and Donna Zaccaro-Ullman worked as a television producer.

Significance

For many women and for some men Ferraro's 1984 campaign for the vice presidency was a watershed, a defining moment in their lives. Never before had a woman been chosen for such a high office by a major political party. During and after the campaign, Ferraro received thousands of letters from women, young and old, who saw her campaign as a symbol of equality, recognition, and opportunity for American women. Gloria Steinem, one of America's most respected feminists, noted during the campaign that "In the long run, the importance of the Ferraro factor may be the talent and dreams it unleashes in others." As an attorney in private practice after the campaign, Ferraro found time to encourage numerous women candidates by raising funds through public appearances on their behalf. Within a decade of the 1984 election, California, the largest state in the union, had chosen two women to represent the state in the United States Senate. By 2007 there were sixteen women senators and about eighty women representatives in the House, in contrast to the seventeen women in Congress when Ferraro was first elected in 1979. Nancy Pelosi had become the Speaker of the House of Representatives, and Hillary Rodham Clinton, senator from New York, was one of the leading candidates for the Democratic Party's presidential nomination for 2008. It would be too much to claim that these advances that women had made by the early twenty-first century were due primarily to Ferraro's pathbreaking 1984 campaign, but in the 1980's and after, she was, and remained, a symbol of the political empowerment of American women. Significantly but not surprising given her own history and accomplishments, in 2007 Ferraro endorsed Senator Clinton for president. Ferraro died in March of 2011 after a 12-year battle with multiple myeloma. Ferraro was honored as a "trailblazer" in a speech by President Obama. In 2013, a public school in Queens, New York was renamed Geraldine A. Ferraro Campus in her honor.

Eugene Larson, updated by Micah L. Issitt

Further Reading

Adams, James Ring. "The Lost Honor of Geraldine Ferraro." *Commentary* 81 (February, 1986): 34-38. This article explores the press and media coverage Ferraro received during the 1984 campaign and concludes that part of the press resorted to sensationalism but some of the media failed to adequately delve into Ferraro's controversial family history.

Blumenthal, Sidney. "Once Upon a Time in America." *The New Republic*, January 6, 1986. In this important article, Blumenthal explores Ferraro's past and her family history and notes that, in spite of her claims, there are numerous criminal connections to both her and her husband's history.

Drew, Elizabeth. *Campaign Journal.* New York: Macmillan, 1985. Drew covered the 1984 election campaign for *The New Yorker* magazine. Her comments on Ferraro's campaign are insightful, including the observation that some exit polls indicated that Ferraro's controversial candidacy lost votes for the Democratic Party.

Ferraro, Geraldine. *Ferraro: My Story.* New York: Bantam Books, 1985. Ferraro, with the assistance of Linda Bird Francke, writes primarily of the 1984 vice presidential campaign and the various vicissitudes that she experienced. It also covers more superficially her earlier life, particularly her political career.

_____, and the Rev. Jesse L. Jackson. "What We Learned the Hard Way." *Newsweek*, December 26, 2006. Ferraro and Jackson discuss their own national candidacies and what changed between the 1980's and 2006.

_____, and Catherine Whitney. *Framing a Life.* New York: Scribner, 1998. Ferraro writes of her early life, including the sacrifices that her mother, Antonetta, made for her after her father died. She also discusses the Italian American stereotypes that were evident in the 1984 campaign and the heights that the daughters of immigrants could attain in the United States in the late twentieth century.

Ferraro, Susan. "What Makes Gerry Run?" *The New York Times Magazine,* March 22, 1992. The author, no relation to the subject, discusses the early stages of the 1992 New York Democratic senatorial campaign in which Ferraro was attempting a political comeback. She also summarizes Ferraro's story since 1984.

"Geraldine Anne Ferraro." In *Women in Congress, 1917-2006*. Washington, D.C.: Government Printing Office, 2006. A brief summary of Ferraro's congressional career.

Witt, Linda, Karen M. Paget, and Glenna Matthews. *Running as a Woman: Gender and Power in American Politics*. New York: Free Press, 1993. A journalist, a political scientist, and a historian collaborated on this sweeping narrative of the experiences of female candidates in American politics. Throughout this work, Ferraro's political career serves as one of the key case studies. The book contains numerous references to Ferraro's 1984 campaign, her career outside public office, and her heroic efforts to encourage the political aspirations of other female Democratic candidates during the 1990 election year.

Heather Fong

Law enforcement officer

Born: 1956; San Francisco, California
Areas of achievement: Law enforcement

Heather Fong is best known for being the first woman to head the San Francisco Police Department and for being the first Asian American woman to head a police department in a major United States city.

Early Life
Heather Jeanne Fong was born in the North Beach area of San Francisco, California, in 1956. Her father, Lum Fong, immigrated to the United States from the Ho Chung village of Chung Shan County in the Guangdong province of southern China; her mother, Mabel, was born in the United States to Chinese parents. Fong, her parents, and her older sister Eileen led a quiet life in Oakland, California, where Lum Fong owned and ran a Chinese grocery store.

The family only spoke Cantonese at home, and Fong's parents emphasized the importance of learning their cultural heritage. Fong studied Cantonese at Saint Mary's Chinese School, a large institution of more than five hundred students, offering a kindergarten-through-twelfth-grade education, including Mandarin and Cantonese language classes. In addition to taking language classes at Saint Mary's Chinese School, Fong attended Saint Rose Academy, an all-girls high school in San Francisco. While there, her interest in law enforcement was sparked for the first time by a police officer's visit to the school, and she began to consider police work as a career.

In 1975, Fong attended the University of San Francisco, earning her BA in 1979. Her college years were busy: She was in the Air Force Reserve Officers' Training Corps (ROTC), and she was a police cadet. While still in school, Fong graduated from the San Francisco Police Academy. She began her career as a police officer in 1977.

Life's Work
As a police officer, Fong proved herself to be a dedicated civil servant very early in her career. During Fong's first year with the San Francisco Police Department, she was assigned to the Golden Dragon Restaurant massacre case, in which sixteen people had been shot in Chinatown gang crossfire. The police chief brought Fong onto the case because of her Chinese-language skills, which proved to be invaluable in the investigation. Fong spent many days transcribing and translating the hours of taped conversations from the Golden Dragon case. Her diligent work ethic came to the attention of the police chief and her

Heather Fong (Wikimedia Commons)

fellow officers. From that point on, until her retirement in 2009, Fong moved rapidly through the department ranks.

In 1979, Fong was promoted to police academy instructor and was given the officer-of-the-year award by the department. She served in this capacity until 1983, when she accepted the position of child-abuse investigator. Three years later, Fong was promoted to the department's police planning and community outreach program, where she stayed for six years. Fong spent only one year as a youth inspector in 1992 before being promoted to lieutenant in 1993, and only one year as a lieutenant before being promoted to captain in 1994. As captain, Fong worked with the special-operations division. A promotion came again in 1998, when Fong was given the position of commander. In 2000, Fong became the deputy chief of the police department and was assigned to the Field Operations Bureau and the Administration Bureau. She became the assistant chief in 2003, the interim chief in January 2004, and finally chief of police for the San Francisco Police Department in April 2004.

> *"Police officers do their jobs, but we have to understand that it's not always enforcement. Sometimes it's intervention to be able to refer people to services to help them."*

Fong frequently faced harsh criticism during her tenure as San Francisco's police chief, and her fellow officers accused Mayor Gavin Newsom of appointing her for political reasons. Fong was also disparaged when she backed Newsom's decision to discipline officers in response to a controversial videotape made by the officers for the department's holiday party, purportedly showing sexist, homophobic, and racist material.

There were additional complaints within the department that she was uncommunicative with officers under her command, and she was challenged regarding her choices of assignments. Morale was said to be low in the department, and duty planning and implementation poor. During this time, San Francisco also had a poor homicide arrest rate compared to other US cities, which critics saw as a direct result of an inadequately functioning police department. Following Fong's retirement in 2009, there was public criticism of her $275,000 annual pension, the highest on record at a time when the city was facing a budget crunch.

Despite the ongoing complaints against her, Fong was lauded for the long hours she devoted to her job, her detail-oriented work, and her incorruptibility. To many in the Asian American community, she was a heroine. In 1988, she was given the Women Warriors award by the Pacific Asian American Women Bay Area Coalition (PAAWBAC). Fong received the Outstanding Public Service award from the Asian Pacific American Community Center in 2003. In 2009, the PAAWBAC again commended her with the Leadership, Courage, and Commitment award. She also received the Women of Achievement award from the Legal Momentum organization in 2009. Fong retired at the age of fifty-five.

Fong served as the Department of Homeland Security Assistant Secretary for State and Local Law Enforcement from November 17, 2014 to the end of the Obama administration.

Significance

Fong's life is significant for leading the way for women and Asians in the San Francisco Police Department and in law enforcement in the United States in general. Her professional ambition and integrity made her a model for minorities in police work and other civic fields, as she successfully utilized both her American upbringing and her Chinese heritage in her dealings with San Francisco's diverse citizens. In Fong's time as police chief, she also helped improve the reputation of her department in the public eye. Many view Fong as a pioneer in leadership roles for women, noting her successes in a male-dominated profession.

Jocelyn A. Brown

Further Reading

Garvey, John. *San Francisco Police Department: Images of America*. Mount Pleasant: Arcadia, 2004. Print. Provides a history of the San Francisco Police Department from 1849 to 2004.

Thoshinsky, Peter. *Blue in Black and White*. New York: Turner, 2005. Print. Chronicles life as a police officer in San Francisco; includes photographs and provides valuable insight into the operations and daily life of the San Francisco Police Department.

Wachs, Benjamin. "The Chief Is In: Is She Accountable?" *SF Weekly*. SF Weekly, 7 Aug. 2008. Web. 19 Jan. 2012. Brings to light the controversy surrounding the hiring of Fong as chief of the San Francisco Police Department.

Benjamin Franklin

Statesman, scientist, and philosopher

Born: January 17, 1706; Boston, Massachusetts
Died: April 17, 1790; Philadelphia, Pennsylvania
Area of Achievement: Politics, philosophy, science, writing

Franklin helped shape most of the important political, social, and intellectual developments in eighteenth-century America. He became a veritable symbol of the United States by the end of his life, both at home and abroad, and he remains an influential folk hero.

Early Life

Among Benjamin Franklin's English ancestors, one had owned a bit of land only twelve miles from the English ancestral seat of the Washingtons. Franklin's father, Josiah, had repudiated the Church of England and left England for Boston in the 1680s; Franklin's mother's forebears had arrived somewhat earlier. When Franklin was born in 1706, the modest household was already teeming with children, for he was a tenth son–and, incidentally, the youngest son of the youngest son for five generations back. The salient facts of Franklin's life were extraordinary from the start.

Although his father was a struggling tradesman (a candle maker and soap boiler), there was much in the way of reading, thinking, and discussing as well as hard work in his home. Franklin learned to read when very young, and by the age of twelve he had progressed through the Bible, the works of John Bunyan, Plutarch's *Parallel Lives* (105–15), and certain essays of Daniel Defoe and of Boston's Cotton Mather. He had very little formal schooling, and his family could not afford to send him to Harvard College.

Instead, an effort was made to bring him into the family business. He disliked the work, and he hated the smell. At that point, an older brother, James, returned from London, where he had been trained as a printer. Thus, the restless, bright, bookish twelve-year-old Benjamin Franklin was apprenticed to his high-spirited brother, who in 1721 started a newspaper, *The New England Courant*. It was the fourth newspaper in the colonies. These years were supremely important in shaping the man who later became so famous. He learned a trade that would bring him profits and prominence. He had access to many books,

Benjamin Franklin (Metropolitan Museum of Art)

especially those loaned by patrons and friends. He discussed and debated matters with men who loitered in the shop and also with friends after hours. The principal subjects were the two that would be commonly avoided centuries later: religion and politics. He worked hard at learning to write and he experienced the thrill of seeing his first piece, an anonymous letter to the editor, in print. When the pugnacious James got into trouble with the authorities and was jailed, his brother, then sixteen, functioned as the paper's editor.

The brothers often quarreled, and the younger Franklin, a mere apprentice, was often treated severely. He resented this and decided to run away, arriving in Philadelphia in October 1723, munching on a large roll, with one Dutch dollar and a copper shilling in his pocket. The scene became a memorable passage in the memoir he later wrote, which included the fact that his future wife happened to see him and laughed at the ridiculous sight he made. He soon found work, for he was an excellent printer, and he soon found adventure as well. An eccentric governor of the province, William Keith, proposed that Franklin go to England to purchase equipment for a new printing business Keith hoped would outdo all competition. He would send letters of credit and letters of introduction.

Franklin was in London by Christmas of 1724, but no letters came from the governor. The eighteen-year-old did find work, however, in a printing house, and as always he read intensively and grappled with ideas. After setting type for a religious book, he became convinced that the author was all wrong. In response, Franklin composed and printed a pamphlet that set forth a radical refutation. He later regarded this as a mistake, but it did gain him some attention and some new acquaintances, a few of them prominent writers of the day.

> *"Love your Enemies, for they tell you your Faults."*

Franklin returned to Philadelphia in 1726 and was soon employed again in his old shop. Before long, he left the shop to form a new business with a partner, on credit. By dint of very long hours of work, ingenious planning, and excellent workmanship, they survived–barely. Then the partner wanted to leave, and Franklin, borrowing money, bought him out. By July 1730, he was the sole proprietor of a promising business, which included the printing of a newspaper begun the year before, *The Pennsylvania Gazette*. Six weeks later, he married Deborah Read, the daughter of his first landlady. Though she was uneducated (thus never an intellectual companion), she was frugal, industrious, and loving. Franklin, at twenty-four, had become a solid Philadelphia burgher.

LIFE'S WORK

The foundation of Benjamin Franklin's renown was his success as a businessman. Both he and Deborah worked very hard, and they lived frugally for some time. It was, however, more than routine drudgery, for new projects were always appearing: Franklin established a stationery shop; Deborah collected and prepared rags for the paper makers; he imported books in both English and foreign languages; he printed almanacs for those who compiled them, and then decided to compile his own. *Poor Richard's Almanack*, begun in 1732 and published between 1733 and 1758, was ultimately to become the best known of the many that were printed in eighteenth century America. Franklin enjoyed borrowing and reworking phrases from his reading and sometimes wrote new adages, which delighted his readers. For many, he and his fictional wise man, Richard Saunders, became one. The central themes of Richard's concern were thrift, industry, and frugality, and Franklin at the time appeared to be practicing what "Poor Richard" preached.

Political connections quickly became an important feature of Franklin's business success. He printed much of the provincial government's work: laws, records of legislative voting, and even the new paper currency in favor of which Franklin had argued in his first political pamphlet, *A Modest Enquiry into the Nature and Necessity of a Paper Currency* (1729). He became clerk of the Pennsylvania Assembly in 1736. The following year, he secured an appointment as postmaster for Philadelphia, a position that gave him immediate access to the latest news–very helpful in his newspaper business. Later, he was deputy postmaster general for all the colonies (1753–74), and under his administration the governmental department showed a profit. He was always heavily involved with public affairs and often managed to influence their course.

It was during his years as a businessman that Franklin's remarkable flair for civic improvement by private initiative appeared. In 1727, he founded a discussion group, or club, of tradesmen, clerks, and mechanics, which he called the Junto. Often Franklin would first propose to his friends at the Junto for discussion an idea for a public project, and then follow his proposal with an article in his newspaper. Soon the project would be under way. He was prominent in the founding of a circulating library, a fire company, a hospital, and an academy that evolved into the University of Pennsylvania, among many other projects. Ever the keen observer of daily life in his beloved city, he was always alert to possibilities for improvement.

Franklin was also a particularly astute observer of nature, and this ultimately led him to the forefront of certain branches of the sciences of his day. On an early transatlantic voyage, he kept careful records of temperatures, of the flora and fauna of the sea, of the positions of the Moon and the stars; later he made a map of the Gulf Stream. He believed that knowledge must be useful, and actual inventions came out of many of his studies, including the improved Franklin stove, bifocal spectacles, a glass harmonica (a musical instrument for which even Wolfgang Amadeus Mozart wrote music), and other gadgets.

His main interest, though, was electricity. His famous kite experiment in 1752 demonstrated the identity of lightning and electricity and gave him an international reputation. He was, as always, interested in practical application, which in this case became the lightning rod. Nevertheless, he was also responsible for naming the

Franklin and his son performing the kite experiment. (Wikimedia Commons)

concept of polarity, negative and positive, to describe the behavior of electricity.

In 1748, Franklin was able to retire from business, expecting to devote himself to his favorite scientific pursuits. Public affairs, however, became the dominant force throughout the remainder of his life. When the threat of war with France led to a gathering of delegates at Albany in 1754, Franklin was there representing Pennsylvania. He proposed a plan for an intercolonial union that the Albany Congress approved, only to see it rejected by both the various colonial governments and the imperial authorities in London. Franklin always believed that if these governments had not been so shortsighted, the American Revolution might have been avoided. In 1757, as a result of a quarrel between the Pennsylvania Assembly and the proprietors of the colony, he was sent to London as spokesman for the assembly, the members of which wanted the authorities there to intervene. In this he achieved a partial success. While in England, he received honorary degrees from St. Andrews and Oxford. He was very happy in England and seriously considered a permanent move, but he came home to Philadelphia in 1762.

Another political quarrel in Pennsylvania led to Franklin's return to England in 1764, where he soon became involved in efforts to forestall the new imperial policies toward the colonies, which Americans regarded as outrageous. For ten years, Franklin was torn between his profound pride in America and things American, and his enthusiasm for English culture. As the foremost American of his day, he was looked to for the preservation of American rights: He became an agent for Georgia, New Jersey, and Massachusetts, as well as the Pennsylvania Assembly. As Anglo-American relations deteriorated, Franklin revealed in private his growing conviction that the American colonists' claims were sound and that their resistance was justified, while he continued to make every diplomatic effort possible for accommodation.

Early in 1774, however, news arrived of the destruction of tea at Boston Harbor, in an act known as the Boston Tea Party. This was quickly followed by a mighty personal attack on Franklin, occasioned by his part in obtaining and circulating certain letters written by Governor Thomas Hutchinson of Massachusetts, the contents of which inflamed opinion against Hutchinson and led to a petition for his recall. Franklin was dismissed by the royal government from his postal appointment and subjected to a searing public humiliation before a committee of the Privy Council (January 1774). For another year he tried in many ingenious ways to achieve a reconciliation, but to no avail. He sailed for America in March 1775.

When Franklin arrived home, the Continental Congress, which had first convened during the preceding fall, was now into its second session at Philadelphia. The deliberations were becoming extremely anxious because the unthinkable had happened: Actual fighting had broken out with British soldiers at Lexington and Concord. Franklin was made a member of the congress the day after he arrived, and he immediately undertook important work. He drew up a plan of colonial union, something similar to an early version of a national constitution. He organized a post office and became postmaster general. He served on a number of important committees, including one that in 1776 was to draft the Declaration of Independence. He was, at the age of seventy, the oldest signer. Toward the end of that year, he was sent by the congress, along with Arthur Lee and Silas Deane, to solicit French support for the American cause.

Franklin was well known in France. He had visited that country before, but more important was his reputation as a scientist, writer (Poor Richard's witticisms had been translated), and apostle of the latest ideas of the Age of Reason. He played the part well, with fur hat and simple clothes, a genial manner, and appropriate bons mots (witticism), and he exuded the spirit of liberty–a veritable backwoods Socrates spreading the truths of nature. Following the American victory at Saratoga (October 1777), the French became receptive to American suggestions, and by February of 1778, France had become a formal ally. This meant that France was now at war with Great Britain.

Franklin became the sole American ambassador in September of 1778 and, as always, found many interests beyond his principal work. He managed, nevertheless, to keep French-American relations good; France provided America with material aid, an army, and, in the crucial autumn of 1781, a navy. After the British defeat at Yorktown (October 1781), peace negotiations with Britain began. Franklin was joined by John Adams and John Jay in the final talks, but on several occasions the wily old Philadelphian's role was decisive. It was an excellent treaty for Americans, gaining them a formal acknowledgment of independence and generous boundaries.

When Franklin returned to Philadelphia in September 1785, he was nearly eighty years old. Yet he was chosen president of the executive council of Pennsylvania, and he became the president of an antislavery society. He was chosen as a Pennsylvania delegate to the Philadelphia Convention, which drew up the US Constitution in 1787, and he gave his prestigious support to its ratification. His last public act was signing a petition to Congress for the abolition of slavery. He died on April 17, 1790.

Significance

Benjamin Franklin's life was so varied and his achievements so diverse that it seems as though there were several Franklins, though one tends to overlap the other. The most familiar is the successful businessman who rose from humble circumstances to dine with kings, substantially by his own efforts. His life symbolized the rags-to-riches success of a self-made man, a theme of great importance in American thought. His version of his life, as presented in the didactic *The Autobiography of Benjamin Franklin* (1791) and in the sayings of Poor Richard, stressed thrift, industry, and frugality, which were important elements of his own Puritan heritage, rendered in secular, easily understood forms. His zest for useful knowledge became the main style of American science and technology, yet he had great respect for learning and for intellectual curiosity, and he believed that educational opportunity was indispensable for a great future nation.

He was civic-minded from the start. He demonstrated what could be done by private, voluntary community effort to care for human needs, but he also stressed the importance of alert participation in the prevailing political system. His style was egalitarian, tolerant, and democratic before such a style was expected and common; yet he understood well the importance of dignity and deference in human affairs. Americans, during his later years, repudiated kings and hereditary aristocrats, but they also yearned for heroes. Franklin provided them with a hero unlike any other known before.

Richard D. Miles

Further Reading

Aldridge, Alfred Owen. *Benjamin Franklin: Philosopher and Man*. Philadelphia: Lippincott, 1965. Print.

Cohen, I. Bernard. *Franklin and Newton*. Cambridge: Harvard UP, 1966. Print.

---. *Science and the Founding Fathers: Science in the Political Thought of Jefferson, Franklin, Adams, and Madison*. New York: Norton, 1995. Print.

Conner, Paul W. *Poor Richard's Politics: Benjamin Franklin and His New American Order*. New York: Oxford UP, 1965. Print.

Crane, Verner W. *Benjamin Franklin and a Rising People*. Boston: Little, 1954. Print.

Franklin, Benjamin. *The Autobiography of Benjamin Franklin*. Ed. Leonard W. Labaree et al. New Haven: Yale UP, 1964. Print.

Granger, Bruce I. *Benjamin Franklin: An American Man of Letters*. Ithaca: Cornell UP, 1964. Print.

Isaacson, Walter. *Benjamin Franklin: An American Life*. New York: Simon, 2003. Print.

Lopez, Claude-Anne. *Mon Cher Papa*. New Haven: Yale UP, 1966. Print.

Middlekauff, Robert. *Benjamin Franklin and His Enemies*. Berkeley: U of California P, 1996. Print.

Morgan, Edmund S. *Benjamin Franklin*. New Haven: Yale UP, 2002. Print.

Srodes, James. *Franklin: The Essential Founding Father*. Washington, DC: Regnery, 2002. Print.

Stourzh, Gerald. *Benjamin Franklin and American Foreign Policy*. Chicago: U of Chicago P, 1954. Print.

Van Doren, Carl C. *Benjamin Franklin*. New York: Viking, 1938. Print.

Ruth Bader Ginsburg

Associate Justice of the Supreme Court (1993-present)

Born: March 15, 1933; Brooklyn, New York City
Area of Achievement: Law, activism

As an attorney and a law professor, Ginsburg was a leader in the legal movement seeking to enhance the rights of women. Ruth Bader Ginsburg was the second woman named to the Supreme Court.

Early Life

Ruth Bader Ginsburg (BAY-dur GIHNZ-burg) was born in Brooklyn on March 13, 1933. She was raised in the city and educated in its public schools. Her mother, who died of cancer the day before her graduation from high school, was a significant influence on her, encouraging her to work hard on her education. She attended Cornell University in New York, where she met her future husband, Martin Ginsburg. Both began their legal studies at Harvard Law School, where she was one of few women in her class. When her husband was hired by a major New York law firm, she transferred to Columbia University Law School. There she graduated as a member of the law review, tied for first in her class. She then served as a law clerk for two years. One of her professors strongly urged that she be chosen for a highly prestigious Supreme Court clerk position, but this was a not a position open to women at that time. For the same reason, in spite of her stellar academic credentials, Ginsburg was unable to find a job with a major law firm in New York. Consequently she took a position teaching at Rutgers University Law School in 1963, where she first became interested in gender discrimination law. While there, she cowrote the first casebook in that field. In 1972, she joined the Columbia Law School faculty and became head of the Women's Rights Project created by the American Civil Liberties Union.

Life's Work

When Ginsburg began to work with the Women's Rights Project, there were a large number of laws, both state and federal, that treated men and women differently, often to the disadvantage of women. She challenged many of these laws, and she was successful getting them rewritten.

Ruth Bader Ginsburg (Wikimedia Commons)

Her work contributed significantly to the advancement of women's rights.

In 1980, Ginsburg was appointed to the Federal Court of Appeals for Washington, D.C., by President Jimmy Carter. While on this court she developed a reputation as being a moderately progressive judge, one who would interpret the law in a liberal fashion but not seek to push rapid change. In that vein, while on this court, she published an article criticizing the Supreme Court's 1973 decision in *Roe v. Wade* (the decision that overturned existing laws banning and regulating abortion) for going too far, too fast and for not focusing only on the rights of the woman.

In 1993, when Byron R. White, who was appointed by John F. Kennedy, retired, President Bill Clinton was given the opportunity to fill the vacancy. At that time there were no Jewish justices on the Court; indeed there had not been one since Abe Fortas stepped down from the Court in 1969. It took the president some time to decide on a nominee, but he eventually chose Ginsburg. She was easily confirmed by the U.S. Senate, winning her seat by a vote of ninety-six to three.

Since Ginsburg has joined the Court, she has become a member of its "liberal" bloc. Analyses of her decisions show she has tended, in non unanimous decisions, to vote

> ### Championing Women's Rights
>
> As a woman in a field then dominated by males, Ruth Bader Ginsburg felt the sting of gender bias, and she spent much of her professional life fighting it. As a professor and a leader of the American Civil Liberties Women's Rights Project, she participated in a number of lawsuits challenging laws that discriminated against women. As project director, she argued six cases involving women's rights before the U.S. Supreme Court, winning five. She also submitted a number of amici curiae briefs in support of other litigants. Her basic argument was that such laws violated the "equal protection" clause of the U.S. Constitution, and, like laws that distinguish people on the basis of race, they should be treated with "strict scrutiny," which usually means they would be declared unconstitutional. If the Court was unwilling to take that position, she would argue that most legal distinctions between men and women were based on stereotypes and, hence, were invalid because they fit no rational purpose. In 1996, she wrote the majority opinion in *United States v. Virginia*, the case in which the Supreme Court decided that Virginia Military Institute must admit women.

with such justices as John Paul Stevens, David Souter, and (fellow Clinton appointee) Stephen Breyer. Those with whom she has tended to disagree most have been Justice Samuel Alito and her former colleagues on the Court of Appeals, Clarence Thomas and Antonin Scalia. As a member of the "liberal" bloc, she has voted with the majority in the case invalidating a Texas law that prohibited private sexual relations between consulting adults of the same gender. She has also made it clear that she considers laws seeking to restrict access to abortions to be unconstitutional. To a degree greater than some of her colleagues, she has supported the rights of the accused against the power of the state in cases of criminal law.

Because of the conservative ascendancy on the Court, Ginsburg often votes with the minority. For instance, when the majority of the Court held that large punitive damages in lawsuits are unconstitutional, she voted in the minority. She also voted with the minority when the Supreme Court upheld California's "three strikes and you're out" law, and she did the same in a case in which the majority took the position that made it difficult for citizens to effectively pursue pay-discrimination lawsuits. She also voted with the dissenters in *Bush v. Gore*, the case that determined the outcome of the 2000 presidential contest. Because she tends to vote with the minority a significant amount of the time she has, relatively speaking, written fewer opinions of the Court (majority opinions) and more dissenting opinions than many of her colleagues. In 2012, Ginsburg became the oldest still-serving member of the Supreme Court.

Two important twenty-first century decisions saw her siding with the majority. First, in the case called *King v. Burwell*, Ginsburg voted to uphold the 2010 Affordable Care Act – commonly called Obamacare. Then, in 2015, Ginsburg voted in *Obergefell v. Hodges* to legalize same-sex marriage in all 50 states. Ginsburg had previously exhibited her support for the idea of gay marriage by performing same-sex marriages, and she argued forcefully during the case's proceedings. She has also authored important majority opinions for the Court, including *United States v. Virginia*, *Olmstead v. L.C.*, and *Friends of the Earth Inc. v. Laidlaw Environmental Services, Inc.*

> "*Dissents speak to a future age. It's not simply to say, 'My colleagues are wrong and I would do it this way.' But the greatest dissents do become court opinions and gradually over time their views become the dominant view. So that's the dissenter's hope: that they are writing not for today but for tomorrow.*"

Ginsburg's first book, *My Own Words* was published in 2016, debuting on the New York Times Best Seller List for hardcover nonfiction at number 12. The book is a collection of her speeches and writings dating back to her time in eighth grade.

Although she has had philosophical differences with some of her peers on the bench, she has been able to maintain good personal relationships with many of them. For instance, though she and Sandra Day O'Connor (the first woman appointed to the Supreme Court) did not always vote the same, they became good friends. The Ginsburgs also have a close personal relationship with the Scalias, though the two justices disagree often in their votes.

SIGNIFICANCE

Ginsburg has had significant impact on American life as a role model, a leader in the women's rights movement, and as a judge. When she entered Harvard Law School, a female lawyer was a rarity. She excelled in the field, and now women make up about 30 percent of the legal profession. Her role in the crusade for greater legal equality for women has been compared to Thurgood Marshall's role in legal integration. She is also the first Jewish woman to attain the position of justice of the United States Supreme Court. In interviews, Ginsburg has accused the Supreme Court of having a poor record in ruling on women's issues. She cited the 2014 case of *Burwell v. Hobby Lobby* in which the Hobby Lobby corporation refused to insure birth control for female employees because of religious beliefs on the part of the corporation's owners. Ginsburg delivered a dissenting opinion based on her belief that corporations should not be allowed to cite religious belief as this right is afforded only to persons. She is known as a jurist who carefully builds on existing law to extend it in liberal directions. As both an attorney and a judge, she has been an intelligent and effective spokesperson for equality for all under the law.

David M. Jones, updated by Micah L. Issitt

FURTHER READING

Baer, Judith. "Advocate on the Court: Ruth Bader Ginsburg and the Limits of Formal Equality." In *Rehnquist Justice: Understanding the Court Dynamic*, edited by Earl Matz. Lawrence: University Press of Kansas, 2003. Evaluates her approach to equality for women, comparing it to other feminist theories.

O'Brien, David M. "Judicial Legacies: The Clinton Presidency and the Courts." In *The Clinton Legacy*, edited by Colin Campbell and Bert A. Rockman. New York: Chatham House, 2000. Discusses Clinton's philosophy of judicial appointments and how Ginsburg fit into it.

Strum, Philippa. *Women in the Barracks: The VMI Case and Equal Rights*. Lawrence: University Press of Kansas, 2002. Discusses the movement to integrate women into the formerly all-male Virginia Military Institute. Contains material on Ginsburg's role, both as an attorney and as a Supreme Court justice.

Tushnet, Mark. "Ruth Bader Ginsburg's Equal Protection Clause." In *A Court Divided: The Rehnquist Court and the Future of Constitutional Law*. New York: W. W. Norton, 2005. Describes Ginsburg's judicial philosophy; also contains biographical materials.

AL GORE

Vice president (1993-2001), environmentalist, Nobel Peace Prize winner

Born: March 31, 1948
Area of Achievement: Government and politics

Gore, both as politician and activist, underscored the need for public concern, discussion, and debate on issues of technology, consumption, and the environment. In 2007 he was awarded the Nobel Peace Prize for his work on global warming. In 2000, he received a majority of the popular vote for president of the United States but was not permitted to take office after the U.S. Supreme Court decided against a further recounting of damaged ballots in Florida.

EARLY LIFE

Al Gore was born and raised in Washington, D.C., where his father was serving as a representative from Tennessee's Fourth Congressional District. When the younger Gore was only four years old, his father was elected to the Senate. While Gore spent many summers on the family

Al Gore (Wikimedia Commons)

farm near Carthage, Tennessee, he lived and attended private schools in Washington.

Gore graduated from Harvard University with a degree in government in 1969 and entered the US Army, intending to serve in Vietnam despite his opposition to the war. While he had comparatively safer duty as a reporter for a military newspaper, simply being in Vietnam was dangerous. Gore was one of the very few sons of Washington politicians to serve in the war zone. After Vietnam, he attended Vanderbilt University and took graduate courses in religion. Not satisfied with this area of study, he switched to the Vanderbilt law school. He also worked as a reporter for the Nashville *Tennessean* while pursing his graduate education.

LIFE'S WORK
At age twenty-eight, Gore quit law school to run for the congressional seat his father had once held. As a border-state Democrat, Gore represented his district's moderately conservative views but sought to establish progressive credentials by developing expertise in arms control and the protection of the environment. He served four terms in the House until Tennessee's senior senator, Republican Howard Baker, retired in 1984. Gore then won his seat in the Senate. He broadened his policy credentials by developing expertise in modern technology, especially the Internet (before the advent of the World

Wide Web).

Four years later, in 1988, Gore ran for president. Although he won a number of southern Democratic primaries, he was not able to win the New York primary and realized he could not win the party's nomination with so many candidates vying that year. His showing was good enough to support a future run for the presidency, although his son's serious car accident kept him from running in 1992. In 1992, Gore published his *Earth in the Balance*, which became the first best seller published by an incumbent senator since John F. Kennedy wrote *Profiles in Courage* in the 1950s.

Bill Clinton, who would become US president in 1993, made an unusual decision by picking Gore, a southern moderate from an adjacent state, as his running mate in 1992. Still, Gore's service in Vietnam mitigated some of the concern over Clinton's lack of service in the same conflict. Upon his election as vice president, he expanded his previous policy expertise into the arena of reorganizing the federal bureaucracy and produced a major report on the subject in 1995. In line with a growing trend to make the vice presidency a more important office, Gore became the most actively involved vice president in the history of that office.

In 2000, Gore was heavily favored for the Democratic presidential nomination, easily overcoming a challenge from former US senator Bill Bradley of New Jersey. He defeated Bradley in every primary. In the general election, Gore ran a strong campaign and showed his policy expertise in each of the three debates with his Republican opponent, George W. Bush. While the experts rated Gore's performance as superior, Bush went into the debates with low expectations but performed well enough to make slight gains in the polls. Bush made additional mistakes, including failing to disclose early in the campaign that he had been arrested in 1976 for drunk driving. This disclosure on the last weekend before the election damaged Bush's candidacy greatly, leading to his loss of the popular vote by more than a half million.

Unfortunately for Gore, the election was not decided by popular vote but by the electoral college, where a majority of the electoral votes organized by states selects a president. Normally, the popular and electoral votes produce the same result, but in 2000, Florida's popular vote was very close. Gore led early in the evening, but Bush pulled ahead after midnight. Later, Bush's lead fell to just a few hundred votes, staying there until certification, now in the hands of Florida state officials. Some critics of this election have argued that because the most important of these officials were Republican, they had acted to "protect" Bush's lead.

Gore has the unfortunate distinction of being one of only four former candidates for president, all Democrats, who won the popular vote for office but lost the election in the electoral college. (In 2016, Hilary Clinton joined this group after her race against Donald Trump.) Two candidates, Andrew Jackson and Grover Cleveland, ran for office at a later time and won their respective presidential elections. Another candidate, Samuel Tilden, abandoned electoral politics and became a social critic and activist for progressive causes. Gore's career has resembled that of Tilden.

The fairness of the election was challenged. A recount of all the ballots likely would have produced a narrow victory for Gore, based on a subsequent unofficial recount conducted by a consortium of national news organizations. Soon after the vote, pollsters found that thousands more Floridians had intended to vote for Gore, and not for Bush. Many voters had cast their ballots incorrectly, thereby unknowingly voiding their own ballots or voting for the wrong candidate. A full recount and a complete judicial review of the various challenges in the courts would have helped to determine the outcome of the elections and given credibility to the electoral system.

However, in an unprecedented move, the U.S. Supreme Court intervened in the election controversy and stopped further counting of the votes. After a narrow 5–4 decision, the Court claimed the authority of the equal protection clause of the Fourteenth Amendment and argued that the Florida Supreme Court incorrectly allowed the recounting of some but not all ballots. This decision has been widely criticized by both conservative and liberal legal scholars. In effect, it was the court system, and not the voters (via the electoral college), that selected Bush for the presidency. After the Court decision, Gore gave a gracious concession speech and served the remainder of his term as vice president.

> "The very first words that we, the American nation, spoke were right here in Philadelphia. You know those words: 'We the people.' It wasn't, 'We the conglomerates.' It wasn't, 'We the corporations.' It was, 'We the people.'"

SIGNIFICANCE

Gore remained in the public realm after his work in electoral politics as a college lecturer, writer, and environmental activist. His book on climate change, *An Inconvenient Truth: The Planetary Emergency of Global Warming and What We Can Do about It* (2006), was a best seller and stirred public debate about the rapid changes to Earth's climate patterns. The book was made into an Academy Award–winning documentary film. For his work to raise awareness about global warming and climate change, he was awarded the Nobel Peace Prize in 2007. He shared the award with the United Nations' Intergovernmental Panel on Climate Change.

Also in 2007, Gore published *The Assault on Reason*, which argued against the trend in US politics that ignores facts and analyses in policymaking. He further argues in the book that, at the expense of democracy, television threatens public discourse because it is focused on entertainment and, through powerful gatekeepers that include the corporate-owned news media, it presents a one-sided perspective and interpretation of the world. The Internet, he argued, is an interactive medium that could change that threat by keeping public discourse and debate alive.

In 2013, Gore announced that Current TV, a cable news network that he cofounded in 2005, was being sold to the Al-Jazeera news network. Gore remains involved in environmental activism and politics, splitting his time between homes in San Francisco and Nashville.

In 2016, Al Gore met with president-elect Donald Trump at Trump Tower in New York to discuss climate change. This as significant, since Trump had previously made comments suggesting global warming was a hoax. After the meeting, Gore related that: "I had a lengthy and very productive session with the president-elect. It was a sincere search for areas of common ground. I had a meeting beforehand with Ivanka Trump. The bulk of the time was with the president-elect, Donald Trump. I found it an extremely interesting conversation, and to be continued, and I'm just going to leave it at that."

Richard L. Wilson

FURTHER READING

Alvarez, R. Michael, and Bernard Grofman. *Election Administration in the United States: The State of Reform after Bush v. Gore*. New York: Cambridge UP, 2014. Print.

Dionne, E. J., Jr., and William Kristol, eds. *Bush versus Gore: The Court Cases and the Commentary*. Washington, DC: Brookings Institution, 2001. Print.

Downie, Leonard, Jr., ed. *Deadlock: The Inside Story of America's Closest Election*. New York: Public Affairs, 2001. Print.

Fishman, Steve. "Al Gore's Golden Years." *New York* 46.15 (2013): 32–86. *Academic Search Complete*. Web. 5 Dec. 2013.

Hosansky, David, ed. *The Environment A to Z*. Washington, DC: CQ P, 2001. Print.

Issacharoof, Samuel, Pamela S. Karlan, and Richard H. Pildes. *When Elections Go Bad: The Law of Democracy and the Presidential Election of 2000*. New York: Foundation P, 2001. Print.

Rakove, Jack N, ed. *The Unfinished Election of 2000: Leading Scholars Examine America's Strangest Election*. New York: Basic, 2001. Print.

Sabato, Larry J., ed. *Overtime! The Election 2000 Thriller*. New York: Longman, 2002. Print.

Wells, Charley. *Inside Bush v. Gore*. Gainesville: UP of Florida, 2013. Print.

Nikki Haley

Governor of South Carolina (2011-2017) and Ambassador to the United Nations

Born: January 20, 1972; Bamberg, South Carolina
Areas of Achievement: Government and politics

Upon being elected governor of South Carolina in 2010, largely with strong backing by the Tea Party movement, Nikki Haley broke historical gender and ethnic barriers and also became the youngest governor in the United States.

Early Life

Nimrata Nikki Randhawa Haley was born Nimrata Nikki Randhawa to Dr. Ajit and Raj Randhawa in Bamberg, South Carolina. Her father was a biology professor at Voorhees College, and her mother had studied law and education before establishing Exotica International, an upscale-clothing business. When Nikki was thirteen years old, she handled bookkeeping and taxes for Exotica International after school. She obtained a BS in accounting from Clemson University and worked as an accounting supervisor in Charlotte, North Carolina, until returning to the family business as its chief financial officer and helping it become a multimillion-dollar operation.

While at Clemson, Nikki met her husband, Michael Haley. She converted from Sikhism to his Methodist religion, although she embraces both. The couple has two children, Rena and Nalin.

Life's Work

Nikki Haley became active in local politics and business organizations while working for Exotica International. She served on local chambers of commerce and took on leadership positions for a variety of civic organizations, including the Lexington County Republican Party, National Association of Women Business Owners, and the Magnolia Junior Women's Society of Lexington.

In 2004, Haley, a fiscal conservative, successfully challenged Republican Larry Koon for his longtime seat as representative of Lexington County's Eighty-Seventh District in the South Carolina General Assembly. She was elected again for two more terms, based on her strong support for tax reform and other conservative measures. In 2006, she won the Strom Thurmond Excellence in Public Service and Government Award from the South Carolina Federation of Republican Women.

Nikki Haley (Wikimedia Commons)

Haley successfully ran for governor in 2010, backed by former Alaska governor Sarah Palin, the Tea Party movement, former Massachusetts governor Mitt Romney, and other Republicans; however, her Tea Party support waned in 2012 when she endorsed Romney for president in South Carolina's Republican presidential primary. She was elected for a second term as Governor of South Carolina in 2014. Haley was asked to deliver the Republican response to Barack Obama's State of the Union Address in January of 2016, leading to widespread speculation that Haley may be tapped to serve as vice president in the case of a Republican win in the 2016 presidential election. When the 2016 election came, Republican nominee Donald Trump chose Mike Pence as his running mate.

In November 2016, President Trump nominated Haley for the position of U.S. Ambassador to the United Nations, which she accepted. She was confirmed in the Senate by a vote of 96-4 and was sworn in in January 2017. As U.N. Ambassador, Haley affirmed the United States' willingness to use military force in response to further North Korean missile tests in the wake of the 2017 North Korea crisis. Haley's tenure as Ambassador was noted for its high degree of visibility.

On March 30, 2017, Haley stated that the U.S. would no longer focus on forcing Syrian President Bashar al-Assad to leave power. This was a policy shift from former president Barack Obama's initial stance on Assad. On April 5, speaking to the U.N. Security Council a day after the Khan Shaykhun chemical attack, Haley said Russia, Assad, and Iran "have no interest in peace" and attacks similar to this would continue occurring should nothing be done in response. A day later, the U.S. launched 59 Tomahawk cruise missiles toward the Shayrat Air Base in Syria. Haley called the strike a "very measured step" and warned that the U.S. was prepared "to do more" despite wishing it would not be required.

> "I think it's very important to get ego out of the room. I think it's important to realize it takes two hands to clap - stop the pointing, stop the blame game. I think we've seen enough of that, I think the country is tired of it. I think they want to see Washington function, they want to see action."

Haley tendered her resignation as the U.N. Ambassador in October 2018, which President Trump accepted.

Significance

As the youngest governor in the United States, Nikki Haley set several other major precedents for South Carolina. She was the first woman and the first Indian American, or member of any ethnic minority, to serve as governor of that state. She was also the first female Republican gubernatorial candidate in South Carolina and the second Indian American governor in the United States. Haley received an honorary doctorate in public service from the University of South Carolina

Sally Driscoll, updated by Micah L. Issitt

Further Reading

Campo-Flores, Arian, and Daniel Stone. "Woman on the Verge." *Newsweek* 12 July 2010: 32-36. Print. Profiles Haley during her gubernatorial campaign, with emphasis on the support from former Alaska governor Sarah Palin and the Tea Party movement.

Haley, Nikki. *Can t Is Not an Option: My American Story.* New York: Sentinel, 2012. Print. An autobiography emphasizing the role of Haley's Indian heritage and upbringing in her career choices.

Pal, Amitabh. "Extreme Makeover, GOP Style." *Progressive* Oct. 2010: 28-30. Print. Compares and contrasts the careers of Haley and Louisiana governor Bobby Jindal in relationship to their conversions to Christianity from the Hindu and Sikh religions.

Alexander Hamilton

Politician and founding Father

Born: January 11, 1755 or 1757; British Leeward Islands
Died: July 12, 1804; New York City, New York
Areas of Achievement: Government and politics, military

Hamilton served as aide-de-camp to Washington during the American Revolution and was a delegate to the Philadelphia Convention of 1787 and signer of the Constitution. An early advocate of a strong national government, he coauthored The Federalist and was the first secretary of the U.S. treasury.

Early Life

Alexander Hamilton was the illegitimate son of a Scottish ne'er-do-well and a woman previously arrested for adultery. He was born in 1755, although at times he claimed that his birth year was 1757. Hamilton spent his early years in abject poverty on the Caribbean island of his birth, Nevis. After his mother's death, he worked for a merchant family on St. Croix, where he flourished, as his unusual abilities brought him to the attention of his employers. Hamilton quickly rose to be something more than a clerk but less than a partner. By age sixteen, he was giving orders to ship captains, making decisions on when cargoes should be sold, and firing and hiring company lawyers. When not working, he studied on his own.

In 1773, Hamilton's employers, recognizing his precocious genius, sent him to the mainland for his first formal education. From 1773 to 1774, he lived with Elias Boudinot, a future president of the Continental Congress, and studied at a Presbyterian academy in Elizabethtown, New Jersey. In this period, Hamilton socialized with such future patriots and political leaders as William Livingston, Richard Stockton, Philip Schuyler, and Henry Brockholst Livingston. In 1774, Hamilton entered Kings College (now Columbia University) as a sophomore. In 1775, he

Alexander Hamilton (Wikimedia Commons)

anonymously published a pamphlet supporting the patriot cause; this was Hamilton's first political activity.

Life's Work

In March, 1776, Alexander Hamilton dropped out of college to become an artillery captain in the New York militia. He quickly came to the attention of senior officers, and in 1777 he joined George Washington's staff. Hamilton's relationship with the general was complex. The childless Washington often treated Hamilton as the son he never had. Hamilton, whose father was never present in his life, revered Washington, but at the same time he felt stifled working for "The Great Man," as his staff officers called him. As Washington's aide-de-camp, Hamilton had a unique view of the war and the politics of the revolution. It was during this period that he became a committed nationalist, as he saw the states squabbling over issues while the national army went without adequate food and other provisions.

The young Hamilton was short, slim, and not particularly athletic. He was brilliant as an administrator but hardly suited to frontline command. Yet he longed for the opportunity to achieve battlefield glory. This desire strained his relationship with Washington, and in February, 1781, he resigned his position. In July, Hamilton returned with his rank of lieutenant colonel to command a battalion, and at Yorktown he was finally given his opportunity for combat glory. Hamilton led his battalion in a brief and heroic assault on a British position. He was thrilled with his exploit but bitter that Congress never saw fit to award him a medal for his heroism. Shortly after the victory at Yorktown, Hamilton returned to civilian life.

In 1780, Hamilton was married to Elizabeth Schuyler. His father-in-law, General Schuyler, was one of the richest men in America and a powerful politician in New York. This family connection eliminated the taint of his illegitimate birth. In April, 1782, he began preparing for a career as a lawyer, and in July he was admitted to the bar. At first, Hamilton was ambivalent about his new profession, writing to the Marquis de Lafayette that he was "studying the art of fleecing my neighbours." Hamilton quickly threw himself into his law practice and was soon representing many of the wealthiest men in his state. Many of his clients were former Loyalists who sought to regain property taken during the revolution, yet Hamilton had few scruples about representing his former enemies. Between 1783 and 1789, he was involved in massive litigation over huge land claims in upstate New York. He also represented banks, shippers, and merchants. Hamilton's fundamentally conservative nature was reflected by his clients and his law practice.

During this period, Hamilton ventured into politics. The New York legislature chose him as a delegate to the Continental Congress (1782, 1783, 1787, 1788) and to the Annapolis Convention of 1786. Through his political connections, he served a short time as a collector of taxes for the Congress. In 1787, Hamilton was also elected to the New York legislature. With the exception of his election to the convention called to ratify the Constitution, this was the only popular election Hamilton ever won. Although a brilliant political theorist, his personal style prevented him from being a popular candidate.

> *"The sacred rights of mankind are not to be rummaged for among old parchments or musty records. They are written, as with a sunbeam, in the whole volume of human nature, by the hand of the divinity itself; and can never be erased or obscured by mortal power."*

The Annapolis Convention of 1786 was called to negotiate a trade agreement among the American states under the Articles of Confederation. The convention

Duel between Aaron Burr and Alexander Hamilton. (Wikimedia Commons)

failed: Most of the states did not bother to send delegates. The meeting at Annapolis led to a call for another convention, however, to be held in Philadelphia the following year. That convention would write the Constitution.

Hamilton was one of three delegates from New York to the Philadelphia Convention of 1787. He received the unanimous support of the state legislature. Even his political enemies (and he had many by this time) believed that Hamilton was one of the ablest men in the state. At the beginning of the convention, a fellow delegate wrote that "Colo. Hamilton is deservedly celebrated for his talents. He is a practitioner of the Law, and reputed to be a finished Scholar. . . . His manners are tinctured with stiffness, and sometimes with a degree of vanity that is highly disagreeable." While haughty and arrogant, Hamilton was also exceedingly handsome, with auburn hair, deep blue eyes, and a charming smile.

At Philadelphia, Hamilton was limited in his effectiveness. The other two New York delegates, John Lansing and Robert Yates, were opposed to a strong national government, which Hamilton supported. Thus, Hamilton was able to participate in debates, but his votes on the developing document were canceled by the rest of New York's delegation. In his first major speech, Hamilton argued for an extremely strong central government and a narrow and limited role for the states. Hamilton asserted his belief "that the British Govt. was the best in the world: and that he doubted much whether any thing short of it would do in America." He argued that the "hereditary interest of the King" prevented the dangers of corruption in England and that, for the American chief executive, "the English model was the only good one on this subject." His plan of government, which never received the support of any other delegates, called for a chief executive to serve for life and the appointment of state governors by the national government. This speech has led Hamilton's detractors to conclude that he was a monarchist. While that is perhaps an exaggeration, it is clear that Hamilton did favor a lifetime chief executive and that he leaned toward ruling over the people, rather than the people ruling themselves.

On June 29, Hamilton left the convention, in part because it was not headed in the direction he favored and in part because Yates and Lansing had outvoted him on most issues. Hamilton also wanted to return to his political base in New York and to the Continental Congress. Early in July, however, Yates and Lansing left the convention, and three days later, Hamilton returned. For the rest of the summer, Hamilton moved in and out of the convention. The rules of the convention required that each state have at least two delegates present to vote on the emerging document. Thus, Hamilton could debate but not vote. His most important contributions came in the debates that took place in September and in his work on the committee of style. At the end of the convention, he persuaded his fellow delegates to sign the document, even though New York as a state was not represented under the convention rules.

After the convention, Hamilton actively supported the new Constitution. In collaboration with fellow New Yorker John Jay and with Virginian James Madison, Hamilton planned and wrote a series of essays collectively known as *The Federalist* (1787-1788). All three authors wrote under the pen name Publius. Of the eighty-five separate essays, Hamilton wrote fifty-one and collaborated on another three. Madison's contributions, which included the famous numbers 10, 14, and 51, ended when he left New York in March, 1788, while Jay's writings were limited by illness. Hamilton continued the project without Madison and Jay, producing the last twenty-one essays on his own, including the powerful number 78, which explained the role of the judiciary in the constitutional system. *The Federalist* was written to convince New York voters to support the Constitution, but this goal was not really achieved. The majority of those elected to the New York ratifying convention opposed the Constitution. Neither the essays of Publius nor Hamilton's own speeches at the ratifying convention convinced the delegates to support the Constitution. Ultimately, New York ratified it by a slim three-vote margin, because a number of opponents of the Constitution concluded that with the ratification in Virginia and Massachusetts they had no choice but to ratify. While it was not persuasive in New York, *The Federalist* is generally considered to contain the single most important contemporary analysis of the Constitution and has been cited repeatedly by scholars and courts in the twentieth century.

With the organization of the new government, Hamilton became the nation's first secretary of the treasury. In his first two years in that office, Hamilton organized the nation's finances, established a mint and a system of creating money, and convinced the Congress and the president to support a national bank. He attempted to create a national program to support manufacturing and economic development, but this was defeated.

Hamilton's *Report Relative to a Provision for the Support of Public Credit* (1795), presented to the Congress in January, 1795, laid out a program for putting the nation on a sound financial footing. Hamilton urged that the national government pay off all foreign and domestic debt incurred by the Congress and the states during the revolution and confederation period. Two aspects of this report were particularly controversial. Hamilton recommended that all bondholders receive the face value of their bonds. This meant that speculators who had purchased war bonds at far below their original value would reap great profits, while those who had actually risked their money to support the American Revolution would not even get their original investment back. Hamilton also recommended that the national government pay off all unpaid state war debts. This proposal offended Virginia, which had paid off most of its debts and did not want to have to pay the debts of other states as well. Congressmen from states with small debts, such as Georgia, North Carolina, and Maryland, also opposed this plan. Representatives from states with large debts, including South Carolina, New York, and Massachusetts, naturally supported the plan.

Hamilton's goals in his debt-funding plan were not to aid one section of the nation and harm another. Nor did he seek to enrich speculators at the expense of patriotic investors who were forced, because of a postwar depression, to sell their bonds at low prices. Hamilton simply sought to put the nation on a sound economic footing.

Nevertheless, high motives and sound economic policy were not enough to push through his proposal, and Congress adopted it only after much political maneuvering, which included an agreement to move the nation's capital from New York City closer to Virginia. Besides offering some political advantages, the Virginians hoped that the move would stimulate economic development in the Chesapeake region.

The creation of the Bank of the United States was Hamilton's second major accomplishment as secretary of the treasury. In the cabinet, Secretary of State Thomas Jefferson and Attorney General Edmund Randolph both opposed the bank. Congressional opposition was led by Madison, Hamilton's former collaborator on *The Federalist*. Hamilton's arguments in favor of the bank were more than economic: They were also constitutional. He asserted that the Constitution needed to be read broadly, and he argued that Congress must have the power to go beyond the specific "enumerated powers" in the Constitution through the "necessary and proper clause" of the document. In the cabinet debate, Hamilton prevailed, and Washington signed the bank bill into law.

Hamilton's "Report on Manufactures," delivered to the Congress in December, 1791, argued in favor of stimulating manufacturing in the nation through tariff and tax policies. Hamilton's report detailed the types of manufacturing needed, including iron, leather, textiles, sugar, gunpowder, paper, and books. The report anticipated an America in which manufacturing, not agriculture, would be the dominant economic activity. This report was unacceptable, however, to the agrarian America of the 1790's.

In the cabinet, Hamilton proved a tireless and ruthless advocate of expanding national power. He came close to accusing Jefferson of treason when the secretary of state publicly indicated his disagreement with Hamilton. As a cabinet official, Hamilton helped organize the Federalist Party to support his economic and political policies. In 1794, he advocated the use of massive military force against hard-pressed western farmers who opposed his policy of taxing the producers of whiskey. Hamilton's role in the Whiskey Rebellion, was, in the end, almost comical. He led a large army into western Pennsylvania, where a handful of farmers were arrested and then released. Hamilton once again sought military glory, but this time he appeared to be an oppressor of the people; instead of glory, he won contempt.

In 1795, Hamilton left Washington's cabinet for the private practice of law. He quickly became one of the most successful attorneys in New York. In 1798, he became inspector general of the army when it appeared that a war with France was likely. This was his last public position. Once again, however, military glory eluded Hamilton, and he returned to law after the crisis with France ended.

In his law practice, he was enormously successful, with clients begging for his services. In 1802, Hamilton earned nearly $13,000, an incredibly large sum for the period. Most of his law practice centered on marine insurance, banking law, and other litigation tied to commerce. Hamilton remained involved in politics, but his aggressive personal style and his penchant for intrigue served only to undermine the Federalist Party that he had helped to build in the early 1790's. Hamilton's public and private attacks on John Adams did little except to aid the fortunes of the Democratic-Republicans led by Jefferson and Aaron Burr. In 1804, he vigorously opposed Burr's attempt to gain the governorship of New York, so Burr challenged him to a duel, which took place on July 11. Hamilton once again had an opportunity for glory on the field of "combat." Once again, however, he was unsuccessful. He died, on July 12, of his wounds.

Significance

Alexander Hamilton was one of the great figures of the revolutionary era. He was brilliant, charming, and a first-rate administrator. Yet he was also vain, overly ambitious, arrogant, and insecure over his status and place in the world. Hamilton's influence was undermined by his inability to get along with other leaders of the age. He was also something of a misfit.

Reared in the West Indies, Hamilton was a monarchist when he first came to America. Although he quickly joined the patriot cause, his political views, as expressed in the Constitutional Convention and in Washington's cabinet, were almost always anti-Republican; he had less faith in representative government than any of the other Founding Fathers. More than most public figures of the period, Hamilton favored a strong chief executive, if not a king. He was similarly out of step with America in his grandiose plans for the nation's economy. Nevertheless, his contributions to American politics, economics, and constitutional theory make him a towering figure of his age.

Paul Finkelman

Further Reading

Bowen, Catherine Dinker. *Miracle at Philadelphia: The Story of the Constitutional Convention, May to September, 1787*. Boston: Little, Brown, 1966. Probably the best narrative history of the convention, and especially appropriate for high school and undergraduate students. Includes good details on convention delegates.

Brookhiser, Richard. *Alexander Hamilton, American*. New York: Free Press, 1999. Brookhiser provides an appreciation and assessment of Hamilton, demonstrating why he was one America's most important Founding Fathers.

Chernow, Ron. *Alexander Hamilton*. New York: Penguin Books, 2004. A comprehensive and meticulously detailed biography, offering new information about Hamilton's ancestry, personality, and relationships with George Washington, Thomas Jefferson, John Adams, and Aaron Burr. Chernow calls Hamilton "the father of the American government," the Founding Father who set the United States on a course of liberal democracy and capitalist economy.

Cooke, Jacob E. *Alexander Hamilton: A Biography*. New York: Charles Scribner's Sons, 1982. A short, readable biography by one of the nation's leading Hamilton scholars. An excellent place to begin research on Hamilton.

_____, ed. *Alexander Hamilton: A Profile*. New York: Hill & Wang, 1967. Contains essays on Hamilton by a wide range of scholars, with articles both favorable and unfavorable to Hamilton.

Emery, Noemie. *Alexander Hamilton: An Intimate Portrait*. New York: G. P. Putnam's Sons, 1982. Much like the James Thomas Flexner biography, although this volume gives more attention to Hamilton's later life.

Flexner, James Thomas. *The Young Hamilton: A Biography*. Boston: Little, Brown, 1978. A superbly written study by the author of a leading biography of George Washington. Focuses on Hamilton's early years and on his psychological development. A fascinating, accessible study.

Hamilton, Alexander. *The Reports of Alexander Hamilton*. Edited by Jacob E. Cooke. New York: Harper & Row, 1964. Contains Hamilton's reports on public credit, the Bank of the United States, and manufacturers. Also contains Hamilton's constitutional arguments in favor of the bank. The reports are models of lucidity and can be read by students, nonspecialists, and scholars.

Hamilton, Alexander, James Madison, and John Jay. *The Federalist*. Edited by Henry B. Dawson. New York: J. and A. McLeon, 1788. Reprint. Cambridge, Mass.: Belknap Press, 1961. Various editions are available in both paperback and clothbound formats, generally including introductions by major scholars. *The*

Federalist papers reveal much of Hamilton's political philosophy, although they should be read with care because they were originally written to gain support for the Constitution and not as political theory.

Harper, John Lamberton. *American Machiavelli: Alexander Hamilton and the Origins of U.S. Foreign Policy*. New York: Cambridge University Press, 2004. Focuses on Hamilton's influence on American foreign policy, placing Hamilton's character, personality, and vision in relation to the Renaissance diplomat and thinker Machiavelli.

Mitchell, Broadus. *Alexander Hamilton: A Concise Biography*. New York: Oxford University Press, 1976. An excellent one-volume study by one of Hamilton's major biographers. Mitchell is also the author of a more elaborate two-volume study of Hamilton. This book covers the same ground, but with less detail.

LEARNED HAND

Jurist

Born: January 27, 1872; Albany, New York
Died: August 18, 1961; New York City, New York
Area of Achievement: Law

During a career on the federal bench spanning more than half a century, Hand became one of the most respected and honored jurists in the United States. His commitment to tolerance and rigorous thought helped transform and modernize American law in the twentieth century.

EARLY LIFE

Learned Hand (LUR-nehd hand) was the second of two children born to Samuel Hand and Lydia Coit Hand. Learned Hand, who had dropped Billings from his name when he was thirty years old because it sounded too "pompous," came from a distinguished legal family. His paternal grandfather, Augustus Cincinnatus, was a prominent New York attorney, active in the Democratic Party in the late nineteenth century. His older cousin, Augustus, was a lawyer and judge and served for many years on the same federal bench as Hand. Hand's father served a term on the highest state court in New York, the Court of Appeals.

Hand received his early education at a small private school, the Albany Academy, in New York. In 1889, following his cousin Augustus by two years, he enrolled at Harvard College. There he studied philosophy under one of the most distinguished groups of scholars of that time George Santayana, Josiah Royce, and William James. His intellectual and literary gifts were evidenced by his election to Phi Beta Kappa and by his being chosen commencement orator at his baccalaureate in 1893. He stayed on at Harvard for another year, receiving a master's degree in philosophy.

Though strongly attracted to an academic career in philosophy, Hand again followed his cousin, entering Harvard Law School in 1894. At this time the law school was in the middle of what has been described as its "Golden Age": Teachers such as Christopher Langdell, James Bradley Thayer, and James Barr Ames were revolutionizing the study of law through their casebook approach, and in the process were laying the foundation for the transformation of many traditional legal doctrines. In this atmosphere of intellectual ferment, Hand flourished, becoming one of the first editors of the *Harvard Law Review* and being graduated with honors.

Following his admission to the New York bar, Hand practiced law in Albany for the next five years. In 1902 he moved to New York City, where he spent the next seven years in what he described as the "dull and petty" work of a New York law firm. His move to New York City was

Learned Hand (Wikimedia Commons)

perhaps also motivated by the fact that he now had a family to support. On December 6, 1902, Hand married Frances Amelia Fincke, a graduate of Bryn Mawr College. They had three daughters: Mary Deshon, Frances Lydia, and Constance.

Hand's lifelong love of the outdoors and hiking (including walking to work every day until his death) was reflected in his looks and physique. Of medium height and stockily built, he had a large, noble head highlighted by rugged features, bushy eyebrows, and dark, piercing eyes. On the bench, he was known for his quick temper, but appropriate apologies were made just as quickly. He did not suffer fools gladly, yet few jurists could be more tolerant. His demeanor was serious but not solemn, and while he craved company and good conversation, he would also have periods of melancholy and brooding. Hand also had a streak of playfulness he enjoyed dressing up as an Indian chief for his grandchildren's amusement, expertly mimicking William Jennings Bryan, and singing ribald sea chanteys or Gilbert and Sullivan melodies.

> "*If we are to keep our democracy, there must be one commandment: Thou shalt not ration justice.*"

LIFE'S WORK

Hand began his judicial career in 1909. President William Howard Taft was eager to improve the quality of the federal judiciary, and on the recommendation of Attorney General George W. Wickersham and a number of prominent New York attorneys, Hand was appointed to the federal District Court for Southern District of New York, the lowest level of the court system. Five years later, Hand was joined on this court by his cousin Augustus. During his tenure on the district court, he became a skilled trial judge and an expert on the intricacies of commercial and corporate law.

In 1912, while serving on the federal bench, Hand ran for, and lost, the position of chief judge of the New York Court of Appeals. It was of dubious propriety for a sitting judge to seek an elective office, and Hand compounded this mistake by running as a Progressive (in the election that year, Hand supported Theodore Roosevelt's unsuccessful bid for the presidency on the Progressive, or Bull Moose, Party ticket). In so doing he incurred the wrath of the regular Republicans and their leader, Taft. Taft never forgave Hand his political apostasy, and during the 1920's Taft, as chief justice of the United States, used his considerable influence to prevent Hand's elevation to the High Court.

Hand's judicial accomplishments were, however, at last recognized in 1924, when President Calvin Coolidge appointed him to the U.S. Court of Appeals for the Second Circuit (including New York, Connecticut, and Vermont), replacing Judge Julius M. Mayer. During Hand's tenure on the Second Circuit, he served with some of the most distinguished jurists in the nation. Thomas Walter Swan and Charles Edward Clark were both former deans of Yale Law School, and Jerome Frank headed the Securities and Exchange Commission during the New Deal. Clearly Hand's greatest pleasure, though, was being joined once again by his cousin and closest friend, Augustus, on the same court in 1927.

Over the next twenty years, the Second Circuit Court of Appeals became one of the busiest and most respected federal tribunals in the nation. The measure of Hand's influence was the fact that, by the 1930's, the court was being referred to as "Learned Hand's Court." Unlike the U.S. Supreme Court, which could choose which cases to hear and therefore dealt with far fewer cases, the circuit court would handle an average of some four hundred appeals a year, involving a wide range of public (constitutional) and private law issues. The latter would involve questions concerning copyright law, patent law, antitrust regulation, admiralty law, contracts, torts, and trusts and estates (among others).

Given the relative obscurity of most of the work done by the federal judiciary below the Supreme Court level, it was not surprising that Hand's leadership and legal influence were recognized mainly by the bar and bench. In May, 1944, however, he was invited to give an address at the annual "I am an American Day" celebration in Central Park. His short speech "The Spirit of Liberty" was greeted with tremendous enthusiasm. Reprints of the work appeared nationwide, and glowing articles in newspapers and magazines introduced Hand's wisdom and style to the general public. During these years, he was also active in a number of professional organizations: He was one of the founders and early leaders of the American Law Institute. The institute was created to simplify segments of the vast body of American law by codifying and restating the thousands of state and federal court rulings, along with relevant legislation, to provide "model" codes of law for future legislative bodies and judges. Hand's specific contributions to the institute included his work on the *Model Penal Code* and the *Restatement of Conflicts of Law, Restatement of Torts*.

Throughout his career, Hand was proposed and considered for elevation to the Supreme Court but never nominated. Why this was so will never be known with absolute certainty. He had the support of the nation's bar, and at least three Supreme Court justices Oliver Wendell Holmes, Jr., Harlan Fiske Stone, and Felix Frankfurter all strongly thought that Hand should join them. Taft's hostility probably accounts for the 1920's. After that it seemed to be a combination of factors geography, politics, and age that prevented his appointment. In 1951, Hand officially retired from the Court of Appeals, though in fact he continued to sit on the court off and on for the next ten years. In 1952, a collection of his writings and speeches was published under the title of his 1944 address, *The Spirit of Liberty*. This and the publication of his 1958 Holmes lectures at Harvard University on the Bill of Rights helped spread his fame to the general public even further. Three years later, on August 18, 1961, Judge Hand died of heart failure in New York City.

Significance

It is difficult to assess fully a judicial career that lasted more than half a century. In large part, Hand's achievement was his work: more than two thousand opinions, along with his articles and speeches. His role on the middle level of the federal judicial pyramid gave him the freedom and scope to apply his vast erudition and wisdom, but precluded as well any major impact on American constitutional development. However, from his work a number of themes emerge that reflect both the man and the times. Of immense importance was his contribution to the transformation of private law (contracts, torts, and so on) in the twentieth century. Like his friend Justice Holmes, Hand believed that the law did and should reflect changing social and economic conditions. Industrialization in America in the late nineteenth and early twentieth centuries brought with it not only increased business and commercial activity but also expanded governmental authority, as well as a host of social and economic problems. Hand's opinions speak to the necessity of the law to adjust to these changes for the betterment of society. In this essentially optimistic vision, he shared many of the beliefs common to the Progressive reform movement that appeared during the first part of the twentieth century.

Another element of Hand's legacy was his passion for tolerance and his commitment to the protection of the human liberties embodied in the Bill of Rights. He believed that freedom to express different thoughts and ideas, even unpopular ones, and respect for all persons were both essential to the preservation of democracy. In this, Hand mirrored (and led, to the extent possible for a lower federal court judge) the growing concern by the judiciary for civil liberties and civil rights issues that began in the 1920's and reached its zenith with the landmark decisions of the Supreme Court under Chief Justice Earl Warren in the 1950's and 1960's.

Finally, Hand's opinions and writings reflected the ambivalence within both the legal community and American society concerning the role and function of judges. The dilemma, simply put, was how to balance on one hand the recognition that judges can, and possibly should, actually make law, and on the other the necessity for a judiciary that is independent yet responsive to the citizenry. While Hand accepted the necessity and freedom of judges to adapt the law to fit changing times and circumstances, he spoke for that school of thought that first appeared in the early part of the twentieth century (and that became more popular in the 1970's) that urged judicial "restraint," especially when dealing with some legislative action or constitutional interpretation. In so doing, he was embraced by liberals and conservatives, judicial activists and "restraintists," alike. That he could be so many things to so many people is a mark of his greatness.

Robert M. Goldman

Further Reading

Blasi, Vincent. *Ideas of the First Amendment*. St. Paul, Minn.: Thomson/West, 2006. Provides information about how leading constitutional thinkers, including Hand, have interpreted the First Amendment.

Carrington, Paul D. *Stewards of Democracy: Law as a Public Profession*. Boulder, Colo.: Westview Press, 1999. Focuses on the role of lawyers, including Hand, in American political history.

Gilmore, Grant. *The Ages of American Law*. New Haven, Conn.: Yale University Press, 1977. A brief and extremely readable survey of the development of American law. A useful introduction to the context of legal thought and practice within which Hand worked.

Griffith, Kathryn P. *Judge Learned Hand and the Role of the Federal Judiciary*. Norman: University of Oklahoma Press, 1973. A detailed and critical analysis of Hand's judicial and legal philosophy. Griffith's early chapters on Hand's life and his world are probably the best introduction to these aspects.

Hand, Learned. *The Bill of Rights*. Cambridge, Mass.: Harvard University Press, 1958. The Oliver Wendell Holmes, Jr., Lectures delivered by Hand at Harvard in 1958. Constitutes Hand's most complete statement of his view of the judicial process and the necessity for judges to exercise restraint in their role as guardians of individual and human rights. One of the classic statements of the "judicial restraint" philosophy.

---. *The Spirit of Liberty*. Edited by Irving Dillard. New York: Alfred A. Knopf, 1952. A collection of Hand's extrajudicial writings and speeches, including his famous speech "The Spirit of Liberty." The introduction by Dillard is indeed a "personal appreciation" rather uncritical, indeed almost worshipful.

Schick, Marvin. *Learned Hand's Court*. Baltimore: Johns Hopkins University Press, 1970. A detailed and brilliant study of the Court of Appeals for the Second Circuit during the years that Hand sat on the court. Focuses on the work of the court, the relationships among the judges, the impact of the CA2, as it came to be known, other federal courts, and most important, how Hand's brilliance was able to influence the other judges.

Shanks, Hershel, ed. *The Art and Craft of Judging: The Decisions of Judge Learned Hand*. New York: Macmillan, 1968. A collection of forty-three decisions taken from Hand's almost two thousand opinions written on the bench. Most of the forty-three deal with public law issues. The introduction by Shanks is interesting because it includes details not generally known about Hand (for example, that his close friends called him "B," not for the Billings name that he dropped, but for "Bunny").

White, G. Edward. "Cardozo, Learned Hand, and Frank: The Dialectic of Freedom and Constraint." In *The American Judicial Tradition*. 3d ed. New York: Oxford University Press, 2007. This chapter is part of a larger study of important American judges and is especially interesting in linking Hand with his friend Benjamin Cardozo.

Patrick Henry

Attorney and politician

Born: May 29, 1736; Studley, Colony of Virginia
Died: June 6, 1799; Brookneal, Virginia

Expressing his libertarian ideas through a uniquely powerful oratory, Henry was a principal architect of the American Revolution. He is especially remembered for his poignant words before the revolutionary convention in Virginia in 1775: "Give me liberty, or give me death!"

Early Life

Patrick Henry was born in Hanover County, Virginia, the second son of John Henry, a well-educated Scotsman from Aberdeen, and Sarah Winston Syme, the young and charming widow of Colonel John Syme. Henry's early years were characteristic of a farm boy in colonial Virginia. Hunting and fishing were consuming enthusiasms for him, although he also received a sound education (focused on mathematics and the Latin classics) from local schoolmasters, his uncle Patrick Henry (a minister), and his father.

At the age of fifteen, he was apprenticed as a clerk in a country store. A year later, he joined his older brother as a partner in a similar venture, which, however, failed. Meanwhile, Henry had fallen in love with Sarah Shelton, the daughter of nearby landowner John Shelton, and the two were married in the fall of 1754. The young couple took up residence on a small farm that had been given to them by Sarah's father. For three years they eked out a marginal existence, but worse was to come. In 1757, their house was destroyed by fire. Destitute, they moved into the large tavern owned by Sarah's father at Hanover Courthouse, where Henry for a time supported himself

Patrick Henry (Wikimedia Commons)

and his family, now including four children, by helping manage the tavern for his father-in-law.

By all accounts, Henry was a charming and convivial taverner, but there is otherwise little in his life to this point to foretell the kind of impact he would have on American history. Proximity to a busy provincial courthouse and frequent association with those who came and went there must have inspired his latent abilities, for by the age of twenty-four he had resolved upon becoming a lawyer. The normal course for a young man of such ambitions would have been to apprentice himself to an established lawyer who had attended one of the Inns of Court of London (there were no law schools in the American colonies; the first would be established in 1779 in Virginia at William and Mary College).

Henry, however, attempted his project through a program of self-study and, miraculously, succeeded within a year. His board of examiners was headed by the illustrious brothers Peyton and John Randolph. Impressed more by the force of natural genius he displayed in his examination than by his spotty knowledge of law, they admitted him to the bar. Their somewhat reluctant confidence was more than justified, for within three years, Henry had become a successful lawyer. Having handled some 1,125 cases, most of which he won, he was, at the age of twenty-seven, poised to enter the arena of history-making events.

Life's Work

The case that catapulted Patrick Henry to widespread recognition as a bold political spirit with a singular gift for oratory was the Parson's Cause of 1763. In colonial America, as in England, the Anglican Church was supported by general taxation, and in Virginia, salaries for the clergy were tied to the price of tobacco. A 1758 act of the Virginia legislature had fixed the nominal price of tobacco for this purpose at two pence per pound. Since this was far less than the actual commodity value of tobacco, the clergy petitioned King George III and his Privy Council to overrule the act. George did indeed overrule the act, thereby allowing the Virginia clergy to sue for back pay.

Henry was engaged to handle the defense in the pivotal case brought by the Reverend Mr. James Maury. The youthful attorney's argument asserted that the 1758 law was just and that in overturning it, the king was acting as a tyrant. The jury of sturdy farmers was so impressed that it awarded the plaintiff Maury only a penny in damages. Henry's fame soon spread throughout Virginia, thereby laying the ground for his entry into the forefront of colonial politics.

> "*Is life so dear or peace so sweet as to be purchased at the price of chains and slavery? Forbid it, Almighty God! I know not what course others may take; but as for me, give me liberty or give me death!*"

In May, 1765, Henry entered the House of Burgesses, only a few weeks after Britain had passed the notorious Stamp Act. On his twenty-ninth birthday, only ten days after taking his seat as a representative, he proposed a number of resolutions against the Stamp Act, based on the assumption that only colonial legislatures had the right to levy colonial taxes. A lean six-footer, with plain angular features and dark, deep-set eyes, the somewhat ungainly and roughly dressed young legislator climaxed his defense of the resolutions with the threatening words (as reported by Thomas Jefferson), "Caesar had his Brutus, Charles the First his Cromwell, and George the Third—" whereupon, interrupted by cries of "Treason!" Henry concluded, "may profit by their example. If this be treason, make the most of it." His daring speech galvanized the House of Burgesses into adopting his resolutions, and Virginia became an example to the other colonies in the rising resistance to taxation without representation.

Over the next few years, Patrick Henry's fame and authority as a revolutionary leader increased, as from his seat in the House of Burgesses he continued to oppose British encroachment upon the autonomy of the colonies. In September, 1774, he served as a member of the First Continental Congress that met in Philadelphia to deal with new British coercive measures imposed in the aftermath of the Boston Tea Party. Some six months later, he was an organizer of the revolutionary convention convened in Richmond to decide how Virginia should respond to the worsening situation, and it was in this setting, on March 23, 1775, that he made the speech that served as a call to arms for the colonies in the coming struggle. Arguing for the need to raise armed forces immediately, he concluded, "Is life so dear or peace so sweet as to be purchased at the price of chains and slavery? Forbid it, Almighty God! I know not what course others may take, but as for me, give me liberty, or give me death!"

"Give me liberty, or give me death!" (Library of Congress)

Swayed by the dramatic impact of this speech, the members of the convention authorized the formation of companies of militia, one of which was led by Henry himself in May to demand restoration of the gunpowder seized from the Williamsburg magazine by the Loyalist governor, Lord Dunmore. Although he succeeded, he was not cut out for military leadership. After a short appointment as a regimental commander, and burdened by grief for the death of his wife, he resigned his commission and returned home on February 28, 1776.

His absence from public life was only brief; in May, he took part in drafting the new constitution of Virginia, and on June 29 he was elected the first governor of the newly constituted commonwealth, a position in which he served for three years (retiring in 1779) and to which he was re-elected for two years in 1784. Meanwhile, he had married again, to Dorothea Dandridge, and had taken up residence on a huge tract of land in the mountainous western area of the state. A representative of the Virginia legislature from 1786 to 1790, he declined a nomination to the Constitutional Convention, while from his legislative seat he bitterly opposed Virginia's adoption of the Constitution in 1788, fearing its restrictive effect upon the sovereignty of the states, particularly those of the South. His vehement and sustained opposition was insufficient to prevent adoption, but it did prompt a general recognition of the need for constitutional amendments, leading to the framing of the first ten amendments; the Bill of Rights passed in 1791.

From 1790 to 1795, Henry returned to private law practice. The last years of his life were spent in semiretirement at his Red Hill plantation in Charlotte County. He refused the positions of both secretary of state and chief justice offered to him in 1795 by George Washington, but, increasingly reconciled to the principles of Federalism in his last years, he agreed in 1799 to run for the Virginia legislature once again. Elected, he did not live to serve his term, dying on June 6, 1799.

Significance

The American Revolution was produced by heroic talents and energies that together achieved critical mass; within this process, the oratory of Patrick Henry was catalytic in effect. In an era of great public speakers, it was his voice in particular that provided a rallying cry for the colonial patriots at critical moments, especially in 1765, during the Stamp Act controversy, and, ten years later, on the eve of the battles of Lexington and Concord. His oratory was legendary in its own time. Characterized, according to contemporary accounts, by extraordinary dramatic nuance and force, it stands as an enduring example of the power of an individual speaker to influence large-scale events.

Henry's resistance to the principles of Federalism in later years is also indicative of a deep strain both in his character and in American society. Born in a picturesque but still largely "wild" region of Virginia, his first love was the land–its topography and vegetation, its creatures, and its seasons. The concept of liberty for him was rooted in a deep respect for nature and the individual autonomy nurtured by the frontier environment. His opposition to British rule and to federal authority should be seen as the two sides of a single coin. His anti-Federalist speeches in the Virginia assembly were a main influence behind the passage of the Bill of Rights. Yet the same kinds of sentiments divided the nation half a century later on the issue of states' rights–a controversy that even the Civil War did not eradicate.

In many ways, Henry's achievements are the stuff of which American legends have been forged. Son of colonial Virginia, self-made forensic genius, patriot, and lifelong spokesman for individual rights, even at the expense of national unity, his life is part of the national mythology of America, and his famous words "Give me liberty, or give me death" have etched themselves on the national psyche.

Charles Duncan

Further Reading

Axelrad, Jacob. *Patrick Henry, the Voice of Freedom.* New York: Random House, 1947. A book for the general reader, somewhat dated in approach but useful for its economical account of Henry's career and its informative commentary on contemporary historical events.

Beeman, Richard R. *Patrick Henry: A Biography.* New York: McGraw-Hill, 1974. A solid, thoroughly researched, academic history. Beeman's vision of Henry is somewhat deconstructionist; he is not the legendary hero but a man more characteristic of his times. Beeman deals especially well with the less celebrated aspects of Henry's career, such as his role as governor and administrator.

Campbell, Norine Dickson. *Patrick Henry, Patriot and Statesman.* New York: Devin-Adair, 1969. The value of this work lies in its sense of the living presence of history as well as in the occasional emphatic detail produced by devoted research.

McCants, David A. *Patrick Henry, the Orator.* New York: Greenwood Press, 1990. An analysis of Henry's oratory within its historical and political contexts.

Mayer, Henry. *A Son of Thunder: Patrick Henry and the American Republic.* New York: Franklin Watts, 1986. A substantial, well-researched, and absorbing biography that places Henry in the context of his time. Emphasizes his roots in the "evangelical revolt" against Virginia's aristocratic establishment.

Mayo, Bernard. *Myths and Men: Patrick Henry, George Washington, Thomas Jefferson.* Athens: University of Georgia Press, 1959. A collection of perceptive commentaries on the major leadership of the American Revolution. The essay on Henry is valuable as an economical, balanced overview of the issues of scholarship and historiography surrounding his biography.

Meade, Robert Douthat. *Patrick Henry.* 2 vols. Philadelphia: J. B. Lippincott, 1957-1969. The most comprehensive biography of Henry to appear in the twentieth century, likely to become the standard authoritative reference work. Meade's coverage of his subject is meticulous, based on definitive research into all aspects of Henry's private and public life.

Tyler, Moses Coit. *Patrick Henry.* Boston: Houghton Mifflin, 1887. A masterpiece of nineteenth century historiography, the first modern biography of Henry, and best for the general reader. The worshipful view of Henry, though old-fashioned, is deeply sincere.

Vaughan, David J. *Give Me Liberty: The Uncompromising Statesmanship of Patrick Henry.* Nashville, Tenn.: Cumberland House, 1997. Vaughan's book is divided into three sections. Part 1 provides an overview of Henry's life, part 2 describes his character traits, and part 3 assesses his legacy.

Willison, George F. *Patrick Henry and His World.* Garden City, N.Y.: Doubleday, 1969. Probably the best all-around general study. Willison's title is appropriate; the coverage of background historical material is thorough and illuminating. The book is well-paced, admirably written, and spiced with colorful, often amusing anecdotes.

Mazie Hirono

Representative (2007-2013) and Senator (2013-present) from Hawaii

Born: November 3, 1947; Fukushima, Japan
Areas of achievement: Government and politics

Mazie Hirono began her political career in the state of Hawaii and was elected to represent Hawaii's Second Congressional District in the US House of Representatives in 2006, achieving reelection in 2008 and 2010. A naturalized citizen born in Japan, she became the first Asian-born woman to be elected to the US Congress.

Early Life

Mazie Keiko Hirono (MAY-zee KAY-koh hee-ROH-noh) was born November 3, 1947, in Japan's Fukushima prefecture, the second child of Laura "Chie" and Matabe Hirono. When Hirono was a young child, her parents separated due to her father's drinking and gambling habits, and her mother took the children to live with their grandparents for several years. In 1955, Hirono immigrated to the United States with her mother, a US citizen, and older brother; her grandparents and younger brother followed two years later. She became a naturalized US citizen in 1959. The family struggled to survive in Hawaii, and Hirono herself began to work at the age of ten. Despite the financial hardships her family faced, education was a

Mazie Hirono (Wikimedia Commons)

priority for Hirono. After attending Kaahumanu and Koko Head Elementary Schools as well as Niu Valley and Jarrett Middle Schools, she graduated with honors from Kaimuki High School.

Hirono attended the University of Hawaii in Manoa, graduating with a bachelor's degree in psychology in 1970. She had intended to become a social worker, but her participation in political activities while at university, including protesting the Vietnam War, kindled her interest in a political career. After becoming involved in organizing for the Democratic Party, she coordinated the campaigns of state representatives Carl Takamura and Anson Chong, assisted Chong during his term, and served as an assistant researcher for James Wakatsuki, the Speaker of the Hawaii House of Representatives. Following these experiences, Hirono attended Georgetown University Law School in Washington, DC, earning her JD in 1978. Returning to Hawaii, she served as deputy attorney general, specializing in antitrust cases, and practiced law privately as well.

Life's Work

In 1980, Hirono was elected to the Hawaii House of Representatives, succeeding Takamura as representative for a district comprising several neighborhoods of Honolulu. During her seven terms in office, she introduced more than one hundred bills that became laws and was named Legislator of the Year by the Hawaii Leaseholders Equity Coalition. She was a member of the House Women's Caucus and served as chair of the Committee on Consumer Protection and Commerce from 1987 to 1992.

> "I bring quadruple diversity to the Senate: I'm a woman; I'll be the first Asian woman ever to be elected to the U.S. Senate; I am an immigrant; I am a Buddhist. When I said this at one of my gatherings, they said, 'Yes, but are you gay?' and I said, 'Nobody's perfect.'"

Hirono was elected lieutenant governor of Hawaii in 1994, serving two terms under Governor Benjamin J. Cayetano. In this role, she promoted civil-service reform, particularly reform of the workers' compensation system, and boosted the tourism and technology industries. A strong supporter of education, she worked to develop the Pre-Plus program, which built preschools and provided early childhood education to children from low-income households. She also served as chair of the Hawaii Policy Group of the National Commission on Teaching and America's Future. In 2002, Hirono ran for governor of Hawaii but lost to Republican candidate Linda Lingle, the former mayor of Maui. Hirono remained politically active despite this loss and founded the Patsy Mink Political Action Committee, an organization named after the first Asian American congresswoman and devoted to supporting female, pro-choice Democratic candidates for political office.

In 2006, Hirono again ran for office, seeking a position in the US House of Representatives. Defeating Republican candidate Bob Hogue by a significant margin, she became the representative for Hawaii's Second Congressional District and took office in 2007. At that time, women made up less than 20 percent of the total membership of the House, and Hirono became one of the few representatives of Asian descent and one of only two Buddhists in Congress. She succeeded in winning reelection in both 2008 and 2010.

While serving in the House, Hirono worked toward reforms in areas such as education, renewable energy, and the environment. Hirono served on a number of committees, including the Committee on Education and the Workforce and the Committee on Transportation and

Infrastructure, and was a member of many caucuses, including the House Democratic Caucus, the Congressional Lesbian, Gay, Bisexual, and Transgender Equality Caucus, and the Congressional Asian Pacific American Caucus. She was elected to serve on the House Democratic Steering and Policy Committee in 2010.

In 2012, Hirono was the Democratic nominee for the U.S. Senate seat being vacated by the retirement of Daniel Akaka. Hirono won the election, defeating Linda Lingle in a rematch landslide victory by 63% to 37%. Hirono was sworn in on January 3, 2013, by the Vice President of the United States Joe Biden. Hirono was the only person of Asian ancestry serving in the U.S. Senate from 2013 until 2017 when senators Tammy Duckworth and Kamala Harris were sworn in representing the states of Illinois and California respectively. Although Brian Schatz joined the Senate a week before she did, making him Hawaii's senior senator, her six years in the House of Representatives makes her the dean, or longest-serving member overall, of Hawaii's congressional delegation.

Hirono announced in May 2017 that she had been diagnosed with stage 4 kidney cancer, which had spread to her seventh rib. The cancer was discovered following a chest x-ray in April before some minor eye surgery. Her right kidney was removed surgically on May 17, 2017, with a Cyberknife procedure to treat the rib lesion. Hirono returned to the Senate on May 22, 2017.

During the Brett Kavanaugh Supreme Court nomination hearings in early 2018, Hirono became an outspoken defender of Christine Blasey Ford after Ford publicly accused Kavanaugh of sexual assault. After the Judiciary Committee's announcement that hearings would continue, Hirono told reporters, "Guess who's perpetuating all of these kind of actions? It's the men in this country... And I just want to say to the men in this country: Just shut up and step up." On November 6, 2018, Senator Hirono won re-election with 69.3% of the vote.

Significance
Throughout her career in public office, Hirono has supported a variety of progressive causes and promoted reforms in areas such as health care and education, influencing policy in her home state of Hawaii and elsewhere in the United States. As the first female immigrant from Asia to be elected to Congress, Hirono has called attention to the underrepresentation of both Asian Americans and immigrants in the federal government.

Seung-Kyun Ko

Further Reading
Beazley, Lisa. "Mazie Hirono." *Hawaii Woman* Nov. 2002: 40–41. Print. A profile tracing Hirono's early childhood life and her difficulties coping with hardship and adjusting to life in Hawaii.

Boylan, Dan. "The Immigrant Congresswoman." *Midweek* 21 Mar. 2007: 36+. Print. A discussion of Hirono's political career and attempts to assist others in their campaigns for positions in the Hawaii legislature.

Flanagan, John. "Mazie Hirono: Her Past, Present and Future." *Star-Bulletin* [Honolulu] 1 Dec. 2002: D3. Print. An interview about Hirono's personal experiences and political career.

Charles Evans Hughes

Chief justice of the Supreme Court (1930-1941)

Born: April 11, 1862; Glens Falls, New York
Died: August 27, 1948; Osterville, Massachusetts
Areas of Achievement: Law, government and politics, diplomacy

As chief justice of the United States, Hughes supported legal decisions that provided constitutional protection for suffrage (voting rights), the freedom of speech, the freedom of religion, the freedom of the press, and the right to political dissent. As secretary of state he focused on four areas: disarmament, reparations and war debts, and U.S. relationships with the Soviets and with Latin America.

Early Life
Charles Evans Hughes was the only child of David Charles Hughes, an evangelical Baptist minister, and Mary Catherine Connelly, a woman who combined intelligence with pious discipline. When Charles was six years old, he convinced his parents that he should be educated at home because he was impatient with his slower classmates at school. By the time he was ten, however, he was back in public school, and in 1876 he entered Madison University (Colgate). Two years later, finding Madison too provincial for his interests, he transferred to Brown University, from which he was graduated at the top of the class in 1881. In 1884, he was graduated from Columbia

Charles Evans Hughes (Library of Congress)

University Law School. He married Antoinette Carter in 1888. She was the daughter of one of the partners in a New York law firm for which Hughes worked after leaving Columbia. The couple had four children; the eldest was the only boy.

After graduation from law school, Hughes devoted himself to the practice of law for twenty years. He became a law partner by the time he was twenty-five, and within a few years he had made himself financially secure. During this period he gave no thought to public life, but in 1905 he came to the public's attention when he accepted a position as special counsel to the New York legislature investigating the unfair rates of gas and electricity and insurance fraud. Hughes's investigative reports brought him almost unanimous praise from New York City newspapers. Indeed, he became so popular that, in an attempt to shore up the popularity of the Republican Party, President Theodore Roosevelt pushed party members to nominate Hughes for mayor of New York City. Hughes declined the nomination, thereby causing a rift between himself and Roosevelt that would last the rest of Roosevelt's life. However, as a result he was established as a prominent, albeit reluctant, public figure. In his early forties, Hughes was launched on a career of public service that would occupy the rest of his life.

LIFE'S WORK

In 1906, the Republican Party desperately needed a popular figure to run for governor of New York against the powerful, ambitious journalist William Randolph Hearst. The Republicans sought a candidate who, in contrast to the ruthless Hearst, would be perceived as committed to principled government. They chose Hughes, and this time he accepted and by the narrowest of margins defeated Hearst. He proved to be an effective, popular governor. He was responsible for reform legislation that was to have a long-term effect on the state of New York. He established, for example, public service commissions that regulated utilities and railroads. As a result, service became better and more impartial and rates fairer, while employees for the first time were able to secure safety provisions in their contracts. The eight-hour workday gained acceptance, and the first workers' compensation laws were established.

"When we lose the right to be different, we lose the privilege to be free."

Again, with this progressive record as governor, Hughes had attracted the attention of the national Republicans, particularly that of the Republican president, William Howard Taft. Taft nominated Hughes for a seat on the Supreme Court of the United States, and Hughes accepted and was confirmed as a justice on the Court in 1910.

He came to the bench when the country was struggling with the issue of constitutional centralization, and he was to play a significant role in settling that issue. Centralization meant placing more power in the hands of the federal government while taking it from the states. Among other factors, the increased complexity of commerce made centralization a necessity, and Hughes's legal decisions were decisive in establishing the limits of state and federal control. Ostensibly, he used the federal authority of interstate commerce to defend decisions that produced Progressive policies. He wrote and supported opinions that regulated working hours, equal accommodations on railroads for black citizens, nonwhite representation on trial juries, equal access to employment for nonnative citizens, trials in locations free from community passions, and numerous other liberal opinions.

Hughes remained on the Court for six years. While on small matters he might render a conservative opinion, on large issues he supported the expansion of federal powers in defense of individual liberties. He did not hesitate in striking down state statutes that he perceived to be in conflict with the Bill of Rights. By 1916, Hughes's brilliant reputation on the Supreme Court had become so distinguished that the Republican Party once again prevailed on him to run for office, this time for president of the United States. He resigned from the bench and ran against the popular incumbent, Woodrow Wilson. Hughes lost. It is fair to say that this was the least satisfactory episode in a distinguished career; Hughes was not a good campaigner, lacking the intense partisanship necessary to run for the presidency. He had no success in moving masses of people to follow him. He had a weak and internally feuding political organization. Most important, the Progressive wing of the Republican Party under Theodore Roosevelt's leadership was only lukewarm in its support.

Four years later, the nation elected Republican Warren G. Harding as president. Hughes became Harding's secretary of state. The stolid, provincial Harding had no coherent foreign policy of his own; as a result, responsibility for such decisions fell squarely on Hughes. Clearly, he was up to the task. Few secretaries of state in the history of the United States can be called his equal. None was more intelligent. Few possessed his imagination, his administrative skills, or his genuine idealism. Indeed, many diplomatic scholars consider Hughes to be one of the three top secretaries of state the nation has ever had. His influence was indelible, even though lesser individuals were left to implement his goals.

Hughes's long-term influence was most noteworthy in four areas: disarmament, reparations and war debts, and the United States' relationships with the Soviets and with Latin America. In November of 1921, Hughes invited representatives of the world's nations to Washington, D.C., to consider ways of reducing national tension in the Western Pacific. The conference became known as the Washington Conference on Naval Disarmament. It was Hughes's plan to reduce tensions around the world, particularly in the Western Pacific, by getting the governments of Great Britain, Japan, and the United States to reduce the size of their naval forces. In an opening speech that both astonished and pleased the delegates to the conference, the secretary of state presented a specific plan for this reduction. In addition to setting limits on tonnage levels for the navies of the world (the French proved the most reluctant to concede on this score), Hughes sought to reduce the militarization of various islands in the Pacific controlled by the national powers. He also pushed for the sovereignty and integrity of China, its right to commercial equity, and Japan's abandonment of expansionism on the Asian mainland. Within fifteen years, all the treaties that resulted from the Washington Conference were either being ignored or abrogated, but for a brief moment in history Hughes's "noble experiment" had influenced international relations.

The matter of reparations and war debts, which was closely related to disarmament in Hughes's mind, also required his attention. After the close of World War I, the victorious Allies (and in particular the French) were seeking huge financial reparations from Germany for losses suffered in the war. Hughes convinced the European Allies that they neither would, nor could, get Germany to pay such reparations, and that continued insistence on these payments would only exacerbate the volatile and unstable condition of postwar Europe. To balance the various claims against the German government, Hughes proposed a more realistic payment schedule and the acquisition of an international loan for Germany that would enable it to stabilize its currency and generate the money necessary to meet reparation payments. At the same time, he convinced Congress that it was necessary to extend the payment schedule and reduce the interest requirements on debts owed the United States by its allies. These reparation and refunding policies lasted for only a few years between World War I and World War II, but they did bring a more rational, tranquil policy to an otherwise chaotic situation.

In Russia, the Communists came to power in 1917, but the United States refused to recognize the Soviet government as a legitimate regime. Many in the United States Senate, however, argued that it was in the United States' interest to resume diplomatic relations with Moscow. It was, they argued, the de facto regime, and as such should be recognized; moreover, recognition would encourage the resumption of trade and promote the United States' commercial interests. Hughes held fast against recognition, arguing that the Soviet revolution was on prima facie grounds both illegal and immoral, because its coming to power abrogated international bona fide agreements between legally established governments. What is more, he held, any assumed economic advantage is problematic, and at best hazardous. As long as the Communists make and encourage worldwide revolution among legally

Coolidge cabinet. Hughes is seated third from left. (Library of Congress)

constituted governments, he argued, the United States has a responsibility not to participate in policies that could legitimate the revolution. As long as Bolsheviks refused to recognize international legal obligation, recognition of this regime can only be a disservice to legitimate democratic governments that continue to meet their international responsibilities.

The last, and in many ways the most important, policy in Hughes's tenure as secretary of state was initiated when he first entered office and lasted throughout his term as secretary. Working together with Sumner Welles, he forged an American policy toward Latin America that was much less interventionist than the policies of administrations that had preceded him. This policy was the beginning of what was later to be called the Good Neighbor Policy. Essentially, the Good Neighbor Policy meant fewer American marines controlling United States interests in Latin America. "I utterly disclaim as unwarranted," he declared, "[superintending] the affairs of our sister republics, to assert an overlordship, to consider the spread of our authority beyond our domain as the aim of our policy and to make our power the test of right in this hemisphere.... [Such assertions] belie our sincere friendship, ... they stimulate a distrust ... [and] have no sanction whatever in the Monroe Doctrine." In reality, however, such nonintervention was only partially implemented under Hughes's leadership. The marines were withdrawn from Nicaragua and the Dominican Republic, but not from Haiti and Panama, where the secretary argued that in the latter two countries it was premature and contrary to the United States' "special interests."

Hughes stepped down from his position as secretary of state in 1925; three years later he was a judge on the Court of International Justice, and in 1930 he accepted his last important public position as chief justice of the United States under Herbert Hoover's presidency.

Constitutional scholars are almost unanimous in assessing Hughes as one of the greatest chief justices in Supreme Court history. He served for eleven years, and during that time his legal leadership was dynamic and progressive, never static and protective. Some of his opinions on economic matters were conservative, but on matters of citizens' welfare his positions represented progressive activism. He argued in support of the government's right to determine an equitable balance between the interests of business and the interests of labor. Expressly, he defended the right of Congress to regulate collective bargaining agreements in interstate commerce. The benchmark decision on this issue was the Wagner Labor Relations Act, which paved the way for supporting legislation on the matter of minimum wages and the hours of work required per day. In addition, Hughes led a unanimous court in declaring President Roosevelt's National Recovery Act of 1933 (NRA) unconstitutional (the Court argued that the act allowed code-fixing; that is, it allowed independent nongovernmental agencies to set wages, prices, and working hours). In other words, Roosevelt's NRA appointments from business and industry were prevented from setting codes of competitive commerce between the states, and Congress could not turn over its legislative responsibility to the executive branch of government in this area, Hughes argued.

As a general rule, Hughes supported the expansion of federal power as an instrument for the protection of personal liberty. He upheld, for example, the right of states to fix prices (*Nebbia v. New York*, 1934), the right of the federal government to regulate radio frequencies (*Federal Radio Commission v. Nelson Bros.*, 1933), the right of women to the same minimum wage afforded men

(*Morehead v. Tipaldo*, 1936), and the right of citizens to set aside private contracts under certain hardship constraints.

In the arena of civil liberties, the chief justice was no less supportive of the government's constitutional right to intrude where it can be shown that the Bill of Rights has been abrogated. He argued that the state of Alabama had denied due process to a black man because he had been denied an attorney (*Powell v. Alabama*, 1932). He supported the reversal of the notorious *Scottsboro* decision (a case of rape against a group of young black men) by declaring that blacks cannot be excluded from jury service merely by virtue of their color (*Norris v. Alabama*, 1935, and *Patterson v. Alabama*, 1935). He maintained that such exclusion denied "equal protection of the laws" as provided in the Fourteenth Amendment. In a case anticipating by sixteen years the famous *Brown v. Board of Education* (1954) school desegregation case, he held that qualified black students must be granted admission to an all-white law school (*Missouri ex rel. Gaines v. Canada*, 1938). As in *Brown*, the Hughes Court declared that separate facilities for blacks was not equal; that is, separate is not equal, and the plaintiff Gaines had not received "equal protection of the laws."

Over the course of Chief Justice Hughes's term on the bench, he supported legal decisions that provided constitutional protection for suffrage (voting rights), the freedom of speech, the freedom of religion, the freedom of the press, and the right to political dissent. Hughes's record on civil liberties can only lead one to agree with Samuel Hendel's observation that he had a "greater fondness for the Bill of Rights than any other Chief Justice."

SIGNIFICANCE

The magnitude of Hughes's service to the country was so widespread and pervasive that it is difficult to know just where the emphasis should be placed. In fact, the wise course is to avoid placing undue emphasis on any specific aspect of his numerous accomplishments, but rather to review the traits of character that he brought to every public position he held. His strong sense of social interest led him throughout his life to fight institutional dishonesty in all of its forms. He was never reluctant to employ the legal leverage of the judiciary against what he perceived to be the injustices of institutional forms of government, business, and industry. On the bench he was always reluctant to impede social reform with a "judicial veto." His conception of a justice's role was as a principled libertarian; in particular, a member of the judiciary must be prepared to employ the law in defense of the citizen's individual rights against the inevitably unfair advantages of powerful national institutions. Understandably, corporations, industry, and government will exercise the initiative necessary to make their efforts worthwhile and successful. In return, individual citizens have the right, through their legislative representatives, to see to it that they do not fall victim to the aspirations of these powerful organizations. It is the role of the judiciary to establish a balanced fairness between collective interests and public liberties.

Hughes not only had the role of jurist; he also represented the most powerful of all institutions, the government itself. In this role, however, he acted with restraint and with an eye to the common good. Because he was an individual with a scrupulous moral sense, an unshakable commitment to fidelity and honor, and the intellectual powers to match, he was never willing to sacrifice long-term ideals for short-term expediencies. Thus, it seems proper to argue that Hughes was a "futurist" and as such endures as one of America's most gifted and distinguished secretaries of state.

Donald Burrill

FURTHER READING

Friedman, Richard D. "Switching Time and Other Thought Experiments: The Hughes Court and Constitutional Transformation." *University of Pennsylvania Law Review* 142, no. 6 (June, 1994): 1891-1984. A comprehensive scholarly examination of the Hughes court.

Glad, Betty. *Charles Evans Hughes and the Illusions of Innocence: A Study in American Diplomacy*. Urbana: University of Illinois Press, 1966. In this study of U.S. diplomacy between the two world wars, Hughes is the centerpiece. Schooled in mainstream nineteenth century American culture, Hughes formulated U.S. foreign policy throughout the era. It is Glad's contention that Hughes's moral puritanism often led to optimistic illusions. Glad's ideological generalizations are not always convincing.

Hendel, Samuel. *Charles Evans Hughes and the Supreme Court*. New York: King's Crown Press, 1951. This is a case-by-case study of Hughes's judicial career, a careful, detailed assessment and evaluation that has become a source book for much legal scholarship on Hughes's Supreme Court opinions.

Hughes, Charles Evans. *The Autobiographical Notes of Charles Evans Hughes*. Edited by David J. Danelske and Joseph S. Tulchin. Cambridge, Mass.: Harvard University Press, 1973. It is difficult for writers not to sketch Hughes as larger than life. Reading his own notes affords an opportunity to assess his own words; this work reveals the man both directly and indirectly.

---. *Our Relations to the Nations of the Western Hemisphere*. Princeton, N.J.: Princeton University Press, 1928. Hughes's analysis of the United States' relationship to Canada and Latin America: his assessment of the Monroe Doctrine, the recognition of governments, and the United States' role in honoring Central American treaties and supplying military arms and financial loans to foreign powers. Particularly interesting is the section in which he sets forth the conditions that he believes justify intervention in Latin American affairs.

---. *The Supreme Court of the United States*. New York: Columbia University Press, 1928. A historical account of the role of the Supreme Court. Ostensibly, the Court's task as the "supreme tribunal" is to interpret the intentions of the nation's legislatures. Hughes argues that it is the Court's role to balance state and national priorities and to determine the rights of citizens against common social interests.

Louria, Margot. *Triumph and Downfall: America's Pursuit of Peace and Prosperity, 1921-1933*. Westport, Conn.: Greenwood Press, 2001. Examines the activities of the three secretaries of state during the presidential administrations of Warren G. Harding, Calvin Coolidge, and Herbert Hoover, describing their efforts to preserve world peace and security. The second part of the book focuses on Hughes.

Perkins, Dexter. *Charles Evans Hughes and American Democratic Statesmanship*. Boston: Little, Brown, 1956. A smoothly written account of Hughes's political and legal career from his start in New York City to his retirement from the post of chief justice of the United States. Throughout, Perkins attempts to portray Hughes as a brilliant, principled individual striving to balance the ideals of liberalism and conservatism in the art of statesmanship.

Pusey, Merlo J. *Charles Evans Hughes*. 2 vols. New York: Macmillan, 1951. One of the best and most exhaustive works on Hughes. Beginning with his childhood in Glens Falls, New York, and ending with his fight against Franklin D. Roosevelt's attempt to "pack the Supreme Court" in 1938, it is a standard text on Hughes. Especially valuable for its interviews with Hughes at the end of his illustrious career: Pusey had the good fortune to interview him many hours a week over a two-and-a-half-year period.

Ross, William G. *The Chief Justiceship of Charles Evans Hughes, 1930-1941*. Columbia: University of South Carolina Press, 2007. Describes the political, economic, and cultural forces that transformed American society and the Supreme Court during Hughes's tenure as chief justice.

DANIEL KEN INOUYE

Soldier, Representative (1959-1963), and Senator (1963-2012) from Hawaii

Born: September 7, 1924; Honolulu, Hawaii
Died: December 17, 2012; Bethesda, Maryland
Areas of achievement: War, government and politics

Because of his Japanese American heritage, Daniel Inouye was not drafted into the US military in World War II. However, he voluntarily joined the US Army, served heroically, and lost his right arm as a member of the 442nd Regiment, which operated chiefly in Italy. He later became the first congressional representative for Hawaii in the US House of Representatives and, beginning in 1963, has served as a US senator from that state.

Daniel Ken Inouye (Wikimedia Commons)

Early Life

Daniel Ken Inouye is the son of Hyotoro Inouye and Kame Imanaga and the grandson of Asakichi Inouye, a native of Yokoyama, Japan, who came to the Territory of Hawaii in 1899 to work on a sugar plantation. Inouye's family lived in a Japanese section of Honolulu, and during his childhood, their family life blended Japanese and American customs. Inouye and many of his friends were known as *nisei*, or American-born children of Japanese immigrant parents.

On Sunday morning, December 7, 1941, as the Inouyes were preparing for church, a radio broadcast informed them that Japan had bombed the Pearl Harbor naval base, which was on the island of Oahu, where the Inouyes lived. Any Japanese Americans living on Hawaii and on the mainland were considered possible spies for Japan and classified 4-C, "enemy aliens." Initially they could not be drafted into the US military, although some of them were quite willing to serve. The following September, Daniel, who had enrolled as a premedical student at the University of Hawaii, was not accepted as a military volunteer. After sending petitions to President Franklin D. Roosevelt, patriotic Japanese Americans who wished to serve learned that the president had established the 442nd Regimental Combat Team, made up of Japanese American soldiers. Inouye and over sixty other premedical students volunteered but found that they would only be accepted if they withdrew from the medical program at their university.

Life's Work

After joining the military, Inouye learned that the federal government was confining many Japanese Americans in communities that were essentially concentration camps. He developed great respect for the military trainees who had opted for duty even though they had come from these degrading camps. After training at Camp Shelby in Hattiesburg, Mississippi, Inouye's unit was sent in June 1943 to Italy for the Rome-Arno campaign. Over the course of the war, Inouye realized that the people he was fighting were not simply the enemy; they were frightened young men who missed their families.

Inouye's unit was called to southern France to assist in locating and freeing the Lost Battalion, a battalion of Texan soldiers that had been surrounded by German troops. In the struggle, Inouye was struck by a bullet that was deflected by two silver dollars he had strapped to his chest. He received a battlefield commission in recognition of his actions. He later suffered his most serious injury as a second lieutenant in Italy in April 1945, the same day that his commander submitted a request that he be promoted to first lieutenant. The troops had to attack a ridge on which the Germans had built a fortification that came to be known as the Gothic Line. Struck in the stomach, Inouye continued to lead his men while sustaining many other injuries. However, due to Inouye's perseverance and use of hand grenades, his platoon was able to make significant advances. Inouye was carried off the field, and his shattered right arm was later amputated above the elbow.

Daniel Inouye's United States Senate Career

One of Inouye's early efforts in the Senate helped enact the Immigration Act of 1965, which shifted the immigration pattern in the United States from one favoring Europeans to one more beneficial to Asians and Latin Americans. He delivered the keynote address at the Democratic National Convention of 1968 in Chicago. In 1973, his questioning during the hearings investigating the Watergate scandal earned this quiet and unassuming man the attention and respect of millions of Americans. In 1976–77, he was chosen to be the first chairman of the Senate Intelligence Committee.

In his defense of minorities, Inouye has sometimes gone beyond what were considered acceptable bounds. As a member of the Committee on Indian Affairs, he helped several tribes gain reparations from the government. He unsuccessfully attempted to pass an appropriation to build schools for North African Jews in France. His interest in the Philippines, a territory of the United States for many decades (like Hawaii), led him to defend former President Ferdinand Marcos even when the majority of his Democratic colleagues favored the removal of Marcos from power.

He served on several subcommittees of the Commerce Committee, and in 2009 succeeded Robert Byrd as leader of the Appropriations Committee. His popularity with Hawaiians has never been in doubt. As of 2010, he had been elected overwhelmingly nine times as one of Hawaii's senators. Upon Byrd's death in 2010, Inouye achieved the position of current senator with the longest service.

Inouye visits with sailors aboard the frigate USS Gary during the his goodwill trip to forward deployed naval forces stationed in Yokosuka, Japan. (Wikimedia Commons)

Inouye remained in military service until 1947, spending much of his time in a hospital. For his heroic actions, he was awarded a Distinguished Service Cross to complement the Bronze Star, Purple Heart, and other medals he had already earned. Soon after his amputation, a nurse refused to do simple tasks for him, telling him that he must learn to live with only one arm. Although he first resented her seeming lack of attention, he realized that she was teaching him a valuable and necessary lesson. While hospitalized, he met another wounded soldier with whom he would later work in the US Congress, Bob Dole of Kansas.

> "*The philosophy of the Constitution, and the Bill of Rights is not simply to grant the majority the power to rule, but is also to set out limitation after limitation upon that power. Freedom of speech, freedom of the press, freedom of religion; what are these but the recognition that at times when the majority of men would willingly destroy him, a dissenting man may have no friend but the law.*"

Returning to civilian life, Inouye reentered the University of Hawaii to study economics and government. He married Margaret Shinobu Awamura, with whom he later had one son, Daniel. In 1950, he received his bachelor's degree from the University of Hawaii. Two years later, he completed a law degree at George Washington University.

From 1954 to 1959, Inouye served as a Hawaiian Territorial Representative, even acting as majority leader for a time. Longstanding efforts to make Hawaii a state succeeded in 1959, and Inouye, a Democrat, was elected as Hawaii's first member of the US House of Representatives. When Senator Oren E. Long decided not to seek reelection in 1962, he endorsed Inouye, who won the election and began an exceptionally long career as US senator.

A further military honor was bestowed on Inouye in 2000. He was one of a group of nisei veterans of the 442nd Regimental Combat Team whose Distinguished Service Crosses were converted to Congressional Medals of Honor.

In 2006, Inouye's wife, Margaret, died after nearly fifty-seven years of marriage. Two years later, he married Irene Hirano, the president of the US-Japan Council and the president and chief executive of the Japanese American National Museum in Los Angeles.

Significance

Inouye's life and career are especially significant in US political history because he was the first Japanese American elected to the House of Representatives as well as the first Japanese American elected to the Senate. He has striven to serve his nation with excellence in both the military and the federal government, despite the fact that loyal Americans of Japanese descent had been deeply mistrusted and even treated like enemies by their own nation. Inouye is also remarkable for his persistence and willingness to continue performing effective governmental work very late in his life.

In his work as a legislator, Inouye has worked to improve conditions for Hawaii, including measures designed to better shipping practices and encourage tourism for the state. Over the years, he has assisted people of many backgrounds, including those of Japanese heritage, American Indians, Jews, other Asians, and Central Americans. Inouye is also well known for having sharply opposed federal assistance to the Nicaraguan *contras* (rebel groups) that was being promoted by the Central Intelligence Agency in the 1980s, warning US citizens that portions of the US government were pursuing alleged national interests in an unchecked and unlawful way. He also served on the Senate Select Committee on Secret Military Assistance to Iran and the Nicaraguan Opposition, which involved an investigation of government and military officials accused of going against congressional decisions in their covert funding of Nicaraguan contras.

In his eighth term as senator, Inouye continued to work on behalf of courageous but neglected individuals. He was an early advocate of the James Zadroga Health and Compensation Act to support the health needs of New York City first responders exposed to toxins during the September 11, 2001, terrorist attacks. The US Senate passed the bill in December 2010.

Robert P. Ellis

Further Reading

"About Dan." *Dan Inouye: United States Senator for Hawaii*. Dan Inouye, n.d. Web. 31 Jan. 2012. Offers biographical information about Inouye, including a timeline, a record of his military medals and commendations, and other awards and committees with which he has been associated.

Elving, Ronald D. "The Quiet Insider: Hawaii's Daniel Inouye Wields a Private, Personal Power." *Congressional Quarterly Weekly Report* (Apr. 1988): 1–3. Print. Discusses Inouye's behavior, attitude, and demeanor in the Senate.

Slavicek, Louise Chipley. *Daniel Inouye*. New York: Chelsea, 2007. Written for young adults. Offers a good summation of Inouye's career.

Smith, Larry. *Beyond Glory: Medal of Honor Heroes in Their Own Words*. New York: Norton, 2003. Includes a chapter summarizing Inouye's military career and awards.

Marí-Luci Jaramillo

Educator and diplomat

Born: June 19, 1928; Las Vegas, New Mexico
Area of Achievement: Education; diplomacy

Jaramillo worked hard to finance her education, eventually earning a doctorate and rising to become the U.S. ambassador to Honduras. During a career spanning nearly half a century, she was a grade school teacher, university instructor, and university administrator, as well as a staunch advocate for the power of learning.

Early Life

Marí-Luci Jaramillo (mah-REE LOO-see har-ah-MEE-yoh) was the second of three children born to Mauricio Autuna Jaramillo, the owner of a shoe shop originally from Durango, Mexico, and his wife Elvira Ruiz Jaramillo, a New Mexican native. As a child, Marí-Luci shined the handcrafted shoes in her father's store, and after graduating from high school she worked at a variety of jobs in order to afford college tuition at New Mexico Highlands University. After her freshman year, however, she married a schoolteacher and dropped out of the university. She gave birth to three children—Ross, Richard, and Carla—before eventually divorcing. Eager to continue her education, Jaramillo returned to the workforce, taking jobs as a waitress, parachute seamstress, and housecleaner, and she saved enough money to return to New Mexico Highlands University, from which she graduated magna cum laude in 1955 with a bachelor's degree in education and minors in English and Spanish.

From 1955 to 1965, Jaramillo taught in elementary schools in Albuquerque and Las Vegas, New Mexico. At the same time, she continued her studies, earning a master's degree with honors from New Mexico Highlands University in 1959. Between 1962 and 1964, she was a language arts consultant to the Las Vegas school system. In 1965, she began teaching at the University of New Mexico, from which she earned her Ph.D. in 1970. At this university she served successively as assistant director of Latin American education (1965-1969), assistant director of minority instruction (1969-1972), chairman of the Elementary Education Department (1972-1975), and professor of education (1976-1977). Under the auspices of the U.S. Agency for International Development, Jaramillo traveled throughout Central and South America during the 1960's and 1970's, presenting teacher training and school development workshops. She also wrote many articles for educational journals, gave countless lectures on the subject of teaching, and participated in the production of several training films.

Life's Work

In 1977, based on the strength of her work in the Latino community, President Jimmy Carter nominated Jaramillo to be the ambassador extraordinary and plenipotentiary of the United States to Honduras. She and her second husband (they would later divorce) lived in Tegucigalpa, the

> **Influence of Jaramillo's Travels in Latin America on Her Teaching**
>
> During the late 1960's and early 1970's, Marí-Luci Jaramillo was heavily involved in New Mexico University's Cultural Awareness Center. Under the aegis of the United States Agency for International Development, she represented the university's Latin American educational programs and was an informal ambassador for the United States before she became formal ambassador to Honduras in 1977. Fluent in Spanish and English, she visited every Central American country, as well as Venezuela, Colombia, Ecuador, and Argentina. At her stops in each nation she held teacher-training workshops focusing on education in general and school development in particular.
>
> In the course of her career, Jaramillo's concepts of education changed. When she first began, she believed that if people were educated, they would be able to succeed in the world, as she had. However, from her travels she discovered this was not a universal truth: Many highly educated people, for a variety of reasons—primarily political and economic—were denied the opportunity to participate in the social system. She incorporated the information she had obtained from her travels into her lectures, articles, and training sessions. Jaramillo counseled students to learn the importance of economics and to study the business world and the workings of politics and government in order to understand the economic and political systems and make them work to their advantage. She stressed the necessity of voting and the importance of making individual voices heard.
>
> For Jaramillo, understanding cultural differences was as important as knowing teaching techniques or finding the proper educational materials, especially for teachers of English as a second language. Teachers, she maintained, have to be committed to promoting positive activities in and out of classrooms in order to ease cultural conflicts. Educators must become keen cultural observers, divorcing themselves from preconceived notions, while teaching in humanistic ways not only English but also the way of life that the language represents.

Honduran capital, until 1980. During her tenure as ambassador, Jaramillo was in charge of six governmental agencies, oversaw five hundred Peace Corps volunteers, and attended to the needs of some two thousand Americans living in Honduras. After Carter left office in 1980, Jaramillo returned to the United States and worked until 1981 as the deputy assistant secretary for inter-American affairs at the U.S. Department of State in Washington, D.C. In 1982, she returned to the University of New Mexico as special assistant to the president and associate dean of the College of Education, and she continued to teach, specializing in English as a second language, women's studies, and minority education with a particular emphasis in Latino learning. In 1985, she became the university's vice president for student affairs.

Two years later, Jaramillo left the University of New Mexico for a job in private industry. Stationed in San Francisco, California, she served as regional vice president for the Princeton, New Jersey-based Educational Testing Services (ETS), a company that develops and administers tests for universities and professional organizations throughout the world. She later was named the company's assistant vice president of field services, administering eight ETS offices throughout the United States. In 1993, under U.S. President Bill Clinton, she worked in the Pentagon as a minority recruiter for the U.S. Department of State. Jaramillo retired in 1995 and returned to live in her hometown of Las Vegas, New Mexico, where she continued to advocate for a variety of educational, minority, and human rights causes.

> "*My tone was: work in a friendly atmosphere. That's what I wanted; productive work, but in a human environment; in a place where people want to work and work hard, and they're going to get a pat on the shoulder when they do good work.*"

Significance

Marí-Luci Jaramillo pursued learning in an era when few Latinas took courses after high school, and she became a staunch advocate of education, particularly for women and minorities. A highly respected teacher and educational author, Jaramillo was associated with many organizations throughout her long career. She was a member of the National Association of Latino Elected and Appointed Officials, the National Association for Bilingual

Education, the Latin Americanista Association, Bilingual Children's Television, the Diversity External Advisory Council of the Los Alamos National Laboratory, and the McGraw-Hill Broadcasting Corporation's La Raza Films Coordinating Committee. She has also been a member of the board of trustees of the Tomás Rivera Center at Claremont University in California, the Children's Television Network, and the board of directors of the New Mexico Highlands University Foundation.

Jaramillo has often been honored for her efforts on behalf of education, minorities, and women. In 1986, she received the Harvard Graduate School of Education Anne Roe Award for her contributions to education and women's professional growth. In 1988, the Miller Brewing Company named her one of America's most outstanding Latino educators; *Hispanic Business* magazine named her one of the one hundred most influential Hispanics in the United States. The Mexican American Women's National Association gave Jaramillo its Primera Award in honor of her appointment as the first Latina to serve as U.S. ambassador to Honduras. She also received an award from the American Association for Higher Education for outstanding leadership in education in the Latino community.

Jack Ewing

Further Reading

Dorman, Shawn, ed. *Inside a U.S. Embassy: How the Foreign Service Works for America.* Dulles, Va.: Â Potomac Books, 2009. A general study that lists Foreign Service personnel typically found at U.S. embassies and explores the duties of American diplomats and ambassadors with examples from around the world.

Grogan, Margaret, and Charol Shakeshaft. *Women and Educational Leadership.* Hoboken, N.J.: Jossey-Bass, 2010. An examination of the contributions of women to the field of education, and how they have changed the concept of what it means to be a leader.

Jaramillo, Marí-Luci. *Madame Ambassador: The Shoemaker's Daughter.* Tempe, Ariz.: Bilingual Press, 2002. An autobiographical memoir charting Jaramillo's rise from poverty to U.S. ambassador to Honduras, university teacher and administrator, corporate spokesperson, and respected educational advocate.

---. *To Serve Hispanic American Female Students: Challenges and Responsibilities for Educational Institutions.* Claremont, Calif.: Tomás Rivera Center, 1987. This brief work encapsulates many of Jaramillo's concepts of minority and Latina education, emphasizing teamwork, cultural integration, and a strong foundation of activities in and out of the classroom.

MacDonald, Victoria-Maria, ed. *Latino Education in the United States: A Narrated History from 1513-2000.* Basingstoke, England: Palgrave Macmillan, 2004. An overview of the domestic state of education for Latinos over five centuries, as told in the words of those who experienced it first hand, and the impact of Latino culture on the United States.

Reardon, Vince. *Legacy: Passing on Cherished Values in a Values-Starved World.* n.p.: L.P., 2010. Presents the stories of twenty-five men and women, including Jaramillo, who have demonstrated particular sets of values and contributed to making the world a better place.

Barbara Jordan

Representative from Texas (1973-1979)

Born: February 21, 1936; Houston, Texas
Died: January 17, 1996; Austin, Texas
Area of Achievement: Government and politics, civil rights, oratory, law, education

The first African American elected to the Texas senate since Reconstruction, Jordan went on to become a member of the U.S. House of Representatives. She mesmerized the nation during televised coverage of the House Judiciary Committee's investigation considering the impeachment of President Richard M. Nixon.

Early Life

Barbara Jordan was born to Benjamin Jordan, a warehouse clerk and part-time clergyman, and Arlyne Patten Jordan. Barbara was raised in a time of segregation and Jim Crow laws. She lived with her parents, her two older sisters, Bennie and Rose Marie, and her grandfathers, John Ed Patten and Charles Jordan.

Jordan's outlook on life as well as her strength and determination can be attributed to the influence of her maternal grandfather, John Ed Patten, a former minister who was also a businessman. While assisting him in his junk business, Jordan learned to be self-sufficient, strong-willed, and independent, and she was encouraged not to settle for mediocrity. Her determination to achieve superiority was quickly demonstrated in her early years.

Jordan spent most of her free time with her grandfather Patten, who served as her mentor. They would converse

Barbara Jordan (Library of Congress)

about all kinds of subjects. His advice was followed and appreciated by the young girl, who adoringly followed him every Sunday as he conducted his business. He instilled in her a belief in the importance of education. Every action, every aspect of life, he stated, was to be learned from and experienced.

With her grandfather's advice in mind, Jordan embraced life and education. She showed herself to be an exemplary student while attending Phillis Wheatley High School in Houston. A typical teenager, Jordan was active in school clubs and other extracurricular activities. She also led an active social life during her years at Phillis Wheatley. It was during her high school years that Jordan was inspired to become a lawyer. She was drawn to the legal profession during a career-day presentation by the prominent African American attorney Edith Sampson. Moved by Sampson's speech, Jordan became determined to investigate law as a possible area of study.

Jordan received many awards during her high school years, particularly for her talent as an orator. Her skill in this area was rewarded in 1952, when she won first place in the Texas State Ushers Oratorical Contest. As part of her victory package, she was sent to Illinois to compete in the national championships. She won the national oration contest in Chicago that same year.

The year 1952 began a new stage in Jordan's education. She was admitted to Texas Southern University after her graduation from high school. It was here that she truly excelled in oration. She joined the Texas Southern debate team and won many tournaments under the guidance and tutelage of her debate coach, Tom Freeman. He was also influential in urging her to attend Boston University Law School. At law school, she was one of two African American women in the graduating class of 1959; they were the only women to be graduated that year. Before 1960, Jordan managed to pass the Massachusetts and Texas Bar examinations. Such a feat was an enviable one. She was offered a law position in the state of Massachusetts, but she declined the offer.

Jordan's impoverished background seemed far behind her. With the continued support of her parents and grandfathers, she opened a private law practice in Houston in 1960. She volunteered her services to the Kennedy-Johnson presidential campaign. She organized the African American constituents in the black precincts of her county. Her efforts were successful. The voter turnout was the largest Harris County had ever experienced. Jordan's participation in such a history-making event demonstrated her talents for persuasion and organization. These skills, coupled with her education and intellect, were to become her assets in all her future endeavors. Jordan's political career was born as a result of the Kennedy-Johnson victory of 1960.

> "*My faith in the Constitution is whole; it is complete; it is total. I am not going to sit here and be an idle spectator to the diminution, the subversion, the destruction of the Constitution.*"

LIFE'S WORK

The decade of the 1960's witnessed Jordan's emergence in the political arena. The 1960's was a period of transition and hope in American history. With the election of the first Roman Catholic president and the epic changes brought on by the Civil Rights movement, it was a time of change. Jordan was determined to be part of that change. After becoming the speaker for the Harris County Democratic Party, she ran for the Texas House of Representatives in 1962 and 1964. She lost on both occasions. Undeterred, Jordan ran for a third time in the newly

> ### "Bound Together by Common Spirit"
>
> Barbara Jordan's reputation for eloquence was evident when she gave the keynote speech before the Democratic National Convention in 1976.
>
> Now we must look to the future. Let us heed the voice of the people and recognize their common sense. If we do not, we not only blaspheme our political heritage, we ignore the common ties that bind all Americans. Many fear the future. Many are distrustful of their leaders, and believe that their voices are never heard. Many seek only to satisfy their private work wants. To satisfy private interests. But this is the great danger America faces—that we will cease to be one nation and become instead a collection of interest groups: city against suburb, region against region, individual against individual; each seeking to satisfy private wants. If that happens, who then will speak for America? Who then will speak for the common good?
>
> This is the question which must be answered in 1976: Are we to be one people bound together by common spirit, sharing in a common endeavor; or will we become a divided nation? For all of its uncertainty, we cannot flee the future. We must not become the "New Puritans" and reject our society. We must address and master the future together. It can be done if we restore the belief that we share a sense of national community, that we share a common national endeavor. It can be done.
>
> There is no executive order; there is no law that can require the American people to form a national community. This we must do as individuals, and if we do it as individuals, there is no President of the United States who can veto that decision.

reapportioned Harris County. She became one of two African Americans elected to the newly reapportioned eleventh district. Jordan was elected to the Texas state senate. She became the first African American since 1883 and the first woman ever to hold the position.

Jordan impressed the state senate members with her intelligence, oration, and ability to fit in with the old boys' club. She remained in the state senate for six years, until 1972. During her tenure, she worked on legislation dealing with the environment, establishing minimum wage standards, and eliminating discrimination in business contracts. She was encouraged to run for a congressional seat. She waged a campaign in 1971 for the U.S. Congress. While completing her term of office on the state level, Jordan achieved another first: In 1972, she was elected to the U.S. House of Representatives. Jordan served briefly as acting governor of Texas on June 10, 1972, when both the governor and lieutenant governor were out of the state. As president pro tem of the Texas senate, it was one of her duties to act as governor when the situation warranted. Despite his being present for all of her earlier achievements, Jordan's father did not live to see her take office as a member of the House. He died on June 11, 1972, in Austin, Texas. His demise spurred Jordan to continue her work.

Having already caught the attention of Lyndon B. Johnson while a member of the Texas state senate, Jordan sought his advice on the type of committees to join. She became a member of the Judiciary and the Ways and Means committees. Little did she know that the Judiciary Committee would evolve into a major undertaking. Jordan's membership in the House was to be one of the many highlights of her political career.

The 1974 Watergate scandal gave Jordan national prominence. Her speech in favor of President Richard M. Nixon's impeachment was nothing short of oratorical brilliance. Her eloquence was considered memorable and thought provoking. Her expertise as an attorney was demonstrated in 1974 when she spoke about the duty of elected officials to their constituents and the United States Constitution. Despite her personal distaste for an impeachment, Jordan insisted that Nixon be held accountable for the Watergate fiasco. A Senate investigation, she believed, was warranted. Her televised speech was the center of media attention and critique for days to come. She sustained her reputation for eloquence during the 1976 Democratic National Convention. During her tenure in the House, she introduced bills dealing with civil rights, crime, business, and free competition as well as an unprecedented plan of payment to housewives for the labor and services they provide. Jordan's popularity was at its zenith when talk of her running for the vice presidency was rampant among her supporters. She shrugged off the suggestion, stating that the time was not right.

It was discovered in 1976 that Jordan suffered from knee problems. The ailment was visible during her keynote address when she was helped to the podium to give her speech. She admitted that she was having problems

Jordan sitting on the House Judiciary Committee during the Watergate hearings. (Wikimedia Commons)

with her patella. The damaged cartilage in one knee made it difficult and painful for her to walk or stand for long. Her brilliant oration was not hampered by her muscle weakness during the delivery of her speech in 1976. She opted not to run for reelection in 1978 and entered the educational field.

During his presidency, Jimmy Carter offered Jordan a post in his cabinet. Political rumors persist that she would have preferred the position of attorney general to Carter's suggestion of the post of secretary of the Department of Health, Education, and Welfare. Since Carter was firm in his offer, Jordan opted to refuse the offer rather than settle for something she did not want. Such an attitude is indicative of her childhood training and upbringing.

Jordan was offered and took a teaching post at the University of Texas in Austin. She taught at the Lyndon Baines Johnson School of Public Affairs. In addition to her instructional duties, she also held the positions of faculty adviser and recruiter for minority students. She continued to hold these positions into the early 1990's. In addition, Governor Ann Richards of Texas appointed her to serve as an adviser on ethics in government.

Jordan received innumerable honorary degrees. Universities such as Princeton and Harvard bestowed honorary doctorates on her. She received awards touting her as the best living orator. She was one of the most influential women in the world as well as one of the most admired. She was a member of the Texas Women's Hall of Fame and hosted her own television show. At the 1988 Democratic National Convention, Jordan gave a speech nominating Senator Lloyd Bentsen as the party's vice presidential candidate. She delivered the speech from the wheelchair she used as a result of her battle with multiple sclerosis. In 1992, she received the prized Spingarn Medal, which is awarded by the National Association for the Advancement of Colored People (NAACP) for service to the African American community.

Significance

Jordan's rise from poverty to prominence through diligence and perseverance in the fields of law, politics, and education is a model for others to follow. During an interview with the Black Entertainment Television channel in February of 1993, Jordan maintained that circumstances of birth, race, or creed should not inhibit an individual from succeeding if he or she wishes to achieve greatness. As an individual who was born poor, African American, and female, and who was most likely lesbian, Jordan demonstrated the truth of her assertion, and her life is a portrait of success highlighted by a series of significant "firsts" and breakthroughs.

Jordan's honorary doctorates from Princeton and Harvard substantiate her dedication to education and excellence. As an African American woman from the South, Jordan broke one barrier after the other. She maintained her integrity and dignity while in political office. Her defense of the Constitution during the Watergate era as well as her dedication to the field of education continue to be examples to those entering the field of law and education.

Jordan denied that her life's achievements were extraordinary. Her modesty was part of her upbringing. She endeavored to live a life that she believed would benefit the country. One of the reasons she refused to run for reelection in 1978 was her need to serve more than a "few" constituents in her district. She wished to serve them in addition to the masses. As she stated in her resignation, "I feel more of a responsibility to the country as a whole, as contrasted with the duty of representing the half-million in the Eighteenth Congressional District." She maintained that anyone may succeed with the proper attitude. In 1978, Jordan believed that her legislative role and effectiveness had ceased and that her most effective role in the global community was in the field of instruction. A new challenge presented itself, and Jordan was eager to confront it.

Despite the effects of her long illness, Jordan demonstrated that race, socioeconomic status, and societal barriers may be overcome and dispelled as roadblocks to success. She gave interviews, lectures, and commencement addresses almost up to the time of her death in 1996.

Annette Marks-Ellis

Further Reading

Browne, Ray B. *Contemporary Heroes and Heroines*. Detroit, Mich.: Gale Research, 1990. A collection of biographical profiles on men and women who have made major contributions to American life. Includes a fine piece on Jordan and her career.

Famous Blacks Give Secrets of Success. Vol. 2 in Ebony Success Library. Chicago: Johnson, 1973. A collection documenting the lives and achievements of black luminaries. The excerpt on Jordan traces her political achievements through 1973.

Fenno, Richard F. *Going Home: Black Representatives and Their Constituents*. Chicago: University of Chicago Press, 2003. Follows the careers of Jordan and three other African American members of the U.S. House of Representatives to examine their visions of constituent representation.

Holmes, Barbara A. *A Private Woman in Public Spaces: Barbara Jordan's Speeches on Ethics, Public Religion, and Law*. Harrisburg, Pa.: Trinity Press International, 2000. Comprehensive analysis of Jordan's speeches, focusing on how her private moral views informed her public career.

Jordan, Barbara, and Shelby Hearn. *Barbara Jordan: A Self-Portrait*. Garden City, N.Y.: Doubleday, 1979. Jordan's autobiography traces her life from childhood to her political career in the House of Representatives.

Ries, Paula, and Anne J. Stone, eds. *The American Woman: 1992-93*. New York: W. W. Norton, 1992. This book is one in a series of reports documenting the social, economic, and political status of American women. Includes profiles and articles on Jordan as well as female political contemporaries such as Governor Ann Richards of Texas and Senator Nancy Kassebaum of Kansas.

Sherman, Max, ed. *Barbara Jordan: Speaking the Truth with Eloquent Thunder*. Austin: University of Texas Press, 2007. Includes several of Jordan's major political addresses, including one on the erosion of civil liberties and another on the constitutional basis of impeachment. The enclosed DVD contains footage of her delivering some of these addresses.

United States House of Representatives. *Commission on the Bicentenary. Women in Congress, 1917-1990*. Washington, D.C.: Government Printing Office, 1991. Compiled to honor the bicentennial of the House of Representatives, this work provides biographical sketches of the various women who have served in Congress, beginning with Jeannette Rankin in 1917 and continuing through the women serving in 1990.

Robert F. Kennedy

U.S. Attorney General (1961-1964) and Senator from New York (1965-1968)

Born: November 20, 1925; Brookline, Massachusetts
Died: June 6, 1968; Los Angeles, California
Areas of Achievement: Government and politics, law

Kennedy served his brother U.S. president John F. Kennedy as an able and active attorney general. He passionately advocated justice and equality for minorities and the poor in the United States. Like his brother nearly five years earlier, Kennedy was assassinated during his campaign for the presidency.

Early Life

Robert F. Kennedy was born on 131 Naples Road in Brookline, Massachusetts. He was the seventh of nine children born to Joseph Patrick Kennedy and Rose Fitzgerald Kennedy; both of Kennedy's parents came from distinguished Irish Roman Catholic families of Boston. Rose's father had been the mayor of Boston, and Joseph Kennedy himself was an able financier who earned millions of dollars while still young.

When Kennedy was four, the family moved to the New York City area, where Joseph, believed that he could be more in touch with financial dealings than he was in Boston. Kennedy first attended school in Bronxville, New York, where he was remembered as a nice boy but not an outstanding student. A constant admonition from his mother in his youth was to read more good books a suggestion he followed. From his father's advice and guidance in Kennedy's boyhood, the youngster learned values to which he would firmly adhere all of his life. Joseph's goal was for his children always to try their hardest at whatever they were doing. The father could abide a loser, but he could not abide a slacker.

Robert F. Kennedy (Wikimedia Commons)

Kennedy's position as the seventh child in his family also affected the development of his personality. His older brothers, Joseph P. Kennedy, Jr., and John F. Kennedy, were ten and eight, respectively, when Kennedy was born. After these oldest boys' births, the Kennedys had had four daughters. Although friendly and playful with his sisters, Kennedy sought the attention and approval of Joe, Jr., and John. To this end, the little boy developed himself as an athlete, mostly by determination, because he was of small stature. Even as a grown man, Kennedy was considerably shorter than his brothers. Kennedy attained a height of five feet ten inches, but his slightly stooped carriage sometimes made him look even smaller. He also appeared somewhat frail, although he was muscular and physically active all of his life. He had also inherited the Kennedy good looks; he had deep-blue eyes, sandy-brown hair, and handsome, angular facial bones. He was also shy as a boy.

The Kennedys reared their children as Roman Catholics; of all the boys, Kennedy was the most religious as a youth and as an adult. He served as an altar boy in St. Joseph's Church, Bronxville.

In 1936, Kennedy's father, was named by President Franklin D. Roosevelt as ambassador to the Court of St. James (London, England), and the family moved abroad. The number and physical beauty of the Kennedy children caused them to be public favorites in England. They all received press coverage, were presented to royalty, and attended British schools.

When World War II began in 1939, Joseph, Sr., sent his family home for their safety. Kennedy then attended preparatory schools, including Milton Academy, to gain admission to Harvard; although his grades were not extremely high, he was admitted in 1944. He distinguished himself most at Harvard on the football squad. He was too small to be an outstanding football player, but by hard practice and a will to succeed, he did make the varsity team. Among his teammates, he found friends, several of whom he kept throughout his life. These men attest that Kennedy was always deeply loyal to his friends.

With the United States' entry into World War II, Kennedy joined the U.S. Navy but did not see battle because of the combat death of his brother, Joe, Jr., a pilot. When he was discharged from the service, Kennedy finished his interrupted Harvard education and entered the University of Virginia Law School.

While in law school, Kennedy was introduced to his sister Jean's college roommate, Ethel Skakel. Skakel came from a wealthy Catholic family and was also a vibrant, athletic young woman. She and Kennedy were married in June of 1950, while he was still a law student. The couple would have eleven children, the last of whom was born after Kennedy's death at the hands of an assassin in 1968.

Life's Work

Kennedy's political career dates from 1946, when he helped manage his brother John's congressional campaign in Massachusetts. In 1952, when John ran for the Senate, his younger brother was his campaign manager. Between these campaigns, Kennedy also worked in the federal government. He served as a legal assistant to Senator Joseph McCarthy in 1953, when congressional inquiries were being made into so-called un-American activities. McCarthy's investigations focused on subversive, communist activities in the United States. Kennedy also served, in 1954, on the John McClellan Committee of the United States Senate, which was investigating organized crime in the United States. Among the groups under the committee's scrutiny was the powerful Teamsters Union, headed by Jimmy Hoffa. Kennedy displayed relentlessness in questioning Hoffa and in his determination to uncover the corruption in the Teamsters Union. Some of the press viewing the committee's hearings believed Kennedy to be too rude and harsh in his persistent examination of witnesses, especially Hoffa. The term "ruthless" became attached to Kennedy's name; it was, his closest friends and advisers believed, a misnomer. His aggressiveness in the Senate hearings demonstrated his strong desire for success and meaningful achievements in public service.

Kennedy achieved more national recognition when he managed John's campaign for the presidency in 1960. Kennedy worked feverishly on John's behalf; he passionately believed in John's ideas for the United States. When the campaign ended after a long night of waiting for election returns, Kennedy was exhausted but exuberant. He was thirty-five years old, and his brother had just been elected the first Catholic president of the United States.

In announcing his cabinet members in the weeks following his election, John wished to include his brother as the attorney general. In private discussions, Kennedy showed reluctance; he feared that people would charge John with nepotism. Finally, Kennedy was persuaded to accept the cabinet position.

> "What we need in the United States is not division; what we need in the United States is not hatred; what we need in the United States is not violence and lawlessness, but is love, and wisdom, and compassion toward one another, and a feeling of justice toward those who still suffer within our country, whether they be white or whether they be black."

Kennedy proved himself to be a good choice for attorney general. He was John's close adviser in many critical instances. The two worked on controlling the volatile civil rights demonstrations that came close to tearing the United States apart in the early 1960's. Some lives were lost in the civil rights battle for freedom of education, public accommodations, and voting rights in the South, but more may have been sacrificed if the Kennedy administration had not intervened with negotiations (and sometimes with federal troops) at critical junctures.

Another tension-fraught moment during which Kennedy aided his brother was the Cuban Missile Crisis. In October of 1962, U.S. surveillance had determined that Soviet nuclear missiles were being established on secret bases in Cuba. For thirteen days, the president, his cabinet, and his advisers met to discuss their possible reactions to these missiles, for they could not let them be fully installed. While some cabinet members and military leaders advocated an invasion of Cuba, a bombing of the island, or both, John Kennedy was determined not to begin a war that could easily lead to a nuclear confrontation. During these thirteen days, Robert Kennedy was one of the leading proponents of a naval quarantine of Cuba. This was the method of protest that John did follow. The result of the quarantine was that Soviet ships, bringing in more missiles and installation equipment, turned back. The United States also removed some of its own missiles from Turkey to appease the Soviets. President Kennedy was greatly relieved that his advisers advocating war had not convinced him.

Tragedy then entered the Kennedy presidency: John was assassinated on November 22, 1963, in Dallas, Texas. Many Americans suffered and mourned, but none so deeply as Robert. His associates in the Justice Department noted his sullenness and depression in the months following John's death. Robert had spent almost all of his political career working on John's campaigns and projects; Robert had never held an elective office at this point in his life. He was spiritually allied to John's plans for the United States, and he was lost without his brother.

At first, Kennedy remained attorney general under President Lyndon B. Johnson, to ease the transition of administrations. In 1964, however, when a Senate seat was vacant in New York, Kennedy decided to seek that office. His running was welcomed by people who believed that he would continue John's work. Yet some New Yorkers were upset that Kennedy was a Massachusetts native seeking office in their state. To those people opposed to Robert Kennedy's campaign, his supporters reviewed his life as a boy in New York. The campaign was a success; Kennedy became a U.S. senator when he defeated the Republican Kenneth Keating. When Kennedy took the oath of office to begin his work as a senator, his younger brother, Edward, was present as a senator from Massachusetts.

Kennedy proved to be an energetic and outspoken senator (a role not usually assumed by a freshman). He worked hard to see that his late brother John's civil rights legislation was passed. Kennedy also toured in many nations during the first years after John's death, and he was always greeted with great enthusiasm and admiration wherever he went. In these travels abroad, as well as in his extensive touring throughout the United States, he was astonished at the deep poverty and endless discrimination under which many people suffered. He began to advocate more strongly legislation providing government aid and training for such groups as rural blacks, inner-city blacks,

Kennedy speaking to a crowd outside the Justice Department. (Library of Congress)

migrant farmworkers, and American Indians. Some people who disliked Kennedy accused him of visiting the poor for his own publicity, but many of those who traveled with him said that he was genuinely moved by and truly sympathetic to the plight of the lower classes in the United States. He often said that he knew he had been born into the privileges of a wealthy family, and he felt a real obligation to help those so much less fortunate than he.

In 1966, American opinion of the expanding conflict in Vietnam supported President Johnson's policy to fight hard and subdue the Communists. Kennedy, however, began to advocate negotiations and political compromises as the only sensible way of bringing the war to an end. He more openly opposed President Johnson's policies in the months that followed, when American forces heavily bombed North Vietnam. The years 1966 to 1968 (and beyond) were marked by intense domestic debate, particularly centering on opposition to the increasingly bloody and costly war in Vietnam. Kennedy became involved in the effort to negotiate quickly an honest and just settlement of the war. To this end, he struggled for several months with the decision of whether to run for the presidency. Kennedy believed that President Johnson's military escalation to defeat North Vietnam was a doomed and tragically wrong policy. Roundly criticized both by political opponents and by large numbers of citizens, Johnson decided not to run for reelection; he announced this decision to the American people on March 31, 1968. Kennedy had declared that he would seek the Democratic Party's nomination to run for president earlier that same month.

With Johnson out of the race, Kennedy began to campaign intensely for an office that he believed he could win. His one formidable opponent was the Democratic senator Eugene McCarthy of Minnesota, also an antiwar activist. McCarthy defeated Kennedy in an Oregon primary for Democratic voters in late May. Kennedy, however, surged back with a win in the California primary, held in the next week. As Kennedy left a platform at the Ambassador Hotel in Los Angeles after thanking his campaign workers for his California success, he was assassinated. He died in a Los Angeles hospital on June 6, 1968, at age forty-two.

SIGNIFICANCE

Kennedy's untimely and tragic death robbed the United States of one of its most dedicated and compassionate public officials. In office or not, Kennedy was always advocating equal rights, a decent education, adequate housing, and freedom from hunger for all Americans. He particularly befriended migrant farmworkers and American Indians, at a time when few national leaders were speaking on behalf of these minorities. Kennedy showed deep personal sympathy for the poor people he visited across the nation and vowed to end their degradation and suffering.

Kennedy did not live to see an end to suffering among America's poor or to see an end to the tragic war in Vietnam. Yet he left behind him many scores of admirers who believed in his social policies and who advocated justice and decent lives for all Americans. Kennedy's greatness lies not only in the struggles he entered during his lifetime but also in the inspiration he gave people to help their fellow Americans in need.

Patricia E. Sweeney

FURTHER READING

Halberstam, David. *The Unfinished Odyssey of Robert Kennedy*. New York: Random House, 1969. A very detailed account of Robert Kennedy's pursuit of the Democratic Party's nomination for the presidency.

Halberstam begins with Kennedy's opposition to Johnson's war policies and proceeds to the night of his assassination, ending rather abruptly and inconclusively.

Kennedy, Rose F. *Times to Remember*. Garden City, N.Y.: Doubleday, 1974. A mother's clear and detailed remembrances of her married life and her nine children. Rose Kennedy is candid on the childhood faults of Robert, as well as his admirable traits. She also deals openly with the assassinations, how she learned of them, and their effect on her family.

Palermo, Joseph A. *In His Own Right: The Political Odyssey of Robert F. Kennedy*. New York: Columbia University Press, 2001. Describes Kennedy's political and personal transformation during his years in the U.S. Senate, from 1964 until his death in 1968. Palermo explains how in these years, Kennedy became a more passionate, compassionate, and effective leader who attracted a growing legion of admirers.

Plimpton, George, ed. *American Journey: The Times of Robert Kennedy*. New York: Harcourt Brace Jovanovich, 1970. A fascinating book of candid interviews on Kennedy's personal life and political career. Plimpton and Jean Stein interviewed the mourners aboard Kennedy's funeral train. Included are recollections by relatives and political allies, as well as spectators watching the train pass by.

Schlesinger, Arthur M. *Robert Kennedy and His Times*. Boston: Houghton Mifflin, 1978. An extensive account of Kennedy's life, filled with countless details of his work and recreation. Emphasizes Kennedy's work with Senate committees in the 1950's and his tenure as attorney general in the early 1960's. Schlesinger especially wishes to refute critics of Kennedy's methods and policies.

Sorensen, Theodore C. *The Kennedy Legacy*. New York: Macmillan, 1969. Sorensen, a leading American historian and Kennedy adviser, thoroughly outlines Kennedy's political stances and plans for action, most of which he supports. The author also compares John and Robert Kennedy, analyzing their similarities and differences.

Talbot, David. *Brothers: The Hidden History of the Kennedy Years*. New York: Free Press, 2007. Examines the inner life of the Kennedy presidency, focusing on the roles of both Robert and John within the administration. Includes information on John's efforts to avoid war and Robert's quest to find his brother's assassin.

Thomas, Evan. *Robert Kennedy: His Life*. New York: Simon & Schuster, 2000. Thomas, a *Newsweek* magazine editor, presents a thorough biography containing a great deal of new information based on his access to Kennedy's colleagues, oral histories, and newly declassified documents.

Vanden Heuvel, William, and Milton Gwirtzman. *On His Own: Robert F. Kennedy, 1964-1968*. Garden City, N.Y.: Doubleday, 1970. Both authors were close friends of their subject, and theirs is a powerful, forceful study. They also show much of the inner workings of American politics. They fully present Kennedy as an unselfish proponent of justice for all Americans.

Witcover, Jules. *Eighty-five Days: The Last Campaign of Robert Kennedy*. New York: G. P. Putnam's Sons, 1969. Like Halberstam, Witcover describes Kennedy's last run for public office the presidency. Unlike Halberstam, however, Witcover continues through the assassination and the funeral (perhaps because he was at both events). The author tries to maintain a balance between Kennedy's strong points and his shortcomings.

ROBERT M. LA FOLLETTE

Representative (1885-1891), Senator (1906-1925), and Governor of Wisconsin

Born: June 14, 1855; Primrose, Wisconsin
Died: June 18, 1925; Washington, D.C.
Area of Achievement: Law; politics

As governor of Wisconsin and a U.S. senator, La Follette combined a strong sense of social justice with an intense commitment to principles as a leader of the reform movement in politics from 1900 to 1925.

EARLY LIFE

Robert M. La Follette (lah-FAW-leht) was born in Primrose township, Dane County, Wisconsin, a few miles from Madison. His father, Josiah, died before Robert was a year old; in 1862 his mother, née Mary Ferguson, married John Z. Saxton of Argyle, a prosperous merchant and Baptist deacon. La Follette attended school in Argyle until 1870, when he returned with his family to the La Follette family farm in Primrose, where he assumed much of the responsibility for operating the farm. In 1873, a

Robert M. La Follette (Library of Congress)

year after his stepfather's death, he began preparatory courses at the Wisconsin Academy in Madison and entered the University of Wisconsin in 1875. He did not distinguish himself in academics but built a reputation as a brilliant speaker and a popular student who financed his education by purchasing and publishing the student newspaper, the *University Press*. Following graduation, he took law courses at the University, read in a Madison attorney's office, and courted his University of Wisconsin classmate Belle Case, whom he married in December, 1881.

La Follette established a legal practice in Madison in 1880; he entered politics the same year with his election to the office of district attorney for Dane County. His warm personality and speaking ability made him popular, and he was easily reelected in 1882. He was elected to the first of three consecutive terms in the United States House of Representatives in 1884, even though he did not have the backing of Republican state bosses. The youngest member of Congress when he entered the House in 1885, La Follette was a fairly regular Republican during his three terms there. He strengthened his political hold on his congressional district by supporting legislation he saw as beneficial to farmers, including assiduous support of the McKinley Tariff of 1890. In spite of his strong political base, he was the victim of an imbroglio over a law requiring English-language instruction in Wisconsin schools. While La Follette had nothing to do with the state law, he was caught in a backlash against Republicans and was defeated in 1890.

La Follette returned to his legal practice in Madison. The clean-shaven, square-jawed lawyer with piercing eyes and upswept, bushy dark hair (which added inches to his five foot five inch frame) built a reputation for dynamism in jury trials. At the same time, he strove to fulfill his political ambitions by establishing, within the Republican Party in Wisconsin, an organization to challenge the control of state bosses, notably U.S. senators John C. Spooner and Philetus Sawyer. By 1897, the La Follette organization had adopted a popular program that grew out of the economic depression that began in 1893: corporate regulation, equity in taxation, and the democratization of the political system through direct primary elections. Refused the gubernatorial nomination by state Republican conventions in 1896 and 1898, La Follette persevered in winning support; in 1900 he was elected governor of Wisconsin and assumed office in January, 1901.

LIFE'S WORK

As governor for two full terms and part of a third, La Follette successfully converted Wisconsin into a so-called laboratory of democracy. The transformation, however, did not take place immediately. When he entered office with the intention of redeeming his campaign pledges of a direct primary law and railroad tax legislation, he encountered persistent opposition from the state legislature. The lack of reform accomplishments in his first term led to a sweeping campaign in 1902 not only for his own reelection but also for the election of state legislators who would follow his program. In subsequent sessions, the legislature passed the primary election and railroad tax laws and set up a railroad rate commission. Moreover, La Follette so firmly established the direction of reform politics in Wisconsin that his followers would control state offices for years after he left the governorship. A few weeks after the legislature convened in January, 1905, La Follette was elected to the United States Senate. He left Wisconsin at the end of the year, after securing passage of the railroad rate commission law, and was sworn into the Senate on January 4, 1906.

La Follette made an immediate impact on the Senate. Although unsuccessful in promoting major reform legislation in early sessions, he received widespread attention for pressing for more stringent regulation of railroads and for his attack on the "Money Trust" while filibustering against a monetary bill proposed by Senate Republican leader Nelson W. Aldrich. His national reputation was further enhanced by his frequent Chautauqua speaking tours around the country (which began while he was governor of Wisconsin) and by the attention accorded him by reform journalists such as David Graham Phillips and Lincoln Steffens; the latter proposed a La Follette presidential campaign in 1908 on an independent ticket. While eschewing such a campaign, La Follette successfully assisted Progressive candidates in several states in their congressional races, thus establishing a solid core of reform-minded colleagues for the ensuing Congress. To publicize his causes (and with the hope of a solid financial return), he initiated *La Follette's Weekly Magazine* in January, 1909; he would continue the venture until his death, although it was more a financial liability than a success and was reorganized as a monthly in 1914.

> "*Publicity, discussion, and agitation are necessary to accomplish any work of lasting benefit.*"

La Follette and his new Senate allies challenged the Taft administration on several important issues and effectively established themselves as an insurgent wing of the Republican Party. By leading Senate Progressives in opposition to the 1909 Payne-Aldrich Tariff and in pressing for conservation measures and a program of direct democracy, La Follette earned the hostile attention of President William Howard Taft, who worked hard to unseat the Wisconsin senator in his 1910 bid for reelection. La Follette won easily and returned to Washington in 1911 determined to reconstruct the Republican Party along liberal lines. As much as any individual, he was responsible for the ideological split in the GOP that led to the formation of the Progressive Party in 1912. He was not the presidential nominee, however, as most of his supporters in the National Progressive Republican League (which he had founded in January, 1911) deserted him to support the popular former president Theodore Roosevelt; his candidacy was further impaired by a temporary breakdown he suffered while delivering a speech in February, 1912, before the annual banquet of the Periodical Publishers' Association in Philadelphia. He refused to endorse any candidate in 1912, but his speeches and magazine articles were generally supportive of the Democrat Woodrow Wilson.

La Follette's influence declined in the Democratic-controlled Senate of the early Wilson administration. While he supported some Wilson labor measures and managed to steer his La Follette Seamen's Act through Congress in 1915, he was critical of the president's blueprint for the Federal Reserve System, appointments to the Federal Trade Commission, and policy on racial segregation in the federal government. His greatest opposition to Wilson came in the area of foreign policy. Sharply critical of Wilson's increased military spending in 1915-1916, La Follette argued that such expenditures increased the profits of corporations at the expense of taxpayers and, ultimately, American security interests. Using the same argument, he voted against American entry into World War I and remained a leading antiwar spokesperson throughout. He also led fights for free speech and against censorship laws, and proposed new taxes on war profits to pay for the prosecution of the war. He voted against the Versailles Treaty in the Senate, characterizing it as reactionary in its treatment of the Soviet Union and in reinforcing colonialism in Ireland, India, and Egypt.

In the conservative Republican era that followed the war, La Follette fashioned a new political constituency among the farm and labor groups that emerged in political affairs in the early 1920's. Reacting to an agricultural depression and what many saw as an antilabor atmosphere, groups such as the American Federation of Labor, the railroad brotherhoods, the Nonpartisan League, and the American Farm Bureau Federation formed an alliance that resulted in the Conference for Progressive Political Action in 1922 and the Progressive Party in 1924. In a zealous campaign against Republican "normalcy," La Follette and Burton K. Wheeler, Progressive candidates for president and vice president, respectively, polled 4.8 million votes, approximately one in every six cast. La Follette's health was poor during this campaign, which was his last. He died of a heart attack on June 18, 1925, and was buried at Forest Hill Cemetery in Madison four days later.

SIGNIFICANCE

La Follette's campaigns, full of vitriol directed against "the interests" as opposed to "the people," largely reflected the Populist roots of mid-western Progressivism. In La Follette's view, the most obvious villain was large-scale corporate capitalism; his ideal was an open, competitive economic system he consistently championed the

La Follette addressing the Chautauqua assembly in Decatur, Illinois. (Library of Congress)

cause of individuals as voters, consumers, and small-business persons. His political solutions included a roster of Populist planks: the direct election of U.S. senators, direct primary elections, the graduated income tax, and public ownership of railroads, among others.

In opposing corporate growth, La Follette fought a losing battle against modernization; he was also responsible, however, for labor and agricultural programs that eased the adjustment of some groups to modern conditions. In addition, an important facet of the "Wisconsin Idea" he initiated as governor was the modern use of expert panels and commissions to make recommendations on legislation and regulatory activities. His reliance on faculty members of the University of Wisconsin (such as economists John Commons and Richard Ely) not only enhanced the university's reputation but also served as an example to reformers in other states.

Nicknamed Fighting Bob La Follette, the senator possessed notable personal characteristics that made him a symbol of the movement he led. His dynamic, aggressive style was complemented by a fearless quality that enabled him to challenge the leadership of his own party and to risk his career in opposing World War I. When engaged in a cause, his intensity was so great that he suffered several physical breakdowns during his political career. This combination of qualities contributed to a remarkable Senate career; in 1957, the Senate voted to recognize La Follette as one of the five outstanding members in Senate history.

Richard G. Frederick

Further Reading

Burgchardt, Carl R. *Robert M. La Follette, Sr.: The Voice of Conscience.* Foreword by Bernard K. Duffy. New York: Greenwood Press, 1992. Describes the political views of La Follette.

Conant, James K. *Wisconsin Politics and Government: America's Laboratory of Democracy.* Lincoln: University of Nebraska Press, 2006. Conant provides a history of the state's Progressivism, including the policies implemented during La Follette's gubernatorial administration.

La Follette, Belle Case, and Fola La Follette. *Robert M. La Follette: June 14* and *1855-June 18, 1925*. 2 vols. New York: Macmillan, 1953. Written by La Follette's wife and daughter. As an "insiders'" account, the book naturally tends to lack objectivity, but it is strengthened by the authors' intimate understanding of the subject. In addition, the book is meticulously researched and ably written with a wealth of detail.

La Follette, Robert M. *La Follette's Autobiography: A Personal Narrative of Political Experiences.* 1913. Reprint. Madison: University of Wisconsin Press, 1963. Originally published by La Follette as a campaign document for the 1912 presidential election. La Follette provides a detailed narrative of his political thought and activities, as well as his antagonism toward Theodore Roosevelt.

Margulies, Herbert F. *The Decline of the Progressive Movement in Wisconsin: 1890-1920.* Madison: State Historical Society of Wisconsin, 1968. Margulies finds that the Progressive movement in Wisconsin was well into decline before World War 1. He details how internal divisions among the Progressives (largely over La Follette's political tactics) led to their defeat by conservatives.

Thelen, David P. *The Early Life of Robert M. La Follette, 1855-1884.* Chicago: Loyola University Press, 1966. A brief examination of La Follette's formative years in Wisconsin, to his 1884 election to Congress.

---. *The New Citizenship: Origins of Progressivism in Wisconsin, 1885-1900.* Columbia: University of Missouri Press, 1972. Demonstrates how La Follette came into a movement already under way in Wisconsin in the late 1890's. The book is particularly good in its treatment of the social and political milieu in which reform ideas grew, largely out of issues of the 1893-1897 depression; these issues caused a "new civic consciousness" to develop among politicians and voters of diverse backgrounds.

---. *Robert M. La Follette and the Insurgent Spirit*. Boston: Little, Brown, 1976. Incisively relates La Follette's career to the course of Progressive insurgency in the Republican Party from the late 1890's to the 1920's. Thelen clearly delineates La Follette's positions and contrasts them with those of regular Republicans and Wilsonian Democrats.

Unger, Nancy C. *Fighting Bob La Follette: The Righteous Reformer*. Chapel Hill: University of North Carolina Press, 2000. Biography in which Unger weaves the story of La Follette's family life with his career accomplishments.

Weisberger, Bernard A. *The La Follettes of Wisconsin: Love and Politics in Progressive America*. Madison: University of Wisconsin Press, 1994. A description of the La Follette family and their political views.

BELVA A. LOCKWOOD

Lawyer and social reformer

Born: October 24, 1830; Royalton, New York
Died: May 19, 1917; Washington, D.C.
Area of Achievement: Law, social reform

Lockwood obtained passage of federal legislation giving women equal pay for equal work in government service in the United States. She also was the first woman granted the right to plead cases before the U.S. Supreme Court and was a committed activist for women's rights.

EARLY LIFE

Belva Ann Bennett was the second of the five children of Lewis Bennett and Hannah Green Bennett. She attended country schools and completed her education by the age of fifteen. Her father's opposition to her educational ambitions, as well as a lack of funds, led her to begin a career in teaching. She taught school for four years before marrying Uriah McNall, a local farmer. The young couple moved to the country near Gasport, where Belva gave birth to a daughter, Lura. When her husband died in a sawmill accident in 1853, Belva returned to school to further her education in order to support herself and her child.

Belva McNall sold the farm and entered Gasport Academy. She also continued to teach school. As a teacher, she experienced at first hand inequities toward women when she was offered half the salary paid to male teachers. Angry and upset, she left her daughter with her parents and entered Genessee College, where she studied law, political economy, and the U.S. Constitution. On June 27, 1857, she received a bachelor of science degree from the college that was to become Syracuse University.

In 1857, Belva McNall became headmistress of Lockport Union School, where her daughter studied. For the next four years, she supervised the staff, taught courses, and, despite conservative disapproval, encouraged gymnastics, public speaking, nature walks, and skating for young women. She also taught at the Gainesville Female Seminary and later became proprietor of the Female Seminary in Oswego, New York. In 1866, while in her middle thirties, Belva McNall, with her daughter Lura, left for Washington, D.C. Her profession was still teaching, but she had political ambitions that would eventually take her far beyond the classroom.

In 1867, Belva McNall opened a school of her own.

Belva A. Lockwood (Library of Congress)

On March 11, 1868, she married Ezekiel Lockwood, a dentist and former Baptist minister. Their only child, Jessie, died in infancy. Ezekiel Lockwood assumed the administrative duties of his wife's school so that she could pursue a law degree. Denied admission to Columbia, Georgetown, and Harvard because she was not only a woman but also a married one, Lockwood was finally accepted at the National

University Law School. She completed her studies in 1873 but was awarded her diploma only after she petitioned President Ulysses S. Grant, the school's ex officio president, to intervene on her behalf. Her husband, who had continued to supervise her school in Washington, was finally forced to close it because of his ill health. He died in 1877.

Life's Work

After judicial rules were changed and women were allowed to practice law in the District of Columbia, Belva Lockwood was admitted to the bar on September 24, 1873. She then embarked on a distinguished career in law. When one of her cases came before the Federal Court of Claims that winter, Lockwood was refused, because she was a woman, the right to plead a case. Her petition for admission to the Supreme Court of the United States (1876) was denied on the basis of custom, but Lockwood would not admit defeat. She petitioned Congress to pass a Declaratory Act or Joint Resolution "that no woman otherwise qualified, shall be debarred from practice before any United States Court on account of sex."

> "*I do not believe in sex distinction in literature, law, politics, or trade - or that modesty and virtue are more becoming to women than to men, but wish we had more of it everywhere.*"

Reasoning that if women had the right to practice law they were entitled to pursue legal matters through the highest courts in the country, Lockwood pushed enabling legislation through Congress. By means of energetic lobbying, and with the support of such pro-suffrage senators as Aaron A. Sargent of California and George F. Hoar of Massachusetts, Lockwood secured the passage of the Lockwood Bill, which permitted women to practice before the Supreme Court. On March 3, 1879, she became the first woman to be admitted to the Bar of the U.S. Supreme Court. Three days later, she was admitted to the U.S. Court of Claims.

A year later, on February 2, 1880, in a striking demonstration of her commitment to racial equality, Lockwood appeared before the Supreme Court of the United States and made a motion that Samuel R. Lowery, an African American, be allowed to practice before the Supreme Court. Lowery, who was the principal of the Huntsville Industrial University in Alabama, became the first black southerner to practice law before the Supreme Court of the United States.

Lockwood became a familiar sight in Washington as she pedaled throughout the city on "Challenge No. 2," an English tricycle that she introduced to the nation's capital. She rode the vehicle to the Capitol, the courts—wherever her work led her. By 1890, Lockwood was well established in her law career, specializing in pension and claims cases against the U.S. government.

It was this specialty that led her to one of the greatest legal triumphs of her career. The Cherokee Indian Nation secured Lockwood to represent it in claims against the U.S. government related to an 1891 treaty involving the sale and purchase of more than eight million acres of land known as the Cherokee Outlet. Lockwood was entrusted with defending nearly fifteen thousand Cherokee clients. After reviewing the numerous treaties and statutes that governed the history of the Cherokees, she filed a petition to uphold the claim of her Indian clients.

On March 20, 1905, the case of the Eastern and Emigrant Cherokees against the United States was decided before the Court of Claims. Following an impassioned argument by Lockwood, the chief justice agreed that the United States had broken and evaded the letter and spirit of its agreement with the Cherokees. Nevertheless, although he decreed that the Cherokees recover certain amounts due in the account rendered by the government, he could not bring himself to allow the full interest on those amounts. The case was appealed to the Supreme Court, where, on April 30, 1906, Lockwood again argued for the Indians and their rights. The court agreed and awarded the Cherokees five million dollars.

As a feminist, Lockwood did much to further women's rights. In 1867, she was one of the founders of Washington's first suffrage group, the Universal Franchise Association. During the 1870's and early 1880's, she was active in the Washington conventions of the National Woman Suffrage Association (NWSA). In January, 1871, Lockwood presented a memorial to the U.S. Senate on "The Right of Women to Vote."

Lockwood addressed congressional committees and drew up innumerable resolutions and bills that would help bring equality to women in the United States. She circulated a petition at the meetings of the National and American Woman Suffrage Associations in New York that hastened the passage, in 1872, of legislation giving women government employees equal pay for equal work. In 1873, she represented a woman in a divorce case, charging the defendant with drunken-ness, cruel treatment, desertion, and refusal to support. She won the case for her client, obtaining the decree of divorce and alimony with costs. Later, in 1896, as a member of a committee of the District Federation of Women's Clubs, she helped Ellen Spencer Mussey and others secure passage of a law liberalizing the property rights of married women and equal guardianship of their children in the District of Columbia. In 1903, she proposed the inclusion of woman suffrage clauses in the statehood bills for Oklahoma, Arizona, and New Mexico, which were then under consideration.

In 1872, Lockwood spoke at Cooper Union in New York on behalf of Victoria Woodhull's candidacy for president of the United States. Lockwood herself was nominated for president in 1884 by women representing the National Equal Rights Party. Her platform reflected her commitment to civil rights, temperance, and feminism. She encompassed equal rights for all, including African Americans, Indians, and immigrants. She advocated curtailment of the liquor traffic, reform in marriage and divorce laws, and universal peace. She flourished a banner inscribed on one side with the words "Women's Rights" and on the other with the word "Peace."

Although Lockwood's campaign alienated many members of the organized suffrage movement, including Susan B. Anthony, it generated much public interest. Astonishingly, she won the electoral vote of Indiana and half that of Oregon, nearly captured New Hampshire, and made a respectable showing in New York. A second campaign four years later was less successful. Her political aptitude was recognized by President Grover Cleveland, who sent her as the U.S. delegate to the Congress of Charities and Correction in Geneva, Switzerland.

Increasingly committed to the cause of world peace, Lockwood put much of her energy into peace organizations after the 1880's. One of the earliest members of the Universal Peace Union, Lockwood served at various times during the 1880's and 1890's on the union's executive committee and the editorial board of its paper, the Peacemaker, as a corresponding secretary and vice president, and as one of the union's chief lobbyists. She was the union's delegate to the International Peace Congress of 1889 and its successors; served as the American secretary of the International Bureau of Peace, founded in Berne in 1891; and served on the nominating committee for the Nobel Peace Prize. In all these organizations, she agitated for the arbitration principle as a means of settling world problems.

Lockwood remained politically active into her later years. She continued lecturing well into her eighties and even campaigned for Woodrow Wilson. In 1909, she was awarded an honorary LL.D. degree by Syracuse University, and in 1913, she was presented with an oil portrait of herself by the women of Washington, D.C. The portrait now hangs in the Art Gallery of the National Museum.

Following the death of her daughter Lura in 1894, Lockwood's financial fortunes collapsed, and her last years were spent in ill health and relative poverty. She died at George Washington University Hospital in 1917 and was buried in the Congressional Cemetery in Washington. The funeral service held in the Wesley Chapel of the Methodist Episcopal Church recalled the triumphs of her life, and the newspapers recorded her history. A scholarship was established in Lockwood's name, and a bust of Lockwood was unveiled by the Women's Bar Association of the District of Columbia to commemorate the seventy-fifth anniversary of her admission to the Supreme Court.

SIGNIFICANCE

Legally and socially, Belva A. Lockwood scored important victories for women. Marriage, she concluded, should be a civil contract in which property rights were equal. She rebelled against the law in the District of Columbia that could compel a man to support his illegitimate child but could not compel him to support his wife and his legitimate children. She worked for the reform of probate law and recognition of the rights of widows and orphans. Single-handedly, Lockwood moved the U.S. Congress to open the highest court to women lawyers. She fought for civil rights for all Americans. Up to the day she died, she worked for world peace.

Over the years of her practice, Lockwood gave aid, advice, and encouragement to women from all parts of the country who were attempting to become attorneys-at-law. Lockwood's hard-won battles, confidence, and fortitude are an inspiration to women throughout the world.

Diane C. Vecchio

FURTHER READING

Curti, Merle. *Peace or War*. New York: Garland, 1972. Curti discusses Lockwood's pacifism and her efforts to advance peace on the national and international scenes.

Fox, Mary Virginia. *Lady for the Defense: A Biography of Belva Lockwood*. New York: Harcourt Brace Jovanovich, 1975. A useful, relatively recent treatment of Lockwood's life and work.

Klebanow, Diana, and Franklin L. Jonas. *People's Lawyers: Crusaders for Justice in American History*. Armonk, N.Y.: M. E. Sharpe, 2003. Contains short biographical chapters on ten civil rights attorneys, including Lockwood. Features a biography of her life and career, a chronology of key events in her life, a review of her major cases, and an annotated bibliography.

Norgren, Jill. "Lockwood in '84." *Wilson Quarterly* 26, no. 4 (Autumn, 2002): 12. Examines Lockwood's 1884 presidential campaign, describing her personal life and career and her opinions of woman suffrage.

Stanton, Elizabeth Cady, et al., eds. *History of Woman Suffrage*. New York: Arno Press, 1969. Contains informative accounts of the NWSA's Washington conventions, 1870 to 1874, in volumes 2 through 4 (1882-1902) and useful chapters on the District of Columbia in volumes 3 and 4.

Stern, Madeleine. *We the Women*. New York: Schulte, 1963. This work contains the most complete account available of Belva Lockwood's life. Stern discusses, at length, Lockwood's most celebrated court cases, including her own quest to practice before the Supreme Court. This is the best source to consult regarding Lockwood's commitment to women's rights, civil rights, and pacifism.

Whitman, Alden, ed. *American Reformers*. New York: H. W. Wilson, 1985. A brief but fairly thorough account of Lockwood's life, highlighting her women's rights and peace activism.

HUEY LONG

Governor of Louisiana (1928-1932) and senator (1932-1935)

Born: August 30, 1893; Winnfield, Louisiana
Died: September 10, 1935; Baton Rouge, Louisiana
Area of Achievement: Politics, economic reform

As a governor and a senator, Long joined a sincere concern for the economic plight of the common people with an overwhelming desire to realize his ideas and plans to fashion a political career of great accomplishment for both good and ill.

EARLY LIFE

Huey Pierce Long was the second son of seven children born to Huey Long, Sr., and Caledonia Tison Long. All the children would receive at least part of a secondary education, an achievement insisted on by their mother. The Long family was not poor, as later stories would claim, chief among them told by Huey Long himself. The elder Long was actually a moderately prosperous farmer whose wealth consisted of land, crops, and animals rather than actual cash.

From his earliest days, Huey Long was restless and energetic; he would undertake any prank to be the center of attention. He read widely, chiefly in history, the works of William Shakespeare, and the Bible, but his favorite book was Alexandre Dumas, *père*'s *The Count of Monte Cristo* (1844-1845); he was impressed by the hero's tenacious quest for power and revenge.

In school, Huey was able and demonstrated early his remarkable memory. He often gained his wishes through sheer boldness and manipulation, as when he convinced the faculty to promote him a grade on his own

Huey Long (Library of Congress)

recommendation. In 1910, Huey left school without graduating. He worked for a while as a salesman, and he met his future wife, Rose McConnell, at a cake-baking contest. They were married in 1913 and had three sons and one daughter. In 1914, Huey entered Tulane Law School in New Orleans as a special student; he did not pursue a formal degree but instead concentrated on the courses needed for the bar exam, which he passed in 1915.

As a lawyer, Long took cases protecting the economic rights of the common folk, such as workers' compensation claims. He became convinced of the need to redistribute wealth and found precedence for this particularly in the Bible, which enjoined the periodic remission of debts and readjustment of riches.

Early in his twenties, Long looked much as he would for the remainder of his life. He was not quite six feet tall and generally weighed around 160 pounds; as he grew older, he had a tendency to become heavier. His face was full, even fleshy, with a round, prominent nose, dark eyes, a wide mouth, and a dimpled chin. Depending on his mood, his appearance could be comical or impressive. His reddish-brown hair was unruly, and he often ran his fingers through it while speaking; one strand usually drooped over his forehead. His most notable characteristic was his unbounded energy: constantly in motion, he ran rather than walked and spoke with an intensity that kept his listeners spellbound.

Long delighted in his courtroom battles, but early in life he had already settled on the path he intended to follow: state office, the governorship, the Senate, the presidency. In 1918, he decided that he was ready to begin.

> "*I know the hearts of the People because I have not colored my own. I know when I am right in my own conscience. I do not talk one way in the cloakroom and another way out here. I do not talk one way back there in the hills of Louisiana and another way here in the Senate.*"

LIFE'S WORK

In 1918, Louisiana was a state ruled by a few, powerful interests: a handful of large corporations, chief among them Standard Oil; the banks and railroads; and the remnants of the old plantation aristocracy. The average citizen earned little, received few services, traveled on wretched dirt roads, and sent his or her children to ill-funded schools. This was the situation that Long was determined to change.

He ran for a position on the State Railroad Commission, a regulatory body much like modern public service commissions. A tireless campaigner, Long spoke widely and also began the use of circulars short, vividly written handbills stating his views and attacking his opponent. He would make brilliant use of this technique throughout his career, always writing the copy himself, using a pithy style that appealed to the voters.

Elected to the Railroad Commission, Long vigorously attacked the dominant force in Louisiana political and economic life, the giant Standard Oil Company. In speeches, commission hearings, and circulars, he detailed the improper influence the company had on Louisiana state government, and, in 1921, Long was found "technically guilty" of libeling the state's governor. His fine was nominal, but his position as champion of the common folk of Louisiana was firmly established. In 1923, he ran for governor.

He had none of the traditional supporters a candidate of that time was careful to recruit: no banks, no sugar barons, no railroads, no corporations, no political machine. The small, elite group that had dominated Louisiana politics for a century was against Long, and Long was fundamentally hostile to their rule. He was opposed by the only large corporation then in the South Standard Oil and by the region's only true big city machine the Old Regulars in New Orleans.

With such a combination against him, it is not surprising that Long lost in 1923, but the size of his vote revealed that Huey Long and his ideas of economic and political reforms had substantial approval across the state. This fact was evident in 1924, when he was reelected to the Public Service Commission (the new name of the Railroad Commission) by an 80 percent majority. When he ran again for governor in 1928, he won decisively, and his victory signaled a new day for Louisiana.

As governor, Long moved to implement programs that would benefit the majority of Louisiana residents: paved roads and highways, public bridges, free textbooks to students (not schools, thus bypassing the church-state controversy in largely Roman Catholic Louisiana), and increased taxes on corporations and business to pay for these programs. Remarkably, most of his agenda was enacted during his first year in office, a tribute to his own personal magnetism, his brilliant political skills, and his immense popular support. His enemies were repulsed, rather than convinced, by this support. When Long asked the legislature for a tax on the huge profits of Standard Oil, the result was an effort to impeach him in April, 1929. The charges, many of them absurd, were all rejected. After the impeachment fight, Huey Long was stronger than ever; he secured a tax on Standard Oil and expanded the reach of his programs.

It was during this time that his political strength and the efforts of his enemies combined to undermine much of the idealist nature of Long. Realizing that his opponents would use any tactics to destroy him and wreck his programs, he came to believe that he must crush his adversaries, leaving them no option but to join him or face extinction. It was also at this time that the fabled Long machine came into being: a powerful institution that reached into every parish in Louisiana, able to dispense jobs, help friends, harm foes, and, most important, get out the vote. One by one, the existing political factions were absorbed; the last to submit was the once-mighty Old Regular machine in New Orleans, which finally yielded to Long in the mid-1930's.

Long became known as the Kingfish, a name adopted from the popular "Amos and Andy" radio program. It perfectly suited his style of leadership: a combination of low comedy and high political acumen. His opponents sneered at him as a buffoon, only to realize too late that they had underestimated the Kingfish.

In 1930, Long's term as governor ended with an impressive list of accomplishments: paved roads and public bridges, better hospital facilities, the expansion of Louisiana State University into a nationally recognized educational institution, more and better public education, free schoolbooks, improved port facilities and an airport for New Orleans, and, symbolic of it all, a new state capitol building. Typically, the construction was a modern, up-to-date skyscraper, visually demonstrating how Huey Long had brought Louisiana into the twentieth century.

Unable to serve a second term as governor, Long was elected to the United States Senate in 1930, but for the remainder of his life, Long remained the effective, if not official, chief executive of Louisiana, commanding special sessions of the legislature whenever he pleased and ordering passage of the laws he desired. This heavy-handed, unmasked expression of power was the most unpleasant aspect of Long's career; apparently he had reached the conclusion probably confirmed by the impeachment battle that his enemies had forced him to employ any means, however questionable or undemocratic, to achieve his high-minded and progressive ideals.

Long used the Senate to espouse with fervent intensity his plans to redistribute wealth in the United States. Pointing out that a minority of the population owned the majority of the riches, Long urged taxes that would limit both earned and inherited wealth and spread the wealth among everyone. Every Man a King was his slogan, and he used it as the title of his 1933 autobiography. Spread the Wealth clubs were organized throughout the country to support the Long program.

Long supported Franklin D. Roosevelt for president in 1932, but the honeymoon with Roosevelt soon ended. The president moved too slowly for Long, and Long was often an annoyance, sometimes a threat to the president, who was trying to hold a Depression-shaken country together. Long made some positive efforts increasing federal banking insurance, for example but was generally opposed to Roosevelt's plans as being too timid and too superficial. He grew more open in his plans to defeat Roosevelt in 1936 by supporting a Republican or third-party candidate, then sweeping into office himself in 1940 as the only man who could save the country.

While involved in national affairs, Long remained closely connected with events in Louisiana. He had his selected governor summon sessions of the state legislature to pass bills that Long wrote, rushed through committee, and shepherded through the final vote. His efforts were increasingly aimed at overawing his opponents; during the 1934 mayoral elections in New Orleans, he ordered out the state militia to control the balloting. Such high-handed techniques, combined with his vitriolic attacks on the popular Roosevelt, began to erode his support. Undeterred, he pressed onward. In 1934, he had a series of radical measures introduced into the Louisiana legislature, which were a preview of what he soon hoped to attempt on a national level. His consistent theme had not changed: He urged economic opportunity for all, but his reliance on brute power had greatly increased.

There had always been strong, indeed violent, opposition to Long in Louisiana. He had fought too many entrenched interests and helped too many of the poor and oppressed for it to be otherwise. Now this opposition began to organize and become dangerous. The Square Deal League raised an armed force that seized control of the Baton Rouge jail in early 1935; it dispersed only after a siege by the state militia. Later that year, the Minute Men of Louisiana formed, claiming to have ten thousand members, all ready to end the rule of the Kingfish, by murder if necessary.

It was in such a climate of violence that Huey Long's life and career ended. On the evening of September 8, 1935, Long was confronted in the state capitol by a young doctor, Carl Austin Weiss, who apparently hated Long for both personal and political reasons; there is no evidence that he was part of any organized plot. Weiss fired two shots at Long and was immediately gunned down himself by Long's bodyguards. The wounded Long was rushed to the hospital. An operation to save him failed, and on September 10, 1935, Huey Long died. His last words were, "God, don't let me die. I have so much to do."

SIGNIFICANCE

In his 1928 race for governor, Long gave a speech that so well expressed his political philosophy that he reprinted it later in his biography, *Every Man a King* (1933). He began by referring to Henry Wadsworth Longfellow's poem "Evangeline," and then continued:

> But Evangeline is not the only one who has waited here in disappointment. Where are the schools that you have waited for your children to have, that have never come? Where are the roads and highways that you send your money to build, that are no nearer now than ever before? Where are the institutions to care for the sick and disabled? Evangeline wept bitter tears in her disappointment, but it lasted through only one lifetime. Your tears in this country, around this oak, have lasted for generations. Give me the chance to dry the eyes of those who still weep here!

The bright side of Huey Long's career and legacy was that he answered the needs of the people of Louisiana for the schools, roads, institutions, and services that they so desperately needed. He broke a century-old tradition of rule by the few and wealthy, and he made the government benefit all the people.

On the dark side, however, he turned the state legislature into his personal tool and the state government into an extension of the Long machine. His supporters have insisted that he was driven to these tactics by the implacable opposition of his foes. There is truth to this; Huey Long was intensely despised and feared by many in Louisiana, often for the good that he had done. Long was not the first popular leader to use questionable methods to obtain worthwhile ends.

During his career, Huey Long was passionately loved and hated; he was called both a fascist and a friend of the common man. His enemies admitted his political brilliance; his friends acknowledged his irregular methods. His many accomplishments have never resolved some basic questions: Was he the best leader to arise in Louisiana, or its worst political disaster? Had he lived, would he have proven to be a national figure of genius or the architect of a homegrown fascist state? These puzzles have no answer or too many answers and the life and career of Huey Long remain an American enigma.

Michael Witkoski

FURTHER READING

Brinkley, Alan. *Voices of Protest: Huey Long, Father Coughlin, and the Great Depression.* New York: Alfred A. Knopf, 1982. Helps to place Long in the context of the economic and social situation of the 1930's, when the country was wracked by depression and a number of theories competed with Share the Wealth and Roosevelt's New Deal as solutions to the United States' economic problems.

Cortner, Richard C. *The Kingfish and the Constitution: Huey Long, the First Amendment, and the Emergence of Modern Press Freedom in America.* Westport, Conn.: Greenwood Press, 1996. Examines Long in relation to freedom of the press.

Davis, Forrest. *Huey Long: A Candid Biography.* New York: Dodge, 1935. Reprint. Ann Arbor, Mich.: University Microfilms, 1969. A contemporary portrait of Long, this biography is more balanced than most produced at the time. Davis used his extensive interviews with Long.

Dethloft, Henry, ed. *Huey P. Long: Southern Demagogue or American Democrat?* Lexington, Mass.: D. C. Heath, 1967. Part of the Problems in American Civilization series and contains essays and articles by a variety of authors, including Huey Long and historians such as T. Harry Williams and V. O. Key, Jr. A good source for sampling the intense emotions that Long and his program could arouse.

Deutsch, Hermann. *The Huey Long Murder Case.* New York: Doubleday, 1963. While this work concentrates on Long's assassination, it does provide some helpful background on his political career, especially in relationship to the Louisiana legislature.

Hair, William Ivy. *The Kingfish and His Realm: The Life and Times of Huey P. Long.* Baton Rouge: Louisiana State University Press, 1991. A biography of Long that looks at the range of his power.

Long, Huey. *Every Man a King*. New Orleans, La.: National Books, 1933. Reprint. Chicago: Quadrangle Books, 1964. This reprint of Long's 1933 autobiography was edited with an excellent introduction by T. Harry Williams. The autobiographical section can be lean on facts and naturally stops with Long in midcareer, but it offers a fascinating glimpse of his energetic personality.

Opotowsky, Stan. *The Longs of Louisiana*. New York: E. P. Dutton, 1960. A general biography of the Long family and their roles in state, regional, and national politics. It clearly shows that, while Huey Long was the most brilliant politician of his family, others shared some of his gifts.

White, Richard D., Jr. *Kingfish: The Reign of Huey P. Long*. New York: Random House, 2006. Well-researched and readable biography recounting the details of Long's life and political career.

Williams, T. Harry. *Huey Long*. New York: Alfred A. Knopf, 1969. This is the definitive biography of Long, unlikely to be surpassed. Williams worked extensively with contemporaries of Long, including many members of the Long organization, who spoke remarkably freely. The book is excellently researched and extremely well written; it is a classic of modern American biography.

JOHN MARSHALL

Chief Justice of the Supreme Court (1801-1835)

Born: September 24, 1755; Germantown, Colony of Virginia
Died: July 6, 1835; Philadelphia, Pennsylvania
Area of Achievement: Law, politics

During his long tenure as chief justice of the United States, Marshall used his considerable intelligence, personal charm, and political skills to make the Court the chief arbiter of constitutional doctrine, firmly establishing what had been the weakest branch of the national government as an equal with Congress and the executive.

EARLY LIFE

John Marshall was the eldest of fifteen children. His father was a planter of moderate means who in time became a wealthy leading citizen of Virginia and later of Kentucky, serving in numerous official capacities in both states. Through Mary, the Marshall family was connected to most of the important families of Virginia. Growing to manhood among the landed gentry molded John Marshall's character, yet his too casual and occasionally sloppy appearance was at odds with his background. John Marshall's education was a typical blend, for the sons of southern colonial gentry, of intermittent and limited formal instruction by tutors in the classics and informal instruction by his parents in reading, writing, and elementary mathematics. The few books in the family library included several on law and served as Marshall's introduction to the subject; from his family's participation in state and local government, he learned about politics.

Only nineteen years old in 1774, when the chain of events beginning with the Boston Tea Party led to the American War of Independence, John Marshall followed his father's example and enthusiastically took the patriots' side in the quarrel with England. He was a popular first lieutenant in the local militia when the fighting started but followed his father into the Continental army as soon as it was formed. He served with distinction until independence was nearly won, rising to the rank of captain and becoming something of a hero. He fought in several

John Marshall (Wikimedia Commons)

battles, was wounded, and was with George Washington at Valley Forge.

During a lull, while stationed in Virginia, Marshall studied law and other subjects for three months at the College of William and Mary in Williamsburg. His law teacher was George Wythe, one of the most respected colonial lawyers, with whom Thomas Jefferson, Marshall's cousin, had also studied. Although short, Marshall's legal education was better than most, because there were no law schools in America. The College of William and Mary was one of the few to offer any law classes as part of the undergraduate curriculum. Most lawyers learned only by self-study while working as a clerk in a practicing attorney's office. During these months of study, he also met and began courting Mary Willis Ambler, known all of her life as Polly.

Marshall had passed the bar examination and received his license to practice from Governor Thomas Jefferson in August of 1780. He returned to Oak Hill in Fauquier County, the family estate, to begin his career. In April of 1782, Marshall was elected to represent his county in the House of Delegates. In the state capital, Richmond, Marshall was introduced to a world beyond that of the country lawyer and landed gentry, and his ambition to be part of it was fired. Marshall renewed his courtship of Polly Ambler, whose family now lived in Richmond, and they were married on January 3, 1783, when he was twenty-seven and she was nearly seventeen. Marshall decided to move to Richmond to practice and became a leading member of the bar within three years.

LIFE'S WORK

The man who had joined the mainstream of Virginia's affairs was a commanding, lean figure, six feet in height, black-haired, with a nearly round face and strong, penetrating black eyes, complimented by a smile that seemed to disarm everyone. Honest, capable of sustained hard work, and possessed of a probing intellect, Marshall was also a gregarious man who loved games and athletic activity and who radiated a captivating friendliness. By nature, he was a gracious person, although he did not have a polished manner. As happened with so many patriots who actively participated in the military and political events of the War of Independence, Marshall had acquired a deep sense of nationalism from his travels through the former colonies and the comradeship of men from all parts of the emerging nation. The fact that this new nation should survive and prosper became a concern of Marshall for the remainder of his life.

> "*The people made the Constitution, and the people can unmake it. It is the creature of their own will, and lives only by their will.*"

Marshall worked hard to build his Richmond practice. He held various official positions with the state and local governments but refused any that would seriously interfere with his private law work. A major reason was Polly's poor health after 1786. Their second child died shortly after birth, and then Polly miscarried a few months later. The shock of these two tragedies brought on a nervous breakdown from which Polly never totally recovered. For the remainder of their long married life and through the eight children yet to come, Polly could not abide crowds or noise. It was necessary to have servants to perform the routine household duties, and Marshall personally did the family marketing.

The condition of the nation worried Marshall throughout the 1780's. He thought the national government was too weak to protect the new nation from foreign threats or to restrain state governments from abuses of power. For this reason, he wholeheartedly supported the work of the Constitutional Convention of 1787 to create a "more perfect union." Elected as delegate to Virginia's special convention to decide whether to adopt the new national constitution, he spoke strongly for it. Once the issue was favorably resolved, however, and the new national government instituted under the leadership of his idol, George Washington, Marshall's attention returned to the practice of law.

Marshall refused all offers of appointment to national office, including the cabinet, until 1797, when he accepted what he thought would be a short-term diplomatic appointment from President John Adams. When Marshall returned to the United States in July of 1798, he was feted as a national hero for his part in what had become known as the XYZ affair. George Washington persuaded him to capitalize on his public recognition and run for a seat in the House of Representatives. Washington had persuaded him to agree to leave his lucrative private practice by convincing him that the republic was in danger from the development of political factionalism.

In the conventional wisdom of his day, Marshall believed that political factions were a threat to the smooth and stable operation of a republican government. Factionalism stirred up the masses to interfere in the affairs of government, best left to the better educated and propertied gentry, who alone could be expected to function from motives of civic virtue and on the basis of practical common sense. Although willing to fight for fundamental principle, Marshall was a man who otherwise believed in moderation and compromise on matters of policy; he saw that political polarization, if unchecked, would eventually destroy the nation. In Congress, he became the leading House spokesperson for President Adams's moderate Federalist administration. In recognition of his service he was promoted to secretary of state in 1800, and, when the Federalists lost the election that year, to chief justice of the United States in 1801. Marshall would remain chief justice until 1835, the year he died.

The Supreme Court in 1801 had serious problems with low public esteem, low pay, poor morale, and rapid turnover of justices. The Court had developed no corporate sense of identity. Marshall's first innovation was to persuade the justices not to give their written opinions *seriatim*—that is, each justice writing his own. Instead, in most cases Marshall persuaded the justices to confer until they reached a consensus so that a single opinion could be issued for the majority. Marshall correctly reasoned that the Court's decisions would be much more authoritative if the majority spoke with one voice. The institution of this practice was the single most important reason for the rise of the Supreme Court to equality with the other branches of government. To facilitate the development of collegiality, he also encouraged the justices to lodge at the same Washington, D.C., inn during the one-to two-month yearly sessions.

A distinctive feature of the American system of government is the power of its courts to declare actions by other parts of the government unconstitutional. This power, called judicial review, had not yet been exercised except by some state courts (with mixed results) when Marshall became chief justice. The first instance of the power's use arose out of the fury of President Jefferson and his party over the famous Midnight Appointments of President Adams in 1801, in the case of *Marbury v. Madison* (1803). The case involved a request that the Supreme Court issue a writ of *mandamus* (a court order) to Secretary of State James Madison. The Court's decision, written by Marshall, first lectured Jefferson and his party on their failing in the practice of principles of good government and then announced that the writ of *mandamus* requested in this case could not be issued because section 13 of the Judiciary Act of 1789, which gave the Court the power to issue the writ, was unconstitutional.

This self-denial by the Court was a shrewd political maneuver. In its first big constitutional case under Marshall, the Court had exercised judicial review and declared an act of Congress unconstitutional, and there was nothing anyone could do about it. It was also a brave act in the face of the enormous anti-judiciary bias of the Jeffersonians. Although the Court did not declare another act of Congress or the president unconstitutional during Marshall's tenure, it did so for state laws on a number of occasions. Thus, the practice as well as the principle of judicial review was established.

After 1805, the political pressure on the Court decreased, partly because the government's attention was increasingly focused on foreign affairs and partly because, under Marshall, the Court had acquired greater respect and, therefore, greater independence. The work of the Court now centered more on two objectives: the supremacy of the national government and the preservation and protection of rights. The two were directly related in Marshall's view.

The point in establishing the supremacy of the federal Constitution, statutes, and treaties over the states was to counter the threat to inalienable rights from abuses of power by the states. Marshall perceived this as the most serious threat of all. For example, the Constitution prohibited the states from interfering with the obligations of the parties to a contract, yet many states were doing just that in numerous ways. In a long line of cases interpreting the "contract clause," Marshall's court fashioned from it a powerful defense of the private citizens' right to whatever property they had come by honestly. In the famous trial of Aaron Burr for treason, Marshall interpreted the Constitution to prevent the charge of treason from becoming an instrument to punish political enemies.

In *Gibbons v. Ogden* (1824), Marshall's court struck down a law creating a steamboat monopoly, not only because it infringed on federal power to regulate interstate commerce, but also because the Constitution's framers had given the commerce power to Congress in order to establish the whole of the United States as a free trade area and the steamboat monopoly violated freedom of commerce. The issue of slavery presented a serious problem for Marshall; on one hand, the slave owner's property right had to be protected, like any other property right, but on the other hand, Marshall thought that black slaves had the same rights as white people. It seemed to him that the only solution to this dilemma was the

American Colonization Society. This organization hoped to remove all black slaves from the United States to Liberia, Africa.

The Jackson years disheartened Marshall. He hated the viciously partisan character assassinations of the Jackson campaign, and he feared that universal manhood suffrage, a major Jacksonian goal, could only result in politicians pandering to the prejudices of the common people. He also believed the states' rights orientation of the Jackson appointees to the Court threatened all of his work to establish the supremacy of the Constitution, guarantees of rights, and the restraint of state uses of power.

As Marshall increasingly saw himself as a relic of the past, he found it necessary to compromise on some issues to save at least something of his work. When Polly died in 1831, he was desolate and felt very much alone. There were, however, some positive moments. When Jackson stood up for the supremacy of the national government in 1832 against South Carolina's attempt to nullify a national tariff, Marshall relented somewhat in his dislike of the old general. Although unable to stop Georgia from brutally removing the Cherokee Indians from the state and humiliated at seeing the state of Georgia flout the Supreme Court's decision forbidding the removal—the Court had no means of enforcing it and the president would not—a remedy was provided. President Jackson's Force Bill, passed by Congress in connection with the Nullification Crisis, provided the Court with its own officials to enforce future decisions.

In 1835, Marshall was seventy-nine when he suffered a spinal injury in a stagecoach accident from which he never fully recovered. He also suffered from serious liver trouble. When told that his time was short, he put his affairs in order and, on July 6, 1835, he died.

SIGNIFICANCE

Marshall built better than he knew. He was mistaken in his beliefs about political parties and the superior governing abilities of the gentry, but practices he established for the Court and many of his judicial doctrines are still important. Supreme Court majorities continued after Marshall generally to speak with one voice. His example of collegial leadership remains the standard for chief justices. The defense of property rights based on the contract clause and his interpretation of the commerce clause contributed significantly to the legal environment necessary for the free enterprise economic system to flourish. Treason remains only a crime and not a weapon against the enemies of whatever politicians are in power.

In raising the visibility and authority of the Supreme Court to a position of equality with the other branches, Marshall created a potent force for political stability within the American system of government. This was his most important achievement. The government's ability to correct its mistakes through the Supreme Court's exercise of the power of judicial review inspires confidence and trust in all levels of the system. The Supreme Court became the guardian and final arbiter of the Constitution, establishing the primacy of the constitutional principles of the nation's founders. In 1801, when John Marshall became chief justice, none of this was certain to evolve, but the fundamentals were all in place when he left, thirty-four years later. During that time, he wrote 519 of the Court's 1,106 opinions, including 36 of the 62 involving major constitutional questions. John Marshall had a major hand in creating the most balanced and equable judicial system in the world.

Richard L. Hillard

FURTHER READING

Baker, Leonard. *John Marshall: A Life in Law*. New York: Macmillan, 1974. A good biography of Marshall's professional life; includes some private matters as well. Explains many details about how Marshall and the legal system in his time worked. Also explains his reasoning in his Supreme Court decisions.

Baxter, Maurice G. *Daniel Webster and the Supreme Court*. Amherst: University of Massachusetts Press, 1966. A superb and scholarly examination of the relationship between Daniel Webster, one of the leading constitutional lawyers of his day and a Marshall supporter, and the development of judicial doctrine by the Supreme Court during much of Marshall's tenure as chief justice.

Beveridge, Albert J. *The Life of John Marshall*. 4 vols. Boston: Houghton Mifflin, 1916-1919. Detailed and wonderfully told story, yet sadly lacking in balance, making Marshall seem a heroic savior of his nation against arch-villains. Even so, these four volumes are still the starting point for Marshall scholarship.

Faulkner, Robert K. *The Jurisprudence of John Marshall*. Princeton, N.J.: Princeton University Press, 1968. Definitive examination of the political philosophy of Marshall. Traces the origins to a mix of the theories of John Locke, American nationalism, and the respect for landed gentry typical of the classical Romans, especially Cicero.

Horwitz, Morton J. *The Transformation of American Law: 1780-1860*. Cambridge, Mass.: Harvard University Press, 1977. Mentions Marshall only briefly. Probably the best one-volume legal history of the era to date. Emphasis is on the transformation of English law in the colonies into a modern national legal system and how this transformation aided economic development.

Newmyer, R. Kent. *John Marshall and the Heroic Age of the Supreme Court*. Baton Rouge: Louisiana State University Press, 2001. Focuses on Marshall's legal philosophies, analyzing some of his Supreme Court decisions and placing his beliefs in historical context. Describes how Marshall's experiences as a soldier in the Revolutionary War, his legal career, and his childhood in Virginia influenced his constitutional thinking.

---. *The Supreme Court Under Marshall and Taney*. New York: Thomas Y. Crowell, 1968. A succinct but thorough and perceptive study of the Marshall Court in the context of the people and events of the times. The Marshall chapters concentrate on Marshall as chief justice, and little of his personal life is included.

Robarge, David. *A Chief Justice's Progress: John Marshall from Revolutionary Virginia to the Supreme Court*. Westport, Conn.: Greenwood Press, 2000. Focuses on the formative influences in Marshall's life before he joined the U.S. Supreme Court, including his upbringing in Virginia, military service, legal career, and experiences as a federalist and diplomat.

Simon, James F. *What Kind of Nation: Thomas Jefferson, John Marshall, and the Epic Struggle to Create a United States*. New York: Simon & Schuster, 2002. Describes how Marshall, a proponent of federalism, and Jefferson, an advocate of states rights, engaged in a lengthy competition to determine the direction of the newly created United States.

Stites, Francis N. *John Marshall: Defender of the Constitution*. Boston: Little, Brown, 1981. This is an excellent short biography of Marshall. Well researched and carefully written, it brings together in a reasonable synthesis the voluminous scholarship available on Marshall.

THURGOOD MARSHALL

Lawyer, judge, and Supreme Court justice (1967-1991)

Born: July 2, 1908; Baltimore, Maryland
Died: January 24, 1993; Bethesda, Maryland
Areas of Achievement: Civil rights; Government and politics; Law

Marshall had a long and distinguished career as an attorney representing the National Association for the Advancement of Colored People (NAACP) and as a federal judge. His nomination as a Supreme Court justice in 1967 marked the first appointment of an African American to sit on the highest court in the United States.

EARLY LIFE

Thurgood Marshall was born in 1908 in Baltimore, Maryland. His ancestors included a great-grandfather who was a slave in Maryland in the mid-nineteenth century. Marshall's paternal grandfather fought as a freedman in the Union Army. The grandfather took the name Thoroughgood, which was later given to Marshall. At seventeen,

Thurgood Marshall (National Archives and Records Administration)

Marshall entered Lincoln University in Pennsylvania, a historically black school. After graduation, he began attending Howard University Law School in 1931. His application to the University of Maryland Law School was rejected, presumably on racial grounds.

Marshall was deeply influenced by Howard's president, Charles Hamilton Houston. One of Houston's goals was to challenge the principle of "separate but equal" education for African Americans, an aim that would be realized—with a direct contribution by Marshall himself—some twenty years later. Marshall graduated magna cum laude with his law degree in 1933. As a young lawyer in his twenties, Marshall gained national attention when he won a court case that granted a black student admission to the same law school that had turned Marshall himself down, the University of Maryland.

LIFE'S WORK

In 1936, Marshall became a lawyer for the National Association for the Advancement of Colored People (NAACP). In 1940, he won his first victory before the Supreme Court (*Chambers v. Florida*, a case that reversed the convictions of three African American men charged with murder of a white man). This was the first of twenty-nine Supreme Court cases that he would win before becoming a judge himself.

Marshall's writings during these years reflect his dedication to equal rights for all racial groups. His 1939 article "Equal Justice Under the Law" appeared in *The Crisis*, the publication of the NAACP. During World War II, the *Lawyers Guild Review* published his article calling for direct governmental action to stop discrimination against African Americans. Similarly, during the Korean War, Marshall wrote (again in *The Crisis*) about discriminatory practices involving African American servicemen in zones of combat.

Marshall's role in the watershed 1954 U.S. Supreme Court decision *Brown v. Board of Education*, which outlawed segregation in public schools, established his importance in the Civil Rights movement. Seven years elapsed before his potential as a federal judge was to be recognized. After *Brown v. Board of Education*, Marshall continued to express his views on how its integration goals should be handled. From the outset, he supported gradual implementation. In the first months of 1956, however, a faction in Congress (spearheaded by southern legislators) challenged the Supreme Court's use of its constitutional authority. Marshall took his defense of the 1954 ruling into the very southern areas that were resisting integration. At a North Carolina rally of the NAACP, he reaffirmed that, although circumstances in each local setting would require local negotiations on *how* integration would be achieved, there was to be no question that it *would* be achieved.

Opponents of integrated schools still tried to rally resistance to the 1954 ruling. Some contended that integrated schools would lead to an increase in marriages between African Americans and whites. Marshall's counterpoint was that marriage—unlike tax-supported education—was a matter of personal choice, over which legislators and judges had little say. Although controversy continued, Marshall had some satisfaction when, in its 1967 decision in *Loving v. Virginia*, the Supreme Court declared laws prohibiting racial intermarriage unconstitutional. By that time, Marshall had joined the federal judiciary, first as a circuit court judge and then, in the very year of *Loving v. Virginia*, the Supreme Court itself.

President John F. Kennedy appointed Marshall to the

Holding a poster against racial bias in Mississippi in 1956, are four of the most active leaders in the NAACP movement, from left: Henry L. Moon, director of public relations; Roy Wilkins, executive secretary; Herbert Hill, labor secretary; and Marshall, special counsel. (Library of Congress)

Marshall's Role in *BROWN V. BOARD OF EDUCATION*

The 1954 U.S. Supreme Court decision *Brown v. Board of Education* marked a turning point in the history of civil rights in the United States. Thurgood Marshall, then chief counsel for the National Association for the Advancement of Colored People (NAACP), argued the case before the high court. In a unanimous decision on May 17, 1954, the court ended the longstanding, legally recognized principle of "separate but equal" education for white and black students in public schools.

Oliver Brown and other African American parents in Topeka, Kansas, sued the school system for refusing to allow them to enroll their children in white schools. With the help of the NAACP, the parents challenged an 1879 Kansas law that permitted but did not require separate schools for black and white pupils. Marshall and other NAACP attorneys prepared to present *Brown v. Board of Education* to the Supreme Court by carefully studying legal precedents set in previous cases to determine which elements offered the greatest chance of success. They studied in particular failed desegregation lawsuits. Ultimately, Marshall's arguments before the court were successful and, in one history-making case, he helped break down racial barriers that had been challenged unsuccessfully in earlier cases. Those barriers fell by logical extension of the *Brown v. Board of Education* precedent in the decades that followed.

U.S. Court of Appeals Second Circuit in New York in 1961. For four years, Marshall served as an appellate judge until Kennedy's successor, Lyndon B. Johnson, appointed him U.S. solicitor general. During his service in this post, Marshall won fourteen of nineteen cases in which he served as representative of the government. It is widely believed that Johnson viewed this appointment as an interim step toward history-making integration in all levels of education and government: the appointment of the first African American to the Supreme Court.

After being nominated by Johnson, Marshall's appointment to the Supreme Court was confirmed on August 30, 1967. Although the Senate vote showed strong support (sixty-nine in favor, eleven opposed), the confirmation process was considerably more drawn out than the two previous confirmations of Arthur Goldberg and Abe Fortas.

Marshall's early years on the Supreme Court aligned him with the then-majority liberal wing: Chief Justice Earl Warren and justices William Brennan, William Douglas, and Fortas. Until the years of the Nixon presidency ushered in a conservative reorientation of the Supreme Court, Marshall was able to maintain his reputation for liberal-leaning positions. Marshall's vote helped bring about victories for liberal causes during the 1960's. These included First Amendment freedom of speech issues and cases supporting protection of the underprivileged.

> "*America must get to work. In the chilled climate in which we live, we must go against the prevailing winds. We must dissent from the indifference. We must dissent from the apathy. We must dissent from the fear, the hatred, and the mistrust. We must dissent from a nation that buried its head in the sand waiting in vain for the needs of its poor, its elderly, and its sick to disappear and just blow away. We must dissent from a government that has left its young without jobs, education, or hope. We must dissent from the poverty of vision and timeless absence of moral leadership. We must dissent, because America can do better, because America has no choice but to do better.*"

As late as 1989, Marshall continued to encourage jurists to recognize that racial equality and civil rights remained a major challenge for their profession. In his remarks before the Second Circuit Judicial Conference, a speech titled "The Future of Civil Rights," Marshall drew attention to the need for conscious cooperation between the legislative and judicial branches in pursuing civil rights legislation and protecting ground gained over the previous two and a half decades.

A major issue that may have influenced Marshall's decision to retire from the Supreme Court in 1991 was the longstanding debate over the death penalty. In a number of cases before the court, Marshall had registered his opposition to capital punishment. He was particularly disturbed by procedures (which varied from state to state) governing last-minute stays of execution. What might have been a crowning blow was his dissenting vote in a capital punishment case (*Payne v. Tennessee*) delivered on June 27, 1991, the very day that Marshall announced his retirement. Marshall died less than two years later, on January 24, 1993.

Significance

Marshall stands as an important symbol of the Civil Rights movement within the judicial system. He made a major stand for integration as the chief counsel for the NAACP and lead attorney in the landmark *Brown v. Board of Education* case. Later, he personally integrated the Supreme Court. His work had a far-reaching impact on American society throughout the second half of the twentieth century and beyond.

Byron Cannon

Further Reading

Ball, Howard. *A Defiant Life: Thurgood Marshall and the Persistence of Racism in America.* New York: Crown, 1998. Well-documented, authoritative biography of Marshall, organized by issues, including civil rights, affirmative action, First Amendment freedoms, and discrimination in the U.S. military.

Tushnet, Mark V. *Making Civil Rights Law: Thurgood Marshall and the Supreme Court, 1936-1961.* New York: Oxford University Press, 1994. Focuses on Marshall's involvement as an attorney representing African American interests in defining and defending civil rights.

---. *Making Constitutional Law: Thurgood Marshall and the Supreme Court, 1961-1991.* New York: Oxford University Press, 1997. Offers a review of Marshall's position on several major issues, such as school desegregation and capital punishment, while on the Supreme Court.

_____, ed. *Thurgood Marshall: His Speeches, Writings, Arguments, Opinions, and Reminiscences.* Chicago: Lawrence Hill Books, 2001. This collection of primary documents (and a personal interview done in 1977), some aimed at the broader public and published in journals, others delivered before an audience of peers in the legal profession, covers a wide range of issues.

Vilma Socorro Martínez

Lawyer, activist, and ambassador

Born: October 17, 1943; San Antonio, Texas
Area of Achievement: Law; activism; diplomacy

Martinez was the first female president of the Mexican American Legal Defense and Educational Fund (MALDEF) and has enjoyed an illustrious career as a Latino civil rights attorney, labor attorney, and the first female ambassador to Argentina.

Early Life

Vilma Socorro Martínez (soh-KOH-roh mahr-TEE-nehz) was born to Salvador, a construction worker, and Marina Martínez in San Antonio, Texas, on October 17, 1943. She grew up in a Spanish-speaking household and did not learn English until she entered school. Her family served as a source of strength and support throughout her youth.

During Martínez's childhood, Texas was openly segregated. As a result, she faced blatant discrimination in many public and private institutions. In her youth, Martínez was denied entry into some public parks, and at movie theaters, she and other Mexican Americans were relegated to seats in the back. Throughout her schooling, she weathered insults from other children about her Mexican heritage. Martínez even experienced discrimination from her high school counselor, who encouraged her to

Vilma Socorro Martínez (Wikimedia Commons)

go to a trade school rather than a university, even though she was an honors student.

At age fifteen, while still in high school, Martínez had the opportunity to volunteer at the law firm of Alonso Perales, a well-known Texas civil rights attorney, who became a role model for her. This internship, coupled with her experience of discrimination, influenced her decision to enter the law profession so that she might improve the lives of other Latinos.

LIFE'S WORK

In 1964, Martínez earned an undergraduate degree in political science from the University of Texas at Austin. At the suggestion of a professor, Martínez applied to East Coast law schools in order to escape the discrimination she faced in Texas. She earned her L.L.B., a professional law degree, in 1967 from Columbia University School of Law.

Upon graduation, Martínez took a position with the National Association for the Advancement of Colored People (NAACP) Legal Defense Fund. In that capacity, she served as counsel for the petitioner in the landmark employment-discrimination case *Griggs v. Duke Power Company* (1971), which was heard before the U.S. Supreme Court, and informed former President Richard M. Nixon's Executive Order 11625, mandating nationwide affirmative action. In *Griggs v. Duke Power Company*, the Supreme Court ruled that employers could not use aptitude tests as the sole criterion for employment or advancement if those tests disproportionately affected minorities.

In 1970, Martínez took a position as an equal-opportunity counselor with the New York State Division of Human Rights. There, she was instrumental in drafting employee-rights legislation. After a year, she joined Cahill Gordon and Reindel, a prestigious New York City firm, where she specialized in labor law. During these early years of her career, Martínez married Stuart Singer, a fellow attorney, and they had two sons, Carlos and Ricardo.

After six years, Martínez had established a reputation as an excellent attorney and an advocate for underrepresented minorities. In 1973, at just twenty-nine years old, she was offered the position of general counsel and president of the Mexican American Legal Defense and Educational Fund (MALDEF), a move that would define her career for the following nine years and make MALDEF one of the most powerful civil rights organizations in the country for years to come. At MALDEF, she litigated

Martínez and MALDEF

Vilma Socorro Martínez was the first female president of the Mexican American Legal Defense and Educational Fund (MALDEF) and the first woman in the nation to lead a civil rights organization. Under her leadership, MALDEF focused on fund-raising so that the organization could grow and expand in scope.

Martínez also brought Chicana issues out into the open by encouraging MALDEF to work beyond the male-dominated agendas. Within MALDEF, she instituted the Chicana Rights Project (CRP), which operated from 1974 through 1983 and was funded by the Ford Foundation. The CRP advocated on behalf of women on issues related to employment, education, immigration, housing, reproductive rights, and childcare.

During Martínez's presidency, she fought to include Mexican Americans in the Voting Rights Act. In spite of protests from the conservative groups and the National Association for the Advancement of Colored People (NAACP), Martínez and MALDEF convinced Congress in 1975 to extend to Mexican Americans the protections and provisions guaranteed by the Voting Rights Act.

Under Martínez's leadership, MALDEF filed the *Plyler v. Doe* (1982) case, which challenged a Texas law that denied free public education to children of parents who lacked legal documentation. Martínez and fellow attorneys argued that children who grew up and lived in the United States for years were, in effect, American. In June, 1982, the court ruled that the Texas law was unconstitutional and that the state must extend free public education to children of undocumented immigrants.

By the time of Martínez's departure in 1982, MALDEF had established relationships with corporate sponsors and been awarded many grants. Martínez's leadership created a strong foundation for MALDEF, which eventually became one of the nation's largest nonprofit organizations.

precedent-setting cases before the Supreme Court and established a fund-raising platform that allowed the organization to expand its client base in the years following her presidency.

Martínez's expertise was highly prized in the political realm. Between 1975 and 1981, she volunteered her consulting services to the U.S. Census Bureau, which subsequently added "Hispanic" as an ethnic category. This addition to the census helped reconfigure electoral districts and empower Latino voters. In 1976, California governor Jerry Brown invited Martínez to join the board of regents of the University of California, and she served as a board member and chairperson through 1990. From 1977 to 1981, she also served on an advisory board to President Jimmy Carter's administration reviewing ambassadorial appointments around the world.

In addition to her work on labor and civil rights issues, Martínez served as an adviser on many boards and committees, including President Bill Clinton's Advisory Committee for Trade Policy and Negotiations. She was appointed to the advisory boards of Columbia University School of Law and the Los Angeles Philharmonic Association. Martínez also served on the boards of corporations such as Anheuser-Busch and Shell Oil Company.

In 1982, Martínez left MALDEF to become a partner with Munger, Tolles, and Olson, a well-known Los Angeles firm. She specialized in labor disputes and commercial litigation. While in Los Angeles, she was hired in 1994 by the Los Angeles Unified School District to fight Proposition 187, which sought to deny public education to children of undocumented immigrants. Martínez halted Proposition 187 at the state level, and after the intervention of MALDEF and other civil rights organizations, in 1998, the federal courts deemed nearly all of Proposition 187 unconstitutional.

On July 24, 2009, the U.S. Senate confirmed Martínez as the ambassador to Argentina. She was both the first woman and the first non-career ambassador appointed to the position. Highlighting a strengthened bilateral relationship between the U.S. and Argentina, closer cooperation in areas of mutual interest, and milestones such as the successful joint NASA–CONAE project that launched the SAC-D satellite into space, Ambassador Martínez ended her tenure in Argentina on July 4, 2013, and she was awarded the Order of May in the grade of Grand Cross (the highest honor awarded by Argentina to a foreign national) in recognition for her tenure and for her work on behalf of improving mutual cooperation and understanding.

Significance

Committed to civil rights, Martínez used her legal training to create and promote legislation that would improve the lives of Latinos and other minorities, particularly in the areas of education, labor, and political participation. By serving as MALDEF's first female president and turning it into one of the most influential civil rights organizations in the United States, Martínez proved herself to be a trailblazer for all women as well as Latinos.

Mary Christianakis

Further Reading

Flores, Lori A. "A Community of Limits and the Limits of Community: MALDEF's Chicana Rights Project, Empowering the 'Typical Chicana,' and the Question of Civil Rights, 1974-1983." *Journal of American Ethnic History* 27, no. 3 (July, 2008): 81-110. A detailed historical account of the Chicana Rights Project and Martínez's role in Chicana feminism.

Meier, Matt S., and Margo Guttierez. *The Mexican American Experience: An Encyclopedia.* Westport, Conn.: Greenwood Press, 2003. Martínez is profiled and her work with MALDEF is discussed in this useful reference work.

Telgen, Dian, and Jim Kamp, eds. *Latinas!: Women of Achievement.* Detroit, Mich.: Visible Ink Press, 1996. This volume documents the contributions of Latinas in the United States, including Martínez.

Harvey Milk

Politician and gay rights activist

Born: May 22, 1930; Woodmere, New York
Died: November 27, 1978; San Francisco, California
Area(s) of achievement: Politics; Social reform

One of the first openly gay political office holders in the United States, Milk was elected to San Francisco's Board of Supervisors in 1977. He was assassinated one year later by an aggrieved former police officer.

Early Life

Harvey Bernard Milk was born and raised in Woodmere, Long Island, not far from New York City. Woodmere was a prosperous suburb and home to a large Jewish population. Milk's grandfather, Morris Milk, owned a department store and helped organize Woodmere's first

Harvey Milk (Wikimedia Commons)

synagogue. His father inherited the family business, and young Harvey worked in the store when he was a teen. He was a good student in high school but not an outstanding one; Milk was a class clown, voluble and quick-witted. After graduating in 1947, Milk moved upstate to attend the New York State College for Teachers (later SUNY Albany), where he majored in mathematics.

Life's Work

After graduating from college, Milk joined the United States Navy and served for four years, first as a diving officer aboard a submarine and later as a diving instructor. He left the military, in part, because his sexuality was becoming a cause for rumors and official concern. Milk returned to New York, and worked a number of jobs over the next several years into the 1960s—first as a high school teacher, and later in various positions in finance in Manhattan. Milk was by nature conservative; his upper middle-class upbringing taught him the importance of minding social manners and distinctions, and he worked hard to keep his sexual orientation a secret from his friends and family. Homosexuality was not only censured in early 1960s, it was still criminalized. Milk's homosexuality was a complication, at odds with the worldview that he had inherited and that he was still largely attached to. He naturally and regularly came into contact with men who led far more bohemian lives than his own. There was a thriving and increasingly visible gay underground in New York City in the 1960s, and the most visible, most progressive gay men were also those who openly questioned middle-class values; they sometimes even came into conflict with the police. One of Milk's boyfriends, Craig Rodwell, was involved with the Mattachine Society—an early, clandestine gay rights organization—and was arrested for "indecent exposure" in a gay cruising area. Milk felt obliged to break off their relationship, feeling that Rodwell was too radical.

> "*I* ask for the movement to continue, for the movement to grow, because last week I got a phone call from Altoona, Pennsylvania, and my election gave somebody else, one more person, hope. And after all, that's what this is all about. It's not about personal gain, not about ego, not about power — it's about giving those young people out there in the Altoona, Pennsylvanias, hope. You gotta give them hope."

In 1964, Milk worked for the campaign of the conservative Republican presidential candidate, Barry Goldwater. He also began dating a new boyfriend, Jack McKinley, who was only sixteen years old when the two first met. Milk worked over the next few years as an insurance actuary, a financial analyst, and a business manager for a theater company. McKinley worked as an actor and a stage manager for increasingly important productions, culminating in *Hair* and *Jesus Christ Superstar*. It was McKinley's involvement in the theater that first brought Milk to San Francisco with the national tour of *Hair* in 1969. Milk, for all his conservatism, had remained restless throughout the 1960s. He was unhappy in his work, and he moved frequently from one job to another. His encounter with San Francisco, then the burgeoning center of the counter-culture, affected him profoundly. Milk underwent a kind of conversion experience; his values changed. Externally, he began to grow his hair long, to wear blue jeans, and even to sport hippie beads. He settled in San Francisco permanently in 1972, opening a camera store on Castro Street, the center of the growing gay community in San Francisco.

It wasn't long before Milk entered local politics. Although he was influenced by the hippie movement, he was a small business owner, and he had a good deal of worldly experience and savvy. Interested both in issues relevant to the gay community (like poor police relations) and policies that affected his business, Milk decided to run for a seat on San Francisco's Board of Supervisors in 1973. Although he lost that race (he came in tenth place out of 32 candidates) he won a majority of votes from residents of the Castro District and established himself as a community leader. In 1975, he ran again, this time for the position of city supervisor. This time around, he decided to cut his hair and wear suits; he also stopped using marijuana. He lost again, but by a much smaller margin. In 1977, Milk campaigned a third time, securing a seat. By 1977, the gay community had become an economic powerhouse in San Francisco, with the Castro Village Association—a group of local business owners that was established by Milk—representing over 90 thriving businesses. Milk campaigned on a number of progressive issues and built alliances with organized labor, but he was not considered a grave threat to business interests, either.

Developments on the national stage played a role in shaping local politics in San Francisco. Anita Bryant, a fundamentalist Christian singer who had become a conservative political activist, spearheaded a national public relations campaign to oppose—and vilify—the gay community and to question the progression of social toleration and gay rights legislation. An essential part of Bryant's message was that homosexuals were pedophiles; a television ad that ran in Florida warned that Dade County was becoming a "hotbed of homosexuality" and that gay men enjoyed "cavorting" with "little boys." The Anita Bryant campaign was significant in helping to shape the nascent Christian conservative Right as a powerful political movement. Ironically, her campaign was at least as important for the reaction that it galvanized. Thanks to Anita Bryant, supporting gay rights became an essential part of mainstream liberal politics where it hadn't been before. By 1977, politics in San Francisco—as in other localities—was pursued in the context of these ideological developments. When Milk was sworn in as the first openly gay man to win a public election in the United States, it made national headlines.

Also newly elected to the board was a former police officer, Dan White. White was often at loggerheads with Milk, with Diane Feinstein, who at that time was the president of the board, and with George Moscone, San Francisco's liberal mayor. Milk's first act was to sponsor a bill outlawing discrimination on the basis of sexual orientation in San Francisco. The only member of the board to oppose it was Dan White, who nevertheless went on the record stating that he supported gay rights.

White suffered from mental illness, including depression, and he was prone to emotional decision-making. In early November, 1978, he resigned in anger from his position on the board; just days later, he asked to be reinstated. He likely would have been, but for the fierce political maneuvering of the liberal faction on the board—including Milk—who vociferously opposed his reinstatement. On November 27, 1978, White climbed through a basement window at City Hall, thus avoiding the metal detectors at the entrance, and he shot and killed both Mayor Moscone and Harvey Milk. Diane Feinstein first appeared on national news making the announcement that the two men had been killed.

White was convicted on manslaughter charges rather than murder. The aftermath to the trial and conviction revealed the high degree of tension that existed between the city's gay population and the city's police. These tensions exploded in the so-called White Night riots. Immediately following the announcement of the jury's decision, Diane Feinstein, who was then the acting mayor of San Francisco, denounced the verdict. A few hours later, about 3,000 protesters swarmed City Hall; some attempted to burn the building to the ground. Several police cars were set on fire. The following night, the police retaliated against the gay community. Wearing riot gear, hundreds of police officers stormed gay bars in the Castro District, where they grabbed patrons at random and began to beat them. The people in the bars and in the streets fought back fiercely. By the early morning hours, sixty-one police officers and over a hundred others had been treated in city hospitals for wounds received in the riots. In 1985, eighteen months after his release from prison, Dan White committed suicide.

Significance

The story of Harvey Milk was first told in Randy Shilts's biography, *The Mayor of Castro Street* in 1982. Since then, he has been celebrated in at least two major motion pictures, an Oscar-winning documentary called *The Times of Harvey Milk* (1984) by Robert Epstein and a biopic called *Milk* (2008) that was directed by Gus Van Sant. *Milk* received eight Academy Award nominations and won two. Harvey Milk changed the world. At a time when many gay men were still nervous about coming out of the closet, Milk made the much bolder step of running for political office as an openly gay man. He encouraged gay men to be open to their friends and families; that was the only way, he felt, that the LGBTQ community would obtain dignified treatment, legal protections, and equal rights. Milk's career, his murder, the events of the aftermath, and the national attention that was focused on all these, made gay and lesbian issues a part of the country's political dialogue for the first time. Milk was a pioneer and an exemplar for subsequent openly gay and lesbian politicians; the life of Milk also holds lessons that everyone, not just aspiring politicians or gays and lesbians, can take to heart. The historian John D'Emilio, speaking on the twentieth anniversary of Milk's death, characterized these lessons well when he said, "The legacy that I think he would want to be remembered for is the imperative to live one's life at all times with integrity."

D. Alan Dean

Further Reading

Faderman, Lilian. *Harvey Milk: His Lives and Death.* New Haven, CT: Yale University Press, 2018.

Milk, Harvey. *An Archive of Hope: Harvey Milk's Speeches and Writings.* Berkeley, CA: University of California Press, 2013.

Shilts, Randy. *The Mayor Of Castro Street : the Life and Times of Harvey Milk.* New York: St. Martin's Press, 1988.

Patsy Mink

Patsy Mink (Wikimedia Commons)

Representative from Hawaii (1965-1977, 1990-2001)

Born: December 6, 1927; Paia, Hawaii
Died: September 28, 2002; Honolulu, Hawaii
Also known as: Patsy Matsu Takemoto Mink
Area of Achievement: Government and politics, women's rights

Patsy Takemoto Mink was the first woman of color elected to Congress. She served in the US House of Representatives as a congresswoman from Hawaii's At-Large District from 1965 to 1977. From 1990 to 2002 she represented Hawaii's Second Congressional District. President Jimmy Carter appointed Mink assistant secretary of state for the Bureau of Oceans and International Environment and Scientific Affairs. As an advocate for equality, she drafted the Title IX amendment of the 1972 Higher Education Act.

Early Life

Patsy Matsu Takemoto Mink was a third-generation Japanese American born to Suematsu and Mitama Tateyama Takemoto on the island of Maui, in what was then the US Territory of Hawaii. Patsy Takemoto's father worked as a civil engineer. Her mother's family had worked on a Maui sugar plantation. Education was extremely important to her family; her father graduated from the University of Hawaii in 1922 and her mother was educated at Maunaolu Seminary in Makawao.

Takemoto was elected student body president of Maui High School in 1944, where she became class president and valedictorian. She began her college career at Wilson College in Chambersburg, Pennsylvania, before transferring to the University of Nebraska–Lincoln. While at the University of Nebraska, Takemoto successfully campaigned to racially integrate the dormitories. She transferred once more to the University of Hawaii at Manoa, graduating in 1948 with a bachelor's degree in zoology and chemistry.

She enrolled in law school at the University of Chicago and graduated with a JD in 1951. At law school she met and married geologist John Mink. They settled in Honolulu in 1952 and Patsy opened a law practice while raising their daughter Gwendolyn. She also lectured on business law at the University of Hawaii.

> **Passage of the Title IX Amendment of the Higher Education Act**
>
> The Title IX Amendment of the Higher Education Act of 1972 was renamed the Patsy T. Mink Equal Opportunity in Education Act by President George W. Bush on October 29, 2002, to honor Mink's diligent campaigns for equal rights for all citizens. Title IX of the Education Amendments of 1972 was written and introduced by Congresswoman Mink with support from Representative Edith Green, who chaired the subcommittee on Higher Education. Title IX was an amendment to the Civil Rights Act of 1964, forbidding discrimination based on color, race, or national origin. The amendment ended gender discrimination in all higher education activities, including collegiate athletics, and protected the rights of minorities. Title IX was passed with energized support from the women's movement, which sought equality in all activities receiving federal contracts and funding, especially hiring practices.

LIFE'S WORK

Mink began her political career in 1954, when she founded the Oahu Young Democrats. She was an attorney for the territorial House of Representatives in 1955. A year later, Mink was elected as a territorial Representative and served in the House of Representatives until 1958. She then ran for territorial Senate, where she served two terms, from 1958 to 1959 and from 1962 to 1964. In 1959, Hawaii was given US statehood. Mink made a bid for US House of Representatives but lost the election. In 1965, however, she was elected congresswoman from Hawaii's at-large district and served until 1971. She was the first Asian American to serve in Congress. She served that district for six consecutive terms. Mink was a member of the Committee on Education and Labor (1965–77), the Committee on Interior and Insular Affairs, and the Budget Committee. Congresswoman Mink introduced the Early Childhood Education Act legislation to establish funding for federal programs to improve childhood education from pre-school through kindergarten. The legislation she introduced supported bilingual education and special education, provided for student loans, and supported the Head Start program and goals of the Great Society.

Seeking to open doors for women, Mink wrote the Title IX Amendment of the Higher Education Act of June 23, 1972, which amended Title IX of the Civil Rights Act of 1964. With the passage of this law, gender discrimination was prohibited in federally funded institutions. Women gained many more opportunities in higher education and school athletics.

Opposing the war in Vietnam and seeking solutions to end the conflict, Mink ran for US president as an anti-war candidate in the Oregon Democratic primary in 1972. Her two essential early political causes were improvements in public education at all levels and the search for an end to racial and gender discrimination. She further combined her goals by introducing the Women's Educational Equity Act in 1974. This legislation, passed by Congress as part of a larger education bill, established federal protection from gender discrimination against women in education and aimed at ending gender stereotyping in elementary and secondary public schools. This act provided $30 million to promote gender equity in schools, expand career opportunities for women, and erase sexual stereotypes.

Serving on the Interior and Insular Affairs Committee, in addition to her educational reform work, Mink supported the needs and development of the Trust Territory in the Pacific, a territory formerly made up of more than two thousand Pacific islands. Mink was also chair of the Subcommittee on Mines and Mining and co-authored the Surface Mining Control and Reclamation (Strip Mining) Act of 1975 (vetoed in 1975, although a similar version became law in 1977) in addition to the Mineral Leasing Act of 1976. Both measures promoted conservation.

Mink ran for a Senate seat in 1976 but the Democratic primary was won by Spark Matsunaga. However, Mink was appointed assistant secretary of state for the Bureau of Oceans and International Environmental and Scientific Affairs by President Jimmy Carter on March 28, 1977, serving until May 1, 1978. From 1978 to 1981 she was president of Americans for Democratic Action, a political lobby committed to progressive reforms.

After stepping down from her role in the State Department, Mink returned to Honolulu, where she was elected to the Honolulu City Council from 1983 to 1987. She also served as chairwoman of the council from 1983 to 1985. Mink was unsuccessful in her run for governor of Hawaii in 1986 and mayor of Honolulu in 1988. However, she did renew her political career when she was reelected to the US House of Representatives in 1990, representing Hawaii's Second District.

She served on the Committee on Education and Labor and the Government Operations Committee. She was also appointed to the Natural Resources and Budget Committees and worked long hours in Washington, D.C. as an effective and diligent congresswoman, often in concert with her husband, John, a consulting hydrogeologist in Hawaii and the Pacific area.

Mink, who strongly believed in gender equality, cosponsored the Gender Equity Act of 1993. She continued to crusade for women's rights by forming the Democratic Women's Caucus in 1995. She pursued reforms in education, labor relations, and health care, desiring passage of a universal health care plan allowing all Americans regardless of economic backgrounds to receive medical coverage and care. Mink served on the Education and Workforce subcommittee on Oversight and Investigations (1997–99). After the terrorist attacks on September 11, 2001, Mink supported the protection of civil liberties and individual privacy while protecting national security.

> "It is easy enough to vote right and be consistently with the majority... but it is more often more important to be ahead of the majority and this means being willing to cut the first furrow in the ground and stand alone for a while if necessary"

Mink served in Congress until her death in 2002 at age seventy-four. She was honored with a state funeral in Hawaii's State Capitol rotunda and buried in the National Cemetery of the Pacific at Punchbowl in Honolulu. Because 2002 was a reelection year for Mink and her name remained on the November 2002 ballot, she was posthumously re-elected. In a special election after her posthumous re-election, Democrat Ed Case succeeded Mink in the 107th Congress and subsequently won a full term from 2003 to 2005 in the 108th Congress.

SIGNIFICANCE
Mink championed equal rights for all US citizens. She was an advocate for civil rights, Title IX, women's equality, and educational reform. As the first Asian American woman in the US House of Representatives, she opened doors for other female politicians to follow. Her contributions to Title IX (1972) and the Women's Educational Equity Act (1974) remain great legislative triumphs for social equality. Patsy Mink was an especially bright, skillful, and compassionate representative of Hawaii in the nation's capital, admired by all who knew her. In 2014 she was posthumously awarded the Presidential Medal of Freedom by President Barack Obama.

Barbara Bennett Peterson

FURTHER READING
Baker, Christina Looper, and Christina Baker Kline. *The Conversation Begins: Mothers and Daughters Talk About Living Feminism.* New York: Bantam Books, 1996. Profiles Mink and her daughter. Their entries appear as first-person recollections of themselves and each other.

Leavitt, Judith A. *American Women Managers and Administrators.* Westport, CT: Greenwood, 1985. Print. Briefly outlines Patsy Mink's career contributions.

Matsuda, Mari J. *Called From Within: Early Women Lawyers of Hawaii.* Honolulu: U of Hawaii P, 1992. Print. Describes Patsy Mink as a pioneering female lawyer.

Office of History and Preservation. *Women in Congress, 1917–2006.* Washington, DC: US Government Printing Office, 2006. Print. Offers a full description of Patsy Mink's service in the US Congress.

RALPH NADER

Consumer advocate, activist, and presidential candidate

Born: February 27, 1934; Winsted, Connecticut
Area of Achievement: Activism; Government and politics

Since the publication of his scathing book about the automobile industry in 1965, Ralph Nader has been America's most recognizable consumer protection activist. He has formed more than 30 public interest groups. Nader's bid for the presidency in 2000 as an independent was widely seen as tilting the election to George W. Bush.

EARLY LIFE
Nader was born on February 27, 1934, in Winsted, Connecticut. The son of Lebanese immigrants, Nader graduated magna cum laude from Princeton University in 1955 and earned his law degree at Harvard Law School in 1958. He was admitted to the Connecticut Bar in 1959

Ralph Nader (Wikimedia Commons)

and became a lawyer in Hartford. He also taught history and government at the University of Hartford from 1961 to 1963, when he left conventional law and moved to Washington.

In 1964 Nader became a consultant for the US Department of Labor, and on the side he worked as a freelance writer for *The Nation* and *The Christian Science Monitor*. He also served as an unpaid adviser to a US Senate subcommittee studying the potential role of the federal government in the automobile industry.

Life's Work

Nader's interest in automobile safety began during his years at Harvard, when he first explored a possible link between a car's engineering design and serious accidents. His article "The Safe Car You Can't Buy" was published in *The Nation* 1959. The ideas in this article would provide the foundation for Nader's groundbreaking book, *Unsafe at Any Speed: The Designed-In Dangers of the American Automobile*, published in 1965. Nader's main target in the book was General Motors' Corvair, which Nader argued had a faulty rear suspension system making it prone to rollovers. Though GM vehemently denied Nader's claims, *Unsafe* became a bestseller and lead to a Senate investigation. The National Traffic and Motor Vehicle Safety Act, giving the federal government more power in setting automobile safety standards, passed in 1966.

Nader's success in forcing auto safety gave him the clout to take on other industries. He organized a group of young lawyers, researchers and college students that would be nicknamed "Nader's Raiders." The Raiders investigated several corporations and industries, as well as government agencies, for potential wrongdoing. The work of Nader's team was linked to the passage of the Wholesale Meat Act of 1967. Two years later, Nader formed his first public interest group, the Center for Study of Responsive Law.

Nader and his supporters investigated the Federal Trade Commission in 1969, accusing the agency of being an unresponsive bureaucracy. The Raiders went after other government entities in similar fashion, issuing critical reports on the Interstate Commerce Commission and the Food & Drug Administration (FDA). In 1970, the Occupational Safety and Health Administration (OSHA) was formed as a result of Nader's findings. During the early 1970s, Nader and his Raiders published several reports and books on topics such as air and water pollution, nursing homes, pesticides and land development.

Nader continued to form watchdog organizations, including the Center for Auto Safety and Project on Corporate Responsibility. One of the most notable groups he founded was the Public Interest Research Group (PIRG), a team of 13 attorneys investigating and filing lawsuits based on consumer and environmental concerns. PIRG quickly transformed into a grassroots advocacy organization, and chapters began popping up at colleges and universities around the country. Thirty-five states had PIRGs as of 2003.

In 1971 Nader formed Public Citizen, an advocacy group pushing for tighter product regulations and consumer protection laws. Under Nader's leadership, Public Citizen successfully fought to ban Red Dye #2 from food products, urged Congress to adopt vehicle fuel economy standards, pushed the banning of the pesticides DDT and DBCP, and called for more non-smoking seating in airplanes. Public Citizen also filed a lawsuit successfully alleging that President Nixon's firing of Watergate prosecutor Archibald Cox was illegal.

Nader resigned as president of Public Citizen in 1980 to devote more time to other projects, including his new magazine, Multinational Monitor, which publishes stories critical of multinational corporations. Nader maintained a lower profile during the 1980s, but continued to write books on consumer issues and encourage

Americans to get involved in activism. In 1988 he returned to the public spotlight with his support of California's Proposition 103, which rolled back auto insurance rates.

Nader first entered presidential politics in 1992, when he campaigned as an independent write-in candidate in the New Hampshire primary. Nader admitted even at that time that he didn't have any interest in becoming president. He was simply running as a protest candidate, to show his lack of enthusiasm for the Republicans and Democrats on the ballot. As expected, Nader received few votes. But his foray into politics was only beginning.

In the next few years, Nader received publicity for his opposition to the North American Free Trade Agreement (NAFTA) and the General Agreement on Tariffs and Trade, two free-trade initiatives Nader argued would threaten American jobs and safety. In 1996, Nader made a more focused run for the presidency, this time taking the banner of the Green Party, a party known for its strong environmental interests. Nader ran as the "anti-establishment" candidate, refusing to take financial contributions, and making little impact in the general election.

> "*We must strive to become good ancestors.*"

Nader returned as the Green Party's presidential nominee in 2000, and this time he ran a more spirited campaign. Nader traveled all around the country and spent $7 million while addressing issues such as the environment, labor wages and corporate mergers. His goal was to earn at least 5 percent of the popular vote, which would have qualified the Greens for federal election funds in 2004. Nader fell short, winning only about 3 percent, but his candidacy was believed to be a factor in Democrat Al Gore's loss to Republican George W. Bush. Nader ran as an independent candidate in 2004 and was again accused of drawing potentially decisive votes from the major party candidates. Nader mounted another presidential run in 2008, but garnered less than half a percent of the popular vote.

Significance

Nader's work as a consumer advocate, along with his frequent television appearances and his books, made him a household name in the twentieth century, and he was generally a well-liked figure in the mainstream. His campaign for the presidency in 2000, however, was extremely controversial because it was thought to draw votes away from the Democratic candidate. Such rifts between the mainstream of the Democratic party and its more progressive wing were to become a familiar feature in the twenty-first century, perhaps most evidently in the fight for the Democratic nomination that was waged in the 2016 primary between Hillary Clinton and Bernie Sanders.

Matt Pearce

Further Reading

Nader, Ralph. *The Ralph Nader Reader.* (Forward by Barbara Ehrenreich.) Seven Stories Press, New York: 2000.

Vsych, Jurgen. *What Was Ralph Nader Thinking?* Wroughten Books, 2008.

Sandra Day O'Connor

Supreme Court Justice (1981-2006)

Born: March 26, 1930; El Paso, Texas
Area of Achievement: Law

O'Connor served as an Arizona state legislator and judge before becoming the first female justice on the Supreme Court of the United States in 1981.

Early Life

Sandra Day O'Connor was born Sandra Day in El Paso, Texas, and brought up on a rustic cattle ranch in southeastern Arizona. The oldest of three children, Sandra Day's early life was marked by hard work and academic excellence. She was reading by age four, and by age ten, she was riding horses, repairing fences, and driving tractors. She also developed studious habits as a youngster, reading the many magazines and books provided by her parents. Encouraged to value education by her college-educated mother, Ada Mae Wilkey Day, Sandra was sent to live with her maternal grandmother to attend a private girls' school in El Paso. Between the ages of six and fifteen, O'Connor typically spent summers with her parents on the ranch and school months away from home. Hard-working and self-reliant, she graduated from public high school in El Paso, Texas, at the relatively young age of sixteen.

O'Connor went immediately on to college, entering Stanford University in California, where she completed both her undergraduate and law degrees by the time she

Sandra Day O'Connor (Wikimedia Commons)

was twenty-two. She attained magna cum laude status for her B.A. degree in economics, and she ranked in the top 10 percent in her law school's graduating class. One of the few women in the law school, she was chosen to be a member of the Society of the Coif, an exclusive honor society for superior students. She also served on the editorial staff of the highly regarded *Stanford Law Review,* and while there she met two fellow students who would play important roles in her life: John O'Connor III, whom she would marry, and William H. Rehnquist, with whom she would serve on the U.S. Supreme Court for more than twenty-five years.

Life's Work

After completing law school, Sandra Day O'Connor planned to practice law and interviewed with several of the traditionally all-male private law firms in California. Despite her strong academic credentials, the only offer she received was to serve as a legal secretary. She turned that offer down, and began what was to become an extraordinary career in public service. She served briefly as deputy attorney for San Mateo County, California, before moving to West Germany because of her husband's Army assignment. On returning to the United States, she proceeded to have and rear three sons, while maintaining a busy schedule of volunteer activities in Phoenix, Arizona. Still unable to secure a law firm position, she started a small private practice in Phoenix and became active in Republican Party politics in her county. Devoted to public service, she became one of Arizona's assistant attorney generals in 1965 and then a state senator in 1969. At age forty-two, O'Connor became the first woman to hold the majority leader position in a state senate.

Although she enjoyed the respect of her senate colleagues and the support of her constituents, O'Connor opted for the intellectual challenge of the judiciary over the political demands of the legislature. She successfully sought election in 1974 as a state trial judge, and four years later she was appointed by Governor Bruce Babbitt to the Arizona Court of Appeals. As both a state legislator and a judge, she developed a reputation as an extremely diligent, intelligent, and fair-minded public servant. Influenced in her youth by her father, Harry Day, who had an intense dislike for Franklin D. Roosevelt and the policies of the Democratic Party, O'Connor became a loyal Republican Party activist, serving on the Arizona committee to reelect President Richard Nixon in 1972 and working for Ronald Reagan's presidential nomination in 1976. Her judicial temperament, fidelity to the Republican Party, impressive academic credentials, and impeccable moral character made her a prime candidate for a federal court appointment.

No woman had served on the Supreme of the United States for the nearly two hundred years since its opening session in 1789. In fulfillment of a campaign pledge to appoint a qualified woman to the U.S. Supreme Court, President Ronald Reagan nominated Sandra Day O'Connor on July 7, 1981, to become the 106th justice in the Court's history. This historic decision by President Reagan followed a three-month-long search headed by Attorney General William French Smith, who, ironically, had been a partner in one of the California law firms that had refused to hire O'Connor years before. Despite some questions that were raised about her relatively brief experience as an appellate court judge, and some concern about her views on abortion rights, her nomination was enthusiastically supported by both conservatives and liberals. O'Connor impressed members of the Senate Judiciary Committee with her careful and prudent approach to controversial legal issues, asserting her strong conservative belief that judges ought to restrain themselves from injecting personal values into their judicial decisions. Her merit on full display, she was confirmed by the U.S. Senate by a vote of 99 to 0 in September of 1981. O'Connor's womanhood, for so long an obstacle to career advancement, now provided the occasion for her rise to the pinnacle of the legal profession.

O'Connor served for twenty-five years as a distinguished and highly respected associate justice of the Supreme Court. As a new member of the Court in 1981, she immediately impressed colleagues with her disciplined work habits and dignified yet congenial manner. Shortly after arriving, she initiated an aerobics class in the Supreme Court gymnasium for all women employees, which she attended faithfully for many years. Although slowed by a bout with breast cancer in 1988, O'Connor maintained one of the most grueling work schedules of any justice throughout her career on the court. Exceedingly well-prepared for each case, she was noted for asking incisive questions during the Court's oral argument and for producing written opinions expeditiously. She also was active off the court, regularly attending Washington, D.C., social events with her husband, arranging family skiing trips, and lecturing widely on legal topics.

> "Society as a whole benefits immeasurably from a climate in which all persons, regardless of race or gender, may have the opportunity to earn respect, responsibility, advancement and remuneration based on ability."

On the Supreme Court, O'Connor had a significant influence on many of the most controversial social and political issues of her time. She developed a reputation as a pragmatic justice who wrote moderately conservative judicial opinions. On the nine-member Court, she often cast the deciding vote, repeatedly discovering some reasonable middle-ground position between her more ideological liberal and conservative brethren. As a result, for much of her tenure, O'Connor was characterized as perhaps the most powerful woman in America, one whose vote would shape public policy in the areas of abortion rights, religious liberty, affirmative action, federalism, and women's rights.

In one of her most important rulings, O'Connor defined the standard for state abortion regulations. Rejecting both the arguments of conservatives that the Constitution does not prevent states from prohibiting early-term abortions and the arguments of liberal feminists that states could place no constitutional restrictions on a woman's right to choose an abortion, she ruled in *Planned Parenthood of Southeastern Pennsylvania v. Casey* (1992) that states could regulate abortion up to the point that these restrictions become an undue burden on the woman seeking the abortion. O'Connor's deciding vote in this case maintained early-term abortion as a constitutional right even while allowing states to impose some conditions. In *Stenberg v. Carhart* (2000) she again cast a deciding vote in striking down a state law that banned a controversial ("partial birth") late-term abortion procedure as insufficiently protective of the mother's health. However, to underscore O'Connor's importance in casting pivotal votes, in 2007, with O'Connor retired and replaced with a more conservative justice, the Supreme Court upheld a similar federal ban on "partial birth" abortion.

In the controversial area of religion, O'Connor was typically a voice of moderation. Against liberals who advocate a virtually total separation of religion from state activities and against conservatives who argue that the Constitution allows more active government support of religion, O'Connor articulated the position that a government policy violates the Constitution only if it intends, or appears, to endorse religion. In a case from 2002 involving public vouchers given to parents who used the money to send their children to parochial schools, O'Connor cast the decisive fifth vote ruling that vouchers did not violate the Constitution so long as the parents, and not the parochial schools, were the primary recipients of the government money.

O'Connor actively participated in moving the Court to a more conservative stance on affirmative action, even while defending such programs against more conservative justices who would abolish them in all circumstances. In a case that displayed her sensitivity to discrimination against women as well as her support for some types of affirmative action programs, she argued in *Johnson v. Transportation Agency of Santa Clara* (1987) against the complaint of a white man who was passed over for a skilled job in favor of a woman who, though well qualified, scored slightly lower on an interview score. At the time, none of the 237 skilled positions in the agency was held by a woman. For O'Connor, this was sufficient evidence that the county had discriminated against women. In subsequent cases, she sought to limit government affirmative action programs to those circumstances in which they serve a compelling interest. In 2003 O'Connor cast the deciding vote in *Grutter v. Bollinger* (2003), ruling that state universities may use race-conscious affirmative action programs when admitting students to

O'Connor being sworn in as a Supreme Court Justice by Chief Justice Warren Burger. Her husband John O'Connor looks on. (National Archives and Records Administration)

achieve the compelling interest of a "diverse" student body.

O'Connor was the only one of her colleagues on the Court to have been an elected state legislator. This fact, combined with her fundamentally conservative values, made O'Connor a strong advocate of limits on the power of the federal government over the states. Her conservative views on Federalism emerged in such important decisions as *Gregory v. Ashcroft* (1991), in which, writing for the majority of the Court, O'Connor ruled that Missouri's constitutional requirement of a mandatory retirement for judges did not violate the federal Age Discrimination in Employment Act. Similarly, in *New York v U.S.* (1992), O'Connor's majority opinion declared that the federal government could not order state governments to assume ownership of nuclear waste if they failed to create adequate disposal sites as required by federal law. She also believed in restraining the power of the federal government even where women's rights may be compromised. In 2000 she joined a ruling to strike down the Violence Against Women Act, a federal law that would have allowed victims of sexual violence to bring civil suits against their attackers in federal court. Her views on federalism also shaped her rulings on capital punishment. Her rulings generally sided with the states in limiting death row appeals, though she did rule in *Atkins v. Virginia* (2002) that states may not execute the mentally retarded.

O'Connor's long-standing commitments to judicial impartiality and restraint and to state sovereignty came into question when she cast a deciding vote in the controversy surrounding the presidential election of 2000. The Supreme Court, splitting five to four in *Bush v. Gore* (2000), ordered Florida to stop a recount of disputed ballots, resulting in the election of the Republican candidate, George W. Bush and the defeat of the Democratic candidate, Al Gore. O'Connor rejected the Florida Supreme Court's order for a recount, a vote that some critics viewed to be inconsistent with her abiding belief in state sovereignty. She, along with four of her Republican colleagues on the Court, withstood public criticism for participating in what many saw as an unprecedented, and partisan, intrusion of the Supreme Court into the election of a president.

On women's rights legal issues, O'Connor stood forcefully for the principle that the Constitution mandates gender equality and that civil rights laws should be interpreted to protect women against discrimination in education and employment. As a state senator, she supported the Equal Rights Amendment. In 1993, Justice O'Connor wrote an opinion for a unanimous court in *Harris v. Forklift Systems* (1993) that made sexual harassment in the workplace easier to prove, and in 1999, in *Davis v Monroe County Board of Education* (1999) she cast the decisive fifth vote holding school officials liable for preventing student-on-student sexual harassment. Although she was not a liberal feminist, O'Connor's efforts to preserve a woman's constitutional right to choose abortion, her votes on the Court to end discrimination against pregnant workers, and her opposition to the exclusion of women from men's private clubs demonstrated her commitment to gender equality.

In one of her last cases, *Hamdi v. Rumsfeld* (2004), O'Connor confronted the problem of individual rights in wartime, and the scope of the president's powers in war. Writing for a divided court, in an opinion she later called one of her most important, she ruled that "a state of war is not a blank check for the President when it comes to the rights of the Nation's citizens."

In her last years on the Supreme Court, O'Connor managed to write three books, including a memoir of her formative years on the Arizona ranch. She announced her retirement from the Supreme Court on July 1, 2005, at the age of seventy-five, and she continued to serve until her replacement, Samuel Alito, was sworn in on January 31, 2006. After leaving the Court, she continued her public service as a member of the Iraq Study Group in 2006, as chancellor of the College of William and Mary, and as a leading advocate for an independent judiciary at national and international conferences. In 2009 she was awarded the Presidential Medal of Freedom by President Barack Obama. O'Connor serves on the Board of Trustees of the National Constitution Center in Philadelphia, and serves as an Honorary Chair of Justice at Stake, a judicial reform organization. O'Connor published a book, *Out of Order: Stories from the History of the Supreme Court,* in 2013.

Significance

O'Connor's pathbreaking rise to the Supreme Court was a significant moment in the greater transformation of women's lives in American society during the last half of the twentieth century. Her celebrated nomination to the Court, applauded by people of all political views, reflected the growing consensus that women were deserving of high governmental office and that they had been unjustly excluded from these positions for far too long. Her appointment to the Court also coincided with the increase in popularity of conservative political ideas in the 1980s, a trend to which she contributed.

O'Connor's accomplishments go beyond the circumstances of her appointment. On the Court, she influenced many important areas of American law, often casting pivotal votes in highly controversial cases. Scholars have proposed that O'Connor lent a uniquely feminine perspective to cases heard by the Court, marked in part by her consistent ability to see both sides of complex issues and her tendency to forge a reasonable compromise that is consistent with her basic conservative values. Other scholars argued that several of the justices became noticeably more receptive to arguments in favor of gender equality after O'Connor's arrival on the Court. O'Connor was joined by a second woman justice after President Bill Clinton nominated Ruth Bader Ginsburg to fill a vacancy on the Supreme Court in 1993.

Although women continue to be underrepresented in political office, O'Connor retained a unique public profile as one of the most popular and easily recognized Supreme Court Justices ever. Her determination to succeed in the predominantly male world of law and politics and her ability to combine motherhood and family with a career dedicated to public service made her a positive role model for many young women.

Philip R. Zampini, updated by Micah L. Issitt

Further Reading

Biskupic, Joan. *Sandra Day O'Connor.* New York: HarperPerennial, 2005. The best full-length biography, covering her personal life and professional career. Very well-researched by a skilled journalist and written in an engaging style.

Greenburg, Jan Crawford. *Supreme Conflict.* New York: Penguin Press, 2007. A journalist's account of the political battles over the direction of the Supreme Court during the George W. Bush administration. The book offers a behind-the-scenes look at the politics of judicial appointments, with much to say about O'Connor's importance, the drama surrounding her retirement, and the search for her replacement.

Maveety, Nancy. "Justice Sandra O'Connor: Accommodationism and Conservatism." In *Rehnquist Justice: Understanding the Court Dynamic,* edited by Earl Maltz. Lawrence: University Press of Kansas, 2003. A scholarly analysis of O'Connor's jurisprudence and critical role on the Supreme Court.

O'Connor, Sandra Day. *The Majesty of the Law.* New York: Random House, 2003. A collection of the justice's reflections on the Supreme Court, legal history, individual justices, the role of women in law, and the legal profession.

_____, and H. Alan Day. *Lazy B.* New York: Random House, 2002. A memoir, coauthored with her brother, of her formative years on the cattle ranch in Arizona during the 1930s. Reveals some of the pleasures and pains of Depression-era ranch life that would shape O'Connor's worldview.

Tushnet, Mark. *A Court Divided.* New York: W. W. Norton, 2005. An analysis of the Supreme Court during the tenure of Chief Justice William H. Rehnquist. The author, a professor of law, focuses on the internal divisions among the justices and illustrates O'Connor's pivotal role in many policy areas.

Thomas Paine

English-born American political philosopher

Born: January 29, 1737; Norfolk, England
Died: June 8, 1809; New York City, New York
Area of Achievement: Politics, philosophy, writing

Paine was a participant in both the American and French Revolutions, and, through his writings, he attempted to foment revolution in England as well. He was interested in the new scientific ideas of his age, spent considerable energy on the design of an iron-arch bridge, and tried to resolve the age-old conflicts between science and religion by espousing Deism.

Early Life

Thomas Paine's father, Joseph Pain (Thomas later added an "e" to his name), was a Quaker stay maker. Working as a craftsman, he provided whalebone corsets for local women. Paine's mother, Frances Cocke, the daughter of a local attorney, was an Anglican who was older than her husband and of difficult disposition. Because a daughter died in infancy, the Pains then concentrated all of their efforts on their son.

Thomas was taught by a local schoolmaster from the age of seven to thirteen and then apprenticed to his father to learn the trade of a stay maker. This was clearly not entirely to his liking, as he managed at one point to run away and spend some time at sea. Upon his return, he practiced his craft in various places in England. In 1759, Paine married Mary Lambert, but his wife died a year later. Dissatisfied with his occupation, he tried others, including a brief stint at school teaching and perhaps also preaching. Still seeking his niche in the world, Paine returned home for a time to study for the competitive examination to become an excise collector. He passed the exam and obtained positions collecting customs revenues from 1764 to 1765 and from 1768 to 1774. He was twice dismissed from his posts for what higher authorities saw as laxity in the performance of his duties. The second dismissal came after Paine participated in efforts to obtain higher wages for excisemen, during the course of which he wrote a pamphlet, *The Case of the Officers of the Excise* (1772).

The time he spent on these endeavors, as well as his arguments, contributed to the loss of his position. Paine was married to Elizabeth Ollive in 1767, and, while

Thomas Paine (Wikimedia Commons)

continuing as an exciseman, he also helped her widowed mother and siblings run the family store. By 1774, the business was in bankruptcy, Paine and his wife had separated, and he was without a government position, with little prospect of regaining one. It was at this point in his life that Paine, so far a failure at everything he had tried to do, obtained a letter of introduction from Benjamin Franklin and moved to America.

Life's Work

Thomas Paine arrived in the colonies at an auspicious moment. A dispute over "taxation without representation," simmering between England and its colonists since the passage of the Stamp Act in 1765, had led to the Boston Tea Party and then to the passage of the Coercive (or Intolerable) Acts (1774). Paine obtained a position as editor for the new *Pennsylvania Magazine*, published in Philadelphia. Meanwhile, American feelings had boiled over, and the Revolutionary War had begun. As an author, Paine had finally found where his true talents lay. In January of 1776, he wrote *Common Sense*, a pamphlet attacking the king, advocating independence, and outlining the form of government that should be adopted. The work was a tremendous success, a consequence of its timely arguments as well as its clear, forceful language.

Reprinted in numerous editions, passed from hand to hand, it reached an audience of unprecedented size. At age thirty-nine, Paine had at last achieved a measure of success. He went on to become the leading propagandist of the American Revolution.

During the war, Paine served as secretary to a commission on American Indian affairs and as secretary to the Committee for Foreign Affairs of the Second Continental Congress. He resigned under pressure from the second position during a bitter political debate over the actions of Silas Deane. He later served as a clerk for the Pennsylvania Assembly and participated in a diplomatic venture to France, seeking additional help for the fledgling nation. He is best known, however, for his continued efforts to promote the American cause. By 1783, he had written a total of sixteen *Crisis* papers as well as other pamphlets. In the *Crisis* papers, with ringing language meant to stir the soul and bolster the war effort, he appealed to patriotic Americans to rally to the cause.

As the war came to a conclusion, Paine turned his efforts to providing some measure of financial security for himself. He appealed to the national Congress and a number of state legislatures for compensation for his previous literary efforts on behalf of the American cause. He was ultimately granted a small pension by Congress, land by the New York legislature, and money by the Pennsylvania government. The Virginia legislature refused to come to his aid after he wrote a pamphlet, *The Public Good* (1780), arguing that all the states should cede their Western land claims to the national government. In this work and others, Paine's talents were utilized by those who wanted to bolster the powers of the central government. In 1786, he wrote a pamphlet, *Dissertations on Government, the Affairs of the Bank, and Paper Money*, in which he defended the Bank of America, chartered by Congress and the state of Pennsylvania as an instrument to raise money for the government and to aid commerce. In the course of this work, he condemned paper money, maintaining that anything but gold or silver was a dangerous fraud.

Always interested in science and new technology, he also busied himself with designing an iron-arch bridge that would be able to span greater distances than was possible with existing methods. Unable to obtain sufficient money or interest for his project in the United States, he left for France in 1787 and from there made several trips to England, primarily to raise support for a workable model.

Paine arrived in France just as the French Revolution began to unfold, although this drama did not at first engage his attention. With the publication of Edmund Burke's *Reflections on the Revolution in France* (1790), Paine again took up his pen for a radical cause, producing, in two parts, *The Rights of Man* (1791, 1792). Whereas the conservative Burke emphasized the value of traditions and claimed that all change should come about gradually, Paine argued for government based on consent, defended revolution as a corrective remedy for unjust government, suggested ways to bring revolution to England, and proposed an early form of social welfare. The second part of *The Rights of Man* led to his being tried and convicted in absentia in England for seditious libel. Paine barely escaped arrest by the English authorities and took passage to France, where he became intimately involved in the course of the French Revolution.

> "*Whatever is my right as a man is also the right of another; and it becomes my duty to guarantee as well as to possess.*"

When Paine returned to France in 1792, it was as an elected delegate to the French assembly. There he was caught up, and ultimately overcome, by the tide of the revolution. Paine associated with the political representatives of the middle and upper classes, with literary figures, and with those who spoke English, never having mastered French sufficiently to converse without a translator. Despite his attacks on monarchy in his previous writings, the depths of French radicalism, the swiftness of change, and the quick trial and execution of the king all went beyond what he could support.

Associated with the Girondist faction of French politics and an object of increasing anti-foreign sentiment, Paine was arrested after the Jacobins achieved power; he subsequently spent ten agonizing months in jail while prisoners around him were carted off to the guillotine. Once the virulence of the revolution ran its course, Paine seemed less of a threat to those in power. As a result, a new American minister to France, James Monroe, was able to appeal for his release from prison, arguing that Paine was an American, rather than English, citizen.

While in prison, Paine began the last work for which he achieved fame, or, in this case, infamy: *The Age of Reason* (1794). The first part of this book was an attack on religion and a defense of Deism, while the second part was specifically aimed at Christianity and included numerous pointed refutations of biblical passages. It was a work that sparked in rebuttal many pamphlets in England and the United States and was also the source of much of the hostility directed against Paine in later years.

Paine's spell in prison had undermined his health and warped his judgment, although he had never been astute in practical politics. Remaining in France, even though after 1795 he was no longer a member of the French assembly, he wrote a pamphlet attacking George Washington and meddled in American foreign policy. In 1802, after an absence of fifteen years, he returned to the United States, taking up residence in, among other places, Washington, D.C., and New York City. He wrote letters and a few pamphlets, but he was anathema to the Federalists and a political liability to the Republicans. He died on June 8, 1809, in New York City, and his body was taken to the farm in New Rochelle, which the New York government had given him years before, and buried. Some time after his death, his bones were clandestinely dug up by an Englishman who took them off to England hoping to exhibit them; they ultimately disappeared.

SIGNIFICANCE

Thomas Paine said that his country was the world, and his life illustrates the truth of this statement. His numerous pamphlets and books zeroed in on the main issues of his time, while the clarity and strength of his language have given his works an enduring appeal. He wrote in support of freedom from arbitrary government and against what he saw as outdated religious superstitions. In addition, he was an active participant in two major revolutions, as well as a friend and acquaintance of major figures in three countries. He was also the center of some controversy, at times difficult to tolerate, exhibiting a disinclination to bathe, a lack of care about his apparel, a propensity to drink, and a tendency to impose on the hospitality of friends for months, and even years, at a time. He was a complex and interesting individual who sparked debate in England, America, and elsewhere among his contemporaries—debate that has continued among historians since his death.

Paine's interest for Americans, though, stems primarily from his authorship of *Common Sense* and the *Crisis* papers. He has frequently been described as the right person in the right place at the right time. The first pamphlet sold 120,000 copies in three months and went through twenty-five editions in 1776 alone. It met the needs of the moment and substantially helped push Americans toward independence. In it, Paine attacked monarchy as being "ridiculous" and George III for being the "Royal Brute of Great Britain." He thought it absurd for England, an island, to continue to rule America, a continent. Paine maintained not only that it was "time to part" but also that it was America's obligation to prepare a refuge for liberty, "an asylum for mankind." After independence was declared, Paine, in the first of his numerous *Crisis* papers, noted that in "times that try men's souls," the "summer soldier" or the "sunshine patriot" might "shrink from the service of his country," but the true patriot will stand firm, conquer tyranny, and obtain the precious prize of freedom.

These stirring words, more than anything else he did or wrote in his long and controversial life, assured Paine's place in history. Simply put, he was the most important propagandist of the American Revolution. As such, his later sojourns in England, France, and ultimately back in the United States constitute merely an interesting postscript to his real contribution to American history.

Maxine N. Lurie

FURTHER READING

Aldridge, Alfred Owen. *Man of Reason: The Life of Thomas Paine*. Philadelphia: J. B. Lippincott, 1959. This scholarly work, based on research in England and France, attempts to give a fair assessment of a complex man. Although the book at times is laudatory, Aldridge basically sees Paine's life as a tragedy.

Conway, Moncure Daniel. *The Life of Thomas Paine*. 2 vols. New York: G. P. Putnam's Sons, 1892. The best nineteenth century biography, written by the first scholar to do extensive research on Paine. This is still a useful work. Conway also published a collection of Paine's writings.

Dorfman, Joseph. "The Economic Philosophy of Thomas Paine." *Political Science Quarterly* 53 (September, 1938): 372-386. Examines the economic ideas expressed in Paine's major pamphlets and his other ideas that had economic implications, downplaying their radicalism.

Edwards, Samuel. *Rebel! A Biography of Tom Paine*. New York: Praeger, 1974. This is a popular biography that covers all of Paine's life. It defends the achievements of Paine's early years, emphasizing his radicalism, but is more critical of the older Paine, noting his eccentric behavior. Edwards accepts as fact some scandalous stories about Paine.

Foner, Eric. *Tom Paine and Revolutionary America*. 1976. Rev. ed. New York: Oxford University Press, 2005. This scholarly biography of Paine concentrates on his American years and on his radicalism. Foner analyzes Paine's political and economic thought and emphasizes the degree to which he was consistent throughout his life.

Fruchtman, Jack, Jr. *Thomas Paine: Apostle of Freedom.* New York: Four Walls Eight Windows, 1994. An insightful biography. Fruchtman maintains that Paine was a pantheist who saw God's handiwork in nature and in humanity's struggles to improve the common good.

Hawke, David Freeman. *Paine.* New York: Harper & Row, 1974. One of the most complete biographies of Paine. Hawke downplays Paine's radicalism, noting that he frequently was only reflecting the ideas of his times, and emphasizes the degree to which he wrote pamphlets for pay. This is a scholarly work that portrays Paine with all of his faults.

Jordan, Wintrop D. "Familial Politics: Thomas Paine and the Killing of the King, 1776." *Journal of American History* 60 (1973): 294-308. This article discusses the appeal of *Common Sense* and its significance in preparing the way for a republic by attacking the idea of monarchy in general and the "brute" King George III in particular.

Keane, John. *Tom Paine: A Political Life.* London: Bloomsbury, 1995. A comprehensive biography of Paine, who is depicted as a generous, farsighted enemy of hypocrisy and injustice, who also could be conceited and dogmatic.

Paine, Thomas. *The Complete Writings of Thomas Paine.* Edited by Philip S. Foner. New York: Citadel Press, 1945. An accessible and well-prepared edition of Paine's works. Foner also edited a paperback edition of Paine's major pieces.

RACHEL PAULOSE

Indian-born lawyer

Born: March 12, 1973; Kerala, India
Area of achievement: Law

Soon after Rachel Paulose was named US Attorney for the District of Minnesota at an unusually young age, she was forced to resign because of criticisms of her management style and accusations of political bias. She nevertheless continued to be employed as a lawyer for the federal government, taking a position with the Securities and Exchange Commission in 2011.

EARLY LIFE

Born in India in 1973, Rachel Paulose is the daughter of Joseph Paulose, a school administrator, and Lucy Paulose, the CEO of an electronics company. Paulose's maternal grandparents, Daniel and Sara Kunjummen, had immigrated to the United States in the 1960s, and her parents moved to the United States soon after her birth. Although raised primarily in Ohio, Paulose moved with her family to Minnesota when she was seventeen.

Paulose attended the University of Minnesota, graduating summa cum laude. Afterward she enrolled at Yale Law School. In addition to serving as editor of the *Yale Journal of Law and Feminism*, she was a board member of both the Asian American Students' Association and, as a devout and conservative Protestant, the Yale Law Christian Fellowship.

> *"The greatest reward is seeing the impact we have on people's lives."*

LIFE'S WORK

Paulose began her legal career in 1997 as a law clerk for the US Court of Appeals for the Eighth Circuit. From 1998 to 1999, she served as a trial lawyer in the US Attorney General's Honors Program, the Justice Department's recruiting program for entry-level attorneys. After working as an assistant US attorney from 1999 to 2002, she spent the next two years in private law firms, first in Washington, DC, and then in Minneapolis, Minnesota. After she successfully represented the Republican Party in an election lawsuit, Paulose's communication skills and charismatic personality attracted the attention of influential leaders of the party.

In January 2006, Paulose left the private sector and returned to the Justice Department. After briefly serving as senior counsel to Acting Deputy Attorney General Paul McNulty, she was promoted to special assistant to Attorney General Alberto Gonzales, in the administration of President George W. Bush. On February 17, 2006, Gonzales appointed Paulose to serve as the US Attorney, or federal prosecutor, for the District of Minnesota. Her nomination was confirmed by the US Senate in August 2006. Paulose became the first woman, and at thirty-three the youngest person, to hold this position. She pledged to enforce the law vigorously, emphasizing the need for robust prosecution of illegal pornography and corruption among elected public officials.

Shortly after Paulose's confirmation, Democratic legislators accused the Attorney General's office of firing eight federal prosecutors for partisan and ideological reasons. Some Democrats were hostile toward Paulose, claiming her more liberal predecessor had been pressured to resign. These critics also objected to the fact that her nomination occurred "out of committee," meaning without a hearing or committee vote, as part of a rarely utilized "discharge resolution." In addition, there were criticisms regarding her swearing-in ceremony, which took place before three hundred people at the St. Thomas School of Law in Minneapolis. After a local television station criticized the event as too extravagant, resembling "a coronation," a spokesperson for Paulose replied that the event only cost taxpayers approximately two hundred dollars.

Soon after Paulose took over management of the Minnesota US District Attorney's office, several employees complained that her management style was authoritarian, and objected to her frequent use of biblical quotations on the job. On April 5, 2007, three of the office's top lawyers voluntarily reverted to lower positions to avoid working under Paulose's supervision. Paulose's defenders argued that the three attorneys were partisan liberals who were either unable or unwilling to cooperate with an aggressive supervisor determined to bring the office more in line with the policies of the Bush administration.

Criticisms of Paulose's actions continued to grow. The *Los Angeles Times* reported allegations that she had removed an assistant US attorney because he was a strong supporter of the voting rights of Native Americans. On September 24, 2007 the *Washington Post* reported that Paulose was under investigation for allegedly making racist remarks and mishandling classified information. On November 19, 2007, Paulose resigned her position and returned to Washington, DC, to work as an official for the Department of Justice.

The following year, she accepted a position as senior trial counsel for the US Securities and Exchange Commission in Miami, Florida. Paulose's resignation did not end the controversy over her work as a federal prosecutor. The US Office of Special Counsel (OSC) investigated the circumstances for her earlier dismissal of a lawyer, and on December 3, 2008, it released a report stating that there "were reasonable grounds to believe that a prohibited personnel practice had occurred that warranted corrective action." Although the dismissed lawyer was given compensation for lost wages, Paulose was never personally accused of any wrongdoing. The *New York Times*, moreover, reported that the OSC official responsible for the report was investigated for having possibly "mixed politics with official business."

Significance

Paulose has always been recognized as an outstanding lawyer. Following her appointment as US attorney, she became caught up in the polarized political climate of the late 2000s. It has been speculated that she was promoted too quickly, without the administrative experience necessary to manage a US attorney's office successfully. Nonetheless, her appointment as a federal prosecutor in Minnesota represented a landmark for women in the history of the state's judicial system.

Thomas Tandy Lewis

Further Reading

Iglesias, David, and Davin Seay. *In Justice: Inside the Scandal That Rocked the Bush Administration*. Hoboken: Wiley, 2008. Discusses the partisan rancor within the US judicial system during the second term of US President George W. Bush.

Minutaglio, Bill. *The President's Counselor: The Rise to Power of Albert Gonzales*. New York: Rayo, 2006. Print. Provides information on Paulose's tenure as US attorney for Minnesota.

Shenon, Philip. "Amid Turmoil, US Attorney Will Shift to Headquarters." *New York Times*. New York Times, 20 Nov. 2007. Web. 27 Mar. 2012. Summarizes the controversy concerning Paulose's work in Minnesota.

Colin Powell

American general and statesman

Born: April 5, 1937; New York City, New York
Area of Achievement: Government and politics

The first African American to achieve the highest-ranking position in the US armed forces, Powell successfully organized and supervised US military operations in the Gulf War of 1991 and served as secretary of state in the early stages of the invasions of Afghanistan and Iraq. He was forced to resign as secretary of state following intense criticism by previously supportive conservatives over bureaucratic infighting concerning the future course of the Iraq War.

Colin Powell (Wikimedia Commons)

EARLY LIFE

Colin Powell was born in New York City to Luther Powell and Maud McKoy, immigrants from Jamaica who came to the United States in the 1920s. Both worked in Manhattan's garment district. Their first child, a daughter, was born in 1931. Five and a half years later Powell was born. The Powells moved from Manhattan to the Bronx in 1940 and settled in Hunt's Point, an ethnically mixed working-class section of the city. Powell's boyhood friendships reflected that ethnic mixture, which may have contributed to his attitudes toward race.

Powell attended neighborhood public schools. The New York City school system was then among the strongest in the country, and although Powell did not stand out scholastically, he benefited from the high quality of his teachers. In high school he took the college preparatory program and as a senior applied for admission to New York University and to the City College of New York (CCNY). Admitted to both, he elected to attend CCNY, at that time the only free public university in the United States.

City College was a remarkable school. It attracted first- and second-generation students from every immigrant group arriving in New York. Its alumni flocked to graduate and professional schools in greater numbers than from any other undergraduate institution. Powell began as an engineering student but switched to geology when, as he put it, he could not "visualize a plane intersecting a cone in space." The highlight of Powell's university career was his service in the Reserve Officers' Training Corps. There Powell found himself in his element. He enjoyed every aspect of his military training and became a member of the Pershing Rifles, an elite military fraternity. He graduated in June of 1958, his degree in geology less important to him than his commission as a second lieutenant in the US Army.

LIFE'S WORK

A few days after graduation, Powell traveled to Fort Benning, Georgia, for five more months of military training, including attendance at the Infantry Officer Basic Course. He volunteered for and successfully completed Ranger School and Airborne (parachute) training. His first full duty assignment was in Germany as a platoon leader in the Second Armored Rifle Battalion of the Forty-Eighth Infantry. As all of Powell's later fitness reports confirmed, he was an able and adaptable officer from the beginning of his military career. His record was typical of officers on the fast track, that is, officers who earn early promotion because they have been identified as more talented than their contemporaries.

On his return from Germany, Powell was assigned to the Fifth Infantry Division at Fort Devens, Massachusetts. While there, he met Alma Johnson, a young woman who worked as an audiologist with the Boston Guild for the Hard of Hearing. Johnson and Powell began dating and were married shortly before he received orders for Vietnam.

> "*There are no secrets to success. It is the result of preparation, hard work and learning from failure.*"

Powell served two tours of duty in the Vietnam War. After Vietnam, Powell served in a variety of military and political positions. His crucial introduction to the civilian side of senior leadership occurred when he was awarded a White House Fellowship in 1972. These fellowships are awarded on a competitive basis to a select group of young professionals. Powell's assignment as a White House Fellow was to the Office of Management and Budget (OMB) under Caspar Weinberger, later to be secretary of defense.

After his fellowship year, Powell received assignments of increasing responsibility. During his service as Ronald Reagan's national security adviser, Powell continued to impress those with whom he was working, among them Vice President George H. W. Bush.

George H. W. Bush became president in January 1989, and Powell was selected to be the chair of the Joint Chiefs of Staff. His new job did not involve the direct command of troops. Troops are controlled by what are called unified and specified commanders. The Joint Chiefs chair is the head of the Joint Chiefs of Staff and the principal military adviser to the president and secretary of defense. The chair is given immense power and influence. Powell determined to use this influence to prevent unwise military entanglements—the lesson of Vietnam—and to promote his conception of the size and organization of the US military establishment in the wake of the collapse of the Soviet Union.

Powell's greatest achievement as chair of the Joint Chiefs was the successful organization and implementation of the Persian Gulf War of 1991. Powell was instrumental in insisting to his superiors that the military and political objectives be clearly defined. Moreover, he worked closely with General H. Norman Schwarzkopf, the operation's field commander, to ensure that the strategy of attack did not involve costly frontal assaults on fortified positions. In January 1991, air attacks began against Iraq and Iraqi forces. A ground assault was launched in February. Four days of fighting were sufficient to clear Kuwait of the invaders and destroy most of Iraq's heavy armored divisions. Bush, Secretary of Defense Dick Cheney, and Powell halted the war immediately thereafter to prevent further slaughter of Iraqi forces.

The 2000 election brought George W. Bush to the presidency. Bush, essentially inexperienced in foreign affairs, needed a person of stature to become secretary of state. He turned to Powell, who accepted Bush's offer. Powell's new job was announced in December of 2000.

As secretary of state, Powell found that the Defense Department (DOD), under Donald Rumsfeld, and the president's more immediate foreign policy staff, under National Security Adviser Condoleezza Rice, did not agree with his approach to foreign and defense policy. Powell's underlying policy in the wake of the Soviet collapse was to expand alliances and trade, especially with Russia and China. He believed that economic growth and security would foster peaceful solutions to international disputes and rivalries. The White House and the DOD, however, favored more aggressive extensions of American power. Powell prevailed in the first nine months of his tenure, because in the absence of war the DOD had a relatively small role in the making of foreign policy.

American foreign policy changed, however, with the September 11, 2001, terrorist attacks on the World Trade Center and the Pentagon. The United States immediately began its invasion of Afghanistan to destroy the Taliban and al-Qaeda and to find Osama Bin Laden, al-Qaeda's leader at the time. Also, many in the Bush administration wanted to depose Hussein, the Iraqi dictator, who was said to be preparing weapons of mass destruction for use in the already unstable Middle East or for delivery to terrorists to use against the United States. Although Powell warned Bush privately against this new foreign policy, he publicly supported it. Some of his biographers believe that his penchant for obeying orders accounts for the apparent contradiction. Whatever the reason, his great prestige in the United States and around the world would, in the end, help Bush develop support for the invasions of Afghanistan in the fall of 2001 and of Iraq in March 2003.

As secretary of state, Powell's major role in the Iraqi invasion was to promote the development of an international coalition, first to support American military action in the invasion and subsequently to assist in the rebuilding of Iraq after the defeat of its forces. Powell's warnings to Bush had been correct, however. As the Iraqi operation bogged down, its supporters in the White House and the DOD became increasingly hostile to Powell. The public saw intense bureaucratic infighting, and Powell was asked to resign by the president's chief of staff, Andrew Card, in November 2004, effective at the end of Bush's first term.

After his second retirement, Powell continued to lecture, write, and promote moderate Republican policy. He remained influential in the foreign policy sphere, most notably in successfully opposing Senate confirmation of John R. Bolton as ambassador to the United Nations. Despite being a Republican, he endorsed Barack Obama for president in 2008 and 2012.

By the time that the 2016 presidential race had been narrowed down to Republican candidate Donald Trump and Democratic candidate Hillary Clinton, however, Powell had not voiced an endorsement for either presidential hopeful. At the same time, as both Trump and Clinton's campaigns became increasingly marked by scandal, Powell was involuntarily forced into the fray during the debate surrounding Clinton's use of a private e-mail address and server during her tenure as secretary of state between 2009 and 2013. As part of her defense of the action, Clinton had argued that she had taken advice from Powell that had led her to this decision. In

Civilian and military officials pose for a group photograph prior to discussing U.S. military intervention in the Persian Gulf during Operation Desert Shield. Powell is seated second from left. (Wikimedia Commons)

sign that racism was on the decline, at least in the military and at the federal level of government. Third, Powell's tenure also led to a restoration of public confidence and pride in the US armed forces and to increased confidence among military members themselves. The defeat and bitterness of Vietnam were lessened in the celebration of the Persian Gulf War victory. For this, some of the credit belongs to Powell. His policy on force reductions was appropriate, given the collapse of the Soviet Union, and was a step toward a more realistic and affordable military policy for the United States. Finally, Powell's insistence that military objectives be defined and attainable made national foreign policy more realistic.

Robert Jacobs

September 2016, the release of Powell's e-mails by both the State Department and hackers revealed that he had in fact talked with Clinton about his use of a personal computer, but he continued to defend his actions, highlighting that he had not used a private server; the release of the e-mails also disclosed some of his feelings about the presidential candidates.

In the 2016 presidential election, though he did not run, Powell received a total of three electoral college votes. This was part of a movement dubbed the "Hamilton Electors," where Republican electors attempted to vote for a more moderate Republican than the party's chosen candidate, Donald Trump. Ten electors defected, but after three votes were invalidated by their respective states, Powell received three (all from the state of Washington) and John Kasich, Ron Paul, Bernie Sanders, and Faith Spotted Eagle received one each.

SIGNIFICANCE

Powell's career was marked by four major achievements and one significant failure. First, he achieved the highest military rank of any African American before him. To have an African American at the very top of the military chain of command was considered a good thing for the armed services, considering that the ranks of the US armed forces are disproportionately black. Second, he was the first African American to be secretary of state. Powell's success could be read, as many have argued, as a

FURTHER READING

Beinart, Peter. "Why Colin Powell Endorsed President Obama." *Daily Beast*, 29 Oct. 2012, www.thedailybeast.com/articles/2012/10/29/why-colin-powellendorsed-president-obama.html. Accessed 18 Oct. 2016.

"Biographies of the Secretaries of State: Colin L. Powell." *Office of the Historian*. US Dept. of State, n.d., history.state.gov/departmenthistory/people/powellcolin-luther. Accessed 18 Oct. 2016.

DeYoung, Karen. *Soldier: The Life of Colin Powell*. Knopf, 2006.

Millett, Allan R., Pater Maslowski, and William B. Feis. *For the Common Defense: A Military History of the United States from 1607 to 2012*. Simon, 2012.

Powell, Colin L. "A Conversation with Colin Powell: What Startups Need to Know." Interview by Dan Schawbel. *Forbes*, May 2012, www.forbes.com/forbes/welcome/?toURL=http://www.forbes.com/sites/danschawbel/2012/05/17/colin-powell-exclusive-advice-for-entrepreneurs/& refURL=https://www.google.com/ &referrer=https://www.google.com/. Accessed 18 Oct. 2016.

---. *It Worked for Me: In Life and Leadership*. HarperCollins, 2012.

_____, with Joseph E. Persico. *My American Journey*. Random, 1995.

Roth, David. *Sacred Honor: A Biography of Colin Powell*. HarperCollins, 1993.

Schwarzkopf, H. Norman. *It Doesn't Take a Hero*. Bantam, 1993.

Steins, Richard. *Colin Powell: A Biography*. Greenwood, 2003.

Walsh, Deirdre. "Hillary Clinton's Emails with Colin Powell Released." *CNN*, 8 Sept. 2016, www.cnn.com/2016/09/07/politics/hillary-clinton-colinpowell-emails/. Accessed 18 Oct. 2016.

Woodward, Bob. *The Commanders*. Simon, 1991.

---. *The War Within: A Secret White House History 2006–2008*. Simon, 2012.

JEANNETTE RANKIN

Representative from Montana (1917-1919, 1941-1943)

Born: June 11, 1880; Missoula County, Montana
Died: May 18, 1973; Carmel, California
Area of Achievement: Government and politics, peace advocacy, women's rights, social reform

Rankin devoted her life to women's rights and advocating peace. She was the first woman elected to the U.S. Congress and the only member to vote against the entry of the United States into both world wars.

EARLY LIFE

Born in a ranch house near Missoula, Montana, Jeannette Rankin was the eldest of seven children. Her father, John Rankin, the son of Scottish immigrants, moved into Montana in the late 1860s. After prospecting for gold, he settled in Missoula, became a builder and contractor, and played a central role in the town's political and economic development. Jeannette's mother, Olive Pickering, migrated from New Hampshire to Missoula in 1878 and served the town as its schoolteacher until her marriage to John Rankin the following year. John developed a lucrative business and purchased a ranch for cattle raising and farming.

The Rankin family was close-knit and loving but fostered each member's individuality. Evenings were often spent in lively discussion and hearing stories of gold prospecting and Indian warfare in the Montana Territory. The family was also very religious, and its beliefs formed the values by which Rankin lived her entire life.

Although she loved to read, public school bored Rankin. She found more satisfaction in learning practical skills from her parents. From her mother, she learned sewing, and she became an expert seamstress. She studied carpentry with her father and constructed a sidewalk in downtown Missoula.

Rankin entered Montana State University in 1898, but her college experience was as frustrating as her earlier schooling had been. Because the university was located in Missoula, the change of scenery that she desired was impossible, and because the campus was regional, little opportunity existed to meet students from diverse backgrounds. Moreover, she frequently complained that her classes were uninteresting. She completed her studies, was graduated in 1902, and for a short time taught school.

Looking for something more challenging than teaching, Rankin drifted from one job to another, dressmaker, sawmill supervisor, and furniture builder. In 1904, she visited her brother at Harvard College in Boston. She found the city exhilarating but was shocked by the slum conditions and the extent of poverty, overcrowded dwellings, and poor health among working class residents. Repulsed by what she witnessed, Rankin committed herself to social work.

LIFE'S WORK

In 1908, Rankin enrolled in The New York School of Philanthropy to study social issues and social work. After completing the program in 1910, she secured

Jeannette Rankin (Library of Congress)

employment in a Spokane, Washington, children's home. At that time the state of Washington was considering woman suffrage. Volunteering her services, she distributed leaflets, canvassed voters door-to-door, and delivered speeches in favor of the state suffrage amendment. Washington granted women the right to vote in November, and her participation sparked an enthusiasm that placed Rankin on a crusade for woman suffrage and social reform.

Rankin returned to Montana in December, 1910, for the Christmas holidays and learned that her home state had scheduled debate on a suffrage amendment for January. She quickly organized the Equal Franchise Society, requested and received an invitation from the state assembly to speak on behalf of the amendment, and presented a well-received argument for woman suffrage. Although the amendment was not passed until 1913, Rankin was instrumental in its eventual victory.

Having gained a taste for social reform politics, Rankin became a member of the National-American Woman Suffrage Association (NAWSA) and joined organizations in several states. By autumn of 1914, she had lobbied and spoken before the legislatures of ten states, marched in rallies in major cities, and petitioned Congress for a national woman suffrage amendment. Rankin was quickly becoming a national personality.

In 1914, war erupted in Europe. Although the United States was not yet involved, Rankin feared that it might be unable to remain neutral. War, she reasoned, would shift the public's attention from social issues and slow the movement for woman suffrage. While in New York, Rankin helped to form the Women's Peace Party in January, 1915, and lobbied Congress to stay out of the European conflict. Although she spent the next summer in Montana organizing "good government clubs" designed to eliminate corruption and to increase women's rights, she devoted most of her time to speaking and writing against American entry into World War I.

In 1916, the likelihood of war led Rankin to take the boldest step of her career. Against the advice of Republican Party leaders, she announced her candidacy for election to the U.S. House of Representatives. Her personal platform reflected her professional goals an amendment to the U.S. Constitution for woman suffrage, child protection laws, social justice, and good government. She was most demanding regarding continued American neutrality. Her antiwar views, which most Montana voters shared, brought her victory in November. Rankin was the only Republican to win office in Montana that year and the first woman in American history to take a seat in the U.S. Congress.

Rankin took the oath of office on April 1, 1917, but the warm welcome she received did not last long. On April 5, the House of Representatives commenced debate on the entry of the United States into the Great War. Special attention was focused on Rankin. She symbolically represented all women in the nation. Her vote for or against war would be interpreted as a woman's ability to deal with political crises.

The House debated the war resolution throughout the night. Rankin chose to remain silent but listened intently to the heated arguments. Tensions rose as opponents of war were jeered, hissed, and verbally branded as unpatriotic. When the House voted, Jeannette Rankin rose to her feet. "I want to stand by my country," she said, "but I cannot vote for war. I vote no." She found herself in the minority. Three hundred seventy-four representatives supported the resolution, while only fifty voted against war. On April 7, President Woodrow Wilson declared war on Germany.

> "*We're half the people; we should be half the Congress.*"

Hannah Josephson stated in her biography *Jeannette Rankin, First Lady in Congress* (1974) that Rankin was warned before the vote that she might lose reelection because of her antiwar stance. Her opposition to war was far more important to her than her concern for reelection. The public's response was swift. Rankin was labeled unpatriotic and a disgrace to women nationwide. Even the National-American Woman Suffrage Association claimed that her vote against war would lose supporters for a constitutional suffrage amendment. Rankin later said that her vote against war was the most significant one she ever made. Women, she believed, had to take the lead to end war.

Once the nation was committed to war, Rankin supported American troops, worked in Congress to protect civil liberties, and pushed for social reform. She championed legislation authorizing the government to hire more women workers, to provide financial relief to families of soldiers, to improve conditions for imprisoned women, and to guarantee food, clothing, shelter, and health care for children living in poverty. She participated in congressional debates on a federal amendment for woman

Rankin at a parade for the suffrage movement. (Library of Congress)

suffrage, which Congress finally sent to the states for approval in 1918. As her term in the House of Representatives ended, however, Rankin's antiwar vote resurfaced and caused her defeat for reelection.

During the twenty years that followed, Rankin toured the nation promoting feminist issues. She worked with the National Consumers' League, which advocated federal child labor laws, better working conditions, and increased women's rights. Most of her energy, however, was directed toward achieving international peace.

The horrors of World War I still vivid in her mind, and believing that social justice could never be attained as long as money was spent on defense and warfare, Rankin helped to form the Women's International League for Peace and Freedom and volunteered her services to numerous other peace organizations. She campaigned against Reserve Officers Training Corps programs on college campuses. She was a central figure at the Conference on the Cause and Cure for War, participated in the Peace March on Chicago, lobbied congressmen to introduce legislation to outlaw war, and advocated the creation of a National Peace Party to challenge both Republicans and Democrats in state and federal elections. As the 1930s drew to a close and the prospect for another world war seemed likely, Rankin intensified her efforts.

In November, 1940, at age sixty, Rankin was again elected to Congress on a peace platform. She proposed bills to prevent the sending of U.S. troops abroad and to require a national vote before war could be declared. Neither measure passed, but she persisted throughout 1941. Despite Japan's attack on Pearl Harbor on December 7, Rankin stood for peace regardless of personal consequences. On December 8, Congress voted for war. This time, Rankin cast the only vote in opposition. As before, Rankin received the brunt of public criticism and was not reelected the following year.

Until her death in 1973, Rankin traveled the world. The extent of global poverty and injustice she witnessed intensified her belief that only in a peaceful world could social problems be resolved. Based on this view, she condemned America's war in Vietnam throughout the 1960s. In January, 1968, she participated in an antiwar march on Washington. The Jeannette Rankin Brigade, so named by her admirers, petitioned Congress to end the war and "heal a sick society at home."

Significance

Rankin pressed her demands for an end to war, the protection of civil liberties, and the direct popular vote on critical national issues. She never realized her dream to end war, but she was responsible, directly or indirectly, for the creation of many laws. Her efforts contributed to voting rights for women, support for dependents of service members, free postage for members of the armed forces, retention of citizenship for women who marry noncitizens, child labor and protection laws, and women's rights. Throughout her life she spoke on behalf of labor, for child welfare, for social justice and greater democracy, and against racial prejudice. She further advocated multimember congressional districts, a unicameral Congress, direct election of the president, and the restructuring of the U.S. military into a purely defensive force. Her two elections to Congress opened avenues for women nationally in politics and business. Although she was labeled an idealist and was criticized severely for her antiwar position, Rankin possessed the courage to remain true to her convictions and dedicated her life to the betterment of American society and the human race.

Kenneth W. Townsend

Further Reading

Dedication of the Statue of Jeannette Rankin. Washington, D.C.: Government Printing Office, 1986. This publication includes a biographical sketch of Rankin and speeches given by prominent political figures in remembrance of her advocacy of women's rights and an end to war. Included is a time line of Rankin's life and accomplishments.

Josephson, Hannah. *Jeannette Rankin, First Lady in Congress*. Indianapolis, Ind.: Bobbs-Merrill, 1974. Although many prominent and influential women with whom Rankin worked receive limited attention and the broad context in which Rankin operated is somewhat vague, Josephson has presented a complete, well-researched biography. The author's twenty-year personal relationship with Rankin makes the work most insightful and revealing.

Libby, Frederick J. *To End War*. Nyack, N.Y.: Fellowship, 1969. Libby surveys the patterns of antiwar thought and peace organizations in twentieth-century America.

Lopoch, James L., and Jean A. Luckowski. *Jeannette Rankin: A Political Woman*. Boulder: University Press of Colorado, 2005. In this political biography, Lopoch and Luckowski portray Rankin as a talented, driven, and deeply divided person.

Noble, David W. *The Progressive Mind, 1890-1917*. Rev. ed. Minneapolis, Minn.: Burgess, 1981. This work provides an overview of the intellectual foundations of the Progressive Era and the evolution in thought of Progressives themselves. One chapter devoted exclusively to women of the period adequately highlights the feminist movement.

Smith, Norma. *Jeannette Rankin: America's Conscience*. Helena: Montana Historical Society Press, 2002. Smith, a friend of Rankin, wrote this biography based on interviews she conducted with her friend in the 1960s.

CONDOLEEZZA RICE

Diplomat, educator, and U.S. Secretary of State (2005-2009)

Born: November 14, 1954; Birmingham, Alabama
Area of Achievement: Business, diplomacy, education, government and politics

Rice was the first African American and also the first woman to occupy a number of high-ranking positions in academia and government. Under President George W. Bush, she served as national security adviser and then secretary of state, during which time she played a key role in shaping U.S. foreign policy.

Condoleezza Rice (Wikimedia Commons)

EARLY LIFE

Condoleezza (KAHN-doh-LEE-zuh) Rice was born in Birmingham, Alabama, the only child of John Wesley Rice, Jr., a high school guidance counselor and Presbyterian minister, and Angelena Ray, a teacher. Her mother was a musician, and Rice's unusual first name derives from the Italian musical term "con dolcezza," meaning" with sweetness." During Rice's childhood, Birmingham was one of the most segregated cities in the South. The family lived in the black middle-class neighborhood of Titusville. Rice's parents were determined that segregation should not hold their daughter back, however, and saw education as an important tool. She was given books and studied the piano, French, Spanish, ballet, and figure skating. Her mother taught her at home for a year, and when Rice started school in 1961 she was able to skip first grade. Encouraged by her parents to excel, Rice became an exceptional student and a musical prodigy. On a trip to Washington, D.C., at the age of twelve, Rice reportedly said that one day she would be in the White House.

During the late 1950s, the dawning of the Civil Rights movement triggered a wave of racially motivated violence in Birmingham. The Titusville neighborhood was frequently targeted, and Rice's father joined a nightly armed patrol. In 1963, a Ku Klux Klan firebomb attack on the Sixteenth Street Baptist Church killed four young girls attending Sunday school; one of the victims was a friend of Rice. The next year, the family moved to Tuscaloosa, Alabama, where Rice's father was appointed dean of students at Stillman College. Rice continued to attend segregated schools but became the first African American to study at the music conservatory at Birmingham Southern College. The family moved again in 1969 when John took the post of administrator at the University of Denver.

In Denver, Rice attended an integrated school for the first time. After skipping seventh grade, she completed high school at the age of fifteen. Her parents persuaded her to enroll in the University of Denver as a piano performance major. Although she was a talented pianist who performed with the Denver Symphony Orchestra, Rice was aware of her limitations as a performer. This conviction led her to abandon her dreams of becoming a concert pianist. A new direction appeared after she took a class with Josef Korbel, a Soviet Union specialist from Czechoslovakia. Korbel was the father of Madeleine Albright, who became the first female U.S. secretary of state. Rice grew fascinated by Cold War politics and changed programs to study political science and Russian history.

After graduating at the age of nineteen, Rice earned a master's degree in government and international studies at the University of Notre Dame in Indiana. She then was offered a position at Honeywell, but the company restructured before she could start work. She gave piano lessons for a time until her mentor Korbel suggested she return to academia. Rice began a Ph.D. program at the University of Denver. Her dissertation examined the relationship between the Communist Party and the army in Czechoslovakia.

LIFE'S WORK

Rice received her doctorate at the age of twenty-six and was the first woman to be offered a fellowship at Stanford University's Center for International Security and Arms Control. In fall, 1981, she was hired to teach political science. She was a popular teacher and received awards for teaching excellence. An expert on the Soviet Union, Rice published a book titled *The Soviet Union and the*

Rice speaks with Brett Kavanaugh, second from left, President George W. Bush and Andy Card, second from right, aboard Air force One. (Wikimedia Commons)

Czechoslovak Army, 1948-1983: Uncertain Allegiance (1984). Another book, *The Gorbachev Era,* co-edited with Alexander Dallin, appeared in 1986.

Rice held fellowships at the Council on Foreign Relations and the Hoover Institution and was also wooed by Harvard, Yale, Columbia, and the Massachusetts Institute of Technology. She also began to move in political circles and served as an informal campaign adviser to Democrat Gary Hart during his 1984 presidential campaign. Although Rice's father had registered as a Republican in 1952 when Democrats in Alabama would not register African Americans to vote, Rice herself registered as a Democratic in 1976 in order to vote for Jimmy Carter. She changed her affiliation to Republican when she became disappointed with Carter's response to the 1979 Soviet invasion of Afghanistan.

> "The essence of America - that which really unites us - is not ethnicity, or nationality or religion - it is an idea - and what an idea it is: That you can come from humble circumstances and do great things."

In 1984, at a faculty lecture and dinner, Rice met foreign policy expert Brent Scowcroft, then head of President Ronald Reagan's Commission of Strategic Forces. Scowcroft was named national security adviser by George H. W. Bush when he was elected president in 1988. The next year, Scowcroft appointed Rice to the National Security Council as director of Soviet and East European affairs. She later became senior director and advised the president on international matters, helping to draft American foreign policy during the unification of Germany and the collapse of Communism in Eastern Europe.

After two years in that post, Rice left her White House job to return to Stanford. In 1993, at age thirty-eight, she was appointed provost of the university, the first African American, first woman, and youngest person ever to hold that position. Faced with the unpopular task of reducing the university's budget deficit, Rice drew criticism for what some perceived as her inflexible stance. Her decision to withdraw Affirmative action when deciding tenure also brought her into conflict with women and minorities. Rice's individualistic approach was reflected in her involvement as a founding board member of the Center for a New Generation, which ran after-school programs for at-risk children offering tutoring, music lessons, and college preparatory courses. In 1995, Rice co-wrote a book with Philip Zelikow titled *Germany Unified and Europe Transformed: A Study in Statecraft*. Keen to gain business experience, Rice joined the boards of directors of a number of major corporations.

Rice remained on close terms with the Bush family. On a visit to the family's summer home in Kennebunkport, Maine, she became friends with George W. Bush, with whom she shared an interest in sports, particularly football. When Bush, then governor of Texas, decided to make a bid for the presidency, Rice left academia to lead his team of foreign policy advisers. In January, 2001, soon after Bush took office, he named Rice his national security adviser, making her the first woman to hold this position. Rice influenced significantly the Bush administration's foreign policy. She also led the response to the terrorist attacks on the United States on September 11, 2001. After this event, the focus of American foreign policy shifted onto the Middle East and the war on terror was declared. Less than a month after the attacks, U.S. forces invaded Afghanistan, which it accused of providing a base for the Islamic fundamentalist group al-Qaeda. Rice also was an early proponent of the U.S. invasion of Iraq.

In April, 2004, Rice was called to testify before a special panel set up to investigate the events of September 11. Displaying customary poise, she fielded questions as to whether, as national security adviser, she had ignored warnings that could have prevented the attacks. When Bush was reelected, Colin Powell resigned as secretary of state. Rice assumed the post on January 26, 2005, becoming the first African-American woman to hold that position. A spokeswoman for the Bush regime, Rice developed the concept of transformational diplomacy to meet the new challenges of the twenty-first century and preempt threats to the United States.

As Bush's second term went on, Iraq descended into civil war and U.S. troops stationed there became the target of attacks by insurgents. As it also emerged that the threat of weapons of mass destruction in Iraq had been exaggerated, the administration and Rice in particular came under heavy criticism. As a close confidante of Bush, Rice also was criticized by some for her allegiance to an administration with a poor record on race relations. In 2009, when Bush left the White House, there was speculation about Rice's future political ambitions. Nevertheless, she returned to her position as political science professor and senior fellow at the Hoover Institution at Stanford. Rice also joined the New York-based Council on Foreign Relations, a public policy think tank focusing on globalization and free trade issues.

SIGNIFICANCE

Rice's career took her from the segregated South during the civil rights era into academia and political office, spheres dominated by white men. One of the most powerful and influential women in America during her time as secretary of state and national security adviser, Rice was involved in major foreign policy decisions made during the post-Cold War period and the aftermath of the September 11 attacks. She attributed her accomplishments primarily to hard work and strong family and religious values. Rice was named a fellow of the American Academy of Arts and Sciences and has been awarded a number of honorary doctorates.

Christine Ayorinde, updated by Micah L. Issitt

FURTHER READING

Bumiller, Elisabeth. *Condoleezza Rice—An American Life: A Biography.* New York: Random House, 2007. This authoritative political biography draws on extensive interviews with Rice, her colleagues, and family.

Felix, Antonia. *Condi: The Condoleezza Rice Story.* New York: Newmarket Press, 2002. A readable and informative portrait of Rice based on interviews with family, friends, and colleagues.

Kessler, Glenn. *The Confidante: Condoleezza Rice and the Creation of the Bush Legacy.* New York: St. Martin's Press, 2007. Based on interviews with Rice and her aides, this is a critical examination of Rice's rise to power and her role as policy maker.

Mabry, Marcus. *Twice as Good: Condoleezza Rice and Her Path to Power.* Emmaus, Pa.: Rodale Press, 2007. Provides a detailed examination of Rice's background and political career and is especially good at uncovering the woman behind the public image.

Rice, Condoleezza. *Extraordinary, Ordinary People: A Memoir of Family.* New York: Three Rivers Press, 2010. Chronicles Rice's life from childhood, through adolescence, to her appointment as secretary of state in 2000.

---. *No Higher Honor: A Memoir of My Years in Washington.* New York: Broadway Paperbacks, 2011. A comprehensive look at the foreign policy strategy carved out by President George W. Bush and his aides during Rice's tenure as secretary of state.

FELISA RINCÓN DE GAUTIER

Mayor of San Juan, Puerto Rico (1947-1969)

Born: January 9, 1897; Ceiba, Puerto Rico
Died: September 16, 1994; San Juan, Puerto Rico
Area of Achievement: Government, women's rights, infrastructure reform

The first female mayor of San Juan, Rincón de Gautier is best known for leading a number of city-wide social reforms and public works. In addition to transforming the city of San Juan, Rincón de Gautier dedicated her political career to social causes such as women's suffrage, child care programs, and services for the elderly.

EARLY LIFE

Felisa Rincón de Gautier (feh-LEE-sah reen-COHN deh GOH-tee-ehr) was born on January 9, 1897, to Rita Marrero Rivera de Rincón, a teacher, and Enrique Rincón Plumey, a lawyer. When she was six years old, her mother gave up teaching to raise a growing family. However, her parents both stressed the importance of education and etiquette for women. As a lawyer and lover of philosophy, Enrique invited artists, politicians, and poets to stay in his home. As a result, Rincón de Gautier and her siblings were familiar with classic texts, which later informed her work in public affairs.

When Rincón de Gautier was eleven years old, her mother died while giving birth to a daughter, Rita. Unable to care for eight children on his own, Enrique asked Rincón de Gautier to drop out of school to care for her siblings and the family home. However, this setback did not hinder Rincón de Gautier's education. After graduating from high school at a later date, she went on to study pharmacy.

In her early twenties, Rincón de Gautier began to show an interest in politics. In 1917, the passage of the Jones Bill made Puerto Ricans citizens of the United States. This bill and the active women's suffrage movement in the United States brought an increased interest in women's suffrage in Puerto Rico. In 1921, when the Nineteenth Amendment granted U.S. women the right to vote, the women's suffrage movement in Puerto Rico began to gain momentum. Rincón de Gautier was introduced to suffragist Ana Roque while unsure about openly supporting a woman's right to vote. Inspired by Roque's words, Rincón de Gautier's dedication to social reform and improving the status of Puerto Rican women was solidified.

In 1932, when Puerto Rican women were granted the right to vote, Rincón de Gautier not only defied her father by registering to vote but also by becoming actively involved in politics as a representative for the Liberal Party. Her first political action was registering women to vote and to join the party.

As Rincón de Gautier's involvement in politics taught her more about the hardships of women and the poor, she decided that she wanted to help. In 1934, she moved to New York City, where she learned the art of fashion design and mastered her sewing skills. Rincón de Gautier brought these skills back to Puerto Rico where she opened a dress shop called Rincón de Gautier's Style Shop and employed Puerto Rican women who otherwise would have worked in sweatshops.

LIFE'S WORK

While managing her dress shop, Rincón de Gautier continued her political activism by working for the Liberal Party. The party asked her to run for the senate in 1936, but because of her father's protests, she turned down the offer. In 1938, Rincón de Gautier and her political counterparts left the Liberal Party over their diverging perspectives and formed the Popular Democratic Party (PDP). The PDP was much more focused on mobilizing the working class and poor, which would later inform Rincón de Gautier's social reform projects during her twenty-two years as mayor of San Juan.

While working for the PDP, Rincón de Gautier met and fell in love with the party's secretary, Jenaro Gautier. In March of 1940, she and Jenaro were married and instead of taking a honeymoon they stayed in San Juan, moving into the PDP's offices to work on the upcoming elections. That same year, Rincón de Gautier was asked to be the president of the San Juan Committee of the Popular Democratic Party. In this position, she was able to gain political power that was rarely granted to women.

In 1944, Rincón de Gautier was asked to run for mayor of San Juan but declined because of Jenaro's disapproval. However, in 1946, after the resignation of the current mayor, Rincón de Gautier was asked again and this time she accepted the position. Her first act as mayor would lay the foundation for her many successful public works that would win San Juan the title of All-American City in 1959. Her first day as mayor, Rincón de Gautier visited the Public Works Department on a mission to clean up the slums of San Juan. In addition to cleaning up the city, she created a Public Housing Authority to decrease homelessness. In her twenty-two years as mayor, she initiated the construction of schools, hospitals, and sanitation facilities, and created new programs to help underprivileged people.

Rincón de Gautier was responsible for increasing government accessibility to the people. In her first term, Rincón de Gautier opened City Hall to the public on Wednesdays. During that time, any resident of San Juan could visit City Hall and share complaints in an open forum. Rincón de Gautier's openness with the public earned her the familiar title DoÃ±a Fela and did not stop with the forums. After two years in office, she hosted a large party with gifts for the underprivileged children of San Juan on the Feast of the Three Kings (January 6). Later, she would become widely known for flying in a planeload of snow each year for children's Christmas parties.

During her twenty-two years as mayor, Rincón de Gautier traveled widely on behalf of the U.S. Department of State. She was awarded many honors, including the Woman of the Americas award given by the United Women of America. Beginning in 1960, Rincón de Gautier's political opponents organized negative campaigns and accusations in order to oust her from office. Wearied by these campaigns and accusations that resulted in a politically charged court trial, she retired in 1968.

Rincón de Gautier's political work did not end when she retired. Until she was ninety-five years old, she remained a member of the U.S. Democratic National Committee, serving as a delegate at national conventions. In 1994, Rincón de Gautier suffered a heart attack and died in a San Juan nursing home.

Rincón de Gautier's Work for Women's Rights

Felisa Rincón de Gautier was a pioneer for the rights of Puerto Rican women. Despite her father's strong opinions that women should not vote or participate in politics, Rincón de Gautier became a politician and champion of women's rights. While she was not active in the early movement to grant Puerto Rican women suffrage, Rincón de Gautier defied her father by being the fifth woman in line to register to vote once that right was granted. That same day, she became the official representative of the Liberal Party and not only worked to register women to vote but also encouraged them to advocate for themselves. Furthermore, as one of the first women to hold a political office, Rincón de Gautier established many programs that contributed to the liberation of Puerto Rican women. One such program was a preschool program called Escuelas Maternales, which eventually became a model for Operation Head Start in the United States. This program not only provided women with jobs but also allowed women with small children to pursue employment. Rincón de Gautier's commitment to quality childcare would allow women to become self-sufficient, moving them toward liberation and empowerment. Programs such as these, as well as Rincón de Gautier's own success, provided Puerto Rican women with the tools and inspiration to seek leadership roles in their own lives and country.

Significance

During a time when women around the world were discouraged and often banned from political leadership, Rincón de Gautier's successful political career paved the way for other female Puerto Rican political leaders. Beloved by her followers and the people of San Juan, Rincón de Gautier revolutionized city government and advanced the city of San Juan. In addition, her commitment to helping the underprivileged and reforming government resulted in the dedication of a Felisa Rincón de Gautier Museum and Foundation in San Juan and a Felisa Rincón de Gautier Institute for Law and Public Policy in New York City.

Erin E. Parrish

Further Reading

"Felisa Rincón de Gautier." In *Latinas in the United States: A Historical Encyclopedia*, edited by Vicki L. RuÃz and Virginia Sánchez Korrol. Bloomington: Indiana University Press, 2006. Succinct but thorough biography of Rincón de Gautier, covering her life and influence on Puerto Rican politics and women's rights.

Gruber, Ruth. *Felisa Rincón de Gautier: The Mayor of San Juan*. New York: Thomas Y. Crowell, 1972. The first extensive biography on Rincón de Gautier, this book includes details on her public and personal lives.

LaCossit, Henry. "The Mayor Wears Flowers in Her Hair." *Saturday Evening Post* 226, no. 47. (May, 1954): 38-169. While slightly dated, this article not only provides biographical details about Rincón de Gautier but also provides insight to her public works and social reforms as they were happening.

Norris, Marianna. *Dona Felisa: A Biography of the Mayor of San Juan*. New York: Donn, Mead, 1969. While written for a juvenile audience, this book captures the influence Rincón de Gautier's social reform works had on the citizens of San Juan.

Margaret Chase Smith

Representative (1940-1949) and senator (1949-1973) from Maine

Born: December 14, 1897; Skowhegan, Maine
Died: May 29, 1995; Skowhegan, Maine
Area of Achievement: Government and politics, diplomacy, military affairs, women's rights

As the first leading American stateswoman to be elected in her own right to both houses of the U.S. Congress, Smith focused her attention on improving the status of women, military preparedness, and defense of free speech and democratic values.

Early Life

Margaret Chase Smith was born in a mill-and-factory town in west-central Maine that provided a small-town atmosphere in which her parents George Emery and

Margaret Chase Smith (Wikimedia Commons)

Carrie Murray Chase reared their six children. Margaret was the eldest of the four who survived. Her father, a barber from Irish and English background, was a hard-working family man whose own father had fought in the Civil War before taking his position as a Methodist minister in Skowhegan. Her mother took jobs occasionally to supplement the family income while instilling in her children the importance of family life and independence.

While pursuing a commercial course of study in high school Smith worked as a clerk in the local five-and-dime store, was employed as a telephone operator, and was hired to record tax payments in the town books during her senior year. She shook hands with President Woodrow Wilson on her senior class trip to Washington, D.C. After her graduation from Skowhegan High School in 1916, Smith taught in the one-room Pitts School outside Skowhegan. Seven months later she returned to Skowhegan to accept a full-time telephone operator's job for Maine Telephone and Telegraph Company.

In 1919, she began an eight-year job at the town's weekly newspaper, *The Independent Reporter*, which Clyde Smith (her future husband) co-owned. Rising to circulation manager, she continued to meet influential people and cultivate her skills in public relations. She drew on these skills in 1922, when she organized the Skowhegan chapter of the Business and Professional

> **Declaration of Conscience**
>
> On June 1, 1950, U.S. senator Margaret Chase Smith denounced the often vicious anti-Communist attacks and smear campaigns of Senator Joseph McCarthy and some of her other colleagues in a Declaration of Conscience she delivered before the Senate, which included the following remarks.
>
> "I think that it is high time for the United States Senate and its members to do some soul-searching—for us to weigh our consciences—on the manner in which we are performing our duty to the people of America—on the manner in which we are using or abusing our individual powers and privileges.
>
> "I think that it is high time that we remembered that we have sworn to uphold and defend the Constitution. I think that it is high time that we remembered that the Constitution, as amended, speaks not only of the freedom of speech but also of trial by jury instead of trial by accusation. Whether it be a criminal prosecution in court or a character prosecution in the Senate, there is little practical distinction when the life of a person has been ruined.
>
> "Those of us who shout the loudest about Americanism in making character assassinations are all too frequently those who, by our own words and acts, ignore some of the basic principles of Americanism: • The right to criticize; • The right to hold unpopular beliefs; • The right to protest; • The right of independent thought.
>
> "The exercise of these rights should not cost one single American citizen his reputation or his right to a livelihood nor should he be in danger of losing his reputation or livelihood merely because he happens to know someone who holds unpopular beliefs."

Women's Club. Smith was named president of the Maine Federation of the Business and Professional Women's Clubs the following year. In 1928, she served as Office Manager for the Daniel E. Cummings Company, a Skowhegan woolen mill. Her early working experiences not only taught her how to get along with people but also instilled in her a respect for working people that influenced her subsequent prolabor record in the United States Congress.

> "*My creed is that public service must be more than doing a job efficiently and honestly. It must be a complete dedication to the people and to the nation with full recognition that every human being is entitled to courtesy and consideration, that constructive criticism is not only to be expected but sought, that smears are not only to be expected but fought, that honor is to be earned but not bought.*"

In 1930, Smith married Clyde H. Smith, a respected and experienced Maine politician who was twenty-two years her senior. From 1930 to 1936, she supported his energetic public career while learning the basic skills for campaigning and public service. During this period, she also served as a member of the Maine Republican State Committee. Clyde Smith was elected to the United States House of Representatives in 1936. Margaret Smith served as his secretary in Washington, D.C., until his death in April, 1940.

LIFE'S WORK

Smith won a special election in the spring of 1940 to fill her husband's vacated seat in the House of Representatives. As a candidate for the succeeding full term in office, Smith scored an impressive electoral victory in the September general election. Her eight years as the congresswoman from Maine's Second Congressional District were highlighted by her interest in military affairs. In her first term she broke with the Republican Party and voted for the Selective Training and Service Act to draft men for the upcoming war. She was the only member of the Maine delegation to vote for Lend Lease in 1941 and she broke with her party to support a bill to arm American merchant ships. In 1943 she was appointed to the House Naval Affairs Committee, which was later merged into the Armed Services Committee.

Many of Smith's concerns focused on the status of women in the civilian workforce and in the military. In 1944, she was appointed by Secretary of Labor Frances Perkins to serve as technical adviser to the International Labor Organization, which explored the role of women in employment planning after World War II. Smith worked to improve the status of women in the military by introducing the Army-Navy Permanent Nurse Corps Bill to grant women permanent status in the military. This bill was signed into law by President Harry S. Truman in April of 1947. Smith toured the South Pacific naval bases and sponsored legislation that would permit women to serve overseas during war. She gained passage for the Women's Armed Services Integration Act of 1948, which gave women equal pay, rank, and privileges. Her desire to see the United States exert leadership in world affairs enabled her to support U.S. membership in the United Nations and the European Recovery Plan.

Senator Smith favored domestic legislation to improve the conditions of the working class and women. She helped to defeat the Tabor Amendment, which had proposed to halve the funds designated for community service programs such as child care. In 1945 and 1949 she cosponsored a proposed Equal Rights Amendment, which did not get the necessary two-thirds majority votes in Congress to be submitted to the states for ratification. She voted with the Democrats against the Smith-Connally Anti-Strike bill. In economic matters she opposed a bill to freeze the social security tax and voted for federal pay raises. In 1947 she voted against a Republican proposal to cut President Truman's budget. That same year she voted with her party in supporting the Taft-Hartley Act, which placed specific limits on labor. She had been named chair of the Maine State Republican Convention in 1944 to prepare her to chair the national Republican Party conference in 1967.

Smith ran for election to the U.S. Senate in 1948, winning by a record plurality. Though her opponents charged her with being a party maverick by calling attention to the votes that she cast contrary to her party, she produced a House voting record that aligned with her party 95 percent of the time. Her election to the United States Senate in 1948 made her the first woman in United States history to be elected in her own right without prior service by appointment to serve in the U.S. Senate and the first woman to be elected to both houses of Congress. Her four terms in the Senate from 1948 to 1972 acquainted her with six presidents, among whom were Dwight D. Eisenhower and John F. Kennedy.

Smith is sworn in as a representative from Maine. (Library of Congress)

In 1949, Senator Smith began a daily newspaper column, Washington and You, which was syndicated nationally for five years. She was named to the prestigious Senate Republican Policy Committee. She won the Associated Press award for Woman of the Year in politics in 1948, 1949, 1950, and 1957. She delivered her famous Declaration of Conscience speech on June 1, 1950, as a response to the abuses of Senator Joseph McCarthy's inquisitions into Communism in the United States. She courageously opposed McCarthy's negativism and demeaning of Americans at a time when most Republicans in the Senate were either too afraid to oppose him or somewhat supportive of his extremist anti-Communist activities. Her Declaration of Conscience speech still has appeal as a defense of American values and the importance of free speech to the maintenance of American democratic processes.

Smith traveled to Florence, Italy, in 1950 as U.S. delegate to the UNESCO conference. She was also appointed as a lieutenant colonel in the U.S. Air Force Reserve. After winning reelection to the Senate in 1954 she embarked on a twenty-three nation world tour to see how U.S. foreign aid money was being used. She interrupted her trip to return to the United States to cast her censure vote on McCarthy. In 1956, Senator Smith campaigned for Eisenhower, the Republican presidential candidate.

She debated in his defense with Eleanor Roosevelt on CBS television's *Face the Nation*. As someone who enjoyed new experiences, Smith had by this time been the first woman to ride on an American destroyer in wartime, spend a day on an aircraft carrier at sea, and in 1957 to fly as a passenger in a F-100 jet fighter that broke the sound barrier.

In 1960, Smith won a hotly contested election over another female candidate, the first time two women had run against each other for a Senate seat. That same year she won *Newsweek* magazine's press poll rating as Most Valuable Senator. On resuming her duties in the Senate, she agonized over her vote on Kennedy's Limited Nuclear Test Ban Treaty. Her concern for national security won out in her vote against both the treaty and most of her party. Her vote put her on the same side as Barry Goldwater, who became the Republican Party presidential nominee for 1964. Although Smith was touted as a potential candidate for vice president in 1964, she earned the distinction that year of becoming the first woman nominated for president by a major U.S. political party.

She supported the 1964 Civil Rights Act using her influence in the Republican Conference to keep the provision barring sex discrimination in employment in Title VII intact. Smith won an unprecedented fourth term for a woman to the Senate in 1966. In 1967 she was elected chair of the Conference of Republican Senators. The next year she had to miss her first roll-call vote in her thirteen years in Congress because of hip surgery. She held the record for 2,941 consecutive roll-call votes. In the remaining two years of her tenure in the Senate, Smith cast important votes against President Richard M. Nixon's nominations of Clement F. Haynesworth and G. Harold Carswell for the U.S. Supreme Court. Demonstrations protesting the Vietnam War, especially on college campuses, led her to make her second Declaration of Conscience speech on June 1, 1970.

In her final campaign for reelection to the Senate in 1972, Smith was defeated by her Democratic opponent, William D. Hathaway. During her Senate career she served on the powerful Armed Forces, Appropriations, Government Operations, and Rules Committees and showed strong support for the space program as a charter member of the Senate Aeronautical and Space Committee. She also sponsored legislation for government support of medical research. Senator Smith used her considerable influence to look out for the seafaring interests and industries of the state of Maine and to cast votes on issues critical to the well-being of the Republican Party and the future course in world politics for the United States. After she left public office, Smith focused on a second career as a visiting professor and lecturer with the Woodrow Wilson National Fellowship Foundation and at numerous college and university campuses.

Significance

In the course of her career, Smith received ninety-five honorary doctoral degrees and more than 270 other awards and honors. In 1989, she was awarded the Presidential Medal of Freedom, the nation's highest civilian honor. The Northwood Institute, Margaret Chase Smith Library in Skowhegan, Maine, was dedicated in 1982 to serve as a congressional research library and archives. This library houses the papers, political memorabilia, and documents that Smith accrued in her thirty-two years in Congress. In 1990 she was honored by the dedication of the Margaret Chase Smith Center for Public Policy at the University of Maine.

Smith's long and distinguished public service career furthered the interests of national security, especially military affairs. She pioneered legislation to further the status of women in domestic issues, in the military, and internationally. She was a model of decorum and earned a reputation for integrity, honesty, and independence of judgment. As a servant of the people in Congress, she put first priority on her duties in office. She campaigned vigorously and did not accept campaign contributions.

Willoughby G. Jarrell

Further Reading

Fleming, Alice. *The Senator from Maine*. New York: Thomas Y. Crowell, 1969. This is a well-written book highlighting the life of Margaret Chase Smith from childhood through her work in Congress. Somewhat historically fictionalized, the book is suitable for grades six through eight.

Gould, Alberta. *First Lady of the Senate: Life of Margaret Chase Smith*. Mt. Desert, Maine: Windswept House, 1990. This work, written for younger readers, reviews the public career of Margaret Chase Smith. The author emphasizes Smith's personal values, public integrity, independent judgment, and contributions to public life.

Graham, Frank, Jr. Margaret *Chase Smith: Woman of Courage*. New York: John Day, 1964. This readable biography describes Smith's professional life in the Senate. The author emphasizes her accomplishments as a woman in national politics at that time, an arena dominated by men. Presents clear explanations of how the U.S. government works.

Meisler, Stanley. "Margaret Chase Smith: The Nation's First Woman Senator Reflects Back over a Capitol Life." *Los Angeles Times*, December 8, 1991, p. M3. A brief interview with Smith in which she reminisces about her experiences as a politician in Washington, D.C. Places her accomplishments within the context of women's efforts to gain greater political representation during the 1990s.

Sherman, Janann. *No Place for a Woman: A Life of Margaret Chase Smith*. New Brunswick, N.J.: Rutgers University Press, 2000. Thoughtful, wellresearched biography that examines the impact of Smith's gender on her political career.

---. "'They Either Need These Women or They Do Not': Margaret Chase Smith and the Fight for Regular Status for Women in the Military." *Journal of Military History* 54 (January, 1990): 47-78. A scholarly analysis of Smith's stance on the issue of equitable status and treatment for women in the military. Amplifies her views on a topic that continues to generate interest among U.S. military leaders and the general public.

Smith, Margaret Chase. *Declaration of Conscience*. Edited by William C. Lewis, Jr. New York: Doubleday, 1972. This book, composed by Smith with the assistance of her legislative aide, William C. Lewis, Jr., focuses on her three decades of public service. It contains important source material including the text of her famous speeches and other important legislative statements.

Witt, Linda, Karen M. Paget, and Glenna Matthews. *Running as a Woman: Gender and Power in American Politics*. New York: Free Press, 1993. A journalist, a political scientist, and a historian collaborated on this sweeping narrative of the experiences of female candidates in American politics. Written from the vantage point of the so-called Year of the Woman in 1992, the book contains various references to Smith's trailblazing efforts in Congress and a telling assessment of public opinion regarding her chances of becoming president in 1964.

SONIA SOTOMAYOR

Supreme Court Justice (2009-present)

Born: June 25, 1954
Area of Achievement: Law, social issues

Sotomayor is the first Hispanic-American Supreme Court justice. She started her life in the housing projects of New York City but went on to attend Yale Law School and become a federal district and circuit court judge, before being nominated to the nation's highest court.

EARLY LIFE

Sonia Sotomayor (SOH-toh-mah-YOHR) was born into a working-class household to her Puerto Rican-born parents. Her father died at a young age, and her mother greatly stressed the importance of education. Sotomayor's mother pushed both her and her brother Juan to do well in school, and both did, with Juan becoming a doctor. Sotomayor went to parochial schools for her elementary days and then attended the well-known high school Cardinal Spellman. She finished there as the valedictorian and was accepted into Princeton University.

Sotomayor struggled at Princeton, in part because she

Sonia Sotomayor (Wikimedia Commons)

felt out of her element and in part because she had not been exposed to some of the things that Princeton took for granted, such as discussion of ancient literature. It did not help that Sotomayor found the whole experience overwhelming. Overcoming her anxiety, she asked for extra help and challenged the marginalization of Latin American culture at the university. She soon began to improve and ultimately won an award as the top undergraduate. Sotomayor had been interested in the law since an early age, and so she turned her attention to law school.

Sotomayor decided to attend Yale Law School and was awarded a scholarship. She was mentored by Yale's general counsel (who also taught at the law school), which was very beneficial. She graduated in 1979 and then moved to New York City, joining the bar in 1980. Sotomayor joined the New York County District Attorney's Office and moved up the ladder to prosecute felonies. In 1983, she left that office, formed her own law firm, and finally joined a corporate law firm to gain experience in civil law.

Sotomayor had made quite an impression upon her boss at the New York County's District Attorney's Office and he recommended her to be on several public agencies and panels. From this background, she came to the attention of New York's Democratic senator at the time, Daniel Patrick Moynihan, who had an agreement with his Republican colleague allowing Moynihan to select some of the district judgeships even though there was a Republican in the White House. Unlike Sotomayor's later confirmation hearings, these early hearings were without controversy, and she was unanimously approved.

LIFE'S WORK

Sotomayor's real work began once she was a district court judge. She was a bit unusual on the district court bench for a number of reasons. She was one of only a handful of women in her judicial circuit, and she was the first Puerto Rican woman to serve on the federal district bench at all. She did not want to gain attention for the wrong reasons, but did have some well-known cases come through her courtroom. Those included the 1994 Major League Baseball strike, in which she issued a preliminary injunction that had the effect of ending the strike. She also ruled to allow *The Wall Street Journal* to print White House counsel Vince Foster's suicide note in 1993.

After five years on the district court bench, President Bill Clinton selected Sotomayor for the Second Circuit Court of Appeals. While little in her background caused controversy, even in 1997 some observers thought that Sotomayor was being groomed for the Supreme Court.

Sotomayor's Supreme Court Confirmation Hearings

Sonia Sotomayor was nominated for the Supreme Court in May, 2009, and her confirmation hearings began in July. Some of the delay was attributed to scheduling issues and the fact that Sotomayor met a number of the senators in one-on-one meetings. Ideological lines formed somewhat predictably. Democrats favored her (Sotomayor was nominated by a Democratic president, Barack Obama), while Republicans argued that she was an "activist judge." In the hearings, the Republicans focused on a comment Sotomayor had made after a 2001 speech in which she suggested that a "wise Latina woman" had a distinct advantage in deciding a case over a white man who lacked similar life experiences. Sotomayor defended her comment as an attempt to inspire her audience (she was giving a lecture on diversity at the University of California at Berkeley) and as a rhetorical device, and linked her words to a quote by Sandra Day O'Connor, the first female Supreme Court justice.

Thus, certain senators were quite probing of the judge in her confirmation hearings. The vote on her nomination was delayed and did not occur until sixteen months after her nomination.

After joining the Second Circuit, Sotomayor wrote nearly four hundred majority opinions and was widely viewed as a centrist judge. Several of her opinions and some opinions in which she joined the majority drew attention either at the time or later during her Supreme Court confirmation hearings. These include a case in which the court upheld a state ban on nunchucks and another concerning affirmative action, in which Sotomayor voted with the majority to allow a city to retry a promotion board when not enough minorities were promoted. She drew the notice of football fans in 2004 when she overturned a lower court ruling and held that the National Football League was allowed to ban college running back Maurice Clarett from the draft because he did not meet the league's age requirement.

Besides serving as a district and circuit court of appeals judge, Sotomayor also taught at New York University School of law and Columbia Law School. Her decade of service on the circuit court of appeals, while shorter than that of some justices, is comparable to that of Justice Clarence Thomas and longer than the circuit court tenures of some other current justices, including Antonin Scalia.

> *"I am reminded each day that I render decisions that affect people concretely and that I owe them constant and complete vigilance in checking my assumptions, presumptions and perspectives and ensuring that to the extent that my limited abilities and capabilities permit me, that I reevaluate them and change as circumstances and cases before me requires. I can and do aspire to be greater than the sum total of my experiences but I accept my limitations. I willingly accept that we who judge must not deny the differences resulting from experience and heritage but attempt, as the Supreme Court suggests, continuously to judge when those opinions, sympathies and prejudices are appropriate."*

Sotomayor was nominated for the Supreme Court when Justice David Souter stepped down in 2009. She was confirmed after a somewhat testy confirmation hearing. While on the court, she generally has voted with its liberal wing and thus has not varied much from her predecessor. She has, however, been very active in asking questions from the bench, something that other newly appointed justices sometimes have avoided early in their tenures.

Sotomayor also was questioned about several cases, including one in which she ruled against white firefighters in a reverse discrimination case; her decision was notable, as it had been overruled by the Supreme Court just days before her hearings. Sotomayor defended her decision as being correct based on the precedents in effect at the time. The full Senate ultimately confirmed her appointment by a vote of 68-31.

As a justice, Sotomayor's rulings and opinions have been used to strike down controversial anti-immigration legislation, and Sotomayor's ruling in the *United States v. Jones* case of 2013 was used to justify federal rulings against the federal collection of digital data. Sotomayor and the court's other two female justices were the dissenting minority in the case of *Burwell v. Hobby Lobby* in which the court ruled that private companies could cite religious beliefs in denying employees certain type of health benefits. Sotomayor published a memoir of her life, *My Beloved World,* in 2013, which received critical praise.

Significance

Sotomayor is significant as the first Hispanic justice on the Supreme Court and one of the few justices who rose from poverty to the high court. Her appointment makes her the third woman on the court and one of the relatively few modern-era justices who have served in all three levels of the federal judiciary (district court, circuit court of appeals, and Supreme Court). None of the justices she joined on the high court has that distinction. Sotomayor has received numerous honorary doctorate degrees during her career, including degrees from Princeton, Yale, Howard, and New York University. Princeton University awarded her the Woodrow Wilson Award for civic service in 2013.

Scott A. Merriman, updated by Micah L. Issitt

Further Reading

Felix, Antonia. *Sonia Sotomayor: The True American Dream.* New York: Berkley, 2010. Relates how Sotomayor became a Supreme Court justice and discusses her background, including her childhood in poverty in New York City.

McElroy, Lisa Tucker. *Sonia Sotomayor: First Hispanic U.S. Supreme Court Justice.* Minneapolis, Minn.: Lerner, 2010. Although aimed at a relatively young audience, this biography covers all the pertinent topics. Very readable and accessible.

Salkin, Patricia E., ed. *Pioneering Women Lawyers: From Kate Stoneman to the Present.* Chicago: American Bar Association, 2009. Stoneman was the first female lawyer in New York in 1886 and Albany Law School hosts a symposium in her honor. This work collects speeches given there on a wide variety of female pioneers in law, including some judges.

Sotomayor, Sonia. *My Beloved World.* New York: Alfred A. Knopf, 2013. Chronicles Sotomayor's early life and education up until 1992. Avoids discussion of her legal philosophy or politics, focuses more on her personal and professional life.

Terris, Daniel, Cesare Roman, and Leigh Swigart. *The International Judge: An Introduction to the Men and Women Who Decide the World's Cases.* Foreword by Sonio Sotomayor. Waltham, Mass.: Brandeis, 2007. This introduction to those who try the world's cases includes a foreword by Sotomayor and profiles of some of the judges.

Adlai E. Stevenson II

Governor of Illinois (1949-1953)

Born: February 5, 1900; Los Angeles, California
Died: July 14, 1965; London, England
Area of Achievement: Law, politics, diplomacy

Although unsuccessful in his repeated bids for the presidency, Stevenson inspired a new generation of liberals who would write the agenda for the New Frontier and Great Society during the 1960's. He brought to the American political scene an all too uncommon blend of integrity, high intelligence, and humane values.

Early Life

Adlai E. Stevenson was born in Los Angeles, where his father, Lewis Stevenson, managed the Hearst mining and newspaper interests. Stevenson's family, however, was based in Bloomington, Illinois, and the marriage of his parents had united the town's leading Republican and Democratic families. The Stevensons and their relatives had long been active in Illinois political affairs. His great-grandfather, Jesse Fell, was a founder of the Republican Party and a political confidant of Abraham Lincoln. His grandfather, after whom he was named, was an Illinois Democrat who had served as Grover Cleveland's vice president during the 1890's.

This family history influenced Stevenson's formative years. In 1906, his family returned to Bloomington, where his father owned and managed several farms, became a noted agricultural reformer, and was active in state and national politics. Consequently, Adlai became acquainted with such political giants as William Jennings Bryan and, most notably, Woodrow Wilson, whose moral vision and internationalism became guideposts for his subsequent political career. Although he enjoyed a happy childhood in Bloomington, he became an indifferent student in the town's primary and secondary schools. This idyllic period was shattered in December, 1912, when he accidentally shot and killed his cousin. Stevenson was so shattered by the tragedy that he could never speak of it until it became part of the 1952 presidential campaign.

In 1916, Stevenson attended Choate School in Connecticut to prepare for the entrance examinations for Princeton University. He entered Princeton in 1918 and was graduated four years later with average grades. He was very active in student affairs and was managing editor of *The Princetonian*. At his father's insistence, Stevenson enrolled at Harvard Law School, where he was miserable; his grades declined accordingly. In 1926, he completed his legal training at Northwestern Law School. During this period, he met with Supreme Court Justice Oliver Wendell Holmes, Jr., which proved to be one of the most satisfying experiences of his life.

By this time, Stevenson had decided to make law his life's work. He had been seriously considering becoming a newspaper publisher, and he enjoyed working on the school press at Choate and Princeton as well as editing the family's Bloomington newspaper. In 1926, Stevenson made one last effort in the newspaper business by getting a job as a reporter for the International News Service to enter the Soviet Union and obtain an interview with Foreign Minister Georgi Chicherin. Stevenson traveled by train from the Black Sea through Kharkov and Kiev to Moscow, and his observations of life under the Bolshevik regime colored his attitude toward the Soviet system for the remainder of his life.

In 1927, Stevenson became a member of a prestigious Chicago law firm, and in the following year, he married Ellen Borden, a Chicago heiress with literary interests. They had three sons, Adlai III, Borden, and John Fell and established a home in the small community of Libertyville, Illinois.

Adlai E. Stevenson II (Library of Congress)

Life's Work

In 1929, the United States suffered the greatest economic contraction in its history, with devastating social, economic, and political consequences. In 1932, voters turned to the Democratic Party under Franklin D. Roosevelt, who promised the country a "new deal." Stevenson became one of the New Deal's bright young attorneys who swarmed into Washington, D.C., to write, enact, and administer myriad administration programs. In 1933, he served as special counsel to the Agricultural Adjustment Administration under George Peek; then, a few months later, he joined the Alcohol Control Administration as special counsel to handle price codes and tax problems following the repeal of Prohibition. During the course of his brief service, Stevenson became acquainted with such figures as George Ball, Alger Hiss, James Rowe, and Tommy Corcoran, who played significant roles in American history.

Although Stevenson had left government service, he became increasingly active in politics. In 1930, he had joined the Council on Foreign Relations, where he honed his oratorical skills on behalf of Wilsonian internationalist principles. In 1939, he joined the Committee to Defend America by Aiding the Allies to counter the isolationist mood of the country. His support of Roosevelt's mobilization efforts, including the "destroyer deal" and the Lend-Lease program, reflected his belief that Great Britain was fighting the American fight against totalitarian aggression.

After the United States entered World War II in December, 1941, Stevenson became assistant secretary of the Navy under his close friend Frank Knox, a Republican newspaper publisher from Chicago. Stevenson handled the press, wrote Knox's speeches, and promoted desegregation of the Navy. In 1943, he led a mission to Italy to plan the Allied occupation of that country. As the war concluded, he was made a member of the United States Strategic Bombing Survey and then became assistant secretary of state under Edward L. Stettinius and James F. Byrnes, Jr. Finally, he became press officer of the United States delegation to the United Nations conference at San Francisco in 1945.

These posts served as a proving ground for Stevenson's meteoric rise in Illinois and national politics during the late 1940's and the 1950's. In Illinois, the incumbent Republican governor had been compromised by corruption in his administration, and Democratic boss Colonel Jacob M. Arvey of Cook County needed strong reform candidates to capture the state house and the Senate seat. Arvey selected Stevenson for governor and Paul H. Douglas for the Senate. In 1948, Stevenson campaigned as a political amateur and pledged honest government. He won by more than 500,000 votes, helping to bring in not only Douglas but also President Harry S. Truman in one of the country's greatest political upsets. This victory made Stevenson one of the "class of '48," a group of moderates and liberals who would dominate national politics into the 1970's.

Although his political career led to the breakup of his marriage, Stevenson was an effective liberal governor during a period of anticommunist hysteria known as McCarthyism. Stevenson appointed businessmen, Republican and Democratic, to state positions, terminated commercial gambling, placed the Illinois state police on civil service, built new highways, streamlined state government, and increased education appropriations. On the debit side, however, was his failure to persuade the state legislature to enact a permanent fair employment practices commission and to authorize a state convention to revise an archaic state constitution.

> "*My definition of a free society is a society where it is safe to be unpopular.*"

As a result of his gubernatorial performance, Stevenson became a favorite for the Democratic presidential nomination in 1952. The Democrats had been in power since 1933, and the party's domestic record and Cold War policies made it vulnerable to a conservative attack. The Truman administration, in fact, had become so unpopular that the president declined to seek reelection. Instead, Truman placed strong private and public pressure on Stevenson to make the race. The problem was that Stevenson did not want the position; he wanted to be reelected governor of Illinois. Moreover, he believed himself to be too inexperienced for the office. Stevenson's hesitation led to the charge that he was indecisive, which was to haunt him for the rest of his career. In the end, he was nominated for president in a movement that came as close to a draft as any in the twentieth century.

The 1952 campaign between Stevenson and General Dwight D. Eisenhower, an enormously popular war hero, became a classic confrontation. Behind in the polls from the beginning, Stevenson pledged to "talk sense" to the American people and offered no panacea for the nation's troubles. His position on the issues revealed him to be a moderate liberal on domestic matters and a cold warrior in foreign affairs. His penchant for writing his own

Stevenson shows aerial photos of Russian missiles in Cuba to the United Nations Security Council in the presence of USSR ambassador Valerian Zorin. (Wikimedia Commons)

speeches, his wit and erudition, his use of Lincolnian and Holmesian anecdotes, and his humility charmed millions of voters. When his opponents condemned him for appealing to intellectuals, he responded, "Eggheads of the world, unite! You have nothing to lose but your yolks!"

Although the early stages of the campaign showed promise, a number of factors combined to bring the Stevenson effort to a bitter conclusion. Stevenson's humor, intellectualism, and Hamlet-like posturing before the nominating convention made many voters suspect that he did not lust for the office. Moreover, the Republican attack of "K1C2" (Korea, communism, corruption) proved to be very effective with the voters. Stevenson's entanglement with the Hiss controversy did nothing to refute the charge that he was "soft on communism." Additionally, his support for federal over states' rights on the tidelands issue cost him significant support in such states as Louisiana, Texas, and California. The coup de grace to the campaign, however, proved to be Eisenhower's pledge to "go to Korea" and bring that stalemated conflict to an end. On election day, Stevenson lost by more than 6.6 million votes, including the electoral votes of four southern states.

Stevenson declined to disappear from public view during the 1950's. He became a world traveler, met world leaders, and solidified his credentials in foreign affairs. He also maintained a rigorous speaking schedule at home, campaigned for Democrats in the congressional elections of 1954 and 1958, and published several books on contemporary issues. In 1956, he was renominated for president by his party and campaigned on the theme of a "New America." Although he proved to be more liberal on civil rights than was Eisenhower, he badly mishandled the *Brown v. Board of Education* (1954) decision, which struck down segregation. Seeking to prevent national divisiveness on this issue, he declared that he would not use federal troops to desegregate public schools. He later recovered somewhat by pledging to enforce the decision if it was defied by state authorities. More controversial, however, were his proposals to end the draft and nuclear testing. Whatever chance he had for success was undermined in late October and November, 1956, by the Suez Canal and Hungarian crises. The electorate declined to change leaders, and Stevenson lost by an even greater margin 35,590,472 votes to 26,029,752.

By now, Stevenson's career had crested. In 1960, die-hard Stevenson loyalists made a "last hurrah" for their hero at the Democratic National Convention in Los Angeles, but the party turned to John F. Kennedy and a younger generation for leadership. Following Kennedy's narrow election victory, Stevenson hoped to be appointed secretary of state, only to be bitterly disappointed by his nomination for ambassador to the United Nations. Kennedy softened the disappointment by making the position cabinet-level and promising Stevenson a role in the National Security Council.

Stevenson's expertise in world affairs and his relationships with world leaders made him a popular and effective representative for the United States. His confrontations with his Soviet counterpart, Valerian Zorin, were tough and dramatic. In April, 1961, Stevenson's prestige tumbled when he denied that the United States had aided the Bay of Pigs invasion in Cuba by Cuban exiles. When President Kennedy took full responsibility for the incident, Stevenson was badly embarrassed and contemplated resignation. This action was averted when Kennedy promised to keep him fully informed of foreign policy decisions and even to seek his counsel.

This led to Ambassador Stevenson's superb performance in October, 1962, over the Cuban Missile Crisis when he successfully challenged Zorin's denial of Soviet insertion of missiles inside Cuba. His calm presentation of the evidence and his vow to wait until "hell freezes over" for the Soviet response won for him great praise at home and abroad. Unfortunately, this bravura performance was tarnished by administration insiders who leaked to journalists that Stevenson had acted the role of appeaser toward the Soviets. Although Stevenson and the Kennedy administration denied the story, it once again reinforced the public's perception of Stevenson's passivity.

Stevenson clearly was unhappy serving under Kennedy and Lydon B. Johnson. His admirers encouraged him to resign with a denunciation of their foreign policies, but he could not bring himself to take that step. While he did criticize Johnson's intervention in the Dominican Republic in 1965, he continued to support the containment, limited war, and collaborative aspects of American diplomacy developed during the Truman administration. He even supported basic American policies in South Vietnam. On the afternoon of July 14, 1965, Stevenson collapsed and died of a heart attack on a street in London.

Significance

Stevenson had acquired the reputation of a political loser, but his career should elicit admiration rather than contempt. He brought to public life the highest ideals and standards and never wavered in their defense. He did not seek easy answers to complex issues. He was an enigmatic political leader, a man who sought the nation's highest office yet appeared indifferent when it was within his grasp. It has been said that Stevenson lacked the ruthlessness to become president, but it may also be that he wanted the office on his terms. It seems ironic that he received his highest accolades not from his fellow citizens but from the people of the world who saw him as the best that America could produce.

A politician's success can be measured in many ways. Stevenson's "New America" campaign of 1956 anticipated much of the social and economic legislation of the New Frontier and Great Society in the 1960's. He inspired and brought into the political system millions of voters who had never before participated. He stood up to McCarthyism and practiced a disciplined civility in politics to which all politicians should aspire.

Stevenson belongs to the tradition of pragmatic reform characteristic of the twentieth century. His admirers saw him as a political leader with a moral vision for economic and social justice at home and abroad. In foreign affairs, he represented the tradition of Wilsonian internationalism, with its respect for international law, collective security, nuclear arms limitation, and human rights. He was, at heart, an optimist, a gentle and wise man who believed in strong and compassionate government and the nurturing of democratic principles throughout the world.

Stephen P. Sayles

Further Reading

Brown, Stuart Gerry. *Adlai E. Stevenson, a Short Biography: The Conscience of the Country*. Woodbury, N.Y.: Barron's Woodbury Press, 1965. A popular biography by a Stevenson admirer. Based on secondary sources as well as interviews with the subject and his friends and colleagues.

Cochran, Bert. *Adlai Stevenson: Patrician Among the Politicians*. New York: Funk and Wagnalls, 1969. Interprets Stevenson's life and career within the context of upper-class reform dating to the Gilded Age. Includes commentary on the role of intellectuals in the Cold War era.

Johnson, Wallace, and Carol Evans, eds. *The Papers of Adlai E. Stevenson, 1900-1965*. 8 vols. Boston: Little, Brown, 1972-1979. Correspondence and papers dealing with the life and career of Stevenson. Reflects his wit, intelligence, and character. A significant source of primary materials for students of post-World War II politics.

Liebling, Alvin, ed. *Adlai Stevenson's Lasting Legacy*. New York: Palgrave Macmillan, 2007. Collection of essays by Eugene McCarthy, Adlai Stevenson III, Arthur Schlesinger, Jr., and others examining Stevenson's past and current social significance.

Martin, John Bartlow. *Adlai Stevenson and the World: The Life of Adlai Stevenson*. Garden City, N.Y.: Doubleday, 1977. A scholarly two-volume biography of Stevenson by a longtime friend and associate. Volume 1 covers the formative years through the 1952 presidential campaign. Volume 2 discusses Stevenson's political decline and his influence in world affairs. A sympathetic portrait.

Ross, Lillian. "A Man for All Seasons." *Vogue*, November, 2003, 136-140. A profile of Stevenson surveying his career before he ran for the presidency in 1952, the 1952 election, and Ross's admiration for his writing.

Severn, Bill. *Adlai Stevenson: Citizen of the World*. New York: David McKay, 1966. A popular biography useful for readers with little background in modern American political history. An admiring treatment.

Stevenson, Adlai E. *Call to Greatness*. New York: Harper and Brothers, 1954. A candid nonpartisan assessment of the United States' position in world affairs during the 1950's. Emphasizes the destabilizing impact of nationalist and independence movements in the developing world. Urges Americans to be more mature in their hopes and aspirations for a stable and peaceful world order.

---. *Friends and Enemies: What I Learned in Russia*. New York: Harper and Brothers, 1959. Commentary on Stevenson's observations while in the Soviet Union in 1958. Notes that the Soviet regime is here to stay but states that the Soviet Union and the United States can maintain a peaceful coexistence. Typical of Stevenson's elegance of expression and clarity of style.

Whitman, Alden, and *The New York Times*. *Portrait Adlai E. Stevenson: Politician, Diplomat, Friend*. New York: Harper & Row, 1965. Drawn largely from the files of *The New York Times*. A flattering account of Stevenson's career, especially from his Illinois gubernatorial campaign until his death. Views Stevenson as a great, but flawed, man and emphasizes his growing estrangement from the Kennedy and Johnson administrations.

NORMAN THOMAS

Presidential candidate and political reformer

Born: November 20, 1884; Marion, Ohio
Died: December 19, 1968; Cold Spring Harbor, New York
Area of Achievement: Politics, religion

Often called "the conscience of America," Thomas ran six times for president on the Socialist Party ticket and became one of the greatest critic-reformers of politics in the United States.

EARLY LIFE

Norman Thomas was born in Marion, Ohio, the home of U.S. president Warren G. Harding, where he earned pocket money by delivering the *Marion Star*. He was the eldest of six children of the Reverend Welling Thomas, a Presbyterian minister whose father, also a Presbyterian minister, had been born in Wales. Norman's mother, Emma Mattoon, was also the child of a Presbyterian clergyman. The Thomas household was Republican in politics, devout in religion, and conservative in conduct, opposed to dancing, card-playing, and Sunday merrymaking. Emma Thomas was acknowledged by the family as its dominant force, emphasizing a keen sense of personal and social responsibility that her firstborn practiced all of his life.

Norman Thomas (Library of Congress)

After his 1905 graduation from Princeton University as valedictorian of his class, Thomas took his first fulltime job as a social worker at New York City's Spring Street Presbyterian Church and Settlement House, located in a poverty-stricken area. In 1907, he became assistant to the pastor of Christ Church in Manhattan. There he met Frances Violet Stewart, active in Christian social service and born into a moderately wealthy family of financiers. They were married September 1, 1910, and led a notably happy marital life, in their turn having six children and fifteen grandchildren.

From 1910 to 1911, Thomas attended the heterodox Union Theological Seminary. There he was most impressed by the writings of Walter Rauschenbusch, one of the leading figures of the Social Gospel movement, who argued that the ethical precepts of Jesus did not harmonize with the selfish materialism of a capitalist society.

Thirty years later, Thomas wrote, "Insofar as any one man ... made me a Socialist, it was probably Walter Rauschenbusch." Ordained in 1911, Thomas became pastor of the East Harlem Presbyterian Church and chair of the American Parish, a federation of Presbyterian churches and social agencies located in immigrant neighborhoods. In 1912, he declared, "The Christian Church faces no more burning question than the problem of making brotherhood real."

Life's Work

The agonies of World War I crystallized Thomas's social radicalism. He came to consider the war an immoral conflict between competing imperial powers, and in January, 1917, he joined the Fellowship of Reconciliation, a religious pacifist group with a commitment to drastic social reform. Thomas came to regard resistance to the war as a clear choice of individual conscience over the dictates of an amoral state. His uncompromising pacifism led him to support Morris Hillquit, the socialist candidate, who ran on an antiwar platform in the 1917 New York City mayoral race.

Thomas joined another pacifist, Roger Baldwin, in the 1917 establishment of the Civil Liberties Union, later renamed the American Civil Liberties Union. In the spring of 1918, he resigned from his church and the parish, aware that his radicalism was jeopardizing these institutions' chances for outside financial assistance. In October, 1918, he applied for membership in the American Socialist Party; he was motivated, he recalled later, by "grotesque inequalities, conspicuous waste, gross exploitation, and unnecessary poverty all around me."

The party was led by three talented people: Victor Berger, Morris Hillquit, and Eugene V. Debs. The first two were its theoreticians and tacticians, but it was the populist, pragmatic Debs (1855-1926) who became American Socialism's greatest leader until Thomas's ascendancy. Debs grounded his convictions on emotional rather than philosophic premises: He had an evangelical devotion to social justice, a generous and sensitive temperament, sincerity, warmth, and an intuitive understanding of popular opinion.

In the 1920 election, Debs received 920,000 votes, but they were largely a tribute to his courage for having chosen imprisonment (from 1918 to 1921) to dramatize his pacifism; membership in the Socialist Party was down that year, from a 1912 peak of 108,000 to 27,000. During the 1920's several conditions combined to keep the American Socialist Party's numbers and influence low: a dominant mood among the electorate of economic conservatism and intense nativism; hostility to organized labor by all three branches of government; a number of failed strikes; and the 1919-1920 Red Scare mass arrests of radicals and labor leaders by the Department of Justice under Attorney General A. Mitchell Palmer. When Senator Robert M. La Follette campaigned for the presidency in 1924, he refused to run solely as the socialist candidate, preferring to call himself a Progressive. Nevertheless, the Socialist Party energetically supported his campaign; 855,000 of La Follette's 3,800,000 votes were cast on socialist levers.

"*For I can assure you that in any war, even if it does not become a world war, I do not think there will be a victor who can do much. There may be one less badly off than the other. One side or the other may have sued first for peace. The destruction will be so great, the moral erosion of the experience will be so great, that it is idle to think you'll find liberty, walking serenely among the corpses of the dead and the agonies of the dying. There are other things to do than that if we want democracy and freedom to live; there have to be other things to do than that.*"

Thomas began his long career of seeking public office in 1924, running as a New York gubernatorial candidate on both the socialist and Progressive tickets. Ironically, he had risen to socialist leadership at a time when many people were leaving the party. More ironically, the income his wife inherited from her conservative father enabled him to crusade for his causes on a full-time basis. He admitted that in this instance, "the critic of capitalism was its beneficiary."

By the mid-1920's, Thomas was the consensual choice to succeed Debs who had never regained his health after his three-year imprisonment, and who died in 1926 as the leader of American Socialism. In 1928, he was chosen the party's presidential candidate the first of six such nominations; he received 267,000 votes. In 1932 he was to poll 885,000; in 1936, 187,000; in 1940, 100,000; in 1944, 80,000; in 1948, 140,000.

Thomas attracted the deep affection and admiration of many people, often including ideological opponents. His physical appearance was impressive: He stood over six feet two, had strongly marked patrician features, vibrant blue eyes, good manners, and an air of genteel self-confidence. Although a man of dignity, he could communicate warmth and cordiality to a wide range of people. His physical energy was phenomenal until his late seventies, when failing eyesight and disabling arthritis began to plague him. Since he had no hobbies, he focused his unflagging pace not only on campaigning but also on writing sixteen books and scores of pamphlets, maintaining an enormous correspondence, attending countless conventions and committee meetings, and delivering thousands of speeches. Perhaps his only flaw as a leader was his remoteness in contrast to Debs from the rough-and-tumble realities of the American political panorama. When it came to conflicting interests, he was by temperament an educator, moralist, and intellectual rather than an accommodating pragmatist. Since he had no solid prospect of winning public office, he could afford to maintain an incorruptible integrity and the noblest of principles.

Thomas's virtuosity as a public speaker was his outstanding leadership asset. He was a masterful humorist, firing quick barbs at his targets. In 1932 he asked his listeners not to fix on Herbert Hoover as the person solely responsible for their economic suffering, since "such a little man could not have made so big a Depression." As for Harry S. Truman, he "proves the old adage that any man can become President of the United States." Perhaps the best-known Thomas anecdote recounts a meeting he had with President Franklin D. Roosevelt in 1935. When Thomas complained to Roosevelt about a particular New Deal measure, the president retorted, "Norman, I'm a damn sight better politician than you." Responded Thomas, "Certainly, Mr. President, you're on that side of the desk and I'm on this."

In 1932, with the country deeply mired in the Great Depression and capitalism seriously shaken, the Socialist Party hoped for a presidential vote of more than two million. The socialist platform anticipated New Deal programs on many issues, demanding federal appropriations for public works, reforestation, and slum clearance, increased public housing, a six-hour day and five-day working week, old-age pensions, health and maternity insurance, improved workmen's compensation and accident insurance, adequate minimum wage laws, and a compulsory system of unemployment compensation with adequate benefits derived from both government and employer contributions.

Contrary to socialist expectations, the combined popular vote for all minority party candidates in 1932 barely exceeded one million, and Roosevelt embarked on an ambitious program to save capitalism by implementing a vast amount of social welfare legislation. Thomas consistently chided the New Deal for what he regarded as its lack of any consistent underlying philosophy, for its opportunistic, helter-skelter improvisation and experimentation. This very pragmatism and daring, however, endeared Roosevelt to the majority of the electorate much to Thomas's frustration. In his *The Politics of Upheaval* (1979), the historian Arthur Schlesinger, Jr., considers that in the 1930's Thomas's "essential contribution . . . was to keep moral issues alive at a moment when the central emphasis was on meeting economic emergencies. At his best, Thomas gave moving expression to an ethical urgency badly needed in politics. . . ."

The 1930's witnessed an increasingly dangerous world situation, with Adolf Hitler's Germany, Benito Mussolini's Italy, and, late in the decade, Francisco Franco's Spain threatening the peace. Under the guise of opposing fascism, communists in both Europe and the United States wooed liberals and radicals to form a united, "popular front." Thomas temporarily flirted with the notion of such international solidarity in his 1934 book, *The Choice Before Us*. A 1937 trip he took to Europe, however, during which he witnessed communist attempts to control Spain's Loyalist government through shabby betrayals and observed Stalin's purge trials of his former comrades, reaffirmed Thomas's mistrust of totalitarian communism and his conviction of its basic incompatibility with democratic socialism. The Moscow-Berlin Pact of August, 1939, outraged him as "a piece of infamy." Thomas made certain that, from 1939 on, the United States Socialist Party would vigorously oppose communism, even when the Soviet Union was America's ally during World War II.

In the late 1930's and early 1940's, Thomas's lifelong pacifist sentiments were in agonizing conflict with his detestation of fascism and strong sympathy for the Spanish Republicans locked in civil warfare with Franco's Falangists. Thomas tried to solve this dilemma by backing aid for the Spanish government while opposing direct United States intervention on behalf of Great Britain and France after World War II had erupted in September, 1939. By late 1941, the Socialist Party's noninterventionist foreign policy, combined with Thomas's often acerbic criticism of the New Deal's socioeconomic program, had alienated many former members and well-wishers. Even though the party fielded presidential tickets through 1956, it was never to recover its health from these losses. By the 1944 presidential campaign, Thomas's insistence on maintaining the fullest measure of civil liberties even amid a world war, and his opposition to the Allied demand on Germany and Japan for unconditional surrender had cost

Thomas at a peace rally in Washinton, D.C., 1940. (Library of Congress)

him much of his previous popularity: His vote total proved the lowest of his six national appeals.

In the 1948 presidential election, Thomas's main target was former vice president Henry Wallace, who had left the Democratic Party to run as an antimilitarist, radical candidate for president on the Progressive ticket. Thomas became convinced that the Progressive Party was controlled by communists, with Wallace serving as a naïve front man capable of such self-damning errors as describing the Soviet Union as a "directed democracy." When Thomas received less than 100,000 votes despite a spirited campaign, he became convinced of the futility of socialist attempts to attract nationwide electoral support, and renounced further office seeking. In 1952 and 1956, the party ran a Pennsylvania state legislator, Darlington Hoopes, for the presidency. He received twenty thousand votes in 1952, two thousand in 1956; no socialist has since sought the presidency.

With his buoyant energy and sparkling mind, Thomas remained dynamically active through the 1950's and early 1960's. He resigned from various official posts in the Socialist Party in 1955, at the age of seventy-one, but remained its most magnetic advocate. The major party candidate to whom Thomas was most sympathetic during this period was Adlai E. Stevenson, with whom he shared a Princeton background and eloquent speech making. The American statesman with whom he disagreed most vehemently was John Foster Dulles, Dwight D. Eisenhower's secretary of state, also a fellow Princetonian as well as fellow Presbyterian. Thomas scorned Dulles's appeasement of demagogic Senator Joseph McCarthy; the bellicosity of his opposition to mainland China; his dismissal of Eleanor Roosevelt from the United States delegation to the United Nations; and his discharge of liberals and socialists, no matter how talented, from foreign service posts.

Thomas remained a morally consistent critic-commentator on American politics to the end of his life. He voted for John F. Kennedy in 1960 and Lyndon B. Johnson in 1964, but with little enthusiasm for either candidate. In the former year, his favorite was an old friend, Hubert H. Humphrey, who lost the Democratic nomination to Kennedy. The Bay of Pigs fiasco shocked Thomas into an outraged telegram of protest, and thereafter he remained lukewarm through Kennedy's one thousand White House days, favoring the president's graceful style and careful separation of state from church, but worried about the moderate, cautious nature of Kennedy's liberalism. He voted for Johnson mainly to vote against the right-wing Barry Goldwater.

Though plagued by arthritic legs and a minor heart ailment, Thomas maintained a strenuous lecturing, debating, and writing schedule in the early 1960's, keeping in the fast lane of what his friends called the "Thomas Track Meet." The only debating opponent who succeeded in spoiling his usually good temper was William F. Buckley, Jr., whom he regarded as a cold-blooded imperialist and self-righteous reactionary. Thomas's preferred activity during his last years was spending several consecutive days as guest-in-residence on a college or university campus, not only lecturing but also making himself available as casual participant in bull sessions with students and faculty. On lecture platforms he would sometimes limp slowly to the podium, leaning on his cane, then address his audience with the opening line, "Creeping Socialism!"

By his eightieth birthday in late 1964, Thomas was cast in the role of Grand Old Man, admired and loved for his integrity, dignity, intelligence, and wit, given standing ovations at his appearances. When he returned to his birthplace for a birthday tribute, the local paper printed one letter critical of Thomas's opposition to American military involvement in Vietnam. He was relieved, saying, "I feel better not to be too respectable." In 1966, he shocked his oldest grandson, a pastor, by permitting *Playboy* to interview him at considerable length. Thomas expressed a frequent regret of his old age: that he had seen the American working class becoming increasingly middle-class in its materialism; this "dilution of labor's down-the-line militancy has been one of the greatest disappointments in my life." In 1965, ophthalmologists diagnosed his retinal arteriosclerosis; by 1966 he was legally blind, bent by his arthritis, and in pain much of the time. He never complained, however, and his voice retained its booming roar. He finished dictating his twenty-first book, *The Choices*, four weeks before his death in a nursing home a month after his eighty-fourth birthday.

Significance

Thomas devoted a long, honorable life to urging a largely uninterested American public to share his vision of Democratic Socialism as a solution to social inequities and injustices. He served as a goad and gadfly in the Socratic tradition of appealing to his country's good sense and conscience. Some of the social welfare and civil rights legislation he sought was enacted into law during the administrations of Roosevelt and Johnson with Thomas given no or scant credit for having championed it. His great hope of building a strong socialist movement in the United States was never realized, and he left his party, under circumstances beyond his control, weaker at his death than when he had joined it in young adulthood.

However, Norman Thomas's life can justly be called an extraordinary success story. He was a patrician moralist who maintained an unswerving passion for social justice, devotion to civil liberties, sympathy for the poor, deprived, and disabled, hatred of war's wasteful slaughter, and faith in the ultimate wisdom of a free people. Profoundly reasonable and fair in temperament, he found expression for his evolving views first in humanitarian Christianity, then in a muted, non-Marxist Socialism. The personal esteem he gained was extraordinary: Thomas became not simply an adornment to hundreds of liberal and left-democratic causes but also an admirable member of the pantheon of great American dissenters that includes Henry Clay, Daniel Webster, Debs, La Follette, and Martin Luther King, Jr.

Gerhard Brand

Further Reading

Bell, Daniel. *Socialism and American Life*. 2 vols. Princeton, N.J.: Princeton University Press, 1952. An incisive, lucidly written historical and sociological analysis, particularly useful for describing the background and development of Marxist socialism in the United States.

Duram, James C. *Norman Thomas*. Boston: Twayne, 1974. A concise study of Thomas's books and pamphlets, with comprehensive notes and references.

---. "Norman Thomas as Presidential Conscience." *Presidential Studies Quarterly* 20, no. 3 (Summer, 1990): 581-590. Duram offers another look at Thomas's significance in the realm of American politics, specifically the presidency.

Harrington, Michael. Review of two Thomas biographies in *The Reporter* 25 (November 9, 1961): 64-66. A leading young socialist whom Thomas befriended portrays him as a representative of the American Protestant drive for social justice and moral improvement.

Kutulas, Judy. *The American Civil Liberties Union and the Making of Modern Liberalism, 1930-1960*. Chapel Hill: University of North Carolina Press, 2006. This history of the formative years of the American Civil Liberties Union also discusses Thomas's work with the organization.

Rosenberg, Bernard. "The Example of Norman Thomas." *Dissent* 11 (Fall, 1964): 415-422. A review of two Thomas biographies. Rosenberg cogently analyzes Thomas's place in contemporary American society and urges fulfillment of Thomas's vision of a better world.

Seidler, Murray B. *Norman Thomas: Respectable Rebel*. Syracuse, N.Y.: Syracuse University Press, 1967. A scholarly biographical-critical study that focuses on Thomas's successes and failures as leader of the Socialist Party.

Swanberg, W. A. *Norman Thomas: The Last Idealist*. New York: Charles Scribner's Sons, 1976. A vivid, well-written biography that emphasizes the warmth and courage of Thomas's character. Includes many illustrative photographs, but often gets so immersed in details that it loses sight of the larger ideological terrain.

Thomas, Norman. "When Cruelty Becomes Pleasurable." In *Hiroshima's Shadow*, edited by Kai Bird and Lawrence Lifschultz. Stony Creek, Conn.: Pamphleteer's Press, 1998. Thomas's essay is included in this anthology of literature critical of the atomic bombings of Hiroshima and Nagasaki by the United States.

Walker, Samuel. *In Defense of American Liberties: A History of the ACLU*. 2d ed. Carbondale: Southern Illinois University Press, 1999. This history of the American Civil Liberties Union explores Thomas's role in the organization's development and mission.

EARL WARREN

Chief Justice of the Supreme Court (1953-1969)

Born: March 19, 1891; Los Angeles, California
Died: July 9, 1974; Washington, D.C.
Area of Achievement: Law

The U.S. Supreme Court under Warren's leadership reached landmark decisions that struck down existing practices in the areas of racial segregation, limitations on political association, voting apportionment, the investigation of criminal suspects, and other controversial issues.

Earl Warren (Library of Congress)

EARLY LIFE

Earl Warren was born in Los Angeles. His father, Methias Warren, was a Norwegian immigrant who had come to the United States during his adolescence and for many years worked as a railroad car mechanic; the boy's mother, Christine Hernlund Warren, was of Swedish ancestry. Ethel Warren, Earl's sister, was four years older than he. In 1896, the family moved to Bakersfield. As a boy, Warren raised animals and worked at various jobs on the Southern Pacific Railroad; his best subjects in school were history, English, and French. His interest was aroused in 1903 when a deputy marshal killed two lawmen and was later tried in a local court; Warren saw the trial and also watched other trials. Although his father encouraged him to consider a career in engineering, Warren was intrigued by the examples of courtroom advocacy he had seen. By the time he completed high school, he had saved some eight hundred dollars, which he used to meet his expenses when he entered the University of California, Berkeley.

Warren's academic record was acceptable, if not outstanding; after his third year, he was allowed to take courses at the university's law school. He received a bachelor's degree in 1912, and two years later he was awarded his law degree. He was graduated at about the middle of his class and was not selected to serve on the school's *Law Review*. For some time thereafter, he practiced in a local law office; on the United States' entry into World War I, he joined the Army, serving as a bayonet instructor. After a period of service that took him to Fort Lee, Virginia, he was discharged in 1918 with the rank of first lieutenant in the infantry. He then began work for the city attorney in Oakland. In 1925, he became the district attorney for Alameda County, an area just east of San Francisco.

Slightly taller than six feet, Warren weighed more than two hundred pounds; he had a strong build, though in later years he had to struggle somewhat to control his girth. His features were often described as typically Scandinavian: He had a long face with a straight nose and clear blue eyes, his complexion was fair, and he had blond hair that eventually became gray. Throughout his adult life he wore glasses, in time favoring those with rounded, dark-rimmed frames.

Although hitherto he had not seriously concerned himself with women, Warren became deeply attached in 1921 to Nina Palmquist Meyers, whom he met at a morning swimming party. An attractive young widow whose husband had died shortly after their son was born, she returned Warren's affection; after a lengthy courtship, they were married in 1925. Over a period of seven years, two sons and three daughters were born to them, and Warren, as a proud father, became an archetypal family man, constantly concerned with his children's education and well-being.

LIFE'S WORK

Warren became widely known for his relentless pursuit of lawbreakers, notably bootleggers, and he took vigorous action against gambling and vice. In 1931, Raymond Moley, an important political observer and later adviser to President Franklin D. Roosevelt, called Warren "the most intelligent and politically independent district attorney in the United States." On some cases Warren went to great lengths to obtain convictions; controversy arose in 1936, during his investigation of a shipboard homicide on the SS *Point Lobos*. Four defendants, who allegedly were Communist sympathizers, were brought to trial on evidence obtained partly through electronic eavesdropping and prolonged interrogation in the absence of defense counsel. Ultimately they were found guilty of second-degree murder. Violent crime affected Warren's life directly, as well: In 1938, his father was beaten to death at his home in Bakersfield. The assailant was never found.

Later that year, Warren was elected attorney general for the state of California; his tenure in that office was characterized by the same zeal he had displayed in local law enforcement. In 1939, drawing on an extended legal definition of the state's coastal waters, he directed a major raid on the *Rex*, an offshore gambling ship. He also became involved in politics: He opposed the nomination of a noted legal scholar to the California Supreme Court, partly because of the latter's purported relations with the Communist Party. Claims of national security were invoked in 1942, when Warren supervised the forcible relocation of about 110,000 Japanese Americans; he depicted them as potential saboteurs and collaborationists. Although somewhat later many others denounced this measure, until the last years of his life Warren contended that it was necessary in view of the military situation at that time.

Warren's politics were Republican, but his positions on social issues had a wide appeal to voters at large. He campaigned for governor in 1942 and was elected overwhelmingly; four years later, under California's cross-filing system, he won the primaries of both major parties. In 1950, he became the only person to be elected to a third term as governor of that state. He supported measures to expand the state's educational system; he also advocated prison reform and improved mental health care. He was acutely conscious of the financial hardships imposed by medical expenses, which he and his family had incurred during periods of hospitalization; in 1945 he urged, unsuccessfully, that the state enact a form of health care insurance. In 1949, he signed a bill requiring that women receive equal pay for work performed on an equal basis with men.

Because of his demonstrated political appeal and the growing importance of California and the Western states in national politics, there were Republican political strategists who looked to Warren as one of the party's possible standard-bearers. In 1948, the Republican nominee for president, Governor Thomas E. Dewey of New York, chose Warren as his vice-presidential running mate. He campaigned with some vigor, and even after Dewey's unexpected defeat, some of the California governor's supporters held out hopes for the next election. At that time, however, Dwight D. Eisenhower announced his candidacy and in short order obtained the Republican nomination; he was then elected president by a convincing margin. In 1953, after the sudden death of Chief Justice Frederick M. Vinson created a vacancy on the U.S. Supreme Court, Eisenhower offered the position to Warren.

A major issue that Warren, and his colleagues, had to confront was the troubled question of racial segregation; in a landmark decision that he wrote for a unanimous Court, Warren found that public facilities described as "separate but equal" were inherently unequal and therefore were in violation of the Constitution. The case of *Brown v. Board of Education* (1954) overturned rulings ultimately based on a decision of 1896; once judicial decisions had eliminated distinctions on this level, a new era in racial relations was opened.

Political concerns also came before the Supreme Court, notably in connection with the government's efforts strictly to limit Communist and other left-wing activities. On constitutional grounds, Warren and his colleagues resisted such measures. On one Monday in June, 1957, the Court handed down four separate decisions restricting powers to investigate individuals' political backgrounds or to cite political affiliations as grounds for the termination of employment.

Warren believed that the most important case to come before him was *Baker v. Carr* (1962), which challenged Tennessee's system of electoral apportionment as unduly favoring lightly populated rural districts. The Court's decision, written by Justice William J. Brennan, effectively established that federal judicial power could be exercised to ensure equal representation for voters participating in state elections. In another case, *Reynolds v. Sims* (1964), Warren wrote the opinion of a majority of justices in holding that both houses of the Alabama legislature had to be elected on an equal and proportional basis.

Rather different, and unsettling, questions arose when Warren became chair of the commission that investigated the assassination of President John F. Kennedy. Although originally he had been reluctant to take this position, Warren conscientiously supervised the collection of evidence; after the commission's report was issued in 1964, he stoutly defended its conclusion that Lee Harvey Oswald had acted alone in killing the president.

Chief Justice Warren had often come under attack for the Court's decisions; desegregation and reapportionment had been denounced as intrusions on states' rights, in areas not hitherto subject to the Court's rulings. Several U.S. senators contended that decisions upholding individual liberties actually were concessions to the communists. Opposition arose in many quarters: In 1957, Warren resigned his membership in the American Bar Association in protest against lack of support from that organization. The militantly anticommunist John Birch Society mounted a widespread campaign calling for Warren's impeachment. During his later years on the Court, Warren became associated with controversial decisions affecting the rights of criminal suspects, for which he was castigated by many.

Members of the Warren Commission present their report on the assassination of President John F. Kennedy to President Lyndon Johnson. (Wikimedia Commons)

> "I believe the preservation of our civil liberties to be the most fundamental and important of all our governmental problems, because it always has been with us and always will be with us and if we ever permit those liberties to be destroyed, there will be nothing left in our system worthy of preservation."

Cases such as *Mallory v. United States* (1957) and *Mapp v. Ohio* (1961) had overturned convictions obtained through improper interrogation or search and seizure without a warrant. *Gideon v. Wainwright* (1963) established the right of the indigent to obtain counsel for their defense during criminal trials. In *Escobedo v. Illinois* (1964), the Court found that the accused has a right to counsel during initial questioning by the police; limitations on the direct investigation of suspects were stated specifically in *Miranda v. Arizona* (1966), a landmark decision that Warren wrote for a majority on the Court. The requirement that, prior to any questioning, the police must inform suspects of their rights under the Constitution established explicit guidelines for the treatment of accused persons but was bitterly attacked by many law enforcement officers and political figures.

Warren sometimes parted company with his fellow justices; thus, he sided with a majority on decisions involving the use of sit-ins to demonstrate for civil rights but dissented in cases in which claims of obscenity were contravened by those of free speech. Weary with advancing age, and in anticipation of his retirement from the bench, in 1968 he offered to resign on the condition that a successor be found beforehand. Although his associate, Abe Fortas, was not confirmed by the Senate and ultimately resigned from the Supreme Court in the wake of a financial scandal, Warren renewed his offer and left the Court when Warren E. Burger was confirmed as chief justice in 1969. The last years of his life were spent writing, traveling, and lecturing; Warren continued to manifest a lively interest in political controversies that affected judicial concerns. He suffered from angina pectoris and coronary occlusion, for which he was hospitalized several times. On July 9, 1974, he died of cardiac arrest at the Georgetown University Hospital in Washington, D.C.

Significance

To friends, associates, and opponents alike, Warren's career in public service posed contrasts and questions that were not readily resolved. During his work in law enforcement, Warren had shown some deference for the rights of the accused, but in exceptional cases he disregarded them; his active role in combating crime, in Alameda County and for the state of California, did not seem to foreshadow his efforts on behalf of individual rights after his appointment to the Supreme Court. In his native state he had denounced communism, and he had carried out sweeping measures against Japanese Americans; as chief justice, he openly championed interpretations of the Constitution that ensured political liberties and promoted racial equality before the law. Although his views had been well within the political mainstream, the transition that later took place could not easily be ascribed to underlying features of continuity in his outlook, or indeed to the changed historical circumstances surrounding cases that arose during his tenure on the Supreme Court.

It was sometimes contended that Warren followed the lead of other justices, such as Hugo L. Black and William O. Douglas, in reaching major decisions, notably those that upheld individual rights. Warren had essentially a practical, rather than an abstract or academic, philosophy of the law; he reached decisions promptly and held fast once he had made them. Other justices, moreover, have readily attested the determined leadership he exercised, even in cases in which he assigned the Court's opinions to others of like mind. While occasionally, as in cases involving pornography, a majority voted against his positions, most major decisions reflected his colleagues' views as well as his own, and often he was able to win over those who wavered.

A final issue concerns the Supreme Court's role in American politics and society. More than any other institution, the Supreme Court brought about racial desegregation, and it prescribed the forms by which criminal suspects are advised of their constitutional rights. Such decisions have tangibly affected the lives of millions. Supporters and critics have described this process as a form of judicial activism, by which the Court's interpretation of the Constitution was applied directly to state and local, as well as federal, concerns. Although opposition often centers on the tenor and content of particular decisions, questions remain as to the nature and scope of the Court's powers within the framework of the Constitution. It is Warren's legacy to have demonstrated the means and range by which the Court might intervene in major questions of American public life.

J. R. Broadus

Further Reading

Kurland, Philip B. *Politics, the Constitution, and the Warren Court*. Chicago: University of Chicago Press, 1970. In a series of lectures that are astringently critical of the Court's actions, Kurland, an important scholar specializing in the Supreme Court, contends that Warren and his colleagues found new and potentially hazardous interpretations of the Constitution.

Levy, Leonard W., ed. *The Supreme Court Under Earl Warren*. New York: Quadrangle Books, 1972. The divergent standpoints of defenders and responsible critics of the Court are presented in this collection of articles by various legal specialists.

Newton, Jim. *Justice for All: Earl Warren and the Nation He Made*. New York: Riverhead Books, 2006. A definitive biography, comprehensively chronicling Warren's life and career and describing the complexities and contradictions of his personality.

Pollack, Jack Harrison. *Earl Warren: The Judge Who Changed America*. Englewood Cliffs, N.J.: Prentice-Hall, 1979. A brisk, favorable account of Warren's life that at each stage evokes the political atmosphere surrounding his work in law and government. The author emphasizes the social and political consequences of decisions handed down by the Warren Court.

Schwartz, Bernard. *Super Chief: Earl Warren and His Supreme Court, a Judicial Biography*. New York: New York University Press, 1983. Warren's sixteen terms on the high court are studied in this massive work by a noted legal scholar. The author reveals the extent to which differing positions and judicial infighting affected the court's deliberations; in the process, Warren's marked capacity for leadership is demonstrated. The unpublished papers of seven justices and a broad range of personal interviews were used in the composition of this work.

Urofsky, Melvin I. *The Warren Court: Justices, Rulings, and Legacy*. Santa Barbara, Calif.: ABC-CLIO, 2001. An examination of the court, including profiles of the justices, discussions of its decisions, and an appraisal of its influence.

Warren, Earl. *The Memoirs of Earl Warren*. Garden City, N.Y.: Doubleday, 1977. This work, which Warren composed during the last four years of his life, published posthumously, depicts Warren's work against crime, his actions as governor of California, and the concerns that guided him in reaching controversial decisions on the Supreme Court. Although not free from special pleading, some portions are lively, and there are also useful statements of his positions on racial issues, criminal investigation, and other important matters.

---. *The Public Papers of Chief Justice Earl Warren*. Edited by Henry M. Christman. New York: Simon & Schuster, 1959. Eleven of Warren's major opinions, from his first five terms on the Supreme Court, are published here, along with other addresses and statements on public issues.

---. *A Republic, If You Can Keep It*. New York: Quadrangle Books, 1972. This brief treatise sets forth, on a rather basic level, Warren's views on the constitution and its place in American history; from time to time he refers to major decisions in which he was involved.

White, G. Edward. *Earl Warren: A Public Life*. New York: Oxford University Press, 1982. This important scholarly examination of Warren's political career and judicial work points to the aspects of continuity and change in his outlook on major issues; the author provides, on a topical basis, a critical assessment of his opinions as chief justice.